International Ha
on the Economics or
Mega Sporting Events

Edited by

Wolfgang Maennig

Department of Economics, University of Hamburg, Germany

and

Andrew Zimbalist

Robert A. Woods Professor of Economics, Smith College, USA

Edward Elgar
Cheltenham, UK • Northampton, MA, USA

Published by
Edward Elgar Publishing Limited
The Lypiatts
15 Lansdown Road
Cheltenham
Glos GL50 2JA
UK

Edward Elgar Publishing, Inc.
William Pratt House
9 Dewey Court
Northampton
Massachusetts 01060
USA

A catalogue record for this book
is available from the British Library

Library of Congress Control Number: 2011939346

ISBN 978 0 85793 026 2 (cased)

Typeset by Servis Filmsetting Ltd, Stockport, Cheshire
Printed and bound by MPG Books Group, UK

Contents

Contributors

Gabriel M. Ahlfeldt Department of Geography and Environment and Spatial Economics Research Centre, London School of Economics and Political Science, UK.

Greg Andranovich Professor of political science and director of the Master of Science in Public Administration program at California State University, Los Angeles, CA, USA. He holds a PhD in political science from the University of California, Riverside, and an MA in economics from George Mason University. His research focuses on urban economic development policy and over the past decade he has published on different aspects of bidding for and hosting the Olympic Games.

Wladimir Andreff Professor Emeritus, University Paris 1 Panthéon Sorbonne, Paris, France, and researcher at the Centre d'Économie de la Sorbonne. He is Honorary President of the International Association of Sport Economists, Honorary President of the European Sports Economics Association, an Honorary Member of the European Association for Comparative Economic Studies, and former President of the French Economic Association. He is the author of eight books and 105 articles in sports economics, his most recent books being *Contemporary Issues in Sports Economics: Participation and Professional Team Sports* (Edward Elgar, 2011), and *Recent Development in the Economics of Sport* (Edward Elgar, 2011).

Robert A. Baade A.B. Diek Professor of Economics, Lake Forest College, Lake Forest, IL,USA and Past President of the International Association of Sports Economists.

Orli Bass Senior Project Officer at the Centre for Critical Research on Race and Identity (ccrri), University of KwaZulu-Natal, Durban, South Africa. She is interested in cities and culture, African identity and cities, and mega events. She is a co-editor of the book, *Development and Dreams: The Urban Legacy of the 2010 Football World Cup* (HSRC Press, 2009).

Robert Baumann Associate Professor in the Department of Economics, College of the Holy Cross, Worcester, MA, USA. He earned his PhD in economics from Ohio State University, which has dominated his coauthors' alma maters on the football field for as long as anyone can remember. He is the author of numerous papers relating to the economic impact of major events.

Urmilla Bob   Associate Professor, Discipline of Geography, School of Agricultural, Earth and Environmental Sciences, University of KwaZulu-Natal, Durban, South Africa.

Dan Brown   University of Cambridge, UK.

Matthew J. Burbank   Associate Professor in political science at the University of Utah, Salt Lake City, UT, USA. His research focuses on citizen participation and urban politics and he teaches courses in American politics, political behavior, and research methods.

Rick Burton   David B. Falk Professor of Sport Management at Syracuse University, Syracuse, NY, USA and author of the historical thriller *The Darkest Mission* (Long Reef Press, 2011). He was formerly the executive director of the Warsaw Sports Marketing Center at the University of Oregon, the commissioner of the Australian National Basketball League and chief marketing officer of the US Olympic Committee. He is a frequent contributor to the *New York Times*, *Sports Business Journal* and *Sport Business International*.

Anton Cartwright   An economist with a special interest in the links between ecological degradation and human poverty. He is a researcher at the African Centre for Cities, University of Cape Town, South Africa, where he convenes the City of Cape Town's Climate Change Think Tank – a partnership between the City of Cape Town, the University of Cape Town and civil society.

Adams Ceballos   Universidad de Concepción, Chile.

Daniel M. Chin   PhD student in economics, University of South Florida, Tampa, FL, USA. He received an MBA from the University of Minnesota, an MS in public management and policy from Carnegie-Mellon University, and BAs in mathematics and economics from the University of Rochester. His professional experience includes work as an analyst at the Federal Reserve Bank, and as an associate portfolio manager at Kenwood Capital Management in Minneapolis.

Dennis Coates   Department of Economics, University of Maryland Baltimore County (UMBC), MD, USA. He has studied the economic impact of sport facilities, sport franchises, and sporting events for 15 years. His research has appeared in numerous academic journals and been cited in a variety of newspaper and news magazines. He is a former president of the North American Association of Sports Economists.

Luiz Martins de Melo   Associate Professor at the Economics Institute of the Federal University of Rio de Janeiro – IE/UFRJ. Formerly Planning Director of FINEP – the Brazilian National Agency for Innovation. He also worked as a technical coordinator of the Rio 2004 Olympic bid. His research fields are innovation financing and the economics of sports. In 1971 he received the Brazilian Sports Merit Order.

Stan du Plessis   Professor of Macroeconomics, Department of Economics, University of Stellenbosch, South Africa, Vice Dean (research) in the faculty of Economics and Management Sciences and Head of Research at the Bureau for Economic Research. He studied at the Universities of Cambridge (MPhil) and Stellenbosch (PhD) and is the President of the Economic Society of South Africa and formerly treasurer and secretary of the African Econometric Society. He was a member of the 'Harvard group' of local and international economists who advised government on policy reform since 2006 and teaches macroeconomics, monetary economics and advanced econometrics, mainly to graduate students. His academic publications have focused on monetary policy and the business cycle but he has also written on the economic impact of the FIFA World Cup, fiscal policy, economic growth, the exchange rate, institutional economics and law and economics. He is a National Research Foundation 'rated' researcher.

Nicolas Eber   LARGE, IEP and EM Strasbourg Business School, University of Strasbourg, France.

Bryan Engelhardt   Assistant Professor in the Department of Economics, College of the Holy Cross, Worcester, MA, USA. He earned his PhD in economics from the University of Iowa. His primary area of research is labor economics, and he has published articles in several top journals including the *Journal of Labor Economics* and the *Journal of Public Economics*.

Arne Feddersen   Associate Professor of Economics in the Department of Environmental and Business Economics, University of Southern Denmark, Odense, Denmark, and study leader of the bachelor's program 'Sports and Event Management'. His areas of research include sports economics, media economics, and applied regional and urban economics. He has published articles in the field of sports economics in several books, conference volumes and scholarly journals including the *Journal of Sports Economics, the International Journal of Sport Finance*, and *Contemporary Economic Policy*.

Ramón Flores   Universidad Carlos III, Madrid, Spain.

David Forrest   University of Salford, UK.

Yingzhi Guo   Professor and supervisor of graduate students in the Department of Tourism, Fudan University, Shanghai, China. She holds a PhD from Chinese Academy of Sciences in 1999 and was a Post Doctorate Fellow of Business Management in Tourist Marketing at Fudan University from 1999 to 2001. She has been a visiting scholar in the Department of Tourism and Hospitality Management, Sejong University in South Korea, and a visiting professor in the Tourism Economics and Marketing Institute, Dresden University of Technology, and the Department of Leisure and Tourism Management, Stralsund University of Applied Sciences, Germany. She is currently a Fulbright visiting scholar from 2011 to 2012 in the USA.

Charles H. Heying   Associate Professor in the Nohad A. Toulan School of Urban Studies and Planning, Portland State University, Portland, OR, USA. He has co-authored a book and numerous articles on the politics and development of Olympic cities. His recent book, *Brew to Bikes: Portland's Artisan Economy*, describes how the transformation from an industrial to a post-industrial economy is being articulated in the trend-setting edges of Portland's artisan production.

Yuansi Hou   Department of Tourism, Fudan University, Shanghai, China.

Brad R. Humphreys   Professor in the Department of Economics, University of Alberta, Edmonton, AB, Canada, where he holds the Chair in the Economics of Gaming. He received his PhD in economics from Johns Hopkins University. His research interests include the economics of sport, the economics of gambling, and the financing of professional sports facilities. He is editor in chief of *Contemporary Economic Policy* and associate editor of the *International Journal of Sport Finance*.

Georgios Kavetsos   An economist in the Department of Social Policy, London School of Economics, London, UK. His main research interests are in the area of behavioural and welfare economics. He has conducted prior research on the impact of hosting major sporting events on measures of subjective well-being and on the impact of stadium proximity on property prices. He is also a member of the editorial board of the *International Journal of Wellbeing*.

Stefan Kesenne   Professor of (Sports) Economics in the Economics Department, University of Antwerp (UA), and at the Human Kinesiology Department of the University of Leuven (KUL), Belgium. He is a member of the Editorial Board of the *Journal of Sports Economics* and of the

European Sports Management Quarterly. In 2007, he published the text-book: *The Economic Theory of Professional Team Sports: An analytical Treatment* (Edward Elgar).

Ruud H. Koning   Professor of Sports Economics at the University of Groningen, The Netherlands. In 1994 he worked on a probability/simulation model of the FIFA World Cup, and since then it has also been applied for the European Cup for country teams. His research interests include competitive balance, betting markets, and home advantage.

Judith Grant Long   Associate Professor of Urban Planning at Harvard University Graduate School of Design, Cambridge, MA, USA. Her research and teaching interests include infrastructure mega-projects, public–private partnerships for urban development, and the intersection of tourism, heritage conservation, and city branding strategies. She is the author of *Public–Private Partnerships for Major League Sports Facilities* (Routledge, forthcoming) and is currently at work on a new book prospectively entitled *Olympic Urbanism*, which analyzes the claim of the Olympic Games as a catalyst for urban redevelopment, based on archival and field research in 15 host cities including Rome 1960 to Rio de Janeiro 2016.

Wolfgang Maennig   Professor in the Department of Economics, University of Hamburg, Germany. Formerly Professor at E.A.P. Paris–Oxford–Berlin–Madrid. He has been a visiting professor at the American University in Dubai, the Federal University of Rio, the Universities Stellenbosch and Istanbul, and the University of Economics, Bratislava. He was also a visiting scholar at the International Monetary Fund, Washington, DC and at the Deutsche Bundesbank. His research on regional economics, sport economics, and real estate economics has been published in numerous academic journals. He has worked as an expert for many bids of large sporting events, for example, the Olympic bids of Berlin 2000, Leipzig 2012, Munich 2018 and the Athletics World Cup Berlin 2009. He was Olympic Champion (rowing, eight with coxwain) at the Seoul Olympics (1988) and president of the German Rowing Federation, 1995–2001. In 2000 he received the Olympic Order.

Boria Majumdar   Senior Research Fellow, University of Central Lancashire, Preston, UK and Adjunct Professor at the University of South Australia. His books include *Twenty Two Yards to Freedom*, *Goalless*, *Once Upon a Furore*, *Olympics: The India Story*, *Sellotape Legacy* (co-author) and several edited collections on the history and politics of sport.

Victor A. Matheson   Associate Professor in the Department of Economics, College of the Holy Cross, Worcester, MA, USA. He earned his PhD in economics from the University of Minnesota. He has published extensively in the field of the economics of collegiate and professional sports including studies of the economic impact of the Super Bowl, the World Cup and the Olympics. He has also worked as a referee in the top professional and intercollegiate soccer leagues in the United States.

Ian G. McHale Senior Lecturer in Statistics at the Salford Business School, University of Salford, UK. Having graduated from the University of Liverpool with a degree in mathematical physics, he studied for his PhD in extreme value statistics at the University of Manchester. Current research interests include statistics in sport and the statistical analysis of gambling-related issues. He was co-creator of the EA Sports Player Performance Index, the official player rating system of the English FA Premier League.

Nalin Mehta Honorary Fellow, Institute of South Asian Studies and Asia Research Institute, National University of Singapore. Dr Mehta is Joint Editor of *South Asian History and Culture*, and Senior Communications Advisor, The Global Fund to Fight AIDS, TB and Malaria, Geneva. His books include *India on Television, Olympics: The India Story*, *Sellotape Legacy* (co-authored), *Television in India* (ed.), *Gujarat Beyond Gandhi* (co-ed.) and *The Changing Face of Cricket* (co-ed.).

Norm O'Reilly Associate Professor of Sport Business in the School of Human Kinetics, University of Ottawa, Canada. A former School Director and Director of the Research Centre (the Institute for Sport Marketing) at Laurentian University, he is an active researcher and has published three books, more than 50 articles in refereed management journals and more than 100 conference proceedings and case studies in the areas of sport management, tourism marketing, marketing, risk management, sport finance, and social marketing. He has also taught at Syracuse University and Stanford University.

Michaela Ölschläger Hamburg Chamber of Commerce, Germany.

Philip K. Porter Professor of Economics, University of South Florida, Tampa, FL, USA. He received a PhD in economics from Texas A&M University and Bachelor's and Master's degrees from Auburn University.

Allen R. Sanderson Department of Economics, University of Chicago, Chicago, IL, USA. His most recent professional journal articles are on the economic impact of universities on their communities and an essay on income and happiness.

Ismael Sanz Universidad Rey Juan Carlos, Móstoles, Spain.

Jeroen Schokkaert   PhD student at LICOS Centre for Institutions and Economic Performance at the University of Leuven (KUL), Belgium. His main research interests are sports, migration and economic development.

Benoit Séguin   Associate Professor in Sport Management, University of Ottawa, Canada, specializing in sport marketing. His research on Olympic marketing, specifically in the area of sponsorship, ambush marketing and the Olympic brand has been published internationally in various journals. He is also a regular professor at the International Olympic Academy and runs its post-graduate programs.

Stephen Shmanske   Department of Economics, California State University, East Bay, Hayward, CA, USA. He has taught economics at CSU East Bay (formerly CSU Hayward) for over 30 years. He is the author of *Golfonomics* and dozens of scholarly articles on sports economics, transport economics, public goods, price discrimination, and applied microeconomics. He is also the Director of the Smith Center for Private Enterprise Studies.

Elmer Sterken   Professor of Monetary Economics and Rector Magnificus, University of Groningen, Groningen, The Netherlands.

Bernd Süssmuth   Since 2010, Full Professor and Chair of the Institute for Empirical Research in Economics and, Econometrics, University of Leipzig, Germany. Studied economics, (major) at the University of Munich and obtained a PhD in economics from the University of Munich (2002). Formerly a post-doc researcher at the University of Modena, Italy, faculty and lecturer at Max Planck Institute for Intellectual Property Munich, assistant professor at the University of Bamberg, TUM Munich University of Technology (habilitation in 2009), and University of California at Santa Barbara (UCSB); and Professor (non-tenured) in the Department of Economics, University of Erlangen-Nuremberg (2009–10). He is also a Research fellow of CESifo Munich; and an editorial board member of Région et Développement.

Kamilla Swart   Associate Professor, Centre for Tourism Research in Africa, Business Faculty, Cape Peninsula University of Technology, Cape Town, South Africa

Johan F.M. Swinnen   Professor of Economics and Director of LICOS Centre for Institutions and Economic Performance at the University of Leuven (KUL), Belgium. His research focuses on institutions and development, transition, political economy, globalization and trade.

Stefan Szymanski Professor of Economics in the Department of Sport Management, University of Michigan, Ann Arbor, MI. He has published extensively in the area of sports economics.

J.D. Tena Universidad Carlos III, Madrid, Spain and University of Sassari, Italy.

Richard Tomlinson Chair in Urban Planning in the Faculty of Architecture, Building and Planning, University of Melbourne, Australia. His research has focused on housing and infrastructure; HIV/AIDS in the context of urban development; urban policy processes and international best practice; the effect of web-based search engines on urban policy perspectives; and mega events and urban economic development. His current research is on the Australian housing market and urban outcomes, and on mega events and urban development. He has been a Visiting Professor at Columbia University, a Visiting Scholar at the Massachusetts Institute of Technology, and a Guest Scholar at the Brookings Institution and the New School University. His research awards include a Robert S. McNamara Fellowship and a Fulbright Scholarship. He has also been a consultant to the South African government (post-apartheid), USAID, the World Bank, European development agencies, NGOs and the private sector.

Henry van Egteren Associate Professor in the Department of Economics, University of Alberta, Edmonton, AB, Canada. He received his PhD in economics from the University of British Columbia. His research interests include environmental economics, the economics of regulation, and law and economics.

Thijs Vandemoortele Postdoctoral researcher at LICOS Centre for Institutions and Economic Performance, University of Leuven (KUL), Belgium. His main research interests are political and economic theory of standards and sports and economic development.

Chun Zhou Department of Tourism, Fudan University, Shanghai, China.

Andrew Zimbalist Robert A. Woods Professor of Economics at Smith College in Northampton, MA, USA and a member of the Five College Graduate Faculty. He received his BA from the University of Wisconsin, Madison and his MA and PhD in economics from Harvard University. He has been a visiting professor at Doshisha University in Kyoto, Japan, at the University of Geneva in Switzerland, at the University of Chile, and at Harvard University. He serves on the editorial boards of various scholarly journals. He has consulted widely in the sports industry for players' associations, teams, leagues, cities, commissions, foundations, film projects, and law firms, and in economic development for international institutions, is a frequent media commentator, and has published 20 books, including *Baseball and Billions* (1992), *Sports, Jobs and Taxes* (1997), *Unpaid Professionals: Commercialism and Conflict in Big-Time College Sports* (1999), *May the Best Team Win* (2003), *National Pastime: How Americans Play Baseball and the Rest of the World Plays Soccer* (2005), *In the Best Interests of Baseball? The Revolutionary Reign of Bud Selig* (2006), *The Bottom Line: Observations and Arguments on the Sports Business* (2006), *Equal Play: Title IX and Social Change* (2007), and *Circling the Bases: Essays on the Challenges and Prospects of the Sports Industry* (2011), and several dozen articles. He did a regular commentary on NPR's *Marketplace* during 2002–05 and contributes opeds frequently to leading newspapers and magazines. He has testified on numerous occasions before the US Congress, state legislatures and city councils. He has served as the Smith College faculty athletic representative for over 10 years.

PART I

INTRODUCTION

1 Introduction: the economics of mega sporting events

Wolfgang Maennig and Andrew Zimbalist

As globalization proceeds, the potential audience for sporting events grows, especially those events that project beyond local or national boundaries. The cumulative television viewership for the 2008 Summer Olympic Games in Beijing, for instance, is estimated to have reached 4.7 billion people, while that for the 64 matches played in the 2006 German World Cup is 26 billion.[1] No one would question the cultural and social significance of such an event. Yet it is also estimated that China spent upwards of $40 billion in preparing for and hosting the 2008 Games. Few would question that such an event also has economic and environmental significance.

It is also true that while no sporting event parallels the Olympic Games in its reach, there are a large and growing number of sporting events with audiences in the tens of millions. These events each have their own design, their own processes for selecting participants and host cities or countries and their own impact on social, economic and environmental conditions.

In former decades, the scholarly analysis of mega sporting events such as the Olympic Games or the Soccer World Cup has been dominated by historians, educators, and philosophers. Today, scholarly analysis of mega sporting events has also turned to consider potential employment and income effects, psychic and marketing benefits, urban branding and transformation, corruptive elements in the bidding processes, among other subjects that are ripe for economic inquiry.

Accordingly, there has been growing attention within governmental and academic circles that seeks to understand the organization as well as the impact of these mega sporting events. But generally the studies and analyses have been isolated in time and place. The present volume seeks to bring together the collective experience and wisdom of those who have organized and studied mega sporting events, so that we may better understand the patterns of these events, the similarities and differences, and to see whether certain lessons may be drawn. Clearly, the hosts of mega events seek benefits for their city, region or nation. In what ways can hosts best plan, prepare and allocate resources and how are the answers to these questions conditioned by the nature of the event and the organizations that sanction it? These are the issues that motivate the present volume. It is our hope that the ensuing chapters will open the door to a better understanding of the role that mega sporting events play in modern society.

PLAN OF THE BOOK

Before we begin to analyze mega sporting events, we must first delineate the terrain that we explore. Therefore, we begin with an attempt to define such events. Part II contains three chapters on the bidding for mega sporting events, with a focus on the Olympic Games. Brad Humphreys and Henry van Egteren (Chapter 3) model the stages of the bidding process for the Olympic Games, demonstrating how the International Olympic Committee (IOC), as a natural monopolist, structures the bidding to maximize the rent it extracts from the staging of the Games. Humphreys and van Egteren clarify that the IOC (and other international sport federations) have every incentive to preserve their natural monopolies – a conclusion that conditions any discussion about a reform program for the future. In Chapter 4, Wladimir Andreff interprets the bidding process as an auction which in the end tends to transfer any rents from mega events to the sporting federations. He concludes that cost overruns, project revisions, delayed completion, and financial deficits are so widespread in mega events that the winner's curse is a common result of the bidding process. From the economic point of view, there might be no problem with such resource transfers from some regions to the worldwide sporting family, as long as it is based on voluntary decisions. Humphreys and van Egteren's analysis, due to principal–agent problems on both sides of the bidding process, tends against a finding of such voluntarism. In their analysis of all 46 bids for the Olympic Winter Games between 1992 and 2014, Arne Feddersen and Wolfgang Maennig (Chapter 5) find that a model including variables such as average distance from the Olympic Village to the sporting venues, the number of hotel beds, as well as GDP and inflation can well predict the decision of the IOC, pointing to a rational, transparent and reproducible selection process – which is contrary to the widespread belief that other, even corruptive, decisive elements are at play. Robert Baade and Allen Sanderson (Chapter 6) provide an analysis of Chicago's failed bid for the 2016 Games. They point out the role of local resistance against mega events as well as to a US-specific factor, that is, the fact that the United States still generates and receives a sharply disproportionate share of Olympic TV revenues. The demands for reform from other members of the Olympic family and the – according to their views unsatisfying – response of the United

States Olympic Committee (USOC) might have hurt the Chicago bid. Their analysis is a warning that timing with respect to geostrategic cycles and the adherence to the relationships and politics within the Olympic Movement are crucial in the host selection process, as they may well dominate the city's or country's objective strengths. Finally, in Chapter 7, Gabriel M. Ahlfeldt, Wolfgang Maennig and Michaela Ölschläger seek to identify how lifestyle and social class, along with spatial and economic factors, condition the response (support or resistance) to the construction of new sports facilities. As such, they offer insight into a central factor in the IOC selection process, that is, the receptivity of the local population to an Olympic bid.

Part III explores important elements around the design of mega events in order to promote their sustainability, and of sports more generally. Anton Cartwright (Chapter 8) starts with the issue of ecological sustainability and maintains that hosts need to be more conscious of the carbon footprint of their event and should compete more in terms of innovative concepts to reduce emissions. Cartwright foresees an ability for mega events to become true catalysts of social and sustainable development. Rick Burton, Norm O'Reilly and Benoit Séguin (Chapter 9) without explicitly referring to ecological or sustainability questions, approach perceptions as the core to any marketing perspective of the stakeholders at mega events. They expose 'on-the-ground' tactics and explain how the concept of 'houses' or hospitality centers plays a central role during mega sporting events. In Chapter 10, Matthew Burbank, Greg Andranovich and Charles Heying analyze the impact of mega events on local politics (as well as how local politics affects the ability to effectively leverage mega events for urban transformation), with particular focus on the US Games in Los Angeles 1984, Atlanta 1996, and Salt Lake City 2002. They affirm that, although the three host city models varied, local community benefits tended to be intangible in all instances. Their conclusion about the ability of even well-run Games to provide a material boost to the city and especially to its lower-income residents is not optimistic. Ruud Koning and Ian McHale (Chapter 11) elaborate on tournament designs which optimize the probability that the best participant wins. Nicolas Eber (Chapter 12), leaning on the experience that doping cases may well endanger the credibility or even the existence of mega sporting events, surveys the economics of doping and of the anti-doping measures that have been proposed. He questions the value of the standard economic approach to doping. Part III closes with Chapter 13, by David Forrest, Adams Ceballos, Ramón Flores, Ian McHale, Ismael Sanz and J.D. Tena. They estimate a random effects Tobit model to predict the number of medals garnered by a country in 14 individual Olympic sports and find that GDP is significant for 12 of these sports, especially in sailing, equestrian, swimming, fencing and cycling events, suggesting an advantage for large developed countries. They propose that sport subsidy policy should focus on development of facilities that can be shared. They also find that hosting an event gives the home country an advantage in competition.

Part IV explores in global terms the economic (and non-economic) impact of mega events and elaborates on the contemporary methods of evaluation. In Chapter 14, Bernd Süssmuth provides a primer on the willingness-to-pay (or contingent valuation) methodology which attempts to identify the psychic value of sporting events to residents in a city. 'Intangibles' are becoming 'tangible', thus a potential target for quantitative economic analysis. Philip Porter and Daniel Chin (Chapter 15) follow with a critique of the standard input–output method that is used in promotional 'studies' under contract with stadium or event supporters. They argue persuasively that the method is completely inappropriate, and is also misapplied, to further the purpose of these promotional studies. Stefan Kesenne (Chapter 16) extends the Porter and Chin critique by showing that cost–benefit analyses (which include opportunity costs), rather than narrow economic impact evaluations, are the proper approach to assessing the welfare implications of stadium building or mega-event hosting.

In Chapter 17, Gabriel Ahlfeldt and Georgios Kavetsos consider the effect of stadiums on nearby property values and introduce a new method to correct for biases in earlier studies. They observe that there are still imperfections and difficulties in the methodology, such as discerning causal direction. Richard Tomlinson and Orli Bass (Chapter 18) discuss the different experiences and substantial challenges in hosting mega events for the BRICS (Brazil, Russia, India, China, and South Africa) countries. In Chapter 19, Jeroen Schokkaert, Johan F.M. Swinnen and Thijs Vandemoortele analyze the relationship between mega sporting events and institutional development, particularly soccer academies, in connection with the hosting of the World Cup in South Africa in 2010. Part IV closes with an econometric analysis of mega-event economic impact by Elmer Sterken (Chapter 20) which controls for the possible endogeneity resulting from growth-oriented countries applying to host mega events. Sterken finds only weak evidence of a possible, modest economic impact from hosting the Summer Games, and no evidence of a positive impact from hosting either the Winter Games or the World Cup.

Part V seeks to evaluate the experience of specific cities and countries in hosting mega events through various case studies. It leads off with a discussion of the history and economics of the Tour de France by Judith Grant Long (Chapter 21). Long argues that until now, when compared to other mega events, the characteristics of the Tour have made it a relative economic bargain for French towns and cities that have hosted legs of the race, but she notes that the cultural and economic forces that have made this true to date may be waning. Robert Baumann, Bryan Engelhardt and Victor Matheson (Chapter 22) begin by summarizing the existing scholarship on the economic effect of mega sporting events and then provide their own evaluation of the impact of the 1994 World Cup on US host cities. They find no significant positive effect. In Chapter 23, Dennis Coates discusses smaller mega events. Coates reviews the existing literature and extends it by statistically studying trade and output effects of several mega events. His findings confirm the prevailing scholarship of little to no economic impact from hosting a mega event. In Chapter 24, Kamilla Swart and Urmilla Bob discuss the development of the academic research agenda in connection with South Africa's hosting of the World Cup in 2010.

Stephen Shmanske (Chapter 25) then provides an econometric analysis of the impact of golf majors on local economies. In particular, he assesses whether hosting the US Open or the PGA Championship has any positive effects on total annual county payroll or payroll in the hotel/motel sector. He finds no statistically significant effects. Yingzhi Guo, Chun Zhou and Yuansi Hou (Chapter 26) then employ surveys of Chinese citizens and factor analysis to evaluate the impact of the 2008 Beijing Olympics on perceptions of the Olympic Games. They generally find positive perceptions along several dimensions that persist through 2010, yet there is little optimism regarding the impact of the Games on employment opportunities, the provision of social services or congestion problems. In Chapter 27, Stan du Plessis and Wolfgang Maennig employ high-frequency data to assess the impact of the 2010 World Cup on South African tourism and find only a modest impact, far below the early projections. They also investigate the awareness effects of mega sporting events, and potential long-term development effects, by using data from electronic social networks.

Nalin Mehta and Boria Majumdar (Chapter 28) narrate the story of the ill-fated 2010 Commonwealth Games in Delhi. Luiz Martins de Melo (Chapter 29) places Brazil's hosting of the 2014 World Cup and 2016 Olympics in the context of the country's economic development and then points out the immense resource costs and challenges it faces as it organizes these games. Finally in Part V, Dan Brown and Stefan Szymanski (Chapter 30) provide a preliminary assessment of the employment impact of the 2012 London Olympic Games.

Part VI presents our concluding chapter, which summarizes the major themes of the book's chapters and looks ahead to the challenges of hosting mega events in the future. Mega events have certainly not lived up to the pro-development claims that characterize the promotional efforts of their backers. This chapter asks what, if anything, can be done to improve the typical hosting experience and what reforms in the sanctioning bodies might be undertaken to facilitate an improved hosting experience.

ACKNOWLEDGMENTS

We would like to express our gratitude to our international contributors for their good work, patience, cheerful cooperation, and willingness to meet the rather strict time demands that we placed on them.

We are also indebted to the Smith College/University of Hamburg Exchange which enabled us to work together for several weeks during June 2011.

Finally, as always, our deep gratitude and love go to our families, Felise, Julius, Shelley, Alex, Ella, Jeff and Mike for putting up with our distractions and anxieties and their steady support and interest in this project.

NOTE

1. See   http://blog.nielsen.com/nielsenwire/media_entertainment/beijing-olympics-draw-largest-ever-global-tv-audience/. See also Baumann et al., ch. 22 in this volume.

2 What is a mega sporting event?

Wolfgang Maennig and Andrew Zimbalist

According to Webster's dictionary, 'mega' is a prefix meaning large or great. It follows that a mega sporting event is a large or great sporting event. Just like beauty, what is great is subjective – it is in the eyes of the beholder. It would be folly to pretend that there is a clear line that demarcates great from normal or ordinary; rather, the magnitude of a sporting event likely falls along a continuum of size, reach or significance.

What are some of the quantifiable indicators that might distinguish a mega from a typical sporting event?[1] The number of participating athletes might be a first criterion to identify a mega sporting event. If the number of athletes is used, the world's largest city marathons with easily more than 25,000 participants are of unique impact. In fact, even according to other criteria mentioned below, the marathons of Boston, New York City, London and Berlin might qualify as mega events.[2]

Two commonly considered standards are attendance at the event and television viewership of the event (Horne and Manzenreiter, 2006). Each standard, in turn, has multiple dimensions: first, the number of attendees and viewers; second, the share of attendees and viewers who come from outside the host metropolitan area (and/or the host country); and, third, the number of TV transmission hours or a combination of transmission duration and spectatorship. Further, to the extent that such information is available and reliable, one might also want to consider the number of people who follow an event on the internet, in printed media or on the radio. Events that attract broader audiences and more awareness will also be events that generate more revenue. Hence, as in most matters, many observers are tempted to decide whether or not an event is considered mega by focusing on a single metric – the revenue it produces.

In sports leagues, regular season games that are primarily of local interest would generally not qualify as mega events. Similarly, golf tournaments other than the majors or tennis tournaments other than the grand slams would probably fall below the mega threshold. Yet it would not take much reflection to realize that some 'regular' events in certain sports may draw broader interest than the capstone events in other sports. For instance, Monday night games during the regular season in the National Football League (NFL) in 2009 enjoyed between 10.2 million and 21.8 million (US) viewers per telecast, while the 2009 National Hockey League

(NHL) Stanley Cup championship series had only between 2.9 million and 8.0 million (US) viewers. By this criterion alone, regular season games in the NFL may be mega events, while the championship finals in the NHL may not be.

Another complication arises when one acknowledges that the viewership for any sporting event will vary considerably depending on the teams or individuals who are competing, and the media outlets that are covering the event. Thus, US ratings for the NHL Stanley Cup series between the Pittsburgh Penguins and Detroit Red Wings in 2009 varied between 2.4 and 4.3 per game, while the 2007 Stanley Cup ratings between the Ottawa Senators and Anaheim Mighty Ducks witnessed ratings between 0.6 and 1.9.[3] Similarly, the US ratings for the US Open Women's Finals in 2009 when Kim Clijsters won was 1.1, while when Serena Williams won in 2008 it was 3.3. As is well known, when Tiger Woods enters and is in contention in a golf tournament, ratings skyrocket. Considering, then, only ratings or attendance, one may conclude that a golfing event with Tiger Woods in contention is a mega event, while the same tournament without him, even if it were one of the four majors, is not.

Further, the place where the event takes place may have an impact. An estimated 4.7 billion viewers – or 70 percent of the world's population – tuned in to watch the 2008 Beijing Olympic Games, an increase of 21 percent over the 2004 Athens Olympic Games with a 3.9 billion audience, and 31 percent over the 3.6 billion who tuned in to the Sydney Games in 2000 (Nielsen, 2008). The special interest of China, the nation with the largest population worldwide, may have had an effect on the TV attendance. Another factor influencing viewership will be the time change between the host country and the larger television markets around the world.

Table 2.1 charts the estimated viewership of a subset of well-publicized sporting events throughout the world. It has to be mentioned, however, that the measurement of TV attendance includes a large element of guesswork, and is subject to measurement error and even manipulation. These issues complicate any effort to make a simple comparison across events, especially when the events are in different countries.[4]

From an economic point of view, mega events might also be separated from normal sporting events by their differential economic impact. Even here, there is no single criterion. On one level, for instance, there is the size of the budget, possibly differentiated into organizing budget and non-organizing budgets (infrastructure, national security, operations, and so on). Then, there is the impact on macroeconomic variables such as employment, income, and tax revenues, and each of these can be reckoned on a national, sectoral, regional or urban level. The general

Table 2.1   Estimated viewership of selected sporting events

Sport	Event	Average US TV rating, 2004–09
MLB	World Series	11.3
MLB	All-Star Game	8.8
NBA	Finals	8.7
NBA	All-Star Game	5.4
NFL	Super Bowl	42.0
NFL	All-Star Game	5.1
NASCAR	Daytona 500	10.4
Horse Racing	Kentucky Derby	8.4
Tennis	Wimbledon Men's Finals	2.9
	Wimbledon Women's Finals	2.6
Tennis	US Open Men's Finals	3.2
Tennis	US Open Women's Finals	2.3
Olympics	Summer (last 6)	16.9
Olympics	Winter (last 5)	18.8
Golf	Masters (highest major)	5.5
NCAA Basketball	Championship Game	12.1
NCAA Football	Championship Game	16.2

conclusion that has come out of the academic literature on such economic impacts of normal sporting events is that a city, county or state should not anticipate a positive economic or fiscal impact from a new sports facility or hosting a sports team. That is, a new sports facility (or sports team) by itself should not be expected to raise employment or per capita income levels in a community. The primary reasons for this outcome are fourfold.

First, despite their large cultural presence, sports teams are modestly sized businesses. In 2007–08, for instance, the average National Basketball Association (NBA) team generated approximately $110 million in revenue. This equals less than 0.02 percent of the disposable income of New York City.

Second, most families have a relatively fixed budget for leisure activities. If a family spends $250 going to a basketball game, it is $250 it does not have available to spend at local theaters, bowling alleys or restaurants. Thus, a good share of money spent at sporting contests is money that is not spent elsewhere in the local economy – one form of entertainment expenditure substitutes for another (the 'substitution effect').

Third, there are generally larger leakages out of the local economy associated with the professional sports dollar. For instance, NBA players earn just under 60 percent of league revenue. The average NBA player earns around $4.9 million in salary. His nominal, federal marginal tax rate is close to 40 percent and he normally has a high savings rate. Fewer than one-third of NBA players make their permanent residence in the same city in which they play (Siegfried and Zimbalist, 2002). Federal taxes, of course, go to Washington and leave the local economy. Savings enter the world's money market, and, generally, also leave the local economy. A significant share of a player's income finds its way back to his hometown. Thus, a higher share of the money spent at entertainment venues other than professional sports stadiums and arenas stays in the city.

Fourth, in the vast majority of cases, arena and stadium projects create a budgetary gap. This is because over the last 15 years approximately 70 percent of the development costs for the average professional sports facility has been publicly funded and the typical lease has shared little facility revenue with local government.[5] When sports facilities create a budgetary gap, this gap must be compensated for by either higher taxes or a reduction of services – either of which puts a drag on the local economy.

In contrast, mega events tend to bring in more dollars from outside the local economy – either because more of the event attendees come from outside the area or outside the country or because television (and corporate sponsorship) rights are sold outside the local area. Thus, the substitution effect for mega events tends to be considerably weaker. Indeed, 'international significance' (Roche, 2000) might be regarded as one of the most important criteria to differentiate between 'mega' and 'normal' sporting events.

Beside stressing the international dimension, modern economic event analysis is not limited to the above-mentioned traditional macroeconomic criteria, but also includes image effects (especially in the form of a possibly improved international perception), ecological effects, as well as psychological and feel-good effects. In sum, mega sporting events are different from other sporting events and subject to economic analysis because of their character as 'short-term events with long-term consequences for the cities that stage them' (Richie, 2000).

The foregoing discussion notwithstanding, it might be observed that it is apparent that some events, such as the Summer and Winter Olympic Games, the Soccer (Football) World Cup, the final game in the Champions League, the NFL's Super Bowl or the Major League Baseball (MLB) World Series, are mega events. Beyond the top half dozen or so events, however, the classification becomes murkier and it is difficult to avoid the conclusion that there is a continuum of events by significance, popularity and revenue generation.[6] After considering the variety and complexity of the possible mega-event identifying factors, it is ultimately difficult not to conclude that where one draws the line between mega and non-mega events is somewhat subjective.

NOTES

1. More qualitatively, several additional criteria may become relevant, such as: the historic number of sporting records achieved at the respective event, tradition (for example, Admiral's Cup, Ascot, Henley, Oxford–Cambridge Boat Race, Wimbledon), the rarity of event frequency, and the marketability of individual sporting success.
2. Of course, it may be problematic to consider the number of participants by itself. Doing so, for example, may lead to the designation of an NCAA (National Collegiate Athletic Association) Division III national championship in track and field as a mega event.
3. In 2011, one ratings point equals approximately 1.16 million US households watching.
4. See Horne (2007) for a list of sporting events and their claimed versus verifiable viewing statistics. Horne claims that true audiences are between a quarter and a third of reported sizes. A different handling of the number of repeats, highlights and delayed showings may contribute to the problems of an international comparison. If one compares the ratings numbers in Table 2.1 with the following estimates of the worldwide television audiences, a good sense of the variability in the figures is apparent:

    *   2006 World Cup Final (300 million viewers);
    *   Euro 2004 Soccer Final (153 million viewers);
    *   2004 Olympic Games: opening ceremony (127 million viewers);
    *   2004 Olympic Games: closing ceremony (96 million viewers);
    *   2004 Super Bowl (95 million viewers);
    *   2004 Olympic Games: men's 100 meters (87 million viewers);
    *   2003 Champions League (67 million viewers);
    *   2004 Olympic Games: men's 200 meters freestyle swimming (66 million viewers);
    *   2004 Formula 1: Monaco Grand Prix (59 million viewers); and
    *   2004 Basketball: NBA finals (25 million viewers).

5. Quantifying the public share in facility construction is complex for a number of reasons, including whether or not the estimate includes land, infrastructure, environmental remediation, maintenance, property and fiscal subsidies, and so on (see, Long, 2002 and Zimbalist and Long, 2006).
6. See, for instance, Coates (ch. 23 in this volume) on the 'not-so-mega' events.

REFERENCES

Horne, J. (2007), 'The four "knowns" of sports mega-events', *Leisure Studies*, **26** (1), 81–96.

Horne, J. and W. Manzenreiter (2006), 'An introduction to the sociology of sports mega-events', in Horne and Manzenreiter (eds), *Sports Mega-Events: Social Scientific Analyses of a Global Phenomenon*, Sociological Review monograph series, Oxford: Blackwell, pp. 1–24.

Long, Judith Grant (2002), 'Full count: the real cost of public funding for major league sports facilities and why some cities pay more to play', PhD dissertation, Department of Urban Planning, Harvard University, April.

Nielsen Media Research (2008), 'Beijing Olympics draw largest ever global TV audience', available at: http://blog.nielsen.com/nielsenwire/media_entertainment/beijing-olympics-draw-largest-ever-global-tv-audience/ (accessed January 22, 2011).

Richie, B.S.R. (2000), 'Turning 16 days into 16 years through Olympic legacy', *Event Management*, **6**, 155–65.
Roche, M. (2000), *Mega-Events and Modernity*, London: Routledge
Siegfried, John and Andrew Zimbalist (2002), 'A note on the local impact of sports expenditures', *Journal of Sports Economics*, **3** (4), December, 361–6.
Zimbalist, Andrew and Judith Grant Long (2006), 'Facility finance: measurement, trends, and analysis', *International Journal of Sport Finance*, **1** (4), November, 201–11.

PART II

BIDDING FOR MEGA EVENTS

3 Mega sporting event bidding, mechanism design and rent extraction

Brad R. Humphreys and Henry van Egteren

1 INTRODUCTION

Economics studies the allocation of scarce resources. The rights to host a mega sporting event such as the Olympic Games and the FIFA World Cup can be thought of as scarce resources that must be allocated to only one among a group of competing cities. Mega sporting events are scarce because they are held infrequently, in most cases only every four years. In economic terms, the non-governmental organizations (NGOs) such as the International Olympic Committee (IOC) or the Fédération Internationale de Football Association (FIFA) that hold the rights to mega sporting events can be viewed as monopoly sellers and the potential host cities or countries can be viewed as competing buyers. This monopoly power further reduces the number of mega sporting events that exist. Many mechanisms to allocate scarce resources, such as the rights to host mega sporting events, exist and each has different properties, implications and characteristics. From an economic perspective, the procedure that awards cities or regions the rights to host mega sporting events such as the Summer or Winter Olympic Games and the World Cup can be understood through the lens of mechanism design theory, the branch of economic theory focusing on how an allocation process should work and the general characteristics of allocation processes.

The basic approach in mechanism design theory is to specify a goal, in this case the awarding of the rights to host a mega sporting event to the 'best' host city or country, determine the conditions under which an appropriate method exists for achieving this goal, and if the conditions exist, specify a form for this allocation method. Instead of analyzing existing allocation methods, mechanism design begins from the premise that many different potential allocation methods exist, and identifies appropriate mechanisms from the set of possible mechanisms based on the specific goal and characteristics of the thing being allocated and the characteristics of the buyers and sellers. In addition, mechanism design focuses on the role played by incentives and private information in the allocation process. Clearly, both incentives and private information are important

17

in awarding the rights to host the mega sporting event. Potential hosts have incentives to award the rights to these events, although these incentives may not be the same. Potential host cities also have private information about their ability and willingness to pay for the rights to host a mega sporting event, and the NGO that holds the rights needs to devise a method to get potential hosts to disclose this information.

Hurwicz (1960) published the seminal paper in mechanism design theory. In this model, agents send messages to each other as part of a communication system that can be interpreted as a general allocation system. A predetermined rule assigns outcomes to every group of received messages. In Hurwicz's general setting many different types of allocation methods, including markets, institutions that operate like markets, and other alternative institutions can be compared, making this a useful framework.

We examine the process through which mega sporting events are awarded from the perspective of mechanism design theory. From this perspective, the sponsoring organization must design an allocation mechanism for awarding the rights to host a mega sporting event to one bidder. In very simple terms, upon which we expand below, the sponsoring organization can be thought of as a principal in the context of principal–agent theory; the principal must contract with one host among a set of potential hosts, who each have different characteristics, for example, willingness to pay, for hosting the mega event. These potential hosts can be thought of as the agents in this principal–agent paradigm; the key feature in terms of mechanism design is that each potential host's willingness to pay for the rights to host the event is private information that cannot be observed by the sponsoring organization. The sponsoring organization wants to award the rights to host the mega sporting event to the host that best matches the principal's objectives. For example, if rent extraction is important to the principal, or sponsoring organization, then the host with the highest willingness to pay should be allocated the event under an optimally designed allocation mechanism.

Several key features associated with the asset being allocated, the rights to host a mega sporting event, are different from those usually considered in the mechanism design literature. First, the sponsoring organizations *must* hold these events, so the asset must be awarded at the end of each bidding sequence. Second, the production associated with the allocation of the rights will take place in the future, and requires a significant amount of future construction of physical capital such as venues and infrastructure. Third, the output of this productive activity, the actual staging of a mega sporting event, involves a public goods aspect. The staging of a successful mega sporting event creates public goods in the form of infrastructure (for example, transit improvements or public sports facilities) that can be enjoyed by the host, but also in the form of prestige, fame, and international stature that can be enjoyed by *all parties* involved with the awarding of the rights to host mega sporting events. It is this latter form of public goods benefits that creates additional incentives for all participants that are not typically examined in mechanism design literature.

Mechanism design provides considerable insight into why the rights to host mega sporting events are awarded in the way they are. We illustrate the application of mechanism design theory to the awarding of the rights to host such events using the awarding of the rights to host the Olympic Games as a specific example. In the following sections, we describe the process through which the IOC awards the rights to host the Olympic Games, interpret this process in light of mechanism design principles, and discuss the implications of the mechanism designed by the IOC compared to alternative mechanisms.

Note that we do not explicitly examine the voting process that formally awards the rights to host the Games to one of the candidate cities. The vote to determine the host is a high-profile event that gets quite a bit of media attention. Feddersen et al. (2008) empirically analyzed the characteristics of winning bids in past votes. While this voting procedure is an important part of the process through which the rights to host the Games are awarded, we focus on the entire process from a mechanism design perspective, and not on individual components of the process.

2 HOW THE RIGHTS TO HOST OLYMPIC GAMES ARE AWARDED

The rights to host the Summer and Winter Olympic Games are awarded by the IOC. The awarding of the rights to host the Games is complex and time consuming. The goal of the process is to determine the best possible host for the Games, based on the objectives of the IOC and the set of potential host cities under consideration.

The procedure by which the rights to host the Olympic Games are awarded is laid out in the Olympic Charter, a set of rules and guidelines that specify how the Games will be allocated and conducted, and how the 'Olympic Movement' will be governed. The 'Olympic Movement' refers to the three types of organizations that govern, regulate, and control the Olympic Games: the IOC, the international organizations that govern individual sports such as FIFA, which are called the 'International Federations' (IFs) in the Olympic Charter, and the National Olympic Committees (NOCs) which regulate Olympic sports and the Games in each country. The IOC membership consists of 115 individuals. The composition of the IOC is specified in the Olympic Charter: 70 IOC members, the largest group, consist of individuals not linked to the NOCs or IFs, and not more than one of these members can come from any one country; 15 IOC members come from the leadership of the IFs or other sport oversight organizations; 15 IOC members come from the leadership of the NOCs, with a maximum of one per country; and finally, 15 IOC members are Olympic athletes elected during the Games. While the Olympic Movement has three constituent parts, the IOC is one of these parts and contains representation from two others, plus the athletes.

The Olympic Charter contains five chapters and 61 articles. The process for awarding the right to host the Olympic Games is defined by Chapter 5, Rule 34 ('Election of the host city'), which, with its by-laws, contains detailed information about the process of awarding the rights to host the Games. This section identifies the IOC as the sole authority for awarding these rights, specifies that potential host cities – called 'applicant cities' in the Olympic Charter – must submit detailed bids describing their plans, specifies that these bids are legally binding, and requires that the government of the applicant cities must guarantee that the bid will comply with the Olympic Charter. Rule 34 also requires that the election to determine the host city must take place in a country with no applicant cities in order to ensure that no pressure is put on the evaluation committee by the hosts of the election.

The Olympic Charter explicitly states that the IOC will not be responsible for the costs associated with hosting the Games ('The IOC shall have no financial responsibility whatsoever in respect of the organization and staging of the Olympic Games', Chapter 5, Rule 37.1) and makes both the NOC of the country hosting the Games and the Organizing Committee of the Olympic Games (OCOG) – the organization that actually produces the Games – jointly and severally responsible for all commitments to the IOC entered into as part of the bidding process. Joint and several liability is the most extensive liability scheme in most legal systems because it makes all parties responsible for all financial liabilities. Chapter 5 also specifies that any profits generated by a host city from the Games (called 'surplus' in the Charter) be 'applied to the development of the Olympic Movement' which implies that the IOC claims the rights to these profits.

The process of awarding the rights to host the Games takes two years from the identification of potential host cities to the actual awarding of the rights to a specific city. The rights to host the games are awarded seven years before the Games take place, so that the host has time to put the necessary facilities and infrastructure in place. The selection process involves[1] two phases, each lasting approximately one year. In Phase 1, prospective

OCOGs and the NOC from that country work together to develop a preliminary bid. In this phase, bidders are called 'applicant cities'. In Phase 2 the group of applicant cities are reduced to a smaller set of candidate cities who will be permitted to develop full bids to host the Games, make formal presentations, and be part of the final voting that determines the site of the Games. In Phase 1, applicant cities interact with the IOC Executive Board, which has the authority to design the process through which the group of applicant cities are reduced to the smaller set of candidate cities and to determine which applicant cities become candidate cities.

In the first phase all applicant cities are required to pay a US$150,000 non-refundable 'candidature acceptance fee' to the IOC and to respond to a detailed questionnaire that asks about all relevant aspects of the Games each applicant city intends to put on. Applicant cities must complete the questionnaire fully, and prepare an applicant file. The questionnaire elicits information on all relevant aspects of a proposed Games, including proposed dates, motivation for hosting the games ('What do you believe would be the long-term benefits for your city/region/country of: bidding for the Olympic Winter Games – irrespective of the outcome of the bid – and hosting the Olympic Winter Games'), the legal environment, public support for hosting the Games, experience hosting other international sporting events, an inventory of sports facilities, accommodation and transportation in the host city, and other factors. Most importantly, the questionnaire elicits detailed information about the financing of the proposed Games in order to assess willingness to pay. For example, the questionnaire contains the following section on financing:

CONTRIBUTIONS FROM PUBLIC AUTHORITIES

Please note that, in the candidature phase, it will be essential for you to obtain, *inter alia*, the following commitments from your public authorities as they are vital to the successful staging of the Olympic Games:

- A commitment to provide all security, medical, customs, immigration and other government-related services at no cost to the Organising Committee (OCOG);
- A commitment to make available all sport and non-sport venues owned by the public authorities to the OCOG either at no cost or at a rental cost to be preapproved by the IOC;
- A commitment to cover any shortfall in the OCOG budget;
- A commitment to undertake and finance the necessary infrastructure developments.

The financial questions clearly seek to identify applicant cities with the highest willingness to pay by the local and national government to host the games as well as the applicant cities with the highest-quality bid. The appropriate fiscal authorities in the host city and country must agree to pay all costs associated with hosting the Games, including cost overruns, as well as make security, medical, and other government provided services available at no cost. These services are costly to provide, so this represents a sizable subsidy to the IOC. In addition, local authorities must agree to build all necessary infrastructure and make all sports facilities available at no cost.

The IOC Executive Board designs the process through which applicant cities are evaluated, evaluates the questionnaires from each applicant city and supplements this information with audits by independent organizations and additional information about the proposed Games. The IOC Executive Board consists of the IOC president, the four IOC vice-presidents, and 10 additional members elected by the IOC. Vice-presidents and elected members serve a maximum of two four-year terms. Elections take place at IOC Sessions. The IOC Executive Board determines which of the applicant cities can move forward to the second phase and become candidate cities. Only the strongest applicant cities, presumably those with the highest willingness to pay for hosting the Games and highest-quality bids, move forward to the second phase, in which the potential host cities advancing to Phase 2 become candidate cities. Candidate cities develop full bids to host the Games in the second phase. In addition, each candidate city must pay the IOC a non-refundable US$500,000 fee in the second phase.

The IOC Executive Board performs additional screening during Phase 2, including evaluation visits to all candidate cities. Phase 2 lasts approximately one year. The bids prepared by the candidate cities are complete plans for hosting the Games, including binding commitments to build the proposed facilities and infrastructure and commitments to adhere to the Olympic Charter. The IOC calls the bids a 'candidature file' and completed files must be submitted to the IOC six months before the rights to host the Games are awarded. Candidature files are binding contracts to host the Games that include complete plans and financial guarantees from the relevant fiscal authorities in each country.

At the end of Phase 2, each candidate city makes a formal presentation of its bid to the IOC Session when it meets to award the rights to host the Games and make other decisions. The Session awards the rights through a voting procedure. The voting proceeds by rounds, and the candidate city receiving the fewest votes in each round is eliminated until one potential host, the winner, remains.

The IOC awarded the rights to host the 2014 Winter Games to Sochi, Russia in 2007. Phase 1 of this process began in July 2005, nine years before the Games will be held, when the NOCs of Russia (Sochi), South Korea (Pyeongchang), Austria (Salzburg), Spain (Jaca), Kazakhstan (Almaty), Bulgaria (Sofia), and Georgia (Borjomi) informed the IOC that they were putting forward applicant cities for the 2014 Games.The pool of applicant cities included a number of multiple bidders for the rights to host the Winter Games. Jaca, Spain was making its fourth consecutive bid; Sofia, Bulgaria bid in 1992 and 1994; Pyeongchang, Korea was making a second consecutive bid, as was Salzburg, Austria. The applicant files were submitted to the IOC in March 2006. The IOC examined the applicant files and solicited information from outside experts for four months, and in June 2006 the IOC Executive Board announced the candidate cities from the Phase 1 group of applicant cities.

From the group of seven applicant cities, three candidate cities were selected for Phase 2: Sochi, Pyeongchang and Salzburg. Phase 2 began in June 2006. Complete candidate files were submitted to the IOC in January 2007, and the rights to host the 2014 Winter Games were awarded to Sochi at the IOC Session held in Guatemala City, Guatemala on 4 July 2007. Salzburg was eliminated in the first round of voting and Sochi won on a vote of 51–47 in the second round.

In the bidding for the rights to host the 2018 Winter Olympics, only three applicant cities were put forward: Annecy, France, Pyeongchang, South Korea, for the third consecutive time, and Munich, Germany. The rights to host the 2018 Winter Games were awarded to Pyeongchang, South Korea in July 2011.

3 AWARDING THE RIGHTS TO HOST THE GAMES AND MECHANISM DESIGN

Clearly, the process through which the rights to host the Games are awarded can be viewed through the lens of mechanism design theory, since a mechanism is simply a set of rules by which agents, here prospective host nations, must interact. As alluded to above, the right to host the Olympic Games has several unique features not found in other standard mechanism design models focused on principal–agent interaction. First, the IOC must hold the Games every four years. The IOC does not have the option of not awarding the rights to hold the Games if no high-quality bids are made. This places a premium on attracting a pool of potential hosts that includes one or more cities that are likely to be able to successfully stage the Olympic Games.

Second, at the time the rights are awarded, the Games will not take place for seven years. Much of the production involved in hosting the Games will take place in the future. Hosting the Games requires a significant amount of capital investment in the form of the construction of venues, housing for athletes, officials, and the media, security, and additional infrastructure for transportation and communication. All venues must be of the highest quality and contain enough seating for the large number of spectators who typically attend the Games, which increases the infrastructure costs. All of this production will take place in the future, after the rights to host the Games are awarded; this enhances the information asymmetries between the IOC principal and the Executive Board middleman and the potential host cities. It also increases the costs associated with awarding the Games to a candidate city that cannot fulfill the promises made in the bid.

The Games have been awarded to a host city that reneged on the bid in recent memory. Denver, Colorado was awarded the rights to host the 1976 Winter Olympics in May 1970. After the terrorist attacks at the 1972 Games in Munich, the security costs associated with hosting the Games increased significantly. Following the tragedy in Munich, the estimated cost of hosting the 1976 Winter Games increased by 300 percent. In November 1972, a referendum on a $5 million bond issue in Colorado to finance the Games failed by a 3-to-2 margin, and on 15 November 1972 Denver withdrew as the host of the Games, just over four years before the Games were to be held. On 5 February 1973 the IOC decided to hold the 1976 Winter Games in Innsbruck, Austria, which had hosted the 1964 Winter Olympic Games. Given the extraordinary costs associated with hosting the Games, and the long time between when the rights to host the Games are awarded and the staging of the Games, and the potential problems created by a host city withdrawing, the principal must pay special attention to attracting a strong pool of potential host cities.

Finally, unlike many other mechanism design settings, the output produced at the end of the process, the Olympic Games, has an important non-market, public good component. The staging of a successful Olympic Games generates accolades in the form of prestige, international stature, fame, and other intangible factors that can be enjoyed by all participants but are not necessarily contractable. These accolades are part of the compensation that all agents associated with staging a successful Games receive, but the importance of these accolades differs across participants. Since these accolades can be enjoyed by all participants in the process, they are non-rivalrous in consumption in that the fact that the IOC enjoys these benefits does not preclude the OCOG and NOC from enjoying these benefits, and non-exclusive in that the IOC cannot stop other agents from enjoying these benefits. That is, these benefits have a public good aspect. The presence of public goods in the production of the Olympic Games generates incentives for the participants that differ significantly from those found in other mechanism design settings.

Also, note that one aspect of the output produced, the quality of the Olympic Games, has a stochastic component. For example, the terrorist attacks at the 1972 Munich Games were random events that significantly reduced the quality of the Games. We know also that the Winter Games are dependent on the weather: poor winter weather, like the conditions at the 2010 Winter Games in Vancouver, could lower the perceived quality of the Games.

In applying mechanism design theory to the awarding of the rights to host the Olympic Games, we posit that the IOC constitutes a hierarchical organization (see Figure 3.1, below). Mookherjee (2006) recently surveyed the application of mechanism design to hierarchical organizations. At the top of this hierarchy sits the IOC, or the Session which is simply a specific set of IOC members that convene to award the rights to host the Games, which can be viewed as a collective principal, or CP (Nielson and Tierney, 2003) in this context. There are many member countries that together constitute 'the principal'. This means that the possibly conflicting objectives of the members of the IOC Session are assumed to be aggregated into a single cohesive view in this analysis. The IOC is the mechanism designer, and determines the rules by which the rights to host the Olympic Games will be awarded to one of the cities that submit bids for these rights. The cities that submit bids for the rights to host the Games can be thought of as producing suppliers, or productive agents, in this context. Potential host cities are producing suppliers because they stage the Games and bear the costs of this activity. The IOC sells the rights to produce the output, so the rights themselves can be thought of as an input into the production of the Olympic Games. These potential host cities can be viewed as agents in the mechanism design process and are located at the bottom of this hierarchical structure.

In the middle of the hierarchy sits the IOC Executive Board. Its multi-person composition suggests that it can be viewed as a collective agent. Further, the IOC, the collective principal, has chosen to allow the IOC Executive Board to design rules by which the agents must interact. Thus, formally, we can view the IOC Executive Board as a delegated collective agent (DCA). We assume that this DCA acts as a single, cohesive entity. Clearly, this may not always be true as there is potential for strategic interaction within and between the collective principal (CP) and the DCA. One way this strategic interaction could be manifested is through instances of corruption on the IOC Executive Board, in the form of side-payments from productive agents to members of the DCA. We shall take up this theme again in a later section.

The awarding of the rights to host the Games contains two phases. Similarly, the IOC's mechanism design process contains strategic interaction at two distinct points. The first point involves strategic interaction between the CP and the DCA and involves elements of hidden action. We call this interaction the CP's game. The DCA undertakes unobservable effort in the evaluation and identification of a high-quality set of candidate cities. The second point involves strategic interaction between the DCA, acting as a principal when viewed from the perspective of the productive agents, and the prospective host cities. This interaction involves elements of both hidden action and hidden information. We call this interaction the DCA's game. Productive agents are endowed with characteristics that define their quality, which is hidden information, and undertake unobservable effort to generate presentations that define the host cities' visions, planned expenditure, and commitment for the Olympic Games.

Mookherjee (2006) points out that many models developed in the mechanism design literature have been developed to analyze this type of hierarchical structure. In one approach, centralization without supervision, the IOC would interact directly with all of the bidding cities when awarding the rights to host the Games. As a mechanism designer, the IOC clearly understands centralization without supervision, and how to design an appropriate mechanism under the conditions that characterize centralization without supervision. The IOC awards the rights to broadcast the Olympic Games through a sealed-bid, first-price auction. On 7 June 2011, the IOC collected sealed bids from three broadcasters, NBC, ESPN/ABC, and Fox Broadcasting, for the rights to broadcast either the next two or the next four Olympic Games. NBC won the rights with a bid of \$4.38 billion for the next four Games. In this setting, the principal decided to interact directly with the agents, the potential broadcasters of the Games, through a standard allocation mechanism. However, in our case, the awarding of the Olympic Games, the mechanism designer has decided to not use centralization without supervision to award the rights to host the Games. Instead, the IOC has designated a monitor, a DCA, in this case the IOC Executive Board, to interact with the group of bidding cities who want to host the Games. The middleman has been delegated authority by the principal to design an incentive mechanism by which the initial group of potential host cities, the applicant cities in the jargon of the Olympic Charter, will be evaluated and also decide which applicant cities move on to Phase 2 and become candidate cities.

An important characteristic of the DCA is that it is a subset of the IOC. This means that some of the diversity in objectives of the DCA, when compared to the CP objectives, is eliminated by picking members from the CP group. An alternative to a DCA composed of IOC members is a DCA made up of non-IOC members regarded as experts in picking prospective host cities.

The DCA, having been delegated authority by the principal, faces all the other agents as a principal, since the DCA designs the rules for the host selection process at Phase 1. Note that this is different from the multiple principal problem in a hierarchy (Dixit, 1996). With multiple principals, each principal writes a separate contract that affects, usually, a common agent. That is, the principals often write incentive contracts to affect different aspects of the agent's welfare. For example, a public utility regulator may specify a price for the agent's output, while an environmental regulator might specify an environmental standard for the agent (Baron, 1985). The principals are involved in a mechanism design game, their welfares are interdependent, and they jointly design the incentive mechanism for the agent, or agents. In the case of the awarding of the rights to host the Olympic Games, the principal determines the rules by which the DCA must act, who then contracts directly with the agents, so at the mechanism design stage, the CP and the DCA do not compete to design a joint mechanism for the agent so the principal does not write rules directly for the agents.

This connection between the CP and the DCA could contain a moral hazard problem. The DCA must exert effort in order to design a mechanism that attracts a pool of potential host cities with a high willingness to pay for hosting the Games and an ability to stage a high-quality event, and eliminates low willingness to pay and low ability to stage cities from the final group of candidate cities, and also exert effort to collect information about the potential host cities. As discussed above, part of the value of the Games is observable, but staging the Games also contains intangibles, or non-market values, that affect this value and are stochastic in nature. Therefore, to the extent that the principal has different objectives from the DCA, for example when the principal has different preferences from the DCA, there is a moral hazard problem in that the DCA may not put forth optimal effort that maximizes the principal's welfare. Clearly, the form the games take is very important, since strategic interaction takes place between the principal and the DCA. The groups of members that constitute the CP and the DCA are not homogeneous and the strategies they use could result in a dissipation of the rents generated by the Games compared to those received by a cohesive group, for example under centralization without supervision. Incentives need to be provided by the IOC to ensure that the DCA pursues a sorting strategy that will guarantee that a winning candidate city capable of making a high payment for hosting the Games and producing a high-quality value Games is among the set of candidate cities that makes it to Phase 2, given that information about the candidate cities' willingness to pay and ability to stage the event is not observable to the principal or to the DCA.

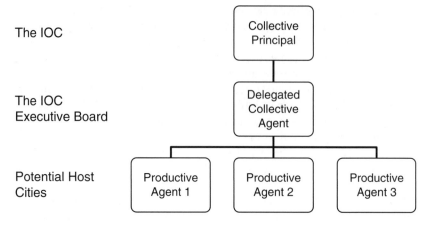

Figure 3.1   The mechanism design framework

Figure 3.1 shows the hierarchical structure and key components of the mechanism design process for awarding the rights to host the Olympic Games. At the top of the hierarchy sits the IOC, the CP that designs the mechanism, which includes the hierarchical structure itself and the incentive structure for the DCA. Below is the IOC Executive Board which plays no productive role in the staging of the Games but has been delegated the authority to interact with the potential host cities. At the bottom are the prospective host cities, which propose to engage in production by paying for and staging the Games.

4   A MODEL OF THE MECHANISM

Given the institutional context described above and the hierarchical structure of the IOC, we can begin to model the specifics of the mechanism. In this section, we describe a model of the process of awarding the rights to host the Olympic Games that reflects this mechanism. Again, the IOC is the designer of this mechanism, which would work as follows.

Nature endows each agent with a quality that determines the private value of the Games to each agent. This is referred to as the agent's type in mechanism design; an agent's type is private information and represents the maximum value of hosting the Games to the productive agent. In this model, we collapse all of the characteristics that define the quality and ability to host a mega event of the host city into a single parameter, the productive agent's type. Higher quality means a greater ability in provision of the Games and also a higher private value for hosting the Games and a higher willingness to pay. This value is realized only if the agent wins the competition to host the Games.

The competition among productive agents for the rights to host the Games is composed of two rounds, corresponding to Phase 1 and Phase 2 of the process described above. Yildirim (2005) models a similar mechanism containing multiple rounds. This competition is designed by the DCA. After effort is undertaken in Phase 1, each productive agent generates a presentation which is observable by all other agents. Effort is not observable and cannot be inferred because the presentation is subject to a random shock, capturing the effects of events beyond the agent's control on the presentation. The presentation represents a commitment on the part of the productive agent to build and pay for venues and provide other capital goods and services at no cost to the principal. At this stage, the DCA determines which productive agents will be allowed to proceed to the second competition, or Phase 2.

In the second competition, after observing the other productive agents' presentations, each remaining productive agent again invests in effort to produce a second presentation, in competition with the remaining productive agents. This presentation is also subject to a random shock, which again means that effort is unobservable. After the presentations are made, the CP chooses a winning presentation from among the candidate cities. This productive agent hosts the Olympic Games. The probability of winning the competition is modeled as a contest success function, similarly to how it is modeled in the sports economics contest theory literature (Szymanski, 2003). We assume that the contest success function can take a logit form in which the probability of winning is a function of the presentations of all the agents in both periods which are themselves a function of cumulative effort and the two random shocks.

Objectives of the Productive Agents

The process of determining a host city is accomplished, in part, by the DCA, the IOC Executive Board and, in part, by the CP, the IOC. The CP has determined that there should be two phases to the selection process and has delegated authority to a collective agent to determine the details of the two phases of the selection process. This DCA determines which agents will proceed from Phase 1 through to Phase 2 of the competition.

In Phase 1, we have seen from the discussion above that the rules designed by the DCA are the same for each agent; there are no agent-specific rules, which are often used for sorting purposes in other settings. The rules require the agents to undertake a variety of tasks each requiring effort in addition to paying a fixed fee. In essence, the DCA imposes both lump-sum costs, in the form of a fee, and variable costs related to effort, on the productive agents. This also occurs in Phase 2, where the lump-sum cost is larger than in Phase 1. Thus, the payoff for the agent involves the expected value of hosting the Games, which is the probability of winning times the agent's type less the payment of two fixed payments, one at each phase of competition, less the costs of effort in each of the two phases. Of course, this is an expected payoff because of the presence of the two random shocks, one in each phase of competition.

Objectives of the DCA

The DCA is interested in choosing two fixed payments to be imposed on the productive agents submitting presentations in both Phase 1 and Phase 2. In order to optimally choose these lump-sum payments, the DCA anticipates the actions of the productive agents, so it would face issues of both hidden action, in the form of effort expended, and hidden information, in the form of the productive agent's type, at this stage. Note that we impose some of the characteristics of the mechanism by suggesting that the DCA is choosing two fixed payments. Of course, we want these payments to be chosen optimally, but we have restricted the mechanism to this form of payment. Ideally, we would like to determine whether this type of payment scheme is optimal, or even whether two rounds of competition are optimal, but for the moment, we simply describe how we might model this particular mechanism.

We assume that the DCA is less interested in monetary payment and more interested in 'accolades' as in Dewatripont and Tirole (1996). Accolades arise as a result of a successful provision of the Games, so they depend on which productive agent is chosen, which in turn depends on the presentation of the productive agent. As mentioned above, all of the claims made in the presentation, which ultimately generate the highest ranking for the presentation, become legally binding. The actual value of the Games is determined by the value contained in the presentation and by a random shock, which arises due to bad weather taking place during the Games, or something like a terrorist attack that is outside the control of the host city. The distribution of this random event is conditional on the effort level of the DCA who can force productive agents to put in place contingency plans to mitigate the negative impact of an adverse random shock on the value of the Games.

The DCA does not wish to share accolades that accrue from the Games. Thus, in taking costly effort, the DCA will choose two fixed costs for the productive agents to ensure that a successful Games generates maximum accolades. Ideally, the DCA would like to consume all of the accolades alone, but the CP also may be interested in this non-market return, and accolades have a public good component that makes them non-rivalrous and non-excludable.

Objectives of the CP

Once the CP chooses a winning productive agent to be the host city, the winning presentation specifies the value of the Games to the players as long as nothing goes wrong during the period when the venues and other capital are put in place and during the hosting of the Games. The CP is interested in maximizing the expected value of the Games, since a successful Games means that it can charge third parties a lot for the television rights, for example. The CP is also interested in accolades and can determine whether or not the DCA receives exclusive or shared benefits. Since there is also a downside risk, generated by the random component, the CP can screen the DCA from adverse publicity. Thus, the CP can induce effort on the part of the DCA by sharing or not sharing the publicity benefits accruing from the Games. This effort level influences the distribution of the random shock that determines the expected value of the Games, or the expected value of the winning presentation.

Characteristics of the CP's Game

The game designed by the CP is played between the CP and the DCA. The CP's game is the first stage of the mechanism design process. The CP moves first, designing the rules of the allocation process. It goes to the end of the game to see how the productive agents will respond to the mechanism designed by the DCA. The principal moves first and solves the moral hazard problem in that the effort level of the DCA is not continuously observable and this effort affects the distribution of the random component of the value of hosting the Games and the effort of the productive agents.

Characteristics of the DCA's Game

The DCA's game is designed by the DCA and played between the productive agents and the DCA. In this game, the DCA faces both hidden information, in the form of the type of the productive agents, and hidden action, in the form of the unobservable effort undertaken by each productive agent. Clearly, there are elements of double moral hazard here as the effort level of the DCA affects the welfare of the agents as well. The agents want the DCA to set tasks that will ensure a high-quality Games, but of course, this is costly for both sides, the DCA and the agents.

The DCA's game involves two stages, Phase 1 and Phase 2, which implies that not all private information is revealed in the first stage. The DCA solves the adverse selection problem, designing a mechanism that gets the productive agents to self-select into two groups, thereby revealing their types, but only imperfectly. However, this sorting does not take the typical format found in the mechanism design literature. Offering type contingent contracts represents one way to solve the adverse selection problem. For example, agents may be offered a menu of contracts consisting of different combinations of premiums and deductibles, or combinations of fixed and variable charges. The agents select the optimum combination given their unobservable type, revealing the private information. In this case, the DCA offers the same rules to all productive agents, and sorts based only on the participation constraint using two groups: productive agents who can pay enough to host a high-quality mega event and productive agents who cannot.

Note that in this game, the number and type of the participating productive agents affects the amount of rent that can be extracted from the winning productive agent. In Phase 1, there could be both high- and low-quality type productive agents in the pool. The presence of low-quality type productive agents can provide an incentive for high-quality agents to bid less than their willingness to pay, since they would only have to bid slightly more than any competing low-quality type agent to advance to Phase 2. By reducing the potential hosts to only high-quality type productive agents in Phase 2, and allowing changes to the bids in Phase 2, the IOC increases the amount of rent that can be extracted from the winning host city. If all the candidate cities in Phase 2 are high-quality type productive agents, and know that they are competing against only other high-quality type productive agents, then they will have an incentive to revise their bid up to their willingness to pay in Phase 2 if their Phase 1 bid was less than their willingness to pay.

Why not use a sealed-bid first-price auction to award the rights to host the Games? It is possible that a low-quality type productive agent could bid and win the rights to host the Games if the IOC did not carefully screen potential host cities. Clearly, if this happened, it would be a nightmare scenario for the IOC to then have to deny the awarding of the Games to the highest bidder in the competition. A sealed-bid first-price auction, or any other common auction method, might not permit the IOC to learn enough about productive agent types to distinguish between types. The fact that the rights to host the Games are awarded long before the Games are held, and staging requires the construction of a significant amount of expensive physical capital, enhanced the importance of correctly distinguishing among types in this process. After awarding the rights to host the

Games, the winning productive agent's true type is only revealed after the venue construction process nears completion. The time required to build venues combined with the requirement that the Games must be held raises the possibility that awarding the Games to a low-quality type productive agent might only be revealed shortly before the Games, precluding a change in venue. The resulting low-quality Games would lead to a significant reduction in the 'accolades' generated by the current Games and also a long-run decline in the revenues generated by the sale of the rights to broadcast future Games, further damaging the IOC.

5   CONCLUSIONS

Analyzing the process through which the IOC awards the rights to host the Olympic Games using mechanism design theory provides insight into the process, and the effects of the process on agents. It also emphasizes the problems faced by the IOC when allocating the rights to host the Games. The games that make up the IOC's mechanism involve both hidden information, in terms of the type of the productive agents, and hidden action, in terms of the effort undertaken by the DCA in the CP's game and by the productive agents in the DCA's game. In addition to the fact that the productive agent's types are unobservable to the IOC, making rent extraction difficult without a properly designed mechanism, the IOC also must award the rights to host the Games every four years, and also must select a host city that is able to deliver the Games proposed in the bid on schedule and as promised seven years in the future. These factors are not commonly faced by other mechanism designers, and cause the IOC to design a mechanism that involves a DCA, the IOC Executive Board, in the process and involved multiple rounds of screening.

Under the current system, the rights to host the Games are awarded to a different city every four years. This requires a new city to undertake extensive construction of facilities for the events and housing for the participants every four years. Many of the venues used in the Olympic Games are much too large for the domestic competitions that will take place in them after the Games have been completed. For example, in Athens, many of the venues constructed for the 2004 Summer Games sit unused, because Greeks have little interest in the sport the venue was designed for, or have crowds that are a fraction of their capacity. The construction of a new set of venues every four years represents a large repeated public outlay for a number of host countries. Why doesn't the IOC grant the rights to host the Games to a permanent location, eliminating the need to build large Olympic venues in multiple locations? As the mechanism design approach makes clear, awarding the rights to host the Games to a permanent location would significantly reduce the prestige generated by staging the Games, and would also change the relationships on the IOC. The NOC of the permanent host country would gain a great deal of power in the IOC, as the control of the venues and the staging of the games would be primarily controlled by the permanent host NOC, not the IOC. This would likely reduce both the revenues earned by the IOC and its prestige as an international organization. While individual host cities and countries would be spared the costs of multiple-bid preparation and the construction costs associated with hosting the Games, the IOC would not benefit from such an arrangement, and would likely be made worse off. It is unlikely that the IOC would willingly agree to an alternative arrangement under which the Games were permanently hosted at one location.

The mechanism designed by the IOC encourages maximum effort on the part of all productive agents who choose to participate (Yildirim, 2005). Maximum effort requires that the participants put significant resources into the preparation of the bids. Preparing a bid to host the Olympic Games can cost millions of dollars, and some potential host countries bid for the rights to host multiple Games. Also, IOC rules on bidding forces participants to obtain legally binding promises to fund the construction of the most lavish facilities possible from the host country's government. The IOC needs to have a large, high-quality pool of productive agents in order to induce each agent to bid an amount equal to the willingness to pay to host the Games. The losers and the winner all expend maximum effort; the resources used to prepare the losing bids results in welfare losses in losing countries, since the resources expended on bid preparation could have been used for other purposes. In addition, potential hosts know that other competitors for the rights to host the Games have an incentive to bid their willingness to pay, which will lead them to promise to provide the maximum possible package of venues and other services possible. If the promised bid package required to win the contest exceeds the minimum required expenditure to host the Games, residents of winning countries could also experience a loss of welfare, since the additional resources required for a winning bid above those required to simply stage the Games could be used for other purposes.

The mechanism also involves two sets of 'collective' players, the CP and the DCA. Nielson and Tierney (2003) have argued that the existence of a CP creates the possibility of strategic behavior between any coalition of principals and, in their case, a single agent. To the extent that preference aggregation is difficult, the agent gains strategic influence. If preferences among the principals are non-homogeneous, the agent again gains strategic influence. The agent may be able to use coalitions of principals to further its agenda. Of course, one could surmise that these same types of strategic interaction problems arise in the case of a collective agent, or, as in our case, a DCA. It is not clear a priori if efficiency is enhanced when a CP creates a DCA. Certainly, there appears to be scope for more strategic interactions among these two groups, but it may be countervailing strategic interaction, playing one group off against another and thereby neutralizing some of the negative effects. This would suggest that the IOC mechanism is optimal, but this remains an open question.

While the mechanism design process described here applies to the awarding of the rights to host the Olympic Games, it can also be applied to the rights to host other mega sporting events. The awarding of the rights to host other such events such as the FIFA World Cup, or the UEFA European Football Championships also involves significant outlay, in the form of new stadium construction, the construction of new or upgraded transportation systems, the construction of new hotels, and other physical capital and infrastructure. These processes involve bids made by prospective host cities or regions that have different unobservable private willingness to pay to host these events. And the rights to host these events are awarded in advance of the actual contests. Since the awarding of the rights to host the Olympic Games also includes similar features, the NGOs who control the rights to host these events face a similar mechanism design problem as the IOC, and this mechanism design model can be applied to the process by which these other rights are awarded.

NOTE

1. If a country has more than one city interested in hosting the Games, there is an earlier phase in which the NOC decides among the competing cities in its country which one will represent the country in the international bidding before the IOC. Thus, in the United States, where there are typically several cities interested in hosting the Summer Games, the entire bidding process for a would-be host city will take more than the nine years implied in the discussion in the text.

REFERENCES

Baron, D. (1985), 'Noncooperative regulation of a nonlocalized externality', *Rand Journal of Economics*, **16**, 553–68.
Dewatripont, M. and J. Tirole (1996), 'Biased principals as a discipline device', *Japan and the World Economy*, **8**, 195–206.
Dixit, A. (1996), *The Making of Economic Policy: A Transaction Cost Perspective*, Cambridge, MA: MIT Press.
Feddersen, A., W. Maennig and P. Zimmermann (2008), 'The empirics of key factors in the success of bids for Olympic games', *Revue d'Économie Politique*, **118**, 171–87.

Hurwicz, L. (1960), 'Optimality and informational efficiency in resource allocation processes', in K.J. Arrow, S. Karlin and P. Suppes (eds), *Mathematical Methods in the Social Sciences*, Stanford, CA: Stanford University Press, pp. 27–46.

Mookherjee, D. (2006), 'Decentralization, hierarchies, and incentives: a mechanism design perspective', *Journal of Economic Literature*, **54**, 367–90.

Nielson, L. and M. Tierney (2003), 'Delegation to international organizations: agency theory and World Bank environmental reform', *International Organization*, **57**, 241–76.

Szymanski, S. (2003), 'The economic design of sporting contests', *Journal of Economic Literature*, **41**, 1137–87.

Yildirim, H. (2005), 'Contests with multiple rounds', *Games and Economic Behavior*, **51**, 213–27.

4 The winner's curse: why is the cost of mega sporting events so often underestimated?
Wladimir Andreff

1 INTRODUCTION

Grenoble taxpayers were not very happy to pay local taxes until 1992 in order to cover the financial deficit from the 1968 Winter Games! The 1976 Summer Olympics in Montreal outperformed the Grenoble Winter Olympics in terms of deficit: the latter was so large that Montreal tax-payers were repaying the debt until 2006, a period of 30 years. After Montreal's financial mess, the number of candidate cities wishing to host such mega sporting events dropped, and since the 1984 Games in Los Angeles the watchword of local Olympics organizing committees (LOOCs) and the International Olympic Committee (IOC) became 'the Games will pay for the Games'. This was incentive enough to trigger an increase in the number of candidates to host the Olympics but not enough to cure the financial deficit disease. After having claimed for seven years that the Games would pay for the Games, the 1992 Winter Olympics in Albertville resulted in a $60 million deficit.[1] Were those three exceptions proving the rule that mega sporting events are usually organized at a reasonable and correctly anticipated cost? Unfortunately not.

In the same vein, when the 2012 Summer Games was awarded to London in July 2005, the expected and advertised cost was about £2.4 billion. By the end of 2008, the cost estimates ranged from £9.4 billion to £12 billion. Some press articles have suggested that the promoters of the London candidature had deliberately underestimated the Olympics bill in order to be awarded the Games. In particular, the London candi-dature file had intentionally underestimated the overall cost in neglecting to account for the VAT, the Paralympics budget and a part of security expenditure. London 2012 promoters of course were neither talking about nor expecting the creation of a new fund in 2008 to cover the rising cost of the Games. There is an impression that having won a harsh struggle in bidding primarily over Paris 2012, London, its authorities, inhabitants and taxpayers are now cursed despite a study based on a contingent valu-ation method which found a positive willingness to pay for hosting the

Olympics by non-London residents – located in the Bath region (Walton et al., 2008). As to the 2014 Sochi Winter Olympics, the city was awarded the Games in June 2007, with an estimated $8.5 billion budget. Since then the budget has skyrocketed. By August 2010, it had already reached $33 billion – a more than threefold increase within three years, with an amount that is larger than the reported cumulative cost of the Winter Olympics in Nagano 1998, in Salt Lake City 2002 and in Turin 2006.

These facts give rise to three long-standing questions to those cities (countries) that apply to host mega sporting events. Why are the actual *ex post* costs of hosting an event predictably much larger than the *ex ante* estimated and expected costs? Consequently, why do the promising prospects exhibited in an economic impact study or a cost–benefit analysis during the candidature usually vanish before the opening ceremony? And thus, why is the initial euphoria of an Olympics (or other mega sporting event) bid followed up with a post-bid curse, post-Olympics disillusion and a substantial bill for the taxpayers of the host city?

Politicians – city mayors, sports ministers, presidents of the Republic, and so on – respond to these questions by making a *tabula rasa* of the past: previous mega sporting events may have shown unexpected extra costs but our candidature is based on a sound economic evaluation and will not be disappointing in any respect. The success story is to come. Most economists are much more sceptical and criticize analytical flaws and methodological tricks that are usually found in economic impact studies and cost–benefit analyses of sporting events. But no one asks why such tricks and flaws are repeatedly reproduced after so many years of published academic criticism. Our contention is that *ex ante* benefit overestimation and more basically cost underestimation are deeply rooted in auctioning the allocation of mega sporting events which so often evolves into a so-called 'winner's curse' – or the misfortune of winning a bidding war. The focus here is on the Summer and Winter Olympics, but the background idea is that the same analysis must be relevant for many mega sporting events which are allocated through an auction as soon as the number of bidders exceeds one, such as FIFA's Soccer World Cup,[2] the Rugby World Cup or UEFA's European football championship (Euro). The hypothesis of a winner's curse has not yet been examined in such a context, though it is sometimes referred to (Leeds and von Allmen, 2002) or further analysed (Swindell and Rosentraub, 2002) with regard to cities bidding to host professional team franchises in North American team sports leagues.

With a view to validating the winner's curse assumption, the chapter starts with a brief overview of the candidature puzzle (Section 2). Then three analytical variants of the winner's curse are presented (Section 3) in order to adopt the one which best fits with the Olympics' centralized monopolist allocation process based on auctioning in a context of asymmetrical information (Section 4). From this pioneering analysis are derived a few indicators that can detect a winner's curse, with emphasis on its major expected outcomes (Section 5). Finally, a preliminary attempt to verify the winner's curse hypothesis with such indices is undertaken for the Summer Olympics from 1972 to 2012 and the Winter Olympics from 1980 to 2014 (Section 6). The conclusion (Section 7) recommends a halt in bidding for the Games, an alternative being to fix an Olympics site once and for all.

2 BIDDING FOR MEGA SPORTING EVENTS: THE CANDIDATURE JIGSAW PUZZLE

The cradle of the winner's curse, if any, lies in bidding to obtain the Olympics, which means that the roots of the curse emerge during a precise time span. First, it must be identified. Let us define the overall sequencing of an Olympiad as follows. In $t - 3$, a city considers the opportunity to participate in bidding for the next Olympics. In $t - 2$, it starts preparing and promoting its candidature in order to have its application ready in due time for the bid (the IOC votes). In $t - 1$, the IOC votes determine the winner which will host the Games. Let us date t the day of the Olympics opening ceremony and $t + 1$ the day of the closing ceremony. Further, assume a post-Olympics economic recession, following growth between $t - 1$ and $t + 1$, occurs up to a date $t + 2$. Let us fix $t + 3$ as the date when all economic and social effects of the Games conclude – taxpayers have finished repaying the debt if any, residents have benefited from sporting and non-sporting infrastructures built up for the Games as well as from positive intangible effects such as feel-good, image and reputation satisfactions. Therefore: $t - 3$ to $t - 2$ is a *preparation* stage for a city's candidature; a simplifying assumption is adopted, that is, this stage does not involve any cost even though some preliminary study may be achieved.

$t - 2$ to $t - 1$ is a *candidature* stage; *ex ante* potential or expected costs are assessed and eventually described in the city's application file submitted first to the country's OC (Olympic Committee) and then to the IOC in $t - 1$. This stage usually lasts six to seven years. It is the stage during which the winner's curse emerges, if any, in the form of an *ex ante* underestimated potential cost c_{t-1}. A bidding city usually commands and finances at least one *ex ante* study regarding the economic impact of hosting the Olympics. Since the cost of such a study is small[3] compared to the expected overall cost of organization, sporting and non-sporting infrastructural investments contained in c_{t-1}, it is neglected in the analysis below.

$t - 1$ to t is an *investment* stage both in organization and (sporting and non-sporting) construction. During this stage the real cost of hosting the Games materializes into an *ex post* actual cost in t, that is C_t, which may or may not differ, from c_{t-1}. Both *ex ante* expected and *ex post* actual costs arc to bc takcn into account when it comes to identifying a possible winner's curse.

t to $t + 1$ is a Games *unfolding* stage which reaches a peak in direct tangible revenues accruing to the LOOC and also a peak of the Olympics economic boom, including sometimes some unexpected last-minute extra costs.

$t + 1$ to $t + 2$ is the time span of the post-Olympics *recession* when local economic activity is slowing down for some months up to one year or so, despite the possibility of modest post-Olympics revenues and intangible social costs and benefits.

$t + 2$ to $t + 3$ is a longer period of time along which all medium- and long-term tangible (paying the debt, using and maintaining sporting and non-sporting facilities) and intangible (local population satisfaction, improved image of the host city, better social cohesion, various social costs and benefits) effects come to an end.[4]

If any supplementary information happens to be published about *ex post* costs after t, it must be picked up for the assessment of a possible winner's curse.

Nearly all bidding cities hire a consulting company or research centre to carry out an *ex ante* economic impact study or an *ex ante* cost–benefit analysis, usually a contingent valuation at this stage. The projected costs and revenues from the Games are a requisite part of the application file remitted to the IOC. A glance at the existing literature shows that *ex post* economic impact and cost–benefit analyses are substantially fewer than *ex ante* studies. Host cities generally do not commission an *ex post* evaluation of the actual costs, revenues and benefits that could reveal too many differences between initial costs and benefits and the *ex post* reality. Thus, the few existing *ex post* studies are mainly due to academic research, for which there is a good reason. When there are both *ex ante* and *ex post* studies for the same mega sporting event, the latter exhibit a disappointing economic outcome. One of the rare events for which one can compare an *ex ante* economic impact study commissioned by the OC (ESSEC, 2007) with an *ex post* economic impact study and cost–benefit analysis with a rigorous methodology (Barget and Gouguet, 2010) is the 2007 Rugby World Cup in France. The results are:

- *Ex ante* economic impact: €8 billion.
- *Ex post* economic impact: €539 million.

- *Ex post* net social benefit (social benefits minus social costs): €113 million.

The aim here is not to discuss the analytical flaws and methodological tricks of economic impact studies and cost–benefit analyses. Most economists do not trust the former and prefer the latter though with some reservations (Crompton, 1995; Porter, 1999; Baade and Matheson, 2001; Hudson, 2001; Johnson et al., 2001; Kesenne, 2005; Walker and Mondello, 2007; Matheson, 2009; Barget and Gouguet, 2010). They raise serious doubts about the excessively optimistic estimates of the *ex ante* studies. Scepticism is widespread among academic economists who generally adopt more rigorous methods to moderate the anticipated net benefits exhibited in studies that will be utilized by bidding cities for the purpose of announcing and promoting their candidature. However, no economist has yet analysed why such overestimation of the positive economic impact of mega sporting events, including their *ex ante* cost underestimation, is so systematically reproduced from one bidding city to the other, and from one Olympiad to the next. This is due to a missing relationship that economists have not yet established between economic impact studies underestimating the costs and overestimating the benefits, on the one hand, and the need for a city to outbid other bidding cities, on the other, that is, to show *ex ante* the biggest expected economic impact or net social benefit, and then to be plagued with a winner's curse.

Moreover, the sceptical assessments of professional economists remain unheeded, or even unheard, by decision makers and city authorities who repeatedly commission *ex ante* economic impact studies, in particular between $t - 2$ and $t - 1$. All city mayors and candidature promoters of bidding cities are eager to obtain a study that will show a positive economic impact derived from hosting the targeted sports events, and are ready to pay a significant amount of money (to a prestigious consultant) to get such a conclusion. Recognizing this, consulting companies obligingly deliver impact studies which exaggerate positive economic spillover, since providing a conclusion that predicts a significant economic impact is a precondition for future selection as a consultant by other cities or countries applying to be potential hosts for some sports event.

Thus, when focusing on methodological weaknesses of economic impact studies, most economists touch a really sensitive issue. However, they do not perceive that methodological shortcomings are deliberate, to support and embellish the application file of a bidding city. Cost underestimation and benefit overestimation are embedded in the process of bidding for the Olympics, and this guarantees that *ex ante* expected costs will be higher than *ex post* actual costs (and anticipated benefits higher than the real ones). In some sense, wrong (that is, overestimating) economic impact studies are a launching pad for the winner's curse. This is why comparing costs publicized during or at the end of the candidature stage with actual organization and investment costs at the end of the investment stage or later, is crucial to check the very existence of a winner's curse and, by the same token, the fallacy of nearly all *ex ante* economic impact studies delivered to cities bidding for a sports event.

Are *ex ante* impact studies and cost–benefit analyses really needed or useful, a relevant question correctly raised by Baade, Kesenne, Matheson and others? One may have some doubts since the result is known in advance: an underestimated initial cost of hosting the sports event and, consequently, a cost overrun resulting in an extra cost to be paid by taxpayers whatever their willingness to pay that was indicated *ex ante*. Our point here is not to assess the accuracy of *ex ante* studies. Nevertheless, if they had sometimes forecast *ex ante* negative or nil economic impact then we would not have suspected them to be so involved in the generation of a winner's curse.

Three final dimensions of the candidature puzzle must be mentioned. First, it is difficult to explain with standard econometric models what are the determinants of bidding success for the Olympic Games. Feddersen et al. (2008)[5] have attempted to do this for Summer Games between 1992 and 2012 with a model comprising 17 variables that should be considered before the IOC votes – the distance of sporting venues from the Olympic village, local weather and unemployment being the most significant variables. The outcome is interesting and, at first sight, surprising. The model correctly predicts the IOC decision for 100 per cent of failed bids. In contrast, it correctly explains only 50 per cent of successful bids. Feddersen et al. include no variable that represents the cost of the Games as publicized by bidding cities. Excluding cost from the model is probably a good econometric choice since cost must not be a priority variable in IOC votes. However, if cost is ignored as an IOC decision criterion, the probability that a successful bidder will be cursed and pay the price for that during the investment stage of the Olympiad is extremely high.

Second, it is not always the least expensive Olympics project that is voted for by IOC members. For instance, Chappelet and Kübler-Mabbott (2008) found that on several occasions IOC votes came as a complete surprise since it was not the best-quality candidature file that had been selected; they identify the 1996 and 2012 Summer Olympics and the 1998, 2006 and 2014 Winter Olympics.[6] Does this mean that IOC voters do not care about the cost of the Games, while bidding cities are very much concerned about it? If so, a winner's curse may be rooted in such an attitude asymmetry.

Table 4.1   Ex ante *cost: comparison between cities bidding for the Summer Olympics ($m)*

Announced Costs 2012	New York	London	Madrid	Paris	Moscow
Overall	10.68	18.25	3.64	8.87	11.86
Investment	7.59	15.79	1.64	6.21	10.07
Operation	3.09	2.46	2.00	2.66	1.79

Announced Costs 2016	Chicago	Tokyo	Madrid	Rio de Janeiro
Overall	3.30	4.07	4.18	9.53
Investment	2.60	2.11	2.35	7.60
Operation	0.70	1.96	1.83	1.93

Sources: Bidding committees.

A third dimension of the candidature puzzle is in line with the previous argument. Very often the bidding city with the highest organization and/or investment cost is eventually successful. Table 4.1 reinforces this assumption with the 2012 and 2016 Summer Olympics. Both London and Rio de Janeiro exhibited the highest investment and overall costs in their bids.

3   THREE VARIANTS OF THE WINNER'S CURSE

According to those sports economists who explicitly refer to the winner's curse, it is defined as 'the tendency of a winning bid to be in excess of the real value of the asset sold in the auction' (Sandy et al., 2004, p. 309) or, in other words, 'since the most optimistic among the potential bidders makes the winning bid, there is a good chance that the actual revenues . . . will be less than that bidder anticipated' (ibid., p. 131). Note that here the winner's curse is merely understood as the result of bidders' behaviour, it is comprehended only as a demand-side triggered mechanism. No specific mention is made of the supply side except that it is a monopoly, like the IOC or FIFA for instance. Leeds and von Allmen (2002, p. 160) comment: 'Economists call this paradox – in which the "winning" city is actually worse off than it would have been had it lost the bid – the winner's curse'. One implication from these definitions is that, on the demand side for an auctioned asset, there must be more than one bidder for the winner's curse to emerge.

Sports economists have placed less emphasis on the supply-side aspect: is there any specific strategy and, derived from it, issues of monopolist organizations such as the IOC, FIFA, UEFA, and so on, that could influence the auction in such a way as to result in a winner's curse? One objective of this chapter is to answer this question as well. Combining the demand- and supply-side dimensions gives rise to analytical problems such as bilateral monopoly,[7] or moral hazard and adverse selection issues in a relationship between one monopoly and several bidders; such issues are related to information asymmetry in principal–agent theory. Since usually more than one city is bidding for the next Olympics, the latter framework is the most relevant given that the IOC is, to some extent, a centralized and private bureaucracy at a global level. Although there are strong rivalries across its members (decision makers, voters), the IOC is not operating, properly speaking, on a competitive supply-side market for the Olympics. It does not sell its exclusive sports event in a genuine market where a fully-fledged market mechanism determines an equilibrium price.

From the very beginning, the winner's curse had been imported into sports economics from auction theory where it was first recognized in 1971 in Western economics literature. In fact, the winner's curse was well known even earlier in centrally planned economies (CPEs) because it was inherent in centralized allocation of inputs and state finance.

The Winner's Curse: 'You Have Won the Bid and Will Lose Money'

The winner's curse hypothesis was first advanced by Capen et al. (1971) to explain the low returns on investments to companies engaged in competitive bidding for oil and gas leases. The impression was that winning bidders had paid too high a price for oil and gas leases (Gilley et al., 1986); they had been cursed. In other words, they had paid an auction price higher than any likely market price and had undertaken too high a cost to be recouped by the revenues of their investment in oil and gas exploitation. Similarly, Gilberto and Varaiya (1989) have provided evidence of a winner's curse to explain large takeover premiums in auctions for failed banks, in sharp contrast to the orthodox view endorsed by the mainstream finance literature.

In all such circumstances, it was noted that in any auction-type setting, where the value of the auctioned object is uncertain but will turn out to be the same for all bidders, the party that overestimates the value of the object is likely to outbid its competitors and win the contest. The items won, however, are more often than not those whose value has been overestimated. Auction winners who fail to recognize this possibility are likely to be cursed by having paid more for an item than its true value. Thus, there is adverse selection in this outcome. The bidding process results in winning bids that produce below-normal or even negative returns, contrary to the theory of rational investment decision. Thaler (1994) stresses the asymmetric information across bidders, which leads to an extreme form of the winner's curse in which any positive bid yields an expected financial loss to the bidder. An increase in the number of other bidders implies that to win the auction, the bid must be more aggressive. Yet the presence of more bidders also increases the chance that the winner will have overestimated the value of the object for sale – suggesting that the bid should be less aggressive.

A parallel can be drawn here with allocation of the Olympics through an auction bid. The IOC, when calling for bids from cities and fixing a deadline for the submission of candidature files, is in a situation that compares with a state or a region calling for bids from companies for oil and gas leases. No one a priori knows the real market value of being selected as the next Olympics host city, not even the IOC. What the IOC looks for is to find a city eager to host the Games and organize them in the best way (that is, the *ex ante* supposedly best project). Thus, the IOC is interested in eliciting aggressive bidding to get the 'best' project because it will benefit from the resulting winner's curse. Bidding cities are exactly in the position that Thaler identifies: if they want to have a chance to host the Games, they must outbid other bidders until the date[8] of allocation (IOC members' vote). Assuming that the IOC chooses the best project from an economic point of view,[9] the winning city is cursed since it has promised to invest and pay excessively to host the Olympics, while the IOC gets a grandiose project for which it will not pay the full price. It appears, first, that the supply side also matters in the analysis of the winner's curse and, second, that adverse selection is likely to allocate the Games to the city proposing the most expensive project. The more a bidding city has underestimated the announced costs for hosting the Olympics, the more the winner's curse will materialize in *ex post* extra costs, and a possible financial deficit, and the more the IOC will enjoy the benefit of a magnificent project without paying its full cost.

Being Cursed on Financial and Second-Hand Markets

Forty years after the article by Capen et al. (1971) the literature about the winner's curse has grown for a very simple reason: the concept has found many applications in financial markets which now comprise the great bulk of the winner's curse literature (Kagel and Levin, 2002). In particular, it is utilized to explain the share value underestimation in initial public offerings (IPOs) and the positive initial returns earned by investors on new issued equities (Rock, 1986; Levis, 1990). Although it is a widespread phenomenon, it has been under the spotlight during IPOs' privatization on new tiny stock exchanges in post-communist transition economies (Andreff, 2000, 2003). Overbidding is also present in different auction mechanisms such as sealed-bid auctions, English auctions, first-price auctions with insider information, blind-bid auctions, and bilateral bargaining games (the last would apply to Olympics bids only if there is one single candidature). Furthermore, one finds sophisticated models and many technicalities that would not easily transfer to analysing city bids for hosting the Olympics.

The winner's curse issue has also been found in second-hand markets, primarily on the market for 'lemons' where the true value of a second-hand car is uncertain and unknown to the purchasers (bidders) while hidden by the seller. Akerlof (1970) has demonstrated that with such information asymmetry the market will lead to adverse selection and the winning purchaser will be cursed. There is even an application of the winner's curse concept in sports labour markets wherein veterans sell their services on the talent market. Cassing and Douglas (1980) have argued that with free agency teams will tend to acquire a biased set of players, those for whom the bidder has overpaid. Because of information asymmetries and uncertainty, bids by potential team owners will not always mirror the true worth of a player, but the team that values correctly has a poor chance of signing a player compared to a team that overestimates the player's value. The latter is cursed.

Since the previous examples do not closely parallel an auction bid for hosting a mega sporting event, the rest of the chapter does not follow this path.

The Winner's Curse in a Context of Centralized Allocation of Investment Funds

In CPEs, investment funds were allocated annually across state-owned enterprises through an auction opened by the central state administration (central planning agency or industrial ministries). It was obviously not a market allocation but a call sent to enterprises to submit investment projects, since the central authorities would finance the best projects. In Yugoslavia until 1956, the Federal Institute for Planning auctioned investment funds every year, collected projects submitted by 'self-managed' enterprises and eventually supported those investment projects which were deemed to be the most efficient and closest to central plan objectives (Neuberger, 1959). The national investment fund was allocated across enterprises that provided the best projects. In the USSR, a national investment fund was distributed by Gosplan across industrial ministries whose job was to allocate their industry investment fund among the enterprises under their tutelage, according to some centralized 'efficiency' criteria (Dyker, 1983). These efficiency criteria, which were used in the Soviet Union until the 1960s, were somewhat debatable with regard to their economic rationale (Andreff, 1993). However, after economic reforms, the criteria for investment decision making came closer to those applied in public enterprises in market economies. In the latter, for each investment project k its discounted net benefit (its social profitability) was calculated that is:

$$B_k = \sum_{t=0}^{N} \frac{R_{kt} - C_{kt}}{(1 + a)^t},$$

where R_{kt} stands for all revenues derived from the investment over its lifetime (from $t = 0$ to N), C_{kt} stands for all investment costs ($C_{kt} = C_0 + C_t + C_{ft}$ with C_0 the initial investment cost, C_t the cost of all further annual investment 'slices' in the case of a pluri-annual investment, and C_{ft} the operational cost of the equipment over its lifetime) and a is the national discount rate fixed by a central planner.[10] In the face of rival projects submitted by enterprises, industrial ministries normally should have stuck to two selection rules:

1. choose an investment project if, and only if $B_k > 0$, for any k; and
2. choose investment project 1, then project 2, then project 3, and so on, until the industry investment fund is exhausted if $B_1 > B_2 > B_3 > \ldots > B_n$. If the ministry investment fund could afford to finance only the first three projects, it would allocate all its investment fund to the most socially profitable projects. Once each enterprise had obtained its own investment fund, it was committed to including the selected investment project (including its costs and revenues) in its own annual plan and to carrying it through.

However, in practice, investment fund allocation did not proceed in such a smooth and theoretical way due to the context of information asymmetry. Each enterprise director was knowledgable about his/her enterprise's existing equipment, technology, production capacity, real costs, the skills and productivity of manpower and, therefore, the time required to achieve the new investment project with the allocated investment fund. In contrast, the industrial ministry (and of course the central planning agency) had only a vague idea, or no idea at all, about the magnitude of the enterprise's internal managerial variables. In such a context, in order to augment its chance of obtaining investment funding, each enterprise was keen not to reveal the true value of its internal managerial variables

– information non-transparency creating a moral hazard situation – and inclined to 'cheat'[11] with regard to the reality of its investment costs and revenues, and the required completion duration of the investment project. It has been demonstrated that cheating on investment projects tended to be the rule rather than the exception in CPEs (Kornaï, 1980; Dyker, 1983; Andreff, 1993):

- enterprises announced an investment and operation cost c_k for project k and not the actual cost C_k, with $c_k < C_k$, in order to augment their chance of obtaining investment funding from the ministry;
- enterprises declared a very optimistic – often completely unrealistic – completion duration for project k; Soviet economies are well known for their unfinished investment building sites resulting from unattainable completion duration; and
- enterprises anticipated overestimated revenue from the investment: $r_k > R_k$, with r_k the *ex ante* announced revenues and R_k the actually expected revenues.

An obvious consequence of investment cost underestimation and investment revenue overestimation is that the social profitability of an investment project k sent by an enterprise to the ministry was somewhat higher than its real social profitability: $b_k > B_k$.

Since all enterprises had adopted such strategic behaviour, central authorities and ministries were confused, and unable to make rational decisions about how and to whom to allocate the national investment fund. Facing a myriad of fabulous investment projects, ministries had a tendency to inflate the number of financed projects in the first year of a five-year plan – overinvestment – which generated a typical investment cycle in CPEs (Bauer, 1978) with fewer investment projects financed by the end of the five-year plan. Indeed, all the projects submitted to a ministry were unrealistic, exhibiting an extraordinary social profitability, unbelievably low costs and a very short completion time. Thus, the aforementioned decision rule 1 eliminated not even one project. Rule 2 eliminated projects that seemed to be the least unrealistic. In such a confused situation, adverse selection was the most common outcome and inefficient or low-efficiency investment projects were financed, including some that were subject to bargaining, lobbying and bribery of the ministry's civil servants in charge of enterprise investment funds.

Generally, enterprises more often cheated by underestimating costs and completion duration than by overestimating investment revenues. Therefore in order to simplify the issue, we shall consider only the costs.

Let us assume that during the auction, a ministry received details of investment projects such as:

$$c_1 < c_2 < c_3 < \ldots < c_k < \ldots < c_n.$$

If it chose the first three, it might well have selected the least efficient or, at least it could not be sure that it had kept the three most efficient ones. If in reality all projects had the same actual cost C^*, it would have meant that $c_1 = C_1 - C^*$ was the investment project for which the *ex ante* cost announced by an enterprise was the most underestimated compared with its actual cost. It follows that $c_2 = C_2 - C^*$ was the second most underestimated project in terms of cost, and $c_n = C_n - C^*$ was the project with the least underestimated cost. The last was nevertheless the one which had no chance of being funded while the first projects 1, 2 and 3 were the most likely to be financed by the ministry although they were the most underestimated, that is, the least feasible in terms of cost and completion duration. Adverse selection is evident.

Now, let us relax the assumption that all projects had the same actual cost C^* but, instead, they had different costs. Then all ministry decision making would depend on the relationship between actual costs and the announced costs $c_1 < c_2 < c_3 < \ldots < c_k < \ldots < c_n$, that is, on the degree of cost underestimation specific to each investment project. Let us imagine that actual costs were indeed such that $C_1 < C_2 < C_3 < \ldots < C_k < \ldots < C_n$ then the risk of adverse selection is difficult to assess exactly but it is minimal. On the other hand, the risk of selecting inefficient investment projects would be quite high if the actual costs C_1, C_2 and C_3 were such that the real social net benefits were B_1, B_2 and $B_3 < 0$, despite *ex ante* announced social benefits b_1, b_2 and $b_3 > 0$ declared by enterprises during the auction. Now, if actual costs were such that $C_n < \ldots < C_k > \ldots < C_3 < C_2 < C_1$, then adverse selection reached its maximum. The latter hypothesis corresponds to a reality where the less efficient an investment project is, the more the enterprise underestimates (hides or cheats about its own inefficiency) its actual costs. Such a hypothesis was more than realistic in Soviet economies because those enterprises submitting the lowest-quality investment projects were more prone to cheat (underestimate costs) than rival enterprises.

The conclusion is that when a centralized organization in a monopoly situation utilizes an auction to proceed with fund allocation to bidding enterprises, adverse selection is highly likely. And the winner's curse lies therein. The ministry is cursed in so far as it has allocated investment funds to less-efficient projects and it will become aware of this when enterprises which have benefited from the fund allocation are unable to complete their investment projects at the announced cost within the announced deadline. The state-owned enterprise, in some way, is also cursed: through cheating, it has submitted an infeasible investment project and, in practice, it will not be able to complete it within the deadline at the *ex ante* announced cost. In the Soviet system, an enterprise which did not satisfactorily complete its plan was normally sanctioned (lower bonuses, fewer honorific rewards, dismissal or even worse under Stalin). In an attempt to avoid sanctions, enterprises also added some bad management practices to informational cheating (Andreff, 1993) known as 'strategic behaviour' in standard economic theory.[12]

When it was lagging behind its annual investment plan time schedule, an enterprise attempted to bargain an extension of its initial investment fund, allocated at the beginning of the year, but which was found to be too short due to cost and completion duration underestimation. First, it bargained with centralized authorities (ministries) to obtain a facilitating revision of its planned objectives: allocation of extra investment funds, extra inputs or manpower, downward revision of plan targets including that the investment project initially submitted would not be completed in due time and so on. Large Soviet enterprises had elaborated a specific strategy based on *tolkachi*. A *tolkach* was an enterprise employee especially engaged to stay in Moscow and canvass relevant ministries with demands for extra investment funds, extra inputs, and downward revision of plan targets. In other words, it was the Soviet variant of lobbying. The *tolkachi* had become (informal) quasi-institutions, in the Soviet economy and, in some sense, they were a product derived, from the enterprise winner's curse. Being cursed by its own cost underestimation strategy, a Soviet enterprise always attempted to obtain extra means for completing its investment project through putting pressure on and attracting the attention of centralized authorities.

Tolkachi were endowed by their enterprise directors with (illicit) secret funds that enabled them to bribe those ministry bureaucrats who were likely to deliver extra investment funds and extra inputs to the enterprise, to address the enterprise's demands as well as those emanating from rival enterprises (also cursed during the auction) and to send the enterprise demand files to decision makers in the Kafka-like universe of a Soviet ministry. It was common practice for Soviet enterprises to corrupt bureaucrats in charge of allocating investment funds and other material means. In a nutshell, with a view to avoiding the worst consequence of the winner's curse consisting in sanctions for plan non-fulfilment, a Soviet enterprise usually resorted to bargaining, lobbying and bribery, the three ingredients of a 'successful' enterprise management in a centralized economy with information asymmetry.

4 THE OLYMPICS CENTRALIZED ALLOCATION PROCESS WITH ASYMMETRIC INFORMATION

There is a similarity between the centralized auction for allocating investment funds in a CPE and the functioning of an auction whereby the Olympics are allocated to a bidding city. However, similar is not identical, even though the selection mechanism of a host city proceeds, in the absence of a genuine market for the Games, with an auction by a (global) centralized authority or organization, that is, the IOC. From the starting point of the comparison, a difference must be underlined. In a CPE, a centralized body offers funds to achieve an investment, then opens an auction for investment projects, and finally allocates investment funds to various enterprises for projects to be achieved within an annual deadline. With the Olympics, the IOC publicizes the task of hosting and organizing the next Games within a precise deadline, then it calls for projects proposals. These proposals are not applications for IOC funding; rather, they are candidates for raising funds from different sources in order to cover the cost of those investments required to host the Games. At the end of an auction, which usually takes several years, the IOC allocates the right to host the Olympics to the most interesting city project. However, the fact that the object of such an auction is not to obtain finance allocated by the IOC but to win the status of being the next host city of the Olympics does not reduce or eliminate the risk of a winner's curse. The risk may be even higher than in a CPE allocation process because the incentive to cheat is much stronger. A city that wants to host the Games commits itself a heavy investment over a six-to seven-year period and then hopes to benefit from the 'Olympics host city' label which provides a unique capacity for collecting and mobilizing finance. The city's financial commitment and concern are approximately a billion dollars to host the Olympics, whereas, in CPEs, enterprise investment was roughly a million roubles, sometimes less.

Now, considered as an auctioneer, does the IOC behave as a central planner or as an industrial ministry allocating investment funds when it opens an auction for the next Games? A weak variant of a central planner model is due to Oskar Lange (1936, 1937), who adapted the Walrasian auctioneer model. The auctioneer announces some price system, enterprises of the planned economy proceed with their economic calculation (profit maximizing under a resource constraint) and then send back to the planner–auctioneer those output and input quantities that maximize their profit. If the quantities supplied and demanded by all enterprises are not equal, the planner revises its price system, then enterprises recalculate their project plans and send revised estimates to the central planner. This iterative process lasts until there is supply–demand equality for all products and resources at equilibrium prices.[13] The auction for the Olympics differs from the Lange model because the IOC initially does not announce any price. Moreover, the explicit or implicit objective of the IOC is not to reach Walrasian equilibrium prices and quantities.

An inverted planning model to Lange's has been suggested by Malinvaud (1967), Manove (1971) and, for operational planning in Hungary, by Kornaï and Liptak (1965). The idea is that the planner announces quantities of output to be produced and inputs to be allocated and enterprises respond, after making their own economic calculation, with prices and costs. The iterations go on until they converge toward equilibrium – the saddle-point theorem. This process is closer to the IOC auction. The IOC, in some sense, announces quantities to be produced – a defined assortment of sporting venues and infrastructure that must be completed and operational within the opening ceremony deadline. In addition, each bidding city adds an optional number of non-sporting infrastructure investments, some required by the IOC, that may facilitate or embellish hosting the Games: transportation, high-tech telecommunications, urban reconstruction, and so on. Does the IOC receive prices and costs from bidding cities? No. It receives candidature files including both number of sporting venues and amount of non-sporting infrastructural investments, and costs (prices) of all those investments and the LOOC expected organization costs. To pursue this comparative analysis, we shall now examine the objectives of the IOC and bidding cities, respectively.

The very existence of the IOC is justified by four responsibilities or objectives, one of which is to elect (choose) every fourth year a host city for the Summer Olympics and the Winter Olympics, and then to supervise its LOOC (Chappelet and Kübler-Mabbott, 2008). Is this objective maximized under some constraint as in the auctioneer–planner model? The constraint is that a bidding city must provide all the required facilities and must commit itself to adhering to an operational budget, which is a minimal precondition for a city to be selected. Are there other conditions that would maximize the IOC objective function? Another one certainly is the best possible quality of the Games which consists of a guarantee of well-functioning and secure sports contests (quality of sporting equipment, distance between Olympic venues and the Olympic village, and so on), an excellent hosting quality (Olympic village, transportation, hotels), overall security, impressive opening and closing ceremonies, high-quality media and telecommunications and, nowadays, an environmental quality, all prerequisites according to the 20 chapters contained in a candidature file. Thus, if the IOC is maximizing something, it is the overall quality of the project which must benefit from worldwide media coverage, leave a grandiose image of each Olympiad, and an unforgettable memory and indelible marks on the host city landscape. With a view to obtaining a grandiose project, it is in the IOC's interest to pave the way for or even fuel overbidding across bidding cities. This is what it clearly started to do after the single candidature of Los Angeles for the 1984 Olympics.

I have intentionally not mentioned the cost of the Games as one of the variables included in the IOC objective function with a view to cost minimization. First, it is more than likely that the cost of the Olympics is not a decisive criterion in the voting of the 104 IOC members. Furthermore, the criterion of minimal cost to some extent clashes with maximizing the desired extravagant quality of the Games. A proof of such a contention is that the IOC often selects the most expensive rather than the cheapest project (see Table 4.1), which means both adverse selection in terms of cost, and that the winner's curse is at work. Afterwards, cost inflation and cost overruns are basic indices of the winner's curse.

The objective function of bidding cities is crystal clear and consists in getting the Games. Therefore, each bidding city must promise fixed quantities of sporting facilities and a variable quantity of non-sporting infrastructure, focusing on their excellent quality since it will be selected or not on these aspects of its candidature. Before Montreal 1976, investment cost and the LOOC operational budget did not matter that much. Since then, and after Los Angeles 1984 demonstrated that the local organizing committee of the Games can end up in the black, the cost dimension of candidatures has become much more significant, though not the major decision criterion. The primary interest of bidding cities is to maximize (and focus on) the qualitative components of their candidature, thereby encouraging ambitious project proposals. After 1984, bidding cities started to take an interest in also demonstrating reasonable or even low costs in parallel with the supposedly unbelievable quality of their candidature. The only way to reconcile an extravagant project with costs that are not exorbitant is, explicitly or implicitly, to cheat, that is, to communicate and to complete the candidature file on the basis of costs that are underestimated by different means (omitting the VAT, the Paralympics budget, and so on). All in all, it is in the interest of the bidding cities to overbid upward with respect to the quality and downward with respect to the publicized cost of their project. Such a strategy compares with that of rival enterprises struggling for the allocation of investment funds in a CPE except that cities are seeking to be awarded the Games, because it is a precondition for mobilizing huge finance necessary for hosting the Olympics. Thus, rival bidding cities are in sync with the principal objective of the IOC, which is to balance outward extravagance with the appearance of reasonable cost.

The parallel with enterprises in CPEs cannot exactly be extended to the completion duration of investments since this was mandatory, but almost never met, in Soviet-type planning. Yet, the completion duration is mandatory and cannot be circumvented in hosting the Olympics – it is not feasible to start up Olympics sports contests if the stadium is not completed – but the IOC's recurrent worries about delayed Olympics building sites can be used as a control variable of the winner's curse. Building delays usually generate cost overruns when it comes to rushing in order to stick to the deadline. Revising building costs upwards (thus revealing the initial cost underestimation) or even giving up some Olympics building to curb skyrocketing costs are also windfall effects of the winner's curse. Another revealing factor is when the LOOC or the host city obtains extra finance or extra public subsidies, for instance, from the government. A financial deficit or an *ex post* lower financial surplus than expected by the LOOC provides further proof of the winner's curse while a sanction of the latter is a bidding city budget deficit which must be covered with a specific post-Olympics taxation. Given all the financial consequences of hosting the Games, one can understand that bidding cities, just like former Soviet enterprises, do not skimp on the means to get the sports event and do not hesitate to engage in lobbying or, in the worst case, in corrupting some IOC voters, that is, the most unscrupulous or greedy members of the IOC.

A last point is that information asymmetry is crucial in the genesis of the winner's curse. A bidding city knows its candidature project down to the tiniest detail, so it is able to communicate in such a way as to emphasize specific aspects of the file, in particular its supposedly extraordinary quality. In contrast, this in-depth knowledge of the candidature file allows the bidding city promoters to play down those less exciting characteristics of the project, namely excessive costs, stark security issues, negative externalities and a possible crowding-out effect. An economic impact study is instrumental in highlighting the best features and blurring the lesser ones. The IOC cannot have a similar in-depth knowledge (information) about each bidding city project and cannot control how accurate or fallacious is the information delivered in the application file, namely about actual costs, externalities, and so on. The Olympics site visits by the IOC representatives are not enough to compensate for information asymmetry between bidding city promoters and the IOC voters – especially since 'the IOC members are renowned for not really taking into account the technical recommendations and focus on their political and personal judgment of the candidatures' (Chappelet and Kübler-Mabbott, 2008, p. 87) when they cast their vote.

5   INDICATORS OF THE WINNER'S CURSE

One can infer from the above analysis some indicators that would enable us to spot and check the existence of a winner's curse resulting from the auction for allocating mega sporting events to a host city:

1. *Unexpectedly higher net social cost or lower net social benefit*   The most convincing index of a winner's curse is a significant difference between *ex ante* and *ex post* net social outcome of a mega sporting event that can be observed in comparing the results of an *ex ante* and an *ex post* cost–benefit analysis of the same event. The winner's curse hypothesis would be confirmed if *ex post* net social cost is significantly higher than *ex ante* net social cost or if *ex post* net social benefit is significantly lower than *ex ante* net social benefit (as with the aforementioned 2007 Rugby World Cup).

A significant difficulty with indicator 1 is that an *ex post* cost–benefit analysis usually is not available or published after each Olympic Games. Therefore, some proxies are required. The three following indicators are consistent with the winner's curse hypothesis although each of them alone is not sufficient to definitely establish a curse. However, if they are recurring from one Olympics to another (like the recurring cost underestimation of Soviet enterprises), one would lean towards the belief that a winner's curse is at work in the Olympics allocation to bidding cities:

2. *Cost overruns*   A first proxy is a recurring difference[14] between *ex ante* cost in the candidature file and *ex post* cost reached on the opening day or after. Let us call it a 'cost overrun index' such as:

    $c_{t-1} < C_t$ (or $c_{t-1} < C_{t+3}$ when data are available for C_{t+3}).

    Given that over a period of six or seven years there is some inflation in any country and that upward cost revisions happen at a more or less clearly defined date and are usually published in current prices, one can accept as a proof consistent with an existing winner's curse a difference of at least 30 per cent between *ex post* actual and *ex ante* anticipated cost. The data to be found are the initial cost in the candidature file in $t-1$, the actual cost at the moment of the opening ceremony C_t and, if one can circumvent data paucity about $t+3$, the actual cost C_{t+3}. Any extra cost or upward cost revision would fuel relevant data for the cost overrun indicator.

An additional remark is necessary about this indicator as well as the next ones. The announced cost c_{t-1} is an official figure and well publicized by the bidding committee in the candidature file and by the IOC. Such *ex ante* cost is not debatable once published. Looking for the actual cost in t or $t + 3$ is obviously less easy and may be cumbersome and boring. Indeed, it is not in the interest of a host city to reveal that the actual cost of the Olympics has markedly surpassed the *ex ante* cost. Thus the genuine *ex post* actual cost is not always much publicized in official documents. Then there is sometimes no other way for researchers than to rely on data published in the press or in documents published without the IOC or the host city stamp.

3. Ex post *revisions in the Olympics project* When there are no data about the *ex post* cost, a second proxy can be used when some significant revisions occur in the Olympics project between $t - 1$ and t. For example, the appearance of a new building in the project which was not included in the candidature file is an explicit index of an initial cost underestimation. Similarly, an upward revision of expenditures linked to one sporting facility or non-sporting infrastructure project between $t - 1$ and t can also reveal the existence of a winner's curse. Or, when a building that was planned in the candidature file happens to be cancelled between $t - 1$ and t, this also reveals an initial cost underestimation: due to the latter the bill skyrocketed after $t - 1$ and the host city has no other way to curb cost overruns than by giving up some building described in the candidature file.

4. *Delayed completion of an Olympics investment* The completion dates of different Olympics facilities which are mentioned in the candidature file simply cannot be missed. Thus, a delayed completion of an Olympics investment merely translates into a time lag between expected and actual completion dates, and in a subsequent final rush in the last weeks before the opening ceremony to complete the unfinished building – which is exactly the investment cycle described for CPEs (Bauer, 1978). A final rush at the very last minute always inflates the actual investment cost.

When none of the three proxy indicators can be fuelled with data or if one wishes to further confirm the existence of a winner's curse, some other variables can be used as proxies. However, they are less significant than the first three indicators:

5. *Extra public subsidy or extra public finance* If the cost of hosting the Olympics was initially underestimated, one way out for the LOOC and the host city is to bargain and obtain additional public finance

or an extra subsidy, for instance from the government or from some regional authorities between $t-1$ and t.

6. *Host city fiscal deficit and debt* When the extra cost of the Olympics project results in a heavy financial burden for the host city its budget plunges into a fiscal deficit and a public debt that has to be repaid over time. The same index may register the transformation of *ex ante* LOOC (or overall) surplus into *ex post* LOOC (or overall) deficit.

7. *A disappointing number of 'foreign' visitors* When the number of 'foreign' (that is, coming from outside the host city or region) visitors in t is lower than expected in $t-1$, then revenues will be lower than expected and, possibly, will increase financial losses.

Two more qualitative indicators may confirm an existing winner's curse: (a) there are clear signs that a bidding city has attempted to influence the IOC voters through lobbying with some IOC members; and (b) since outcome uncertainty about who will host the Games lasts until the IOC votes, and given that some IOC members are less scrupulous and disinterested than they should be, a bidding city can be led one step forward into bribery and corruption that can be taken as a confirmation of a winner's curse. However, lobbying and corruption *per se* are not decisive indicators of a winner's curse. Lobbying and corruption are unfortunately common practices in various economic activities attempting to influence different decision makers, including in some rigged relationships between money and sports such as fixed matches and online sport gambling (Hill, 2009). Spotting lobbyists, even when lobbying is very effective as during the London campaign for the 2012 Olympics (de Rendinger, 2006), is not an easy task and does not alone guarantee the existence of a winner's curse, unless if it is to complement, for instance, a cost overrun or a delayed completion indicator.

6   PRELIMINARY INDICES VERIFYING THE WINNER'S CURSE HYPOTHESIS

This chapter aims to validate the winner's curse hypothesis. Tables 4.2–4 provide some readily available data on the costs of hosting the Olympics that are consistent with this hypothesis. The data gathered in these tables must not be taken at their face value since, as mentioned above, some do not bear an official stamp. The only important point here is to check whether $C_t > c_{t-1}$, *ex post* is higher than *ex ante* cost, meaning that a *cost overrun* had occurred. Data have been collected, when easily available, for the Summer Games since 1972 and the Winter Games since 1980.

Table 4.2 Ex ante *and* ex post *cost of the Summer Olympics*

Host city, year (No. of bidders)	c_{t-i}: *ex ante* cost	C_t: *ex post* cost	After t cost
Munich 1972 (4 bidders)	Overall cost: $2,705m	Investment cost: $1,757m00 LOOC operation cost: $656m00	
Montreal 1976 (3 bidders)	Investment cost: $549.5m00 Olympic stadium cost: $172m	Investment cost: $3,395.6m00 LOOC operation cost: $476m00	Operation: $1,592m Stadium: $1,000m
Moscow 1980 (2 bidders)	Overall cost: $3.7bn Operation cost: $2bn Investment cost: $1.7bn	Overall cost: $9bn	
Los Angeles 1984	No commitment	Overall cost: $1,592m LOOC operation cost: $546m	
Seoul 1988 (2 bidders)	Overall cost: $3.1bn Investment cost: $3,450m	LOOC operation cost: $664m00 Investment cost: $4,063m00	Extra cost: $2bn
Barcelona 1992 (6 bidders)	Investment cost in: 1985: F13bn; 1988: F23.5bn 1990: F35.5bn; 1992: F41.5bn LOOC operation cost: $1,670m Overall cost in 1990: $2,021m	Investment cost: $10,134m00 Overall cost: $9.3bn	Debt: $6.1bn
Atlanta 1996 (6 bidders)		LOOC operation cost: $1793m00 Investment cost: $1,324m00 LOOC operation cost: $1,346m00	
Sydney 2000 (5 bidders)	Overall cost in 1994: $3,428m Investment cost: $2,500m LOOC operation cost: $1,463m New South Wales Invt: $1,220m	Investment cost: $2,601m00 LOOC operation cost: $2,434m00 New South Wales Invt: $1,249m	Overall cost: $6.6bn

Athens 2004 (5 bidders)	LOOC operation cost: $2,162m00 Overall cost: €4.6bn	LOOC operation cost: $2,404m00 Overall cost: €6.0bn (June 2004) Investment cost: $2,170m00	Overall: €9.6bn Invt cost: €13.5bn
Beijing 2008 (5 bidders)	Investment cost: $1,600m00 Invt cost in 2006: $2,800m LOOC operation cost: $786m00 Olympic stadium cost: €300m Overall cost: €2.2bn ($1.9bn) in 2004; $2.4bn in 2006	LOOC operation cost: $1,458m00 Infrastructure cost: $35.6bn Olympic stadium cost: €380m Overall cost: $43–45bn	Infrastr: €29bn
London 2012 (5 bidders)	Overall cost: £3.4bn in 2005; £3.674bn end 2005; £9.3bn in 2007; £10.0bn in 2009 Investment in 2005: £2.664bn; in 2006: €15.0bn LOOC operation 2005: £1,010m; in 2006: £1,900m	Overall in 2011: $19bn (£11.6bn)	

Note: m: million; bn: billion; $m00: in 2000 dollars; Australian dollars for Sydney; F: French francs

Sources: Auf der Maur (1976), Gouguet and Nys (1993), Andreff and Nys (2002), Preuss (2004, 2006), Barget and Gouguet (2010), Zimbalist (2010, 2011), bidding committees, press articles.

Table 4.3 Ex ante *and* ex post *cost of Winter Olympics*

Host city, year (No. of bidders)	c_{t-1}: ex ante cost	C_t: ex post cost	After t cost
Lake Placid 1980 (2 bidders)	Initial operation cost: $47m Investment cost: $129m	LOOC operation cost: $96m	Op. loss: $8.5m
Sarajevo 1984 (3 bidders)	Operation cost: $17.6m	Operaton cost: $20.2m Investment cost: $15.1m	
Calgary 1988 (3 bidders)	Initial overall cost: CAN$500m	Overall cost: CAN$1,000m LOOC operation cost: $636m	
Albertville 1992 (7 bidders)	Initial total cost: F2,933m in 1987: F3,160m; 1991: F11,487m of which operation cost: F3,233m; sports equipment: F714m infrastructure: F8,630m Accommodation cost: F289m	Overall cost: F12bn	Op. loss: $60m (F285m)
		LOOC operation cost: F4,200m sports equipment: F5,755m infrastructure: F7,800m Accommodation cost: F575m	Extra sports equipt cost: F286m
Lillehammer 1994 (4 bidders)	Overall cost in 1988: $1,511m	Overall cost: $1,700m	Op. loss: $343m
Nagano 1998 (5 bidders)	Overall cost in 1992: $450m	Overall cost: $875m	Debt: $11bn
Salt Lake City 2002 (4 bidders)	Operation cost: $400m in 1989; 1996: $1,000m; 1998: $1,300m	Operation cost: $1.9bn	Op. loss: $168m
Turin 2006 (6 bidders)	Investment cost: €3.5bn Operation cost: $660m	Investment cost: €13bn Operation cost: $1,357m	Op. loss: $38m
Vancouver 2010 (3 bidders)	Operation cost: $846m	Operation cost: $1,269m	Op. loss: $37m
Sochi 2014 (3 bidders)	Initial total cost: $8.4bn 2007: $12bn; 2010: $33bn	Investment cost: €1.31bn	

Note: m: million; bn: billion; $00: in 2000 dollars; F: French francs

Sources: Tihi (1983), Jeanrenaud (1999), Andreff and Nys (2002), Chappelet (2002), Elberse et al. (2007), Solberg (2008), Burton and O'Reilly (2009), Barget and Gouguet (2010), Zimbalist (2010, 2011), bidding committees, press articles.

Table 4.4   Summer Olympics: operational and construction cost increases

Olympics	Operational cost			Construction cost		
	1st estimation	Last estimation	Increase %	1st estimation	Last estimation	Increase %
Munich 1972	1968	1974	222	1965	1974	171
Montreal 1976	1972	1977	538	1972	1977	385
Los Angeles 1984	1981	1984	20	1983	1984	3.4
Seoul 1988	1982	1989	82	1982	1989	352
Barcelona 1992	1988	1993	28	n.a.	n.a.	n.a.
Atlanta 1996	1989	1997	51	1989	1997	14
Sydney 2000	1993	2001	68	1990	2001	228

Source: Solberg and Preuss (2007).

There is practically no sign of a winner's curse involved in Los Angeles 1984 (Table 4.2), which is an expected result since the 1984 Olympics was not auctioned, Los Angeles being the only candidate. Nevertheless, it must be recalled that Los Angeles had very little construction expense and the city had agreed to host the Games only on the condition that it took on no financial obligation (Zimbalist, 2011). In the case of Lake Placid 1980, the second bidding city, Vancouver, withdrew a few days before the IOC cast their votes, which may have alleviated the winner's curse. It has been difficult to find enough information comparing *ex ante* and *ex post* costs for Munich 1972, so the conclusion of an existing winner's curse is still not clear. On the other hand, data are not absolutely reliable for Moscow 1980 and Sarajevo 1984. Nearly all other Olympiads show recurring cost overruns consistent with the winner's curse hypothesis and it is already crystal clear for London 2012 and Sochi 2014 as shown in Tables 4.2 and 4.3.

With regard to the Summer Olympics, without commenting on each statistic *per se*, Tables 4.2 and 4.4 show a strong tendency for the Games to end up with a higher *ex post* actual than *ex ante* expected cost. It appears that cost underestimation is often, more due to investment and infrastructure costs than to the LOOC operation cost. If the criterion of a 30 per cent cost overrun in current prices is adopted, the winner's curse is likely to exist for Montreal 1976, Moscow 1980, Seoul 1988, Barcelona 1992, Athens 2004, Beijing 2008, and London 2012. With a 30 per cent extra cost criterion the hypothesis is rejected for Atlanta 1996 and Sydney 2000. In the last two cases, complementary proxies must be meaningful to draw a conclusion.

Turning to the Winter Olympics (Table 4.3), with the same criterion, a winner's curse is recognized for Lake Placid 1980, Calgary 1988,

Albertville 1992, Salt Lake City 2002, Turin 2006, Vancouver 2010 and Sochi 2014. On the other hand, complementary indexes are crucial to draw conclusions about Lillehammer 1994 and Nagano 1998.

The *ex post revisions* indicator can be witnessed for several Games. The most infamous and costly revision probably is the story of the Montreal Olympic stadium roof (Auf der Maur, 1976) which was eventually completed as late as 1985, nine years after the Games, at an almost sixfold increase. Moreover, transforming the velodrome into a *Biodôme* had triggered an additional $1.5 billion cost. In Albertville, the cost of the Courchevel ski-jump has been revised from $13 million up to $26 million, and the La Plagne bobsleigh run from $15 million to $50 million. A $1,346 million expenses targeted at public transportation equipment was eliminated from the initial Albertville LOOC budget. In Sydney, two galleries of the Homebush Bay stadium were forgone due to excessive cost. In Beijing, simplifying the 'Bird's Nest' structure of the stadium is a revision that saved 50 per cent of steel costs; the Olympic swimming pool, eventually assessed as too sophisticated, was streamlined. In Vancouver, the security budget multiplied seven times between 2003 and 2010, from $153 to $1,070 million. The cost of the London Olympic stadium has been revised upwards from $406 million to $850 million while the cost of infrastructures is up by $170 million; the Olympic park has inflated by $1,440 million over its initial $5.3 billion bill. The Rosa Khutor ski resort was added, after the bid, to the Sochi project; it is opportunely financed by Interros, a holding company owned by a rich oligarch, Vladimir Potanin.

Next, consider the *delayed completion* indicator. The Albertville urban project still remains uncompleted. The completion delay of the Centenary Park in Atlanta required additional jobs and overtime work, and thus has generated extra cost. In Athens, a number of building sites lagged behind schedule, in particular the new tramway, a circular motorway and a suburban train to the new airport. In January 2004, only one (the Nikaia gymnasium) of the 33 Olympic sites was ready. Then, there was a final investment rush. The completion of several London Olympic sites, including Wembley stadium, is late and the LOOC is meeting with increasing obstacles to organizing all sports equipment in due time.

As a result, and as usual with the Olympics, extra public finance and subsidies have been obtained by the LOOC. Montreal 1976 received overall $1 billion in public subsidies. Albertville 1992 received extra financial aid from the government in 1987 up to one-quarter of the LOOC budget, and an extra $46 million after the Games, in July 1992. In Sydney, the riding school obtained an operation subsidy of $676,000 per year and the Blacktown Olympic Park $654,000 per year. The city of Athens never stopped raising public loans when preparing to host the Games and this helps to account for the increase in the Greek public debt. The Italian government provided $223 million to the LOOC in 2005 in order to cope with its budget deficit which was apparent as early as 2004.

An LOOC deficit does not emerge as often as it should because extra expenditures are transferred to (or subsidized by) the host city budget and sometimes the region or national government budget. Nevertheless a loss – an operation deficit – has been registered for Munich 1972, Montreal 1976, Lake Placid 1980, Albertville 1992, Lillehammer 1994, Sydney 2000, Salt Lake City 2002, Athens 2004, Turin 2006, Vancouver 2010, and probably though unofficially for Seoul 1988 (Preuss, 2004) and slightly for Atlanta 1996. Given the heavy subsidies collected by Barcelona 1992 (and a subsequent $6.1 billion debt), the $3 million official financial surplus is practically fictitious. The Lake Placid deficit also was not officially visible since it had immediately been covered by an exceptional aid from New York state.

As a consequence, money is taken out of the taxpayers' pocket. The Montreal 1976 debt was reimbursed by taxpayers through an extra local tax ($176 million) and a Quebec provincial special taxation on tobacco ($480 million). Moreover, running Montreal Olympic sporting facilities has created a $13 million annual deficit over 35 years. The city of Barcelona budget had to charge $1.7 billion repayment to taxpayers. The Albertville LOOC deficit reached $60 million and the city's debt was $2,400 per inhabitant; it has been financed by a 4 per cent increase of the local housing tax. Several municipalities of the Tarentaise valley, which hosted the Albertville Games, such as Pralognan, Brides-les-Bains, Macôt, Les Saisies and Courchevel also ended up in debit. The Sydney Games eventually generated a $168 million debt. New South Wales pays $37.3 million per year to operate former Olympic sites.[15] The Australia stadium had not been financed by issuing shares on the stock exchange and is in financial disarray, and the Superdome and the water sports centre are running at a loss. It is estimated that Greek taxpayers will pay for the Games deficit until 2030.

On the Olympics revenue side there are fewer determinants of the winner's curse than on the cost side. One is *ex ante* overestimation of the number of visitors attracted by the Games, in particular foreign visitors. For instance, in Albertville, a substantial share of the printed 800,000 tickets went unsold. One-quarter of Atlanta tickets were left unsold. The number of visitors at the Sydney Games was lower than predicted (Preuss, 2004). However, one cannot find a major source of the winner's curse in missing or lost revenues.

If, by chance, it were not possible to find any sign of lobbying and corruption during the Olympic bids, then we would have a good counterfactual to the winner's curse hypothesis. But lobbying has seemingly become an almost unavoidable strategy to win the bid. Lobbying has a cost, though often unknown (of course unpublicized). In a few cases, some information has filtered through the press: Sydney lobbied and paid about $0.5 million honoraries to overbid Beijing for the 2000 Games. Just before the votes for allocating the 2008 Games, Beijing committed itself to building 10 stadiums in African countries to win over some IOC members from that continent. London also adopted aggressive marketing and lobbying tactics whose effect is considered by some as a major determinant of its winning bid for 2012. De Rendinger (2006) describes in detail the sequencing of London lobbying 'technology': first hunting, then farming, then convincing, then closing, and eventually controlling (some future votes); he mentions that the Paris 2012 candidature did not follow a similar strategy. Moreover, London had opportunely offered $24 million to aid sports participants of poor countries if it won the bid. Such a strategy of course has been called into question in the French press, which asked whether the IOC has not turned itself into a lobby.[16]

With regard to corruption, the Sheridan report published in 1999 has established that Sydney 2000 bribed VIPs to become the Olympics host city. In September 1993, just before the IOC cast its votes, the Australian Olympic Committee had offered $65,000 to two IOC members, representatives of Kenya and Uganda. A peak in bid corruption was reached with the Salt Lake City Olympics (Maennig, 2002, 2005) and the rules of the Games allocation have subsequently been emended. Unveiling naked corruption has triggered a reform of the IOC (Chappelet and Kübler-Mabbott, 2008) and the exclusion of several IOC members such as Augustin Arroyo (Ecuador), Zein el-Abdin Gadir (Sudan), Sergio Santander Fantini (Chile), Jean-Claude Ganga (Congo), Lamine Keita (Mali), and Paul Wallwork (Samoa) in 1999, while the infamous Kim Un-yong (South Korea), a former IOC deputy president, was censured in 1999 and eventually resigned in 2005, under strong pressure. In fact, illicit embezzlements and bribes had already occurred in 1991 when Nagano won the bid over Salt Lake City for the 1998 Winter Olympics. At nearly the same time, suspicion fell on Robert Helmick, a former president of the International Swimming Federation and the architect of the Atlanta victory for 1996. According to Chappelet and Kübler-Mabbott, Seoul's win over Nagano for the 1988 Summer Games had also been plagued with special favours granted to some IOC members.[17]

However, to end on a less pessimistic note, it must be noted that in the most recent bids (namely for the 2018 Winter Olympics), the IOC has attempted to fight the cost underestimation. Each and every investment has to be mentioned and financing has to be secured. Calculations are both in US dollars and local currency and the IOC asks bidding cities for a realistic estimation of miscellaneous and unexpected costs. The outcome of such IOC effort in terms of alleviating the winner's curse remains to be seen in the future.

7   CONCLUSION

It is not feasible to verify the winner's curse as an outcome of *all* Summer and Winter Olympics bids. However, cost overruns, project revisions, delayed completion, financial deficit and debt are so widespread that it is enough to conclude that the winner's curse is more the rule than the exception. In particular, cost overruns are observed in most Games sampled in this chapter. The only host city which at first sight was not cursed, Los Angeles 1984, is the only one which did not have to overbid rival cities, because it was the only candidate following the financial mess of Montreal 1976.

From this derives a policy recommendation: to avoid cost overruns and other bad consequences of the winner's curse, there should no longer be an allocation of the Olympics through auctioning. If such recommendations were to materialize, the suggested practical reform is to fix a site for the Olympics once and for all (from time to time the Greek city of Olympia is mentioned as the proper site), which will avoid any auctioning, overbidding and winner's curse. However, it is not in the interest of the IOC to have just one candidate or always the same (Olympia) since the bid winner – host city – being cursed, and paying the bill for providing magnificent but expensive Games, is the easiest means for the IOC not to pay the actual price for having its mega sporting event hosted.

NOTES

1.   To the best of our knowledge, the Albertville Games were the only instance in which an *ex ante* economic impact study had dared to predict that they would end up in the red (Andreff, 1991). Such *ex ante* warning is somewhat rare in the literature. Let us imagine what might have happened if a consultant had delivered a pre-2005 study to the mayor of London that concluded: 'give up your candidature to the 2012 Games, it is much too expensive'!

2.   Allmers and Maennig (2009) have already shown that no significant net economic benefits can be identified for the FIFA World Cup in France 1998 or in Germany 2006. More in tune with the winner's curse hypothesis, total investment of \$1.35 billion in stadiums for the 2010 World Cup in South Africa was much higher than the \$105 million initially budgeted at the time of the tournament bid in 2004 (du Plessis and Maennig, 2009).

3.   Around \$1 million, but the overall cost of the bid can reach up to \$100 million, not to speak of under-the-table expenses, also neglected here.

4. Except for t to $t + 1$ which lasts two weeks, and a $t + 1$ to $t + 2$ sequence which rarely lasts longer than one full year, all other sequences occur over several years.
5. See also Feddersen and Maennig (ch. 5 in this volume).
6. In fact, Chappelet and Kübler-Mabbott rely on this empirical evidence for introducing an analysis of lobbying, influenced votes, and corruption in the process of allocating the Games. Such misdoings are connected with the winner's curse issue even though they are not the most significant proof of it.
7. If there were just one single bidding city for each Olympics, the situation would be one of a bilateral monopoly. Economic theory has demonstrated since the Edgeworth Box that, in this case, the outcome of negotiations and the precise terms of the transaction will depend on the respective bargaining power (or simply the naked power) of the two bilateral monopolists (the IOC and the single bidding city).
8. The selection process of the host city has evolved in two steps, first across potential bidders in the same country, and then across 'qualified' bidding cities of different countries. This does not change the likelihood of the winner's curse emerging and probably increases the pressure on cities to bid even more aggressively.
9. This assumption is dropped below when we introduce non-economic factors that influence the IOC votes.
10. If R_{kt} were to include social indirect and non-pecuniary benefits while C_{kt} were to include social indirect and non-pecuniary costs, the investment choice would have relied on standard cost–benefit analysis. Soviet enterprises and planners were not concerned about such indirect and non-pecuniary effects.
11. The verb 'to cheat' is used to mean what is seen, in academic terms, as information bias, distorted information and/or information manipulation in the communication between enterprises and the authorities (industrial ministries).
12. This third variant of the winner's curse fits with a public choice approach since the winner is cursed after deliberately underestimating/overestimating public investment decisions while in the first one the winner is cursed simply due to his/her wrong estimation of the magnitude of, say, oil and gas leases and the interest of exploiting them. There is no public choice and no one is cursed deliberately in the latter case.
13. For a modelling of this iterative process, see Andreff (1993).
14. Olympics cost overruns may have various origins – including some exogenous (bad weather, overall skyrocketing inflation in the host country and so on) – not to speak of poor local management of the Olympics project. But if cost overruns recur so regularly that they appear to be the rule in every Olympics rather than the exception, one can conclude that cost overruns are an embedded outcome of a winner's curse (as they were in the process of allocating investment funds in CPEs).
15. A related issue is that some Olympic facilities are no longer used (in particular ski jumps and bobsleigh runs) after the Games. However, it is not a proof of the winner's curse *per se* since the non-use is due to a short (or non-existing) local demand for such facilities though they are required by the IOC.
16. S. Cypel, 'Londres l'a emporté grâce à un lobbying efficace auprès du CIO, sensible à ses promesses', *Le Monde*, 8 July 2005 (London has won thanks to an efficient lobbying by the IOC which is sensitive to its promises).
17. Bribing an IOC member may pertain to other mega sporting events than the Olympics. It was recently alleged in the press that Issa Hayatou, Cameroon's IOC member, took a \$1.5 million bribe to vote for Qatar to host the 2022 FIFA World Cup.

REFERENCES:

Akerlof, G. (1970), 'The market for lemons: qualitative uncertainty and the market mechanism', *Quarterly Journal of Economics*, **89**, 488–500.
Allmers, S. and W. Maennig (2009), 'South Africa: economic scope and limits', in N.J.

Rao and A.S. Sidoya (eds), *Economics of Sports*, Hyderabad: ICFAI University Press, pp. 186–213.

Andreff, W. (ed.) (1991), *Les effets d'entraînement des Jeux Olympiques d'Albertville: Retombées socio-économiques et innovations dans le domaine du sport en région Rhône Alpes*, PPSH 15, CNRS, Lyon and Grenoble.

Andreff, W. (1993), *La crise des économies socialistes. La rupture d'un système*, Grenoble: Presses Universitaires de Grenoble.

Andreff W. (2000), 'Privatisation and corporate governance in transition countries: beyond the principal–agent model', in E.F. Rosenbaum, F. Bönker and H.-J. Wagener (eds), *Privatization, Corporate Governance and the Emergence of Markets*, London: Macmillan, pp. 123–38.

Andreff, W. (2003), 'Twenty lessons from the experience of privatisation in transition economies', in Y. Kalyuzhnova and W. Andreff (eds), *Privatization and Structural Change in Transition Economies*, London: Palgrave, pp. 29–59.

Andreff, W. and J.-F. Nys (2002), *Économie du sport*, Que sais-je?, no. 2294, Paris: Presses Universitaries de France.

Auf der Maur, N. (1976), *Le Dossier olympique*, Montréal: Editions Québec Amérique.

Baade, R. and V. Matheson (2001), 'Home run or wild pitch? Assessing the economic impact of MLB All Star Game', *Journal of Sports Economics*, **2**, 307–27.

Barget, E. and J.-J. Gouguet (2010), *Evènemens sportifs. Impacts économique et social*, Bruxelles: De Boeck.

Bauer, T. (1978), 'Investment cycles in planned economies', *Acta Oeconomica*, **21**, 243–60.

Burton, R. and N. O'Reilly (2009), 'Consider intangibles when weighing Olympic host city benefits', *Sports Business Journal*, September, 7–13.

Capen, E., R. Clapp and W. Campbell (1971), 'Competitive bidding in high-risk situations', *Journal of Petroleum Technology*, **23**, 641–53.

Cassing J. and R.W. Douglas (1980), 'Implications of the auction mechanism in baseball's free agent draft', *Southern Economic Journal*, **47**, 110–21.

Chappelet, J.-L. (2002), 'From Lake Placid to Salt Lake City: the challenging growth of the Olympic Winter Games since 1980', *European Journal of Sport Science*, **2**, 1–21.

Chappelet, J.-L. and B. Kübler-Mabbott (2008), *The International Olympic Committee and the Olympic System*, Abingdon: Routledge.

Crompton, J.L. (1995), 'Analysis of sports facilities and events: eleven sources of misapplication', *Journal of Sport Management*, **9**, 14–35.

De Rendinger, A. (2006), *Jeux perdus. Paris 2012, pari gâché*, Paris: Fayard.

Du Plessis, S. and W. Maennig (2009), 'South Africa 2010: initial dreams and sobering economic perspectives', in U. Pillay, R. Tomlinson and O. Bass (eds), *Development and Dreams. The Urban Legacy of the 2010 Football World Cup*, Capetown: HSRC Press, pp. 55–75.

Dyker, D. (1983), *The Process of Investment in the Soviet Union*, Cambridge: Cambridge University Press.

Elberse, A., C. Anthony and J. Callahan (2007), 'The Vancouver Olympics', *Harvard Business*, October.

ESSEC (2007), 'Les retombées économiques de la Coupe du Monde de rugby 2007 en France', Étude pour le Comité d'organisation France, April 27.

Feddersen, A., W. Maennig and P. Zimmermann (2008), 'The empirics of key factors in the success of bids for Olympic Games', *Revue d'Économie Politique*, **118**, 171–87.

Gilberto, S. and N. Varaiya (1989), 'The winner's curse and the bidder competition in acquisitions: evidence from failed bank auctions', *Journal of Finance*, **44**, 59–75.

Gilley, O., G. Karels and R. Leone (1986), 'Uncertainty, experience and the winner's curse in OCS lease bidding', *Management Science*, **32**, 673–82.

Gouguet, J.-J. & J.-F. Nys (1993), *Sport et développement économique*, Paris: Dalloz.

Hill, D. (2009), 'How gambling corruptors fix football matches', *European Sport Management Quarterly*, **9**, 411–32.

Hudson, I. (2001), 'The use and misuse of economic impact analysis', *Journal of Sport and Social Issues*, **25**, 20–39.

Jeanrenaud, C. (1999), *The Economic Impact of Sports Events*, Neuchâtel: CIES.
Johnson, B.K., P.A. Groothuis and J.C. Whitehead (2001), 'The value of public goods generated by a major league sports team', *Journal of Sports Economics*, **2**, 6–21.
Kagel, J.H. and D. Levin (2002), *Common Value Auctions and the Winner's Curse*, Princeton, NJ: Princeton University Press.
Kesenne, S. (2005), 'Do we need an economic impact study or a cost–benefit analysis of a sport event', *European Sport Management Quarterly*, **5**, 133–42.
Kornaï, J. (1980), *The Economics of Shortage*, Amsterdam: North-Holland.
Kornaï, J. and T. Liptak (1965), 'Two-level planning', *Econometrica*, **33**, 141–69.
Lange, O. (1936, 1937), 'On the economic theory of socialism', *Review of Economic Studies*, **4** (1, 2), 53–71, 123–42.
Leeds, M. and P. von Allmen (2002), *The Economics of Sports*, Boston, MA: Addison Wesley.
Levis, M. (1990), 'The winner's curse problem, interest costs and the underpricing of initial public offerings', *Economic Journal*, **100**, 76–89.
Maennig, W. (2002), 'On the economics of doping and corruption', *Journal of Sports Economics*, **3**, 61–89.
Maennig, W. (2005), 'Corruption in international sports and sports management: forms, tendencies, extent and countermeasures', *European Sport Management Quarterly*, **2**, 187–225.
Malinvaud, E. (1967), 'Decentralized procedures for planning', in E. Malinvaud and M.O.L. Bacharach (eds), *Activity Analysis in the Theory of Growth and Planning*, London: Macmillan, pp. 170–208.
Manove, M. (1971), 'A model of Soviet-type economic planning', *American Economic Review*, **61**, 390–406.
Matheson, V. (2009), 'Economic multipliers and mega-event analysis', *International Journal of Sport Finance*, **4**, 63–70.
Neuberger, E. (1959), 'The Yugoslav investment auctions', *Quarterly Journal of Economics*, **73**, 88–115.
Porter, P. (1999), 'Mega-sports events as municipal investments: a critique of impact analysis', in J. Fiszel, E. Gustafson and L. Hadley (eds), *Sports Economics: Current Research*, Westport, CT: Praeger, pp. 61–74.
Preuss, H. (2004), *The Economics of Staging the Olympics. A Comparison of the Games 1972–2008*, Cheltenham, UK and Northampton, MA, USA: Edward Elgar.
Preuss, H. (2006), 'The Olympics', in W. Andreff and S. Szymanski (eds), *Handbook on the Economics of Sport*, Cheltenham, UK and Northampton, MA, USA: Edward Elgar, pp. 183–96.
Rock, K. (1986), 'Why new issues are underpriced', *Journal of Financial Economics*, **15**, 187–212.
Sandy, R., P.J. Sloane and M.S. Rosentraub (2004), The *Economics of Sports: An International Perspective*, Basingstoke: Palgrave Macmillan.
Solberg, H.A. (2008), 'Impacts from mega events: what do we know so far?', Trondheim Business School, September 30.
Solberg, H.A. and H. Preuss (2007), 'Why mega sports events become more expensive than planned', European Association for Sport Management (EASM) conference presentation, Turin, 12–15 September.
Swindell, D. and M.S. Rosentraub (2002), 'Negotiating games: cities, sports, and the winner's curse', *Journal of Sport Management*, **16**, 18–35.
Thaler, R.H. (1994), *The Winner's Curse: Paradoxes and Anomalies of Economic Life*, Princeton, NJ: Princeton University Press.
Tihi, B. (1983), 'XIV Zimske Olimpijske Igre kao factor razvoja Sarajevskog regiona, Bosne i Hercegovine i sire zajednice', Sarajevo: Ekonomski Institut, Sarajevo.
Walker, M. and M.J. Mondello (2007), 'Moving beyond economic impact: a closer look at the contingent valuation method', *International Journal of Sport Finance*, **2**, 149–60.
Walton, H., A. Longo and P. Dawson (2008), 'A contingent evaluation of the 2012 London Olympic Games', *Journal of Sports Economics*, **9**, 304–17.

Zimbalist, A. (2010), 'Is it worth it? Hosting the Olympic Games and other mega sporting events is an honor many countries aspire to – but why?', *Finance and Development*, March, 8–11.

Zimbalist, A. (2011), 'Economic impact of the Olympic Games', in S.N. Durlauf and L.E. Blume (eds), *The New Palgrave Dictionary of Economics Online*.

5 Determinants of successful bidding for mega events: the case of the Olympic Winter Games

Arne Feddersen and Wolfgang Maennig

1 INTRODUCTION

> For cities, a successful bid is still in reach, but a thorough commitment to the important relationships and politics within the Olympic Movement is necessary. Timing and prevailing politics will be most important to a successful bid, not the city's strengths or merits. (Hahn, 2010)

For some – or even many – observers, the citation might hit the bull's eye. From the point of view of sports, the statement is a clue to its values and principles. Decisions for Olympic host cities should be taken in order to ensure the best and fairest conditions for the competing athletes, to strengthen the diffusion of Olympic values, and to ensure a sustainable worldwide promotion of (Olympic) sports, to name some of the most important targets. If Hahn were correct, the 'hard factors' for example, sporting facilities and infrastructure, political stability, financing, climate, public support, all extensively described in the bid books and evaluated by the International Olympic Committee's (IOC) Commission, would be of reduced importance.

The process of deciding who will host the Olympic Games has so far attracted relatively little attention in economic analyses. Schauenberg (1992) analyzes the voting procedure for the 1996 Olympic Games and reveals some 'irrationalities'. Swart and Bob (2004) identify factors such as accountability, political support, relationship marketing, ability, infrastructure, bid team composition, communication and exposure, and existing facilities as decisive for a successful bid. However, these determinants are not submitted to any empirical test. Westerbeek et al. (2002), after asking 135 respondents[1] about the importance of 69 items, identify by factor analysis decisive factors that they (also) call accountability, political support, relationship marketing, ability, infrastructure, bid team composition, communication and exposure, and existing facilities. The problem, which is a general problem with factor analysis, is that the naming of such factors is somewhat arbitrary. For example, the Westerbeek et al. (p. 317) 'accountability' factor includes the 'ability to identify key target markets of importance to the event owners' and 'to have an established and recognized presence in the marketplace as a bidding organization'. The 'political support' factor includes 'financial stability of the city'. Beside the problem of interpreting factors, it is hardly possible to quantify the items they encompass. Thus, if an applicant city wishes to enhance its competitive position, it remains unclear which items should be modified. Furthermore, having spent much effort on improvements, it is hard to measure whether the city's ranking for that item has really appreciated.

Feddersen et al. (2008) use a multivariate binary logistical regression model that is suitable for analysis of the IOC's yes/no decision for the Olympic Games. They find that the distance of sporting venues from the Olympic Village, local temperatures and unemployment rates – possibly a proxy for general economic stability in the country of the bidding city – are significant determinants in explaining the IOC's decision for the Summer Games. Poast (2007) uses rank-ordered conditional logit estimation on bidding city characteristics from 1959 through 2005. Analyzing both Summer and Winter Olympics, he concludes that the IOC's only systematic tendencies when selecting a host city are to maintain continental diversity in hosts and to take into consideration the economic performance of the candidate country.

The remainder of this contribution, which is based on the methodology by Feddersen et al. (2008), is organized as follows. Section 2 sketches the history of the bids and the awarding of the Games. Section 3 presents the data, the estimation model and the results of the econometric analysis and, finally, Section 4 closes with a conclusion.

2 THE HISTORY OF BIDS FOR THE OLYMPIC WINTER GAMES

While the modern Olympic Games were founded in 1894 and first staged in 1896 in Athens, winter sports played a minor role during the first decades of the modern Games. Figure skating was part of the sporting program of the 1908 Olympics in London and together with ice hockey part of the 1920 Olympics in Antwerp. During the seventh Olympic Congress the IOC decided to implement a winter sport event held in association with the 1924 Summer Olympics in France. This event was originally called 'Semaine Internationale des Sports d'Hiver' (International Winter Sports Week) and then was designated by the IOC as the first Olympic Winter Games in retrospect during its 26th Session in May 1926. Until 1992, the Winter Olympics had been staged every four years in the same year as the Summer Games were held.[2] Starting with 1994, the Winter Olympics are still held every four years, but two years after the according Olympic Summer Games.

Table 5.1 provides an overview of the years and locations in which the

Table 5.1   History of bids for the Olympic Winter Games

Selection	Olympics	Host city	Contenders
1921	1924	Chamonix	–
1926	1928	St. Moritz	Davos, Engelberg
1929	1932	Lake Placid	Bear Mountain, Denver, Duluth, Lake Tahoe, Minneapolis, Montreal, Oslo, Yosemite Valley
1933	1936	Garmisch-Partenkirchen	Montreal, St. Moritz
	1940	Garmisch-Partenkirchen/St. Moritz/Sapporo[a]	–
1939	1944	Cortina d'Ampezzo[b]	Montreal, Oslo
1946	1948	St. Moritz	Lake Placid
1947	1952	Oslo	Cortina d'Ampezzo, Lake Placid
1949	1956	Cortina d'Ampezzo	Colorado Springs, Lake Placid, Montreal
1955	1960	Squaw Valley	Garmisch-Partenkirchen, Innsbruck, St. Moritz, Karachi
1959	1964	Innsbruck	Calgary, Lahti
1964	1968	Grenoble	Calgary, Lahti, Lake Placid, Oslo, Sapporo
1966	1972	Sapporo	Banff, Lahti, Salt Lake City
1973	1976	Innsbruck (Denver[c])	Sion, Tampere, Whistler
1974	1980	Lake Placid[d]	–
1978	1984	Sarajevo	Gothenburg, Sapporo
1981	1988	Calgary	Cortina d'Ampezzo, Falun
1986	1992	Albertville	Anchorage, Berchtesgaden, Cortina d'Ampezzo, Falun, Lillehammer, Sofia
1988	1994	Lillehammer	Anchorage, Östersund, Sofia
1991	1998	Nagano	Aosta, Jaca, Östersund, Salt Lake City
1995	2002	Salt Lake City	Östersund, Québec, Sion, *Graz, Jaca, Poprad, Sochi, Tarvisio*
1999	2006	Turin	Sion, *Helsinki, Klagenfurt, Poprad, Zakopane*
2003	2010	Vancouver[e]	Pyeongchang, Salzburg, *Andorra la Vella, Harbin, Jaca, Sarajevo*
2007	2014	Sochi	Pyeongchang, Salzburg, *Almaty, Bordschomi, Jaca, Sofia*
2011	2018	Pyeongchang	Annecy, Munich

Table 5.1   (continued)

Notes: Cities in italics were not shortlisted by the IOC but have been recognized as official applicant cities.
a.   At first Sapporo was selected to be the host, but Japan had to give back the Games. The IOC then decided to give the Winter Olympics to St. Moritz, but due to controversies between Switzerland and the IOC, the Games were withdrawn again. Finally the IOC gave the 1940 Winter Olympics to Garmisch-Partenkirchen. Because of the Second World War the Winter Games were finally canceled.
b.   Canceled due to the Second World War.
c.   The IOC had chosen Denver in 1970, but the citizens of Colorado rejected the Games and Innsbruck was installed as host in 1973.
d.   Vancouver withdrew before the vote.
e.   Bern withdrew before the vote.

Sources: Lyberg (1996) and Schollmeier (2001).

Olympic Winter Games have been held, the year of the IOC's bid decision and the unsuccessful applicant cities. In the period from 1924 to the end of the Second World War, some three cities applied for each of the Winter Games. The exceptions were the 1924 Games with Chamonix as the only 'applicant' and the 1940 Winter Games which were given to Garmisch-Partenkirchen.[3] For the 1932 Winter Games, a record number of eight cities applied, although all of the bidding cities – with the exception of Montreal – were located in the USA. Today, only one city from every nation is allowed to bid.

After the Second World War and until the 1992 Winter Games, at minimum three cities applied for each of the Winter Games, with some exceptions like the 1948 and 1980 Winter Games which had fewer applicants. In a third phase from 1992, the number of bidding cities (and thus the competition) increased, complicating the election process according to the Hare method. The repercussions of the IOC corruption scandal of Salt Lake City led to fundamental changes[4] with division of the application process into two phases, in order to provide greater transparency and to reduce the bidding costs. In the first 'applicant city phase' – usually between ten and eight years before the Games – every city nominated by its National Olympic Committee may participate in the competition. Some eight years before the Games and about a year before the selection, after an evaluation the number is restricted to a smaller group of 'candidate cities'. The trend toward more bidding cities might have come to a halt, since for the 2018 Olympic Winter Games only three cities entered the competition.

3   EMPIRICAL ANALYSIS OF OLYMPIC BIDS, 1992 TO 2018

Data and Descriptive Analysis

We shall consider all cities that placed bids for the seven Winter Olympic Games from 1992 to 2018.[5] Since the introduction of the two-stage procedure ('applicant city phase', 'candidate city phase'), some cities were not awarded the status as a 'candidate city' and, thus, were eliminated from the voting by the IOC Session. As the decision whether a city will be short-listed or not is also made by the IOC – albeit not by the IOC's supreme organ (IOC Session) – all 'applicant cities' are considered as failed bids in our empirical analysis.[6] Hence, the dataset consists of the election procedure for eight Olympic Winter Games with a total of 48 individual bids. Out of these 48 cities, which have been officially recognized by the IOC as applicant cities, 36 are located in Europe, and six each are from North America and Asia.[7]

Data for the empirical analysis are taken from the bid books of the cities in question and from the reports of the IOC Evaluation Commission, and relate to the year in which the IOC made its decision. In the case of incomplete data or macroeconomic data not included in the bid documentation, data from the World Bank were used. In cases in which data provided by the bid books and the IOC Evaluation Commission differ, the latter – most recent – source was used.

Based on the questionnaire for applicant cities published by the IOC in the candidature acceptance procedure,[8] the variables *ALTITUDE*, measuring the altitude above sea level of the bidding city (measured in 100 meters), *SNOW*, measuring the average snow height in centimeters in the relevant period and *PRECIPITATION*, measuring average precipitation in the relevant period are included. As all applications for the Winter Games originate from cities with a similar climate, we do not include a variable indicating the climate zone as Feddersen et al. (2008) do for the Summer Games.

The share of venues already existing at the time of the application is also a required item in the IOC questionnaire. The IOC seems to worry about sprawling construction periods and costs and nominally prefers completed and adequate facilities. Thus, we include the proportion of already completed venues requiring no further modification (*VEXIST*), measured as a share of the total number of Olympic sporting facilities. The sign of the variable *VEXIST* is expected to be positive. Besides the accommodation of the athletes, coaches, and team officials in the Olympic Village, additional persons (for example, officials from the IOC and the

International Federations, media, spectators) need accommodation. The variable *BEDS* stands for the number of available hotel beds within 50 minutes of traveling time around the Olympic Village. The sign of this variable is expected to be positive.

Furthermore, following conventional wisdom, the IOC seems to prefer locally concentrated Games. This idea is tested by including the average distance from the Olympic Village(s) to the sporting venues in kilometers (*DIST*). Moreover, some applications contain more than one cluster of sport venues. This is especially the case if large cities with adjacent winter sport regions apply for the Winter Olympics. In most cases the indoor events (for example, figure skating, speed skating, ice hockey, ceremonies) are staged in (large) arenas in the main Olympic city, while outdoor events (for example, alpine skiing, cross-country skiing, ski jumping) are hosted in a mountain-based second venue cluster.[9] To test for any IOC preference for local concentration, we include the number of planned Olympic Villages (*NOVILL*).The expected sign is negative for both *DIST* and *NOVILL*. Additionally, the distance from the Olympic center to the nearest international airport might be important for the logistics of the Olympic Winter Games. Thus, a variable measuring this distance is included (*DISTAIR*) which is expected to have a negative sign.

Conventional wisdom also suggests that the IOC has a preference for continental variety, even if no official rule for rotating the host cities among continents exists. Since the first three Olympic Winter Games after the Second World War were staged in Europe (St. Moritz 1948, Oslo 1952, Cortina d'Ampezzo 1956), the Games have only been held on the same continent (Europe) for two consecutive Games twice. To cover this 'implicit' continent rotation, two dummy variables were tested. The first dummy variable takes a value of one if a bidding city is located on the same continent as the host city of the previous Games (*ROTATION1*) and zero otherwise. The second dummy variable counts the number of Games held on continents other than the applicant's continent (*ROTATION2*). In addition, conventional wisdom also suggests that the IOC acknowledges persistency or stamina of a city if a bid fails.[10] Thus, a dummy variable that takes a value of one if a city applied consecutive times was included (*CONSECAPP*). Following conventional wisdom, the expected sign of this variable is positive.

In order to test for socio-economic determinants which might proxy the potential of the bidding city to organize the Games in a technically and financially stable manner, we also include the national purchasing-power-adjusted per capita GDP in constant 2000 US$ as defined by the World Bank, the inflation rate (*INFLATION*) and the population size of the applicant city (*POPCITY*). As Feddersen et al. (2008) showed that

Table 5.2   Descriptive statistics of bidding cities for the Olympic Winter Games, 1992–2018

Variable	Median		Mean		Minimum	Maximum
	Successful	Unsuccessful	Successful	Unsuccessful	Successful	Successful
ALTITUDE	1,273	754	1,154	766	316	1,830
TEMP	−4.20	−2.50	−2.69	−2.84	−7.70	4.50
PRECIPI-TATION	36.00	36.00	53.49	39.82	16.30	122.60
SNOW	70.00	48.00	85.21	61.10	50.00	140.50
VEXIS	33.33	46.15	42.59	45.94	14.28	88.88
NOVILL	2.00	2.00	1.57	1.79	1.00	2.00
POPCITY	350,000	57,000	363,587	479,101	22,000	921,485
GDP	24,215	16,885	21,678	16,046	2,644	33,369
INFL	3.00	4.00	5.29	12.49	1.00	16.00
CORRUP	7.00	7.00	6.63	6.24	2.50	9.20
BEDS	87,316	30,000	102,220	44,592	36,000	300,000
DIST	16.54	25.00	18.89	26.45	5.90	33.18
DISTAIR	69.00	90.30	79.50	101.89	29.50	170.00

Sources: World Bank Group (2011).

the development status or the life expectancy of the applicant countries is highly correlated with the GDP, we did not test these variables.

Finally, corruption might be an important factor in the IOC selection process. Poast (2007) and Feddersen et al. (2008) employ the Corruption Perception Index (CPI) from Transparency International as an independent variable in a model of the IOC voting behavior. The index ranges from 0 to 10, with 10 being a complete lack of perceived government corruption, 0 indicating extremely pervasive government corruption. Poast (2007, p. 85) emphasizes the use of the CPI as reasonable because members of local Olympic organizing committees interact closely with local government officials. However, a low CPI (that is, widespread corruption) could also be regarded by the IOC as a sign of instability in the political and economic system of the bidding country. In this case a negative effect of high corruption would be expected. Thus, the effect of the variable *CORRUP* is theoretically unclear.

Table 5.2 contains the mean and the median of our variables and displays differences between the successful and unsuccessful bidding cities. The number of Olympic Villages (*NOVILL*) and the share of the existing venues (*VEXIS*) do not differ between the two groups at first sight. Ambiguous results can be found for the number of inhabitants of the city (*POPCITY*), the inflation rate (*INFL*), the *PRECIPITATION*, and the

Table 5.3 Point biserial correlation coefficients (*PBIS*) between the
endogenous variable (HOST) and exogenous variables

Variable	Coefficient of correlation
ALTITUDE	0.3144
TEMP	0.0525
PRECIPITATION	0.1634*
SNOW	0.1942
VEXIS	−0.0823
NOVILL	−0.0904
POPCITY	−0.0458
GDP	0.1847
INFL	−0.0620
CORRUP	0.4140***
BEDS	0.4238***
DIST	−0.1848
DISTAIR	0.0032

Note: The coefficients of correlation are computed using a point biserial correlation test
due to the dichotomous character of the endogenous variable. *** $p < 0.01$; ** $p < 0.05$;
* $p < 0.10$.

average temperature (*TEMP*). According to the descriptive comparison,
successful cities are located in higher altitudes and tend to have more
snow, higher GDP per capita, more hotel beds, and smaller distances
between the Olympic Village(s), competition venues, and the airports than
the unsuccessful cities.

Table 5.3 displays the point biserial correlation coefficient (PBIS)
between the endogenous binary variable (*HOST*) and the exogenous variables. Seven exogenous variables exhibit a PBIS with an absolute value of
0.15 at least: *ALTITUDE, PRECIPITATION, SNOW, GDP, CORRUP,
BEDS,* and *DIST.*

Table 5.4 displays the (classic) coefficient of correlation between the
exogenous (continuous) variables. All coefficients of correlation have
absolute values below 0.50 with the exception of the correlation between
GDP and *CORRUP* (0.59). Combined with the next highest correlations
between the variables *GDP* and *DIST* (0.48) and *PRECIPITATION* and
INFL (0.47), no systematic problems with multicollinearity are indicated.

Binary Choice Model

Our dependent variable *HOST*, the outcome of the election process by
the IOC, is a binary variable which takes the value of one if city *i* wins

Table 5.4 *Correlation coefficients between the exogenous variables*

	ALTITUDE	TEMP	PRECIPI-TATION	SNOW	VEXIS	NOVILL	POPCITY	GDP	INFL	CORRUP	BEDS	DIST	DISTAIR
ALTITUDE	1.000												
TEMP	0.184	1.000											
PRECIPI-TATION	0.016	0.201	1.000										
SNOW	0.317	−0.033	0.040	1.000									
VEXIS	0.164	0.082	−0.026	0.087	1.000								
NOVILL	−0.091	0.407	0.062	−0.111	0.068	1.000							
POPCITY	−0.250	−0.039	−0.192	−0.235	0.054	0.047	1.000						
GDP	0.107	−0.175	0.055	0.169	−0.141	−0.174	−0.294	1.000					
INFL	0.100	0.178	0.473	−0.129	0.044	0.044	−0.020	−0.273	1.000				
CORRUP	−0.210	−0.222	0.102	0.135	−0.136	−0.066	−0.231	0.587	−0.167	1.000			
BEDS	0.150	0.240	0.126	0.147	−0.172	−0.145	−0.059	0.122	0.133	−0.020	1.000		
DIST	0.012	0.019	0.060	0.014	0.013	−0.134	−0.249	0.477	−0.194	0.407	−0.025	1.000	
DISTAIR	−0.086	−0.243	0.039	−0.015	−0.157	−0.032	−0.241	0.343	−0.135	0.427	−0.115	0.332	1.000

the right of hosting the Olympic Winter Games in campaign j and zero otherwise, calling for the use of a binary regression approach. Given the nature of the host city election process, resulting in just one selected city per bidding campaign, the event of a successful bid is rare in our dataset (eight out of 48). To deal with such an asymmetric distribution, we use a complementary log-log model (Greenberg, 2003, p. 667).

$$HOST_{ij} = f(ALTITUDE_{ij}, TEMP_{ij}, PRECIPITATION_{ij}, SNOW_{ij},$$

$$VEXIST_{ij}, NOVILL_{ij}, POPCITY_{ij}, GDP_{ij}, INFL_{ij}, CORRUP_{ij}, BEDS_{ij},$$

$$DIST_{ij}, DISTAIR_{ij}, ROTATION_{ij}, CONCECAPP_{ij}).   (5.1)$$

Table 5.5 contains the estimation results, whereas the standard errors are adjusted for clusters, which are represented by the eight campaigns for the Olympic Winter Games. The model shows an appropriate goodness of fit. The McFadden pseudo R^2 has a value of 0.678 and the Cox–Snell R^2 has a value of 0.457. Furthermore, the LR statistic is significant at the 1 percent level. Overall, 10 of our 14 exogenous variables turned out to be significant and all coefficients show the expected sign.

First, the altitude has a positive impact on the probability of winning a bid. Adding 100 meters of altitude and holding the remaining independent variables at their means will raise the winning probability by 7.3 percentage points, showing that mountain regions with higher altitudes might be advantaged. Regarding the weather variables, *TEMP* is insignificant, while *PRECIPITATION* and *SNOW* are significant at the 1 percent level and 5 percent levels, respectively. One additional centimeter of snow will raise the winning probability by 0.4 percentage points. One additional millimeter of average precipitation during the time period of the Games decreases the probability by 0.5 percentage points.[11] This might indicate that the IOC dislikes potential disturbances and time delays for outdoor competitions. Regarding the variables representing the organizational concept, the share of existing venues (*VEXIS*) is significant at the 1 percent level, while the number of Olympic Villages (*NOVILL*) turned out to be insignificant. According to the marginal effect, an increase of the share of already existing facilities by one percentage point from 50 to 51 percent yields an increase in the probability of a successful bid by 0.3 percentage points. The significant coefficient of the variable *DIST*, displaying the average distance between the facilities and the Olympic Village implies a decrease in the probability of winning the bid by 2.4 percentage points if *DIST* increases by one kilometer. Conventional wisdom on the IOC's preference for concepts with short distances between the venues and the

*Table 5.5   Determinants of success of bids for the Winter Olympics:
complementary log-log model*

	Coefficients	Marginal effects
CONSTANT	−25.384*	
	(13.788)	
ALTITUDE	1.162***	0.073
	(0.365)	
TEMP	−0.081	−0.005
	(0.164)	
PRECIPITATION	−0.075***	−0.005
	(0.025)	
SNOW	0.063**	0.004
	(0.032)	
VEXIS	0.041***	0.003
	(0.014)	
NOVILL	−2.392	−0.150
	(2.529)	
POPCITY	0.115*	0.007
	(0.065)	
GDP	−0.049	−0.003
	(0.247)	
INFL	−0.043***	−0.003
	(0.010)	
CORRUP	2.300***	0.144
	(0.692)	
BEDS	0.089***	0.006
	(0.019)	
DIST	−0.384***	−0.024
	(0.133)	
DISTAIR	−0.020**	−0.001
	(0.010)	
ROTATION2	0.126	0.008
	(0.122)	
CONSECAPP	2.395	0.146
	(1.772)	
McFadden's R^2	0.678	
Cox–Snell R^2	0.457	
LR	29.316***	

Note: Standard errors are in parentheses. Marginal effects are average marginal effects.
Coefficients displayed are log odds. *** $p < 0.01$; ** $p < 0.05$; * $p < 0.10$.

Olympic Village seems to be confirmed. This result is similar to the findings by Feddersen et al. (2008), who also found a significantly negative relationship between the average distance and the winning probability for bids for Summer Olympics. Furthermore, a larger distance to the next international airport (*DISTAIR*) has a negative impact on the winning probability (minus 0.1 percentage point per kilometer). Confirming the results for the Summer Olympics by Feddersen et al. as well, the number of available hotel beds within 50 minutes of traveling time around the Olympic Village (*BEDS*) shows a significantly positive impact: 1,000 additional beds can be translated into a rise in the winning probability of 0.6 percentage points.

Neither *ROTATION1* nor *ROTATION2* showed a significant impact on the winning probability. Combined with the finding from Feddersen et al., who found identical results using the same variable definitions for the Summer Olympics, strong evidence against the existence of an implicit preference of continent rotation by the IOC members could be isolated.[12] Furthermore, based on the insignificant coefficient of *CONSECAPP*, the hypothesis of no systematic influence of consecutive applications cannot be rejected.

Finally, all socio-economic variables are significant at the 1 percent level with only two exceptions. *POPCITY* turned out to be significant on the 10 percent level only, while *GDP* is insignificant at all conventional significance levels. On the basis of the reduced statistical significance, the population of the bidding city has a positive impact on the winning probability, while the marginal impact is small. Additional 100,000 inhabitants will increase the winning probability by 0.7 percentage points. A rise in inflation by one percentage point will lower the winning probability by 0.3 percentage points. One additional point of the CPI (*CORRUP*), which can be translated into a smaller level of corruption in the observed country, will increase the winning probability by 14.4 percentage points. The wealth of a nation as measured by the GDP per capita does not seem to influence the decision of the IOC but a preference for stability – proxied by a low inflation rate and low corruption – can be attested. A further test of the goodness of fit of an estimated binary regression model is provided by evaluation of the success of the prognosis. The classification table shown in Table 5.6 illustrates the overall explanatory power provided by our regression model. It correctly predicts the result of failures in the application process in 97.5 percent of all cases, and correctly predicts success in 87.5 percent of cases, respectively. The only mistake of our model appears when predicting the outcome of the bid campaign for the 1992 Winter Olympics. According to our model, Cortina d'Ampezzo would be the winner of the IOC election instead of Albertville.

Table 5.6   *Explanatory power of the model of determinants of success of bids for Olympic Winter Games*

		Predicted by the model		Percentage
		Negative decision	Positive decision	
IOC decision	Negative decision	39	1	97.50
	Positive decision	1	7	87.50
Total				95.83

4   CONCLUSIONS

This chapter examined the probability of success of bids on the basis of quantified determinants. The analysis is based on a total of 48 bids for the Winter Olympics between 1992 and 2018.

Ten of our variables turned out to have a significant effect on the decision of the IOC, none displaying an unexpected sign. The significance of the altitude (+), the average precipitation (–) and snow levels (+) of the bidding city mirror the preference for stable and good winter sport conditions. The signs of the extent of already existing sporting venues (+) and of the population size of the bidding city (+) may indicate an IOC preference for sustainable concepts and/or low financing risks. The average distance from the Olympic Village to the sporting venues as well as to the airport (–), and the number of hotel beds (+) indicate the importance to fulfill the extensive needs for accommodation for the Olympic Family, the International Federations, the media, and spectators and for convenience of the athletes and officials. Turning to socio-economic determinants, the signs of inflation and of our corruption variable indicate an IOC preference for political/economic stability in the host country. The GDP per capita, the number of Olympic Villages, as well as variables which proxy any preference for continental rotations did not exhibit any significant effect.

About 96 percent of the predictions in the sample were correct, a goodness of fit (or statistical error) which is well within the bounds of reliable models. Our model points to a rational, transparent and reproducible IOC selection process, based on climate of the bidding cities, conceptual issues of the bid, and economic/political stability in the host country. We do not find evidence for Hahn's (2010) hypothesis, mentioned in our introduction, that other effects, such as timing are most important.

Nevertheless, his idea of the importance of prevailing politics needs further empirical testing. Future studies could also take into consideration the role of the quality of the cities' presentations before the IOC plenum, the personal preferences of IOC members, the public support in the bidding regions, historical, psychological and lobbying/'public relations' related factors. In addition, it would be interesting to elaborate on potential 'best practices' (ibid.) and in a more systematic way than we have done with our model as well as on potential cycles in the IOC's (geo)strategy, which in the period of writing this chapter seemed to be inclined to explore 'new territories'.

NOTES

1. Westerbeek et al. (2002) use a sample of 135 event owners and organizers which includes experience in organizing the Olympic Games, the Commonwealth Games, Formula One Grand Prix and the World Power-Lifting Championships, among others.
2. In 1940 and 1944 the Olympic Games were canceled due to the Second World War.
3. Initially, the IOC awarded the Winter Games to Sapporo (Japan), but Sapporo gave back the Games. The IOC then designated St. Moritz as the host city, but it also gave them back. The IOC then decided to award the Games to Garmisch-Partenkirchen.
4. For a description and an economic analysis of the corruption involved in the Salt Lake City scandal and the institutional changes afterwards, see Maennig (2002).
5. Bid books prior to the 1992 Games provide significantly less information.
6. During the bid procedure for the 2010 Winter Olympics, Bern withdrew its bid after being shortlisted due to a negative referendum. Since no IOC decision was made, this bid was eliminated from our dataset.
7. So far, no city from Africa, Australia or South America had launched an application.
8. For an example, see IOC (2009), p. 87.
9. Examples are the Winter Olympics in Turin 2006 and Vancouver 2010.
10. This stamina effect is often cited as a reason for the success of Pyoenchang in its 2018 bid. On the other hand, the Swedish city of Östersund also applied for three consecutive campaigns (1994, 1998, 2002) but always failed.
11. Nevertheless, this does not translate to more than an increase of 16.75 percent probability of winning if precipitation changes from the maximum to the minimum.
12. On the occasion of his July 2011 trip to Japan, IOC president Jacques Rogge stated: 'There is a perception that there is an automatic rotation of continents. This is not the case' (N.N., 2011).

REFERENCES

Feddersen, A., W. Maennig and P. Zimmermann (2008), 'The empirics of key factors in the success of bids for Olympic Games', *Revue d'Économie Politique*, **118**, 171–87.
Greenberg, S. (2003), *Whitaker's Olympic Almanack: The Essential Guide to the Olympic Games*, London: A & C Black.
Hahn, J. (2010), 'Positioning and politicking: keys to Olympic bid success', available at: https://portfolio.du.edu/portfolio/getportfoliofile?uid=166207 (accessed 30 September 2011).
International Olympic Committee (IOC) (2009), '2018 Candidature Acceptance Procedure', Lausanne: IOC.

Lyberg, W. (1996), *Fabulous 100 Years of IOC: Facts, Figures and Much, Much More*, Lausanne: IOC.

Maennig, W. (2002), 'On the economics of doping and corruption in international sports', *Journal of Sports Economics*, **3** (1), 61–89.

N.N. (2011), 'Jacques Rogge was delighted', *Sport Intern*, **43**, 17 July, p. 1.

Poast, P.D. (2007), 'Winning the bid: analyzing the International Olympic Committee's host city selections', *International Interactions*, **33** (1), 75–95.

Schauenberg, B. (1992), 'Die Hare-Regel und das IOC. Irrationales Abstimmungsverhalten bei der Wahl von Atlanta zum Austragungsort der Olympischen Sommerspiele 1996?', *Schmalenbach Business Review*, **44** (5), 426–44.

Schollmeier, P. (2001), *Bewerbungen um Olympische Spiele: Von Athen 1896 bis Athen 2004*, Cologne: Deutsche Sporthochschule.

Swart, K. and U. Bob (2004), 'The seductive discourse of development: the Cape Town 2004 Olympic bid', *Third World Quarterly*, **25** (7), 1311–24.

Westerbeek, H.M., P. Turner and L. Ingerson (2002), 'Key success factors in bidding for hallmark sporting events', *International Marketing Review*, **19** (3), 303–22.

World Bank Group (2011), 'Data Query System', available at: http://data.worldbank.org/ (accessed 14 July 2011).

6 An analysis of the political economy for bidding for the Summer Olympic Games: lessons from the Chicago 2016 bid

Robert A. Baade and Allen R. Sanderson

1 INTRODUCTION

Rather from a simple change of heart, a way to deflect attention away from growing city-hall corruption scandals, or responding to the business community's offering to front the bidding costs, in the summer of 2005 Mayor Richard M. Daley suddenly suggested that Chicago might consider seriously 'going for the gold' – competing for the right to host the 2016 Summer Olympic and Paralympic Games.[1] Thus Chicago was to join Houston, Philadelphia, San Francisco, and Los Angeles to vie for the United States Olympic Committee's (USOC) endorsement. The USOC subsequently selected San Francisco, Los Angeles and Chicago as the three applicant cities. Owing to local financial and political issues, largely surrounding funding for a stadium that could serve both the Olympics and the San Francisco 49ers' football franchise, San Francisco withdrew its bid, leaving only Chicago and Los Angeles for the USOC to consider. In a close vote, the USOC chose Chicago on April 14, 2007, as the United States' candidate city.[2]

On June 4, 2008, the International Olympic Committee (IOC) chose four of the seven applicant cities – Chicago, Madrid, Rio de Janeiro, and Tokyo.[3] Sixteen months later (October 2, 2009), at the IOC session in Copenhagen, Rio de Janeiro was selected on the third ballot.

The selection of a host city for the Olympic Games by the IOC reflects both the political and economic character of the event. The IOC must project an objectivity and fairness in making its selection, the political dimension, while pursuing the 'rent-seeking' characteristic of all monopolists, the economic dimension. The political economy that defines IOC behavior as it relates to the selection process can be illuminated through a case study. The purpose of this chapter is to use Chicago's bid to host the 2016 Summer Olympic Games to provide insight into IOC decision making. Shedding some light on what many view as an opaque process may prove beneficial to applicant and candidate cities as they formulate and execute a winning strategy for hosting the Games.

The chapter is organized as follows. Section 2 identifies and analyzes IOC political motivations. The IOC functions as a monopolistic supplier, but its authority comes by courtesy of the international community. Capricious decision making, or the perception of such, could undermine that authority. Section 3 discusses the rent-seeking of the IOC, to include the extent to which it relies on the Summer and Winter Olympic Games and broadcast revenues to finance its operation. Section 4 explores the IOC and USOC dispute regarding broadcast revenues. Section 5 focuses on the character of Chicago's bid in pursuit of the 2016 Summer Olympic Games. Finally, conclusions and policy implications are delineated in Section 6.

2   THE POLITICS OF THE INTERNATIONAL OLYMPIC COMMITTEE

Voting members of the IOC ultimately select the host city for the Summer and Winter Olympic Games. A candidate city's chances of successfully bidding for the Games are enhanced through obtaining information and understanding the criteria, to include strategic interests and concerns that guide the IOC selection process. The strategic response of a National Olympic Committee (NOC) to its perception of the IOC's evaluative process is amenable to game-theory analysis. A logical predicate to that analysis is to consider IOC motivations in choosing a host. The IOC, as noted in the introduction, must give the impression of objectivity and transparency if it is going to maintain its authority. The IOC must represent the wishes and desires of the international community, and as those evolve so must the IOC. Maintaining transparency can be advanced through following a standard selection process; an articulation of a set of criteria that govern the selection of a host city; and assembling an IOC membership involved in the selection process that represents the world. An analysis of each of these items follows.

The selection process has been codified in the *Olympic Charter*, which is subject to periodic revision. The Charter currently in force is *Olympic Charter: In Force as from 11 February 2010*. This 104-page document codifies everything from the 'Composition and General Organization of the Olympic Movement' (Chapter 1, Section 1), to 'Rights to the Olympic Games and Properties' (Chapter 1, Section 7), as well as the words that must be used by the host nation's head of state to proclaim an opening of the Games of the Olympiad (Chapter 5, Section 56).[4]

One key to understanding the IOC selection process is to understand the composition and general organization of the 'Olympic Movement'. The *Charter* identifies the three main constituents as: 'the International

Olympic Committee, the International Federations and the National Olympic Committees'.[5] The *Charter* makes clear where ultimate authority resides:

> The Olympic Movement is the concerted, organized, universal and permanent action, carried out under the supreme authority of the IOC, of all individuals and entities who are inspired by the values of Olympism.[6]

Quoting again from the *Charter*:

> Under the supreme authority of the International Olympic Committee, the Olympic Movement encompasses organizations, athletes and other persons who agree to be guided by the Olympic Charter . . .

> Any person or organization belonging in any capacity whatsoever to the Olympic Movement is bound by the provisions of the Olympic Charter and shall abide by the decisions of the IOC.[7]

The *Charter* makes absolutely clear the organizational hierarchy; the IOC is the supreme authority, and the NOCs must play by the rules articulated and agree to accept IOC rulings on all matters relating to the conduct of the Olympic Games.

The values that the IOC embraces and promotes through the Games, the 'Fundamental Principles of Olympism', are also clearly articulated:

> Olympism is a philosophy of life, exalting and combining in a balanced whole the qualities of body, will and mind. Blending sport with culture and education, Olympism seeks to create a way of life based on the joy of effort, the educational value of good example and respect for universal fundamental ethical principles.

> The goal of Olympism is to place sport at the service of the harmonious development of man, with a view to promoting a peaceful society concerned with the preservation of human dignity.[8]

An analysis of Chicago's unsuccessful bid requires an examination of the extent to which the USOC and/or the City of Chicago failed to comply with the values endorsed by the *Charter* and the IOC and/or challenged the supreme authority of the IOC. Generally speaking, from a game-theoretical perspective if an applicant for the Games challenges the organizational structure or fails to abide by the rules, the interests of the applicant and the decision maker are no longer compatible. The selection of a host city that has become an adversary results in a clear reduction of the payoff – economic rent – for the authority. If other applicant NOCs pursue a strategy consistent with that of the adversarial applicant, then the supreme authority may have to concede some power. However, if the other applicants honor the rules of the game and do not challenge the IOC, then the candidate city that does challenge will have to submit an offer that more than compensates the authority for its losses to remain competitive.

There has been at least one instance in recent history where circumstances effectively compelled IOC concessions. In 1978 Los Angeles was the only applicant for the 1984 Summer Olympic Games, and the IOC had to accept the offer that Los Angeles presented or cancel the Games. Faced with that prospect, the IOC was not in a position to use other applicant city bids to compel Los Angeles to improve its 'offer'. It is in no way surprising that the IOC encouraged other applicant city bids even up to a year before the 1984 Games were held. The *Charter* states:

> Any application to host Olympic Games must be submitted to the IOC by the competent public authorities of the applicant city together with the approval of the NOC of the country. Such authorities and the NOC must guarantee that the Olympic Games will be organized to the satisfaction of and under the conditions required by the IOC.[9]

When there is only one applicant city, as was the case for 1984, the applicant city and the IOC share authority as it relates to the conduct of the Games and the sharing of rents from them. The payoffs for the IOC and the NOC in this situation are either zero, the outcome if the applicant city withdraws its bid or the IOC cancels the Games, or some finite return that will depend on the negotiating strengths of the two parties. Both the IOC and NOC would choose to hold the Games as long as the costs they incur are exceeded by the benefits derived if the Games are held. It is safe to say that the IOC did not fare as well for 1984 had there been other applicant cities while the City of Los Angeles fared better than they would have had there been competition to host the Games. This practical observation is made despite the following language in the *Charter*:

> Any surplus incurred by a host city, an OCOG [Organizing Committee for the Olympic Games], or the NOC of the country of a host city as a result of the celebration of an Olympic Games shall be applied to the development of the Olympic Movement and of sport.[10]

'Surplus' is subject to interpretation and practice. The applicant city could reduce costs by providing less in the way of infrastructure than that perceived as appropriate by the IOC. Alternatively, the IOC or the NCO could spend money in ways that are inconsistent with the ideals expressed in the *Charter* but sufficient to eliminate any surplus.

Applicant or candidate cities, all else equal, can improve their chances of being selected when there is more than one applicant city by being 'politically correct' as it relates to espousing the values articulated in

Table 6.1 IOC membership by geographic area

Countries / Statistic	Number of members	Percentage of total
Asia, Australia, Fiji, India, and Indonesia	20	18.2
Canada and United States	5	4.5
Africa to include Morocco but not Egypt	15	13.6
Europe (to include Monaco) and the Commonwealth of Independent States	44	40.0
Central and South America, Aruba, Barbados, Cuba, Mexico, Panama, Puerto Rico	14	12.7
Middle East to include Israel, Egypt, and Turkey	12	10.9
Total	110	99.9

Source: See IOC (2011).

the *Charter* and accepting the IOC's authority. The political dimension, however, also involves things beyond the control of the applicant. The host city is finally determined by a vote during the 'Session'. The Session represents a gathering of all IOC delegates and applicant cities do not determine those who cast a vote. According to the *Charter*, 'the total number of IOC members may not exceed 115'.[11] The *Charter* limits constituency membership:

> . . . a majority of members whose memberships are not linked to any specific function or office, as defined in BLR 16.2.2.5; their total number may not exceed 70; there may be no more than one such member national of any given country, as defined in and subject to BLR 16 . . .,[12]

Presently there are 110 members of the IOC, and Table 6.1 identifies their geographic distribution. As the information recorded in the table indicates, Europe and the Commonwealth of Independent States dominate the composition of the IOC. The smallest representation comes from the United States and Canada. It should also be noted that the IOC is male dominant: only 17.3 percent (19) of the IOC are female. This information is important, and it does suggest that the composition of the IOC does not favor the selection of an applicant city from North America, specifically from the United States or Canada. The argument that the composition of the IOC explains why Chicago was rejected requires further explanation

Table 6.2   Location of the Summer Olympic Games, 1896–2016

Year	Location (city and country)
1896	Athens, Greece
1900	Paris, France
1904	St. Louis, USA
1908	London, UK
1912	Stockholm, Sweden
1916	Scheduled for Berlin, Germany (WWI precluded the Games)
1920	Antwerp, Belgium
1924	Paris, France
1928	Amsterdam, the Netherlands
1932	Los Angeles, USA
1936	Berlin, Germany
1940	Scheduled for Tokyo, Japan (WWII precluded the Games)
1944	Scheduled for London, UK (WWII precluded the Games)
1948	London, UK
1952	Helsinki, Finland
1956	Melbourne, Australia
1960	Rome, Italy
1964	Tokyo, Japan
1968	Mexico City, Mexico
1972	Munich, Germany
1976	Montreal, Canada
1980	Moscow, USSR (now Russia)
1984	Los Angeles, USA
1988	Seoul, South Korea
1992	Barcelona, Spain
1996	Atlanta, USA
2000	Sydney, Australia
2004	Athens, Greece
2008	Beijing, PRC
2012	London, UK
2016	Rio de Janeiro, Brazil

Source: Olympic Host Cities (2011).

given the selection of four North American sites in the last 11 Summer Olympic quadrenniums. The selection of Rio de Janeiro also ignores the relatively small representation of members from South and Central America. A review of the Summer Olympic Games locations during modern times – 1896 to the present to be exact – does not unambiguously suggest a correlation between location and current IOC membership. The location for the Summer Olympic Games is represented in Table 6.2.

Table 6.3   Rank orders by geographic area for IOC representation (current) and successful bids

Geographic area	IOC membership: %	IOC membership rank order	Successful bids % since 1896 (28 in total actually held)[a]	Successful bids rank order[b]
Asia, Australia, Fiji, India, and Indonesia	18.2	2	17.9	2.5
Canada and the United States	4.5	6	17.9	2.5
Africa to include Morocco but not Egypt	13.6	3	0	5.5
Europe (to include Monaco) and the Commonwealth of Independent States	40.0	1	57.0	1.0
Central and South America, Aruba, Barbados, Cuba, Mexico, Panama, Puerto Rico	12.7	4	7.1	4.0
Middle East to include Israel, Egypt, and Turkey	10.9	5	0	5.5

Notes:

a.   Between 1896 and 2016, the IOC designated 31 Summer Olympic Games host cities. Because of the First World War (1916) and the Second World War (1940 and 1944), only 28 Summer Olympic Games were actually held. The statistics recorded in Table 6.3 are for Games actually held.

b.   When ranks are tied the convention is to average the ranks in the ascending order of values for the purposes of computing the Spearman's rank correlation coefficient (Spearman rho).

Table 6.3 combines the information from Tables 6.1 and 6.2 and provides rank orders by geographic area for both representation and successful bids. The information exhibited in the table does not yield a statistically significant Spearman rho or Kendall tau coefficient (this, in part, is attributable to the ties identified with the two rank orders and the small number of observations). While it cannot be concluded that there is a statistically significant relationship in the rank orders, three things are worth noting: First, the very top of the rankings indicates that the selection of a host city favors those countries that have the greatest representation of current IOC members.[13] Second, the frequency of selection of a city from the United States or Canada is far greater than is reflected in the IOC membership of those two nations. Third, selection has favored the developed world.

The bias toward developed countries, however, may be changing. The selection of Rio de Janeiro as the host city for the 2016 Summer Games arguably reflects a growing less-developed country (LDC) voice in global decision making. (The selection of South Africa and Brazil as the host nations for the FIFA World Cups in 2010 and 2014, respectively, bolsters that contention.) This may well be the result of the promise by some groups that hosting a mega sporting event serves as a significant catalyst for economic development. There is ample reason to argue that LDCs may have a greater need for measures that can induce economic growth.[14]

Summarizing the political dimension as it relates to the selection of a host city, a case can be made that it is important for an applicant host city and its NOC to develop a relationship with the IOC to include an operational endorsement of IOC values as articulated in the *Charter*. It also appears to be advantageous for the applicant city to be from Europe, where IOC representation is strongest. Strategically speaking, it is also essential to recognize the hierarchy as it relates to Olympism: the IOC is the supreme authority in all matters relating to the Olympic Games. IOC authority extends to the distribution of rents derived from the Olympic Games, and it would be a strategic mistake, ordinarily, for an NOC to pursue economic rents derived from hosting the Games at the expense of the IOC. A discussion of the 'rent-seeking' by the IOC is discussed and analyzed in the next section.

In addition to the potential geopolitical distribution of IOC voting members, the voting model itself – a series of rounds in which the 100+ delegates choose one favorite, with the city garnering the least votes being eliminated each time – may add complexity and intrigue. Nobel laureate Kenneth Arrow compared many voting systems in terms of their likely impact. His 'impossibility theorem' exposes the flaws in whatever rule is chosen, and the possibility that the consensus best city – or candidate – may not prevail in the end.

In the selection process for the 2012 Games, for example, Madrid received the highest number of votes by far in Round 2 but was eliminated in Round 3, leaving London and Paris to battle each other in the 4th round. In the Copenhagen vote for the 2016 Games, despite what many considered a strong proposal, Chicago was eliminated on the first round:

Round 1   Madrid 28, Rio 26, Tokyo 22, Chicago 18;
Round 2   Rio 46, Madrid 29, Tokyo 20;
Round 3   Rio 66, Madrid 32.[15]

In conjunction with the standard treatment of voting models and blocs is the matter of gamesmanship and integrity. In the former, what one may term 'strategic' or game-theoretic voting or, informally, 'horse-trading', can certainly occur. For example, it was rumored that in the 2016 vote Rio was able to convince some IOC members to vote for Tokyo on Round 1 to ensure that Chicago, which Rio felt would be stronger competition, got eliminated early. With respect to the issue of integrity, the IOC has not been immune to allegations of vote-buying and corruption in the choice of a host city, most recently in the process for the 2002 Winter Games that eventually selected Salt Lake City. More recently still, the IOC's twin, FIFA, has been stung by similar bribery charges with regard to awarding the 2022 World Cup to Qatar.

3 THE ECONOMICS DIMENSION: IOC RENT-SEEKING[16]

The IOC is a monopoly supplier in the market for the Summer and Winter Olympic Games, an entertainment market arguably distinct from all others.[17] The IOC, furthermore, behaves as a monopolist in this distinctive market to include wielding its market power to maximize its well-being. The *Charter* clearly identifies and sanctions IOC rent-seeking:

1. The Olympic Games are the exclusive property of the IOC which owns all rights and data relating thereto, in particular, and without limitation, all rights relating to their organization, exploitation, broadcasting, recording, representation, reproduction, access and dissemination in any form and by any means or mechanism whatsoever, whether now existing or developed in the future. The IOC shall determine the conditions of access to and the conditions of any use of data relating to the Olympic Games and to the competitions and sports performances of the Olympic Games.
2. The Olympic symbol, flag, motto, anthem, identifications (including but not limited to 'Olympic Games' and 'Games of the Olympiad'), designations, emblems, flame and torches, as defined in Rules 8–14 below, shall be collectively or individually referred to as 'Olympic Properties'. All rights to any and all Olympic properties, as well as all right to the use thereof, belong exclusively to the IOC, including but not limited to the use for any profit-making, commercial or advertising purposes. The IOC may license all of part of its right on terms and conditions set forth by the IOC Executive Board.[18]

This language leaves no doubt with regard to the appropriation of revenues relating to the conduct of the Games. Footnote 6 in the *Charter* specifies, furthermore, that 'Games will be organized to the satisfaction of and under the conditions required by the IOC'. It is tautological to say that the said organization maximizes IOC well-being. Finally, the IOC specifies how any surplus generated by a host city, and by extension its NOC, should be used (see note 10 in this chapter). Any surplus is put to a use consistent with IOC objectives and values, and is, therefore, consistent with maximizing its well-being rather than that of the host city or NOC.

Rent-seeking involves not only the appropriation of revenues favorable to the monopolist, but maximizing the revenues made available by the host city through the conduct of the Games. The IOC can be thought of as a contest designer and the applicant cities as contestants. Theoretically, the contestant submitting the highest bid wins the prize, the right to host the Games. (Political and personal considerations, of course, could alter this calculus. Rio de Janeiro's geographic-diversity appeal and Juan Antonio Samaranch's personal plea on behalf of Madrid were sufficient to offset Chicago's likely financial advantage in bidding for the 2016 Olympic Summer Olympic Games.) Rent-seeking viewed from this perspective requires a contest design that maximizes the value of applicant bids. The features of the contest are that it involves multiple stages and that the outcome is winner-take-all. There are actually three stages in bidding for the Games. Applicant cities must first be selected by their NOCs since the Olympics organizational structure emphasizes the relationship between the IOC and the NOCs. Once the NOCs select a city, then the IOC selects candidate sites among the applicant cities submitted by NOCs. The selection of the host city to some degree reflects the nature of the relationship between an NOC and the IOC. This is important to note because tensions between the IOC and an NOC could diminish an applicant city's chances of winning.

Research has revealed a couple of things with regard to the design of contests. There are two theoretical outcomes that are most relevant for this analysis. First, in the case of either linear or concave cost functions as it relates to bidding for the Games, the contest designer – the IOC in this case – maximizes revenues (bids) by adopting a single-prize strategy.[19] The IOC apparently believes that the cost function facing applicant cities is linear or concave, and that perception is arguably correct. If the cost function is shaped primarily by an 'ability parameter' unique to each applicant (the ability parameter is independently distributed, privately processed information), then it appears reasonable to assume that bidding costs decline beyond a certain point, especially for those cities that are generally favored to win. The courting between an NOC and its applicant city very likely promotes a feeling of confidence, particularly when the applicant city is well-positioned to meet IOC infrastructure demands. Beyond the infrastructure needed to accommodate the Games, the costs are relatively small, and this suggests a concave cost function.

A second relevant theory has to do with the likelihood that the winning bid exceeds the value of the Games, the 'winner's curse' for the selected city. Given theory relating to the winning bid, the prevalence of the winner's curse is directly related to the number of bidders – candidate cities – vying for the Olympic Games.[20] Practically speaking the perception of objectivity and transparency in the selection process very likely would be impaired if there were a single-stage contest. Accusations of capriciousness in selecting a host city would likely intensify as the number of applicant cities considered evaluated directly by the IOC increased (witness the controversy surrounding the BCS (Bowl Championship Series) in NCAA (National Collegiate Athletic Association) football in the United States). Allowing the NOCs to select applicant cities from within a nation at a first stage, deflects some criticism to the NOC that would otherwise be directed at the IOC. It is certainly easier to rate the virtue of five cities than 25. The multi-stage contest from the contest designer's point of view, therefore, preserves the financial advantage to the contest designer of more bidders while reducing the number of bids the designer has to consider directly.

It is conceivable, furthermore, that the multi-stage construct encourages higher bids for the Games among candidate cities given their investment at the applicant city stage. The higher the sunk costs for applicant cities, the more financially aggressive they are likely to be at the candidate city stage of the competition in an effort to recoup their costs.

The IOC depends on the Olympic Games to finance its operations, and so maximizing well-being is tantamount to maximizing the difference between revenues and costs from the Games. Broadcast rights and sponsorships are the financial life-blood of the IOC. It has been reported that these two sources account for approximately 85 percent of the Olympic Movement's total income. The three main constituents of the Olympic Movement are the IOC, the International Federations, and the NOCs. The IOC distributes approximately 90 percent of its revenues to the Olympic Movement, retaining the remainder for operational and organizational costs associated with governing the Olympic Movement.[21] Although the 1936 Berlin Olympics were the first Games to be televised, broadcasting did not become a mass phenomenon until 1960 in Rome. The total revenue from broadcasts for the Rome Games was $1.2 million, with European television operators accounting for most of that amount. The IOC received an insignificant amount of that total revenue at that time, about 1 to 4 percent, but the IOC recognized a potential significant revenue source and it took the necessary legal steps to control broadcast rights starting with the 1968 Games in Mexico City.[22] In fact, the IOC amended the Olympic Charter in 1971, Article 21, stipulating that the IOC held the exclusive right to negotiate the television contract and the

Table 6.4   Evolution of the distribution of revenue from television broadcast rights for the Olympic Games

Period \ Entity	IOC share %	Host cities share %
1948–1968	1–4	96–99
1972–1980	10	90
1984–1992	33	67
1996–2004	40	60
2006–2010	51	49

Source: Pena (2009).

distribution of those revenues.[23] Juan Antonio Samaranch recognized the potential importance of the American television market, and following his election as IOC President, broadcast revenue increased substantially as did the IOC's share of that revenue. Jacques Rogge, Juan Antonio Samaranch's successor, if anything bolstered the emphasis on broadcast revenues. Rogge reportedly stated: 'We need spectators at the Games, but the IOC does not insist on 100,000-seat stadiums. The Olympics are primarily put on for television'.[24]

It could be argued that the modern Olympics story is about commerce and money (Barney et al., 2002), and if that assertion is true, then the modern Olympic story is about broadcast revenue and its control. Indeed, it would seem that television and the Olympics were made for one another. Sport has the capacity to attract large audiences, and only the World Cup has the global television appeal of the Summer Olympic Games. Table 6.4 identifies trends relating to the distribution of revenue from television broadcast rights between the IOC and host cities.

The majority of the broadcast revenues originates from the United States, but ironically the share of broadcast revenue from the US peaked for the Moscow Games in 1980, Games that the US boycotted because of the then Soviet Union's Afghanistan incursion. Table 6.5 identifies the amount and share of broadcast revenues accounted for by the US and Europe from 1980 through the Beijing Games in 2008.

Several things are worth noting. First, the share of broadcast revenues emanating from the US has diminished but stabilized to slightly over 50 percent. Second, the percentage of broadcast revenues originating in Europe currently approximates a quarter of all broadcast revenues. Third, the United States and Europe together account for about 75 percent of broadcast revenues, which means that approximately 25 percent originate from the 'rest of the world'. It should not be surprising, perhaps, that Rio

Table 6.5   Dollar revenues and percentage of broadcast revenues accounted for by the United States and Europe from the Olympics, 1980 through 2008

Statistic / Olympics	$ Broadcast revenues (current dollars in millions)	Percent of broadcast revenues originating in the United States	Percent of broadcast revenues originating in Europe
Moscow 1980	101	84.1	7
Los Angeles 1984	286.9	78.6	7.6
Seoul 1988	402	74.6	7.5
Barcelona 1992	631.1	63.5	14.9
Atlanta 1996	898.3	50.7	27.55
Sydney 2000	1,331.6	53	26.2
Athens 2004	1,494	53	26.3
Beijing 2008	1,737	51.4	25.5

Source: Pena (2009).

de Janeiro, as part of the rest of the world, was awarded the 2016 Games given the growing importance of broadcast revenues from places other than the United States and Europe.

4   THE IOC AND USOC DISPUTE REGARDING BROADCAST REVENUES

As established above, broadcast revenues are the financial life-blood of the IOC. Since the IOC distributes 90 percent of its revenues to the International Sports Federations and NOCs, those entities depend on broadcast monies as well. Given that the distribution of broadcast funds is a zero-sum game, the significant portion of broadcast revenues appropriated by the USOC has become a major source of tension not only between the USOC and the IOC, but between the USOC and the 204 other NOCs. Tim Elcombe and Stephen Wenn (2011) have attributed the source of the broadcast-revenue dispute to US Public Law 95–606, popularly known as the 'Amateur Sports Act', promulgated by Congress in 1978. Elcombe and Wenn opined:

> Exclusive rights to the use of Olympic marks and emblems in the U.S. territory granted in the Amateur Sports Act were leveraged by the USOC to obtain amounts of Olympic-generated revenue from the sale of television rights fees and major corporate sponsorships far larger than any of the other National

Olympic Committees (NOCs) recognized by the IOC. This privileged financial position has become a divisive issue for the USOC, IOC, and the world's 204 other NOCs.[25]

The tension between the IOC and the USOC appeared to reach a zenith following a July 8, 2009, announcement by the USOC of its plan to launch the US Olympic Network (USON) in partnership with Comcast Corporation. USON was expected to launch in 2010, and Stephanie Streeter, Acting Chief Executive Officer of the USOC, stated:

> The U.S. Olympic Network will be a dream come true for fans of the Olympic Games, delivering rich year-round content associated with the world's greatest sporting competitions. By bringing the stories, competitions and history of the Olympic Movement into American homes year-round, the USOC hopes to not only inspire a new generation of athletes but also to educated young people about the ideals and values of the Olympic movement. And, we believe strongly that the USON can also serve as a template that can be used in other parts of the world to expand access to the Olympic experience. Plus, the USON's unparalleled year-round exposure of the Olympic brand – already one of the world's most recognized and respected – will generate compelling opportunities for Olympic sponsors to expand their association with the Olympic Games and the Olympic Movement. At the same time, we believe it will enhance interest in and viewership of Olympic-related coverage on broadcast networks. We are excited to work with all of our partners, and everyone associated with Olympic Movement, to establish the USON as the foremost full time channel for Olympic-related content.[26]

The language of the USOC announcement was carefully worded with the intention of placating both the IOC and the other NOCs. The announcement highlighted the 'values of the Olympic Movement', and its use as a 'template that can be used in other parts of world to expand access to the Olympics experience'. The IOC and other NOCs were not buying the USOC claims, and the creation of the USON received swift and pointed criticism from the IOC. The reaction of the IOC was clearly represented through remarks made by IOC Finance Commissioner Chairman Richard Carrion in a *New York Times* interview on July 9: 'They [USOC] do just what they think they want to do, and the Olympic movement be damned. I think it's just unilateral and, frankly, somewhat arrogant'.[27]

Chicago was not involved in the development of the USON or the decision to announce the launch of USON so close to the October 2, 2009, IOC decision date about the host city for the 2016 Summer Olympic Games. The USOC July 8, 2009 announcement regarding the creation of USON undermined Chicago's bid if it was construed as posturing by the USOC in its ongoing dispute with the IOC regarding the distribution of broadcast revenues. Carrion's comments left little doubt about how the

IOC viewed USON. Since other NOCs would be affected negatively by the launch of USON, IOC votes very likely moved away from Chicago to the three other candidate cities.

Punishing Chicago for USOC arrogance could result in some costs to the IOC and the other NOCs. The US market remains the most lucrative, and not awarding the Games to Chicago could diminish IOC revenues for the 2016 Games. It should be noted, however, that Chicago and Rio are each one hour removed from the Eastern Daylight Time Zone in the US; thus it is unclear how broadcast revenues would be affected. Viewership in the US is based on interest in the Games and convenience for viewers as it relates to dramatic effect. Viewers, even if aware of the IOC–USOC dispute, are not likely to allow their viewing to be influenced by it. Sponsorship revenues may be affected as US sponsors may be less inclined to be involved in the Rio Games. That remains to be seen.

The long-term implications are less clear. US cities may be less willing to bid for future Olympic Games given the perception that the risk of securing them has increased. Following New York City's failure to secure the 2012 Summer Olympic Games, USOC chairman Peter Ueberroth indicated that US cities might not bid for the 2016 Olympic Games because it is not worth it. Specifically the dispute revolves around what the IOC and other NOCs perceive as the excessiveness of the share of broadcast revenues and sponsorship revenues appropriated by the US from the Games, 12.75 and 20 percent, respectively. The conventional wisdom appears to be that until that dispute is resolved, the US will not serve as a host for the Summer Games in the future.[28]

Ueberroth's perception of the changed risk–reward profile reflected not only the commonly perceived political antipathy directed toward the US over revenue-sharing, but the inability of the US to 'present a clear partnership between city, state, and federal officials'.[29] Chicago's failed bid likely has bolstered the impression articulated by Ueberroth, and if the US does not bid for future Games that will likely have a negative impact on IOC financial expectations for future Games. Given the fact that the total costs involved for any candidate city in just bidding for the Games will likely exceed $50 million,[30] cities may be less inclined to bid.

On the other hand, the IOC, in awarding the 2016 Olympics Games to Rio de Janeiro, may be anticipating that future revenue streams from the Games will be less dependent upon US and European markets. Future Olympic audiences will be more Asian and South American, and the IOC may benefit long term from developing markets in those parts of the world in which there is a larger potential audience. That strategy, of course, depends on the continued economic development of the world's populous areas, and that is not a certainty.

The USOC–IOC dispute regarding the distribution of revenues from the Olympic Games does not explain entirely Chicago's unsuccessful bid for the 2016 Summer Olympic Games. Chicago's bid was generally considered strong, but in retrospect there were flaws. In the final analysis the bid's strengths were not sufficient to offset USOC mismanagement, particularly as it related to the creation of USON. The next section discusses the history of the Chicago bid and the flaws that led to its failure.

5   CHICAGO'S BID

In a public announcement on May 11, 2006, after nearly a year of informal conversations and deliberations, as well as 2004 comments suggesting it would be folly, Chicago Mayor Richard M. Daley[31] named Patrick G. Ryan, personal friend and founder and chief executive of insurer Aon Corp. as head of an exploratory committee to examine the feasibility of putting Chicago forth as an applicant city for the 2016 Games. In that news conference, Daley stated up-front that the Olympics 'cannot become a financial burden to the taxpayers of Chicago and Illinois'.[32] USOC Chairman Peter Ueberroth, present at the gathering, complemented the mayor's stance: 'The bid process . . . must be 100 percent privately financed – no public money'.[33]

Ryan would later become Chicago 2016 Chairman. And the city and state would later be forced by language in the *Charter* and the standard host city contract to provide $500 million and $250 million, respectively, of taxpayer support as a financial guarantee in the case of cost overruns or revenue shortfalls. But the lack of a complete financial guarantee, and financial exposure for taxpayers, continued to plague Chicago's bid, especially in light of recent cost overruns on other local projects, the precarious nature of the city's and state's budgetary situations, and what most regarded as overly optimistic revenue projections from the Games. (Unlike practices in most nations, the US federal government underwrites a relatively modest portion of the costs of the Olympic Games, leaving host cities and states to shoulder the majority of the financial burden. This has been a sore point with Olympic organizers in the past.) The cost of the bid itself was approximately $80 million, all privately funded, though the economist's notion of opportunity cost looms large – that is, a substantial portion of that money donated by firms and well-heeled bid supporters would certainly have gone to other civic projects instead.

Barely two months later, Chicago unveiled its first Olympic plans – a temporary 80,000-seat facility to be used in conjunction with Soldier Field to offer two venues for opening and closing ceremonies,[34] the Olympic

Village, a new aquatic center, and media center, all along the lakefront and close to the center of the city.

Subsequently, many things changed. Chicago's original slogan, 'Stir the Soul', did not translate well into other tongues, so it was replaced by 'Let Friendship Shine'. The two-stadium concept, not an IOC favorite, was dropped in favor of a larger temporary facility, and one not on the lakefront but in Washington Park on the South Side; the aquatic center, after Daley's visit to Beijing to view the 2008 Games, was moved adjacent to it in Washington Park. But with many venues near the heart of the city, the compact nature remained a strong feature of Chicago's bid throughout.

In Spring 2007, the USOC, in a tight vote, selected Chicago over Los Angeles to represent the United States. Chicago officially became a candidate city in September 2007. The IOC evaluation committee visited each of the four candidates in Spring 2009; each city made its final presentation to the IOC in June, leading up to the final Copenhagen vote on October 2. (One 2008 event of note was the arrest on December 10 of then-governor Rod Blagojevich on federal corruption charges; his predecessor, George Ryan – no relation to Pat Ryan – is currently serving a six-year prison term for corruption. In June 2011 Blagojevich was convicted on 17 counts.)

Any successful sports competition or political campaign contains a mix of skillful planning, good execution, and, frankly, dumb luck. With respect to the latter component, Chicago benefitted by having the 2008 Summer Games in Beijing taint geographical neighbor Tokyo's bid for 2016, just as London's hosting for 2012 affected European entry Madrid. And when Rio de Janeiro was awarded the 2014 World Cup, an international event many in Brazil may regard as more important than the Olympics, that entry may have slipped a notch. On the proverbial other hand, Chicago drew the short straw in terms of the order for the evaluation team to visit each of the candidate cities in early 2009: Chicago was the first city the 13 inspectors visited, and the date was late March in a city known for harsh winters and late springs.

On the political front, Chicagoan Barack Obama's November 2, 2008, victory may have signaled to the international community an abrupt change from the Bush administration.[35] In addition, the continuity provided by the Daley administration, virtually certain to have been in power through 2016, would have reduced the risk for the IOC.

Events and data points in 2008 and the first half of 2009 included:

- Chicago 2016 commissioned a study that purported to show that the Games would produce over $22 billion in economic impact on the city and state, mainly as the result of increased tourism, a figure that was significantly higher – by approximately a decimal place – than others were projecting.

- Formal opposition, anti-Olympics rallies, and public forums sprung up across the city. Preservation groups, community leaders, and those worried about bird sanctuaries, boating, finances or gentrification of some neighborhoods grew in number and intensity. An ad hoc group, no games Chicago, gained some traction as the most organized opposition to Chicago's bid throughout the process, and its leadership even met with IOC officials in Chicago, Switzerland and Copenhagen.
- An ongoing public, private, and legal skirmish between the USOC and the Chicago 2016 committee headed by Ryan continued to fester over an internet domain name. The USOC had used Chicago2016. org as its official website, but a local entrepreneur, Steve Frayne, owned Chicago2016.com. The Chicago Organizing Committee complained about possible confusion over the two sites.
- Public support for the Games, an important variable for the IOC, ebbed and flowed. Polls indicated that Madrid appeared to have strong support among its citizens, and Tokyo residents much less desire for the Games. Chicago surveys indicated strong support in 2008, but then waning enthusiasm from early to late in 2009, when numbers supporting or opposing the Games were about equal among the public. The driving factor in this tepid support appeared to be the mayor's about-face in terms of his promise of using tax revenues and giving virtually unlimited financial guarantees to cover shortfalls. This more than anything else seemed to galvanize local opposition.
- In addition to the dispute between the IOC and the USOC over the latter's proposed television network and revenue-sharing arrangements (see Section 4 above) in the two years leading up to the Copenhagen vote, Chicago also had to contend with leadership turnover and instability with its Colorado partner – the USOC. Removal of the USOC chief executive, installation of a less-experienced acting director, massive layoffs at the organization's headquarters, and the USOC's lack of political savvy and international influence, made its management team less able to assist, and perhaps even turned a potential complementary asset into another liability for Chicago.

In late 2009, leading up to October 2, President Obama initially indicated that Valerie Jarrett, a close adviser, would represent his administration in Copenhagen. That was later supplemented by a decision to add First Lady Michelle Obama to the delegation. (Oprah Winfrey also attended and spoke; Michael Jordan was invited but did not attend.) But as the date drew closer and the pressure mounted, the President decided to attend and speak in Copenhagen as well, though his total time on the ground in Denmark consisted of only a few hours, compared with much longer commitments of time by leaders of the competing delegations.[36]

Chicagoans in general, and the Chicago 2016 committee (at least publicly) were shocked by the lopsided first-ballot trouncing in Copenhagen on the October 2, 2009, vote. Odds-makers and popular websites – in Las Vegas, Toronto and other locations – suggested strongly that Chicago held front-runner status and could count on a tight race in the final round against Rio, a contest pitting the monetary advantages of a US city versus the strong emotional appeal of a South American candidate. 'Miscalculation' was a word frequently employed in hindsight. In a Dewey-Defeats-Truman moment, Jerry Roper, president of the local Chamber of Commerce, said on the eve of the vote: 'In Chicago, if there's one thing we know how to do is count votes'.[37]

Budgetary exigencies, political corruption, and a short-sighted decision to lease the city's parking meters for what many considered a bargain-basement up-front price that galvanized citizens as virtually nothing else in recent memory.[38] Polls showing widespread job disapproval left Mayor Richard M. Daley vulnerable to a re-election challenge in February 2011. (He had won six mayoral elections, receiving 71 percent of the vote in 2007.) The selection of Rio de Janeiro for the 2016 Games was probably the straw that broke the mayor's political back and led to his decision to retire as Chicago's longest-serving major.

6   CONCLUSIONS AND POLICY IMPLICATIONS

Unpredictable or surprising results have marked the Olympic Games. The 'Miracle on Ice' during the 1980 Lake Placid Winter Olympic Games remains a compelling chapter in American sports lore. No one really expected a team of American amateur hockey players to compete with the experienced, powerful Soviet Union team let alone beat them. Not all the upsets occur during actual athletic competition. The 'Debacle on Daley Plaza' – the announcement that Chicago had been eliminated as a contender during the first round of voting to host the 2016 Summer Olympic Games – left Chicagoans gathered on that Plaza on October 2, 2009 stunned and searching for answers for the rejection. What accounted for what many considered a monumental upset? What can be learned from the experience?

Like any unexpected outcome in an athletic competition, the vote outcome in 2009 was years in the making. The preparations by the USOC and Chicago were deficient in ways that were fundamental to winning the delegate vote. The USOC and Chicago failed to convince IOC delegates that the values espoused by the Olympic Movement in putting on the Games matched the principal motivation of the United States. The inability and/or unwillingness of the USOC to develop the essential relationships with IOC officials contributed substantially to the mistrust and tension between the USOC and the IOC. The lack of relationship building can in large part be attributed to the relatively recent instability and lack of experience within the USOC leadership, as noted in Section 5, above. It cannot be ignored, however, that the relationship between Juan Antonio Samaranch, Jacques Rogge's immediate predecessor as IOC head, and the USOC was troubled. That coupled with Samaranch's reported plea for Madrid votes in the first round contributed to Chicago's early exit.

Complementing the difficulties that the USOC had with the IOC, and vice versa, and the tensions between the USOC and the Chicago 2016 committee (and with the Daley administration as well), was the inability of the local 'boots on the ground' – Pat Ryan and his people, Mayor Daley and his underlings – to articulate clearly and communicate effectively with those on whom the burdens (and possible benefits) of the Games would ultimately fall: the citizens of Chicago and their neighborhoods. The ever-shifting literal and financial landscape produced anxiety among the populace and easy fodder for the media. Appearing to rely on 'the Chicago Way', a reference to the well-known tactic of riding roughshod over anyone who dared to question or criticize a decision, as well as producing information only on a need-to-know basis or when cornered, the Chicago 2016 insiders and government officials did not create friends or smooth feathers. This was evident in the press, polls, and general population. While well-intentioned, 'stubborn' and 'arrogant' were familiar criticisms of those leading the charge. In terms of the USOC and Chicago, as well as Chicago and its citizens, there was certainly plenty of finger-pointing and possible blame to go around.

The criticism that the US views the Games as mostly an economic opportunity, 'the commercial Games', exacerbated by the experiences of the 1996 Summer Games in Atlanta, was further embellished rather than negated by the timing of the USOC July 8, 2009, announcement regarding its launch of an Olympics cable network, USON. The USOC decision was viewed as an attempt by the US to maintain, if not increase, its share of broadcast revenues or at least strengthen its hand in upcoming negotiations with the IOC over the distribution of broadcast and sponsorship revenues, the financial life-blood of the IOC. The USOC gambit alienated not only the IOC but the more than 200 other NOCs that in effect share with the USOC broadcast and sponsorship revenues. This alienation surely influenced delegate voting, and Chicago garnered the least votes of any of the four candidate cities in the first round of voting. Chicago may well have been unaware of, and thus victimized by, the USOC action. If so, then the lack of a coordinated strategy between Chicago and the USOC to secure the Games is an indictment of USOC leadership.

Deficiencies in the USOC/Chicago bid do not entirely explain the voting outcome. The delegation representing Rio de Janeiro exhibited acumen in designing and executing a bidding strategy, and that coupled with a shift in economic and political power away from the United States contributed significantly to Rio's success. Clearly the right to host the 2016 Games was not solely Chicago's to lose.

Given the costs of even bidding for the right to host the Olympic Games, minimizing risk requires that cities and NOCs understand the essentials of winning bids. The USOC did little to follow even the most essential ingredients of a recipe for securing the Games, and Chicago's loss was in part at least attributable to USOC mismanagement. A good starting point for future bids by US cities is to ensure that the USOC and the candidate city are following a blueprint that impresses upon delegates the embrace of the values articulated by the Olympic Movement and cultivates vital relationships with the IOC and its delegates. Failure to do so coupled with global economic and political realignment, will result in further disappointment and frustration for the US in bidding for future Games.

The fact that the USOC will not put forth a city for the 2020 Summer Olympic Games may be an admission that much work needs to be done within the US to avoid the embarrassing mistakes that undermined Chicago's 2016 bid.

NOTES

1. Officially the Summer Olympic Games are referred to as the Summer Olympic and Paralympic Games. For ease of exposition, the term 'Summer Olympic Games' will represent the official title.
2. Chicago had bid twice unsuccessfully earlier, in 1952 and 1956.
3. The other three bidding cities were Baku, Azerbaijan; Doha, Qatar; and Prague, Czech Republic.
4. The Olympic Charter can be found online at: http://www.olympic.org/Documents/ Olympic%20Charter/Charter_en_2010.pdf.
5. IOC (2010, p. 9).
6. Ibid., p. 11.
7. Ibid., p. 13.
8. Ibid., p. 11.
9. Ibid., p. 73.
10. Ibid., p. 72. It should be noted that OCOGs and host cities are not the same entities.
11. Ibid., p. 30.

12. Ibid., p. 30.
13. It should be emphasized that the IOC representation is based on the current roster of representatives. The extent to which that representation has changed over time obscures, perhaps vitiates, any correlation between representation numbers and successful bid attempts. A more exacting technique in establishing the relationship between representation and winning bids would require identifying the composition of the IOC at the time the selection occurred for each of the 31 host city designations.
14. It should be noted that the idea that mega sporting events induce a growth in economic activity is not supported by economics scholarship. The popular perception and promise that mega events induce economic growth has trumped research undertaken by academic economists to a significant degree in guiding decision making as it relates to the pursuit of hosting mega events by countries and cities.
15. For an examination of various voting models and their likely outcomes, see Hansen and Sanderson (2009).
16. It should be noted that in the *Charter* the IOC is identified as a not-for-profit entity. Rent as used in this chapter refers to 'well-being' as opposed to profit. The operative assumption is that the IOC functions in a way that maximizes the difference between its total benefit and its total cost. The end to which that difference is used by the IOC is not material to this analysis.
17. While the IOC could be identified as a monopolist as it relates to the conduct of the Olympic Games, in terms of operational structure, it is more akin to a cartel in that there are regional blocs and more than 100 voting members with varying interests.
18. IOC (2010, p. 20).
19. See, for example, Moldovanu and Sela (2001).
20. Theoretically, the winner's valuation of the good varies directly with the number of bidders. Here it is assumed that the number of bidders equal the number of the cities that submit applications at the first stage of the process. The winning bid is conditioned by the bids submitted. The information that each bidder uses might well have a temporal dimension as well, as information on past winning bids is used to condition present bids: a 'first-order statistic' such as the perceived greatest economic impact recorded from the games or the perceived mean economic impact.
21. See http://www.olympic.org/ioc-financing-revenue-sources-distribution.
22. Pena (2009, p. 3).
23. Ibid.
24. Barney et al. (2002, p. 278).
25. Elcombe and Wenn (2011).
26. USOC (2009).
27. NYSportsJournalism.com (2009).
28. SI.com (2011).
29. Newsmax.com (2005, p. 1).
30. See, for example, Zinser (2005) for costs reportedly involved in bidding for the Games.
31. In Chicago politics, the middle initial – M – is a constant fixture to distinguish Richard M. Daley, first elected mayor in 1989, from his father, and former mayor of Chicago for 21 years, Richard J. Daley. Together father and son ruled Chicago from 1955 to 2011 for all but 13 years.
32. Bergen and Washburn (2006, p. 26).
33. Ibid.
34. Soldier Field, home of the Chicago Bears, is the National Football League's smallest stadium, with 61,500 seats, too small for IOC requirements.
35. A McCain victory in 2008 would certainly have diminished the prospects for any US candidate city after Senator McCain led Senate hearings on the 2002 Winter Olympics bribery scandals in Salt Lake City, proceedings that embarrassed IOC leadership, a group not likely to forget that public humiliation.
36. For the 2012 Summer Olympics vote, British Prime Minister Tony Blair spent

considerable time in Singapore in advance of the vote; French President Jacques Chirac went but spent relatively little time there. President George W. Bush stayed away.
37. Belkin (2009).
38. The Mayor leased Chicago's 36,000 parking meters to a private firm. In essence Daley traded a 75-year revenue stream for one payment of $1.15 billion. The City's Inspector General calculated that the present value, market value, of the lease should have been $2.2 billion. In addition the acquiring firm immediately raised meter rates throughout the City, further infuriating the populace.

REFERENCES

Barney, Robert K., Stephen R. Wenn and Scott G. Martyn (2002), *Selling the Five Rings: The International Olympic Committee and the Rise of Olympic Commercialism*, Salt Lake City, UT: University of Utah Press.

Belkin, Douglas (2009), 'Mayor places Olympian bet on Chicago's bid for Games', *Wall Street Journal*, September 30, p. A20.

Bergen, Kathy and Gary Washburn (2006), 'City out to prove Olympic mettle', *Chicago Tribune*, May 11, Section 1, p. 26.

Elcombe, Tim and Stephen Wenn (2011), 'A path to peace: thoughts on Olympic revenue and the IOC/USOC divide', *SAIS Review*, **31** (1), 117–33.

Hansen, John Mark and Allen R. Sanderson (2009), 'The Olympics of voting', *Forbes Magazine*, June 3, available at: http://www.forbes.com/forbes/2009/0622/sports-inter national-olympic-committee-on-my-mind.html (accessed June 3, 2011).

International Olympic Committee (IOC) (2010), *Olympic Charter: In Force as from 11 February 2010*, available at: http://www.olympic.org/Documents/Olympic%20Charter/ Charter_en_2010.pdf (accessed March 18, 2011).

International Olympic Committee (IOC) (2011), 'IOC membership by country', available at: http://www.olympic.org/content/the-ioc/the-ioc-institution1/ioc-members-list/ (accessed March 18, 2011).

Moldovanu, Benny and Aner Sela (2001), 'The optimal allocation of prizes in contests', *American Economic Review*, **91** (3), 542–58.

Newsmax.com (2005), 'U.S. cities may not bid for 2012 Olympics', October 11, available at: http://archive.newsmax.com/archives/articles/2005/10/11/91847.shtml (accessed May 29, 2011).

NYSportsJournalism.com (2009), 'U.S. Olympic TV network draws wrath of IOC', July 9, available at: http://www.nysportsjournalism.com/olympic-tv-battle-7-09-09/ (accessed May 29, 2011).

Olympic Host Cities (2011), available at: http://geography.about.com/od/country information/a/olympiccities.htm (accessed March 18, 2011).

Pena, Emilio Fernandez (2009), 'Olympic Summer Games and broadcast rights', *Latina*, **64**, available at: http://www.revistalatinacs.org/09/art/876_Barcelona/77_144_FernandezEng. html (accessed April 24, 2011).

SI.com (2011), 'IOC–USOC inch toward new revenue-sharing pact', June 8, available at: http://sportsillustrated.cnn.com/2011/more/06/08/ioc.usoc.revenue.talks.ap/index.html (accessed June 27, 2011).

USOC (2009), 'USOC and Comcast partner to launch the U.S. Olympic Network', July 8, available at: http://www.teamusa.org/news/2009/07/08/usoc-and-comcast-partner-to-launch-the-u-s-olympic-network/14101 (accessed May 29, 2011).

Zinser, Lynn (2005), 'Olympic Committee chooses London for 2012 Summer games', *New York Times*, July 6, available at: http://www.nytimes.com/2005/07/06/sports/ othersports/06cnd-olympic.html (accessed May 29, 2011).

7 Support for and resistance against large stadiums: the role of lifestyle and other socio-economic factors

Gabriel M. Ahlfeldt, Wolfgang Maennig and Michaela Ölschläger

1 INTRODUCTION

Local resistance against mega sporting events may play a determining role for the probability of winning a bid (Baade and Sanderson, ch. 6 in this volume). In order to be able to treat the target audience efficiently, it is thus of utmost importance for the officials responsible for the bid to know about motives and socio-economic backgrounds of the resistant and the supporting milieus.

As noted in the so-called 'death-of-class' debate, a one-dimensional view on society along an income ray falls short in accounting for the full diversity of personal tastes, attitudes and values, and consumption preferences. Therefore, new concepts have been developed to classify individuals not only by social class or strata, but on the basis of a broad range of values, attitudes or leisure patterns (Veal, 1993). As a case study which might lead to generalizations towards other sport issues such as mega events, we investigate at the voting-precinct level the 2001 stadium referendum on the Allianz-Arena in Munich where residents were asked about the public provision of a site and the accompanying subsidies for infrastructure for the new home venue of the professional football teams FC Bayern Munich and 1860 Munich. Assuming rationality, the clear majority vote for the project indicates that at city level, public subsidies are overcompensated by a substantial increase in utility of the majority of residents. As there is hardly compelling evidence for positive economic impact of stadium projects (Matheson, 2008), the literature has suggested civic pride, feel-good, happiness and consumption benefits as sources of utility increase (Groothuis et al., 2004; Coates and Humphreys, 2006; Cornelissen and Maennig, 2010; Hilgers et al., 2010; Kavetsos and Szymanski, 2010).

The existing empirical analyses of referendums on stadiums (Coates and Humphreys, 2006; Agostini et al., 1997; Ahlfeldt and Maennig, 2012) and cultural institutions (Rushton, 2005) provide evidence for the relevance of socio-economic and demographic attributes such as age and economic wealth in sharpening residents' consumption preferences. Also, evidence indicates that the expected net utility derived from such consumption amenities varies significantly with the distance to these facilities (Coates and Humphreys, 2006; Dehring et al., 2008; Ahlfeldt et al., 2010). We go beyond the scope of previous studies by employing indicators that capture residents' lifestyle in more detail. Using georeferenced data on probabilities of households belonging to different SINUS milieus, we show that neighborhoods' milieu composition is highly correlated with the share of yes-votes for the project and a quantitatively important determinant of voting decisions. This is an important extension as failure to account for lifestyle-specific preferences may result in biased estimates of proximity effects in the presence of residential sorting with respect to unobserved household characteristics.

2 BACKGROUND AND DATA

The Project

Professional football in the Bavarian capital of Munich is shaped by the two sports clubs TSV 1860 München and FC Bayern München. While the latter was the first team playing at the modern Olympic stadium in the 1972/73 season, TSV 1860 had long stayed at the 'Grünwalder Straße' and only partly switched to the Olympic stadium (N.N., 2007). By the mid-1990s, however, the Olympic stadium also became unpopular with the club directors and fans of FC Bayern München. The stadium no longer met the demands of a modern football stadium. To solve this problem, various plans to renovate the Olympic stadium or to build a completely new stadium for football were discussed (Pauli, 2001). However, the planned renovation of the Olympic stadium fell through because the architect and copyright holder Behnisch withdrew his own renovation plans after numerous misgivings expressed by individuals engaged in the protection of historical monuments, architectural experts, and art historians (Dürr, 2000). Additionally, Germany's bid to host the 2006 Football World Cup was accepted in 2000 and the city of Munich intended to apply to stage the opening game of the tournament.

Eventually, at the beginning of 2001, both FC Bayern München and TSV 1860 München negotiated to construct a new stadium, designed exclusively for football, with about 66,000 seats, as soon as the city agreed on a suitable location (N.N., 2001a). The Munich city council finally opted for the Fröttmaning district in the north-eastern periphery in July 2001

(Dürr, 2001). This was also the time when the architectural competition for the new stadium was opened, which, as a stated objective, put nothing less than the creation of a new landmark for the city of Munich on the agenda. A referendum entitled 'Stadium construction in Fröttmaning – World Cup 2006 football in Munich' on the construction project was scheduled for October 21, 2001 (Hornberger, 2001). It comprised on the one hand the passing of the planning law requirements for the construction of a dedicated football stadium in the location of 'Fröttmaning industrial estate' and the complete absorption of construction costs by the Munich football clubs. On the other hand, the city of Munich would commit itself to provide a municipal plot in the framework of a long-term inheritance rights contract and to contribute to the usual extent to the necessary infrastructure measures (in particular the construction of underground train and road connections) (N.N., 2001c). It should be noted here that this 'usual public contribution' amounted to as much as €210 million, of which the city of Munich provided €107 million (N.N., 2005). The plot itself was valued at about €85 million (170 million DM) (N.N., 2001b).

Finally, a significant majority of 65.7 percent voted in favor of the construction of the new stadium. The result of the vote and the 37.5 percent voter turnout were the highest in a Munich public consultation since their introduction in 1996 (N.N., 2001d, 2001e). In February 2002 the two football clubs, among a range of spectacular drafts from very prominent architects, decided in favor of the model submitted by the architects Herzog & DeMeuron. As a key feature the winning design is characterized by a completely illuminated façade, which adopts the colors of the resident teams FC Bayern and TSV 1860 München and supports the iconic charisma of the arena. Ahlfeldt and Maennig (2010b) provide a detailed discussion on iconic stadiums, including the Munich Allianz-Arena.

Lifestyle Groups and Proxy Variables

To describe the inequality of societies or populations, various approaches such as class, social strata or lifestyle groups are discussed across nearly all social sciences. While the concept of social class is mainly based on observable/objective variables such as income or education, the lifestyle approach includes tastes, behavior, attitudes or values and accounts for different ways of life beyond the class-specific socio-structural variables (Veal, 1993; Mochmann and El-Menouar, 2005; Otte, 2008).

Against this background, the voting behavior on the public consultation on stadium construction in Fröttmaning is likely to have been influenced by lifestyle in two ways. First, selected lifestyle groups can have strong preferences for football consumption. Individuals belonging to such groups spend their leisure time in playing or watching football. Their attitude towards the new stadium is influenced by their direct consumption preferences. Second, highbrow lifestyle groups without any particular football consumption preferences can favor the new construction because of its iconic architecture. Their attitude results from cultural interests and aesthetic sensibility.

In order to capture lifestyle groups, we employ two proxy variable sets based on political party affiliation and the MOSAIC milieu classification scheme. The MOSAIC milieus have been developed for direct marketing applications and correspond to the SINUS milieus by the market research institute Sinus-Sociovision. Accordingly, groups of like-minded individuals are classified into 10 milieus, which can be visualized in a two-dimensional diagram with strata affiliation at the vertical axis and value orientation at the horizontal axis. For this reason socio-economic factors as well as general view of life and attitudes to everyday life or consumption are included (Sinus-Sociovision, 2007a; Otte, 2008). These milieus are labeled:

- *Conservative* Milieu with focus on tradition and values with humanistic sense of responsibility. Prevalently retired academics with high income (Fischer, 2002c).
- *Establishment* Highbrow and high-income milieu with focus on high-level, aesthetic and selected consumption patterns (Fischer, 2002a).
- *Post-Materialist* Highbrow, cosmopolitan, self-conscious and tolerant milieu with individualistic attitudes and without striving for social status (Fischer, 2002e).
- *Modern Performer* Modern, unconventional, performance-oriented milieu comprising young and intellectual people with high income (Fischer, 2002d).
- *Traditionalist* Middle- or lower-class milieu consisting of mainly retired workers or employees with values such as tidiness, decency, or sense of duty (Allgayer, 2002c).
- *GDR-Nostalgic* Older milieu focusing on socialistic values and rejecting capitalism, globalization, and prestigious consumption (Allgayer, 2002a).
- *Middle-Class Mainstream* Status-oriented milieu willing to perform and striving for comfortable, secure life with family and friends (Allgayer, 2003).
- *Consumer-Materialist* Lowbrow milieu with low purchasing power but preference for status-oriented consumption (Allgayer, 2002b).
- *Experimentalist* Stylish milieu with hedonistic attitudes including individuals with modern occupations and high education (Fischer, 2002b).

● *Hedonistic*   Modern, trend-oriented, fun-loving milieu consisting of young workers, employees or apprentices with little purchasing power (Fischer, 2002c).

Data

The area examined in this work refers to the autonomous administrative city of Munich, the capital of the Free State of Bavaria. At the time of the assessment, October 21, 2001, some 1,259,730 inhabitants were living in Munich, in an area of 310.41 km². The municipal area of Munich, within the boundaries of October 2001, was subdivided into various spatial units: 25 municipal districts, 106 constituent districts, and 455 subdistricts. Besides the spatial structuring of the municipal districts, the municipal area could be further fundamentally subdivided into 656 voting precincts or electoral wards at the time of the assessment. However, in the event of smaller ballots, such as a public consultation, a different division of the voting precinct was made for reasons of cost and a lower-than-expected turnout. Accordingly, for the public consultation concerning the building of the new stadium, the municipal area was divided into only 311 voting precincts.

On the occasion of the public consultation on the new stadium in Fröttmaning, 902,061 citizens entitled to vote were called upon to make a final decision. Those eligible to vote were all German nationals or nationals of other EU member states, who had reached the age of 18 on polling day and who had been registered as predominantly resident in Munich for at least three months. Of the 338,225 citizens who took part in the vote, a significant majority of 65.7 percent voted in favor of the construction of the new stadium. This result and the 37.5 percent voter turnout were the highest in a Munich public consultation since their introduction in 1996 (N.N., 2001d, 2001e). The absolute 'yes' and 'no' votes for each voting precinct have been made available by the Munich district administration department. Among the total 311 voting precincts, there were 50 postal vote districts, which cannot be further considered in this assessment because of a lack of spatial classification by the Munich electoral office. The postal vote districts accounted for 60,054 of the total 338,225 votes cast. After the postal vote districts are subtracted, 261 constituencies or polling stations remain in the actual assessment, in which 278,171 Munich voters cast their votes on polling day. All of the data used in this assessment were obtained from the Munich statistics office (N.N., 2001e; München, 2007).

The proxy variable set for lifestyle groups are the MOSAIC milieus which are based on the SINUS milieus. To ascertain these milieus, 250 persons were classified into 10 milieus by qualitative aspects. After that, these persons had to complete a questionnaire with 112 standardized life-style questions. These 112 items were reduced by discriminant analyses to a quantitative milieu indicator comprising 46 items. The detailed allocation algorithm and the lifestyle questions are not published (Otte, 2008). The firm Mirkomarketing-Systeme links the SINUS milieus with its own microgeographic dataset on the structure of consumers. Therefore, certain milieu probabilities are determined (Sinus-Sociovision, 2007b). Detailed information about this process is not provided. In this analysis the milieu probabilities for the 455 Munich subdistricts in 2005 are utilized, which were provided by the local statistical office.

Additional to the lifestyle indicators, data on the demographic structure of the population, such as their age, sex, and the proportion of foreigners to Germany and to the EU, were available and represent the status on September 30, 2001. These data were available at the level of the 656 voting precincts and aggregated to the 261 precincts according to the official register. Furthermore, data of the distribution of purchasing power were obtained from the Munich statistics office (München, 2007). The record of purchasing power was derived originally from a prognosis of the consumer research society Gesellschaft für Konsumforschung (GfK), for the year 2004. Here, 'purchasing power' means the income of a household available for consumer purposes, adjusted for taxes and social security contributions.

The data on purchasing power, party affiliation, and milieu probabilities have been adjusted to the level of the 261 voting precincts using GIS and standard area interpolation techniques (Goodchild and Lam, 1980; Arntz and Wilke, 2007; Ahlfeldt and Maennig, 2012). Our empirical analyses are based on the observation of grouped data on the precinct level since individual data on residents' preferences are not available. Applying the methodology of 'ecological inference' similar to Schulze and Ursprung (2000) and Rushton (2005), we infer the probability of a voter supporting the project, who with respect to the considered characteristics is representative for a precinct. An extensive discussion of the underlying assumptions of ecological inference can be found in Shively (1969), King (1997), or King et al. (2004).

3   EMPIRICAL RESULTS

Milieu Preferences and Neighborhood Composition

While at city level little evidence is available for direct economic effects arising from stadium construction, the literature provides compelling evidence for significant neighborhood spillovers within a range of 3–5 km. Positive effects are found in real estate prices (Carlino and Coulson, 2004; Tu, 2005; Ahlfeldt and Maennig, 2009, 2010a; Ahlfeldt and Kavetsos, 2011) or voting pattern (Coates and Humphreys, 2006). The expected net proximity cost revealed in the Munich stadium referendum (Ahlfeldt and Maennig, 2012) is a notable exception. Coates and Humphreys (2006) argue that, among other reasons, proximity effects of a stadium may arise from residents with different preferences sorting in distinct neighborhoods, which naturally reflects in the spatial pattern of the election outcome. This rationale leads us to begin our empirical investigations by comparing the residential composition in the neighborhoods of the proposed (Allianz-Arena) and the existing (Olympic Stadium) stadiums to the rest of the city. We conduct a series of simple separate regressions of the log of probability of a household belonging to milieu J at precinct $i(PMil_i^J)$ on a constant as well as a dummy variable (IM_i^J) denoting all voting precincts within 3 km in the case of the Olympic Stadium (Olympiastadion) and 4 km in the case of the Allianz-Arena (Fröttmaning). Within these areas, significant proximity effects are revealed in the voting pattern (Ahlfeldt and Maennig, 2012):

$$\log (PMil_i^J) = \alpha_0 + \alpha_1 IM_i^J + \varepsilon_i, \qquad (7.1)$$

where α_0 and α_1 are the coefficients to be estimated and ε_i is the error term. The percentage difference (PD) between the probabilities of belonging to a certain milieu group within a respective impact area and the rest of the city are inferred from the coefficient α_1 according to the standard interpretation in semi-log models.[1]

Also, we provide a first descriptive assessment of heterogeneity in residents' preferences by exploring the (spatial) correlation between the proportion of yes-votes and MOSAIC milieu probabilities. Table 7.1 shows the respective differentials in milieu probabilities as well as the correlation coefficients between the share of yes-votes and the probabilities of belonging to certain MOSAIC milieus (Corr.) for the proposed stadium locations.

From the results of Table 7.1 it is evident that the composition of each neighborhood differs considerably relative to one another as well as relative to the rest of the city. At the same time there are significant correlations between the proportion of yes-votes and lifestyle proxies, pointing to significantly different attitudes towards the project. For example, across precincts the proportion of yes-votes decreases with the increasing probability of belonging to a societal leading milieu (Establishment, Post-Materialist and Modern Performer). These milieus on average seem to oppose the project. In contrast, the two mainstream milieus, Middle-Class

Table 7.1   Residential composition and stadium attitude (MOSAIC milieus)

	PD		Corr.
	Olympic Stadium	Allianz-Arena	
Conservative	−12.20***	0.37	0.266***
Establishment	4.34***	−10.00***	−0.384***
Post-Materialist	4.36	−17.50***	−0.525***
Modern Performer	3.00**	−0.09	−0.294***
Traditionalist	−2.19	5.32	0.536***
GDR-Nostalgic	−2.48	17.83***	0.452***
Middle-Class Mainstream	−10.20***	19.44**	0.432***
Consumer-Materialist	−2.87**	8.88**	0.338***
Experimentalist	10.05***	1.53	−0.131**
Hedonistic	1.97***	1.85	0.008

Note: PD denotes the percentage difference between the probability of a household belonging to a certain milieu within a 3 km (4 km) radius around the Olympic Stadium (Allianz-Arena). Corr. is the correlation coefficient between the share of yes-votes in the Allianz-Arena referendum and the milieu probability across voting precincts.***/**/* denote significance at the 1/5/10% levels.

Mainstream and Consumer-Materialist, as well as the milieus with traditional values (Conservative, GDR-Nostalgic and Traditionalist) seem to support the project. The correlation between yes-votes and the modern milieus, Hedonistic and Experimentalist, is insignificant or has a small value, respectively. Notably, quite a high concentration of residents belong to milieus that have a particularly positive attitude towards the project in the vicinity of the Allianz-Arena. In contrast, within the impact area of the Olympic Stadium we find higher proportions of milieu groups that on average were in relative opposition to the project. Thus the chosen site potentially minimizes local opposition as intended by the authorities, particularly when compared to the considered alternative located close to the Olympic Park. These results, however, do not support the hypothesis of residential sorting with respect to preferences for professional football in the neighborhood of the Olympic Stadium, nor can the opposition to the new stadium be explained by the residential composition in proximity to the Allianz-Arena.

Econometric Analysis

Milieu-specific preferences are investigated in more detail using spatial econometrics in order to reveal lifestyle specific correlations with proportion of yes-votes, conditional on socio-economic characteristics. All models control for proximity effects using two neighborhood dummy variables denoting precincts within the impact areas of the Allianz-Arena and the Olympic Stadium. In addition, by introducing interaction terms with continuous distance measures, proximity effects are allowed to diminish with distance. This specification proved to be efficient after careful evaluation on the basis of parametric and non-parametric estimates (Ahlfeldt and Maennig, 2012). The OLS method was used in Agostini et al. (1997) and Coates and Humphreys (2006) for the empirical analysis of the voting behavior in the consultations concerning American stadium projects. Accordingly, the dependent variable, $pcvy_i$, represents the percentage of 'yes' votes in the respective constituencies i in the Munich public consultation. The explanatory variables are, besides geographic variables capturing proximity effects, the economic and demographic characteristics of the voters in constituency i including the milieu proxy variables. The regression equation is thus:

$$pcvy_i = \alpha + \beta X_i + \varepsilon_i, \qquad (7.2)$$

where X_i is the vector of the explanatory variables (including a constant), β denotes the vector of the unknown parameter to be assessed, and ε_i is the error term.[2]

For almost all estimated models, the standard Lagrange multiplier (LM) test for spatial dependency suggests the appropriateness of a spatial error correction model (Anselin and Bera, 1996; Anselin and Florax, 1996), which indicates spatial autocorrelation of error terms possibly due to omitted variables that are correlated across space (Anselin, 2003).[3] The SAR model corrects for the spatial structure in the error term ε_i as follows:

$$\varepsilon = \lambda W\varepsilon + \mu. \qquad (7.3)$$

Parameter λ corrects for the spatial correlation in the error term (ε); W is a rook contiguity weights matrix; and μ is an independent and identically distributed vector of error terms.

Our baseline specification results excluding milieu proxy variables are presented in Table 7.2. Table 7.3 shows coefficient estimates for milieu variables that are individually introduced into the basic model specifications in separate regressions to avoid collinearity problems. We restrict the presentation of estimation results to the coefficients and standard errors of interest, accompanied by the respective coefficients of determination. Since milieus are defined, among other factors, on the basis of households' economic wealth, we exclude unemployment and purchasing

Table 7.2   Basic models

	OLS	SAR
Proportion population	0.0088***	0.0066***
18–25 years old (%)	(0.0025)	(0.0011)
Proportion population	−0.0038***	−0.0027**
25–35 years old (%)	(0.0012)	(0.0021)
Proportion population	0.0060***	0.0027*
35–45 years old (%)	(0.0020)	(0.0016)
Proportion population 60+	0.0054***	0.0027**
years old (%)	(0.0012)	(0.0011)
Proportion population	0.0067***	0.0023*
male (%)	(0.0015)	(0.0013)
Proportion population	0.0011	−0.00006
EU–foreigner (%)	(0.0012)	(0.0012)
Olympic 4k	0.0662***	0.0530*
	(0.0169)	(0.0318)
Olympic 4k × dist. to	0.0206	−0.0160*
Olympic Stadium (km)	(0.0065)	(0.0088)
Fröttmaning 5k	−0.3170***	−0.3116***
	(0.0320)	(0.0528)
Fröttmaning 5k × dist. to	0.0770***	0.0715***
Fröttmaning (km)	(0.0093)	(0.0123)
Constant	0.0676	0.4246***
	(0.1240)	(0.1096)
R-squared	0.520	0.630

Note: Endogenous variable is share of yes-votes in the OLS and SAR estimates. Olympic 4k (Fröttmaning 5k) denotes precincts within 4 km (5 km) of the Olympic Stadium (Allianz-Arena). Standard errors (in parentheses) are robust for spatial autocorrelation in the SAR model.***/**/* denote significance at the 1/5/10% levels.

power in order to avoid collinearity.[4] Except for the coefficient estimate for the Modern Performer milieu in the SAR model, the coefficients are highly significant in all models. Compared to the unconditional correlation coefficients presented in Table 7.1, however, there are some changes. The milieus, Establishment and Post-Materialist, as well as the traditional milieu, Traditionalist, still oppose the project, but the Conservative, Experimentalist and Hedonistic milieus generally supported the project. The positive attitude of mainstream milieus (Middle-Class Mainstream and Consumer-Materialist) towards new stadium construction remains unchanged.[5]

Our results point out that mainstream lifestyle groups and modern milieus tended to vote in favor of the Allianz-Arena. In contrast, highbrow

Table 7.3   Support for the Allianz-Arena project by MOSAIC milieus

Milieu	OLS	SAR
Conservative (%)	−0.01116**	−0.01211***
	(−0.00432)	(0.00401)
	[0.533]	[0.642]
Establishment (%)	−0.02214***	−0.02150***
	(−0.00345)	(0.00387)
	[0.584]	[0.666]
Post-Materialist (%)	−0.01313***	−0.01411***
	(−0.00108)	(0.00120)
	[0.696]	[0.755]
Modern Performer (%)	0.01608**	0.00786
	(−0.00646)	(0.00513)
	[0.534]	[0.632]
Traditionalist (%)	0.02424***	0.02089***
	(−0.00349)	(0.00328)
	[0.605]	[0.676]
Middle-Class	0.01164***	0.01145***
Mainstream (%)	(−0.00274)	(0.00270)
	[0.557]	[0.652]
Consumer-Materialist (%)	0.03327***	0.03362***
	(−0.00309)	(0.00343)
	[0.661]	[0.726]
Experimentalist (%)	0.01341***	0.01243***
	(−0.00320)	(0.00302)
	[0.559]	[0.652]
Hedonistic (%)	0.05064***	0.04899***
	(−0.00726)	(0.00666)
	[0.606]	[0.693]

Note: Baseline model is in Table 7.2. Standard errors (in parentheses) are
heteroskedasticity robust for OLS and adjusted for spatial dependency in SAR estimates.
Estimations' coefficients of determination are in square brackets.***/**/* denote
significance at the 1/5/10% levels.

lifestyle groups, which include the Conservative, Post-Materialist and
Establishment milieus, opposed the project.[6] In the case of MOSAIC
milieus, all those voting in opposition are upper-middle- or upper-class
milieus. Only the Modern Performer milieu as a highbrow upper-middle-
class milieu shows a weak tendency to support the project – and even this
relationship becomes insignificant when accounting for spatial dependency.
These results confirm the widely held assumption that the preference for
professional football is characteristic for substrata or middle strata. Note,

however, that the traditional socio-economic indicators such as income and rate of unemployment are not statistically significant when accounting for spatial dependency. This is compelling evidence that lifestyle, preferences, tastes and attitudes are not linearly constituted along an income ray.

Furthermore, our results strongly indicate that estimated proximity effects at the projected and the existing stadium locations are not attributable to the composition of residents and their preferences. Proximity effects in the neighborhood of the Allianz-Arena project remain virtually unchanged if milieu characteristics are accounted for. Effectively, the neighborhood is dominated by lifestyle groups that in general supported the project. The location choice therefore seems well considered, confirming that the agenda setter chose an appropriate location in anticipation of lobbying pressure as predicted by theory.[7] Similarly, residential composition does not explain the support of the Allianz-Arena project in the vicinity of the old stadium. In contrast, if lifestyle group composition is taken into account, there are significant localized effects in the neighborhood of the existing stadium even in the SAR models, which otherwise yield insignificant results. This finding reflects that the neighborhood's inhabitants generally belong to lifestyle groups that oppose the stadium (see first part of this section).

4 CONCLUSION

The main findings of our analysis are twofold. First, our results indicate the existence of robust expected proximity cost associated with a professional football stadium, a finding that may well influence future bid concepts on the integration of sports facilities into the urban structures. Note that the traditional socio-economic indicators such as income and rate of unemployment are not statistically significant when accounting for spatial dependency. Note also that proximity effects even become somewhat more pronounced by inclusion of lifestyle proxies. Neither observation is surprising. As noted in the so-called 'death-of-class' debate, a one-dimensional view on society along an income ray falls short in accounting for the full diversity of personal tastes, attitudes and values, and consumption preferences. There is compelling evidence that lifestyle, preferences, tastes and attitudes are not linearly constituted along an income ray. The lifestyle approach used in our empirical study includes tastes, behavior, attitudes or values and accounts for different ways of life beyond the class-specific socio-structural variables (Veal, 1993; Mochmann and El-Menouar, 2005; Otte, 2008).

We conclude that there is compelling evidence for lifestyle-specific heterogeneity in expected net benefits of the stadium project under investigation. We show that the proportion of opponents increases with the probability of belonging to a societal leading milieu (Establishment, Post-Materialist and Modern Performer). In contrast, the two mainstream milieus, Middle-Class Mainstream and Consumer-Materialist, as well as the milieus with traditional values (Conservative, GDR-Nostalgic and Traditionalist) support the project. The correlation between yes-votes and the modern milieus, Hedonistic and Experimentalist, is insignificant or has a small value, respectively.

Our results indicate that mainstream lifestyle groups and modern milieus tended to vote in favor of the Allianz-Arena. In contrast, high-brow lifestyle groups, which include the Conservative, Post-Materialist, and Establishment milieus, opposed the project. In the case of MOSAIC milieus, all those voting in opposition are upper-middle- or upper-class milieus.

Possible explanations range from heterogeneous consumption preferences for professional football over a subjective perception of the value of the stadium architecture to a distinctly perceived opportunity cost of the commitment of public funds. Lifestyle proxy variables contributed significantly to the explanation of the voting outcome, revealing significant relationships where coefficients on standard indicators of economic wealth such as household income or rate of unemployment are not statistically significant when accounting for spatial dependency.

From our results, the clear recommendation emerges that more attention should be paid to specific lifestyle preferences, values and attitudes that potentially influence individual behavior and market outcomes. Our results are interesting when taking into account some of the dominant arguments against sport facilities or mega events, namely the displacement of low-income groups and the relocation of public funds in the discrimination of disadvantaged persons. It seems that those groups are less opposed to sport facilities or mega events. They may have less information about the economic impact of the project or may be more susceptible to the media hype. It seems that the main opposition comes from highbrow lifestyle groups, which may think that they are speaking on behalf of disadvantaged groups. Of course, care should be taken when generalizing from this case study to all cities, stadiums, and mega events.

NOTES

1. $PD = [\exp(\alpha_1)-1] * 100$ (Halvorsen and Palmquist, 1980).
2. We address heteroskedasticity using the standard Whilte/Huber 'sandwich' correction.
3. Another form of spatial dependency emerges from the dependent variable being

endogenous to neighboring observations. This dependency can be dealt with by the application of a spatial lag model. Methodological aspects of spatial error and spatial lag models are covered in Anselin (1988) and Anselin and Bera (1998).

4. Coefficient estimates of control variables are affected only marginally by the altered specifications.
5. The GDR-Nostalgic milieu is not listed due to its lack of relevance in Western Germany.
6. It can be assumed that political parties recruit their voters in certain milieus. For example, the majority of FDP voters are likely to belong to the Establishment. Green Party voters and Post-Materialists are likely to share similar values.
7. The theoretical political economy literature assumes that policy produces efficient outcomes, because politicians tend to base decisions on principles and function efficiently when subject to symmetrical pressures (Grossman and Helpman, 1994).

REFERENCES

Agostini, S.J., J.M. Quigley and E. Smolensky (1997), 'Stickball in San Francisco', in R.G. Noll and A. Zimbalist (eds), *Sports, Jobs, and Taxes: The Economic Impact of Sports Teams and Stadiums*, Washington, DC: Brookings Institution, pp. 385–426.

Ahlfeldt, G.M. and G. Kavetsos (2011), 'Form or function? The impact of new football stadia on property prices in London', SERC Discussion Paper 0087, Spatial Economics Research Centre, LSE, London.

Ahlfeldt, G.M. and W. Maennig (2009), 'Arenas, arena architecture and the impact on location desirability: the case of "Olympic Arenas" in Berlin-Prenzlauer Berg', *Urban Studies*, **46** (7), 1343–62.

Ahlfeldt, G.M. and W. Maennig (2010a), 'Impact of sports arenas on land values: evidence from Berlin', *The Annals of Regional Science*, **44** (2), 205–27.

Ahlfeldt, G.M. and W. Maennig (2010b), 'Stadium architecture and urban development from the perspective of urban economics', *International Journal of Urban and Regional Research*, **34** (3), 629–46.

Ahlfeldt, G.M. and W. Maennig (2012), 'Voting on a NIMBY facility: proximity cost of an "iconic" stadium', *Urban Affairs Review*, **48** (2), 205–37.

Ahlfeldt, G.M., W. Maennig and H. Scholz (2010), 'Erwartete externe Effekte und Wahlverhalten: Das Beispiel der Münchner Allianz-Arena', *Jahrbücher für Nationalökonomie und Statistik*, **230** (1), 2–26.

Allgayer, F. (2002a), 'Zielgruppe DDR-Nostalgische: Das Ideal der alten DDR-Verhältnisse', *media & marketing*, 6/2002, 48–54.

Allgayer, F. (2002b), 'Zielgruppe Konsum-Materialisten', *media & marketing*, 4/2002, 48–55.

Allgayer, F. (2002c), 'Zielgruppe Traditionsverwurzelte: Ruhiger Lebensabend mit der Familie', *media & marketing*, 9/2002, 58–64.

Allgayer, F. (2003), 'Zielgruppe Bürgerliche Mitte: Freundeskreis in Harmonie', *media & marketing*, 1–2/2003, 56–62.

Anselin, L. (1988), *Spatial Econometrics: Methods and Models*, Dordrecht: Kluwer.

Anselin, L. (2003), 'Spatial externalities', *International Regional Science Review*, **26** (2), 147–52.

Anselin, L. and A.K. Bera (1996), 'Simple diagnostic tests for spatial dependence', *Regional Science & Urban Economics*, **26** (1), 237–89.

Anselin, L. and A.K. Bera (1998), 'Spatial dependency in linear regression models with an introduction to spatial econometrics', in A. Ullah and D.E. Giles (eds), *Handbook of Applied Economic Statistics*, New York: Marcel Dekker, pp. 237–89.

Anselin, L. and R.J.G.M. Florax (1996), 'Small sample properties of tests for spatial dependency in regression models: some further results', in L. Anselin and Florax (eds), *New Directions in Spatial Econometrics*, Berlin: Springer, pp. 21–74.

Arntz, M. and R.A. Wilke (2007), 'An application of cartographic area interpolation to German administrative data', *Advances in Statistical Analysis*, **91** (2), 159–80.

Carlino, G.A. and N.E. Coulson (2004), 'Compensating differentials and the social benefits of the NFL', *Journal of Urban Economics*, **56** (1), 25–50.

Coates, D. and B.R. Humphreys, (2006), 'Proximity benefits and voting on stadium and arena subsidies', *Journal of Urban Economics*, **59** (2), 285–99.

Cornelissen, S. and W. Maennig (2010), 'On the political economy of "feel-good" effects at sport mega-events: experiences from FIFA Germany 2006 and prospects for South Africa 2010', *Alternation*, **17** (2), 96–120.

Dehring, C.A., C.A. Depken and M.R. Ward (2008), 'A direct test of the homevoter hypothesis', *Journal of Urban Economics*, **64** (1), 155–70.

Dürr, A. (2000), 'Kein Großumbau des Olympiastadions', available at: http://www.sued deutsche.de/muenchen/artikel/496/1495/ (accessed 10 June 2008).

Dürr, A. (2001), 'Bürger entscheiden über neue Super-Arena', Süddeutsche Zeitung Online, available at: http://www.sueddeutsche.de/muenchen/artikel/913/.

Fischer, R. (2002a), 'Zielgruppe Etablierte: Über allem liegt ein Hauch von Luxus', *media & marketing*, 5/2002, 48–56.

Fischer, R. (2002b), 'Zielgruppe Experimentalisten: Kino statt Fernsehen, Indien statt Ballermann', *media & marketing*, 1–2/2002, 66–72.

Fischer, R. (2002c), 'Zielgruppe Hedonisten: Lust am Leben und am Trash', *media & marketing*, 12/2002, 54–62.

Fischer, R. (2002d), 'Zielgruppe Moderne Performer: Protagonisten der Ich-AG', *media & marketing*, 11/2002, 58–64.

Fischer, R. (2002e), 'Zielgruppe Postmaterialisten: Immer auf der Suche nach Informationen', *media & marketing*, 7–8/2002, 52–8.

Goodchild, M.F. and N.S. Lam (1980), 'Areal interpolation: a variant of the traditional spatial problem', *Geo-Processing*, **1**, 297–312.

Groothuis, P.A., B.K. Johnson and J.C. Whitehead (2004), 'Public funding or professional sports stadiums: public choice or civic pride?', *Eastern Economic Journal*, **30** (4), 515–26.

Grossman, G.M. and E. Helpman (1994), 'Protection for sale', *American Economic Review*, **84** (4), 833–50.

Halvorsen, R. and R. Palmquist (1980), 'The interpretation of dummy variables in semilogarithmic equations', *American Economic Review*, **70** (3), 474–75.

Hilgers, D., W. Maennig and M. Porsche (2010), 'The feel-good effect at mega sport events. Public and private management problems informed by the experiences of the FIFA World Cup', *International Journal of Business Research*, **10** (4), 15–29.

Hornberger, S. (2001), 'München prüft drei Standorte für Stadion', available at: http://www.welt.de/print-welt/article439509/Muenchen_prueft_drei_Standorte_fuer_Stadion.html (accessed 15 May 2008).

Kavetsos, G. and S. Szymanski (2010), 'National well-being and international sports events', *Journal of Economic Psychology*, **31** (2), 158–71.

King, G. (1997), *A Solution to the Ecological Inference Problem: Reconstructing Individual Behavior from Aggregate Data*, Princeton, NJ: Princeton University Press.

King, G., O. Rosen and M.A. Tanner (2004), *Ecological Inference: New Methodological Strategies*, Cambridge: Cambridge University Press.

Matheson, V. (2008), 'Mega-events: the effect of the world's biggest sporting events on local, regional, and national economies', in D. Howard and B. Humphreys (eds), *The Business of Sports*, Vol. 1, New York: Praeger, pp. 81–97.

Mochmann, I.C. and Y. El-Menouar (2005), 'Lifestyle groups, social milieus and party preference in Eastern and Western Germany: theoretical consideration and empirical results', *German Politics*, **14** (4), 417–37.

München, S.A. (2007), *M-Statistik Standarddatensätze und Datenpakete*, Munich.

N.N. (2001a), 'Bayern und Sechzig beschließen Stadion-Neubau', available at: http://www.sueddeutsche.de/muenchen/artikel/102/8094/ (accessed 14 May 2008).

N.N. (2001b), 'Beschlussvorlage des Planungsreferats für den 11.07.2001 – Anlage 6', available at: http://www.solarstadion.de/anlg6jpg.htm (accessed 14 January 2008).

N.N. (2001c), 'Fragestellung des Münchner Bürgerentscheids vom 21.10.2001', available at: http://www.solarstadion.de/be01.htm (accessed 14 January 2008).

N.N. (2001d), 'M-Statistik – Wahlberichterstattung: Stadionneubau in Fröttmaning 2001', available at: http://www.mstatistik-muenchen.de/themen/wahlen/wahlberichterstattung/be/2001/be_stadion.htm (accessed 16 January 2008).

N.N. (2001e), 'M-Statistik – Wahlen und Volksabstimmungen: Bürgerentscheide in München seit 1996', available at: http://www.mstatistik-muenchen.de/sammelordner_monatsberichte/document/monatsberichte/heft4_5_6_2001/heft5/art1/be_mchn.htm (accessed 16 January 2008).

N.N. (2005), 'WM-Tourismus kurbelt in München die Wirtschaft an', available at: http://www.allianzarena.de/de/aktuell/news-archiv/06208.php (accessed 16 January 2008).

N.N. (2007), 'Geschichte der Münchner Löwen', available at: http://www.tsv1860.de/de/verein/klubinfo/index.php (accessed 15 January 2008).

Otte, G. (2008), *Sozialstrukturanalysen mit Lebensstilen*, 2nd edn, Wiesbaden: VS Verlag für Sozialwissenschaften.

Pauli, M. (2001), 'Stadionfinanzierung im deutschen Profifußball: Eine institutionenökonomisch fundierte, modelltheoretische Untersuchung', Dissertation, Universität Paderborn, Paderborn.

Rushton, M. (2005), 'Support for earmarked public spending on culture: evidence from a referendum in Metropolitan Detroit', *Public Budgeting and Finance*, **25** (4), 72–85.

Schulze, G.G. and H.W. Ursprung (2000), 'La donna e mobile – or is she? Voter preferences and public support for the performing arts', *Public Choice*, **102** (1/2), 131–49.

Shively, W.P. (1969), '"Ecological" inference: the use of aggregate data to study individuals', *American Political Science Review*, **63** (4), 1183–96.

Sinus-Sociovision (2007a), 'Die Kartoffelgrafik als Landkarte', available at: http://www.sinus-sociovision.de/2/2-3-3-1.htm (accessed 16 February 2009).

Sinus-Sociovision (2007b), 'Wo die Milieus wohnen – MOSAIC Milieus', available at: http://www.sinus-sociovision.de/2/2-3-3-10.htm (accessed 16 February 2009).

Tu, C.C. (2005), 'How does a new sports stadium affect housing values? The case of FedEx field', *Land Economics*, **81** (3), 379–95.

Veal, A.J. (1993), 'The concept of lifestyle: a review', *Leisure Studies*, **12** (4), 233–52.

PART III

DESIGN OF MEGA EVENTS

8 Can mega events deliver sustainability? The case of the 2010 FIFA World Cup in South Africa

*Anton Cartwright**

1 INTRODUCTION

'*Ke Nako*' – it is time. These are the bold words that ushered in the 2010 FIFA World Cup between 11 June 2010 and 11 July 2010 in South Africa. 'Time for what, exactly?' was never totally clear. It was a football event, but everyone, from politicians to business people, social justice movements and non-governmental organizations (NGOs) hoped that Africa's first hosting of the world's largest mega event would boost their interests. As it transpired the 2010 Football World Cup was declared a success. FIFA awarded the country '9 out of 10 . . . a *summa cum laude*' for its efforts (Blatter, 2010). The criteria for making these judgements vary and are vague, but South Africa became only the third host country since 1930 to attract more than three million paying spectators, the showpiece was responsible for the word '*vuvuzela*' being entered into the Oxford Dictionary of English, and the FIFA World Cup showcased South Africa in a favourable light. For a country such as South Africa where the social fabric has repeatedly been fractured and the future remains highly contested, the opportunity to feel good about itself was not trivial. Aligning behind a single cause provided much needed support for the ongoing effort to build a new and more just society.

South Africa's successful hosting of the 2010 FIFA World Cup was preceded by its efforts on smaller – but none the less significant – events including the 1995 Rugby World Cup, the 2000 Summit on Sustainable Development, the 2003 Cricket World Cup and the 2009 Confederation's Cup. Indeed, the country has a track record as a sophisticated and reliable host of such events. In some senses this is ironic, even painful, against the backdrop of South Africa's patchy delivery of basic services and domestic policy implementation since 1994 (McDonald and Pape, 2002; Bond, 2004): in May 2010 South Africa still grappled with an obdurate housing backlog of 2.1 million units (Cottle, 2010). What the 2010 FIFA World Cup™ demonstrated is that when South Africa's decision makers are united by a common cause (or a common threat) they are capable of much more than has become the accepted norm. In the run-up to the 2010 event, South Africa was repeatedly reminded that failure to honour its guarantees to FIFA on scheduling, security and infrastructure, would see the event given to another country. Adding insult to injury, Australia was bookmarked as the most likely beneficiary of South Africa's potential demise. A more subtle but pressing threat involved appearing incompetent or poorly organized as the world looked on. The combination was enough to ensure that South Africa's elite in business, politics and civil society temporarily suspended their petty conflicts and defence of vested interests, stuck to their promises and in a relatively short time built the stadiums, transport systems and management structures with which to roll out the 30-day extravaganza.

The ability to galvanize action is a feature of mega events, especially those hosted in developing countries. Regardless of whether they generate or cost money in the long term, mega events create windows of opportunity in which countries can achieve the extraordinary and re-imagine and reconfigure structural impediments (social and infrastructural) to development. Once this is recognized, the question becomes, 'What will host countries choose to achieve with this opportunity?' or perhaps more accurately, 'What will they be placed under pressure to achieve?'. Typically this opportunity gets cast in the form of 'legacy projects and infrastructure'. The argument adopted here is for a more ambitious notion of legacy that involves host countries identifying structural deficiencies in their economies and hosting mega events in a manner that contributes to addressing these.

One aspect that received only peripheral attention in the build-up and during the 2010 event, was the contribution – more accurately, the lack of contribution – made by the FIFA World Cup to South Africa's transition to a low carbon green economy. 'What has football got to do with the environment?' you might ask. This chapter argues that South Africa's neglect of the opportunity to transition to a low carbon economy represents a loss of exactly the type of opportunity that mega events are well placed to seize. The chapter proceeds to examine where responsibility for this oversight lies and explores alternative causes for optimism in spite of the missed opportunity.

2   2010 AND SOUTH AFRICA IN CONTEXT

South Africa competed fiercely to host the 2010 Football World Cup™, having lost the right to host the 2006 event through a combination of naivety and dubious circumstances. Competition for mega events appears to have increased in the last decade, in spite of the evidence that it is very difficult to generate a financial profit as host (Cartwright and Cristando, 2008; Kuper and Szymanski, 2009). Hosting the 2010 FIFA World Cup™ cost South Africa's national government ZAR31 billion (US$4.43 billion) and its host cities a further ZAR9 billion (US$1.28 billion) in direct payments. Of this expenditure, ZAR22.9 billion was spent on stadiums and related infrastructure (Cottle, 2010). That the combined cost more than doubled from the original 2007 estimate is perhaps not surprising. Nor should it have been surprising that, in the midst of a global recession, there were far fewer football tourists than originally forecast (309,000 rather than the 485,000 predicted according to Grant Thornton, although these numbers are contested, see du Plessis and Maennig, 2011) or that the ZAR55 billion (US$7.85 billion) anticipated from the event (Grant Thornton, 2008) was never realized. The contribution to GDP was also eventually calculated at much less than the projection in the bid book – 0.54 per cent relative to 3 per cent (Grant Thornton, 2010). Anybody who has reviewed the short-term financial impacts of hosting mega events from Montreal (1976) through Greece (2000), Japan and South Korea (2002), Germany (2006) and back to Vancouver's Winter Olympics (2010) knows that hosts tend not to generate short-term financial windfalls, but also that short-term gains are a poor yardstick by which to measure the impact of these events (Brunet, 1993; Ahlert, 2000; Baade et al., 2002; Abad, 2001; Essex and Chalkley, 2004; Horne, 2004; Zimbalist, 2010). (Table 8.1.)

The conventional understanding is that the benefits go beyond easily measured financial windfalls and include increased international profile, the opportunity to rebrand a country and influence international perceptions of a country favourably, the ability to focus the fiscus on a sudden targeted infrastructure spend with the associated economic multipliers, the potential for a tourism windfall and even the support for social cohesion and nation building. By the same reasoning, however, mega events can have unforeseen negative impacts, most obviously on the environment and on income inequality.

The reality is that mega events do provide a rare hiatus in a country's development; a time when society, the economy and international opinion align in support of a particular country or city. This is not easily quantified, but the extent to which this opportunity is used to create impetus, positive change and a reference point, determines what can be referred to as the 'success' of the event. The Barcelona Olympics was, it is often claimed, used in this manner to reconfigure infrastructure and to accelerate that city's much-needed process of urban renewal (Brunet, 1993; Nello, 1997; Abad, 2001).

Table 8.1   Shifting projections for the 2010 event

	Actual (Rm)[1]	2008 update (Rm)	2007 update (Rm)	Bid book (Rm)
Ticket sales	2,100[2]	6,000	4,600	4,660
Other event expenditure	n/a	132	93	76
Spectator trip expenditure	3,640	8,163	6,894	4,466
Team trip expenditure	n/a	176	161	161
Press and VIP spend	n/a	440	391	290
Sponsorship and rights spend	756	756	756	756
Infrastructure and stadium spend	31,000	17,400	17,400	2,304
TOTAL SPEND	55,000	33,068	30,356	12,713
GDP contribution	20,000[3]	55,714	51,144	21,419
Employment generated (direct)	130,000	415,400	381,327	159,697

Notes:
1. Estimated.
2. Revenue accruing to the LOC (excludes FIFA revenue which is not reported in FIFA financial statements).
3. Estimated at 0.05 per cent by Grant Thornton (2010).

Sources: Grant Thornton (2008); Ndaba (2010); FIFA (2011).

South Africa's decision makers were aware of the precedents, became familiar with the processes followed by cities such as Barcelona, and were committed to ensuring that the 2010 World Cup™ left a legacy that served the country well in the aftermath of the event[1] (Maennig and du Plessis, 2008). To a certain extent they were successful. Collectively the fiscal stimulus provided to the construction sector saved some jobs in the face of the global financial crisis; the 309,000 visiting football tourists spent a combined ZAR3.64 billion (US$0.52 billion) and 95 per cent of these tourists said they would like to return (as reported in post-event surveys) which, it is assumed, together with the impressions created during the 26 billion television viewings of the event, will be good for its tourism sector.[2] In addition, the investment in better transport and security systems that were required of the event, have improved these sectors of the South African economy. What is equally clear, however, is that the World Cup was not used to address either the country's carbon intensity or the origins of this intensity. Appreciating the full extent of this lost opportunity, requires an appreciation of the liability that is the current state of South Africa's carbon-intensive economy, and how this might have been altered by the 2010 Football World Cup™.

3 GREEN GOALS?

That neither the local organizing committee (LOC) nor FIFA saw any need to consider or report ecological impacts from the 2010 event is itself symptomatic of the manner in which Football World Cups are run. In the run-up to the 2010 event, however, the LOC latched onto an idea that had been begun by the Oeko Institute in Germany 2006, and identified the need to score 'green goals' in the planning of the event. The LOC appointed a person to oversee its Green Goal Programme but never supported the brief and the criteria that comprised green goals remained vague and beset by differences of opinion and emphasis between the LOC and the South African Department of Environmental Affairs.

South Africa's economy and society depends heavily on a 'minerals-energy complex' (Fine and Rustomjee, 1996), but needs to transition away from this dependence if it is to retain competitiveness and create employment. The need is increasingly acute in a global economy that is becoming carbon constrained and in which South Africa's extractive industries of mining, forestry and agriculture find themselves a long way down the value chain. In 2006, every dollar of South African GDP (adjusted for purchasing power parity) involved the emissions of 1.66 $kgCO_2$ from fossil fuel combustion (US EIA, 2008).[3] This is more than three times the carbon intensity of the world economy (0.55 $kgCO_2$/\$GDP) and more than four times that of a country such as Germany. As a carbon intensity outlier, South Africa risks losing competitiveness as countries begin accounting for their emissions. Decoupling the economy from emissions is not easy, especially for oil- and coal-producing countries. South Africa has been particularly poor in this regard. Measures for CO_2/GDP decreased 14.9 per cent between 1992 and 2006 in South Africa, compared with a 56.7 per cent decrease in China, 26.8 per cent decrease in the USA and a 21 per cent decrease in Germany over the same period.

It was no surprise, then, that an *ex ante* estimate of the 2010 World Cup™ carbon footprint performed by Randall Spalding-Fecher and others from the company Econ Pöyry in February 2009, produced a large number – 2.7 million tons of CO2-e (Econ Pöyry, 2009). Such estimates are at best indicative: would the lights in a hotel have been on anyway even if World Cup tourists had not been there? Should one include the effects of water vapour emitted by aeroplanes given that this vapour does trap heat in the atmosphere but does not hang around in the atmosphere very long? How many locals will not be commuting or holidaying as a result of the World Cup congestion? As calculations go, however, the Econ Pöyry estimate is as comprehensive and balanced as anyone could have hoped for. While actual emissions from the event can be assumed to be lower than the estimate in the same proportion as visitor numbers were lower than those projected,[4] the projected carbon footprint estimate served as a reference point on the scale of the problem and a guide for remedial actions. In the study, which was the first of its kind to include the emissions arising from international travel, 67 per cent of all emissions were generated by fans' air travel. The balance of accounted emissions comprised inter-city transport, intra-city transport, stadium constructions and material, stadium and precinct energy use and energy use in accommodation. But even if international travel is ignored, the South African World Cup™ appears to have been more greenhouse gas intensive than any preceding Olympic Games or Football World Cup™ (Cartwright, 2010). To understand why this is the case, it is necessary to appreciate that South Africa uses its own particularly dirty coal to generate over 93 per cent of its electricity and that the state-owned company SASOL (formed during apartheid isolation) uses coal to supply 30 per cent of the country's liquid oil, using a process that is responsible for the world's biggest point-source of greenhouse gas pollution at the industrial town of Secunda. It is equally necessary to appreciate that the apartheid space economy deliberately separated people's living place from economic opportunities, that South African cities have very low residential densities, and that these attributes drive up the energy intensity of the economy. There could be no other way, then, but for a World Cup in South Africa to have generated a massive footprint, and to blame the event for this is to confuse symptoms with causes.

4   OFFSETTING THE CARBON FOOTPRINT OF THE 2010 WORLD CUP™

The 2010 World Cup™ carbon footprint should have served not as a project to be offset, but as a marker of the underlying problem, namely the carbon intensity of South Africa's economy and society. It is a problem that represents a grave liability to the economy in an increasingly carbon-constrained world, but once host countries seek to align their hosting of mega events to their meeting of local priorities, it is also a problem with the attributes and structural origins that could have been addressed.

While the opportunity was missed in South Africa, it is useful to reflect on how the 2010 World Cup™ could have gone about the process differently: what would have been involved, who should have been responsible and what might have been the desirable outcome? The ambition needed to reach beyond simple offsets, but the carbon market does provide a useful proxy for what might have been. Offsetting the carbon footprint of the 2010 World Cup™ would have cost roughly ZAR210 million (US$30 million) based on US$11 per ton. This seemingly large sum is in fact less than 1 per cent of the total cost of hosting the World Cup. In practice, South Africa could have marshalled this investment in carbon 'credit' to any carbon-saving programme in the country or region, prioritizing lowest marginal abatement costs, highest social impact or ease of implementation as it saw fit. In the process it would have aligned its expenditure with local priorities and needs while still meeting FIFA demands. This deliberate alignment is one of the key strategies of successful hosts, and one of the definitive oversights of Japan, South Korea and Greece, respectively (Baade et al., 2002; Cartwright and Cristando, 2008; Kuper and Szymanski, 2009).

Had South Africa reduced the 2010 event's footprint by spending this additional money in its planning and construction or through the carbon market, it could have claimed the hosting of the first carbon-neutral mega event in the world, a status that would automatically and instantaneously have seen it reposition itself from climate change laggard to climate change pioneer. It would also have set a watershed precedent for future events. More importantly, had South Africa seen fit to link its hosting of the world's largest mega event to a transition away from a carbon-intensive society, it would have begun the process of changing the structure of its economy and communities. Dow and Downing (2007) point out that the adoption of renewable energy is a catalyst to more sustainable societies, and in South Africa, renewable energy investments that break the current economic dependence on coal and mining are a prerequisite for creating employment, forming more just societies and higher economic growth levels. The World Cup could not have achieved the full extent of the transition required in South Africa on its own, but South Africa is unlikely to face a better opportunity to begin the process than that which was provided by the mobilization of resources, the public's embracing of an international agenda and the collective self-belief that accompanied the 2010 event.

5 UNDERSTANDING SOUTH AFRICA'S MISSED GREEN GOALS

It is of course easy to criticize, especially with the benefit of hindsight.

In a country such as South Africa that still sees the 'environment' as a human construct or a place where rich (predominantly white) people go on long weekends, the two-way causalities between ecological degradation and human development are easily missed, as is the need to break from the minerals-energy complex in favour of a more sustainable economy. In this sense the lack of imagination, the shortage of foresight and the path-dependent economics that saw the 2010 World Cup™ fail in its 'greening' have their origins deep within the prevailing South African psyche. Addressing this while simultaneously preparing to host the world's biggest sporting event would have required a level of systemic sustainability ambition that has no precedents in South Africa, or an explicit brief from FIFA. Indeed, to the extent that FIFA concerns itself with event legacies, this focuses on projects and not systemic or strategic improvements in host countries.

The Football World Cup is unlike the Olympics, and in this sense Barcelona is a misleading benchmark. Not only is the World Cup spread across a country as opposed to being focused in one city, but the influence of FIFA is definitive and leaves host countries, and particularly those host countries in the developing world for which the consequences of failure are greater, with very little influence. FIFA generated revenue of US$3.65 billion from the 2010 event (excluding significant revenue from ticket sales) (FIFA, 2011). It is not surprising, then, that they guard their monopoly of the event fiercely, go out of their way to ensure the protection of 'commercial partners' (sponsors) and insist on a proven blueprint for ensuring that the event delivers its four-yearly windfall. In South Africa, FIFA insisted on the building of five new stadiums (even overseeing the relocation of the stadium within Cape Town), required dedicated upgrades to the country's telecoms capacity and a temporary overhaul of the country's marketing and tax legislation. In the scramble to comply, South Africa's focus narrowed on getting the basic infrastructure in place, ensuring safety and providing transport. In spite of the obvious potential, the 2010 FIFA World Cup™ was not seen by the host country as a time for unprecedented ambition involving systemic changes to its society and the economy.

In the course of the frenetic preparations, the much vaunted 'green goals' passed from the LOC to host cities where, with the notable exceptions of Durban and Cape Town,[5] they were forgotten about in the rush to provide enough public toilets to spectators and mineral water to FIFA officials. FIFA, the LOC and the general public seemed not to mind. Cape Town, Durban and to a lesser extent Port Elizabeth continued to pursue 'green goals' in spite of the lack of support or accountability from the LOC. Cape Town initiated 42 green goal projects, 17 of which continued after the event and claimed to have 'compensated for' 95 per cent of the event emissions; Durban continues with an offsetting tree-planting campaign in the city and, as with Cape Town, installed energy-efficient lighting at stadium precincts. Very few of these efforts, however, were quantified or verified in accordance with carbon accounting practices, and no attempt has been made to aggregate the impact of green goals across host cities. Outside of Cape Town and Durban, remarkably few claims were made or publicity sought around the sustainability of the event. As such, the green goal legacy represents a spatially patchy series of projects conceived of as an adjunct to the event and the host city economies. Collectively the effort fell short of the need to alter the carbon and resource-intensive trajectory of South Africa's economy.

The South African origins of this missed opportunity have been discussed above, but what of FIFA? Did FIFA appreciate that awarding the 2010 World Cup to South Africa would result in such a large emissions footprint? Surely. In that sense, FIFA should take some responsibility for the carbon footprint of an event that it manages on a very short string. This is particularly true given the emissions that arise from the cement, iron and steel used in the construction of the stadiums and other infrastructure on which FIFA insists. FIFA encourages host countries to offset some of their carbon emissions in climate change mitigation projects but does not enter into binding agreements with host countries on these offsets in the same way that it does on matters of security, stadiums and hospitality. FIFA, as an internationally recognized entity, does attempt to offset its own internal carbon footprint arising from its business operations, but it is mildly disingenuous for the organization to imagine that that is sufficient when it goes out of its way to ensure that it regulates almost every other aspect of the event's hosting. For an organization of its profile, influence and financial status, its level of commitment to reducing greenhouse gas emissions in its host countries is both conspicuous and cause for concern. FIFA did nominate Cape Town for the IOC Sport and Environment Award in Doha in 2011 for its Green Goal 2010 Programme, an award that Cape Town won to the acclaim of the city and, ironically, FIFA.

In an ideal world, in awarding the event, FIFA and other organizing bodies would take cognizance of climate change as a pressing global threat and consider the greenhouse gas intensity of aspirant hosts' economies, or at least the commitment of aspirant hosts to running an event in a carbon responsible manner, in addition to conventional criteria. That the *Realpolitik* of international events, and perhaps football in particular, is far from ideal is not news. FIFA's failure to accept significant climate change responsibility, and failure to make the connection between a warming world and the well-being of people (including football-playing people) and its own future, was reiterated in its decision to award the 2018 and 2022 events to two countries (Russia and Qatar) that are almost as carbon intensive as South Africa. As a matter of priority FIFA should be pressured to insist that these countries use the event not to entrench the importance of their respective fossil fuel sectors, but to diversify away from them into cleaner, safer and more sustainable energy sources.

6   A SILVER LINING?

Frustration and regret are legitimate emotions when the extent of the missed opportunity for a transition to renewable energy at the 2010 World Cup™ is understood and appreciated. But it may not be as dire, or as futile, as we imagine. The Football World Cup™ is, apart from being a FIFA-run event, also a truly international and internationalizing event. South Africa is a relatively new member of the international community and some of its tardiness in embracing renewable energy and a more sustainable economy can be attributed to its years in isolation and its lack of exposure to the defining global issues.

To a certain extent this changed in the short month that was the 2010 Football World Cup. South Africans hosted the world, were exposed to new cultures and forced to realize that other countries, some of them little known in South Africa, contained football teams and people that could teach their country a lot – not only about football. One of the ironies of South Africa's years in apartheid isolation is that while the rest of the world understood South Africa to be a regressive pariah, many people within the country told themselves that isolation was somehow fostering innovation, self-sufficiency and progress. This mindset is embedded in the pride in anachronistic industrial behemoths such as Sasol, Denel[6] and Eskom,[7] for example. Redressing this belief and coming to terms with just how far out of line with the global community South Africa is on certain scores, is at once a painful and exciting process and one that was aided by the exposure of the 2010 World Cup™.

In the run-in to 2010 there were written and film documentaries on almost every aspect of the country, including its carbon footprint and sustainability track record. Some people were confused, others offended, but the posing of novel questions led to new understanding and awareness. This included awareness of the ecological impact of mega events, of the links between electricity consumption and global warming, cement and the emission of CO_2. Exposure, in this way, contributed to a process of 'socio-institutional learning' and internationalization that is a prerequisite for any global effort to address greenhouse gas emissions and climate change (Downing and Dyszynski, 2010). It may be considered to be clutching at straws to imagine that this highly intangible product of mega events is significant, and yet it is an underacknowledged and undeniable attribute of mega events and one that took root in South Africa during the 2010 World Cup™.

7 CONCLUSION

The *Realpolitik* that defines the allocation of mega events is far from ideal or perfectly competitive. In the future, however, it is important that aspirant hosts be encouraged to consider the carbon intensity of their proposed event and to compete in terms of the extent to which they will reduce their emissions. In this way mega events could fulfil their potential as levers of positive change. Creating the collective self-belief required for profound change in host countries is one of the great attributes of mega events. Exactly who is responsible for ensuring that these opportunities are grasped – host countries or organizing bodies such as the IOC and FIFA – and how they are grasped, can be debated. In the case of football there is clear scope for FIFA to extend its immense influence so as to ensure that its events not only become less carbon intensive, but that host countries use these events to realize profound domestic changes that will serve them long after the proceedings are over. The default, in which simply hosting the event is considered ambition and success enough, represents a lack of imagination and a missed opportunity, especially in contexts such as climate change where the consequences of replicating business as usual are severe.

NOTES

*   Gratitude is due to Katie Williams for reviewing an earlier version of this chapter.
1. As Adrian Lackay, a spokesperson for the South African Revenue Services (SARS), so aptly stated in the run-up to the event: 'Our approach to the World Cup has been that it was never going to be a revenue raising exercise. Certainly it would be wrong to view the World Cup as a significant contributor in itself. The concessions we had to give to FIFA are simply too demanding and overwhelming for us to have material monetary benefits' (quoted in the City Press News Paper, 6 June).
2. South Africa received just over 1 million more tourists in 2010 than in 2009; a 15 per cent increase that outperformed the world average increase by 8 per cent (Minister Martinus van Schalkwyk, Media Briefing at South African Parliament, Cape Town, 1 March 2011).
3. The figures do not include land-use-based emissions.
4. Interestingly if the events-generated GDP and GDP:CO_2 ratios are applied, the Econ Pöyry ratio remains conservative, although it is obviously not accurate to assume that the hosting of the event was as carbon intensive as the South African economy as a whole, given the contribution of energy and coal mining to the South African economy.
5. Late in 2009 the National Department of Environmental Affairs issued a tender for an organization and projects that could offset the air-travel component of the 2010 World Cup and subsequent events, but then failed to award a contract. Instead host cities, lumped with the loose responsibility, have in some instances focused on the planting of trees.
6. Denel is a South African Arms Manufacturer that is solely owned by the government.
7. Eskom is South Africa's state-owned energy utility and a monopoly.

REFERENCES

Abad, J.M. (2001), 'Economic impact of the Olympic Games on tourism', in *World Tourism Organization and International, Olympic Committee*, Sport & Tourism, 1st International Conference, 22–23 February 2001, Madrid, World Tourism Organization, pp. 69–71.

Ahlert, G. (2000), 'The economic effects of the soccer World Cup 2006 in Germany with regards to different financing', *Economic Systems Research*, **13** (1), 109–27.

Baade, R., J. Vail and V. Matheson (2002), 'The quest for the Cup: assessing the economic impact of the World Cup', Department of Economics, Williams College, Williamstown, MA.

Blatter, S. (2010), Speech given at the closing ceremony of the 2010 Football World Cup, Sandton, South Africa, 12 July.

Bond, P. (2004), *Talk Left, Walk Right*, Durban: UKZN Press.

Brunet, F. (1993), *Economy of the 1992 Barcelona Olympic Games*, Lausanne: International Olympic Committee.

Cartwright, A. (2010), 'Green own goal? The World Cup's carbon footprint and what can and cannot be done about it', in Heinrich Boell Stiftung, *Perspectives*, 29 April, available at: http://www.boell.org.29/web/publications-540.html.

Cartwright, A. and J. Cristando (2008), 'Linking the 2010 Soccer World Cup with local economic development', InWent 2010 – LED Training Module.

Cottle, E. (2010), 'A preliminary evaluation of the impact of the 2010 Fifa World Cup™: South Africa', available at: http://www.sah.ch/data/D23807E0/Impact assessmentFinalSeptember2010EddieCottle.pdf (accessed January 2010).

Dow, K. and T.E. Downing (2007), *Climate Change Atlas*, London: Earthscan.

Downing, T.E. and J. Dyszynski (2010), *Frontiers in Adaptation Economics: Scaling from the Full Social Cost of Carbon to Adaptation Processes*, Oxford: Global Climate Adaptation Partnership.

Du Plessis, S. and W. Maennig (2011), 'The 2010 World Cup high-frequency data economics: effects on international tourism and awareness for South Africa', *Development South Africa*, **28** (3), 349–65.

Econ Pöyry (Randall Spalding-Fecher, Marianne Ramlau and Franziska Sinner) (2009), 'Feasibility study for a carbon neutral 2010 Fifa World Cup in South Africa', Department of Environmental Affairs & Tourism, Pretoria.

Essex, S. and B. Chalkley (2004), 'Gaining world city status through staging the Olympic Games', *Geodate*, **17** (4), 7–11.

FIFA (2011), *Annual Financial Report: 61st FIFA Congress 31 May and 1 June*, Zurich, available at: www.fifa.com/mm/document/affederation/administration/01/39/20/45/web_fifa_fr2010_eng[1].pdf (accessed July 2011).

Fine, B. and Z. Rustomjee (1996), *The Political Economy of South Africa: From Minerals-Energy Complex to Industrialization*, London: Hurst.

Grant Thornton (2008), 'The Business of 2010: How the Numbers Add Up', Media Briefing, 21 November.

Grant Thornton (2010), 'Updated economic impact of the 2010 Fifa World Cup', April.

Horne, J. (2004), 'The global game of football: the 2002 World Cup and regional development in Japan', *Third World Quarterly*, **25** (7), 1233–44.

Kuper, S. and S. Szymanski (2009), *Soccermix: Why England Loses, Why Germany and Brazil Win, and Why the U.S., Japan, Australia, Turkey – and Even Iraq – Are Destined to Become the Kings of the World's Most Popular Sport*, New York: Nation Books.

Maennig, W. and S. du Plessis (2008), 'World Cup 2010: South African economic perspectives and policy challenges informed by the experience of Germany 2006', *Contemporary Economic Policy*, **25** (4), 578–90.

McDonald, D. and J. Pape (2002), *Cost Recovery and the Crises of Service Delivery in South Africa*, London and New York: HSRC Press/Zed Books.

Ndaba, D. (2010), 'When the sun sets on the 2010 World Cup, will the host cities be ready to sweat their new sporting assets', *Engineering News*, 30 July (online publication, accessed August 2010).

Nello, Oriol (1997), 'The Olympic Games as a tool for urban renewal: the experience of Barcelona '92 Olympic Village', in Miquel de Moragas, Montserrat Llinés and Bruce Kidd (eds), *Olympic Villages: A Hundred Years of Urban Planning and Shared Experiences: International Symposium on Olympic Villages*, Lausanna 1996, Lausanne: International Olympic Committee, pp. 91–6.

United States Energy Information Administration (US EIA) (2008) 'International Energy Annual 2008', available at: http://eia.doe.gov/iea/carbon.html.

Zimbalist, A. (2010), 'Is it worth it? Hosting the Olympic Games and other mega sporting events is an honor many countries aspire to – but why?', *Finance and Development*, **47** (1), March 8–11.

9 Stakeholder perceptions of short-term marketing tactics during the Olympics
Rick Burton, Norm O'Reilly and Benoit Séguin

1 INTRODUCTION

Any discussion of mega sporting events and the perceptions created by these events is bound up in the very word 'perception'. By perception we refer to the views and images that a stakeholder holds of a certain entity. In the case of mega events, the stakeholders could be the rightsholder, a sponsor, a media partner, a national sport organization, and so on; while the entity could be the event, a sports federation, sponsorship or a host country.

We take this approach based on perceptions as they are core to any marketing perspective and while perceptions are almost always important to any entity, when we move into the world of mega sporting events there are numerous perceptions in play. As such, when we look at properties like the International Olympic Committee (IOC), football or basketball federations (FIFA and FIBA) or the Rugby World Cup, we must immediately recognize various stakeholders and their public, private and political agendas (Burton, 2003).

Using the Olympics as an example we can suggest that the IOC is charged with caring for and stewarding the Olympic Games (as a brand), while coordinating numerous different sport federations (that is, swimming, gymnastics and athletics) that are heavily invested in caring about the considerations of their individual sport officials and athletes. Likewise, countries (with their National Olympic Committees), regions (with their tourism boards) and individual athletes are all dreaming about the possibility and likelihood of performing on an international stage. Meanwhile, potential or selected host cities are active in enhancing the reputation of their city, state, province, region and ultimately country.

Host broadcasters, such as NBC Sports or CBC, have perceptual goals (if not ratings and profitability concerns), while governments or their respective agencies (including tourism) are concerned with how a mega event enhances their global or party agenda.

The purpose of this chapter is to take a very specific aspect of mega events, their perceptions and their impacts on stakeholders, and to articulate some approaches to the short-term marketing strategies and impacts that organizations seek as part of overall mega-event activations.

2 STAKEHOLDER PERCEPTIONS AND WHY THAT MATTERS

When we talk about short-term impacts and perceptions, the following stakeholders are of interest because of their aggregated spending power or influence:

1. consumers of products and business-to-business customers;
2. sponsors of events, teams, athletes, cities and other entities;
3. tourists;
4. athletes;
5. coaches;
6. administrators;
7. families and friends (different from tourists);
8. media outlets such as broadcasters, websites, bloggers and social networks;
9. governments and government agencies; and
10. public interest groups that consider the holistic impact of mega events.

While the above list may not be completely inclusive, it should provide a sense that significant infrastructures already exist that are impacted from any plan that desires to bring a major event from the discussion or bidding stage to the completed colossus that towers over a city for 17 days (in competitive actuality) or for months and years (in the sense of facilities construction, test events and final preparation). Further, in an age of instant communication and heavy scrutiny of all financial/economic and social performances, these 10 groups cannot take their obligations or fiduciary responsibilities lightly. Each of the above, whether driven by a board, CEO or single customer is weighing up various value equations that help justify the expenditure of time, money or both.

Interestingly, all of the above stakeholders will generally arrive, in one form or another 'on the ground' in the setting of the mega event and immediately begin drawing conclusions tied to a particular entity's appearance, performance, past reputation and current media coverage. Because of this, we shall use this chapter to investigate short-term marketing tactics with the assumption that in the staging of all major events, there comes a day (and hour) when each stakeholder must arrive and assess the work of thousands. In most cases, this is favourable but readers should be aware that since perceptions are not always based on 'facts', that innuendo, rumours and false information often emerge and shape public perception. This is generally seen in the months leading up to an event when stories start to appear that certain facilities or arenas may not be ready for the start of the event.

As an example, in the months prior to the Athens Summer Olympics in 2004, media coverage consistently suggested that the Greek government and host organizing committee were not going to finish on time. More recently, the 2010 Commonwealth Games staged in India were pummelled by reports of unfinished dormitories, deaths of construction workers and a general atmosphere of incompletion, corruption and community apathy.

3   OVERVIEW OF ON-THE-GROUND SHORT-TERM MARKETING TACTICS

As discussed, numerous organizations are interested in mega events for short-term benefits as they provide unique opportunities for changing or enhancing perceptions and because of this, on-the-ground marketing generally places a premium on tactics including hospitality, experiential activations and interpersonal relationship building.

Think for a moment about any special event the reader has ever attended, be it a circus, sporting contest, festival or fair. As 'spectators' arrive they are met with a host of considerations including their first sense regarding the scale of the grounds and their construction; the collection of unique smells from food, animals or other attendees; the colliding of sounds from competition, musicians, vendors or marketers; the inspection of (from looking at but also rubbing shoulders with) other 'guests' and whether any are known personally or by reputation. This sensory rush can disorient some while thrilling others, but there is almost always a point when participants want to reach a place they view as either safe or their own. In most cases, this may be their assigned seat or in festival settings, it may be an area near a stage or a patch of grass where a blanket can be spread out.

Such specificity may amuse contemporary readers, but historically one must remember that ancient contests at the Coliseum in Rome or twelfth-century jousting matches in England brought a range of classes together in close proximity to one another. And not surprisingly, seat-based segmentation offering varying degrees of proximity to the performance or separation from the masses became a critical aspect of early mega events.

Not surprisingly, this segmentation, generally for the benefit of the elite or well connected, continues to this day and often takes on critical forms for assisting with the management of overall perception.

4 'THE HOUSE'

Probably the most common and most effective short-term, on-the ground mega-event marketing tactic is what is known as 'the house'. Although originally founded around the Olympic Games as the Olympic House, the concept – in various forms – has been implemented in a variety of mega-event settings, such as the FIFA World Cup, Formula 1 racing events, film festivals and many more.

In general, the 'house' takes on a few specific forms:

1. National Olympic Committee Houses (for example, USOC House, Swiss House and so on) which are typically hospitality tactics to support families and friends of the athletes, coaches and administrators at the event. In the case of Canada Olympic House, one of the key drivers of its establishment was the feedback from athletes (via a survey) that they were concerned about their parents in foreign countries and that it could impact on their preparation and performance at the Olympic Games.
2. Corporate/Sponsor Houses (for example, Heineken House, Bud House, Visa Olympians Lounge and so on) which are houses that are funded or managed by sponsors who typically have a corporate branding and/or sales objectives. In the case of the well-known Heineken House, it is clearly to sell their product, promote their brand and build loyalty in influencers (Olympic athletes) who then return to their own communities as (hopefully) brand ambassadors.
3. International Sport Organization Houses (for example, IOC House) typically have administrative as well as marketing functions. Meetings are held, events happen, functions take place all based on the objectives of the international organization. Many of these objectives are unique to the mega-event scenario where certain aspects (media interest, stakeholders present and so on) are possible.
4. Government Houses (for example, Canada House, London House and so on) are the last class of houses. These are typically 'quieter' in their marketing approach but have strong administrative functions and may be used by national or local governments for meetings to discuss bilateral agreements between governments, future mega-event bids and so on.

Granted, the concept of 'houses' is not fully inclusive to all of the restricted-access locations that spectators may know about or sense exist. Most mega-event patrons know that they cannot walk out onto the field of play before the competition or go behind the curtain (that is, go back-stage). They know that they cannot go into the locker or changing rooms where the competitors may be readying for athletic battle or practising material to be used on the stage. They know that they cannot go into the areas where lights and microphones are prepared for broadcast usage. Since they are not members of the media, they know that they cannot go into press boxes or photographer pits. In all, the spectator or 'guest' quickly learns about concepts such as 'All Access' passes, VIP passes, Field passes or media credentials.

A growing development, though, has been the creation and management of limited access 'houses' that desire to create the perception that almost all members of certain communities are welcome to enter if they are fortunate enough to know where a 'house' is, when it is open, what can be done in the house (such as purchase merchandise or food) and when the house is closed. An example would be USA House at the Beijing Olympics where American citizens could receive short-term access to a floor of the house for the primary purpose of shopping for Team USA merchandise.

In order to present more on houses and how they work, the authors undertook research on the attendees (families and friends of athletes) at the Canada Olympic House (COH) at the 2008 and 2010 Olympic Games in Beijing and Vancouver, respectively. Also, the authors reviewed different scenarios given that the Beijing COH was situated in a foreign country where neither of Canada's official languages (English and French) was widely spoken. In contrast, the Vancouver COH was a dual site (Vancouver and Whistler) and set up in the athletes' home country.

Case Study: Canada Olympic House 2008 – Beijing

In 2008, the COH Beijing had marketing objectives related to their spon-sors (who funded 100 percent of COH's costs), events hosted by organiza-tions (such as Canadian National Sport Organizations: NSOs) that rented a portion of the space for lunches, dinners or evenings, and hospitality for the athletes, their families and their friends, largely to provide a comfort-able place for the parents and friends of athletes (Canadian TV, free food and beverages, sponsor gifting and so on). A survey of the family and friends, and sport partners, who attended the COH was carried out to determine the success of the COH in pursuing these objectives. In total,

*Table 9.1   COH hospitality values (home away from home) – Beijing
2008*

COH was a 'home away from home'

Answer options	Response frequency	Response count
Strongly Agree	59.3%	227
Agree	22.7%	87
Neither Agree or Disagree	8.9%	34
Disagree	2.3%	9
Strongly Disagree	2.3%	9
Not Applicable	4.7%	18
answered question		383
skipped question		73

La MOC était un 'second chez-moi'

Answer options	Response frequency	Response count
Tout a fait d'accord	64.0%	16
D'accord	28.0%	7
Plus ou moins d'accord	0.0%	0
Pas d'accord	0.0%	0
Pas du tout d'accord	0.0%	0
Sans objet	8.0%	2
answered question		25
skipped question		6

487 of the attendees (39.8 percent response rate), provided data on the survey. The sample was representative by gender, sport, home province, and other demographic variables. Table 9.1 supports the very high level of success of the COH Beijing (the questions are the same but the data differ based on responses in English and in French).

Similarly, as shown in Table 9.2, the attendees found the atmosphere created at COH to be highly appealing.

In terms of usage of the COH, attendees reported many return visits (in some cases as many as 50) to the COH. These are outlined in Table 9.3 and Figure 9.1.

One specific activation tactic/approach was the Family and Friends program which included both web and on-site support for the COH and would help guests find tourist destinations, directions to get around, tickets to events, transportation, special events (Opening and Closing Ceremonies, for example). About 75 percent of guests used this service and it was effective, as indicated in Table 9.4.

Table 9.2   COH hospitality values (atmosphere) – Beijing 2008

I enjoyed the atmosphere at COH

Answer options	Response frequency	Response count
Strongly Agree	64.0%	244
Agree	26.2%	100
Neither Agree or Disagree	3.7%	14
Disagree	1.8%	7
Strongly Disagree	1.3%	5
Not Applicable	3.1%	12
answered question		381
skipped question		75

J'ai apprécié l'ambiance à la MOC

Answer options	Response frequency	Response count
Tout a fait d'accord	80.0%	20
D'accord	20.0%	5
Plus ou moins d'accord	0.0%	0
Pas d'accord	0.0%	0
Pas du tout d'accord	0.0%	0
Sans objet	0.0%	0
answered question		25
skipped question		6

For the events run by the Family and Friends program, there was good uptake by guests, with 55.8 percent of English respondents and 64 percent of French respondents attending an event (as shown in Table 9.5).

The COH Beijing was run by a combination of full-time Canadian Olympic Committee (COC) staff and volunteers. The volunteers comprised two levels, those on the Mission Staff (that is, members of the Canadian Olympic Team) and local volunteers who offered their time to support the Mission staff and the COC staff in running the COH. The model was very effective, according to the guests (as reported in Table 9.6).

Case Study: Canada Olympic House 2010

In 2010, the COH had two sites in each of the two Olympic cities of Vancouver and Whistler. Given the distance and travel logistics between the two sites, the COC was required to manage the two sites in order to provide the athletes, their families and their friends – as well as coaches

Table 9.3   Total number of COH visits – Beijing 2008

		Frequency	Percent	Valid percent	Cumulative percent
Valid	0	12	2.8	2.8	2.8
	1	32	7.4	7.5	10.3
	2	30	6.9	7.0	17.3
	3	36	8.3	8.4	25.8
	4	35	8.1	8.2	34.0
	5	60	13.9	14.1	48.0
	6	37	8.6	8.7	56.7
	7	17	3.9	4.0	60.7
	8	35	8.1	8.2	68.9
	9	7	1.6	1.6	70.5
	10	61	14.1	14.3	84.8
	12	14	3.2	3.3	88.1
	13	3	0.7	0.7	88.8
	14	12	2.8	2.8	91.6
	15	22	5.1	5.2	96.7
	16	2	0.5	0.5	97.2
	20	7	1.6	1.6	98.8
	22	1	0.2	0.2	99.1
	25	2	0.5	0.5	99.5
	30	1	0.2	0.2	99.8
	50	1	0.2	0.2	100.0
	Total	427	98.8	100.0	
Missing	System	5	1.2		
Total		432	100.0		

Note: Most visited between 5 and 15 times, with a few respondents noting very high levels of visit.

and administrators – with the services and support necessary for their hospitality and athlete support objectives.

Operating two COHs in its home country provided additional challenges for the COC. First, the number of people wanting access to the COH increased significantly. This included past national team athletes, previous COC board members or volunteers, high-level sport volunteers (for example, Olympic Summer Sports), sponsors/suppliers and so on. This meant that COH accreditation had to be allocated based on strict criteria and that staff/volunteers working at the front desk of the COH had to be sensitive when managing delicate situations involving stakeholders. Other challenges dealt with the level of services offered in both official

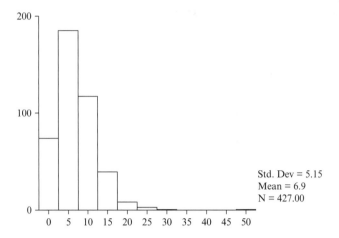

Figure 9.1   Total number of COH visits

Table 9.4   COH hospitality values (website efficiency) – Beijing 2008

I found the information on www.olympic.ca/familyandfriendsprogram website useful and informative

Answer options	Response frequency	Response count
Strongly Agree	19.5%	79
Agree	44.8%	182
Neither Agree or Disagree	10.1%	41
Disagree	0.5%	2
Strongly Disagree	0.5%	2
Not Applicable	25.1%	102
answered question		406
skipped question		50

J'al trouve les renseignements sur le site web www.olympic.ca/programme pour la famille et les amis utiles et instructifs

Answer options	Response frequency	Response count
Tout a fait d'accord	55.2%	16
D'accord	20.7%	6
Plus ou moins d'accord	6.9%	2
Pas d'accord	3.4%	1
Pas du tout d'accord	0.0%	0
Sans objet	13.8%	4
answered question		29
skipped question		2

*Table 9.5   COH hospitality values (attendance at special events) – Beijing
2008*

I attended one of the Family and Friends Program Events at Canada Olympic
House (COH)

Answer options	Response frequency	Response count
Yes	55.8%	212
No	44.2%	168
answered question		380
skipped question		76

J'ai assiste à l'un des événements organises dans le cadre du programme pour la
famille et les amis à la Maison olympique du Canada (MOC)

Answer options	Response frequency	Response count
Oui	64.0%	16
Non	36.0%	9
answered question		25
skipped question		6

languages. While the COC has made significant progress in this area over
the last few Olympic Games, having the Games at home meant high expectations from guests. The COH had to ensure that: staff/volunteers had
an adequate level of bilingualism, guests be greeted in their language of
choice, all information posted or given be in both languages, an adequate
mix of French/English programming including the television feed used
for the dozens of television sets placed throughout the COH, feed coming
from both French and English broadcasters. In other words, the COC had
to provide an environment where both Anglophone and Francophone
would feel at home when at the COH. The choice of the two locations of
COH and operating hours proved to be a challenge as well.

Similar to 2008, the COHs were administered by a combination of
COC staff and volunteers and were highly successful. Some 255 attendees
responded to the survey (a 31.8 percent response rate of all attendees).
The sample was representative by gender, sport, home province, and
other demographic variables. Some changes were noted compared to the
2008 results, including that fewer attended Family and Friends events
at the COH (41 percent) which can likely be explained by being a home
Games. Similarly, 2010 attendees were very satisfied but more critical than
2008 attendees of attributes such as location, opening hours and service
provided, also likely due to 2010 being a home Games.

Table 9.6   COH hospitality values (friendliness of staff) – Beijing 2008

The staff at Canada Olympic House (COH) were friendly

Answer options	Response frequency	Response count
Strongly Agree	56.8%	218
Agree	31.5%	121
Neither Agree or Disagree	4.4%	17
Disagree	3.4%	13
Strongly Disagree	1.6%	6
Not Applicable	2.6%	10
answered question		384
skipped question		72

Le personnel de la Maison olympique du Canada (MOC) était aimable

Answer options	Response frequency	Response count
Tout afait d'accord	92.0%	23
D'accord	8.0%	2
Plus ou moins d'accord	0.0%	0
Pas d'accord	0.0%	0
Pas du tout d'accord	0.0%	0
Sans objet	0.0%	0
answered question		25
skipped question		6

Overall, the 2010 COH was viewed as highly effective by both English and French respondents (see Table 9.7). Furthermore, the atmosphere was also highly positive (Table 9.8).

With respect to the dual-site aspect, most COH attendees took advantage of both houses with 96.7 percent visiting Vancouver COH and 71.7 percent taking in Whistler COH. Similar to 2008, attendees returned often to the COH. Combined responses for both houses are shown in Table 9.9.

Views of COH staff were also very positive (Table 9.10)

Overview of Beijing and Vancouver

While the focus of the authors' research was on Canadian facilities, familiarity with USA House in Beijing (2008) and Russia's Sochi 2014 House in Vancouver (during the 2010 Winter Games) provided additional insight into how the US Olympic Committee (USOC) and Russian Olympic Committee (ROC) viewed the role of those structures. To that

Table 9.7   COH hospitality values (home away from home) – Vancouver 2010

COH was a 'home away from home'

		Response percent	Response count
Strongly Agree		47.0	78
Agree		31.9	53
Neither Agree or Disagree		15.7	26
Disagree		3.0	5
Strongly Disagree		0.6	1
Not Applicable		1.8	3

La MOC était un 'second chez-moi'

		Response percent	Response count
Tout à fait d'accord		66.7	16
D'accord		25.0	6
Indécis		4.2	1
Pas d'accord		0.0	0
Pas du tout d'accord		0.0	0
Sans objet		4.2	1

end, USA House was almost always an exclusive setting with numerous dignitaries and athletes given luxurious settings and a 'safe haven' from the onslaught of Olympic vehicular traffic, human congestion, sensory overload and evident marketing of brands and services. And, while Russia House seemed more accessible, there were definitely security checkpoints and it was clear that certain areas of the structure were off limits to casual visitors.

Table 9.8   COH hospitality values (atmosphere) – Vancouver 2010

I enjoyed the atmosphere at COH		Response percent	Response count
Strongly Agree		59.0	98
Agree		35.5	59
Neither Agree or Disagree		2.4	4
Disagree		1.8	3
Strongly Disagree		0.6	1
Not Applicable		0.6	1

J'ai apprécié l'ambiance de la MOC		Response percent	Response count
Tout à fait d'accord		75.0	18
D'accord		25.0	6
Indécis		0.0	0
Pas d'accord		0.0	0
Pas du tout d'accord		0.0	0
Sans objet		0.0	0

5   VANCOUVER 2010 – NATIONAL SPONSOR ACTIVATION

Another important group of stakeholders around the 2010 Olympic Winter Games were the national sponsors. The domestic (national) sponsorship program of the 2010 Vancouver Olympic Winter Games was the most successful to date raising approximately $756 million in revenue

Table 9.9   COH hospitality values (total visits) – Vancouver 2010

COH Visits

		Frequency	Percent	Valid percent	Cumulative percent
Valid	0	2	0.8	0.9	0.9
	1	13	5.1	5.5	6.4
	2	19	7.5	8.1	14.5
	3	23	9.1	9.8	24.3
	4	29	11.4	12.3	36.6
	5	29	11.4	12.3	48.9
	6	22	8.7	9.4	58.3
	7	15	5.9	6.4	64.7
	8	14	5.5	6.0	70.6
	9	2	0.8	0.9	71.5
	10	37	14.6	15.7	87.2
	11	2	0.8	0.9	88.1
	12	10	3.9	4.3	92.3
	13	1	0.4	0.4	92.8
	14	2	0.8	0.9	93.6
	15	7	2.8	3.0	96.6
	20	3	1.2	1.3	97.9
	22	1	0.4	0.4	98.3
	24	1	0.4	0.4	98.7
	26	1	0.4	0.4	99.1
	30	1	0.4	0.4	99.6
	35	1	0.4	0.4	100.0
	Total	235	92.5	100.0	
Missing	System	19	7.5		
Total		254	100.0		

Descriptive Statistics

	N	Minimum	Maximum	Mean	Std deviation
COH visits	235	0	35	6.82	4.942
Valid N (listwise)	235				

(IOC, 2010). This amount does not include the sums that each sponsor spent on activating or promoting their sponsorship. A number of authors (Eisenhart, 1988; Kuzma et al., 1993) have suggested a ratio of up to 3:1 (that is, for each dollar spent on sponsorship another 3 dollars is spent on activating). Regardless of the ratio used for the Vancouver Games, it is reasonable to assume that total spending by sponsors was well over

Table 9.10   COH hospitality values (helpfulness of staff) – Vancouver 2010

The staff at COH were helpful

		Response percent	Response count
Strongly Agree		63.3	105
Agree		30.7	51
Neither Agree or Disagree		3.6	6
Disagree		1.8	3
Strongly Disagree		0.6	1
Not Applicable		0.0	0

Le personnel de la MOC était d'une aide précieuse

		Response percent	Response count
Tout à fait d'accord		54.2	13
D'accord		45.8	11
Indécis		0.0	0
Pas d'accord		0.0	0
Pas du tout d'accord		0.0	0
Sans objet		0.0	0

$1 billion. In a post-Games study conducted by the authors, sponsors were unanimous in stating that the investment was well worth it (Séguin and O'Reilly, 2011). The 2010 Games were found attractive for national sponsors for a number of reasons. The values associated with the Olympic brand, its wide appeal, the huge audiences delivered (spectators and TV viewers), the belief that the brand is one of the most supported brands in sports (huge equity) and the exclusivity were all mentioned as key benefits of being an Olympic sponsor. But the opportunity to 'connect' with Canadians on a deep emotional level was seen as an opportunity of a 'lifetime' by some. The prospect of playing a role in such an important chapter in Canadian history went beyond marketing value; in many ways it was a sort of nation-building value that provided a huge benefit that could not be replicated in other properties.

The Vancouver Organizing Committee (VANOC) was determined to make the Games an opportunity to touch the soul of a nation, to unite Canadians and to inspire the world. The VANOC brand was in line with these ambitious goals with its essence being: 'a celebration of what's possible in today's Canada – a chance to share the best of ourselves and what we've achieved as a country and a celebration of what's possible for our future – a chance to dream bigger, reach farther, and to create lasting legacies for others' (VANOC, 2006). The activation programs of partners (public and private) played an essential role in branding the experience and bringing the Games to Canadians and making them Canada's Games. The Torch Relay (prior to the Games) and the Games themselves provided countless opportunities for sponsors and non-sponsors to connect with the surge of pride felt by Canadians as the Games got under way.

The Olympic Torch Relay gave selected Canadians of all cultural backgrounds the opportunity to carry the Olympic Flame. The Olympic Torch Relay reached up to 90 percent of the Canadian population within one hour's drive and passed through more than 1,000 communities and places of interest. The Torch Relay played a central role in bringing the Games to Canadian citizens, creating excitement across the country and providing unique opportunity for sponsors/ government to connect with Canadians. For example, as a way to support this opportunity to engage Canadians across the country, the Government of Canada invested $24.5 million to enhance the local festivities that showcase a community's cultural heritage while welcoming the Olympic and Paralympic Flames (Government of Canada, 2011). Two other positive outcomes from the Torch Relay were the ability for companies to showcase their products directly to Canadian consumers from coast to coast and the expanded window of opportunity for marketing the Olympic property. The Relay was a great platform for all sponsors to activate. While only two sponsors had the official rights to the Relay (RBC and Coca-Cola), a number of initiatives remained possible for all Grand National sponsors. The Relay proved to be a unique opportunity for sponsors to develop employee incentive programs as well as provide a highly charged emotional experience to some key business partners. For an official sponsor like RBC, acquiring the rights to the Relay proved to be a cost-efficient investment for the corporation. RBC is deeply involved in local marketing and the Torch Relay went to 1,000 communities. That is 1,000 locations where RBC does business every single day, 1,000 communities where employees were likely filled with pride for having brought the Relay to their community and to their clients. Hence, connecting/engaging employees (current and future) with the Olympics with the goal to increase/drive employee pride were important for all sponsors. Increasing pride in the company was believed to ultimately lead to employee tenure, which, in turn, can lead to client tenure. This was particularly important for those who 'live and die' on the relationships between employees and clients as shown with this quote: 'We are a sales organization and it is all about the relationships we have with our clients, the longer the employee stays with us the better ability we have to impact the client tenure' (Olympic sponsor; Séguin and O'Reilly, 2011). The Olympic sponsorship also provided an opportunity for employers to speak to employees about what they stood for, their commitment to certain values and how they supported Canada and Canadian communities. Many sponsors used their connection to athletes to create a tangible connection with the Olympics.

Consumer experience and national pride were also enhanced during the Games through branded merchandise. By signing the Hudson's Bay Company (HBC) – Canada's oldest and largest national retail brand with 500 stores nationwide – as the official clothing and luggage partner and exclusive merchandise retailer of the Games and Canada's Olympic Team, VANOC ensured that Olympic merchandising would receive unprecedented distribution across the country while reaching a younger audience. During the Games, thousands stood in lines everyday at the Official Super Store in downtown Vancouver, from the time it opened at 9 a.m. until it closed at midnight. Many were hoping to snag the colorful and stylish 'red, knit mittens' which bore the Olympic rings on one side and the maple leaf on the palm. HBC sold more than 3.5 million pairs, making them one of the most visible providers of patriotism during the Games.

When walking around downtown Vancouver the feeling was that if you were not wearing Canadian gear, you visibly were out of place. Even in sections of the city far from the venues and downtown, store windows proudly displayed the 'Go Canada Go' message. The stores, streets and venues were filled with Canadian flags, painted faces, and Canadian hockey jerseys. All of this helped create the amazing atmosphere that surrounded the Games and for sponsors such as HBC (official supplier of Canadian Olympic Team) unprecedented traffic in its Olympic store.

*Figure 9.2   HBC Super Store Downtown Vancouver with VISA signage:
corner of Georgia and Howe*

Cooperation

Cooperation is a theme which was evident when examining both sponsor
activation and ambush marketing. From a sponsor activation point
of view in Vancouver there were several examples of official sponsors
working together in their activation and levering strategies. The HBC
Store downtown at Georgia and Granville contained the official Olympic
Shop for Vancouver apparel. At the Olympic Shop only VISA and cash
were accepted as forms of payment. In addition, there was a large amount
of VISA signage both inside and outside of the store (see Figure 9.2).
Canada Post (see Figure 9.3) and General Mills combined in a similar
manner with large signage displays in downtown Vancouver incorporating
both of their brands.

Official sponsors were not the only collaborators in Vancouver; there
was evidence of non-sponsors working together as well to gain some sorts
of benefits from having the Olympics in Vancouver. Such strategies have
often been referred to as ambush marketing (see Sandler and Shani, 1989;
Séguin and O'Reilly, 2008). The most obvious example of this type of

*Figure 9.3   Activation by Canada Post: Canada Post and General Mills
signage on Canada Post building – Robson Street*

cooperation was among three 'perceived' ambushers: Roots, MasterCard, and Right to Play. In Roots window displays (see Figure 9.4) and signage these three companies joined together to promote their association with each other in a manner that suggested association to the Games or at the very least, used Games-related themes as the base for their campaign. Sears was also involved with at least two other non-sponsors including Timex and MasterCard and one official supplier, Nike, using signage, promotions, and window displays to connect them to the Games. In-store the placement of Timex and SSC signage alongside Sears's 'Sears Welcomes the World' messaging made an obvious connection with the Games. While MasterCard had a similar approach using signage they also combined with Sears on a promotion. While making no direct connection to the Olympics, the use of hockey imagery and the timing suggest an attempt to take advantage of the Games-driven hype over Canadian national hockey as opposed to professional hockey (NHL). Finally, the coordination between Sears and Nike is more complex as it involves an official supplier and less direct collaboration. The Sears building at the corner of Robson and Granville was a prime location and each night Nike used the white

Figure 9.4   Cooperative ambush using Canada pride (Roots, MasterCard and Right to Play)

backdrop of the building to project enormous, topical advertisements for their force fate campaign. While this was not an explicit co-branding exercise by Nike and Sears, the provided picture clearly shows the potentially confusing proximity of the Sears brand to the Nike advertisement. Furthermore, on at least one occasion these advertisements included the Olympic rings in some form thus closely, albeit not directly, associating Sears with the Olympic rings. This leads directly into the next subsection.

Nike Canada

As Official Supplier of high performance sporting goods for Vancouver 2010, Nike Canada was afforded specific rights with regard to their association with the Games. As part of their commitment they provided the jerseys worn by the men's and women's ice hockey teams. These turned out to be immensely popular. On the streets of Vancouver and in venues, beyond just the hockey arena, the jerseys were everywhere, as prevalent, perhaps more so, than the other official clothing provided by HBC. The sheer number of people wearing the jersey was overwhelming and as such the Nike brand was intimately tied to the Games arguably in a way few other sponsors were able to achieve. To support the campaign and capitalize on its success Nike also had an extensive, multidimensional activation and levering strategy. This strategy used social media (that is, Facebook – www.facebook.com/niketraining), nightly, topical projection signage, their retail locations, and television advertisements to emphasize their campaign built around the jerseys and hockey as an expression of what it means to be Canadian. While it could be viewed as a risky strategy which depended to a great extent on the success of the men's and women's ice hockey teams, the explosion of nationalism combined with the gold medal performances of both teams justified their course of action and arguably saw them emerge as a major winner in the sponsorship activation stakes.

While the above reflects well on the Nike marketing department, it leads to questions regarding the potential for overactivation of official sponsors or suppliers. That is, activation which suggests a greater association than is actually the case based on their level of sponsorship. The structure of the Olympic marketing program can, at times, be confusing and numerous studies have posed questions around the ability of consumers to differentiate between various sponsorship levels and their given rights (Sandler and Shani, 1993; Shani and Sandler, 1998; Séguin et al., 2005). As an official supplier Nike Canada was granted fewer rights than both TOP sponsors and National Partners. However, Nike's ability to successfully and fully activate their sponsorship using multiple elements of the communications mix ensured that their presence at the Games equalled or surpassed most of the Worldwide and National Partners. In at least one case, the indirect display of the Olympic rings in Nike's projection signage offered them access to the same benefits only bestowed upon TOP sponsors who paid a significant premium for exclusivity with regards to those rights. While ambush marketing is often viewed and discussed as an outsider (or non-authorized party) trying to access the privileges of those with rights, in this case it is the insider using the ambiguity and confusion around sponsorship structure to potentially undermine other sponsors. The issue of consumer confusion is among the major concerns in relation to ambush marketing and curbing this confusion within the sponsorship program as well as in relation to outsider associations.

6   CONCLUSION/SUMMARY

We started this chapter with a discussion about perceptions and ended by showing very distinct images that were consistent with sophisticated perceptual management. This material should hopefully have provided readers a stronger sense of how different stakeholders view 'on the ground' tactics and how the concept of 'houses' or hospitality centers can play a huge role in shaping the considerations of countries, Olympic committees and sponsors during some of the biggest all-time sporting events. For national sponsors, 'houses' also provide unique opportunities to engage consumers and employees in a meaningful manner through communications cues that activate strong emotional connectors such as national pride and competitive spirit. When used in sync with other communication/ promotion programs such as VANOC's communication strategies, the look of the Olympic Games, national broadcasting and distinct properties such as Canada Olympic House, it provides additional support to the various sponsor activation programs.

REFERENCES

Burton, R. (2003), 'Olympic Games host city marketing: an exploration of expectations and outcomes', *Sport Marketing Quarterly*, **12** (1), 37–47.

Eisenhart, T. (1988), 'Sporting changes zap competitors', *Business Marketing*, 92–7.

Government of Canada (2011), 'Torch Relay', available at: http://www.canada2010.gc.ca/invsts/exprnc/030302-eng.cfm (accessed June 14, 2011).

International Olympic Committee (IOC) (2010), *Olympic Marketing Fact File*, Lausanne: IOC.

Kuzma, J.R., W.L. Shanklin and J.R. McCally Jr. (1993), 'Number one principle for sporting events seeking corporate sponsors: meet benefactor's objectives', *Sport Marketing Quarterly*, **2** (3), 27–32.

Sandler, D.M. and D. Shani (1989), 'Olympic Sponsorship vs. ambush marketing: who gets the gold?', *Journal of Advertising Research*, **29** (4), 9–14.

Sandler, D.M. and D. Shani (1993), 'Sponsorship and the Olympic Games: the consumer perspective', *Sport Marketing Quarterly*, **2** (3), 38–43.

Séguin, B., M. Lyberger, N. O'Reilly and L. McCarthy (2005), 'Internationalizing ambush marketing: the Olympic brand and country of origin', *International Journal of Sport Marketing and Sponsorship*, **6** (4), 216–29.

Séguin, B. and O'Reilly, N. (2008), 'The Olympic brand: ambush, marketing and clutter', *International Journal of Sport Management and Marketing*, **4** (1/2), 62–84.

Séguin, B. and N. O'Reilly (2011), 'Olympic sponsorship and ambush marketing: summary of interviews with Grand National sponsors of the 2010 Vancouver Winter Olympic Games', Report presented to the Canadian Olympic Committee, Toronto.

Shani, D. and D.M. Sandler (1998), 'Ambush marketing: is confusion to blame for the flickering of the flame?', *Psychology and Marketing*, **15**, 367–83.

VANOC (2006), 'Vancouver Sponsor Workshop: The Vancouver 2010 Brand', Vancouver, Canada.

10 Mega events and local politics
Matthew J. Burbank, Greg Andranovich and Charles H. Heying

1 INTRODUCTION

The rise of sport as an instrument of urban development is undeniable as cities pursue consumption-oriented strategies to find or make their place in the global economy (Euchner, 1994; Kuper and Szymanski, 2009; Rosentraub, 2010; Soja, 2010). In large part a consequence of the economic restructuring whose pace quickened over the last three decades of the twentieth century, cities and nations sought to retain competitive positions as the importance of location initially seemed to be lessening under the rapid advance of telecommunications and transportation technologies. When the economic sectors that were gaining employment tipped in favor of services, however, economic development strategies focused on transforming downtown areas and creating new spaces to attract business investment and service-oriented jobs. Public policies focused on the importance of culture in consumption-oriented economic development and urban regeneration strategies have adopted entrepreneurial approaches (Harvey, 1989; Clarke and Gaile, 1998; Judd and Fainstein, 1999; Owen, 2002; Smith, 2007). Cities in the United States had the added constraint of reductions in federal support for urban programs that started in the late 1970s and hit cities especially hard during the 1980s (Caraley, 1992; Eisinger, 1998). These policy changes shifted the political terrain away from the politics of redistribution – fighting poverty and inequality – and toward the politics of becoming more competitive in the global economy.

As cities have pursued this path of building an amenity-rich infrastructure through entrepreneurial policies, a number of thorny questions remain unanswered. Chief among these is whose interests are served by these policy decisions? Pursuing a policy path that regenerates urban centers – in terms not only of the built environment, but also enhancing social and cultural capital and facilitating the processes of democratic politics – presents major challenges to local public officials, city residents and businesses. More often than not the relations between the state, the community and the market are divisive and the process of creating policy often lacks mechanisms for understanding and addressing these divergent interests. Thus, there is greater potential for conflict when public policy decisions are made regarding whether to build or upgrade facilities, where and how to provide new infrastructure for improved accessibility to these facilities, or when trading off the commercial value of sports and entertainment for community-use values when making decisions about land use. In addition to these policy decisions over the built environment, cities also have engaged in unprecedented levels of city marketing to compete in the global economy. City images, and the processes for developing these images, open other avenues for political conflict because images support a powerful narrative and rationale for the allocation of scarce public resources, focusing economic development policy making (Pagano and Bowman, 1997). Although the autonomy of local institutions varies within and across national contexts, there are important local impacts that occur in the pursuit of sports and entertainment development. This chapter is concerned with these impacts, particularly when cities bid for and then host the Olympic Games. After discussing the politics of mega events, we examine the three US cities with recent experience of hosting mega events: Los Angeles, Atlanta and Salt Lake City. Our examination of these cities includes their original reasons for wishing to host the Olympic Games as expressed in the bid process, which allows us to assess images and city marketing, and the legacies in these cities in the post-Olympics period, which permits an examination of the politics of economic development policy making.

2   URBAN IMPACTS OF MEGA EVENTS

Economic development and urban regeneration have become increasingly focused on developing cultural amenities. In the current context of globalization, symbolic representations of lifestyle issues have overlaid the importance of simply rebuilding business centers in central cities which has led to the construction of interchangeable convention centers, renovated waterfronts, entertainment districts, sports stadiums, and upscale shopping areas. Often these developments occur in special zones, or bubbles, offset from a city's neighborhoods but close enough to bring about gentrification, ultimately changing the way people use downtown areas as well as the people who can afford to live there. Elected local officials often look to competitive economic development as an alternative way of raising local revenues because, if the economy grows, taxes do not have to be raised. Decision making for these new consumption-oriented urban landscapes has in many cases shifted away from city council chambers to the more closed venues of city redevelopment agencies or other quasi-public bodies, in part reflecting changes in the nature of public–private financing arrangements. As a consequence, these projects often are developed with limited public participation and input (Sanders, 1992).

The pursuit of mega events provides a way of differentiating cities because, by definition, mega events are unique (Andranovich et al., 2001). Many global sporting competitions, for example, are held only every four years. In addition to the sports themselves, sporting competitions bring global businesses that sponsor the competitions to the host city, providing an unparalleled opportunity for global positioning. The competition to host these mega events is fierce and this competition raises the specter of overselling the potential benefits and understating the potential costs. Because mega events entail bringing in an external event, cities must bid for the right to host. Although hosting the Olympic Games may be appealing to many cities, the requirements to host the Games are substantial and the Olympics are a relatively scarce commodity. In American cities, for example, the bid process involves competing against other US cities to gain the endorsement of the United States Olympic Committee (USOC) and then competing against other cities from around the world to secure the Games from the International Olympic Committee (IOC) (for more on the IOC process, see Humphreys and van Egteren (ch. 3), Feddersen and Maennig (ch. 5), and Baade and Sanderson (ch. 6) in this volume).

The bidding process itself is sometimes used simply to put a city 'on the map', but the timeframe between bidding and hosting provides the chance for intervening events to complicate city politics. The global financial crisis that erupted in 2008 is such an example, as the 2010 Olympic Games in Vancouver, the 2010 World Cup in South Africa and the 2012 Olympic Games in London had a more difficult time than expected attracting corporate sponsors because of these changing economic conditions. But mega events provide another challenge to local politics: winning a bid to host the Olympics puts pressure on a city to complete its event preparations, and this can put stress on the normal planning process, and on the allocation of resources for urban development projects. In the time between awarding the Olympics and their manifestation in the host city, the process of organizing the event pits the longer-term urban future against the shorter-term exigencies of place making for the host city's debut before a global television audience. In this policy environment, the politics of place promotion and the development of the city's amenity infrastructure can lead to the privileging of extralocal interests (Heying et al., 2007).

The potential benefits of hosting the Olympics include tangible benefits such as the development of infrastructure and amenities, city branding and image development, increased tourism and the visitor economy, promotion of trade and business investment, and the enhancement of managerial skills needed to stage future global events. Intangible benefits can include feel-good effects, national or local pride and self-confidence, civic engagement, and the psychological benefits of collective imagination about the future (Süéssmuth et al., 2010; Hilgers et al., 2010; Andranovich and Burbank, 2011). These outcomes are not assured, however, and may not be beneficial to city residents or to the city as a whole (Heying et al., 2005). The outcomes from hosting an event will not be homogeneous and are likely to be contingent on local, regional, national, and international institutions and interests attaching their own meaning to the event's outcomes (Holden et al., 2008).

Still, it is the urban impacts of hosting the Olympics that have the potential to affect urban politics. The overall concern of critics of the Games is that local interests are pushed aside as the interests of corporate sponsors or international sporting bodies are given primacy in policy making (Eisinger, 2000; Jennings, 2000; Lenskyj, 2000, 2004; Shaw, 2008). If these concerns are accurate, hosting the Games provides another mechanism for benefits to be extracted from cities, fostering uneven development and furthering inequalities. In studies of the effects of Olympic urbanization, Rome, Tokyo, Munich, Montreal, Sarajevo, Seoul, Calgary, Barcelona, Lillehammer, Sydney, Beijing and London are host cities that have seen noticeable urban impacts. The regeneration impacts have included automobile and mass transit development, airport expansion, physical rebuilding, expansion of cultural facilities and tourism amenities, and parks and open space development. Simply spending a lot of money, however, does not always lead to successful regeneration. Of the cities mentioned, Tokyo, Barcelona and Beijing were the biggest spenders and spent the most in non-sports development. Liao and Pitts (2006) report that Tokyo spent 97 percent of its budget on non-sports urban development, while Barcelona spent 67 percent and Beijing spent 65 percent. These cities are also examples of cities that were transformed by the Olympic Games, although it might be more accurate to say that these cities used the Olympics to further existing urban development plans. Smith and Fox (2007) call this 'event-themed' rather than 'event-led' regeneration.

Garcia-Ramon and Albet (2000) provide a summary of how the Olympics were used in Barcelona's transformation (see also Calavita and Ferrer, 2000; Monclus, 2011). Barcelona's elected city council played a central leadership role in the design and management of the city's major transformation projects. They adhered to the Town Planning regulations to maintain legitimacy and project coherence. These regulations led to five considerations: the integration of projects within the overall vision for the city; connection and continuity of newly built areas with existing neighborhoods; renovation and rehabilitation of the Old Town area to avoid gentrification and maintain social coherence in the neighborhoods; the use of public spaces in the newly transformed areas to generate identity and foster social and cultural integration; and upgrading peripheral areas via the restoration of squares, arcades, open spaces, and gardens. In addition, this process involved city residents in planning and as volunteers. Barcelona also benefitted from the active role taken by other medium-sized cities in the broader metropolitan area to help balance the 'polarities' of development. Finally, the Olympics provided an opportunity to position Barcelona globally through urban marketing promotional strategies. In sum, Barcelona used the Olympics as an event-themed regeneration strategy and local government, city residents and businesses were able to find common ground in making this happen.

The example of Barcelona illustrates how the Olympics can contribute positively to urban regeneration. Yet, not all host cities have the commitment of national resources or the cooperation of local actors to accomplish such a transformation. In the United States, for example, cities are not likely to see substantial national resources provided for urban regeneration. US cities, however, are still eager to bid for the Olympics and have sought to use the Games to rebuild a city or its image. In the following sections we set out three distinct models of how American cities have used the Olympics as part of an urban mega-event strategy.

3　THE PRIVATE GAMES MODEL: LOS ANGELES 1984

The 1984 Olympics in Los Angeles are the exemplar for the 'private' Games model. The creation of the private model for hosting the Games was not a product of the ideology of city leaders but rather developed from a confluence of city and Olympic politics. The process of bidding for the 1984 Olympic Games began in 1975 with a progrowth group of downtown business leaders and civic notables operating as the Southern California Committee for the Olympic Games (SCCOG). This committee had originally been established after the 1932 Olympics in Los Angeles (LA) and had made several attempts to bring the Games back to the city. As one SCCOG member explained in an editorial in the *Los Angeles Times* newspaper, the committee's motivations for seeking the Games were: (i) to give the city of LA the chance to display its attractions on a global stage; (ii) the opportunity to increase revenues from the influx of new visitors; and (iii) the 'intangibles' that would enhance the city's position in history and contemporary society (Rood, 1977). The SCCOG raised nearly $160,000 from private sources to finance bid activities leading up to selection by the USOC, but it also needed the endorsement of city leaders. Because this effort was occurring when the city of Montreal was going into debt to organize the 1976 Olympics, elected officials in LA were chiefly concerned with avoiding any commitment of public money to bid for or host the Games. Mayor Tom Bradley and the city council were supportive of the bid with the understanding that it would be privately financed.

The Los Angeles bid process was not typical because, following the terrorist attacks at the 1972 Munich Olympics and the financial problems facing Montreal, there were very few cities in the world actively bidding for the 1984 Olympics. Once LA had secured the USOC endorsement, it appeared to be the only serious candidate and the bid committee entered into negotiations with the IOC to establish whether and under what conditions the city would host the Games. The central issue in these negotiations was that the IOC required that the city and the USOC assume financial responsible for staging the Games while elected officials were insistent that the city could not assume financial responsibility. The issue of the financial responsibility of American cities was an especially sensitive one for the IOC because it had already been forced to move the 1976 Winter Games from Denver to Innsbruck after voters in Denver passed a city charter amendment preventing public money from being spent on the Games. What prevented the negotiations from reaching a deadlock was that the LA bid committee offered the alternative of a privately financed Games. By using corporate sponsorship and a portion of the television revenues, the bid committee maintained that it, rather than the city, could be responsible for funding the Games. Although the negotiations were difficult, an agreement was reached after Mayor Bradley publicly threatened to withdraw the city's bid and the IOC agreed to suspend its rule requiring the city government to bear the financial risks. The IOC awarded the 1984 Olympic Games to Los Angeles in October 1978. Shortly thereafter the LA City Council approved modest tourist-related tax increases to provide the city some funds for the Games and at the same time Olympic skeptics on the council had Proposition N placed on the city election ballot. Proposition N was intended to prevent any other public money from being spent on the Games, and it passed easily in November 1978.

The Los Angeles Olympic Organizing Committee (LAOOC) was the nonprofit set up to organize and run the Games. The LAOOC's plan had two essential features: (i) to raise sufficient funds from television revenues, ticket sales, and from a limited number of large corporate sponsors to stage a 'spartan' Games; and (ii) to minimize costs by using existing or temporary facilities whenever possible. The private Games model worked for LA in 1984 in the sense that the Games were staged successfully and the organizing committee produced a $232 million surplus. Politically, the private model also worked in the sense that the insistence by local governments that they avoid financial responsibility meant that the LAOOC was largely free from government control and from the expectation that Olympic money would be used to benefit city residents. Also, while there were some conflicts, the LAOOC plan to limit Olympic-related development helped to avoid political conflicts over the costs and benefits of specific projects (Burbank et al., 2000).

Because of the approach taken by Olympic organizers, the 1984 Olympics did not have a strong impact on the built environment in LA or Southern California. Hosting the Games did help bring some development projects to fruition more quickly, such as completion of the upper deck of LA International Airport and the installation of fiber optics for telecommunications, but these projects would have happened even without the Games. Similarly, the limited involvement of local government in the bid and conduct of the Games meant that the Olympics did not produce any transformative change in LA politics. Efforts by Mayor Bradley to push for development related to the Games in the Sepulveda Basin did exacerbate anti-LA sentiment in the San Fernando Valley. More positively, a substantial portion of the LAOOC surplus was retained and used to fund the Amateur Athletic Foundation (later renamed the LA84 Foundation). This money continues to promote sports competition and sports education throughout Southern California. Perhaps most importantly, the success of the 1984 Olympics brought attention back to LA and helped the city and region develop a sports tourism infrastructure that has become a sizable component of the area's economy.

4   THE URBAN DEVELOPMENT MODEL: ATLANTA 1996

Atlanta's bid for the 1996 Olympics was inspired in part by the success of the 1984 Games. Olympic boosters in Atlanta saw hosting the Games as a way to put the city on the global map. Yet unlike Los Angeles, Atlanta did not have an Olympic bid infrastructure in place ready to be activated nor was there strong support initially from the key actors in the city's power structure. Much of the early work was done by a small group of acquaintances of a local lawyer, Billy Payne, who became the city's Olympic entrepreneur. Payne's group worked to attract the support of members of Atlanta's business and political elite. A key early convert to Payne's cause was Atlanta Mayor Andrew Young. After he left office, Young became chairman of the Georgia Amateur Athletic Foundation (GAAF), an organization formed to promote Atlanta's bid. After the GAAF won the USOC's endorsement, the Atlanta Organizing Committee (AOC) was formed with Billy Payne as president and CEO, Andrew Young as chair, and Gerald Bartels, president of the Atlanta Chamber of Commerce, as secretary. By persuading a number of key business and political leaders that hosting the Games would raise Atlanta's international standing, Payne ensured that the AOC was able to draw on the considerable private resources of Atlanta businesses as well as the political connections of leaders such as Young to support the bid through a demanding IOC competition.

Although there was substantial support for hosting the Olympics during the bidding process, after the Games were awarded in 1990 it became clear that there were conflicting visions for the Atlanta Olympics. For Young and others on the organizing committee, the primary task was to put on a successful athletic event (Newman, 1999, p.153). Atlanta Mayor Maynard Jackson, on the other hand, spoke of the Games as the 'twin peaks of Atlanta's Mount Olympus' with the first peak 'to stage the best Olympic Games ever' and the second peak to 'simultaneously uplift the people of Atlanta and fight poverty in the process' (Roughton, 1991, p.F3). Jackson's more-expansive view reflected the expectations of many, especially inner-city residents, that hosting the Games should also mean improving the city for its residents. The efforts by Atlanta city government to use the Olympics as a vehicle to improve the city for residents, however, were largely unsuccessful. While the nonprofit Atlanta Committee for the Olympic Games (ACOG) had substantial resources for creating Olympic venues, ACOG did not intend to use its resources to promote development 'outside the fences' of those venues. The city government established the Corporation for Olympic Development (CODA) as a vehicle to spearhead development efforts within the 'Olympic Ring' neighborhoods but this organization suffered from a late start, changes in leadership, and a lack of resources. CODA attracted $76 million in public and private funds, but only $8 million of that was spent directly on neighborhood improvement (French and Disher, 1997, p.388). In contrast to LA, the Atlanta Games required more Olympic-related development. Within the city, the development of the Olympic Stadium and the creation of Centennial Olympic Park largely served the interests of ACOG's business partners but resulted in the displacement of as many as 16,000 poor inner-city residents when public housing units were demolished (Burbank et al., 2001, p.112).

The legacy of Atlanta's Olympics is uneven. Certainly, Atlanta was able to raise its global profile as a city capable of staging a complex mega event. The physical legacy of the Games was positive but social costs were extracted from the poor. The Games were instrumental in overcoming political resistance to infrastructure investment. Reversing a 25-year history of failed bond measures, Atlanta voters passed an infrastructure bond totaling $375 million that helped the city to secure state and federal matching funds to reverse years of disinvestment in street, sewer and water systems (Ray, 1995; GAO, 1999). ACOG generated revenues of $1.7 billion, spending roughly a third on local construction and the rest on operations. In addition the federal government contributed close to one billion dollars, with $371 million going to improve Hartsfield International Airport and much of the rest going to other infrastructure. Local and state government added another one billion dollars in matching funds for infrastructure and the private sector contributed $400 million, nearly half of this accounted for by its investment in the mixed-income residential housing that replaced public housing units.

Although there were improvements to the city and region associated with hosting the Games, in a larger sense Mayor Jackson's vision of using the Games to uplift the people of Atlanta and fight poverty did not succeed (Rutheiser, 1996; Keating and Flores, 2000; Burbank et al., 2001, pp. 102–13; Beaty, 2007). In addition, transportation problems, security issues, a controversy over street vendors, and the overt commercialism of the Atlanta Games brought negative publicity. Of course, some organizations in Atlanta did benefit including the quasi-public Georgia World Congress Center, which owns and maintains Centennial Olympic Park, businesses such as Coca-Cola and Turner Broadcasting, and universities such as Georgia Tech, Georgia State, and Clark Atlanta. Yet the hope that poor neighborhoods would benefit was not realized and Olympic development reinforced a legacy of ill will in neighborhoods such as Summerville, Peoplestown, and Mechanicsville that experienced displacement and lost housing (Burbank et al., 2000; Keating and Flores, 2000; Beaty, 2007).

5   THE PUBLIC INVESTMENT MODEL: SALT LAKE CITY 2002

Before being selected by the IOC to host the 2002 Olympics, Salt Lake City had made numerous bids including for the 1972, 1976, 1992 and 1998 Winter Games. The city's earliest bids were mostly to attract attention for the area's ski resorts. After the success of the 1984 Los Angeles Olympics, the idea of using the Games to establish the city's image and promote tourism took hold among political and business leaders. In November 1988, the USOC announced that it was opening the selection process for the 1998 Winter Games. Anchorage had been the USOC's designated city for the 1992 and 1994 competitions but the USOC wanted to make its selection dependent on a commitment to build winter sports training facilities regardless of whether the city was actually chosen by the IOC to host the Olympics. Anchorage balked at this commitment, but Olympic bid proponents in Salt Lake City did not. In response to the USOC actions, the mayor of Salt Lake City convened a new bid committee whose key actors were a small group of local business people and Olympic entrepreneurs who supplied the leadership and resources. The bid committee's immediate challenge was to find a way to get a funding commitment to build Olympic-quality facilities for a ski jump, bobsled track and speed skating oval. Members of the committee approached the state legislature with a plan to divert sales tax revenue that would otherwise go to cities and the state government in order to create a $56 million fund to build sports facilities. A bill to this effect was introduced by the speaker of the Utah House, who was a member of the bid committee, and it passed the legislature overwhelmingly with the provision that the plan be subject to a public referendum. This commitment of public funds by the legislature helped convince the USOC to select Salt Lake City as the US city for the 1998 and, if needed, the 2002 competitions. The public referendum on the sales tax diversion was approved by 57 percent of the voters in November 1989. In contrast to LA and Atlanta, Salt Lake City's bid depended on a commitment of public funding for sports facilities, which was regarded as a public investment to get the Olympics and to promote the winter sports industry. During the debate over the referendum, Olympics proponents made the argument that with or without the Games, this use of public money would be an investment in making Salt Lake City a 'winter sports capital' (Jardine, 1989).

Due to the infusion of public money, Salt Lake City had more public infrastructure in place than either LA or Atlanta. The Salt Lake Organizing Committee (SLOC) was the nonprofit organization responsible for staging the Games, but there were three other state organizations in place. The Utah Sports Authority (USA) was created to build and manage the publicly funded sports facilities, the Utah Athletic Foundation (UAF) was created to assume ownership and operation of those facilities after the Games, and the Utah Sports Advisory Committee was created to provide legislative and local government oversight. While the USA and the UAF were important in the pre- and post-Games periods, respectively, the Utah Sports Advisory Committee did not provide any serious public oversight during the build-up to the Olympic Games and SLOC was able to organize the event in a manner consistent with its goals and largely free from public oversight of its actions. Public officials in Utah were obligated to get involved in the leadership and management of SLOC, however, when media reports began to circulate about the tactics used by the bid committee to get the Games. The Salt Lake bribery scandal, as it became known, prompted investigations by a local ethics commission, the USOC, the IOC, and the US Department of Justice. The negative publicity generated by the bribery scandal prior to the 2002 Olympics illustrated the difficulty of controlling the coverage of an international mega event.

The model of Olympic development in Salt Lake City was more extensive than in the LA model and, in contrast to Atlanta, local government made no attempt to use the Games to address urban inequality. Local governments and Olympic proponents did, however, leverage the Olympic timeline to advance specific projects such as the federally funded construction of a light rail train line in Salt Lake City, a controversial federal land exchange to allow expansion of Snowbasin ski resort, and efforts to link a large private development near downtown Salt Lake City to the Olympics in order to justify the use of additional public money for the development. In the end, the Olympics were conducted with the private resources raised by SLOC, more than $1.3 billion in federal money for transportation and security, and the initial public investment in building winter sports facilities.

The conduct of the 2002 Olympics by SLOC produced an operating surplus of nearly $100 million for the organizing committee. Part of this surplus was used to pay back the public money invested by the state and local governments from the sales tax diversion and to endow a legacy fund for use by the UAF to continue to operate the speed skating oval, ski jump and bobsled track. Although Salt Lake City itself gained little by way of tangible assets from having served as the host city, the city and region did benefit from investments of public and private funds in transportation and tourism-related infrastructure. Furthermore, the city and state have attempted to leverage the Games by assisting in the creation of the Utah Sports Commission as a vehicle for attracting sports-related events to the area as part of the tourist mix. But, as the publicity associated with the Salt Lake Olympic bribery scandal illustrated, the effort to project a new global image for the city produced rather mixed results. Despite the early investment by the city and state to build Olympic facilities to attract the Games, there was very little public investment to carry out a longer-term development strategy based on tourism following the Games.

6   OLYMPIC IMPACTS: WHOSE CITY IS IT?

The impacts of bidding for and then hosting the Olympics are both tangible and intangible, making their assessment complex and open to speculative and sometimes dubious claims during the bidding process. In an assessment of impact studies conducted on the host city experience, for example, Kasimati (2003) found that most of the studies of impacts were conducted prior to the Games being held. In addition, a number of sports economists have shown that a technique commonly used for impact analysis, input–output analysis, is flawed. Porter (1999; Porter and Chin, ch. 15 in this volume) cites the misuse of the technique by event promoters, including the choice of multiplier, choice of impact area, specification of demand, and reliance on dollar measures. Baade (2006) notes that certain errors and omissions in economic impact studies will lead to substantial upward bias in results, and some of these always appear in pre-event studies. Finally, in a post-Games study of the Atlanta and Salt Lake City Olympics, Porter and Fletcher (2008) compare data on retail sales, hotel occupancy, real hotel rates, and enplanements to the pre-event impact studies and find that the economic impacts were minor at best, and that the increase in real hotel rates during the Olympics could be misinterpreted as having greater economic impact than actually occurred in these two cities. While post-Games analyses have been few, the IOC's new commitment to event legacy suggests that future host cities may be held to a general standard. Our research on the impacts of hosting the Games suggests that while there will be no shortage of candidate cities, the pressures of commercialism will continue to push against the needs of communities, and local governments will have a difficult time overcoming these pressures. Since the desire to bid and host the Olympics is created out of local politics and against the backdrop of local spatial practices, it is possible to envision alternative futures for potential host cities, just as we can chart the nuances of difference among the three cities examined in this chapter.

If the host city experience stays on the 'business as usual' path, then we would not expect to see local impacts vary from the typical host city experiences of the recent past. Tangible local impacts can be expected to benefit larger institutions, corporate sponsors and the IOC. Local politicians may derive some added name recognition. Local community benefits will tend to be intangible. This path is not preordained, but the nature of the host city model can go a long way in illustrating the potential for benefits to reach down to all members of the community. In the three cities reviewed here, the host city models varied but in all instances the local impacts were similar in terms of the beneficiaries.

There are two general trajectories that could emerge in future host city experiences: a tighter IOC hold over the Games or a more localized Games. If the IOC tightens its control over the Games, the opportunities for financial elites, developers, the tourism industry, corporate sponsors and international sports federations will be boosted in the host cities. Corporate sponsors are interested in increasing their market share for whatever goods and services they provide and the Olympics are a way to link their corporate brand with the Olympic identity. International sports federations compete with each other and the Olympics provide opportunities to showcase their particular sport. In both instances, external pressures on local economic development will hold greater authority over the pattern of economic development occurring during the run-up to the Games. Property led development emphasizing consumption-oriented amenities will outline the local beneficiaries and the promise for broad-based urban regeneration will be dimmed.

The second trajectory – toward a more localized Games – is more promising for urban regeneration, but requires a great deal of effort prior to bidding. Cities where hosting the Olympics was the catalyst for urban transformation – Barcelona is the most significant example – used the Olympics to push their own vision of how the city should be regenerated. The approach taken in South Africa in the preparation of the Cape Town 2004 bid, which included working directly with communities to determine needs, explicitly linked the Games to those communities disadvantaged by history and the spatial practices of apartheid, and included a model for human development (Hiller, 2000; Swart and Bob, 2004). While an initial effort was made in South Africa to synchronize the World Cup staging with local development needs, unfortunately the follow through and the results were lacking (see Swart and Bob (ch. 24) and Du Plessis and Maennig (ch. 27) in this volume). The lesson is one that is hard earned: host cities continue to show that the Olympics do not automatically translate into urban regeneration for all of the city's people.

REFERENCES

Andranovich, G. and M.J. Burbank (2011), 'Contextualizing Olympic legacies', *Urban Geography*, **32** (6), 823–44.

Andranovich, G., M.J. Burbank and C.H. Heying (2001), 'Olympic cities: lessons learned from mega-event politics', *Journal of Urban Affairs*, **23** (2), 113–31.

Baade, R.A. (2006), 'The economic impact of mega-sporting events', in W. Andreff and S. Szymanski (eds), *Handbook on the Economics of Sport*, Cheltenham, UK and Northampton, MA, USA: Edward Elgar, pp. 177–82.

Beaty, A. (2007), *Atlanta's Olympic Legacy*, Geneva: Centre on Housing Rights and Evictions, available at: http://www.ruig-gian.org/ressources/Atlanta_background_paper.pdf.

Burbank, M.J., G. Andranovich and C.H. Heying (2001), *Olympic Dreams: The Impact of Mega-events on Local Politics*, Boulder, CO: Lynne Rienner.

Burbank, M.J., C.H. Heying, and G. Andranovich (2000), 'Antigrowth politics or piece-meal resistance? Citizen opposition to Olympic-related economic growth', *Urban Affairs Review*, **35** (3), 334–57.

Calavita, N. and A. Ferrer (2000), 'Behind Barcelona's success story: citizen movements and planners' power', *Journal of Urban History*, **26** (6), 793–807.

Caraley, D. (1992), 'Washington abandons the cities', *Political Science Quarterly*, **107** (1), 1–30.

Clarke, S.E. and G.L. Gaile (1998), *The Work of Cities*, Minneapolis, MN: University of Minnesota Press.

Eisinger, P. (1998), 'City politics in an era of devolution', *Urban Affairs Review*, **33** (3), 308–25.

Eisinger, P. (2000), 'The politics of bread and circuses: building the city for the visitor class', *Urban Affairs Review*, **35** (3), 316–33.

Euchner, C.C. (1994), *Playing the Field*, Baltimore, MD: Johns Hopkins University Press.

French, S.P. and M. Disher (1997), 'Atlanta and the Olympics: a one-year retrospective', *Journal of the American Planning Association*, **63** (3), 379–92.

GAO (1999), *Federal Funding of Olympic Games*, Washington, DC: United States General Accounting Office.

Garcia-Ramon, M.-D. and A. Albet (2000), 'Commentary', *Environment and Planning A*, **32** (8), 1331–4.

Harvey, D. (1989), 'From managerialism to entrepreneurialism: the transformation of urban governance under late capitalism', *Geografiska Annaler*, **71** (1), 3–17.

Heying, C.H., M.J. Burbank and G. Andranovich (2005), 'Taking the measure of the Games: lessons from the field', *Plan Canada*, **45** (2), 20–22.

Heying, C.H., M.J. Burbank and G. Andranovich (2007), 'World class: using the Olympics to shape and brand the American metropolis', in Smith (ed.), pp. 101–10.

Hilgers, D., W. Maennig and M. Porsche (2010), 'The feel-good effect at mega sport events', *International Journal of Business Research*, **10** (4), 15–29.

Hiller, H. (2000), 'Mega-events, urban boosterism and growth strategies: an analysis of the objectives and legitimations of the Cape Town 2004 Olympic bid', *International Journal of Urban and Regional Research*, **24** (2), 439–58.

Holden, M., J. MacKenzie and R. VanWynsberghe (2008), 'Vancouver's promise of the world's first sustainable Olympic Games', *Environment and Planning C*, **26**, 882–905.

Jardine, J. (1989), 'We can't have it both ways', *Utah Holidays*, 19 October, 8–9.

Jennings, A. (2000), *The Great Olympic Swindle*, London: Simon & Schuster.

Judd, D.R. and S.S. Fainstein (eds) (1999), *The Tourist City*, New Haven, CT: Yale University Press.

Kasimati, E. (2003), 'Economic aspects and the Summer Olympics: a review of related research', *International Journal of Tourism Research*, **5**, 433–44.

Keating, L. and C.A. Flores (2000), 'Sixty and out: Techwood Homes transformed by enemies and friends', *Journal of Urban History*, **26** (3), 275–311.

Kuper, S. and S. Szymanski (2009), *Soccernomics*, New York: Nation Books.

Lenskyj, H.J. (2000), *Inside the Olympic Industry*, Albany, NY: SUNY Press.

Lenskyj, H.J. (2004), 'Making the world safe for global capital: the Sydney 2000 Olympics and beyond', in J. Bale and M. K. Christensen (eds), *Post-Olympism?*, New York: Berg, pp. 135–45.

Liao, H. and A. Pitts (2006), 'A brief historical review of Olympic urbanization', *International Journal of the History of Sport*, **23** (7), 1232–52.

Monclus, F.-M. (2011), 'Barcelona 1992', in J.R. Gold and M.M. Gold (eds), *Olympic Cities: City Agendas, Planning and the World's Games, 1896–2016*, 2nd edn, New York: Routledge, pp. 268–86.

Newman, H.K. (1999), *Southern Hospitality: Tourism and the Growth of Atlanta*, Tuscaloosa, AL: University of Alabama Press.

Owen, K.A. (2002), 'The Sydney 2000 Olympics and urban entrepreneurialism: local variations in urban governance', *Australian Geographical Studies*, **40** (3), 323–36.

Pagano, M. and A.O. Bowman (1997), *Cityscapes and Capital*, Baltimore, MD: Johns Hopkins University Press.

Porter, P.K. (1999), 'Mega-sports events as municipal investments: a critique of impact analysis', in J. Fizel, E. Gustafson and L. Hadley (eds), *Sports Economics: Current Research*, Westport, CT: Praeger, pp. 61–73.

Porter, P.K. and D. Fletcher (2008), 'The economic impact of the Olympic Games: ex ante predictions and ex post reality', *Journal of Sport Management*, **22** (4), 470–86.

Ray, B.J. (1995), 'Leveraging the mega-event: Atlanta's efforts to boost its infrastructure and host the 1996 Olympics', paper presented at the Urban Affairs Association Annual Meeting, Portland, OR, May 3–6.

Rood, R. (1977), 'Consider, for a moment, the benefits of hosting the Olympics', *Los Angeles Times*, 6 December.

Rosentraub, M.S. (2010), *Major League Winners*, Boca Raton, FL: CRC Press.

Roughton, B. (1991), 'Atlanta Olympics update '91: on journey to '96, Atlanta aims to stage great games and improve itself', *Atlanta Journal Constitution*, 21 July.

Rutheiser, C. (1996), *Imagineering Atlanta: The Politics of Place in the City of Dreams*, London: Verso.

Sanders, H.T. (1992), 'Building the convention city: politics, finance and public investment in urban America', *Journal of Urban Affairs*, **14** (2), 135–60.

Shaw, C. (2008), *Five Ring Circus: Myths and Realities of the Olympic Games*, Gabriola Island, BC: New Society Publishers.

Smith, A. and T. Fox (2007), 'From "event-led" to "event-themed" regeneration: the 2002 commonwealth games legacy programme', *Urban Studies*, **44** (5/6), 1125–43.

Smith, M.K. (ed.) (2007), *Tourism, Culture and Regeneration*, Cambridge, MA and Wallingford, UK: CABI Press.

Soja, E.W. (2010), *Seeking Spatial Justice*, Minneapolis, MN: University of Minnesota Press.

Süessmuth, B., M. Heyne and W. Maennig (2010), 'Induced civic pride and integration', *Oxford Bulletin of Economics and Statistics*, **72** (2), 202–20.

Swart, K. and U. Bob (2004), 'The seductive discourse of development: the Cape Town 2004 Olympic bid', *Third World Quarterly*, **25** (7), 1311–24.

11 Estimating match and World Cup winning probabilities

Ruud H. Koning and Ian G. McHale

1 INTRODUCTION

Without any doubt, the Soccer World Cup is the most important single sports tournament that is organized on a regular basis. Whole nations come to a standstill during games of the tournament (for example, more than eight million Dutch people watched the final of the 2010 World Cup of Netherlands against Spain, 56 per cent of the total population of the Netherlands).

In the run-up to each Continental and World Cup tournament many people take an active interest in discussing the most likely winner. For fans, pundits and the media this question is more of incidental interest while for bookmakers and bettors answering the question has financial implications. As such, in recent years statisticians and econometricians have been in high demand in the gambling industry as odds setters and punters attempt to gain an edge over the competition. Forecasting in sport has attracted growing attention in academia too, with an increasing number of papers appearing in the statistics and economics literature. Of course, academics use their forecasting models not for making money (the ones they publish anyway!), but rather to address other questions such as: is the betting market efficient? (see, for example, Goddard and Asimakopoulos, 2004), the effect of a red card in football (Ridder et al., 1994), or what effect does the tournament structure have on the probability of winning (see, for example, Scarf and Yusof, 2010).

Forecasting winners in academia is not just confined to football. Tennis (McHale and Morton, 2011), golf (McHale and Forrest, 2005), cricket (Scarf and Shi, 2005) and American Football (Boulier and Stekler, 2003) are just some of the individual sports that academics have tried to forecast. Performance at an Olympic Games has been addressed at the country level, and to a lesser extent the individual level. Bernard and Busse (2004) have addressed the question of: what share of the total medals available should a country be expected to win given its economic and demographic characteristics such as population and gross domestic product (GDP). At the individual level, there is a relatively small literature on predicting the long-run progression of winning times and distances at athletic events, for example Robinson and Tawn (1995) use extreme value statistics to model the women's 3,000 metre winning times.

In this chapter, we present a simulation procedure to estimate the probability of a team winning the Soccer World Cup. The simulation uses a forecasting model of match outcome based on the FIFA world rankings and the population size and GDP of the competing teams/countries. We then use the simulation procedure to examine the effect of tournament design on the probability of a team winning the title. Section 2 describes our forecasting model for match outcome and Section 3 presents the data and modelling results. Section 4 describes our simulation procedure and presents our findings on the effect of tournament design and draws on some teams' probabilities of winning the tournament. We conclude with some discussion in Section 5.

2   FORECASTING MATCH RESULTS IN FOOTBALL

Broadly speaking, there are two approaches to modelling the outcome of a football match: Poisson-type models of goals (see, for example, Karlis and Ntzoufras, 2003; McHale and Scarf, 2011) and ordinal outcome models of match outcome (see, for example, Goddard, 2005). Poisson-type models estimate the probability of every possible score-line in a match and are becoming increasingly popular with the advent of betting markets on exact score-lines. It is simple enough to compute the probabilities of winning, drawing and losing by summing the relevant exact score-line probabilities. In contrast, ordinal outcome models predict the probabilities of each outcome directly. In this chapter we adopt the ordinal outcome approach as we are primarily interested in modelling the match outcome rather than the exact score-line, and a small improvement is gained in the lower computing time to run the large number of simulations. Research by Goddard (ibid.) suggests that there is little difference in performance of the two approaches.

To introduce our model, consider a game between team i and j, with the first team playing at home. The outcome is assumed to be generated by a latent regression model. The quality of team i is θ_i, that of team j is θ_j, and the difference in quality is $\theta_i - \theta_j$. The actual outcome of the match depends on difference in quality, and random factors captured by ε_{ij}. These random factors are specific to each specific match. Latent quality difference is now

$$Y^*_{ij} = \theta_i - \theta_j + \varepsilon_{ij}, \tag{11.1}$$

with $\varepsilon_{ij} \sim N(0,1)$. The scale of equation (11.1) is not identified and hence the variance of ε_{ij} is set to 1 without loss of generality. Team i is expected to win if the quality difference is large and positive, and team j is expected to win if it is large and negative. A draw is expected if the quality difference is small. The outcome of the match is denoted by Y_{ij}, with $Y_{ij} = 1$ for a home win, $Y_{ij} = 0$ for a draw, and $Y_{ij} = -1$ for an away win. The latent regression (11.1) relates to the outcomes as follows:

$$\Pr(Y_{ij} = 1) = \Pr(Y^*_{ij} > c_2) = 1 - \Phi[c_2 - (\theta_i - \theta_j)]$$
$$\Pr(Y_{ij} = 0) = \Pr(c_1 < Y^*_{ij} < c_2) = \Phi[c_2 - (\theta_i - \theta_j)]$$
$$- \Phi[c_1 - (\theta_i - \theta_j)]$$
$$\Pr(Y_{ij} = -1) = \Pr(Y^*_{ij} < c_1) = \Phi[c_1 - (\theta_i - \theta_j)]. \tag{11.2}$$

The constants c_1 and c_2 measure home advantage; the probability of a home win if both teams are of equal quality is $1 - \Phi(c_2)$, and the probability of an away win is $1 - \Phi(c_1)$. To identify the parameters, we impose the identifying restriction that average quality is 0: $\Sigma_i \theta_i = 0$ so that teams with a positive θ are better than average, and teams with a negative θ are below average.

Model (11.2) is reasonable for games that have a home team, as is the case for domestic league football. In national team football this is only the case in friendly games and qualification games, however, for games played during tournaments, no particular team except the hosting country plays at home. To deal with this complication, we introduce an additional parameter d, and for tournament games with no home team we have:

$$\Pr(Y_{ij} = 1) = \Pr(Y^*_{ij} > d) = 1 - \Phi[d - (\theta_i - \theta_j)]$$
$$\Pr(Y_{ij} = 0) = \Pr(-d < Y^*_{ij} < d) = \Phi[d - (\theta_i - \theta_j)]$$
$$- \Phi[-d - (\theta_i - \theta_j)]$$
$$\Pr(Y_{ij} = -1) = \Pr(Y^*_{ij} < -d) = \Phi[-d - (\theta_i - \theta_j)], \tag{11.3}$$

and compared to equations (11.2), we impose the restriction $d = c_1 = -c_2$. Because we have information from qualification games (where one team plays at home and one plays away), and from tournament games (where no team has home advantage), the three parameters c_1, c_2 and d are all identified. The quality parameters θ_i and θ_j are identical in models (11.2) and (11.3), and note that d is identified because of the earlier assumption that average quality is 0.

This type of model has been estimated for domestic football by, for example, Clarke and Norman (1995) and Koning (2000). Estimating team strength for each team in a domestic league is reasonable given the relatively small number of teams, and high number of matches. However, for national team football this is simply not a feasible approach as the model contains too many parameters: the number of countries plus three (c_1, c_2 and d), minus one (the restriction that average quality is 0). Given that FIFA has 208 member associations,[1] compared to the 20 teams that compete with each other in most European domestic leagues, the number of parameters is simply too large to estimate with any level of accuracy.

A further complication evident in national team football is that a team's strength will most likely vary through time, more so than for domestic teams. This is a consequence of two factors. First, national teams can select, by definition, national players only. It is not possible to use local drawing power to increase the quality of a national team by hiring talent from abroad. This argument applies with even more force after the Bosman ruling of 1996, when European teams became unrestricted in their ability to hire talent from other EU countries. One can argue (Kesenne, 2007; Koning, 2009) that this has caused concentration of top talent in the big leagues that are best able to market broadcasting rights to generate television income, and are best able to win prize money in the Champions League. For example, Manchester United will remain able to hire the best talent available on the international market in the foreseeable future. Because of that, they will remain a successful team and team strength will remain relatively constant over a large number of games. In contrast, national teams cannot hire talent on the international player market, no matter their commercial value and sportive success. For this reason, the strength of a national team can be expected to change over a relatively small number of games and so information on the quality of national teams has to be more recent than that of professional teams. The second factor compounds the effect of the first factor in that national teams play far fewer matches than domestic teams. For example, the English national team played three qualification games, four games during the World Cup 2010, and six friendlies between 1 September 2009 and 1 September 2010. In the same period, Manchester United played 38 Premier League games, and 10 Champions League games.

A limited number of matches per team, and a large number of national teams (our dataset has 3,623 matches, and 155 different national teams) make it infeasible to estimate a strength parameter for each national team and so the model is parameterized more parsimoniously by assuming that the quality parameter θ is a function of a limited number of observable covariates x: $\theta_i = \beta' x_i$. The number of parameters to be estimated then is the number of covariates plus three (c_1, c_2 and d). Since only difference in quality $\theta_i - \theta_j$ appears in equations (11.2) and (11.3), we can only incorporate differences of covariates as explanatory variables: $\theta_i - \theta_j = \beta'(x_i - x_j)$.

The advantage of this approach to modelling winning probabilities is that the model allows prediction outside of the sample, in the sense that it will give the probability distribution of the three possible outcomes, even if teams i and j have never played each other. Moreover, we can relate sporting success to observable characteristics of both teams, while still allowing for the random nature of the outcome of sports events. Cross-sectional variation in the covariates (and perhaps limited variation over time) is able to identify the regression coefficients β. We should note that only differences of the covariates enter the model so as to ensure there is symmetry in the predictions (the predictions for a match between team i and team j should be exactly the same as those for team j versus team i).

When forecasting national team match results there is an obvious and convenient covariate freely available: the FIFA world ranking of each team at the time a match takes place has proven to be a valuable indicator of team strength and is accordingly included in our model. We include both the ranking position and the ranking points a team has at the time of the game. In addition to rankings information, we mirror work on determining success of a country at the Olympic Games, and experiment with including GDP and population size of each country in our forecasting model.

3   DATA AND MODEL ESTIMATION

To estimate this ordered probit model, we compiled a dataset consisting of outcomes of official FIFA soccer games starting 26 January 2005, ending 26 May 2010 (up to the last match before the World Cup 2010 in South Africa). The dataset consists of every official international match played by national teams. Variables that are included are, among others: the team names, the result after 90 minutes, the result in overtime, type of match (friendly, qualification, or tournament match), and location of the match. To this dataset with scores, we added the position of both teams in the FIFA world ranking, and the number of points on that ranking. The ranking is measured at the end of the month preceding the date of match. Finally, we added one year lagged log-population size and log-GDP per capita of the two countries obtained from the Groningen Growth and Development Centre. Missing values in these two variables caused the dataset to decrease to 3,623 observed matches.

Table 11.1   *Estimation results for model including economic and*
demographic variables (only non-friendly games)

	Estimate	Std error	t-statistic	p-value
c_1	−0.635	0.035	−17.902	0.000
c_2	−0.001	0.033	−0.030	0.976
d	0.361	0.040	9.037	0.000
Δ log-population	0.147	0.014	10.584	0.000
Δ log-GDP per cap	0.178	0.025	7.223	0.000

We present the results of three models: a model based on only the economic and demographic information of the country, a model based only on world ranking information and a model based on all available information. Likelihood-ratio tests showed that the parameter estimates differed significantly between friendly and non-friendly games. For that reason, we report results on non-friendly games only as we are interested in predicting tournament results.

The estimation results of the ordered probit model with log-population and log-GDP per capita as explanatory variables are provided in Table 11.1. First, we interpret the constants c_1 and c_2. If both countries have equal population and equal GDP, the probability that the home team wins is $1 - \Phi(c_2)$, which is 0.49. Similarly, the estimated probabilities of a draw and a home loss are calculated as 0.24 and 0.27 respectively. These estimates compare with frequencies 50 per cent, 23 per cent, and 27 per cent in the sample used.

The effect of population size is significant and positive: countries with a higher population are more successful in soccer games, keeping per capita income constant. Also, countries with a higher GDP per capita are more likely to win their matches against opponents with a lower GDP per capita. Even though soccer is not a particularly capital-intensive sport, resources as measured by national GDP per capita and talent pool as measured by the size of the population matter. Wealthier countries are probably better able to maintain training facilities and youth training programmes that result in high-quality national teams.

The coefficients on population size and GDP per capita are approximately similar, in fact a test that they are equal is not rejected. This result means that an increase in GDP caused by an increase in population produces the same effect as increasing GDP per capita. This can be seen by rearranging our specification: $\alpha \log(pop) + \beta \log(GDP/pop) = (\alpha - \beta)pop + \beta GDP$ and since $\alpha = \beta$, it is actually only GDP that matters.

In Table 11.2 we give the estimation results when world ranking and

Table 11.2   *Estimation results, specification with FIFA ranking (only non-friendly games)*

	Estimate	Std error	*t*-statistic	*p*-value
c_1	−0.754	0.038	−19.658	0.000
c_2	−0.025	0.035	−0.724	0.469
d	0.377	0.042	9.089	0.000
Δ log-world rank	−0.244	0.038	−6.402	0.000
Δ log-points	0.584	0.069	8.521	0.000

Table 11.3   *Estimation results, specification with economic variables and FIFA ranking (only non-friendly games)*

	Estimate	Std error	*t*-statistic	*p*-value
c_1	−0.755	0.038	−19.624	0.000
c_2	−0.022	0.035	−0.631	0.528
d	0.379	0.042	9.097	0.000
Δ log-population	0.038	0.016	2.358	0.018
Δ log-GDP per cap	0.060	0.026	2.278	0.023
Δ log-world rank	−0.205	0.040	−5.109	0.000
Δ log-points	0.577	0.069	8.414	0.000

points on that ranking are used as covariates. Estimates for the c_1, c_2 and d parameters that calibrate the distribution of the three outcomes are similar to the ones in Table 11.1. We enter the ranking covariates as differences after a logarithmic transformation, similar to Klaassen and Magnus (2001). Teams that are higher on the world ranking (and therefore, have a lower rank number) have a higher probability of winning, and also teams with a larger points difference compared to their opponent are more likely to win. Both effects are significant.

In the final specification (Table 11.3) we include all variables. The effects of population size and GDP per capita decrease significantly, as does their significance. However, both coefficients are significantly different from 0, at a 0.05 level of significance. This is a little surprising as one would have thought that the world rankings would sufficiently capture all information on a team's strength and that any advantage from population or GDP gained would already have fed into the rankings through the country results. This bias may be a consequence of a bias in the world rankings themselves. For instance, McHale and Davies (2007) suggest that a bias towards continents where FIFA is trying to increase the popularity of the sport may exist, thus artificially inflating the ranking of teams from Africa and Asia. However, our results demonstrate that the FIFA world ranking captures a lot of the variation in outcomes, as was to be expected, and given that our primary focus is to forecast the match result rather than to determine factors of footballing success, we continue without further comment.

4   FORECASTING TOURNAMENT WINNERS

The forecasting model described above can be used to produce probabilities of each team winning a single match at the World Cup finals. Although of interest, it is perhaps more interesting to infer probabilities of each team winning the World Cup itself. In this section we carry out such an exercise using simulation. Further, we investigate the effect on the tournament-win probabilities of tournament design by experimenting with the tournament structure.

Who Wins the World Cup?

In order to predict the winner of the World Cup, and estimate probabilities of victory for all competing teams, one needs to know the structure of the tournament, not just the identity of the participating teams as is the case when forecasting a single match. The current tournament design for the World Cup is a hybrid of a league and a knockout stage. Figure 11.1 depicts the tournament design as used for the 2010 World Cup.

The 32 teams qualifying for the tournament are split into eight groups of four teams. Each group forms a mini-league and the teams each play three games. As for domestic leagues, teams are awarded 3 points for winning a game, 1 for drawing and 0 for losing. The two teams with the most points in each group progress to the knockout stages. Teams on equal points are separated first by goal difference, then goals scored, then the result between the two teams, and finally, if the two teams cannot be separated, lots are drawn to decide which team progresses to round 2. This last separation is an empirical simplification of the actual FIFA rules. Teams are allocated into the leagues based on seeding (eight teams are granted seed status and these teams are separated from each other), and then by continent.

We use the match outcome probabilities from the model presented in the previous section to simulate the actual tournament. The model specification we use to estimate out-of-sample winning probabilities is the one incorporating log-ranks and log-points only (Table 11.2), because these covariates are updated frequently and are readily available just before the

POT	Group A	Group B	Group C	Group D	Group E	Group F	Group G	Group H
1: seeds	South Africa	Argentina	England	Germany	Netherlands	Italy	Brazil	Spain
2: Asia, Oceania and North/Central America	Mexico	South Korea	USA	Australia	Japan	New Zealand	North Korea	Honduras
3: Africa and South America	Uruguay	Nigeria	Algeria	Ghana	Cameroon	Paraguay	Ivory Coast	Chile
4: Europe	France	Greece	Slovenia	Serbia	Denmark	Slovakia	Portugal	Switzerland

ROUND 2

r2a	a1	b2
r2b	c1	d2
r2c	d1	c2
r2d	b1	a2
r2e	e1	f2
r2f	g1	h2
r2g	f1	e2
r2h	h1	g2

QUARTER FINALS

qf1	r2e	r2f
qf2	r2a	r2b
qf3	r2c	r2d
qf4	r2g	r2h

SEMI FINALS

sf1	qf1	qf2
sf2	qf3	qf4

FINAL

f	sf1	sf2

Note: The top two teams from each group progress to Round 2, where the top game in Round 2 (r2a) is played between the winners of group A (a1) and the runners-up from group B (b2), and so on.

Figure 11.1 Tournament design for 2010 World Cup in South Africa

tournament starts (unlike economic variables such as GDP or population size). The approach to estimate the probability that a certain country wins the World Cup follows Koning et al. (2003) and is as follows.

For the group stages we simulate the match result. In addition we simulate the score since the result alone is sometimes not sufficient to separate the teams when they finish the three games on equal points. We generate the score by randomly selecting a score from the set of match results. An advantage of this approach is that the outcome frequencies are in accordance with the model, and the distribution of goals scored conditional on the outcome of the game is in accordance with scores in recent matches. This procedure is not needed in the knockout stage, although draws are settled on a weighted coin toss according to:

$$\Pr(\text{team } i \text{ proceeds}) = \Pr(i \text{ wins in 90 mins})$$
$$+ \Pr(\text{draw at 90 mins}) \frac{\Pr(i \text{ wins in 90 mins})}{\Pr(i \text{ or } j \text{ win in 90 mins})}.$$

Having estimated the probabilities of a win, draw, or loss in any possible game during the tournament we obtain the probability that a country wins the tournament, as follows:

1. We generate outcomes (win/draw/loss) in the group stage according to the estimated probabilities.
2. Conditional on the final ranking in each group, we know the order of play for round 2. By integrating over all possible opponents, we calculate the probability of reaching the quarter finals, semi-finals, final, and of winning the tournament. This calculation is analytical.
3. We repeat the process 100,000 times (because progression from the group stages is reliant on the simulated results).

The results of the 10 countries with the highest win probabilities are given in Table 11.4. It is expected that the country that leads the world ranking has the highest probability of winning the World Cup and that is what we find. Brazil is by far the favourite at the start of the tournament, if we take only FIFA ranking and points into account. If the World Cup were handed out in a random draw among all participating countries, each country would have a probability of $1/32 = 0.03125$ to win the title. Brazil's estimated winning probability is 12 times as large. Note that the seventh likeliest country (Argentina) has a win probability that is higher than the one of random allocation; that of the eighth likeliest country (France) is already smaller. As a byproduct, the simulation approach also gives probabilities of reaching certain intermediate stages of the tournament.

Table 11.4   Estimated probabilities for 2010 World Cup

	Pr(r2)	Pr(qf)	Pr(sf)	Pr(f)	Pr(title)	Bet365
Brazil	0.935	0.755	0.618	0.437	0.373	0.146
Spain	0.926	0.547	0.418	0.231	0.184	0.175
Portugal	0.798	0.468	0.312	0.122	0.087	0.030
Netherlands	0.876	0.651	0.251	0.104	0.070	0.067
Germany	0.750	0.494	0.306	0.193	0.056	0.067
Italy	0.894	0.609	0.219	0.079	0.050	0.067
Argentina	0.752	0.481	0.291	0.176	0.048	0.109
France	0.715	0.412	0.235	0.129	0.031	0.046
England	0.680	0.397	0.224	0.123	0.030	0.125
Greece	0.608	0.323	0.161	0.075	0.014	0.006

Note: Probabilities shown are the probability of reaching round 2 (r2), the quarter finals (qf), the semi-finals (sf), the final (f) and of winning the title.

Perhaps the toughest test of the accuracy of a forecasting model is to compare the predictions with that of the betting market. The final column of Table 11.4 shows the Bet365 probabilities from the day before the tournament kicked off. In comparison to the bookmaker inferred probabilities of winning the tournament, there are some differences. First, the model estimates that Spain was second favourite by quite some margin to the favourite Brazil, but the bookmakers reversed this and indeed were shown to be correct since Spain won. Further down the list, there are two more notable differences: Argentina and England. In both cases the bookmaker assigns a higher inferred probability of victory compared to the model. However, this can probably be explained in terms of the bookmakers protecting themselves as England is often heavily backed in tournaments so that bookmakers artificially inflate the probability of winning so that they will pay out less money in the event that England were to win. A similar story is likely true of Argentina, although Argentina did have a strong team that had underperformed in the run-up to the tournament and this was reflected in their relatively low world ranking.

Tournament Design and Winning Probabilities

It appears then that a statistical model can give reasonable and certainly informative predictions for individual matches and tournaments. We now turn our attention to the effect of tournament design on tournament result. First, we are interested in the effect of seeding teams. Second, we are interested in the effect the league-knockout hybrid tournament has on

Table 11.5   *Estimated probabilities for 2010 World Cup if the tournament*
           had no seeding

	Round 2	qf	sf	Final	Title
Brazil	0.932	0.812	0.671	0.527	0.396
Spain	0.882	0.719	0.541	0.369	0.226
Portugal	0.812	0.585	0.378	0.213	0.100
Netherlands	0.784	0.540	0.330	0.172	0.074
Italy	0.751	0.490	0.278	0.135	0.053
Germany	0.702	0.427	0.222	0.097	0.034
Argentina	0.685	0.399	0.201	0.084	0.027
France	0.641	0.349	0.162	0.062	0.018
England	0.642	0.350	0.162	0.062	0.018
Greece	0.567	0.268	0.107	0.035	0.008

Note: Probabilities shown are the probability of reaching round 2 (r2), the quarter finals (qf), the semi-finals (sf), the final (f) and of winning the title.

the probability of the strongest team winning the tournament. We investigate these issues by altering our simulation programme to allow for two counterfactual tournament designs:

1. the same structure (league and knockout hybrid) with no seeding, and
2. a round-robin tournament where every team plays every other team once.

The economic theory of tournaments has been well-treated in the literature: see, for example, Szymanski (2003, 2006) and Muelhauser (2006). In this chapter we take an empirical approach and look at the effect of tournament design on the probability of teams progressing through the tournament and of winning the title. Most recently, Scarf et al. (2009) examine the effect of tournament design for the UEFA Champions League and attempt to identify the most exciting tournament structure according to various measures of outcome uncertainty. Other authors (Bojke, 2007; Koning 2007; Ryvkin and Ortmann, 2008) have adopted a forecasting/ simulation approach to assess the impact of tournament design on various measures of outcome uncertainty.

In Table 11.5 we give the title probabilities if there was no seeding (seeding is used by FIFA as a way to give an advantage to the better teams – the top eight teams are separated during the group stages). By comparing these probabilities with the ones obtained using the actual draw

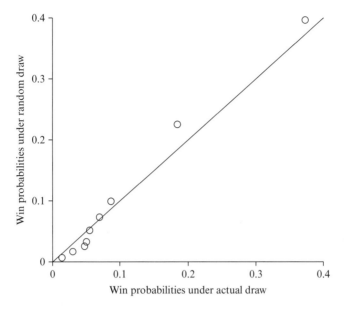

Figure 11.2   Comparison of win probabilities under actual draw and random draw (no seeding)

(Table 11.4), we can get an understanding of the effect of seeding at the World Cup 2010. Figure 11.2 shows the probabilities under the actual draw versus the probabilities under a random draw.

The figure shows that the very top teams (Brazil, Spain, Portugal and the Netherlands) experience a slight disadvantage as a result of the seeding policy, while teams seeded 5 to 8 experience a slight improvement in their chance of winning the tournament. It may be that very strong countries are hurt by seeding as it is more likely that they have to beat at least one other strong country (of these four) to win the title. If there was no seeding, it is possible that, for example, Brazil, Spain and Portugal meet earlier and eliminate each other, increasing the probability for Netherlands to win the title.

Next, we give win probabilities of a tournament in a round-robin format in Table 11.6. By playing more matches, quality differences are magnified and top contenders are more likely to win. One bad performance (or an unlucky draw by the random number generator) is not punished by being eliminated from the tournament. Figure 11.3 shows the tournament win probabilities under the actual draw plotted against the tournament win probabilities under a round-robin format. The figure shows how the round-robin tournament structure would very much increase the

Table 11.6   Estimated probabilities for a 2010 World Cup had the tournament structure been a round-robin format

	Pos. 5	Pos. 4	Pos. 3	Pos. 2	Title
Brazil	0.008	0.023	0.073	0.239	0.654
Spain	0.036	0.084	0.187	0.408	0.253
Portugal	0.128	0.195	0.253	0.163	0.050
Netherlands	0.160	0.202	0.185	0.088	0.024
Italy	0.166	0.163	0.121	0.049	0.011
Germany	0.125	0.101	0.064	0.026	0.003
Argentina	0.116	0.081	0.051	0.014	0.003
England	0.073	0.048	0.025	0.006	0.001
France	0.072	0.053	0.022	0.004	0.001
Greece	0.026	0.013	0.006	0.001	0.000

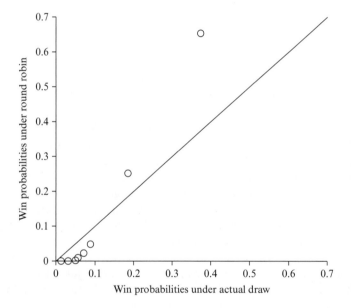

Figure 11.3   Comparison of win probabilities under actual draw and a round-robin tournament

probability of the strongest teams winning the title. Of course, such a tournament design is not practical as it would take 16 weeks to play if each of the teams played two games per week.

Finally, Figure 11.4 summarizes the effect of the three different tournament structures on the probability of winning the title for the top five

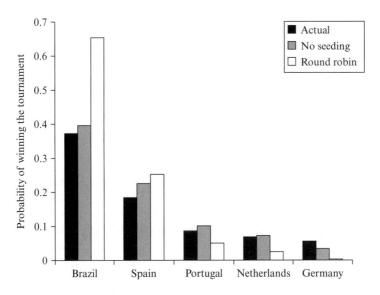

Figure 11.4   Probability of winning the World Cup 2010 under three different tournament designs

teams. It is clear from the figure that the round-robin format is advantageous to the top two teams at the most recent World Cup, while using the current tournament structure without seedings would help all five of the top teams. Thus, if increasing outcome uncertainty is the objective of the tournament organizers, it appears that they achieved their goal.

5   DISCUSSION

The main purpose of this chapter was to demonstrate how to forecast a football match result, and then use the forecasting model to obtain the estimated probability of a team winning a tournament. We use the procedure to experiment with the effect of two alternative tournament designs and answer two specific questions: what is the effect of seeding, and what is the effect of the league-knockout hybrid tournament structure?

Our results suggest that seeding in the 2010 tournament did not help the strongest teams, seeded 1 to 4, but did help the teams seeded 5–8. Further, a round robin would aid only the top two teams, Brazil and Spain. Of course, a round robin among 32 teams would be completely impractical to operate, but nevertheless, it is interesting to see the quantitative difference between the tournament designs – Brazil had an estimated probability of winning the title of 0.373 under the actual tournament structure, but this increased to 0.654 for a round-robin tournament.

Regarding the forecasting model, the statistical significance of the economic variables in our forecasting model that already included the FIFA world rankings was somewhat surprising. It suggests a bias in the ranking itself that should be taken into account when using the ranking to forecast. A thorough analysis of the effect of economic variables and how they drive success on the pitch would need to be more sophisticated. For one thing, our analysis is confined to male soccer, so ideally we would use the relevant size of the male population in a given year. Moreover, if we take the population size as an indicator of the size of the potential talent pool, perhaps we should use the number of players who are registered with their national association. Even though such a measure would underestimate the total number of players, it would mitigate the effect of some outliers in our dataset. For example, China and India are very populous countries that have not been very successful in international soccer.

In closing, we note that forecasting models of match results are an important resource for tournament organizers interested in designing more exciting tournaments – a tournament design that maximizes the probability of the best team winning is probably not of very much interest to fans. Indeed, the best tournament at giving the title to the best team would be no tournament at all – the organizers would just hand the World Cup to the team ranked number one. The effect of tournament design can be investigated looking at the counterfactuals with the methodology presented here.

NOTE

1. Available at: www.fifa.com (accessed 20 June 2011).

REFERENCES

Bernard, A.B. and M.R. Busse (2004), 'Who wins the Olympic Games? Economic resources and medal totals', *Review of Economics and Statistics*, **86** (1), 413–17.
Bojke, C. (2007), 'The impact of post-season play-off systems on the attendance at regular season games', in J. Albert and R.H. Koning (eds), *Statistical Thinking in Sports*, Chapter 11, London: CRC Press, pp. 179–202.
Boulier, B.L. and H.O. Stekler (2003), 'Predicting the outcomes of National Football League games', *International Journal of Forecasting*, **19**, 257–70.
Clarke, S.R. and J.M. Norman (1995), 'Home ground advantage of individual clubs in English soccer', *The Statistician*, **44** (4), 509–21.

Goddard, J. (2005), 'Regression models for forecasting goals and match results in Association Football', *International Journal of Forecasting*, **21**, 331–40.

Goddard, J. and I. Asimakopoulos (2004), 'Forecasting football match results and the efficiency of fixed-odds betting', *Journal of Forecasting*, **23**, 51–66.

Karlis, D. and J. Ntzoufras (2003), 'Analysis of sports data using bivariate poisson models', *The Statistician*, **52**, 381–93.

Kesenne, S. (2007), 'The peculiar international economics of professional football in Europe', *Scottish Journal of Political Economy*, **54** (3), 388–99.

Klaassen, F.J.G.M. and J.R. Magnus (2001), 'Are points in tennis independent and identically distributed? Evidence from a dynamic binary panel data model', *Journal of the American Statistical Association*, **96** (454), 500–509.

Koning, R.H. (2000), 'Competitive balance in Dutch soccer', *The Statistician*, **49** (3), 419–31.

Koning, R.H. (2007), 'Post-season play and league design in Dutch soccer', in P. Rodríguez, S. Kesenne and J. Garcia (eds), *Governance and Competition in Professional Sports Leagues*, Oviedo: Ediciones de la Universidad de Oviedo pp. 191–215.

Koning, R.H. (2009), 'Sport and measurement of competition', *De Economist*, **157**, 229–49.

Koning, R.H., M. Koolhaas, G. Renes and G. Ridder (2003), 'A simulation model for football championships', *European Journal of Operational Research*, **148** (2), 268–76.

McHale, I.G. and S.M. Davies (2007), 'Statistical analysis of the FIFA world rankings', in J. Albert and R.H. Koning (eds), *Statistical Thinking in Sport*, London: Chapman & Hall, pp. 77–90.

McHale, I.G. and D. Forrest (2005), 'The importance of recent scores in a forecasting model for professional golf tournaments', *IMA Journal of Management Mathematics*, **16** (2), 131–40.

McHale, I.G. and A. Morton (2011), 'A Bradley–Terry type model for forecasting tennis match results', *International Journal of Forecasting*, **27**, (2), 619–30.

McHale, I.G. and P.A. Scarf (2011), 'Modelling the dependence of goals scored by opposing teams in international soccer matches', *Statistical Modelling*, **11**, 199–216.

Muelhauser, G. (2006), 'Implications from the theory of contests for modelling and designing sports competitions', in W. Andreff and S. Szymanski (eds), *Handbook on the Economics of Sport*, Chapter 35, Cheltenham, UK and Northampton, MA, USA: Edward Elgar, pp. 342–8.

Ridder, G., J.S. Cramer and P. Hopstaken (1994), 'Down to ten: estimating the effect of a red card in soccer', *Journal of the American Statistical Association*, **89** (427), 1124–7.

Robinson, M.E. and J.A. Tawn (1995), 'Statistics for exceptional athletics records', *Journal of the Royal Statistical Society. Series C (Applied Statistics)*, **44** (4), 499–511.

Ryvkin, D. and A. Ortmann (2008), 'The predictive power of three prominent tournament formats', *Management Science*, **54** (3), 492–504.

Scarf, P.A. and X. Shi (2005), 'Modelling match outcomes and decision support for setting a final innings target in test cricket', *IMA Journal of Management Mathematics*, **16**, 161–78.

Scarf, P.A. and M.M. Yusof (2010), 'A numerical study of tournament structure and seeding policy for the Soccer World Cup Finals', *Statistica Neerlandica*, **65** (1), 43–57.

Scarf, P.A., M.M. Yusof and M. Bilbao (2009), 'A numerical study of designs for sporting contests', *European Journal of Operational Research*, **198**, 190–98.

Szymanski, S. (2003), 'The assessment: the economics of sport', *Oxford Review of Economic Policy*, **19** (4), 467–77.

Szymanski, S. (2006), 'The theory of tournaments', in W. Andreff and S. Szymanski (eds), *Handbook on the Economics of Sport*, Chapter 34, Cheltenham, UK and Northampton, MA, USA: Edward Elgar, pp. 337–41.

12 Doping and anti-doping measures
Nicolas Eber*

1 INTRODUCTION

Doping is for at least one decade a hot topic in the economics of sports.[1] The growing literature in the field is primarily theoretical since empirical investigation is obviously difficult to implement.[2] Economists have applied their usual theoretical tools to analyze the decision by rational athletes whether or not to use performance-enhancing drugs and, then, to define the incentive mechanisms that could lead athletes to refrain from taking drugs.

The economic decision to use drugs has two main features. First, it deals with an *illicit* action since it implies an infringement of the rules. Second, it is a *strategic* decision insofar as it is taken in a context of strategic interactions among a set of contestants. While a Beckerian, 'crime economics' approach focuses on the first aspect, the game-theoretic approach allows us to fully consider the second one.[3] Although some authors have proposed interesting crime economics models (for example, Bourg, 2000; Maennig, 2002), the growing theoretical literature has mainly developed game-theoretic models.[4]

In this survey, we focus on the leading game-theoretic approach and discuss the relevance and the limits of the main results in the recent literature. We explain how the models identify the economic motivations and incentives for athletes to take drugs and we summarize the anti-doping measures that have been proposed.

The key idea of the economic analysis of doping in sport is that athletes are typically involved in a prisoner's dilemma-type interaction (Breivik, 1987; Bird and Wagner, 1997; Eber and Thépot, 1999; Haugen, 2004). The idea is straightforward: doping being a dominant strategy (that is, yielding a preferred outcome regardless of the strategy used by the competitor), each athlete finds it optimal to take drugs; this results in a situation of generalized doping although each athlete would be better off in a dope-free world. However, this basic model does not give a full account of the strategic interaction among athletes, so it has been extended in several ways to incorporate in the analysis the repetition of the game, potential differences in athletes' abilities, the existence of fair-play norms, and so on. These theoretical exercises lead to propositions concerning anti-doping measures whose implementation in the field, however, are difficult.

The structure of this survey is as follows. In Section 2, we recall the basic, prisoner's dilemma (PD), model of doping. Section 3 presents the recent developments of the game-theoretic literature that extend the simple PD paradigm. In Section 4, we summarize the anti-doping measures that have been formulated by economists from their theoretical models and discuss the stakes of the anti-doping policy in the specific context of mega events. Finally, in Section 5, we try to assess objectively the actual added value of an economic approach of the problem.

2 THE BASIC MODEL

As indicated in the introduction, the key idea of the game-theoretic approach is that doping in sports is something like a prisoner's dilemma (Breivik, 1987; Eber and Thépot, 1999; Haugen, 2004). This idea is very simple.

Assume two athletes, A and B,[5] with identical physical abilities and preferences. The strategic variable of the model is the use of drugs by athletes. More specifically, each athlete chooses to dope (D) or not to dope (ND). Of course, athletes are controlled for doping use, with a positive probability of being caught. If an athlete is caught by a doping test, he/she is punished (disqualification, ban for the coming seasons, and so on). In the case where only one athlete is caught, that athlete is disqualified and his/her competitor then receives all the prizes devoted to the winner. If placed in equal conditions (that is, if they are both doped or both undoped), the athletes are assumed to share the market, winning each event with a probability of one half or, over a whole season, each winning half of the events. However, if one athlete dopes while his/her competitor does not, the former is sure to win.

The typical doping game may be represented as in Table 12.1.

As shown in detail in Eber and Thépot (1999) and Haugen (2004), the solution of the game depends on several parameters, especially the prizes, the probability of being caught by a test or the perceived costs of doping. The basic structure of the parameters coming from professional sports, with a very high prize for the winner, a rather low probability for a cheater of being caught, and the manifest low evaluation of the health costs,[6] leads to a prisoner's dilemma, with generalized doping as unique equilibrium. In such a case, the no-doping situation is unstable. Indeed, if both athletes start from the no-doping situation, each one has an interest in switching to doping since it will ensure that he/she wins all the events (instead of winning only half of them if he/she continues not to take drugs). Expecting this behavior from his/her competitor, the other athlete also has an interest

Table 12.1   The doping game

Athlete B	D	ND
Athlete A		
D	A and B share the market but incur a cost for their health and the risk of being caught by a test	A wins for sure (but incurs a cost for his/her health and the risk of being caught by a test) and B is always second
ND	B wins for sure (but incurs a cost for his/her health and the risk of being caught by a test) and A is always second	A and B share the market without incurring the costs of doping

in choosing doping because, in doing so, the latter will be able to share the honors with his/her (doped) competitor instead of being always second if he/she does not take drugs. In such a PD configuration, the potential gain from using drugs *unilaterally* outweighs the costs. Doping is here a dominating strategy, which results in a preferred outcome regardless of the strategy used by the competitor. In game-theory terms, the only Nash equilibrium of the game is (D, D), each athlete choosing to dope.[7]

This basic model shows that the individual incentives to take drugs depend positively on the money at stake (that is, the winner's prize or, more precisely, the spread of the prizes between a first and a second place),[8] and negatively on the perceived costs of doping (expected punishment in the case of a positive test, perceived health costs, and so on) and on the probability of incurring such costs, namely on the probability of being caught by a test.

3   EXTENSIONS OF THE BASIC MODEL

Several extensions of the standard game-theoretic model have been proposed. In particular, there are two straightforward extensions of this basic PD story. First, it can be generalized to more than two athletes, thus becoming a common resource property dilemma (Bird and Wagner, 1997). The key idea is the same: regardless of the number of other athletes who dope, the athlete with a strong taste for victory will find doping optimal; yet, if all athletes dope, they all bear negative health consequences with no significant change in each one's odds of victory. However, in more complex models, the number of participants may have an impact on the equilibrium properties. For example, Ryvkin (2009) develops a model with N players and shows that, as the number of players increases, more severe regulation in the form of an increase in the probability of testing or in the penalty is required to sustain the no-doping equilibrium.

The second possible extension deals with the repetition of the basic PD game. In such a dynamic game, punishments, reputation effects or information-gathering aspects play a key role and lead to several specific effects, such as an 'end-of-career' effect. Indeed, it may be more difficult to find incentives and credible punishments for older athletes since they are closer to the end of the game. Such athletes will not suffer from a ban as strongly as young athletes for whom a two-year ban could be particularly impeding.[9] Since competition is multi-generational in the sense that younger athletes compete with older ones, systematic strong incentives to take drugs for the latter lead to more incentives to the former in order to be rapidly competitive.

Recent extensions of the basic model are more specific and allow an analysis of the potential heterogeneity in abilities among athletes and with fair-play norms.

Heterogeneity among Athletes

Berentsen (2002) shows that the PD nature of the doping game is strongly linked to the assumption that athletes are of equal ability. Specifically, Berentsen analyzes the more general case where athletes are not necessarily characterized by identical physical abilities. In such a case, the game is no longer of a PD type, but has an equilibrium in mixed strategies with unexpected properties. In particular, the favorite (more talented) player is more likely to take drugs than is the underdog; yet, for some parameter values, he/she is less likely to win with doping opportunities than without.[10]

Berentsen and Lengwiler (2004) analyze an evolutionary doping game with two types (strong and weak) of athletes. They look at the dynamics of the population and identify the conditions under which cycles may arise, with drugs being used for a while and not at other times.

Fair-play Norms

Athletes generally share some kind of *fair-play norms* that may tend to make them refrain from doping.[11] The importance of such norms has been fully recognized by Bird and Wagner (1997, p. 755): 'the only real hope for ending the practice of doping lies in the norms of fair competition among the athletes'. Eber (2008) recently showed that the incorporation of fair-play norms into the analysis of the basic performance-enhancing drug game may lead to a substantial modification in the very nature of the game, switching it from a PD to a coordination ('stag-hunt') game characterized by two (pure-strategy) equilibria: a 'bad' – doping – equilibrium but also a 'good' – no-doping – one. The idea is straightforward. Assuming that athletes care about unfair advantage or disadvantage due to doping, that is, dislike the competition being unfairly distorted by doping, they may find it rational to take drugs if their competitor does so, but, because of the guilt they feel if they win with the help of drugs against an honest competitor, they also may find it rational not to take drugs if they are sure that the competitor does not. In such a framework, 'fair-play' athletes appear as 'conditional cooperators': guided by fair-play values, they do not take drugs if they expect their competitors not to do so, but they do take drugs when they expect others to do the same. Hence, the main problem for athletes becomes to coordinate their intentions about using drugs, and communication among athletes may then have a key role.

Although the theoretical arguments about fair-play norms may be appealing, important caveats should be stressed. The main one concerns the fact that the coordination on the good (no-doping) equilibrium may be unlikely if not impossible in very large-scale contests such as worldwide athletic competitions.[12] As shown by Eber (2011), increasing the number of contestants in the doping game implies generally that: (i) the individual gain from unilateral cheating is higher, (ii) fair-play values need therefore to be stronger to have a no-doping equilibrium, (iii) it is more likely that the least-fair players will not be fair players enough to sustain the no-doping equilibrium, and (iv) the coordination on the good equilibrium is much more difficult.

Summary of the Theoretical Results

Other recent game-theoretic models have extended the standard framework to account for the re-awarding of the prize in the case where the winner is caught doped and the loser is not (Curry and Mongrain, 2009), the complementarity of doping with other, legal, inputs such as training (Kräkel, 2007; Ryvkin, 2009; Gilpatric, 2011) or the features of the auditing regime (Curry and Montgrain, 2009; Stowe and Gilpatric, 2010).

A lot of models are now available. In each of them, the equilibrium properties depend crucially on the parameter values. Thus, as in other fields of economics (for example, industrial organization (see Fisher, 1989), we might be left with the feeling that the overall conclusion of the game-theoretic analysis is simply that a lot of different things *can* happen.

4 SUMMARY OF THE PROPOSED ANTI-DOPING MEASURES

In spite of its limits, all the above theoretical literature has led to normative insights, identifying anti-doping measures that should be put forward in order to improve the efficiency of the fight against doping. We shall summarize these policy recommendations, with a simple distinction between external and internal regulation systems, and then discuss the stakes of the anti-doping policy in the specific context of mega events.

External Regulation

This is the simple regulation system with an external institution that has the task of preventing doping by monitoring athletes and punishing those who are detected as cheaters.[13] From the economic analyses of doping behavior, the fight against doping should obviously be organized so as to alter athletes' economic incentives to use drugs. It deals with both lowering the gains from doping (for instance, by reducing the spread of the prizes between a first and a second place) and increasing the expected costs (for instance, with more frequent monitoring and more severe financial penalties but also with prevention in order to make the athletes more sensitive to the potential health costs).

Several authors put forward solutions specifically designed to reduce the economic incentives to doping. Eber and Thépot (1999) argued that what is needed is a *global* reform of the competitive sports encompassing lower spreads in the prizes from events,[14] fewer events during the season, an improvement of the test system and more prevention. According to Maennig (2002, 2009), the crucial point is to increase the expected costs of doping and the simpler and more effective way to do that is to increase the financial penalties;[15] more precisely, Maennig (2009, p. 350) argues that 'to implement such policies competition associations or organizers would require athletes to contractually agree to penalties of this kind before competitions'. He also stresses, in line with the deferred compensation models, that part of the sponsoring revenues could be paid in funds which would be paid out at the end of a sporting career and could serve to pay any penalties for doping offenses during the career. Berentsen (2002) proposes a ranking-based, punishment scheme: in his two-athlete model, the winner risks a sanction S_1, the loser a sanction S_2, with $S_1 > S_2$.[16] Berentsen shows that this ranking-based punishment scheme is more effective than the International Olympic Committee (IOC) sanction scheme because it makes it easier and cheaper (fewer tests) to reach the no-doping equilibrium. This suggests that only winners (and not losers) should be tested after the competition. In a similar vein, Curry and Mongrain (2009) and Stowe and Gilpatric (2010) underline the merits of differential monitoring schemes, where contestants are audited based on either their initial position or their final ranking.[17]

Of course, all these propositions, based on the basic idea of directly reducing the economic incentives to doping, may be difficult to implement and probably insufficient to deter athletes from using drugs. Indeed, as long as athletes are prepared to sacrifice their health for a gold medal (see the Goldman survey mentioned in note 6), finding a commensurate penalty system is simply not feasible.[18]

Internal Regulation

Bird and Wagner (1997) note that, in the context of a common property resource problem, a centralized enforcement system based on written rules applied by an external institution works well only when behavior is easy to observe and the central authority can easily impose appropriate sanctions. Emphasizing that this condition is far from being satisfied in the case of doping, they argue that informal self-enforcement institutions would be far more efficient than formal regulatory measures.[19] Bird and Wagner propose a 'peer monitoring' system that they call the 'drug diary' system.

The system proposed by Bird and Wagner relies on the principle that no drugs would be explicitly forbidden but that athletes are obliged to publish a 'drug diary' in which they record all the drugs they take. Doping would then be defined as the secret use of any undeclared drug (including 'harmless' drugs). The athletes are randomly tested for substances not mentioned in the diary. If a substance not mentioned is found, the athlete is considered as 'doped' and is then sanctioned. In that system, the definition of doping becomes a matter for each athlete: as noted by Bird and Wagner (1997, p. 757), 'the term doping would now refer not to the use of a drug on a negative list but to any drug used in secret'. In fact, all drugs used to increase performance in such a way that athletes would be ashamed to admit it is classified as doping.

According to Bird and Wagner, this system has several virtues. Generally speaking, it encourages honesty, transparency, and equal access to doping, that is, the development of athletic norms against unfair use of drugs. Moreover, it helps to resolve three main problems with the negative-list system. First, it no longer advertises drugs. Second, it does not encourage the development of new drugs, since no substances are forbidden. Third, the system may be implemented by the athletes themselves.[20]

Indeed, Bird and Wagner additionally advocate a collegial enforcement system according to which any two athletes who are currently registered by the sports association are allowed to demand a drug diary test of any third registered athlete. The test could be demanded at any time and there would be sanctions for false accusations in order to prevent frivolous challenges intended only to impeach other competitors. According to Bird and Wagner (p. 759), 'a system in which athletes are allowed to challenge one another's integrity in public creates a situation in which mutual trust and respect are beneficial'. Thus, the collegial enforcement system may encourage the development of internalized norms of fair competition.

Although the theoretical arguments of Bird and Wagner, in the spirit of the work of Ostrom, may be appealing, there are obvious practical limits to their propositions. In particular, the drug diary system may become profoundly unfair as soon as athletes have different ethical values with respect to doping. In other words, the drug diary system could be efficient only if all the athletes share the same values. If this were not the case, the system would accept 'certifying' an athlete who chooses to use all the possible performance-enhancing drugs and who has the 'courage' to declare or even claim it. Thus, the system would favor unscrupulous people who cynically declare the use of performance-enhancing drugs, to the detriment of both dope-free athletes and doped athletes who do not want to claim the use of drugs. As for the collegial enforcement system, it rests on suspicion and informing and this seems far from the fair-play norms put forward by Bird and Wagner. In spite of these potential shortcomings, the authors have recently reiterated their confidence in their 'drug diary system' (Castronova and Wagner, 2009).[21]

A 'peer monitoring' system is also put forward by Berentsen et al. (2008). They advocate a system of monitoring where losers 'blow the whistle' if they consider that they suffered from an unfair defeat due to the cheating of the winner. The winner is then tested only if he/she is accused by the losers and there is a penalty for false accusations.[22] Berentsen et al. show theoretically that if punishment for cheating is sufficiently large, such a system improves the efficiency of the anti-doping fight, with less cheating and lower costs in terms of test frequencies. But again, as for the Bird–Wagner proposition, the approach relies both on suspicion and informing and on the assumption of a good knowledge by the losers of doping practise by the winner.

In a somewhat similar vein, other authors have focused on the key role of athletes' values. In a field study on Norwegian athletes, Tangen and Breivik (2001) classify different types of athletes. They show that two types of athletes with winner-oriented preference systems, based on a Lombardian[23] or Machiavellian ethic, were willing to dope and actually used doping means to a much greater extent than fairness-oriented, Coubertinian, athletes. Such results plead for the general principle that what is fundamentally needed is the development among top-level athletes of a new system of preferences based on fairness-oriented values. In this respect, placing more emphasis during the education of athletes on the pleasure in attaining one's goals, the joy of an honest victory, and so forth, is crucial (Bourg, 2000, p.176).

Moreover, in the multiple equilibria context that may arise in the case where athletes share fair-play norms (Eber, 2008, 2009), preplay communication, with for example meetings on the issue of doping, may facilitate the coordination on the no-doping equilibrium and formal agreements of athletes on anti-doping rules may then serve as a useful coordination device. In this respect, the promotion by the International Cycling Union (UCI) of an 'anti-doping charter' is clearly valuable, though again obviously not sufficient.[24]

The Specific Case of Mega Events

There are lively debates about the stakes of the anti-doping policy in the specific context of mega events. In particular, what is the influence of doping on the credibility and the value of mega events? It is sometimes argued that doping scandals generate bad publicity and may undermine spectator interest significantly, but it is not clear that the interest of fans actually declines following doping affairs. In the standard economics framework, the attractiveness of a sporting event/show depends merely on the balance of the competition and the level of performance. In such a framework, a configuration of generalized doping may even have a positive impact on the event value since, if generalized, doping probably has a weak influence on the competitive balance of the contests but leads obviously to greater performances. Moreover, mega-event organizers can publicize both very intensive effort (and expenses) in the anti-doping fight and very low figures concerning the prevalence of doping.

Thus, it seems that the impact of doping on the value of mega events is an empirical question, but data are scarce and often lead to controversial interpretations. For instance, it is not clear whether the television audience from the Tour de France has really suffered from doping scandals. While the audiences remain at a high level and the organizer (Amaury Sport Organisation) continues to earn large profits, some have noticed a drop in audiences in the years following important doping scandals.[25] Moreover, the fact that mega events should lead to very high incentives to dope and, hence, a very high prevalence of doping is also clearly not corroborated by the data since organizers can boast about very low rates of positive cases in their events.[26]

To sum up, it seems that both directions of the causation between doping and mega-events value are very difficult to assess and further empirical work is needed to know whether: (i) the very high incentives from mega events lead to more doping, and (ii) doping scandals undermine the credibility and the value of the mega events. As noted by Preston and Szymanski (2003, p. 621) about cheating in sport in general (sabotage, doping, match-fixing), 'it is not clear how much cheating has to occur before interest in the sports starts to suffer, but there certainly does not seem to be any clear evidence that scandals related to cheating have reduced interest'. In some respects, the accelerating value of broadcast rights is even a sign of an increasing value of the events.

CONCLUSION

Many theoretical models have been proposed. In each of them, the equilibrium properties depend crucially on parameter values that are difficult if not impossible to estimate empirically. Given this, it is not surprising that, for the time being, none of the recommended measures in this literature emerges as a plausible definitive solution to the challenge of the anti-doping fight.

This somewhat pessimistic assessment of the extant scholarship may cast some doubt on the actual added value of the economic approach.[27] On this point, there are two polar views. The first one is definitely optimistic and argues that if current models are unsatisfactory, it simply implies that further research is needed to achieve a better understanding of the system and, then, more accurate policy recommendations.[28] The contrasting view is much more skeptical about the potential value of the contribution of economic science. Assessing the value of microeconomic theory, Rubinstein (2006) makes a parallel between economists' models and 'fables' and argues (p. 882) that 'as in the case of a good fable, a good model can have an enormous influence on the real world, not by providing advice or by predicting the future, but rather by influencing culture' (in the sense of conventions that influence the way people think and behave).[29] But it is not so clear that this idea applies to the specific case of doping in sports because, perhaps more than in any other fields, the parameters of the models are very difficult to estimate empirically,[30] the behavior of actors is basically unobservable, and few if any of the propositions coming from the theoretical analysis seem, at least for the moment, to have real operational usefulness.

NOTES

*   I would like to thank Wolfgang Maennig and Andrew Zimbalist for helpful comments and suggestions.

1.   For overviews, see, for example, Preston and Szymanski (2003), Eber (2006), Dilger et al. (2007), Sharpe (2009) and the policy section of the special issue on the economics of sports in *Economic Analysis and Policy*, December 2009 (vol. 39, no. 3).

2.   See, however, Dilger and Tolsdorf (2005, 2010), Pitsch et al. (2007) and the psychological research on doping attitudes by Petroczi et al. (2008, 2010).

3.   Note that the recent developments in the literature (Kräkel, 2007; Curry and Mongrain, 2009; Stowe and Gilpatric, 2010; Gilpatric, 2011) consider cheating in contests in general, doping appearing only as one among many examples. Other examples include sabotage in labor (Chen, 2003) or rent-seeking contests (Konrad, 2000), fraudulent accounting in business (Berentsen and Lengwiler, 2004) or scientific fraud in academics; all these cases deal with a highly competitive situation (of the 'winner-takes-all' type) in which participants use illegal means in order to improve their relative positions.

4.   Another interesting approach has been proposed by Strulik (2007). Strulik develops a socio-economic model and studies the social dynamics of doping, identifying the conditions for the emergence of a 'doping culture'.

5.   The two-player model fits duel sports well (boxing, tennis, and so on). It also applies to team sports (where the decision of the team manager is whether to dope or not his/her team) and to other individual sports such as cycling or athletics when dominated by two clear leaders. In any event, the logic of the basic model may easily be generalized to more than two athletes (see Bird and Wagner, 1997).

6.   A large majority of professional athletes are clearly characterized by a high preference for the present and a very strong preference for winning. In 1995, Chicago physician and author Bob Goldman surveyed 198 US top-level athletes on the following question: 'You are offered a performance-enhancing substance, with two guarantees: (1) You will not be caught. (2) You will win every competition you enter for the next five years, and then you will die from the side effects of the substance. Would you take it?'. More than half of the respondents (52 percent) answered yes! (Without the side-effects, only three declared that they would not take the drug!)

7.   Note that a direct consequence of this theoretical analysis is the prediction about the prevalence of doping that nearly every athlete in elite sports is doped.

8.   As put forward by Eber and Thépot (1999), the PD logic in the doping game comes from the strong incentive for an athlete to switch from a second place half of the time to the first place for sure, and such an incentive is due to the spread of the prizes between the first and the second place. It is worth noting here that the reduction of the incentives to dope does not necessarily mean a lowering of the money at stake in professional sports but rather a leveling of the distribution of money between contestants, that is, a reduction of the 'winner-takes-all' feature of professional sport contests.

9.   This end-of-career problem may be spectacularly illustrated by recent positive cases concerning older athletes and by the fact that, in the panel of 64 world-class sprinters studied by Dilger and Tolsdorf (2005), athletes who had been tested positively were significantly older (by about 3 years).

10.   This counterintuitive result comes from the assumption that performance-enhancing drugs are more effective for the weak player. It follows that the more talented is then incited to take drugs more frequently so as to counter the powerful effect of drugs for the less talented. Yet, in some cases, the higher probability of doping use by the more talented is not enough to outweigh the greater effectiveness of drugs for the less talented so that finally the former is less likely to win than in the case without doping.

11.   As put forward by Bird and Wagner (1997, p. 752): 'athletes are typically thought of as bound together in a tightly knit community with strong preferences for (or at least familiarity with) normatively approved behavior and "fair play"'.

12.   Note, however, that decision making is not strictly simultaneous and that some

information may come from the course of a season. For instance, there could be within-country testing during Olympic trials that would inform competitors from other countries prior to the Olympics what their opponents are doing.

13. In the present context, this institution is obviously the World Anti-Doping Agency (WADA) whose credibility and, hence, independence is another important problem, in some respects reminiscent of the credibility/independence problem of central banks in the conduct of monetary policy (Eber, 2002).

14. Note, however, that an athlete may have a very inelastic response to differential prize money in part because the athlete ultimately depends more on endorsement and collateral income than on prize money. Of course, these outside sources of income may be very sensitive to behavioral transgressions by the athlete; if so, it would imply that narrowing the prize spread may not matter anyway.

15. Note that the Anti-Doping Code of the IOC envisages fines of up to US$100,000.

16. The IOC punishment scheme is not ranking based, so that $S_1 = S_2$.

17. Stowe and Gilpatric (2010) also stress the advantage of 'correlated' (rather than independent) audits even though they themselves note (p. 10) that 'correlated audits require the capacity to audit all contestants, which may be infeasible'.

18. Even the fact that an athlete may go to jail for doping (as in Italy) could be insufficient.

19. Note that this idea of the relevance of informal rules as a response to a common property resource problem is of course not restricted to the specific problem of doping but has also been stressed in the context of natural resources by 2009 Nobel Prize winner Elinor Ostrom.

20. Except, of course, that the testing must still be administered externally.

21. Castronova and Wagner (2009) are even more explicit about their doubts concerning the negative-list system: 'The then- (and tragically still-) current method of publishing a list of banned substances and enforcing the list can *never, ever* work' (p. 342; original italics), or: 'the idiocies of the enforcement system ensure that all athletes are doped to the four winds' (p. 344).

22. Specifically, the whistleblower must transfer a monetary payment to the controller when accusing the winner of using performance-enhancing drugs and this monetary payment is lost if the test is negative but returned to the whistleblower if it is positive.

23. In reference to Vince Lombardi, the famously tough football coach, to whom has been attributed the well-known quote 'winning isn't everything, it's the only thing'.

24. The UCI requests that all ProTour cyclists sign a charter saying they are not involved in doping and agreeing to pay a year's salary (on top of a two-year ban) if found guilty of drug use. Note that the UCI cannot force riders to sign, but will publish on its website a list of those who have signed the charter, showing therefore also those who are reluctant to sign it.

25. For example, the average audience figures from the Tour de France French television broadcasts dropped from 5.1 million in 1997 to 3.6 million in 1998 just after the Festina affair, and from 4.2 million in 2005 to 3.6 million in 2006 in the wake of the Puerto operation. Since then, audience figures have stabilized around the level of 3.6 million. (An average of 3.6 million people watched the race in 2010.)

26. For example, as a result of the doping tests conducted during the Beijing Olympic Games in 2008, there were only 10 positive results from approximately 5,000 urine samples. Annual WADA reports provide figures for positive tests around 2 percent (for example, 1.97 percent of adverse findings in A-samples out of the 223,898 tests conducted in 2007).

27. Other approaches of the anti-doping policy include psychological research on doping attitudes (Petroczi et al., 2008, 2010) or ethical debates about whether one should allow performance-enhancing drugs in sport (Savulescu et al., 2004; Kayser et al., 2007). It can be noted that, in both cases, there are practically no references to the economic literature.

28. For example, this is the point of view defended by Sharpe (2009, p. 354) who argues that 'more theory is needed' and concludes his essay on the economics of doping with

the following optimistic conjecture: 'economic theory already has available to it the appropriate analytical tools; it merely remains to apply them to the case at hand'.

29. A related, though less pessimistic, viewpoint is proposed by Gilboa (2010) who points out that, when applying and evaluating rational choice models, social scientists in general and economists in particular should be careful to distinguish between the paradigm and the theories. Although the latter may have poor descriptive and predictive power and may even be refuted, the former can still be a useful tool as a general system of thought.

30. The fact that it is necessary to know the parameters of the theoretical model for drawing relevant policy issues is a debatable point. It can be argued that the process can rely on the regulator regarding whether the doping rate is above a threshold (acceptable) value and then changing the policy parameters (number of tests, financial penalties) accordingly.

REFERENCES

Berentsen, A. (2002), 'The economics of doping', *European Journal of Political Economy*, **18**, 109–27.

Berentsen, A., E. Bruegger and S. Loertscher (2008), 'On cheating, doping and whistleblowing', *European Journal of Political Economy*, **24**, 415–36.

Berentsen, A. and Y. Lengwiler (2004), 'Fraudulent accounting and other doping games', *Journal of Institutional and Theoretical Economics*, **160**, 402–15.

Bird, E. and G. Wagner (1997), 'Sport as a common property resource: a solution to the dilemmas of doping', *Journal of Conflict Resolution*, **41**, 749–66.

Bourg, J.-F. (2000), 'Contribution à une analyse économique du dopage' [Contribution to an economic analysis of doping], *Reflets et perspectives de la vie économique*, **39**, 169–78.

Breivik, G. (1987), 'The doping dilemma – some game theoretical and philosophical considerations', *Sportwissenschaft*, **17**, 83–94.

Castronova, E. and G. Wagner (2009), 'Sports rules as common pool resources: a better way to respond to doping', *Economic Analysis and Policy*, **39**, 341–4.

Chen, K.-P. (2003), 'Sabotage in promotion tournaments', *Journal of Law, Economics, and Organization*, **19**, 119–40.

Curry, P. and S. Mongrain (2009), 'Deterrence in rank-order tournaments', *Review of Law and Economics*, **5**, 723–40.

Dilger, A., B. Frick and F. Tolsdorf (2007), 'Are athletes doped? Some theoretical arguments and empirical evidence', *Contemporary Economic Policy*, **25**, 604–15.

Dilger, A. and F. Tolsdorf (2005), 'Karriereverläufe und Doping von 100m-Läufern', in H. Kossbiel and T. Spengler (eds), *Modellgestützte Personalentscheidungen 8*, Mering, Germany: Rainer Hampp, pp. 103–17.

Dilger, A. and F. Tolsdorf (2010), 'Doping und Wettbewerbsintensität', *Schmollers Jahrbuch*, **130**, 95–115.

Eber, N. (2002), 'Credibility and independence of the World Anti-Doping Agency: a Barro–Gordon-type approach to antidoping policy', *Journal of Sports Economics*, **3**, 90–96.

Eber, N. (2006), 'Doping', in W. Andreff and S. Szymanski (eds), *Handbook on the Economics of Sport*, Cheltenham, UK and Northampton, MA, USA: Edward Elgar, pp. 773–83.

Eber, N. (2008), 'The performance-enhancing drug game reconsidered: a fair play approach', *Journal of Sports Economics*, **9**, 318–27.

Eber, N. (2009), 'Doping and fair play', *Economic Analysis and Policy*, **39**, 345–7.

Eber, N. (2011), 'Fair play in contests', *Journal of Economics*, **103**, 253–70.

Eber, N. and J. Thépot (1999), 'Doping in sport and competition design', *Louvain Economic Review*, **65**, 435–46.

Fisher F. (1989), 'Games economist play: a noncooperative view', *RAND Journal of Economics*, **20**, 113–24.

Gilboa, I. (2010), *Rational Choice*, Cambridge, MA: MIT Press.

Gilpatric, S. (2011), 'Cheating in contests', *Economic Inquiry*, **49** (4), 1042–53.

Haugen, K. (2004), 'The performance-enhancing drug game', *Journal of Sports Economics*, **5**, 67–86.

Kayser, B., A. Mauron and A. Miah (2007), 'Current anti-doping policy: a critical appraisal', *BMC Medical Ethics*, **8** (2) (electronic journal).

Konrad, K. (2000), 'Sabotage in rent-seeking contests', *Journal of Law, Economics, and Organization*, **16**, 155–65.

Kräkel, M. (2007), 'Doping and cheating in contest-like situations', *European Journal of Political Economy*, **23**, 988–1006.

Maennig, W. (2002), 'On the economics of doping and corruption in international sports', *Journal of Sports Economics*, **3**, 61–89.

Maennig, W. (2009), 'Pecuniary disincentives in the anti-doping fight', *Economic Analysis and Policy*, **39**, 349–51.

Petroczi, A., E. Aidman and T. Nepusz (2008), 'Capturing doping attitudes by self-report declarations and implicit assessment: a methodology study', *Substance Abuse Treatment, Prevention and Policy*, **3** (9) (electronic journal).

Petroczi, A., E. Aidman, I. Hussain, N. Deshmukh, T. Nepusz, M. Uvacsek, M. Toth, J. Barker and D. Naughton (2010), 'Virtue or pretense? Looking behind self-declared innocence in doping', *PLoS ONE*, **5** (5) (electronic journal).

Pitsch, W., E. Emrich and M. Klein (2007), 'Doping in elite sports in Germany: results of a www survey', *European Journal for Sport and Society*, **4**, 89–102.

Preston, I. and S. Szymanski (2003), 'Cheating in contests', *Oxford Review of Economic Policy*, **19**, 612–24.

Rubinstein, A. (2006), 'Dilemmas of an economic theorist', *Econometrica*, **74**, 865–83.

Ryvkin, D. (2009), 'Contests with doping', Working Paper, Florida State University.

Savulescu, J., B. Foddy and M. Clayton (2004), 'Why we should allow performance enhancing drugs in sport', *British Journal of Sports Medicine*, **38**, 666–70.

Sharpe, K. (2009), 'The economics of drugs in sport', *Sport in Society*, **12**, 344–55.

Stowe, J. and S. Gilpatric (2010), 'Cheating and enforcement in asymmetric rank-order tournaments', *Southern Economic Journal*, **77**, 1–14.

Strulik, H. (2007), 'Riding high – success in sports and the rise of doping cultures', Working Paper, University of Hanover.

Tangen, J.O. and G. Breivik (2001), 'Doping games and drug abuse. A study of the relation between preferences, strategies and behavior in connection to doping in Norwegian sports', *Sportwissenschaft*, **31**, 188–98.

13 Explaining and forecasting national team medals totals at the Summer Olympic Games

David Forrest, Adams Ceballos, Ramón Flores, Ian G. McHale, Ismael Sanz and J.D. Tena

1 INTRODUCTION

At the start of each Olympic Games it has become something of a sport in itself for economists to issue forecasts of how many medals each country will win. Among authors referenced below who have employed their academic work to produce public forecasts have been Andreff and Andreff, Bernard and Busse, Johnson and Ali, Maennig and Wellbroch, and Forrest et al. Each of these research groupings has succeeded in generating significant media attention, a reflection that, while the Olympic Charter might insist that competition is among individual athletes, in practice national medals totals are the focus of considerable interest and strong prestige is perceived to attach to countries that finish well. Indeed, during the Cold War, which country secured the more medals appeared to be one of the major fronts on which America and Russia fought for global reputational supremacy.

Now, forecasts may be fun; but, aside from providing benchmarks for the *ex post* assessment of performance, they appear to offer little social utility since real outcomes are known soon enough in any case. Their real significance is therefore that they provide unusually public out-of-sample testing of underlying models which employ data from previous Games to try to further understanding of how medals totals are determined.

Ideally, understanding the reasons behind the distribution of medals would yield implications for policy, both at the level of the individual country and globally (for the International Olympic Committee: IOC). For the individual country which aspires to raise its level of performance, estimation of what is essentially a medals production function should be at least a useful starting point. And, from the perspective of global policy, modelling should illuminate the mechanisms that yield what appears to be gross inequity in the distribution of medals. Groot (2008) pointed out that, in proportion to population, India should win nearly four times as many medals as the United States. In fact, in the 2008 Games, India won three medals and America claimed 110. For India, this was actually an improvement on 2004.

Econometric analysis of how many medals countries win extends as far back as Grimes et al. (1974); but the dominant reference in the current literature is Bernard and Busse (2004), a contribution which appeared in a very high-profile journal. Our starting point is therefore their highly influential model though we note that similar models were developed contemporaneously by Andreff (2001) and Johnson and Ali (2004).

2   BERNARD AND BUSSE

The Bernard and Busse (2004) model is based on the underlying proposition that a country's share of medals depends on the amount of sporting talent it has relative to other participating countries. In turn, talent is a function of resources, represented by population and real GDP. A higher population is likely to provide more candidates who could, potentially, become world-class sportspersons while a high income raises the probability that those with that raw ability will transform, or be transformed, into international competitors. This proposition leads to their specification that the share of medals won by a country i at the (Summer) Games of year t (M_{it}) will depend on its population (N_{it}) and on its real per capita gross domestic product (per capita GDP) in US dollars ($(Y/N)_{it}$). They add dummy variables to represent Olympics *host* countries and countries which had the status of command economies (either within the *sovietbloc* or as *otherplanned* economies such as Cuba and China), since these appeared to have performed consistently well given what would be expected purely on the basis of their population and income levels. Estimating over data from 1960–96, they reported results from the following:

$$M_{it} = f[\log N_{it}, \log(Y_{it}/N_{it}), host_{it}, sovietbloc_{it}, otherplannedeconomy_{it},$$
time dummies]   (13.1)

where the time dummies control for the population and income levels of other countries competing at Games t.

The principal econometric issue in the panel data analysed was the large mass point at $M_{it} = 0$: a large proportion of countries which send athletes to a Games fail to win any medals at all (we note, for example, that countries as populous as Bangladesh, Ghana and Pakistan failed to collect anything from Beijing, 2008). This was addressed by Bernard and Busse estimating a Tobit model. The Tobit model, designed for datasets with censored observations, assumes that the same factors which influence the probability of winning at least one medal similarly affect the medal shares among those countries which do win at least one; in the present context this assumption appears uncontroversial.

Results from Tobit estimation, with and without random effects, were reported; but there was no fixed-effects model. This is understandable because some countries *never* achieved a medal and the country fixed effects for each of them would then be estimated as minus infinity (Lui and Suen, 2008). Even without this technical problem, there would be a very large increase in the number of parameters to be estimated from including fixed effects when employing a dataset with so many cross-sectional units (over 150 countries). Fortunately, however, using random instead of fixed effects (which could be problematic if country effects were correlated with the covariates) does not appear to be a major issue, since Lui and Suen found little difference when they applied a similar model as Bernard and Busse to a narrower dataset, generated by medal performances at the Pan American Games (where, over time, all countries for which full information was available, had in fact won a medal at least once).

The principal practical issue was what to do about the boycott years of 1980 and 1984. The Russian-hosted Games of 1980 was subject to a political boycott by the United States and all its major allies (other than Great Britain). Unsurprisingly, this was followed by the Soviet bloc absenting itself from the following Games, which, unfortunately for the IOC, had been scheduled in an American city. These two boycotts certainly changed the shape of the respective medals tables; but it could be argued that the model of medal shares should still work when the set of participating countries is smaller since the underlying model proposes that relative population and relative income should still drive relative success among participants (the effect of the weight of population and income missing from the observed set of countries being collected in the time dummies). Indeed, Bernard and Busse report results with and without 1980 and 1984 in the dataset and coefficient estimates are very similar. However, an exception is that on *host*, which falls substantially when the boycott years are excluded, implying that Russia and America benefited disproportionately in terms of medal wins when their major rival failed to take part in 'their' Games. This appears to us a good reason for Bernard and Busse having presented a preferred specification with the boycott years in fact excluded since, otherwise, general hosting effects might have been overestimated.

Results were that all coefficient estimates were positive and those on log population and log per capita income were not significantly different from each other. The similarity in coefficient estimates on these two variables implied that there would have been no material difference in findings had the product of population and per capita real GDP (that is, total GDP) been included instead of the two separate variables: it proved not to matter whether a given national income level is achieved predominantly through high population or predominantly through high mean income. Rather, sheer weight of GDP was driving medal shares. Roughly, a 1 per cent increase in GDP was associated with an increase of 1.25 percentage points in medal share (note that this estimate may be biased downwards a little, in terms of reflecting global inequality in sporting achievement, to the extent that some countries are excluded from the sample at some Games and may not have participated simply because they had too few economic resources to have an acceptable chance of winning a medal). Host effects were estimated to add 2.4 percentage points to medal share and Soviet bloc countries were estimated to have 'overperformed', relative to their GDP, by 6.1 percentage points.

The authors commented that their specification was spartan and were therefore not surprised that, while the model was successful in identifying key structural determinants of levels of achievement, the fit was inadequate for it to be fit for purpose from a forecasting perspective. They therefore reported a final version of the model, to incorporate a lagged dependent variable which captured a strong tendency to persistence in medal score (this necessitated the deletion of observations from 1988 because medal shares in the preceding Olympics had been distorted by a boycott). Coefficient estimates on log population and log per capita income and on the hosting and political systems dummies remained significant, with those on the first two terms still insignificantly different from each other. That on the extra term proved highly significant and large in magnitude (0.73). It improved fit principally by eliminating serious underprediction of medals totals for the very highest-performing countries. Estimation of this version of the model on the 1996 cross-section then yielded forecasts for 2000, issued *ex ante*, which appeared satisfactory. It may puzzle the reader of their article that Bernard and Busse did not calculate long-run impacts from population and per capita GDP, exploiting the estimate of the coefficient on this lagged dependent variable. However, we would be sceptical over whether the model could capture adequately the dynamics of success given the relatively small number of time points observed and that these are from two non-adjacent subperiods, up to 1976 and from 1992.

The Bernard and Busse paradigm has been the starting point for most subsequent work to have investigated degrees of Olympics success. There have been refinements. For example, Andreff et al. (2008) lag the population and per capita terms by one Olympiad (four years), on the grounds that extra resources cannot produce more output (medals) in the very short run, and also add regional dummies. Johnson and Ali (2004) present an ordered probit model in which it is the individual athlete that is the unit of analysis (with covariates still defined at country level). Lui and Suen (2008) find that Poisson modelling of country medals count provides good fit and they also experiment with the addition of life expectancy and education variables to the model. Andreff and Andreff (2011) extend the analysis to the Winter Olympics. All of these adaptations yield interesting conclusions but the stylized facts identified by Bernard and Busse remain robust: population and per capita income are the major identified determinants of medal wins (though it should be acknowledged that the latter appears to prove more influential than the former in the case of the Winter Games) and hosts and planned economies tend to deliver relatively enhanced performance.

3 BUILDING ON BERNARD AND BUSSE

Within its own terms, Bernard and Busse was a highly successful contribution and it confirmed, in general terms, that inequalities in the distribution of international sporting success, at least in respect of the Olympics, for the most part merely reflected inequality in the distribution of economic resources. This has value for some aspects of the debate within international sporting politics. For example, it implies that a fast-growing economy like that of China can hope for a quick increase in its performance level but that, if the bulk of poor countries are to progress, this will require specific measures to be taken by sport itself. For example, Groot (2008) reviews a proposal that countries should be allocated entitlements to send given numbers of competitors to the Games; Olympic committees in poor countries, with insufficient resources or athletic talent to use up their quotas, could then sell their surplus places to rich countries, engineering a transfer of resources to be used to develop talent in the vendor nations.

For individual countries, policy implications from the model are, however, thin. Influence over the values of the principal covariates are beyond the scope of those responsible for national sports policies, and drawing conclusions from the results is difficult given ambiguity over why each of the covariates possesses predictive power.

For example, total GDP is concluded to be the principal determinant of medal shares. But the mechanism through which GDP exerts its influence is unclear. For example, a high per capita income might be a means to government affording resources to train elite sportspeople to a high standard or it might, either or as well, affect performance by raising health and nutrition standards such that there is a large number of recreational players from which future champions can emerge. Again, hosting effects could reflect government allocating more resources to winning success because there is a greater payoff in terms of prestige when it is in the spotlight as host. Alternatively, hosting effects overall could be no more than a reflection of the home advantage noted to exist for most sports whatever the level of competition. Even the reason for the superior propensity of communist and planned economies to generate extra medals is not obvious. Tcha (2004) points out that Eastern bloc countries might have targeted a higher number of medals than other countries with similar population sizes and income levels either because the benefits to them were greater (perhaps one might speculate that an authoritarian political system may measure benefits with more weight given to the preferences of the rulers than the ruled) or because the cost of medals was lower (in a command economy where athletic talent can be directed into environments offering intensive training).

In short, the impacts from GDP and population and political system have been identified and measured in the literature; but the framework discussed above begs many questions concerning the mechanism through which each covariate exerts its influence. Our research programme therefore takes the Bernard–Busse contribution as a starting point for investigations that aim to raise understanding of how the distribution of medals is determined.

Possible routes to developing the Bernard–Busse model further are to add covariates and to disaggregate by type of country and by individual sport. We report below our work on each of these three approaches. Disaggregation by rich country/poor country, and by sport, are innovatory features of this chapter and the exercises seemed to yield insights which enriched understanding of the pattern of medals across nations.

4   ADDING COVARIATES

In Forrest et al. (2010), we reported a model we had estimated as the basis of the medals forecasts that we issued before the start of competition at the 2008 Beijing Games. We regressed medal share of country i at the Games of year t on its share of the total GDP of all countries in the sample for that Games and its share of the total population of all countries in the sample for that Games. This specification is similar to Bernard and Busse in that it presumes that total GDP is a key determinant of medal share. It differs in measuring income in shares rather than in absolute terms; the advantage is that this obviates the need for time dummies to capture the income levels of other competing nations.

This change is one of presentation but does not represent substantive development of the Bernard–Busse framework. We sought development by introducing two new covariates.

The first was a new dummy variable to represent the situation where country i, competing at Games t, was going to be the new host, four years later. The introduction of this *futurehost* variable was inspired by an impression from the raw data that the next host had often done well relative to its previous performances (though we discovered subsequently that Clarke, 2000, had already noted this tendency, and that Maennig and Wellbroch, 2008, had, contemporaneously with us, incorporated a future host variable in their own modelling).

Future hosts are awarded the Games six years in advance. At the intermediate Games, its athletes do not benefit from home advantage. If they still 'overperform', this would suggest that government might already be modifying sports policy, for example by shifting resources (from the overall sports budget or elsewhere) into elite training programmes, with the intention of achieving sporting success at its own Games. If it is already receiving a payoff at the intermediate Games, high achievement at its hosted Games is likely to be in part the result of government investment in the generation of medals rather than simply a product of home advantage. The inclusion of *futurehost* was therefore an attempt to illuminate the reason for the significance of *host* itself.

The other covariate we added was a measure of government expenditure on sport. If such a measure could be collected, it would have direct policy relevance because it would facilitate estimation of the marginal cost of winning a medal. Its impact on the coefficient estimates on the dummy variables for host and political system would likewise illuminate the mechanisms by which host countries and communist countries have reached elevated levels in the medals table.

Sadly, it does not appear possible to collect consistent panel data showing government expenditure on sport, or of any component of government spending on sport, for a sufficient number of countries. We therefore had to resort to a 'rough' proxy. The United Nations data on public expenditure by country divide public expenditure into nine broad categories, of which one is 'recreational, cultural and religious affairs' (United Nations, 2000). This category includes sport. Of course, it also includes many spheres little related to sport. We were encouraged by finding from EUROSTAT that, for the five European countries which reported a breakdown of this broad category expenditure year by year from 1990, the proportion of it accounted for by the sport subcategory was strikingly consistent across countries and over time (at 35 per cent). While recognizing that this European group might not be an adequate representation of all countries, we were sufficiently encouraged to introduce the additional covariate, *recspendshare*, the share of a country in the total public expenditure on this function of government by all countries in the sample for the particular Games. The public expenditure figures were based on the mean of the available annual figures from the period since the preceding Games. Data were collected from the series *Government Financial Statistics*, published by the International Monetary Fund.

The Tobit model we estimated was therefore:

$$M_{it} = f(gdpshare_{it}, populationshare_{it}, host_{it}, futurehost_{it}, sovietbloc_{it},$$
$$otherplannedeconomy_{it}, recspendshare_{it}). \tag{13.2}$$

It should be noted that including measures based on total GDP and on population is equivalent to Bernard and Busse including GDP per head and population since, if the value of any two of the variables is given, the third is determined arithmetically. In a specification such as (13.2), the Bernard–Busse proposition that it is only the product of per capita GDP and population that matters is tested by examining whether the coefficient estimate on the population variable is zero.

Equation (13.2) was estimated only over the Games from 1992 to 2004 because the United Nations data on public expenditure began to become available only from 1990. Further, many countries took considerable time to comply with lodging of the relevant statistics with the International Monetary Fund. Consequently our estimation was based on only 196 country-year observations and then with the caveat that there was an unquantifiable risk of selection bias since the compliance of countries with the reporting regime might be correlated with relevant unobserved country characteristics.

Nevertheless, the results were interesting. It was unsurprising that positive effects from GDP, host status and (in our case, former) membership of the Soviet bloc were all confirmed. But the two new covariates played additional roles. The coefficient estimate on *futurehost* was strongly significant and of similar magnitude to that on *host* itself. The coefficient estimate on the recreational spending variable was significant at just outside the 5 per cent level.

As noted above, public forecasting exercises provide effective out-of-sample testing of the efficacy of underlying models. Our forecasts were based on the underlying model including the two new covariates (but supplemented, as in Bernard and Busse, by a lagged dependent variable) and our published assessment of the forecasts (Forrest et al., 2010) demonstrated that the new covariates did indeed improve the performance metrics.

In common with other forecasters, we had our failures. Japan was a significant loser in the 2008 Games, recording 25 medals (compared with 37 in 2004). This we had not anticipated. Our forecast was 35. Other forecasters also failed to signal Japan's slide in the medals table. For example, Johnson and Ali (2008) predicted 37.

On the other hand, our model picked out the three largest shifts in the distribution of medals from 2004: the surge of China and of Great Britain, and the slump of Russia.

China, the host, finished second to the United States in number of medals, up from 63 in 2004 to 100 in 2008. Johnson and Ali (2008) had called 90 and Andreff et al. (2008) 80. However, in this case, our 'superior' performance was accounted for only by an ad hoc adjustment to forecasts based on speculation that there would be an 'extra' effect from interaction between *host* and *otherplannedeconomy*.

Great Britain increased its number of medals from 30 to 47. We had predicted 44, compared with 28 (Johnson and Ali), 34 (Andreff et al.) and 38 (Maennig and Wellbroch). Clearly, our forecast, like that of Maennig and Wellbroch, benefited from the inclusion of the new variable *future-host* in the underlying model. Great Britain received the same boost as in-sample estimation had revealed previous future hosts to have obtained. It is perhaps suggestive that Great Britain had responded to the award of the Games by allocating substantially more resources to training Olympic competitors: it had spent £70 million on its World Class Performance Programme in the four years prior to Athens, 2004, but £235 million in the four years prior to 2008 (Nevill et al., 2009). It is plausible that other hosts had responded in the same way.

Russia was the biggest loser in Beijing, its medals total declining from 92 to 72. Our forecast (74) had anticipated this, as had that of Maennig and Wellbroch (78), whereas Johnson and Ali predicted 95 and Andreff et al., 96. Johnson and Ali also reported severe overprediction for countries such as Bulgaria, Hungary and Poland, suggesting that forecasters' success may be very sensitive to how they model the role of political system for countries which are former but no longer members of the Soviet bloc.

Overall, our forecasts proved good enough for us subsequently to reestimate our underlying model with Beijing observations included. This allowed a much bigger sample size because compliance with reporting of recreational spending had become much more widespread by 2008 (indeed, it was only because of this that we had been able to issue forecasts for most countries at Beijing, 2008; a conspicuous exception was Cuba).

In this new experiment, exploiting more observations, and with a broad range of countries represented, the result on the recreation spending variable was considerably strengthened. The variable was now strongly significant. Explanatory power was further increased by entering it as a quadratic, showing decreasing returns to spending on 'recreation'. The magnitude of the effects may be illustrated by considering the cases of Germany and Great Britain.

Germany and Great Britain are similarly sized European countries but, according to the most recent data, Great Britain accounts for a larger share (7.3 per cent) of 'world public expenditure' on 'recreation'. From our results, a one percentage point increase in spending share would increase expected medals for Germany by 1.8 but, given diminishing returns, by only 1.4 for Great Britain (we assume that the total number of medals available is the same as in Beijing). Recall, however, that recreation spending is much broader than sport. One might speculate that medals would be calculated to be much 'cheaper' to engineer were the whole of any increase in recreational spending to be allocated to sport (rather than just the 35 per cent typical in Europe).

An interesting feature of our results, estimated over 1992–2008, is that the coefficient estimate on *gdpshare* falls somewhat when the recreational spending variable is included in an otherwise identical model (0.57 to 0.45). This suggests that part, but only part, of the explanation for the role of GDP in general is that richer countries devote more public resources to sport. On the other hand, the coefficient estimate on the dummy variable signifying former membership of the Soviet bloc barely moves according to whether *recspendshare* is included in the model. This may indicate that it was the communist system itself, rather than a tradition of high spending on sport, that accounted for the high achievement of the sports systems developed in the days of the Soviet bloc.

These conclusions must be regarded as tentative because of uncertainty over how well our recreation spending variable proxies public spending on sport. Clearly it would be better to use a more focused measure of expenditure on sport but this is unlikely to become available in the foreseeable future given the very large number of countries for which it would be required. However, Li et al. (2009) sought to overcome this obstacle by taking one very large country and subdividing it by province. They traced the geographic origin of each Chinese gold medallist in the 2004 Games and then applied a Bernard–Busse type model, relating the number of medals accruing to a province to its population and per capita income. They then added a measure of public expenditure on sport in that province. The coefficient estimate was not only positive, strong and significant but it also removed altogether the role accorded to per capita income. Thus richer provinces win more Olympic medals in China, but this is only because richer provinces devote more public resources to sport. This is a stronger result than from our international analysis but the caveat should be made that expenditure in China might be more productive of medals than in other countries. Li et al. point out that in no other country can a child be removed from primary school and placed in an intensive sports academy where academic studies are neglected.

Nevertheless, their results and ours together come close to confirming the ability of governments to raise medals performance by allocating more resources to sport. More refined assessment of the marginal cost of medals is likely to be gained in the future (though we would note that research needs also to address the question of how to evaluate marginal benefit). Further insight would likely be gained if country studies were able to investigate whether, in the long run, it is more efficacious to concentrate resources on the elite or on the recreational sports sectors.

5   DISAGGREGATION BY COUNTRY

Research to date has been dominated by attempts to estimate world medals production functions. There is a risk here that excessive aggregation will lead to a failure to reveal that different countries face different obstacles to progress towards any aspirations they may have to win more medals. For example, rich and poor countries may be positioned on different production functions rather than occupy different positions on the same production function.

In our next experiments, we distinguished between rich and poor countries, defined by whether they were members of the OECD at the end of our data period (which was 1992–2008). A total of 32 countries were allocated to the OECD subsample. The model specification was as in (13.2) and we estimated both static and dynamic versions of the model (the dynamic adds a lagged dependent variable).

Important differences appeared between the two groups of countries (the same pattern was found when we based the comparison on groups of countries with incomes above and below the mean). For the OECD group of countries, the population variable was decisively insignificant, as in the aggregated results. The GDP variable was positive and significant but became insignificant in the presence of the recreational spending variable when the dynamic version of the model was estimated. These results suggest that, within the club of affluent countries, relative performance at the Games is influenced by size of economy but the effect of GDP is mediated to an important extent through how much resource is allocated to recreation. Within this group, it appears to be the case that public expenditure plays a key role in determining position in the medals table.

For the poorer countries, the findings were very different. The coefficient estimate on *gdpshare* was positive and strongly significant (and much larger in magnitude than for the OECD subsample), but that on *populationshare* was negative and strongly significant. The implication is that large developing economies achieve more medals if their size is based more on relatively high living standards than on sheer numbers in the population. Further, the role of total GDP is related closely to the affluence of the population. Large numbers of people in a country are likely to provide large numbers in the right tail of the distribution of sporting talent but, if living standards are low, too few will be healthy enough and rich enough to begin participating in sport in the first place. Disaggregation therefore reveals that the mechanism by which GDP influences medals is different between rich and poor countries. In poor and middle-income countries, GDP may largely be proxying health, nutrition and access to recreational sports opportunities.

The recreation spending variable is nevertheless still significant in the non-OECD estimates. But, it is weak in the dynamic model, capturing that increases in expenditure on recreation will have only a marginal payoff in poor countries in the short run. Our interpretation is that it takes time to build success in relatively poor countries because the stock of sports capital needs to be built. By building sports capital, government can influence long-run performance if it decides that the payoff is worth the investment.

6 DISAGGREGATION BY SPORT

The final experiments we report are based on applying the model sport by sport. We anticipated that significant differences would be revealed among sports in terms of which covariates drove success. For example, participation in some sports requires the provision of expensive assets and, here, in the case of poor countries, there will be few participants from whom world-class practitioners can emerge. The problem will be worse if there is high asset specificity (Lens, 2011, reports that specialist sports academies in the former East Germany are relatively ineffective in producing Olympic medal winners in sports with high asset specificity). Modelling should reveal which areas of sport are most promising if the goal is for a relatively poor country to win more medals.

This time, our dataset is extended to cover 1960–2008 in order to capture adequate numbers of medals in each individual sport. We omit the boycott years of 1980 and 1984 to avoid the potential bias in assessment of hosting effects. The recreational spending variable is dropped because it is unavailable for Games before 1992. Because we now embrace Games either side of the political changes associated with the fall of communism, we add a variable applicable to countries whose territory lay within the Soviet sphere of influence but for which *sovietbloc* is now equal to zero. This is to capture any superior performance associated with persistence in the old ways of organizing sport. However, any such effects are likely to diminish over time as societies converge to the Western European model. Therefore, our term for former Soviet bloc states is set equal to one (if a country is in this category) *multiplied by* the inverse of the square root of the number of Games since it left the bloc. This allows for the decay in performance over time (to be expected given the falls in sports participation documented in Poupaux, 2006) and, while ad hoc, this term *exsoviettrend*, appears to track the data well. Finally, to allow for political fragmentation after 1990, we include a dummy variable for a new country at its first Games. Hence, our model of medal share of country i for sport j at Games t is:

$$M_{ijt} = f(gdpshare_{it}, populationshare_{it}, host_{it}, futurehost_{it}, sovietbloc_{it},$$
$$exsoviettrend_{it}, newcountry_{it}, otherplannedeconomy_{it}). \qquad (13.3)$$

We estimated (13.3) (as a random effects Tobit model) for each sport for which more than 200 medals had been awarded over the data period. Purely team sports were among those not considered: they have generated too few medals for meaningful analysis even in those cases where the sport was included in every Games. The 14 sports for estimation were: athletics, boxing, canoe/kayak, cycling, equestrian, fencing, gymnastics, judo, rowing, sailing, shooting, swimming, weightlifting and wrestling.

For clarity, we note that, for those predictor variables expressed as shares, calculation is with reference to the share among all countries represented in that Games, whether or not they took part in the particular sport j. There is an implicit assumption here that countries which were not in competition for a given sport were absent because no athlete had met the qualifying standard or else they felt they had no chance of a medal.

The GDP variable was significant for 12 of the 14 sports, the exceptions being canoe/kayak and gymnastics. Among the other sports, the coefficient estimates ranged between 0.216 (wrestling) to 1.748 (sailing). Each coefficient estimate shows a 'marginal effect' for a country which is assumed to win at least one medal. For example, for such a country, an increase of one percentage point in its *gdpshare* raises its expected medals' share in wrestling by 0.216 percentage points. For other countries, where there is a lower probability of achieving a positive medal share, the marginal effect is smaller than 0.216 because it is given by the coefficient estimate *multiplied by* the probability that medals' share is positive.

The sports with the steepest relationship between medals won and GDP were found to be (in order) sailing, equestrian, swimming, fencing and cycling. All had coefficient estimates above 1.25. Sailing and equestrian are self-evidently expensive sports requiring substantial investment in yachts and horses, respectively. Champion swimmers are most likely to emerge in countries where the general population is enabled to take up the sport by ready access to a suitably dense network of (expensive) pools. This sort of network will not exist in poor countries (an extreme but illustrative figure quoted by Andreff, 2006, is that Ethiopia had only one swimming pool per 6.2 million inhabitants). Cycling medals are mainly won at the track rather than on the road and cycle tracks are very costly facilities to build and maintain, with no alternative use to help pay for them. These are not promising areas for less affluent countries and their presence in the Olympics contributes disproportionately to the inequality in the distribution of medals.

The 'cheapest' sports appear to be canoe/kayak and gymnastics, where GDP is not even a factor in either case, followed by wrestling and boxing. These represent areas where progress for less affluent countries is more realistic. In three of the cases, a general rather than specific sports venue can be used by participants, making these sports potentially more generally accessible. Aid is provided to the poorest countries by Olympic Solidarity and it might be advised to focus on development of facilities that can be shared among such disciplines.

In Bernard and Busse (2004), weight of population exerts no influence on medal shares independent of total GDP. However, at the level of the individual sport, we detected statistical significance, always positive, for *populationshare* in five of the 14. Weightlifting was the outlier with a coefficient estimate of 1.673. The others were shooting (0.867), boxing (0.819), athletics (0.565) and wrestling (0.512).

All sports require a mixture of skills and favourable physical characteristics for success. In weightlifting, the physical characteristics associated with champions are both relatively important and specific to the sport. Few members of any population will be endowed with the required characteristics and this gives an obvious advantage to larger countries. It could be argued that athletics is similar in some of its events.

Balmer et al. (2003) considered home advantage in athletics, boxing, gymnastics and weightlifting (also team sports, which we do not consider here) by comparing country performance when host relative to performance at other Olympics. They employed data from all Games 1896–1996. Gymnastics and boxing were characterized by clear home advantage, not detectable for athletics and weightlifting. Their interpretation was that hosts secure their extra medals in sports where the outcomes are determined subjectively (as they always are in gymnastics and usually are in boxing). They attributed this to home advantage resulting from officials being influenced by home crowds

We considered 14 sports and were surprised to find statistically significant hosting effects for as many as 13 of them (the exception was fencing). There was some support for Balmer et al.'s ideas to the extent that gymnastics generated the largest coefficient estimate (0.140), followed by equestrian (0.113). Some equestrian events are subjectively evaluated though another factor may be familiarity with the facilities, which can vary idiosyncratically across countries (indeed, in the case of equestrian, the host has some discretion to design the course to suit the strengths of its own team). The smallest significant coefficient was for athletics (0.038).

We were interested, from a historical perspective, in the performance of the *sovietbloc* dummy variable. Analysis at the aggregate level always confirms that communist countries were significantly more successful in winning Olympic medals, taking into account their income and population levels. But analysis by sport reveals that this overperformance was by no means across the board. In fact, for only six of the 14 sports was the coefficient estimate significant at 5 per cent: these were boxing, canoe/kayak, fencing, shooting, weightlifting and wrestling (gymnastics and judo are added if the significance level is extended to 10 per cent). For the other sports, including the highest-profile ones, namely athletics and swimming, communist countries display no evidence at all of elevated success.

The Soviet Union and its client states appear therefore to have secured their propaganda gains from high positions in the medals tables on the basis of specialization in a set of sports characterized by the award of many medals and low costs. The six sports for which the *sovietbloc* variable was significant at 5 per cent included the four 'cheapest' sports, as measured by the coefficient estimates on *gdpshare*, and only one of the more 'expensive' sports (shooting). We note also that the sports in which the Soviet bloc was successful tended to be those practised widely in the military. With their large armed forces, Warsaw Pact members may have found it relatively cheap to find champions to supply competitors in these disciplines. Military participants have featured heavily in the history of the Olympics (Nys, 2006) and further research on the interaction between medal awards and the size of the military might prove informative. Stefan Szymanski suggested to us that part of a peace dividend may actually be fewer Olympics medals.

Naturally, further possibilities exist in the context of models relating medal shares to GDP both for adding covariates (for example, to measure cultural attitudes) and for disaggregation (for example, male–female medals). However, the report on our research programme presented above will, we hope, confirm that building on the standard medals production function will prove useful in improving both forecasting and understanding of the inter-country distribution of those coveted assets, Olympic medals.

REFERENCES

Andreff, W. (2001), 'The correlation between economic underdevelopment and sport', *European Sport Management Quarterly*, **1**, 251–79.

Andreff, W. (2006), 'Sport in developing countries', in Andreff and S. Szymanski (eds), *Handbook on the Economics of Sport*, Cheltenham, UK and Northampton, MA, USA: Edward Elgar, pp. 308–15.

Andreff, M. and W. Andreff (2011), 'Economic predictions of medal wins at the 2014 Winter Olympics', paper presented at the International Association of Sports Economists and European Sport Economics Association Conference on Sports Economics, Prague, May.

Andreff, M., W. Andreff and S. Poupaux (2008), 'Les determinants économiques de la performance olympique: prévision de médailles qui seront gagnées aux Jeux de Pékin', *Revue d'Économie Politique*, **118**, 135–69.

Balmer, N.J., A.M. Nevill and A.M. Williams (2003), 'Modelling home advantage in the Summer Olympic Games', *Journal of Sports Sciences*, **21**, 469–78.

Bernard, A.B. and M.R. Busse (2004), 'Who wins the Olympics: economic resources and medal totals', *Review of Economics and Statistics*, **86**, 413–17.

Clarke, S.R. (2000), 'Home advantage in the Olympic Games', in G. Cohen and T. Langtry (eds), *Proceedings of the Fifth Australian Conference on Mathematics and Computers in Sport*, Sydney: University of Technology, pp. 43–51.

Forrest, D., I. Sanz and J.D. Tena (2010), 'Forecasting national team medal totals at the Summer Olympic Games', *International Journal of Forecasting*, **26**, 576–88.

Grimes, A.R., W.J. Kelly and P.H. Rubin. (1974), 'A socioeconomic model of national Olympic performance', *Social Science Quarterly*, **55**, 777–82.

Groot, L. (2008), 'The contest for Olympic success as a public good', Working Paper 08–34, Utrecht School of Economics, Netherlands.

Johnson, D.K.N. and A. Ali (2004), 'A tale of two seasons: participation and medal counts at the Summer and Winter Olympic Games', *Social Science Quarterly*, **85**, 976–93.

Johnson, D.K.N. and A. Ali (2008), 'Predictions for medal counts at Beijing Olympics', available at: http://faculty1.coloradocollege.edu/~djohnson/Olympics/Beijing2008predictions. pdf (accessed May 26, 2011).

Lens, F. (2011), 'Asset specificity in the promotion of élite sport', paper presented at the International Association of Sports Economists and European Sport Economics Association Conference on Sports Economics, Prague, May.

Li, H., L. Meng and Q. Wang (2009), 'The government's role in China's Olympic glory', *Applied Economics*, **41**, 3313–18.

Lui, H.-K. and W. Suen (2008), 'Men, money and medals', *Pacific Economic Review*, **13**, 1–16.

Maennig, W. and C. Wellbroch (2008), 'Sozioökonomische schätzungen olympischer medaillengewinne', *Sportwissenschaft*, **38**, 131–48.

Nevill, A.M., N.J. Balmer and E.M.Winter (2009), 'Why Great Britain's success in Beijing could have been anticipated and why it should continue beyond 2012', *British Journal of Sports Medicine*, **43**, 1108–10.

Nys, J.-F. (2006), 'Military sport', in W. Andreff and S. Szymanski (eds), *Handbook on the Economics of Sport*, Cheltenham, UK and Northampton, MA, USA: Edward Elgar, pp. 282–6.

Poupaux, S. (2006), 'Soviet and post-Soviet sport', in W. Andreff and S. Szymanski (eds),

Handbook on the Economics of Sport, Cheltenham, UK and Northampton, MA, USA: Edward Elgar, pp. 316–24.

Tcha, M. (2004), 'The color of medals: an economic analysis of the Eastern and Western blocs' performance in the Olympics', *Journal of Sports Economics*, **5**, 311–28.

United Nations (2000), 'Classification of the Functions of Government (COGOF)', M. No. 84, Statistics Division, United Nations, New York.

PART IV

GENERAL STUDIES OF ECONOMIC IMPACT AND METHODOLOGY

14 The econometric analysis of willingness to pay for intangibles with experience good character

Bernd Süssmuth

1 INTRODUCTION

This chapter gives a practitioner's primer of statistic and econometric techniques and their welfare economic foundations as they relate to assessing the intangible value of hosting a mega sporting event. Recently, a young body of literature, using techniques emanating from cultural and environmental economics and marketing science, is concerned with the quantification of intangible economic ramifications of the notoriously and in major parts publicly subsidized hosting of mega sporting events (see eftec, 2005; Barros, 2006; Atkinson et al., 2008; Barget and Gouguet, 2010; Süssmuth et al., 2010). These studies apply in different forms and for different events what has become known as the contingent valuation method (CVM) which assesses positive externalities of the mere hosting of the respective event which are not directly internalized by the market by quantifying the corresponding willingness to pay (WTP) of the concerned taxpayers (Arrow et al., 1993). Besides using CVM as the central technique to survey stated preferences, we also briefly sketch a methodology known as discrete choice or choice-based conjoint analysis and other alternative methods.

Hosting a mega sporting event such as Olympics, the FIFA World Cup, the UEFA Euro, or the Commonwealth Games has the notion of an experience good. An experience good is a good for which consumers cannot assess its value in advance but only upon consumption or from past experience (Nelson, 1970; Ungern-Sternberg and von Weizsäcker, 1985; van der Ploeg, 2002). By this defining characteristic, the assessment and analysis of the value of hosting a mega sporting event requires the application of techniques that deviate from standard techniques used to analyze the intangible value of environmental goods such as the existence of a lake seen from an individual's patio. The latter has the notion of a non-use benefit derived from *not* directly experiencing the good or service under the assumption that, apart from seeing the lake, the individual does not directly use it in the sense, for instance, of going to swim in it. As mega sporting events hosted in one's home country usually are experienced directly by residents of a developed country less than once in a lifetime, the frequency of experiencing the use as well as the non-use value of the event is extremely low (Süssmuth et al., 2010). However, a WTP assessment and analysis is frequently required and run in advance of a mega sporting event in order to assess, for example, whether a country's bid for the Olympics is backed by the public (eftec, 2005; Atkinson et al., 2008). Here we shall take a different perspective by giving a practical guide and highlighting problems of assessing the welfare surpluses of hosting a mega sporting event as well as of identifying determinants of this assessment and of the ability to make an accurate assessment prior to and after the event. The latter will also be of practical use for purely *ex ante*-type studies as they allow a selection on observables, for example, by a corresponding weighting of *ex ante* survey responses.

2   SURVEY SET-UP AND PRELIMINARIES

Representativeness, Stratification and Selection on Observables

Usually, we want our sample to be representative, say for the population of taxpayers in a particular (designated) host country. Having seen many ambitious surveys run not only for a WTP assessment of a nation's hosting of a mega sporting event, but also for visitors' or residents' perceptions of such events, my impression is that a lot of survey-based research is done without a prior commitment to a clear strategy concerning the representativeness of the underlying sample. It is not as though you can fan out into city centers or stadiums trying to get as many filled out questionnaires as possible. A minimum commitment, for example, would be to representatively match the age and gender composition of a population (see, for example, Mandel and Süssmuth, 2011), closely followed by dimensions such as employment, family income, educational background, and residential region. Such a selection based on exogenous criteria is known in the econometrics literature as 'selection on observables'. For the classical example, suppose a known population is composed of 75 percent males and 25 percent females, while your survey efforts produce a 50:50 sample selection in terms of gender. In other words, you 'oversampled' female respondents. Clearly, the criterion 'gender' is known and observable. In order to work with your sample, you have two options: either stratify the sample, that is, drop some female respondents from the sample so as to match the 75:25 share (ibid.), or weight it. The former strategy has the shortcoming of losing observations and possibly violating representativeness criteria in other dimensions such as age. The classical solution, therefore, is to resort to weighting the sample, assigning male respondents a weight of 75/50 and female respondents a weight of 25/50. For further detail on issues of stratification, selection on observable, and weighting of observations, the reader is referred to the comprehensive representation in Cameron and Trivedi (2005, Chapters 14.5 and 24.3). How to deal with the selection on unobservables will be discussed in Section 5 of this chapter.

Online or Offline Queries?

Frequently, institutes in social science survey research such as TNS institutes[1] run online panels which are representative for the respective population and recruit participants both online and offline. Participants in such panels usually have the incentive to get, for example, a free daily newspaper subscription if they participate in an online survey on different topics each quarter of a year. For example, the German section of the internet survey pollster YouGov© maintains a panel of approximately 65,000 participants. These members are invited via email and paid in 'bonus points' which are convertible into cash as soon as a threshold of €50 is reached.[2]

An online query does also not necessarily conflict with one of the central guidelines for WTP surveys of the National Oceanic and Atmospheric Administration (NOAA) panel (Arrow et al., 1993), that is, to conduct face-to-face interviews (see also Whitehead, 2006). This is due to the fact that today the internet is an essential form of communication, while the extensive set of guidelines for CV survey construction, administration, and analysis of the NOAA was compiled in the early 1990s. Going beyond the scope of the present chapter, I am also sure that the near future will most probably show several ways how we can use social networks such as Facebook in this context. There are several papers that document what has become known as the 'warm glow' effect in the context of CVM (see, for example, Andreoni, 1989; Kahnemann and Knetsch, 1992; Nunes and Schokkaert, 2003). Accordingly, survey participants potentially gain some sort of moral satisfaction through the mere act of giving *per se*. This effect relates to concepts such as peer-group pressure, feelings of guilt, and sympathy. It superimposes a 'cold' WTP, in particular, in face-to-face interviews. The fact that the bias induced by a 'warm glow' is pronounced for personal interviews is documented by Schkade and Payne (1994) who analyze verbal protocols of CVM-based studies. These authors find that some respondents vocalize a parallel with charitable contributions when answering the WTP survey in front of an interviewer. We can interpret this finding as lending support to the hypothesis that the 'warm glow' is a relevant bias in personal rather than in online interviews.

Another advantage of an online query is that it allows you to analyze server statistics, in order to assess a potential self-selection bias through drawing participants who tend to be involved in lobbying for the event or, in general, are interested in the mega sporting event. One way to assess such a bias (and maybe counteracting it using, for example, weighting of observations, see previous subsection) is through an 'implicit control experiment'. If you want to run such an experiment and plan to send out invitation emails and/or to distribute (offline) flyers or reminder cards, make sure that they contain only the following information: the URL of the survey's web-page and a note that it would be greatly appreciated if the readers were to participate in a research project – without any further definition of the project. Usually, your survey web tool will then allow you to quantify the termination rate of participants after they are informed about what the survey is actually about (that is, after receiving the first survey page containing, for example, a language choice). If you get to know who drops out after they become aware of the topic, this information can be used for weighting observations from queries that were not terminated.

3   WELFARE ECONOMIC FOUNDATIONS

Consider the following simplified double ledger account of direct government involvement in Germany's hosting of the FIFA World Cup 2006 (Table 14.1) which comprises information and estimates available prior to the tournament and that most colleagues would more or less have agreed on. In order to assess the hosting project as a whole, we actually want a representative sample of taxpayers to evaluate net intangible benefits and costs of a nation's hosting of the cup. By doing so, we assume that educated citizens are informed about spending on infrastructure and other expenditures, amounting to approximately €3.4 billion, and are also able

Table 14.1   Double ledger accounting of direct government involvement: FIFA World Cup 2006

Assets		Liabilities	
Turnover, tourism & other	€1.5bn	Cost of event	€0.1bn
		Widgets	€0.1bn
Long-term benefits (multiplier effects)	€0.5 to €1.0bn	*Gross profit* less	€1.4bn
Intangibles	?	Infrastructure & other	€3.4bn

to anticipate the assets side in a double ledger account of the event. In order to make the hosting a zero-sum game an amount of up to €0.9 billion should be expected in terms of intangibles generated by the mere staging of the event.

What is the microeconomic rationale behind 'backing' the hosting from a welfare economics perspective? In general, the answer covers two aspects. First, in terms of the investment aspect of the undertaking, the question is: what are taxpayers willing to pay for it? Second, in terms of a public subsidizing of the project, the question is: how to compensate citizens in the case of omission? In general, welfare surplus measurement proceeds in two steps: measuring individual surpluses and then aggregating them up to a social welfare measure.

The marginal utility and the monetary value of the marginal utility from the hosting are generally given from:

$$\max U \text{ s.t. } p_i x_i = m \Rightarrow L = U + \lambda(m - p_i x_i), \tag{14.1}$$

where λ denotes the marginal utility of income (utility/€) and p_i gives us the monetary value of marginal utility (€/x_i). From the first-order condition of problem (14.1) we obtain:

$$\frac{1}{\lambda} \frac{\partial U}{\partial x_i} (\text{€}/x_i)$$

as our measure for marginal WTP or, in general, as a measure for implied marginal utility.

The measure is independent of the properties of U. It is insensitive to positive monotone transformations in U. Consumer surplus is defined in these terms. Hence, it can be depicted as integrals of the demand functions for the shown p-interval in the bottom part of Figure 14.1, where x_i is denoted as C on the abscissa.

Obviously, there is more than one demand function shown in the bottom part of Figure 14.1. In fact, there are three of them shown – for the sake of simplicity as linear functions. The one that is defined by bf and denoted as $H(U_1)$, the one that is defined by da and denoted as $H(U_0)$, and finally the one that goes through ba. While $H(U_1)$ and $H(U_0)$ are Hicksian demand functions, the line defined by ba is the Marshallian demand. As can be seen from the top part of Figure 14.1, the Marshallian demand reflects a local price effect that nets the substitution effect and the income effect. In contrast, the Hicksian demand functions are shaped such that their slopes correspond to the substitution effect for a constant level of utility, that is, for U_1, U_0, respectively. Using Sheppard's Lemma and given that we have estimates on the WTP and the willingness to accept (WTA) (how WTA

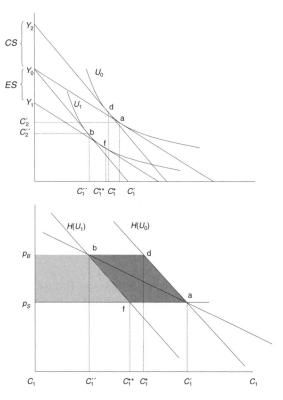

Figure 14.1   Compensated, equivalent, and Marshallian surplus derived from WTP and WTA

can be measured is outlined in the following section), we get measures for both: the compensated surplus (CS) and the equivalent surplus (ES). [3] They are defined as follows:

$$CS = \int_{p_S}^{P_B} H(U_0)\,dp \equiv WTA \qquad (14.2)$$

$$ES = \int_{p_S}^{P_B} H(U_1)\,dp \equiv WTP. \qquad (14.3)$$

From these definitions it is straightforward to approximate the Marshallian surplus, which is the integral under the Marshallian demand function for the interval $p_S p_B$:

$$MS \approx ES + \tfrac{1}{2}(CS - ES) = WTA + \tfrac{1}{2}(WTA - WTP). \qquad (14.4)$$

Although not of direct use in the weighing up of surplus measures against costs, it usually is reported for the sake of completeness in empirical studies of social welfare (see Mandel and Süssmuth, 2011). Note that CS and ES are constructed to give the minimal expenditures (measured in Y units) for reaching U_1, U_0, respectively. In other words, they differ in the considered income effect. How to interpret these measures? In general, if one is faced with a WTP (ES) clearly exceeding the costs of a public project, a subsidy is not justified. In our context, it would make sense to let the market do the allocation and transfer some part of revenues back to the public. The same logic applies the other way around, justifying a subsidy, in particular, in the case of merit goods. If the ES equals costs, balancing a double ledger account as shown in Table 14.1, it is justified that the government pushes up costs using, for example, capital market instruments before the intangibles of hosting the event are realized. In contrast, the WTA (CS), though slightly more complicated to measure (see the discussion in the following section), gives us an upperbound monetary value in the sense of how highly a project is actually valued by the public.

4 CONTINGENT VALUATION IN PRACTICE

The CV Counterfactual and Two Central Sources of Bias

'Contingent' in the CV context refers to the condition of a hypothetical situation that is analogous to the market situation for a particular publicly provided good without the actual existence of such a market. 'Contingent' has the meaning of eventual, possibly, conditional on, or uncertain. In this sense, our result will also be eventual in its nature, that is, contingent upon how well respondents understand the counterfactual market setting with which they are confronted. As an example, consider the following counterfactual used in Süssmuth et al. (2010). In the quarter prior to the start of the 2006 World Cup, a representative sample of subjects was asked a series of questions concerning their general attitude towards soccer, mega events, and the World Cup. It was followed by this counterfactual scenario:

> Suppose that shortly before the beginning of the cup finals, severe doubts on whether Germany can really stage the 2006 World Cup finals are raised. They concern such issues as the weak status of stadium construction and potential terrorist attacks. Therefore, FIFA is tending toward relocating the cup finals to Switzerland, where an ideal infrastructure is ready to stage the matches thanks to early and thorough preparation of the Swiss co-hosting of the 2008 European Cup finals. There is still a chance that the tournament will take

place in Germany, but only if a series of costly safety measures are adopted. However, these previously unplanned measures can only be financed with immediate voluntary contributions from the population. Would you personally be willing to contribute some of your own money to ensure that the finals can be hosted in your home country?

In a series of pre-tests, the questionnaire and, in particular, also scenarios such as the exemplary one above, should be carefully tested. The pre-tests can provide relevant information with regard to participants' understanding and potential caveats of the scenario. For example, a first version of the above counterfactual considered France (the host of the World Cup 1998) as back-up host instead of Switzerland. However, the fact of a historically developed rivalry between Germany and France can bias and obviously did bias the WTP of respondents in the pre-test series. Its traditional status of neutrality and its rather minute territory, therefore, made Switzerland the ideal and realistic candidate for this scenario. According to pre-test runs, respondents should assess the final scenario as realistic and not as far-fetched. This type of bias is referred to as '*hypothetical bias*'. Devising a scenario for a WTA assessment is a rather more difficult task. Respondents can be asked directly for a transfer or rebate of already paid taxes. In the above sample scenario, this transfer would, for example, be due in the case of a realized relocating of the cup finals to Switzerland. Mandel and Süssmuth (2011) is an illustrative study, where such a strategy is followed. Alternatively, a scenario can be constructed based on a hypothetical bet. For example, Rätzel and Weimann (2006) rely on such a strategy. In our example, the participants could imagine that right before the actual relocating of the cup finals to Switzerland, a bet could be placed on this outcome. The final question would then be how high the payoff of the bet must be in order to make the respondent indifferent to the situation where the finals would have taken place in the home country. To capture the broad picture, the sample could be split (by randomly assigning participants in one of two groups) in order to get both estimates for ES and CS based on WTP and WTA measures, respectively, as done in Mandel and Süssmuth.

Pre-tests should not only provide relevant information with regard to participants' understanding and potential caveats of the scenario, but also possible WTP and WTA values and ranges. The latter is of particular importance as the survey should not rely on an unfavorable dichotomous choice framework or open-ended valuation question, but on a closed-ended one, that is, on a valuation question in payment card format (Whitehead, 2006). A payment card strategy is based on pre-tests in which respondents are offered 'cards' indicating monetary amounts to be ascribed to a particular outcome (a successful bid for the Olympics) or the preservation of a certain status quo (no relocation of the cup finals) dependent on the respective counterfactual. From such pre-tests the actual survey's minimum ranges of interval levels can be derived. In order for respondents to see noticeable differences in the intervals they can tick in the survey, such intervals are usually constructed so as to increase proportionally to their starting value. Furthermore, some studies also give respondents the possibility of expressing another (possibly higher, that is, exceeding the payment card) amount. A final standard in CVM studies is to use reminders of budget constraints to minimize the hypothetical bias of respondents.

In addition to bias associated with the hypothetical nature of CV questions, free-riding behavior is an obvious qualification. A respondent may not reveal his/her true WTP for an intangible such as the hosting of a mega sporting event, expecting to benefit from others who are willing to pay for it. This type of bias is referred to as 'free-rider bias'. A number of strategic methods ('incentive compatible mechanisms') have been suggested in the literature to allow respondents to find it in their self-interest to reveal their true WTP. One such mechanism is a so-called 'provision point'. The provision point mechanism is implied by a scenario that states that unless a minimum amount of money (that is, the provision point) is raised, the good or service in question will not be available to anybody. It reduces the incentive to free ride as the respondent risks losing the benefit if a minimum amount of money is not raised. Whether or not it makes sense to actually include a specific minimum amount, money-back guarantee, or a proportional rebate rule in case of excess contributions, is not completely uncontroversial. A provision point can be implied by formulations such as 'can only be financed with immediate voluntary contributions from the population'. Even though, it seems that the profession has not yet reached a consensus on the value added of provision points,[4] such points have the potential to reduce free riding and to increase the proportion of demand revealed in large group, single-shot environments (Rondeau et al., 1999; Poe et al., 2002).

Intentionally Violating the Test–Retest Reliability

If you want to take the experience good notion of a mega sporting event into account, the survey should be re-run after the event. In the above example, Süssmuth et al. (2010), three months after the Cup final, asked the same persons the following 'groundhog day' question:

> About six months ago you were asked in a counterfactual scenario about your willingness to pay for your home country to host the Football World Cup finals.

Now that you have experienced it, imagine yourself back in March: would you change your mind and/or adjust the amount you would be willing to pay?

However, allowing respondents to recall their answers given in the pre-survey, intentionally violates what is referred to as 'test–retest reliability' in the CV context (Reiling et al., 1990, p. 128). According to Reiling et al., a low variability of estimated contingent values of a specific population over time is 'a necessary condition for accurate value estimates'. This holds for a population in which experience of the non-use value is either zero or can be made by every individual in the population with a positive probability. However, it does not apply in the case of Germany 2006. A significant part of the German population have never experienced the hosting of a mega event in Germany, either because they were too young or because they had been born and raised in the German Democratic Republic (GDR) which never hosted such an event. Therefore, Süssmuth et al. (2010) ultimately analyze two different populations. In the pre-survey, one for which at least 20 percent of the population have zero experience and in the post-survey, a population for which everyone experienced the public good benefits. In sum, asking participants for their *ex post* evaluation clearly violates the idea of assessing the test–retest reliability of contingent values, that is, their constancy over time. A meaningful test–retest reliability in the case of mega sporting events can only be achieved for the post-survey's contingent value. However, the latter requires an answer to the delicate question of the appropriate time between first and second administration of the (post-surveys) CV question, which is another controversial issue discussed in the literature and goes beyond the scope of the present chapter, which is primarily concerned with the short-term effects of mega sporting events.

Modern Alternatives and Complementary Approaches to CVM Techniques

This subsection does not give an overview of all alternative approaches with regard to CVM techniques. In fact, I abstract from sketching market observations (revealed preferences on markets) or rather traditional approaches with known shortcomings such as hedonic regressions, alternative/substitution cost approaches, and complementary cost (such as transport cost) approaches (Clawson–Knetsch methods). Most – if not all – of these approaches are not suited for the study of mega sporting events and hence are not used in the prominent studies on such events cited in the introductory section of this chapter. Much more promising approaches in this context are budget games (revealed preferences in the lab), economic jury assessments, and discrete choice or choice-based conjoint analysis. The last is a method that can be combined directly with the CVM approach. A choice-based conjoint analysis confronts respondents with a discrete choice. For example, we could offer participants a choice of winning a prize in a lottery that can take two forms: a flight to and a holiday on some Caribbean island, however, exactly scheduled at the time when a mega sporting event takes place in the participant's home country (at zero additional cost); and the same prize for a time slot outside the timeframe of the event, implying a mark-up payment > 0. This stylized example highlights the potential of this approach to draw inferences on implied welfare surpluses of hosting a mega event and/ or to combine it with CVM-based techniques. In economic jury assessments a body of experts is utilized to estimate the cost of hosting a mega event. McFadden (2009) summarizes the central issues of this approach as being jury selection (participation fees and treatment), sampling noise (jury size), and the incentive compatibility of the WTP elicitation mechanism. Relying on mechanism design techniques in a 'principal–agent econometrics' framework, McFadden finds the optimal jury size for a public project of a small city with 240,000 inhabitants to lie between 65 and 115 jurors. He also calculates optimal participation payments for 30-minute telephone interviews and total costs per juror in the US. Overall, the message of this literature is that participation and truthful responses are attainable in economic juries and surveys. Small and well-rewarded juries (theoretically) suffice to evaluate public projects such as the hosting of mega sporting events. Finally, budget games in the lab may rely on even smaller groups of (mostly student) respondents. The strength of this approach in which many expenditure and revenue categories can be varied simultaneously, lies in its potential to give insights into complementarity and substitutability relationships between competing programs such as hosting a mega sporting event versus installing an education program.

5   ECONOMETRIC ANALYSIS OF WTP MEASURES

Censored Regression and Decomposition of Marginal Effects

As respondents (given a survey design as outlined in Sections 2 and 4) are not allowed to give a negative WTP as an answer, WTP measures are censored left at zero and usually also right due to the upper WTP threshold of the survey's payment card. If both *ex ante* (with corresponding measure WTP1) as well as *ex post* (with measure WTP2) surveys are conducted, this also applies to $\Delta WTP = WTP1 - WTP2$, which will also be censored left at the upper WTP threshold.

The standard censored regression (Tobit) model is given by:

$$y = \begin{cases} y_i^* = \beta'X_i + \varepsilon_i & \text{for } y_i > 0 \\ 0 & \text{for } y_i \leq 0 \end{cases}, \tag{14.5}$$

where:

$$\mu = \beta'X;\ y_i^*|X_i \sim N(\beta'X_i, \sigma^2). \tag{14.6}$$

Corresponding marginal effects (ME) are:

$$\frac{\partial E(y_i|X_i)}{\partial X_i} = \beta\Phi\left(\frac{\beta'X}{\sigma}\right)\left[1 + \frac{\beta'X}{\sigma}\frac{\phi(\mu|\sigma)}{\Phi(\beta'X|\sigma)}\right] \tag{14.7}$$

and

$$\frac{\partial E(y_i^*|X_i)}{\partial X_i} = \beta. \tag{14.8}$$

In this set-up (14.5) to (14.8), Φ and ϕ denote the standard normal cumulative distribution function and probability density function, respectively. σ is the standard deviation given from the conditional distribution of the latent variables y_i^* in (14.6). ME (14.7) is sometimes referred to as 'slope' measuring the effect that a marginal variation in X_i has on the 'non-latent'.

While the marginal effects (14.8) have no direct economic interpretation, the marginal effects (14.7) can be calculated as (i) marginal effects on the uncensored probability, (ii) conditional on being uncensored, and (iii) unconditional expected values (McDonald and Moffit, 1980). In other words, we decompose the effect into a part that measures how a variation in X_i affects whether our observation falls into the positive part of the distribution and a part that gauges the effect on the conditional expectation value in the positive part of the distribution.

Let us consider a sample decomposition run by Süssmuth et al. (2010) for illustrative purposes. Statistic or econometric software packages such as Stata facilitate the decomposition by offering corresponding commands for censored regression models. In the case of Stata v.10 or higher, the corresponding command is dtobit2, for earlier versions it is dtobit. Table 14.2 shows such a decomposition output, where the dependent is an *ex ante* WTP (WTP1) measure, regressed in a Tobit framework on the years of schooling (school) an individual has been educated. There are eight further explanatories considered in the regression that we abstract from in the following interpretation. As can be seen in Table 14.2(c) (italics), reporting marginal effects of the uncensored probability, one year of additional

Table 14.2 Exemplary Stata output for dtobit / dtobit2 ME decomposition command

(a)Marginal Effects: Unconditional Expected Value

Variable	dF/dx	Std err.	z	P>|z|	X_at	95%	C.I.
gew*	4.1415330	2.1012280	1.97	0.049	0 --> 1	0.023203	8.259860
alter	-0.0760026	0.0458560	-1.66	0.097	43.1675	-0.165879	0.013873
school	0.3128102	0.1741135	1.80	0.072	10.4350	-0.028446	0.654066
gdr_sys	-0.0042017	0.0769006	-0.05	0.956	6.6600	-0.154924	0.146521
mann*	0.4168917	1.1091250	0.38	0.707	0 --> 1	-1.756950	2.590740
berlin*	-1.508145	3.0722600	-0.49	0.624	0 --> 1	-7.529660	4.513370
ost*	-1.254633	2.4291140	-0.52	0.606	0 --> 1	-6.015610	3.506340
beruf*	-0.8098345	1.2047740	-0.67	0.501	0 --> 1	-3.171150	1.551480
einko	0.2832560	0.3021828	0.94	0.349	4.0350	-0.309011	0.875523
_cons	-12.3026200	3.5684220	-3.45	0.001	1	-19.296600	-5.308640

(b) Marginal Effects: Conditional on being Uncensored

Variable	dF/dx	Std err.	z	P>|z|	X_at	95%	C.I.
gew*	5.6828920	2.3392040	2.43	0.015	0 --> 1	1.098140	10.267600
alter	-0.0846103	0.0510494	-1.66	0.097	43.1675	-0.184665	0.015445
school	0.3482378	0.1938329	1.80	0.072	10.4350	-0.031668	0.728143
gdr_sys	-0.0046776	0.0856101	-0.05	0.956	6.6600	-0.172470	0.163115
mann*	0.4642137	1.2347400	0.38	0.707	0 --> 1	-1.955830	2.884260
berlin*	-1.8202820	3.4202120	-0.53	0.595	0 --> 1	-8.523770	4.883210
ost*	-1.4475340	2.7042260	-0.54	0.592	0 --> 1	-6.747720	3.852650
beruf*	-0.8995382	1.3412220	-0.67	0.502	0 --> 1	-3.528290	1.729210
einko	0.3153365	0.3364067	0.94	0.349	4.035	-0.344009	0.974682
_cons	-13.6959700	3.9725670	-3.45	0.001	1	-21.482100	-5.909880

Table 14.2 (continued)

(c) Marginal Effects: Probability Uncensored

Variable	dF/dx	Std err.	z	P>|z|	X_at	95%	C.I.
gew*	0.1587360	0.0728057	2.18	0.029	0 --> 1	0.016039	0.301433
alter	-0.0026334	0.0015889	-1.66	0.097	43.1675	-0.005748	0.000481
school	0.0108386	0.0060329	1.80	0.072	10.4350	-0.000986	0.022663
gdr_sys	-0.0001456	0.0026645	-0.05	0.956	6.6600	-0.005368	0.005077
mann*	0.0144456	0.0384302	0.38	0.707	0 --> 1	-0.060876	0.089767
berlin*	-0.0548881	0.1064512	-0.52	0.606	0 --> 1	-0.263529	0.153752
ost*	-0.0444497	0.0841667	-0.53	0.597	0 --> 1	-0.209413	0.120514
beruf*	-0.0280067	0.0417444	-0.67	0.502	0 --> 1	-0.109824	0.053811
einko	0.0098146	0.0104704	0.94	0.349	4.0350	-0.010707	0.030336
_cons	-0.4262753	0.1236428	-3.45	0.001	1	-0.668611	-0.183940

Note: *dF/dx is for discrete change of dummy variable from 0 to 1.

240

schooling increases the probability that an individual has a positive *ex ante* WTP by 1 percent (0.0108). From the reported standard errors and p-values (also italicized), we see that the effect is statistically significant, at least, at the 10 percent level. In Table 14.2(b), we find ME conditional on being uncensored, that is, the marginal effect of the part of the empirical model that is uncensored. We can interpret the corresponding coefficient in the following way. The *ex ante* WTP of an individual with *ex ante* WTP > 0 is increased by one additional year of schooling by about 35 cents (0.3482). Finally, in Table 14.3(a) we find the effect of one additional year of schooling on the unconditional expected value or, in other words, on the overall expected *ex ante* WTP (equation (14.7)) to amount to 31.3 cents (0.3128).

Heckman Correction and Selection on *Ex Post* Observables

The basic idea behind the Heckman selection model – by analogy with Tobit/probit sometimes also referred to as 'Heckit' – is selection on unobservables based on an underlying two-step process. In our context, the latter can be sketched as follows:

$$\left. \begin{matrix} 0 \\ 1 \end{matrix} \right\} \rightarrow Y_{0/1} = \beta'X_i + \varepsilon_i\text{: Support hosting of mega event: yes/no?}$$

$$WTP_i \rightarrow Y_1 = \beta'X_i + \varepsilon_i\text{: How much are you willing to pay for it?}$$

The correction then essentially proceeds in five steps. The first is to set up a binary choice model that models the expected individual consumer surplus level $E(CS_i) = CS_i^*$ as an ordinary least squares (OLS) system and lets the individual weigh up the communicated average surplus from hosting the event CS_i against this latent:

Support hosting:

$$\begin{cases} 0 & \text{for } WTP_i = 0 \leftrightarrow CS_i \leq E(CS_i) = CS_i^* \leftrightarrow CS_i - CS_i^* \leq \varepsilon_i \\ 1 & \text{for } WTP_i > 0 \leftrightarrow CS_i > E(CS_i) = CS_i^* \leftrightarrow CS_i - CS_i^* > \varepsilon_i, \end{cases}$$

where ε_i denotes the standard OLS residual with $\varepsilon_i \overset{i.i.d.}{\sim} N(0, \sigma_\varepsilon^2)$. Defining $Q_i \equiv CS_i - CS_i^*$, this implies

$$\Pr(WTP_i > 0) = \Pr(Q_i > \varepsilon_i). \tag{14.9}$$

In a second step, we use a Probit model to estimate the probability that an individual has a positive WTP for a national hosting of a mega sporting event. The standard normal distribution ensures that the probability is both transformed on the interval [0, 1], that is, $R_\infty \rightarrow [0, 1]$, and monotonically increasing. Hence, by centering:

$$\Pr(WTP_i > 0) = \Pr\left(\frac{Q_i}{\sigma_\varepsilon} > \frac{\varepsilon_i}{\sigma_\varepsilon}\right) = \Phi\left(\frac{Q_i}{\sigma_\varepsilon}\right), \text{ where } \frac{\varepsilon_i}{\sigma_\varepsilon} \overset{i.i.d.}{\sim} N(0, 1). \quad (14.10)$$

In a third step, which may or may not be necessary, we address the problem that most probably $Cov(CS_i, WTP_i) \neq 0$, requiring an instrumental variable (IV) estimator, where instrument Z_i replaces CS_i. It is given by:

$$CS_i = \gamma' Z_i + v_i \text{ with } Cov(Z_i, WTP_i) = 0 \wedge v_i \overset{i.i.d.}{\sim} N(0, \sigma_v^2).$$

Hence, we get

$$\Pr(WTP_i > 0) = \Phi\left(\frac{\tilde{Q}_i}{\sigma_\eta}\right), \quad (14.11)$$

where $\eta_i = \varepsilon_i - v_i$ and $\tilde{Q}_i$ corresponds to Q_i, but is constructed on the base of the instrumented CS_i. Depending on whether endogeneity is an issue, either estimates of $\tilde{Q}_i$ or Q_i (that is, $\hat{Q}_i$) are used in a fourth step to construct an estimator for the inverse Mills ratio, which is simply an additive part in the conditional CS_i relationship, that is, $E(CS_i|CS_i^* > 0)$, that can be expressed as:

$$\hat{\lambda}_i = \frac{\phi(\hat{Q}_i/\sigma_\eta)}{\Phi(\hat{Q}_i/\sigma_\eta)}.$$

In a final step, the actual correction is done by including $\hat{\lambda}_i$ as regressor in a feasible generalized LS estimate. Depending on whether or not the corresponding coefficient (which has the interpretation of a covariance between errors in the OLS relationships of latent and observed variables) is estimated as statistically different from zero, selectivity is an issue or not. As the inverse Mills ratio is not observed, but has to be estimated in the above sketched two-step procedure, we speak about a selection mechanism based on unobservables.

Table 14.3 makes the point for the World Cup 2006 WTP analysis by Süssmuth et al. (2010). The starting assumption is that residents have an expected heterogeneous benefit (CS_i) from the national hosting. They also face an individual shadow price of avoidable costs in case of relocation. This weighing up against the reservation position depends on characteristics such as age (AGE), educational level (EDU), gender (MALE), region (BERLIN, EAST), and employment status (WORK). If this propensity

Table 14.3   *Example of a two-step Heckman correction: WTP analysis for the FIFA World Cup 2006*

	WTP1 indicator	WTP1 amount	WTP2 indicator	WTP2 amount	ΔWTP indicator	ΔWTP amount
BENEFIT	0.719***		0.491***		0.350**	
	(3.03)		(2.93)		(3.03)	
AGE	−0.007*		−0.014***		−0.017***	
	(−1.65)		(−3.79)		(−4.56)	
EDU	0.157***	1.957	0.056	−1.735	0.070	−4.822**
	(2.46)	(0.87)	(0.99)	(−1.12)	(1.23)	(−2.26)
MALE	−0.036	8.638**	0.252**	1.983	0.224*	2.060
	(−0.26)	(1.95)	(2.18)	(0.59)	(1.91)	(0.47)
BERLIN		−11.309*		−5.677		−0.160
		(−1.73)		(−0.67)		(−0.01)
EAST		−2.141		8.243**		10.672**
		(−0.40)		(1.89)		(2.24)
WORK		−2.718		3.226		6.389
		(−0.63)		(1.02)		(1.52)
λ / 100		−296.58		−36.35*		−21.00
		(−1.19)		(−1.79)		(−0.97)
N	500	496	500	496	500	496
− ln L	230.0	411.5	324.2	936.3	311.0	843.3

Notes: WTP1 – *ex ante* WTP, WTP2 – *ex post* WTP, ΔWTP = (WTP2–WTP1), 'indicator' refers to 0/1 decision (Heckit Step I: binary probit); 'amount' refers to actual amount $\in$ [0, 70] or $\in$ [-70, 70] (Heckit Step II); *, **, *** denotes significance at 10, 5, 1% levels; all estimates include a constant; values in parentheses give z-statistics for the censored models, else they represent corrected t-statistics; λ denotes the inverse Mills ratio.

Source: First part of Table 3 in Süssmuth et al. (2010, p. 211).

is correlated with the actual value (WTP), a selectivity problem arises. Süssmuth et al. use the two-step Heckit to test and account for it (Table 14.3). The discrete choice decision is identified by AGE and BENEFIT; that is, these two regressors are excluded from the outcome equation (second step). BENEFIT is a dummy of whether a respondent sees an overall benefit for Germany or not. By this identification in the bivariate model a sort of functional form assumption is made. Accordingly, AGE and BENEFIT are assumed to make individuals more likely to report a WTP $>$ 0. However, it is also assumed that changes in these two variables deter them from reporting higher values. In general, this type of assumption is inevitable for a straightforward procedure such as the Heckit to check whether sample selectivity correction is adequate. The actual check is performed using a test of the estimated coefficient for the inverse Mills ratio ($\hat{\lambda}_i$, which is, as it has been multiplied by a hundredth, denoted as $\lambda/100$ in Table 14.3) with which the Heckit model augments the regression in its second step (Cameron and Trivedi 2005, pp. 550–55). Obviously, selectivity is only relevant, at a 10 percent level of significance, for explaining the final WTP (WTP2). It does not matter for the *ex ante* WTP (WTP1) and the change in WTP (ΔWTP). In the last two cases, resorting to standard censored regression models (see above) is justified.

6   CONCLUDING REMARKS

In this chapter, we followed a bottom-up approach in highlighting central steps, hiccups, caveats, and recent innovations in the econometric analysis of willingness to pay for a national hosting of mega sporting events which represent by their very nature intangibles with an experience good character. The practitioner's primer started from survey design issues. It gave some welfare economic foundations of the method before going into detail of the contingent valuation technique and idiosyncrasies of its application in the context of mega sporting events. Finally the FIFA World Cup 2006 study by Süssmuth et al. (2010) highlighted econometric problems and techniques in the analysis of measured willingness to pay.

NOTES

1. The Taylor Nelson Sofres (TNS) group is a leading group of market research and market information companies that emerged from a merger of five market research companies, originally located in the UK, France, and Australia, in the 1960s.
2. This practice could create a sampling bias by including too many low-income individuals, that is, respondents who respond to the modest monetary incentive. However, given information on income, the classical solution of selection on observables as described in the preceding subsection is applicable.
3. Note that the location of the demand functions differs from the standard textbook case considering a decrease in the price level that is weighed against the status quo position (improvement), while here the withdrawal of hosting a mega event is weighed against the status quo of hosting (deterioration).
4. For a rather optimistic appraisal of provision point mechanisms, see Poe et al. (2002). In contrast, Champ et al. (2002) find no statistically significant difference in WTP assessments with or without a provision point.

REFERENCES

Andreoni, J. (1989), 'Giving with impure altruism: applications to charity and Ricardian equivalence', *Journal of Political Economy*, **97**, 1447–58.

Arrow, K., R. Solow, P. Portney, E. Leamer, R. Radner, and H. Schuman (1993), 'Report of the NOAA Panel on Contingent Valuation', *Federal Register*, **58**, 4601–14.
Atkinson, G., S. Mourato, S. Szymanski and E. Ozdemiroglu (2008), Are we willing to pay enough to "back the bid"? Valuing the intangible impacts of London's bid to host the 2012 Summer Olympic Games', *Urban Studies*, **45**, 419–44.
Barget, E. and J.-J. Gouguet (2010), 'L'accueil des grands événements sportifs: quel impact économique ou quelle utilité sociale pour les régions? L'example de la Coupe du monde de rugby 2007 en France', *Région et Développement*, **31**, 93–117.
Barros, C.P. (2006), 'Evaluating sport events at European level: the Euro 2004', *International Journal of Sport Management and Marketing*, **1**, 400–410.
Cameron, A.C. and P.K. Trivedi (2005), *Microeconometrics: Methods and Applications*, New York: Cambridge University Press.
Champ, P.A., N.E. Flores, T.C. Brown, and J. Chivers (2002), 'Contingent valuation and incentives', *Land Economics*, **78**, 591–604.
eftec (2005), 'Olympic Games Impact Study – Stated Preferences Analysis', Final Report for the Department of Culture, Media and Sport, London.
Kahnemann, D. and J. Knetsch (1992), 'Valuing public goods: the purchase of moral satisfaction', *Journal of Environmental Economics and Management*, **22**, 57–70.
Mandel, P. and B. Süssmuth (2011), 'Size matters. The relevance and Hicksian surplus of preferred college class size', *Economics of Education Review*, **30**, 1073–84.
McDonald, J.R. and R.A. Moffit (1980), 'The uses of Tobit analysis', *Review of Economics and Statistics*, **62**, 318–21.
McFadden, D. (2009), 'Economic jury recruitment and management. Public project evaluation with Manski set-identified selection effects', mimeo, UC Berkeley.
Nelson, P. (1970), 'Information and consumer behavior', *Journal of Political Economy*, **78**, 311–29.
Nunes, P.A.L.D. and E. Schokkaert (2003), 'Identifying the warm glow effect in contingent valuation', *Journal of Environmental Economics and Management*, **45**, 231–45.
Poe, G.L., J.E. Clark, D. Rondeau, and W.D. Schulze (2002), 'Provision point mechanisms and field validity tests of contingent valuation', *Environmental and Resource Economics*, **23**, 105–31.
Rätzel, S. and J. Weimann (2006), 'Der Maradona Effekt: Wie viel Wohlfahrt schafft die deutsche Nationalmannschaft?', *Perspektiven der Wirtschaftspolitik*, **7**, 257–70.
Reiling, S.D., K.J. Boyle, M.L. Phillips and M.W. Anderson (1990), 'Temporal reliability of contingent values', *Land Economics*, **66**, 128–34.
Rondeau, D., W.D. Schulze and G.L. Poe (1999), 'Voluntary revelation in the demand for public goods using a provision point mechanism', *Journal of Public Economics*, **72**, 455–70.
Schkade, D. and J. Payne (1994), 'How people respond to contingent valuation questions: a verbal protocol analysis of willingness to pay for an environmental regulation', *Journal of Environmental Economics and Management*, **26**, 88–109.
Süssmuth, B., M. Heyne and W. Maennig (2010), 'Induced civic pride and integration', *Oxford Bulletin of Economics and Statistics*, **72**, 202–20.
Ungern-Sternberg, T. von and C.C. von Weizsäcker (1985), 'The supply of quality on a market for "experience goods"', *Journal of Industrial Economics*, **33**, 531–40.
van der Ploeg, R. (2002), 'In art we trust', *De Economist*, **150**, 333–62.
Whitehead, J.C. (2006), 'A practitioner's primer on contingent valuation', in A. Alberini and J.R. Kahn (eds), *Handbook on Contingent Valuation*, Cheltenham, UK and Northampton, MA, USA: Edward Elgar, pp. 66–91.

15 Economic impact of sports events
Philip K. Porter and Daniel M. Chin

1 INTRODUCTION

In March 1997 sports economists Robert Baade, Philip Porter and Andrew Zimbalist offered testimony in the trial *Poe v. Hillsborough County*. At issue was the constitutionality of Hillsborough County, Tampa, Florida and the Tampa Sports Authority using their taxing power and credit to build a stadium for the Tampa Bay Buccaneers.[1] Florida law forbids government using either its taxing power or credit in support of private individuals unless such a project serves a 'paramount public purpose'.[2] The trial set the stage for a decade of research by economists into the claims of teams and sporting event sponsors. The National Football League (NFL) in conjunction with Hillsborough County and Tampa City offered testimony from two individuals: one reporting the annual economic impact on the community generated by the presence of the Tampa Bay Buccaneers and the other reporting on research conducted by the Arizona Office of Tourism and the Super Bowl Host Committee about the impact of the 1996 Super Bowl in Phoenix. Tampa was being offered a Super Bowl if they built a new stadium for the team.

Zimbalist's testimony set the stage, describing the NFL, how it obtained monopoly power and could force communities under threat of departure to subsidize team stadium costs. Baade testified that 'professional sports teams generally have no significant impact on a metropolitan economy' and 'sports investments appear to be an economically unsound use of a community's scarce financial resources' (Baade, 1994). Porter testified that hosting a Super Bowl generated no return to the host city.

Both of the NFL expert witnesses used input–output (I–O) models to make predictions about team and event impacts. Team impacts were a simple two-page calculation of team and visitor spending multiplied by a regional multiplier. The source of the data was the Buccaneer team. The multiplier was purchased from one of the companies that sell commercial I–O models. Under questioning the witness could not verify the team's figures or how the multiplier was computed, and his testimony was disallowed as hearsay. This illustrates one of the points made in this chapter: the I–O model is a black box. Data are input by practitioners trained in the use of the model but naive about the configuration of the model. Porter and Fletcher (2008, p. 470) explain:

> The ease and accessibility of computer-driven, regional input–output models has spawned a new industry of regional planners and forecasters. For a negligible fee one can lease a fully automated I–O model for a region as small as a county or MSA. The models are so user-friendly that one need only enter data – for example, an anticipated increase in demand for a product of the region – and the model will predict changes in regional sales, taxes, incomes, or employment . . . [T]he model obscures the underlying assumptions and working principles of the model at the same time it makes using it easy.

The other NFL witness in the *Poe v. Hillsborough County* trial had done considerably more work, surveying visitors at the 1996 Super Bowl and using a full I–O model to conclude that the impact generated by the Super Bowl on the local economy was $305,800,000, of which $143,000,000 came directly from the event visitors. Porter, who published the results of his investigation in 1999, analyzed sales data in Florida and Arizona and found no measurable impact: 'Only one of the eighteen Super Bowl dummies had the anticipated [positive] sign and was significantly different from zero. Two others were negative and significant and the rest were insignificant' (1999, pp. 67–8). The one positive and significant Super Bowl generated only $1,279,000 in new sales. Summarizing the event impact testimony the trial judge said it was hard to believe that the impact was $305,800,000 but that it was even harder to believe that it was zero.[3] This illustrates two additional points made in this chapter. One, impact estimates based on I–O models are an exaggeration of the impact that new demand could generate *even under the best of circumstances*. Two, it is obvious that visitors do attend these events and spend money in the local economy so that something must be going on to offset this if the resulting impact is zero or negative.

Baade's 1994 paper and Porter's 1999 paper were the basis of their testimony. Over the next decade sports economists published more than 40 articles in scholarly journals searching for the economic impact of sporting events or teams. This chapter concentrates on the event literature. Events that have been studied include the FIFA World Cup (Szymanski, 2002; Baade and Matheson, 2004; Hagn and Maennig, 2008, 2009; Allmers and Maennig, 2009; Feddersen et al., 2009; du Plessis and Maennig, 2011), the Olympic Games (Hotchkiss et al., 2003; Atkinson, et al., 2008; Jasmand and Maennig, 2008; Porter and Fletcher, 2008), the Super Bowl (Porter, 1999; Baade and Matheson, 2000a; Coates, 2006), the Daytona 500 (Baade and Matheson, 2000b), Major League Baseball (MLB) All-Star Game (Baade and Matheson, 2001) and the NCAA Final Four (Matheson and Baade, 2004). More recent articles have studied all mega events that occurred in a location over time (Coates and Humphreys, 2002; Coates and Depken, 2006; Baade et al., 2008; Coates and Matheson, 2011) These studies searched for the impact of sporting events in retail or taxable sales, government tax receipts, personal income, hotel occupancy, airport utilization, employment, housing values, and economic growth. Without exception, these authors found no consistent positive impact from a sporting event, often finding the event associated with a negative impact. Baade et al. (2008) conducted an exhaustive study of teams, stadiums and events in Florida and concluded:

> Our detailed regression analysis of taxable sales in Florida over the period 1980 to 2004 reveals that on average mega-events ranging from the World Cup to the World Series have been associated with *reductions* in taxable sales in host regions of $5 to $10 million per month. Likewise, strikes in Major League Baseball, the National Hockey League, and the National Basketball League, each of which has resulted in the cancellation of large parts of entire seasons, appear to have also had no demonstrable negative effect on taxable sales in host cities. (2008, p. 794; emphasis added)

Appendix 15A to this chapter reviews the vast academic literature concerning the economic impact of sports events and sports teams that was unavailable at the trial.

The District Court ruled that certain clauses in the Buccaneer contract giving them revenues not generated by the team did not serve a paramount public purpose. On appeal the Appellate Court ruled that paramount public purpose did not hinge on the return to public spending or the source of the subsidy. It was enough for the Court that voters had chosen to subsidize teams.[4] Without restraint from the courts, wise choices concerning public subsidies to sports teams and events must rely on educating the public and its representatives, and in informing I–O practitioners of the severe limitations of their models in sport event applications.

Explanations for the inaccuracy of I–O analysis fall under three broad categories: crowding-out, substitution, and leakages. Crowding-out occurs when a regional economy is fully (or nearly fully) employed and new demands can only be met by failing to satisfy existing demands; new sources of sales, employment and income simply replace old sources. Substitution occurs when local residents attend the event. The presumption is that these residents would have spent their money locally anyway so that no new demand is introduced. Leakages occur when money spent locally does not circulate in the same pattern as anticipated, but more rapidly flows out of the region.

This chapter explains how hosting a mega event can have a negative impact on the economy. Crowding-out and leakages reduce the impact of visitor demand, they do not eliminate it. Satisfying the new demand must be more lucrative than satisfying the existing demand to entice the regional suppliers to alter their behavior and there is typically some slack in an economy that could, at least temporarily, be put to use. And even if money leaks out more rapidly than was assumed, there was at least the initial level of new demand. In what follows we show that crowding-out leads I–O models to greatly overstate the potential impact of a sporting event. That is, even under the best circumstances the new demand accompanying an event cannot produce the level of impact that I–O models predict. In addition, substitution effects can be negative and of such a great magnitude as to explain the oft-found result that an event is associated with a reduction in economic activity.

The chapter proceeds as follows. Section 2 presents the I–O model in technical detail so that we might uncover and explore its inner workings. Section 3 presents the methods used to construct the I–O model and highlights its long-run nature. Section 4 introduces the concept of crowding-out and focuses on the contrast between the long-run relationships represented in the model and the short-run cash flows associated with a sporting event. Section 5 introduces leakages that render new demand impotent. Section 6 considers substitution and the role of local purchases that can explain the oft-found negative impacts of an event on the local economy. Section 7 concludes.

2   THE REGIONAL INPUT–OUTPUT MODEL

The first practical I–O model was created by Wassily Leontief (1944) and applied to the question of how the end of the Second World War would affect the economy. The model is designed to answer the basic question: what level of output from each sector of the economy is just sufficient to meet the needs of its and other sectors for it as an input and to satisfy final demand? Properly constructed and properly implemented, I–O models can be used to measure the impact of a change in demand. When improperly constructed or implemented, the measures may bear no relation to reality and the predictions, if believed, can prove harmful. Careful use of the model is important.

To make this model operational three critical assumptions are made. First, production is assumed to be characterized by fixed factor proportions – to produce a unit of output j requires a fixed amount of input i. Second, production is characterized by constant returns to scale – if a_{ij} is the amount of input i needed to produce a unit of output j, then to produce n units of j requires na_{ij} amount of input i. The values a_{ij} are called technical coefficients. The third assumption is that prices are constant. This is necessary as it permits: (i) the aggregation of output at a reasonable level – as, for example, measuring agricultural output as the dollar value of peas and carrots, and so on; (ii) defining a unit of real output as 'a dollar's worth' of output; and (iii) estimating the technical coefficients from industry data by observing revenue (as units of output) and purchases (as units of input) from each sector. As such the technical coefficient a_{ij} is the dollar amount of product i needed as an input to produce a dollar of output j.

To illustrate the application of I–O analysis to sporting events we simplify the presentation by assuming there are three sectors to the economy: shelter (hotels), designated S; food (restaurants), designated F; and manufacturing (everything else), designated M. If each sector $j(= S, F, M)$ is to produce enough output, x_j, to satisfy the input needs of all three sectors as well as its final demand, d_j, x_j must satisfy the equation $x_j = a_{jS}x_S + a_{jF}x_F + a_{jM}x_M + d_j$. Subtracting input needs from output leaves an expression for final demand in each sector according to:

$$(1 - a_{SS})x_s - a_{SF}x_F - a_{SM}x_M = d_S$$
$$-a_{FS}x_s + (1 - a_{FF})x_F - a_{FM}x_M = d_F$$
$$-a_{MS}x_S - a_{MF}xF + (1 - a_{MM}) = d_M.$$

In matrix notation this system is expressed as:

$$(I - A)\, x = d, \tag{15.1}$$

where:

I is the identity matrix,

$A = [a_{ij}]\, i, j \in \{S, F, M\}$ is the matrix of technical coefficients,

$x = \begin{bmatrix} x_S \\ x_F \\ x_M \end{bmatrix}$ is a column vector of outputs and

$d = \begin{bmatrix} d_S \\ d_F \\ d_M \end{bmatrix}$ is a column vector of final demands.

In regional impact applications the economy is assumed to be 'open', meaning that purchases and sales of goods may be made outside the region. In this setting the technical coefficients are interpreted as the dollar amount of product i *produced in the regional economy* and needed as an input to produce a dollar of output j and will be less than the total amount needed when some of i is purchased from outside the economy. Similarly, the value of final demand, d_j, may be greater than local demand reflecting sales of local products outside the region. Then, knowing final demand and the technical coefficients, regional output (sales of each sector in dollar values) can be found by solving equation (15.1) as:

$$x^* = \begin{bmatrix} S^* \\ F^* \\ M^* \end{bmatrix} = (I - A)^{-1}d. \tag{15.2}$$

Total regional sales under the assumptions of the model is $Y^* = S^* + F^* + M^*$.

Impact analysis attempts to answer the question: what will be the impact on regional sales if there is a change in demand for the goods produced in the region? Suppose there is a one dollar increase in the demand for shelter in the region, $\Delta d_S = 1$. The region must produce Δd_S more shelter to meet the increase in demand. In turn, producing more shelter increases the demand for shelter, food, and manufacturing from the region as inputs to support the production of Δd_S. This additional demand requires more of S, F, and M and the process continues in an infinite chain of diminishing sales. To determine how much regional sales change (the impact) when there is one more dollar of demand for shelter we solve the equation

$$\begin{bmatrix} S' \\ F' \\ M' \end{bmatrix} = (I - A)^{-1} \begin{bmatrix} d_s + 1 \\ d_F \\ d_M \end{bmatrix}$$

which determines new sales $y' = S' + F' + M'$. $m_s = Y' - Y^* > 1$ is the 'regional multiplier' for an increase in the demand for shelter in the region. Because of the assumptions of constant returns to scale and fixed factor production, the impact of any change in the demand for shelter can be found as $m_S \Delta d_S$. In like manner, the model can be solved to reveal a multiplier for changes in the regional demand for each output.

A numerical example will help.[5] Suppose the coefficient matrix is

$$A = \begin{bmatrix} 0.2 & 0.3 & 0.2 \\ 0.4 & 0.1 & 0.2 \\ 0.1 & 0.3 & 0.2 \end{bmatrix}.$$

That is, as the first column indicates, every $1 of shelter (industry 1's output) produced requires $0.20 of shelter, $0.40 of food (industry 2's output) and $0.10 worth of manufacturing (industry 3's output) as inputs to the production of shelter. If final demand for the region's output is

$$d = \begin{bmatrix} d_s \\ d_F \\ d_M \end{bmatrix} = \begin{bmatrix} 10 \\ 5 \\ 6 \end{bmatrix},$$

then

$$x^* = \begin{bmatrix} S^* \\ F^* \\ M^* \end{bmatrix} = (I - A)^{-1}d = \begin{bmatrix} 1.7 & 0.78 & 0.62 \\ 0.89 & 1.61 & 0.62 \\ 0.55 & 0.70 & 1.55 \end{bmatrix} \begin{bmatrix} 10 \\ 5 \\ 6 \end{bmatrix} = \begin{bmatrix} 24.84 \\ 20.68 \\ 18.36 \end{bmatrix}$$

and total regional sales are $63.88 ($24.84 + 20.68 + 18.36). If

$$d' = \begin{bmatrix} d_S \\ d_F \\ d_M \end{bmatrix} = \begin{bmatrix} 11 \\ 5 \\ 6 \end{bmatrix},$$

then

$$x' = \begin{bmatrix} S' \\ F' \\ M' \end{bmatrix} = (I - A)^{-1}d' = \begin{bmatrix} 26.56 \\ 21.56 \\ 18.91 \end{bmatrix},$$

total regional sales are $67.03 so that the shelter demand multiplier is 3.15. That is, under the assumptions of the model each additional dollar of shelter demanded from the regional economy generates $3.15 of total regional sales. In like fashion, a $1 increase in demand for food increases total regional sales to $66.98 implying that the food multiplier is 3.1, and a $1 increase in demand for manufacturing increases total regional sales to $65.76 generating a manufacturing multiplier of 1.88.

3   ESTIMATING TECHNICAL COEFFICIENTS IN PRACTICE

I–O models are sometimes referred to as econometric models because the technical coefficients are estimated using econometric techniques. For the most commonly used I–O models the procedures used and the results obtained are proprietary information created by firms who in turn sell access to their I–O models. However, sufficient literature exists to outline the process of estimating technical coefficients for general discussion of the application to sport events.[6] Periodically, data are gathered from business firms about the firms' revenue and purchases from each sector designated in the I–O model. These data are correlated to reveal technical coefficients that estimate the dollar amount of purchases firms in sector *i* make from firms in sector *j*.

Two aspects of this estimation are important for sports event applications. First, the coefficients being estimated represent long-run, steady-state relations. For example, over the course of years that comprise the dataset used to estimate the technical coefficients, the hotel sector will have purchased resources from the construction sector (manufacturing in our simple example) as new hotels are built and existing hotels are maintained to offset depreciation. The technical coefficient, a_{MH}, the dollar amount of manufacturing needed to produce a dollar of hotel output, is expected to be quite large as hotels are a capital-intensive industry, but the coefficient approaches zero in the short run as there is little depreciation and no incentive to expand hotel capacity in a region when demand increases only during a short duration event.

Second, the model has no horizon. As data are solicited and averaged over many years when estimating technical coefficients, inputting new demand stimulated by an event into the model is not interpreted as being of short duration. For example, suppose 100,000 visitors come to a region as a result of hosting a Super Bowl and stay an average 3.65 nights. This generates 365,000 new visitor nights of demand in about four days. However, within the model this value is treated in the same way as 1,000 visitor nights every day over the course of a year, year-in and year-out. In the latter case one reasonably expects the hotel industry to respond by building new capacity while in the former case expansion would not happen.

As we develop the model in the context of a sports event, we shall see that crowding-out not only lessens the net impact on demand, but that it also results in phantom measures of demand that greatly exceed the real gross impact. In addition, crowding-out alters the technical coefficients and decreases the associated spending multipliers. However, the user/practitioner, who inputs an estimate of new demand into the black box of the I–O model, is typically unaware of this and could not alter the model even if he/she were.

4 CROWDING-OUT LESSENS REAL CHANGES IN DEMAND, CREATES PHANTOM DEMAND, AND REDUCES THE MULTIPLIER

The I–O model's two critical assumptions, that prices are constant and that production is characterized by constant returns to scale, are both

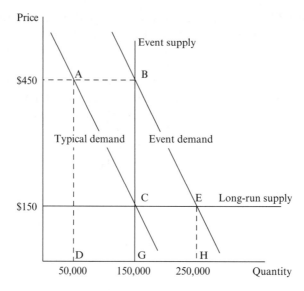

Figure 15.1   Event supply versus long-run supply

violated in the application to one-time only, short duration events. Constant returns to scale is a long-run concept in which all inputs are assumed to be variable and for which an increase in output requires an equal proportional increase in all inputs. If the economy is competitive, a steady increase in demand is met with an expansion of productive capacity and output and the attendant jobs and income that flow from economic expansion. This is what the model simulates. However, no such expansion materializes when the event is short lived.

Consider Figure 15.1 which might reasonably depict regional supply and demand conditions in the hotel industry. Based on long-lasting relations, the hotel industry has a capacity of 150,000 rooms for visitors which is the typical, steady-state level of demand, and competition generates a price of $150 which covers costs including a normal profit for the industry.[7] Under the assumptions of the model, the perfectly elastic long-run industry supply is constant at $150. This implies that were demand to grow steadily and consistently to 250,000 rooms, the industry would respond by building an additional 100,000 room capacity and renting them for $150. These additional 100,000 rooms would require materials, carpenters, plumbers, maids, and so on from the local economy and, in turn, sales of these goods and services would generate additional purchases needed to supply them. The multiplier, if constructed properly, would reasonably approximate the long-run impact of the new demand as follows:

100,000 rooms of net new demand each period in the future and sold for $150 would generate $15,000,000 in new hotel sales each period (area CEGH in Figure 15.1). Given the hotel sales multiplier of 3.15, the estimated impact on the regional economy of 100,000 new hotel rooms demanded is $47,250,000 per period.

But this is not at all what actually happens during a sporting event. Instead of occurring steadily over time, the new demand is concentrated in a few days and supply does not adjust. No new rooms are built, no additional carpenters, plumbers, or maids are hired. Rather the hotel industry responds by raising prices. During the Super Bowl or the Olympic Games this increase is two- to threefold.[8] These higher prices reduce the quantity demanded to the same 150,000 that is typical for the region; new demand has 'crowded out' existing demand. Crowding-out cannot be observed. It comes in the form of local residents or would-be visitors who decide to go elsewhere to avoid crowds and higher prices.

The regional hotel industry increases nominal sales by $45,000,000 as a result of a $300 increase in the price of 150,000 rooms. This amount is subject to taxation. As the underlying cost of providing a room has not changed, this additional revenue accrues to the owners of the hotel as extraordinary profits. Since hotel owners may live anywhere in the world, these profits generate no regional impact. That is, the regional impact is as little as the additional hotel tax with no increase in employment, real regional sales, or regional income.[9]

Consider how the I–O practitioner analyzes this same situation. Armed with a group of survey interviewers who sample event visitors, the practitioner solicits information concerning event visitor spending. The sample would reveal by extrapolation that the 100,000 event visitors would have spent $45,000,000 on hotel rooms (area ABGD in Figure 15.1). The practitioner enters this into the model as new demand that was stimulated by the event. Recall the assumptions of the model that prices are constant and long-run supply adjustments are made to accommodate demand changes. At the assumed price of $150 per room (used to calibrate the model), the model interprets the practitioner's input as if 300,000 new visitors came to the region. This is presented in Figure 15.2 as 'interpreted demand', because demand would have had to increase this much in the long run to generate new hotel revenue of $45,000,000 (equal to area CFIG in Figure 15.2). Since the model interprets this input as a real increase in hotel demand and assumes an appropriate long-run supply response, it also assigns additional materials, carpenters, plumbers, and maids accordingly.

In the immediate period of the event when hotels are already full,

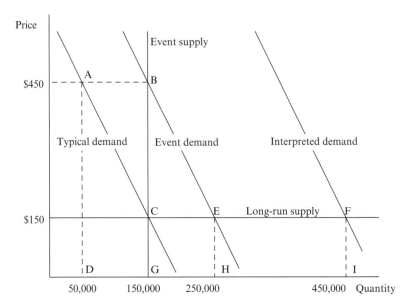

Figure 15.2   Misinterpretation of event demand

the impact of visitors is negligible or zero (event supply in Figure 15.1 is perfectly inelastic). Were the new visitors to come steadily over time, the direct impact would have been $15,000,000 (area CEHG) with additional multiplier effects. Measuring real demand by what visitors spend when prices are high, overstates demand and its attendant impact (area CFIG). Thus, measuring demand when prices have temporarily risen due to crowding-out not only fails to account for what is crowded out, but mistakes nominal price increases requiring no new inputs for real demand increases that do require new inputs.

What happens within the I–O model when prices change can be seen from the structure presented in Section 2. Recall that technical coefficients are the dollar amount of one input required to produce a dollar's worth of another input. When hotel prices rise but other prices do not, the true coefficients change relative to the historical relations hidden in the model. The matrix of technical coefficients in our example,

$$A = \begin{bmatrix} 0.2 & 0.3 & 0.2 \\ 0.4 & 0.1 & 0.2 \\ 0.1 & 0.3 & 0.2 \end{bmatrix}$$

changes to

$$A = \begin{bmatrix} 0.1 & 0.3 & 0.2 \\ 0.2 & 0.1 & 0.2 \\ 0.05 & 0.3 & 0.2 \end{bmatrix}$$

when hotel prices double.[10] The associated hotel multiplier that was 3.15 is now 2.29, a 27 percent decrease. Tourist visitor multipliers fall when the nominal price of the things tourists purchase increase. Of course, the user/practitioner who purchases an I–O model cannot change the model's technical coefficients nor does he/she know what change would be appropriate; the model is a black box.

When demand temporarily increases and there are short-run capacity constraints, prices rise. Several things happen. In the regional economy, higher prices crowd out other spending, offsetting the increase in demand so that the net increase in demand is reduced, perhaps to near zero. The I–O practitioner who surveys event visitors about their spending conflates nominally higher spending with real increases in demand and the I–O model applies a now inappropriately high multiplier to this overstated level of demand. Even if the demand increase were permanent and long run so that crowding-out did not occur and expansion of capacity was possible, the economy would not grow as much as predicted.

5 LEAKAGES: WE DON'T SELL WHAT YOU'RE BUYING

Mega events alter cash flows in ways the model does not recognize. From national income accounts we know that, over time, roughly one-third of income goes to capital and two-thirds to labor. In our hotel example this would imply that $50 of the $150 long-run price of a room goes to debt service and equity returns to the capital supplier and $100 pays for the maids, carpenters and plumbers needed to build and maintain hotels. Most hotels are financed with funds from the international credit markets and owned by shareholders from around the world. The I–O model would recognize this and attribute as much as one-third of the revenue generated by regional hotel sales to leakages in subsequent rounds of spending. That is, the region does not own and sell its hotels, the world does. The region sells maids, carpenters and plumbers. When the price of the hotel room doubles or triples during an extraordinary event, the model does not recognize that the fraction going to owners has risen temporarily. This is the source of the declining multiplier in the previous section.

It is not just the extraordinary profits of the hotel industry that leak out of the local economy during mega events. Many visitors do not stay in the region, preferring to stay in a neighboring region. Their spending does not reverberate in the local economy. Vendors are attracted to the region by the opportunities afforded by the event. For example, the area will require more limousines than the steady-state demand will support so that owner/drivers from surrounding regions will temporarily descend on the region, making sales and departing with the revenue. During the 2005 Super Bowl in Jacksonville, Florida, the city imported cruise ships as temporary hotel rooms, so that even hotel revenues were exported. The NFL Experience and several NFL stores temporarily move to the area during the Super Bowl and entertainment for many of the parties and for the half-time show are imported. The teams bring their own chefs and bartenders. One notable example is provided by Tampa's adult strip clubs:

> Brian Rouleau, executive director of operations for a company that owns a couple dozen strip clubs in several states, including some in Tampa, said they're hiring dancers from as far away as Atlanta and putting them up in local hotels to bolster ranks at Pony Tails, Gold Rush, Pink Pony and Diamond's the week of the Super Bowl.[11]

These and other extraordinary leakages are not addressed by the I–O model which interprets the purchase of limousine services, retail goods, entertainment, hotels, and even lap dancers as being supplied by the local economy. Recall that the surveyors ask visitors: how much will you *spend* while you are in town? This value gets inputted into the model as new demand. The relevant question should have been: how much did the local economy *sell* to you while you were in town? A simple analogy illustrates the point. If, while you are laid over in Dallas waiting to connect to another plane, you order a new $500 suit from a tailor in Hong Kong to be delivered to your home in Tampa, you would honestly answer that you spent $500 while in Dallas, but the impact there would be zero as you did not buy anything from Dallas.

When there is an extraordinary event that attracts vendors to the area, that results in visitors staying outside the area, or that generates excessive profits in key industries owned by investors outside the area, leakages occur that are not part of the day-to-day operation of the local economy and therefore not incorporated into the model. I–O practitioners cannot know where the money is being spent and therefore cannot control for the increased fraction that leaks out.

6 SUBSTITUTION: WE BUY WHAT YOU ARE SELLING

The people who do these studies are very good at two of the four areas of arithmetic – adding and multiplying. And they're not very good at subtracting and dividing. (Allen Sanderson[12])

Substitution occurs when local spending supports some of the new demand. The correction made by I–O practitioners is to not count local demand as it represents money that otherwise would have been spent in the local economy. But, when an event comes to the region and brings its own goods to sell, local spending is diverted to goods the local economy does not produce. That is, local demand for the goods brought to the region by the event must be counted negatively.

Consider the MLB All-Star Game and the associated Home Run Derby. Patrick Rishe produced the economic impact study for the 2005 Major League Baseball All-Star Game in Detroit, Michigan. He notes: '37 percent of the more than 54,000 All-Star and Home Run Derby attendees came from outside of Michigan . . . 63 percent of fans were from Michigan, and 50 percent of those were from metro Detroit'.[13] That is, half the attendees at the All-Star Events are drawn from the local economy and nearly two-thirds from nearby. The All-Star Game in Phoenix, Arizona on 12 July 2011 was preceded by the Home Run Derby on 11 July 2011. Ticket prices for the two events started at $169 and $91 each, respectively, for outfield reserved tickets. Clubhouse and dugout reserved tickets for the All-Star Game are more than $1,000 each ($499 for the Home Run Derby). Chase Field seats 49,033. If we assume that both events sold out and use Rishe's figures that 50 percent of attendees live in the local area, $6,374,290 of local spending (at the lowest ticket prices) will have been siphoned from the local economy because it hosted the All-Star Game. The same is true when local residents purchase tickets to the NFL Experience or goods from the NFL store when the Super Bowl is hosted locally; when a local business rents a high-priced room during an event; or when local advertisers purchase signage in the stadium or ads in the event program from the league.

Substitution is the source of negative impacts. Markets are much more fluid than I–O models recognize. Purchases from one location can be made in another location and paid for in a third location. Economic impact is generated where the product is produced and where the revenue goes, not necessarily where it is purchased. Since Major League Baseball produces the All-Star Game and Home Run Derby and sells tickets, the impact of that sale is realized in New York at the headquarters of MLB. Similarly, the National Football League produces the Super Bowl and the NFL

Experience and sells tickets. The impact of that sale generates revenue and associated impact in New York City. When locals attend these events, it is as though they went to New York and spent money they otherwise would have spent at home and local sales decrease.

7   CONCLUDING REMARKS

IMPLAN[14] and REMI[15] sell fully automated I–O models to private users and train them in the use of the models. Many modern users of the I–O model do not fully understand the inner workings of the model. This is particularly true of those applying the model to short duration events. I–O models are simply inappropriate for sports event modeling.

When extraordinary sports events draw large audiences to a location, existing facilities would be overwhelmed if there were not some mechanism to avoid crowding. Prices ration scarce resources and sports events lead to higher prices at local hotels where capacity cannot be increased in the short run. Surveys of event attendees greatly overstate real changes in demand, because the I–O model is calibrated, and functions, under the assumption that prices are fixed. When a visitor pays twice as much as usual for a room and that value is input into an I–O model as an increase in demand, the model interprets this as two rooms being rented. We call this 'phantom demand'. The model then compounds this error by applying a multiple to the phantom demand that should have decreased in the face of higher prices in some, but not all, sectors. Thus, the use of I–O models to estimate the impact of sporting events greatly overstates the potential of the new demand to generate economic impact.

Higher prices during the event drive others away, crowding them out of the regional economy. Applications of I–O models to sports events uniformly report 'gross impacts' and ignore offsets created by crowding-out. With crowding-out, the real change in demand can be zero. Higher prices for hotels create excess short-run profits for the hotel industry. These profits, like the revenues generated by outside sales to event attendees, leak out of the local economy. Rather than stimulating further rounds of local spending as would happen if the demand were satisfied locally, these leakages do nothing for the local economy.

When a region hosts a sports event they invite the sponsor and others anxious to sell goods into the community. These individuals sell goods not only to the visitors but also to local residents. The event reduces local spending when residents spend money on goods imported for the event. Thus, the combination of phantom demand, exaggerated multiplier, and no accounting for crowding-out, leads to wholly unrealistic exaggerations of the impact of the event. Substitution can make the impact negative.

What is amazing is that I–O studies are not needed. Governments possess data on sales, income, tax receipts, and transportation and hotel utilization. They can easily test whether an event has had any impact by comparing these measures during the event to other times.

NOTES

1. This case was appealed. A summary of the finding can be found at http://caselaw. findlaw.com/fl-supreme-court/1254955.html.
2. Article VII, section 10(c) of the Florida Constitution states: 'Neither the state nor any county, school district, municipality, special district, or agency of any of them, shall become a joint owner with, or stockholder of, or give, lend or use its taxing power or credit to aid any corporation, association, partnership or person'. The law goes on to list exemptions including ports and airports. The law has been amended to include projects that serve a 'paramount public purpose'. See Acton and Campbell (1998) for a review of the findings in the case and Randall (2003) for a review of the broader use of public purpose.
3. Trial transcripts have proven difficult to obtain. This report comes from one of the authors who was present at the hearing.
4. See Acton and Campbell (1998) for a legal analysis of the appellate trial findings in Poe. The appellate court's ruling can be reviewed at http://caselaw.findlaw.com/fl-supreme-court/1254955.html.
5. The example, but not the extensions that follow, is from Chiang and Wainwright (2005, p. 115).
6. See, for example, Miller and Blair (1985, pp. 15–24).
7. For our purposes this can be thought of as average price. Over the course of seasons, hotels lower prices when demand is low to better utilize fixed capacity and raise prices when demand is high to increase revenue and profits and to ration scarce resources. Scheduled maintenance fills the remainder of off-season demand. We maintain the assumption that the hotel industry is fully employed.
8. Porter (1999), and Porter and Fletcher (2008) found that prices nearly tripled during earlier Super Bowls and the Olympic Games. Sport Management Research Institute (2010) reports a doubling of prices during the 2010 Super Bowl in Miami, FL.
9. An owner might live in the region. To the extent that he or she spends more money as a result of the extraordinary profit there is an 'induced effect', equal to the owner's new demand. As most extraordinary profits are saved, the induced effect, if it exists, is not expected to be very large.
10. This formulation assumes the other industries can purchase needed hotel services at times other than during the event when prices are high. If that is the case, while it takes $0.10 of manufacturing to produce $1 of shelter during normal times the same manufacturing will produce $2 worth of shelter during the event. Hence the first column of the coefficient matrix is halved.
11. Available at: http://www.sptimes.com/News/010901/TampaBay/Tampa_plans_to_sack_1.shtml.
12. Available at: http://bleacherreport.com/articles/176232-super-windfall-forecast-debated.
13. A summary can be found at http://www.detroitsports.org/files/All-Star%20economic%20impact%20FINAL.pdf.
14. The acronym stands for *IM*pact analysis for *PLAN*ning.
15. Regional Economic Models, Inc

REFERENCES

Acton, E.C. and M.E. Campbell (1998), 'Public funding of sports stadiums and other recreational facilities: can the deal be "too sweet"?', *Stetson Law Review*, **27**, 877–98.

Allmers, S. and W. Maennig (2009), 'Economic impacts of the FIFA Soccer World Cups in France 1998, Germany 2006, and outlook for South Africa 2010', *Eastern Economic Journal*, **35** (4), 500–519.

Atkinson, G., S. Mourato, S. Szymanski and E. Ozdemiroglu (2008), 'Are we willing to pay enough to "back the bid"?: valuing the intangible impacts of London's bid to host the 2012 Summer Olympic Games', *Urban Studies*, **45** (2), 419–44.

Baade, R.A. (1994), 'Stadiums, professional sports, and economic development: assessing the reality', Heartland Institute Policy Study No.62, Chicago, IL, April.

Baade, R.A. (1997), 'Mariner economic analysis', prepared for Citizens for Leaders with Ethics and Accountability Now, Washington, DC, March 1997.

Baade, R.A., R. Baumann and V.A. Matheson (2008), 'Selling the game: estimating the impact of professional sports through taxable sales', *Southern Economic Journal*, **74** (3), 794–810.

Baade, R.A. R. Baumann and V.A. Matheson (2011), 'Big men on campus: estimating the economic impact on college sports on local economies', *Regional Studies*, **45** (3), 371–80.

Baade, R.A. and V.A. Matheson (2000a), 'An assessment of the economic impact of the American Football Championship, the Super Bowl, on host communities', *Reflets et Perspectives*, **34**, 35–46.

Baade, R.A. and V.A. Matheson (2000b), 'High octane? Grading the economic impact of the Daytona 500', *Marquette Sports Law Journal*, **10**, 401–15.

Baade, R.A. and V.A. Matheson (2001), 'Home run or wild pitch? Assessing the economic impact of Major League Baseball's All-Star Game', *Journal of Sports Economics*, **2** (4), 307–27.

Baade, R.A. and V.A. Matheson (2004), 'The quest for the Cup: assessing the economic impact of the World Cup', *Regional Studies*, **38** (4), 343–54.

Baade, R.A. and V.A. Matheson (2005), 'Striking out? The economic impact of Major League Baseball work stoppages on host communities', Working Paper, 05-07, Department of Economics Faculty Research Series, College of the Holy Cross, Worcester, MA.

Chiang, Alpha C. and Kevin Wainwright (2005), *Fundamental Methods of Mathematical Economics*, 4th edn, New York: McGraw-Hill/Irwin.

Coates, D. (2006), 'The tax benefits of hosting the Super Bowl and the MLB All-Star Game: the Houston experience', *International Journal of Sport Finance*, **1** (4), 239–52.

Coates, D. and C.A. Depken II (2006), 'Mega-events: is the Texas–Baylor Game to Waco what the Super Bowl is to Houston?', International Association of Sports Economists Working Paper Series, 06-06, Limoges.

Coates, D. and B.R. Humphreys (1999), 'The growth effects of sport franchises, stadia, and arenas', *Journal of Policy Analysis and Management*, **18** (4), 601–24.

Coates, D. and B.R. Humphreys (2001), 'The economic consequences of professional sports strikes and lockouts', *Southern Economic Journal*, **67** (3), 737–47.

Coates, D. and B.R. Humphreys (2002), 'The economic impact of postseason play in professional sports', *Journal of Sports Economics*, **3** (3), 291–9.

Coates, D. and B.R. Humphreys (2003), 'The effect of professional sports on earnings and employment in the services and retail sectors in U.S. cities', *Regional Science and Urban Economics*, **33**, 175–98.

Coates, D. and B.R. Humphreys (2004), 'Caught stealing: debunking the economic case for D.C. Baseball', Cato Institute Briefing Papers, 89, 27 October.

Coates, D. and V.A. Matheson (2011), 'Mega-events and housing costs: raising the rent while raising the roof?', *The Annals of Regional Science*, **46** (1), 119–37.

Dehring, C.A., C.A. Depken II and M.R. Ward (2007), 'The impact of stadium announcements on residential property values: evidence from a natural experiment in Dallas–Fort Worth', *Contemporary Economic Policy*, **25** (4), 627–38.

du Plessis, S.A. and W. Maennig (2011), 'The 2010 World Cup high-frequency data economics: effects on international tourism and awareness for South Africa', *Development Southern Africa*, **28** (3), 349–65.

Feddersen, A., A. Grötzinger and W. Maennig (2009), 'Investment in stadia and regional economic development – evidence from FIFA World Cup 2006 stadia', *International Journal of Sport Finance*, **4** (4), 221–39.

Hagn, F. and W. Maennig (2008), 'Employment effects of the Football World Cup 1974 in Germany', *Labour Economics*, **15** (5), 1062–75.

Hagn, F. and W. Maennig (2009), 'Large sport events and unemployment – the case of the 2006 Soccer World Cup in Germany', *Applied Economics*, **41** (25), 3295–302.

Hamilton, Bruce and Peter Kahn (1997), 'Baltimore's Camden Yards ballparks', in Roger G. Noll and Andrew Zimbalist (eds), *Sports, Jobs and Taxes: The Economic Impact of Sports Teams and Stadiums*, Washington, DC: Brookings Institution, pp. 245–81.

Hotchkiss, J.L., R.E. Moore and S.M. Zobay (2003), 'Impact of the 1996 Summer Olympic Games on employment and wages in Georgia', *Southern Economic Journal*, **69** (3), 691–704.

Hudson, I. (1999), 'Bright lights, big city: do professional sports teams increase employment?', *Journal of Urban Affairs*, **21** (4), 397–407.

Jasina, J. and K.W. Rotthoff (2008), 'The impact of a professional sports franchise on county employment and wages', *International Journal of Sport Finance*, **3** (4), 210–27.

Jasmand, S. and W. Maennig (2008), 'Regional income and employment effects of the 1972 Munich Summer Olympic Games', *Regional Studies*, **42** (7), 991–1002.

Johnson, B.K., M.J. Mondello and J.C. Whitehead (2007), 'The value of public goods generated by a National Football League team', *Journal of Sport Management*, **21** (1), 123–36.

Keating, R.J. (1999), 'Sports pork: the costly relationship between Major League Sports and government', Policy Analysis, No. 339, Cato Institute, Washington, DC, April.

Lavoie, M. and G. Rodriguez (2005), 'The economic impact of professional teams on monthly hotel occupancy rates of Canadian cities: a box–Jenkins approach', *Journal of Sports Economics*, **6** (3), 314–24.

Leontief, W. (1944), 'Output, employment, consumption, and investment', *Quarterly Journal of Economics*, **58** (2), 290–313.

Lertwachara, K. and J.J. Cochran (2007), 'An event study of the economic impact of professional sport franchises on local U.S. economies', *Journal of Sports Economics*, **8** (3), 244–54.

Matheson, Victor A. and Robert A. Baade (2004), 'An economic slam dunk or March madness? Assessing the economic impact of the NCAA Basketball Tournament', in John L. Fizel and Rodney D. Fort (eds), *Economics of College Sports*, Westport, CT: Praeger, pp. 111–33.

Miller, Ronald E. and Peter D. Blair (1985), *Input–Output Analysis: Foundations and Extensions*, Englewood Cliffs, NJ: Prentice-Hall.

Noll, Roger G. and Andrew Zimbalist (1997), 'Sports, jobs, and taxes: are new stadiums worth the cost?', *The Brookings Review*, **15** (3), 35–9.

Porter, Philip K. (1999), 'Mega-sports events as municipal investments: a critique of impact analysis', in John L. Fizel, Elizabeth Gustafson and Lawrence Hadley (eds), *Sports Economics: Current Research*, Westport, CT: Praeger, pp. 61–74.

Porter, P.K. and D. Fletcher (2008), 'The economic impact of the Olympic Games: ex ante predictions and ex post reality', *Journal of Sport Management*, **22** (4), 470–86.

Quinn, K.G., P.B. Bursik, C.P. Borick and L. Raethz (2003), 'Do new digs mean more wins? The relationship between a new venue and a professional sports team's competitive success', *Journal of Sports Economics*, **4** (3), 167–82.

Randall, M.M. (2003), 'Note and comment: the different faces of "public purpose": shouldn't it always mean the same thing?', *Florida State University Law Review*, **30**, 529–51.

Rappaport, J. and C. Wilkerson (2001), 'What are the benefits of hosting a Major League sports franchise?', *Federal Reserve Bank of Kansas City Economic Review*, First Quarter, 55–86.

Siegfried, J. and A. Zimbalist (2000), 'The economics of sports facilities and their communities', *Journal of Economic Perspectives*, **14** (3), 95–114.

Siegfried, J. and A. Zimbalist (2002), 'A note on the local economic impact of sports expenditures', *Journal of Sports Economics*, **3** (4), 361–6.

Sport Management Research Institute (2010), '2010 SB XLIV & Pro Bowl Market Analysis & Economic Impact Investigation Final Report', available at: www.southfloridasuper bowl.com/images/cmsimages/2010MarketAnalysisInvestigation6-16-2010.pdf (accessed 9 May 2011).

Szymanski, S. (2002), 'The Economic Impact of the World Cup', *World Economics*, **3** (1), 169–77.

Zimmerman, D. (1996), 'Tax-exempt bonds and the economics of professional sports stadiums', Congressional Research Service, Washington, DC, 29 May.

Zipp, John F. (1997), 'Spring Training', in Roger G. Noll and A. Zimbalist (eds), *Sports, Jobs and Taxes: The Economic Impact of Sports Teams and Stadiums*, Washington, DC: Brookings Institution, pp. 427–51.

APPENDIX 15A

Table 15A.1 Economic impact studies

Author (Year)	Team/event studied	Impact on	Result
Allmers, Maennig (2009)	FIFA World Cup (1998, 2006, 2010)	Hotel stays, income, retail sales	No significant impacts in France (1998). Significant impacts on hotel stays and income in Germany (2006)
Atkinson, Mourato, Szymanski, Ozdemiroglu (2008)	Summer Olympic Games (2012)	Intangible benefits	£2 billion as reported by survey data versus £2.375 billion in announced capital costs
Baade (1994)	Presence of professional teams, stadiums	Income	Of the 36 cities studied, two are significantly impacted by an additional team (one positively and one negatively), and three by an additional stadium (all negatively)
Baade (1997)	Seattle Mariners	Economic activity	$3.8–$5.1 million a year at a cost of $28 million a year
Baade, Baumann, Matheson (2008)	Presence of professional teams, stadiums, mega events in Florida	Taxable sales	With few exceptions, additional teams, stadiums, and mega-events do not have a significant impact
Baade, Baumann, Matheson (2011)	Presence of college teams in Florida	Taxable sales	Men's basketball games have insignificant impact. Football games average $2 to $3 million impact and are marginally significant
Baade, Matheson (2000a)	Super Bowls	Economic activity	An average of $32 million from 1973 to 1997
Baade, Matheson (2000b)	Daytona 500	Taxable sales	About $42 million per race

Table 15A.1 (continued)

Author (Year)	Team/event studied	Impact on	Result
Baade, Matheson (2001)	MLB All-Star Games	Employment, taxable sales	Average loss of 8,000 jobs. For 3 games played in California, an average loss of $30 million in taxable sales
Baade, Matheson (2004)	FIFA World Cup (1994)	Income	Across the 13 host cities, average income was $712 million below trend compared to boosters' claims of $300 million gains
Baade, Matheson (2005)	MLB strikes	Income	Best-guess estimates of MLB teams' economic impacts implied by work stoppages are $16 million and $132 million compared to boosters' claims of $300 million
Coates (2006)	Super Bowl and MLB All-Star Game in Houston	Tax revenues, taxable sales	$5 million in tax revenues from Super Bowl, $1 million from All-Star Game. Insignificant impact on taxable sales
Coates, Depken (2006)	Various sports events in Texas	Tax revenues	Of the coefficients that measure the impact of 24 different sports events, 9 are significantly positive and 4 are significantly negative
Coates, Humphreys (1999)	Presence of professional teams, stadiums	Income	No significant impact on changes in income, and significant negative impacts on levels
Coates, Humphreys (2001)	Work stoppages and relocations	Income	NFL and NBA work stoppages as well as NBA teams that relocate out of a city have no significant impact
Coates, Humphreys (2002)	MLB, NBA, NFL playoff games	Income	No significant impact in the host cities whose teams are in the playoffs
Coates, Humphreys (2003)	Presence of professional teams, stadiums	Earnings, employment	Significantly positive impact in the Amusement and Recreation sector offset by significantly negative impact in other service-oriented sectors

Coates, Humphreys (2004)	Presence of professional teams, stadiums	Income, earnings, employment	'The net economic impact of professional sports . . . in cities that hosted professional sports teams over nearly 30 years, was a reduction in real per capita income over the entire metropolitan area'
Coates, Matheson (2011)	Mega events	Housing rental prices	Of the 18 variables in the most detailed model specification, 12 are insignificant
Dehring, Depken, Ward (2007)	Cowboy Stadium	Housing values	Announcements of stadium location reduced property values by 1.5%
du Plessis, Maennig (2011)	FIFA World Cup (2010)	International tourists	40,000–90,000 versus ex ante forecasts of approximately 400,000
Feddersen, Grotzinger, Maennig (2009)	FIFA World Cup (2006)	Employment, income	No significant impact in urban areas where new stadium construction took place compared to other urban areas
Hagn, Maennig (2008)	FIFA World Cup (1974)	Long-run employment	No significantly positive impact on host cities through 1988
Hagn, Maennig (2009)	FIFA World Cup (2006)	Employment	No significant impact on the cities that hosted games compared to other German cities that did not host games
Hamilton, Kahn (1997)	Camden Yards	Employment, tax revenues	Baltimore Oriole games cost net $11 million a year in lost jobs and taxes, and Baltimore Raven games cost net $12 million
Hotchkiss, Moore, Zobay (2003)	Summer Olympic Games (1996)	Employment, wages	Employment increased by 17% in counties near events compared to the rest of Georgia. Impact on wages inconclusive
Hudson (1999)	Presence of professional teams	Employment	No significant impact based on a sample of 17 cities over 20 years
Jasina, Rotthoff (2008)	Presence of professional teams, stadiums	Employment, wages	Of the 12 employment variables, seven are significant (four positively and three negatively). Of the 12 wage variables, four are significantly negative

Table 15A.1 (continued)

Author (Year)	Team/event studied	Impact on	Result
Jasmand, Maennig (2008)	Summer Olympic Games (1972)	Employment, income	Significantly positive impact on income, and insignificant impact on employment in host regions
Johnson, Mondello, Whitehead (2007)	Jacksonville Jaguars	Intangible benefits	Approximately $36 million
Keating (1999)	Presence of professional teams, stadiums	Role of government	'. . . the results of studies on changes in the economy from the presence of stadiums, arenas, and sports teams show no positive economic impact from professional sports – or a possible negative effect'
Lavoie, Rodriguez (2005)	Work stoppages in sports	Hotel occupancy rates in Canadian cities	Of the 12 city-work stoppage pairs studied, four are significantly negative and the rest insignificant
Lertwachara, Cochran (2007)	Expansion/relocation of professional teams	Income	During a team's first year in a city, per capita income falls by $1,117, and by $13, 901 in the team's first 10 years
Matheson, Baade (2004)	NCAA Basketball Final Four	Income	The 1970–99 Men's Final Fours lost an average of $44 million for the host cities while the 1982–98 Women's Final Fours gained $70 million. Both estimates are highly statistically insignificant
Noll, Zimbalist (1997)	Presence of professional teams, stadiums	Role of government	'Sports facilities now typically cost the host city more than $10 million a year'
Porter (1999)	Super Bowls in Arizona and Florida	Taxable sales	Of the 18 dummy variables accounting for six games and three time intervals, only one is significantly positive

Study	Subject/Event	Variable	Findings
Porter, Fletcher (2008)	Summer Olympic Games (1996), Winter Olympic Games (2002)	Taxable sales, hotel occupancy, airport usage	No significant impacts
Quinn, Bursik, Borick, Raethz (2003)	New stadiums	On-field performance	No significant impact for NBA, NFL, and NHL teams. Significant impact for MLB teams (about 4 percentage points)
Rappaport, Wilkerson (2001)	Presence of professional teams	Employment, tax revenues	30-year net present value of job and tax benefits range from $26 million for an NHL team to $40 million for an NFL team, amounts that are far below the outlays needed to attract a team
Siegfried, Zimbalist (2000)	Presence of stadiums	Net spending/role of government	'. . . the net effect from the sports team is estimated to be virtually zero'
Siegfried, Zimbalist (2002)	Sports spending	Economic activity	'. . . a standard local economic impact multiplier exaggerates the stimulative effect of sports expenditures by over 400%'
Szymanski (2002)	FIFA World Cup	Economic growth	Loss of 2.4% of nominal GDP in host country
Zimmerman (1996)	Presence of stadiums	Role of government	'Economic benefits were overstated by 236% primarily because the reduced spending on other activities . . . was not netted against stadium spending. And no account was taken of losses incurred by foregoing more productive activities'
Zipp (1997)	1995 MLB replacement player spring training	Taxable sales	No significantly negative impact in host counties

16 The economic impact, costs and benefits of the FIFA World Cup and the Olympic Games: who wins, who loses?

Stefan Kesenne

1 INTRODUCTION

After the European dominance in organizing the Football World Cup, FIFA now seeks to capture new markets by moving the sports event to other continents. In 2010, for the first time in its history, the FIFA Football World Cup was organized in an African country. Notwithstanding the initial skepticism, South Africa made it a success. In spite of too large a number of participating teams, playing too many boring games, and the failure of the SA team to qualify for the second round, the World Cup in Africa was a boost to the whole continent's morale and it clearly made many South Africans happy and proud.

Nevertheless, the huge costs of hosting the World Cup have not been covered by the revenues, contrary to the positive economic impact studies that invariably show up when a country applies to host a major sports event. As soon as the vuvuzelas were silenced, the South African government and the city governments faced huge budget deficits, and the country was stuck with too many stadiums that are too large to maintain and run profitably (white elephants).

This is also what Simon Kuper and Stefan Szymanski (2009) concluded in their recent book *Soccernomics* (p. 249): 'It turns out that hosting the World Cup doesn't make you rich, but it does make you happy'. Well, at least it makes many people happy.

In this contribution, I try to explain why economic impact studies contradict cost–benefit analyses of hosting major sports events.

2 ECONOMIC IMPACT STUDIES VERSUS COST–BENEFIT ANALYSES

There is a fundamental difference between an economic impact study (EIS) and a cost–benefit analysis (CBA) of a sports event. An EIS is only registering economic activity, calculating the (additional) money flows that are generated by the organization of a major sports event, and this can be considerable. Building new and expanding existing sports stadiums and hotels, as well as urban regeneration, create value added, income, employment and tax revenue. Apart from many mistakes that are often made in an EIS, such as neglecting crowding-out and displacement effects (see Preuss, 2008, for a good overview of these effects), an EIS does not tell us which flow is a cost and which flow is a benefit, even if none of the above mistakes is made. It is clear, however, that some of these money flows are costs of organizing the event and others are benefits, but, in an EIS, this important distinction is simply not made. Moreover, an EIS does not specify who is bearing the costs and who is running away with the benefits (see Kesenne, 2005). That is probably why FIFA and the IOC relish World Cup and Olympics EI studies.

In order to see this distinction more clearly, let us start from a very simple numerical example of the money flows of an international sports event. Starting from the same data input, we conduct two EI studies, a wrong one and a correct one, and a cost–benefit analysis for the host country. This example does not pretend to represent any real scenario, the only aim is to show the difference between these approaches. Assume that, for the organization of a sports event, the total cost of a new stadium is €10 million, which is financed by the local government. For its construction, 800 workers are employed, of whom 400 were previously unemployed. There is no unemployment benefit system. The average labor productivity is assumed to be the same in every industry of the host country, equal to €12,500. During the event, the local spectators spend €1 million on tickets and €0.5 million on food and drinks. The visiting spectators spend €1.5 million on tickets and €2 million on lodging and catering. The international sports body (such as FIFA or the International Olympic Committee: IOC) receives not only €2.5 million from ticket sales but also €4 million from TV rights and sponsorships. The global tax rate in the host country is 40 percent, but the international sports body is exempted from tax payments in the host country.

A wrong EIS for the host country, which we have seen all too often, will report the results as presented in Box 16.1.

These figures look very nice for the host country. However, because 400 of the hired 800 workers were previously employed, their new employment has created a crowding-out effect of €5 million elsewhere. A second crowding-out effect is caused by the money spent by the local spectators on tickets during the event, because they would have spent the amount of €1 million on other goods and services if the event had not taken place. This implies that other local businesses face a decrease in sales of €1 million. The €0.5 million the locals spend on food and drinks do not change the total sales of local businesses. If the international sports body receives all the revenues from ticket sales, sponsorship and TV rights, there is no

---

BOX 16.1   WRONG ECONOMIC IMPACT STUDY

Income creation:	€15 million
in: construction	10.0
lodging and catering	2.5
ticket sales	2.5
Job creation (15m/12,500)	1,200 jobs
Tax returns (15m × 0.40)	€6 million

BOX 16.2   CORRECT ECONOMIC IMPACT STUDY

Additional income creation:	€4.0 million
in: construction	5.0
lodging and catering	0.0
ticket sales	0.0
other local businesses	−1.0
Additional job creation (4m/12,500)	320 jobs
Additional tax revenues (4m × 0.40)	€1.6 million

---

positive economic impact in the host country from these items. Finally, the positive economic effect to the host country from the visitors' spending of €2 million is also questionable, because fewer regular tourists will visit the host country during the year of the sports event than in other years. In London, 'VisitBritain' chairman Christopher Rodriguez (2010) expects a reduction in the number of foreign visitors in 2012, because regular summer holidaymakers are put off by high prices and large crowds. Therefore, assuming 100 percent crowding-out, another €2 million are lost. So, adding up, the extra income creation is only €4 million and the additional job creation is 320 jobs. The tax returns are €1.6 million. The correct EIS in Box 16.2 shows a different picture.

For simplicity reasons, I have assumed in this example that the sports event does not change the locals' propensity to save. If the locals had paid their tickets fully with their savings, the second crowding-out effect would not occur. But lower savings can have another negative effect on the economy, because it increases the interest rate which hurts investments and lowers the country's production capacity in the long run. This correct study reduced the economic impact considerably, but it still looks

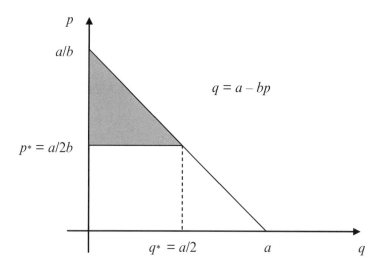

Figure 16.1   The consumer surplus

favorable to the host country. Nevertheless, this result is also misleading because it does not indicate the costs and benefits for the host country.

The objective of a CBA is to decompose the money flows into costs and benefits. On the cost side, it starts from the opportunity cost rather than the actual financial cost. The idea behind the opportunity cost is that the money invested in a sports stadium could have been invested in housing, schools or hospitals where the benefits could have been much higher. The benefit of the best alternative investment is the cost of investing the money in sports stadiums. It is obvious that a strict application of the opportunity cost idea is hardly manageable, because it would imply that all possible alternative investments of the money spent on sports stadiums have to be investigated. Nevertheless, all crowding-out effects should be taken into account. On the benefit side, a CBA also includes the spectators' consumer surplus. A consumer surplus occurs if the willingness to pay for watching sports event is higher than the price the spectator has to pay. In this numerical example, we assume that the consumer surplus is 50 percent of the total expenditures on tickets. This is a consequence of the profit-maximizing price setting by the FIFA or the IOC. Assume that the demand for tickets is given by the linear function: $q = a - bp$. Total revenue is then equal to $R = pq = ap - bp^2$, and the optimal ticket price, with zero marginal cost, is $p^* = a/2b$. Total expenditures on tickets is then $R^* = p^*q^* = a^2/4b$ and the consumer surplus is $CS = a^2/8b = R^*/2$. In Figure 16.1, where the downward-sloping demand curve is drawn, the consumer surplus

---

BOX 16.3 COST–BENEFIT ANALYSIS OF THE HOST COUNTRY

Opportunity cost (5 + 1 + 2 + 0.5)	€8.5 million
Total benefits (2.5 + 0.5)	€3.0 million
Net benefits	−€5.5 million
The winners:	
400 workers	€3.0 million
Local spectators (CS)	€0.5 million
The losers:	
Local businesses	€0.6 million
Local government	€8.4 million
Net effect	−€5.5 million

---

is indicated by the shaded area below the demand curve and above the optimal price level. As can be seen, it is equal to half the amount of money spent on tickets, indicated by the rectangular area $q^* x p^*$. For simplicity reasons, I assume that no consumer surplus is lost for the consumption that is replaced, and that there are no other intangible costs and benefits.

A proper CBA for the host country would report the figures as shown in Box 16.3. The opportunity cost consists mainly of the €5 million that the 400 workers would have produced and earned in other industries if they had not been hired to build sports stadiums. Local businesses lose €1 million that the local spectators have spent on tickets. Furthermore, another €2 million are lost because the regular foreign tourists do not show up during the sports event, and finally also €0.5 million for catering that locals would have spent anyway. So, the total opportunity cost is €8.5 million. The only benefits to the host country in this numerical example consist of the spending of locals and foreign visitors on lodging and catering of €2.5 million added to the consumer surplus of its citizens of €0.5 million. So, the net benefit to the host country is negative and equal to €5.5 million.

It is equally important to know who are the winners and the losers. The winners are the 400 previously unemployed workers, earning now an after-tax income of €3 million. Other winners are the local spectators with their consumer surplus of €0.5 million. Among the losers are the local businesses losing an after-tax income of €0.6 million. The biggest loser, however, is the government, or the taxpayers of the host country, who lose

€8.4 million. So, based on the winner/loser approach, the loss to the host country is again €5.5 million.

However, the big winner from the organization of a major sports event is obviously the international sports body cashing all the revenues from ticket sales, sponsorship and TV rights, which adds up to €6.5 million. Other possible winners in this simplified example are the foreign spectators with their consumer surplus of €0.75 million. So, overall, the net benefit of the sports event is positive and equal to €1.75 million. A global positive result of the organization of the Olympics or the Football World Cup might suggest that the IOC and FIFA should subsidize the host government or, at least, pay taxes in the host country.

3 DISCUSSION

The simple numerical example shows both the misleading character of an EIS and the importance of conducting a careful CBA of a sporting event, in particular for the host country. The organization of the Olympic Games and the World Cup Football is a very profitable business for both the IOC and FIFA. Otherwise, they would have been bankrupt. But this does not mean that the organization of the Olympics or the World Cup is profitable to the host city or country. Over the last decades, only Los Angeles managed to close the Summer Olympics of 1984 without a fiscal loss for the city. LA used many existing sports facilities rather than building new ones, and Peter Ueberroth, the chairman of the US Olympic Committee raised a lot of money selling local sponsorships. Also part of the explanation is that, after the financial disasters of the Summer Olympics in Montreal 1976 and in Moscow 1980, no other city was willing to organize the Olympics in 1984. This put LA in a very strong bargaining position against the IOC and so LA forced the IOC to bear a large part of the costs and claimed a good part of the IOC revenues. The IOC was not in a position to refuse; without the Games in 1984, the IOC would have gone bankrupt because the Olympic Games are its only source of income and, in the early 1980s, the IOC did not have enough financial reserves to survive four years without the revenues from the Olympic Games. Currently, the IOC and FIFA have sufficient financial reserves, thanks to the huge profits from the Olympics and the World Cup over the last decades. Economists have rarely found positive economic effects in a city or a country hosting the Olympic Games or the World Cup, or from building new sports stadiums (see Noll and Zimbalist, 1997; Baade and Matheson, 2002; Hagn and Maennig, 2008; Maennig and Hagn, 2009).

Some economists have argued that one can observe significant positive effects of major sports events on economic growth. The smaller the country or the region under investigation, the more significant the growth of GDP will be (see Sterken, 2006). Large investments in stadiums and infrastructure can have a modest positive growth impact on GDP, in particular during the years preceding the event. Sterken (2008) observed positive growth effects in the host countries from organizing the Olympic Games, but not from organizing the FIFA World Cup. Indeed, the Olympic Games require more investments in sports and other infrastructure than the Football World Cup. However, Szymanski (2002) also observed that during and after the sports event, when all sports investment projects are finalized, the decrease in investments causes the economic growth to turn negative, hereby neutralizing the initial positive growth effect. Unfortunately, the so-called Keynesian multiplier effect works in both directions. Keynesian aggregate demand policy can help an economy to grow, but only if the economy is in a slump with a low degree of capacity utilization and high rates of unemployment. But even then, it does not mean that the benefits of hosting a major sports event are higher than the costs. So, in the final analysis, it is still the taxpayer who pays the bill. The citizens of Montreal paid a special tax for more than 30 years through 2006, to cover the costs of the 1976 Summer Olympics. Also, the current dramatic budgetary deficits of Greece are engendered in part by the huge costs and losses of hosting the 2004 Summer Olympics in Athens.

Often, the argument is heard that the World Cup or the Olympics should not be held responsible for all the cost of building new stadiums and infrastructure, because these facilities can serve the population for many years after the sports event. Even if this is true, it does not change the cost–benefit ratio of the sports event. If it is the opportunity cost that matters, this argument does not hold. If these investments in stadiums or infrastructure would not have been made without the sports event, it implies that they did not enjoy political priority because they were less productive than the best alternative investment, such as in housing, schools or hospitals. These houses, schools and hospitals would have lasted for many years as well, and with higher returns than football stadiums, So, all the money spent on sports facilities is part of the opportunity cost of the organization of the sports event. Moreover, in many host countries, new stadiums or other sports infrastructure had to be demolished immediately after the Olympics (Athens 2004; Beijing 2008) or after the European Football Cup (Portugal 2004). Also, after the World Cup in South Africa 2010, the new football stadiums have been called 'white elephants', and some stadiums will probably be demolished because they are too large to be exploited profitably, or their maintenance costs are so high that it is less costly to simply destroy them with explosives and bulldozers (see Zimbalist, 2010).

Some researchers have also observed and estimated a very high level of total consumer surplus of millions of spectators who can watch the games at home on a free TV network (see Barget and Gouguet, 2008). It cannot be denied that this consumer surplus is real, but this surplus cannot be counted as a benefit to the host country. Mega sporting events, such as the Olympics or the Football World Cup, are broadcast in countries all over the world and can also be watched without having to host them. Also, one should not neglect the negative consumer surplus of, possibly, the majority of the female population who do not like to watch football or any other sport, and have to miss their favorite TV programs or interaction with their spouse during the World Cup and the Olympic Games.

Being short of better arguments to show the profitability of major sports events in the host country, some lobbyists point to the highly speculative and obscure long-term effects on image, future tourism and foreign investments. To the best of my knowledge, no study has ever shown that these long-term effects really exist and can be attributed to hosting the sports event.

Does it mean that it would be desirable for the IOC and FIFA to stop organizing the Olympic Games and the Football World Cup? Certainly not – these are great spectacles where splendid athletes compete for glory, and money, supplying quality entertainment that makes many people happy, thereby encouraged by opportunistic governments offering their population 'bread and circus'. Many South Africans were very happy and proud indeed to host the Football World Cup, even after their national team did not perform very well. Kuper and Szymanski (2009) signal a positive correlation between hosting sports tournaments and happiness, after correcting for many other effects that can influence happiness. The observed gain in happiness seems to last at least a couple of months, but no longer than one year. Perhaps happiness can be good enough a reason to host a major sports event, which might explain why so many governments want to stage the World Cup or the Olympic Games. Also, political lobbying by specific local business interests can play a role. It is indeed up to politicians to decide whether this increase in happiness is worth the high cost of hosting a major sports event, but it is up to economists to inform the population correctly about the negative net benefits of organizing the event, and this cannot be done using an EIS.

4 CONCLUSION

In this contribution, I have tried to show that the so-called economic impact studies of major sports events can be very misleading. I have argued that the costs of the Olympic Games or the FIFA World Cup are always higher than the returns in the host city or country, for the simple reason that the IOC and FIFA keep too much money for themselves, and return to Switzerland leaving the host countries with huge budget deficits.

One suggestion could be that the IOC, and certainly FIFA, should do a better job by sharing their huge profits with the host countries. In any event, in order to help politicians decide whether more happiness is worth the costs, economists should stop fooling the population and the politicians with misleading economic impact studies, and turn to more reliable cost–benefit analyses.

REFERENCES

Baade, R. and V. Matheson (2002), 'Bidding for the Olympics, Fool's Gold?', in C. Barros, M. Ibrahimo and S. Szymanski (eds) (2002), *Transatlantic Sport*, Cheltenham, UK and Northampton, MA, USA: Edward Elgar, pp. 127–51.

Barget, E. and J.-J. Gouguet (2008), 'L'impact économique, touristique et social de la Coupe du monde de rugby 2007', *Revue Espaces*, **256**.

Hagn, F. and W. Maennig (2008), 'Employment effects of the Football World Cup 1974 in Germany', *Labour Economics*, **15** (5), 1062–75.

Kesenne, S. (2005), 'Do we need an economic impact study or a cost–benefit analysis of a sports event?', *European Sport Management Quarterly*, **5** (2), 133–42.

Kuper, S. and S. Szymanski (2009), *Soccernomics*, New York: Nation Books.

Maennig, W. and F. Hagn (2009), 'Large sports events and unemployment: the case of the 2006 Soccer World Cup in Germany', *Applied Economics*, **41** (25), 3295–302.

Noll, R. and A. Zimbalist (1997), 'Sports, jobs and taxes', *The Brookings Review*, **15** (3), 35–9.

Preuss, H. (2008), *The Impact and Evaluation of Major Sporting Events*, London: Routledge.

Rodriguez, C. (2010), SportBusiness.com, September 13.

Sterken, E. (2006), 'Growth impact of major sporting events', *European Sport Management Quarterly*, **6** (4), 375–89.

Sterken, E. (2008), 'Organizing international sporting events like the FIFA World Cup or the Olympic Games positively affects the economy of the host country', *First Quarterly*, **(5)**.

Szymanski, S. (2002), 'The economic impact of the World Cup', *World Economics*, **3** (1), 169–77.

Zimbalist, A. (2010), 'Is it worth it? Hosting the Olympic Games and other mega sporting events is an honor many countries aspire to – but why?', *Finance and Development*, **47** (1), March, 8–11.

17 Outlook, progress and challenges of stadium evaluation

Gabriel M. Ahlfeldt and Georgios Kavetsos

1 INTRODUCTION

The urban economics literature has long been investigating the links between property prices and neighbourhood characteristics. A number of contributions have focused on the impact of schools (Gibbons and Machin, 2003, 2006), airports (Tomkins et al., 1998), transport links (Gibbons and Machin, 2005), and crime (Gibbons, 2004).

Following the nugatory effects associated with mega sporting events and franchises on economic growth, tourism, employment and wages (Siegfried and Zimbalist, 2000), a recent strand of the urban economics literature has focused on the impact sports stadiums have on prices of proximate properties. The main result is that stadiums have a positive impact on the desirability of the location, thus inflating sale and rent prices. However, it is unclear whether this is attributed to fandom, area regeneration/accessibility, the stadium's architectural design, or neighbourhood trends that might be correlated with the effect of the stadium's construction. Moreover, it is often difficult to make cross-study comparisons because of the differences in terms of the data used and the methodology employed.

In this chapter we offer an outlook on the findings of existing studies, suggest two potential methodologies to be used in order to better identify the stadium effect, and present some of the challenges that arise in terms of policy.

2 OUTLOOK OF EXISTING STUDIES

Over the last decade, a number of studies have aimed at identifying stadium effects on property prices. This section presents the findings of the most significant of these.

Carlino and Coulson (2004) study the impact that the existence of a National Football League (NFL) franchise has on a pooled dataset of property rents in 53 of the largest US metropolitan areas. Applying a semi-log hedonic model they estimate that the presence of the NFL franchise increases annual rents by a sizeable amount in the wider metropolitan area, having a more profound increase in cities – an effect they attribute to fandom and civic pride of individuals wishing to relocate to the area, thus pushing rents upwards. Estimation of a wage equation, though, did not return a statistically significant finding for the presence of the NFL, thus offering only limited evidence for a theory of compensating differentials. Coates et al. (2006) challenge these results. In brief, they question the significance of the results following the inclusion of outliers, the existence of unequal observations between cities and the overall lack of additional observations, among other issues. In response, Carlino and Coulson (2006) offer additional evidence and arguments supporting their earlier study. Along the same lines, applying the same methodology as Carlino and Coulson (2004) on property prices rather than rents, Kiel et al. (2010) find that the presence of an NFL franchise does not have a statistically significant effect; although this inconsistency might be attributed to different perceptions owners versus renters have when it comes to the sports franchise.

Feng and Humphreys (2008) study transactions data for properties proximate to the Nationwide Arena and Crew Stadium in Columbus, Ohio, both of which are franchised. Applying a spatial lag hedonic model on a single cross-section of transacted properties, they find a positive effect of both stadiums on proximate property prices.

However, are property prices/rents appreciating mainly because of the property's proximity to a stadium or because of the team using it? Focusing on the construction of the FedEx Field in Maryland, Tu (2005) estimates the effect of the stadium prior to it hosting a franchised team. His semi-log hedonic model results suggest that prices of proximate properties significantly increase following each completion phase of the construction (pre-development, development, and post-development).

Results of European-based studies point towards the same conclusion. Ahlfeldt and Maennig (2009, 2010b) study the impact of the Velodrom and the Max-Schmeling Arena in Berlin. Their studies use growth rates and prices of land values, respectively. Significant aggregated impacts are estimated for the two arenas are estimated in both. Notably though, these stadiums are considered as architectural landmarks, which further induce the effect on prices probably because of the increased identification felt by citizens and fans (Ahlfeldt and Maennig, 2010a).

Ahlfeldt and Kavetsos (2010) study the case of the New Wembley Stadium (home of the English national soccer team) and the Emirates Stadium (home of Arsenal FC), both located in London. The choice of the two stadiums offers an interesting contrast, with the New Wembley being constructed at the same site as the historic Wembley Stadium and benefiting from an impressive architectural design, and the Emirates Stadium being relocated to a modern, though not especially impressive, facility. Applying a semi-log difference-in-differences hedonic model on data from both the Nationwide Building Society and the UK Land Registry they find significant positive effects on proximate properties in both cases, as well as significant anticipation effects. In a pooled cross-sectional analysis of 27 professional sports stadiums in the Greater London area, the same authors find evidence supporting the positive impact of stadiums on proximate property prices (Ahlfeldt and Kavetsos, in press).

Further, it has been documented that even the announcement of constructing a stadium is capable of producing positive spillover effects on property prices. Dehring et al. (2007), for example, study a series of stadium construction announcements in Dallas to host an NFL franchise. Their difference-in-differences methodology suggests that announcements promoting construction have a significant positive impact on property values. Locating the stadium in Arlington did not, however, have similar effects. Along the same lines, Kavetsos (in press) investigates the impact of the announcement of London's successful bid to host the 2012 Olympic Games. Arguing that London had unexpectedly won the bid, thus ruling out any anticipation effects, he finds a positive and significant impact on property prices in host boroughs and up to nine miles away from the main stadium. Despite the fact that the legacy plans of the main stadium did not involve the relocation of a professional sports team at the time, the study is unable to distinguish the estimated effect attributed to the Olympic facilities from that attributed to the regeneration of the Olympic site into a park.

Finally, looking at the impact of stadiums from another perspective, Coates and Humphreys (2006) study precinct-level voting preferences regarding the decision to subsidize the construction or renovation of sports stadiums in Green Bay and Houston, US. The evidence here also points towards an appreciation of property wealth, business trade or fandom, as referenda indicate that precincts proximate to the facilities tend to agree on average with the subsidization plan. Interestingly, Ahlfeldt and Maennig (in press) find the opposite effect when investigating the referendum on the Allianz-Arena in Munich, Germany, indicating that (perceived) proximity cost may vary across sports and countries.

Table 17.1 summarizes the existing evidence on localized stadium impact. It is important to interpret the results against the background of the employed data and methodology. In terms of data, two categories of studies can be distinguished: (a) those investigating a marginal willingness to pay for locating closer to a stadium via property rents or prices,

Table 17.1   Empirical evidence on stadium impact

Study	Country	Stadium	Data / year	Method	Main result
Carlino and Coulson (2004)	US	Cross-section of NFL stadia	Rents / 1993 and 1999	Semi-log model	8% increase in cores
Tu (2005)	US	FedEx Field	Property prices / 1992–2001	Semi-log model and diff-in-diff	13% maximum increase, decreasing with distance. Impact area of 3 miles
Coates and Humphreys (2006)	US	Lambeau Field and new basketball arena	Precinct level referendums (share of 'yes' votes) / 1999 and 2000	OLS	Lambeau Field: 7% increase for proximate properties. Basketball: 18% increase for proximate properties and 27% for further away
Dehring et al. (2007)	US	New stadium to host NFL franchise in Dallas City or Arlington	Property prices / 2004–05	Semi-log model and diff-in-diff	−1.5% announcement effect of construction in Arlington
Feng and Humphreys (2008)	US	Nationwide Arena and Crew Stadium	Property prices / 2000	Log-log model based on OLS, ML and spatial 2SLS	S2SLS result: 1.75% price decrease for every 10% increase in distance between the property and the stadium
Ahlfeldt and Maennig (2009, 2010b)	Germany	Velodrom and Max-Schmeling Arena	Land values / 1992–2005	Diff-in-diff on growth rates and prices, respectively	Aggregated impact of +2.5% (MS Arena) and +15% (Velodrom)

Study	Country	Stadium / Event	Dependent variable / period	Model	Results
Kavetsos (in press)	UK	London 2012 Olympic Stadium and Olympic Village	Property prices / 2001–07	Semi-log model and diff-in-diff	2.3 to 3.2% increase in host boroughs. 2 to 5% increase up to 9 miles
Ahlfeldt and Maennig (in press)	Germany	Allianz-Arena	Precinct level referendum (share of 'yes' votes) / 2001	OLS, spatial autoregressive model (SAR) and binary choice model	SAR result: reduction in share of 'yes' votes of up to 46% compared to the Munich average, declining with increasing distance from the proposed site and tending to zero after about 4.4km
Ahlfeldt and Kavetsos (2010)	UK	New Wembley Stadium and Emirates Stadium	Property prices / 1995–2008	Semi-log model and diff-in-diff	15% increase proximate to New Wembley. 1.7% increase for every 10% decrease in distance to Emirates
Kiel et al. (2010)	US	NFL stadiums	Property prices / 1993 and 1999	Semi-log model	No statistically significant effect
Ahlfeldt and Kavetsos (in press)	UK	Cross-section of 27 London stadiums	Property prices / 2000–07	Semi-log model	Pooled result: 6.6% increase for proximate properties, decreasing with distance up to 3.25km. Individual variations exist when focusing on the functionality of stadiums

Note: Part of this table is from Ahlfeldt and Maennig (2010a).

and (b) those investigating expected utilities of co-location with a new (or renewed) stadium directly expressed in public polls. Category (a) is further distinguished into studies that (a-i) compare price across space at a given time and (a-ii) compare changes in prices across space over time. As we shall argue in the next section, it is difficult to isolate the unbiased stadium effect from property data using the spatial dimension alone (that is, a-i). All studies that conduct a comparison over space and time (that is, a-ii) can be identified by the 'diff-in-diff' methodology in Table 17.1.

3   PROGRESS ON IDENTIFICATION

Framework

The main concern with studies focusing on the impact of sports stadiums on property prices is the ability to generate unbiased estimates in light of unobserved spatial heterogeneity. In this chapter, although we deliberately place our discussion in the context of stadiums due to the increasing importance major sports facilities play in policy, for example, in the realm of neighbourhood renewal, our argument equally applies to any other type of neighbourhood facility with significant local externalities.

The problem can be illustrated within a standard bid-rent framework. At the starting point, we assume that households maximize their utility by trading non-housing against housing consumption. The utility derived from housing consumption depends on the size and quality of the unit they inhabit, but also on the quality of the location where they live. Neighbourhood quality is a composite good that encompasses access to employment opportunities, which may or may not be assumed to be concentrated in the central business district, and a range of location-specific features, including natural amenities (for example, green and water spaces), various environmental externalities (for example, noise and pollution) and the quality of public services (for example, school quality). Sports stadiums are a specific location amenity and residents may derive utility from locating close to the services offered by the facility. As discussed, direct utility effects related to a stadium may be derived from consumption benefits or a 'civic pride' effect and emotional attachments to the sports team(s) hosted in the stadium, among other reasons. In addition, residents living closer to a stadium naturally enjoy transport cost savings due to shorter journeys when attending stadium-related events.

Given competitive markets' mobile residents, utility maximization implies that the utility derived from the proximity to the stadium, as well as to all other location and non-location characteristics of the property, fully capitalizes into households' bid-rent functions. That is, mobility and equal-utility constraint imply that, at least at the margin, any increase in utility be offset by a corresponding increase in rent:

$$r(S, L, F, D) = f[S, L(D)] + F(D), \qquad (17.1)$$

where S and L are vectors of non-location and location-specific property characteristics and $F(D)$ is the monetary equivalent of the utility derived from co-location (F) with the stadium, which is a function of distance to the stadium (D).

As discussed in Section 2, a number of studies have attempted to estimate the function $F(D)$ on the basis of assessed land values or observed property transaction prices. Estimating the true marginal effect of distance to the stadium dF/dD, however, is empirically challenging in practice given that the slope of the bid-rent dr/dD, which can be estimated from the data, is a composite effect of stadium effects and potentially correlated location effects:

$$\frac{dr}{dD} = \frac{dr}{dL}\frac{dL}{dD} + \frac{dr}{dF}\frac{dF}{dD}, \qquad (17.2)$$

where dr/dL and dr/dF are the marginal effects of location quality and stadium functionality on the bid-rent, and dL/dD and dF/dD reflect the change in the amount of the (dis)amenities as one moves away from the stadium. Note that equation (17.2) denotes the total derivative, not implying any particular functional form. In practice, most empirical studies employ a (semi-log) linear approximation for the stadium effect on rents, which may or may not be feasible. In our empirical example below we make use of both a (semi-log) linear parameterization as well as a more flexible specification.

Clearly, bid-rent functions depend on other location characteristics than the distance to a stadium, thus $dr/dL \neq 0$. If these location characteristics are correlated with distance to the stadium, that is, $dL/dD \neq 0$, an estimated marginal effect of stadium distance will be biased. To avoid a bias, a common strategy in the literature has been to hold constant the effect of observable location characteristics by including location characteristics in a regression model, that is, comparing like with like. The problem here is that, no matter how sophisticated the dataset at hand is, it will simply not be possible to observe *all* location characteristics in practice. So effectively, the derivative of bid-rent over stadium distance is a composite of stadium effects as well as potentially correlated location effects that are partially observed (O) and unobserved (U). Hence:

$$\frac{dr}{dD} = \frac{dr}{dF}\frac{dF}{dD} + \frac{dr}{dO}\frac{dO}{dD} + \frac{dr}{dU}\frac{dU}{dD}. \tag{17.3}$$

While in an appropriate empirical set-up $dO/dD \neq 0$ would not be a concern, as differences in observable characteristics can be controlled for, a scenario with $dU/dD \neq 0$ exhibits the risk of severe bias in the estimated stadium effect in either direction. In an empirical specification, this problem corresponds to a correlation of the exogenous regressor with the error term, that is, an omitted variable problem. The degree of bias will depend on the (dis)utility residents derive from proximity to the unobserved characteristics, that is, an increase in $|dr/dU|$, the proportion of unobserved total location characteristics and the correlation of the spatial distribution of these unobserved features with the distance to the stadium, that is, an increase in $|dU/dD|$.

Given that we cannot do anything about $|dr/dU|$ and there is not much we can do about increasing the proportion of observable location characteristics beyond a threshold constrained by data availability, the likelihood of identifying the true stadium effect, in practice, depends on the ability of the researcher to set up a strategy that minimizes $|dU/dD|$. We argue that there are at least two compelling strategies to obtain an unbiased estimate of dF/dD.

One way is to increase the number of stadiums included in the analysis so that the observable and unobservable location quality components become a composite of effects at all locations of m stadiums included in the analysis. Thus, equation (17.3) becomes:

$$\frac{dr}{dD} = \frac{dr}{dF}\frac{dF}{dD} + \sum_m \frac{dr}{dO}\frac{dO}{dD_m} + \sum_m \frac{dr}{dU}\frac{dU}{dD_m}. \tag{17.4}$$

As before, O is not a concern as the related factors can be controlled for in hedonic regressions. If, over the urban area, unobservable features are spatially clustered, but not (entirely) causally related to the location of sports facilities, accidental correlations will cancel each other out at different stadium locations, m. If the number of stadiums m is large enough, these correlations should eventually approach zero so that from the first derivative we can infer the stadium effect, as long as observable location quality is controlled for. Equation (17.4) then simplifies to:

$$\frac{dr}{dD} = \frac{dr}{dF}\frac{dF}{dD} + \sum_m \frac{dr}{dO}\frac{dO}{dD_m}. \tag{17.5}$$

Of course, this does not solve the problem of reverse causality that may arise if sports stadiums are built in high- or low-priced areas on purpose; this is a separate issue that has not been addressed in the literature yet.

The alternative approach would be to make use of a quasi-experimental setting and hold unobserved location effects constant by differentiating them out over time, for example, in case a *new* stadium is (re)built. In practice, this can be done by aggregating observed property price transactions to space–time cells analysed in first difference or by conditioning on location fixed effects in a quasi-panel strategy. The variant of equation (17.3) in this case is:

$$\frac{d(r_{t+1} - r_t)}{dD} = \frac{d(r_{t+1} - r_t)}{d(F_{t+1} - F_t)} \frac{d(F_{t+1} - F_t)}{dD} + \frac{d(r_{t+1} - r_t)}{d(O_{t+1} - O_t)} \frac{d(O_{t+1} - O_t)}{dD}$$

$$+ \frac{d(r_{t+1} - r_t)}{d(U_{t+1} - U_t)} \frac{d(U_{t+1} - U_t)}{dD}. \tag{17.6}$$

To the degree that unobservables (and observables) are time-invariant this approach solves the problem as $d(U_{t+1} - U_t)/dD = 0$ (and $d(O_{t+1} - O_t)/dD = 0$). Given that F_t, the functionality of the stadium before it is constructed, is zero, then by definition equation (17.6) collapses to:

$$\frac{d(r_{t+1} - r_t)}{dD} = \frac{d(r_{t+1} - r_t)}{dF_{t+1}} \frac{dF_{t+1}}{dD}, \tag{17.7}$$

indicating that the rent gradient with respect to distance to the stadium in first difference gives an unbiased estimate of the stadium proximity effect. Again, this strategy offers no solution for reverse causality, that is, if a stadium is built at a particular location due to an effective or anticipated change in rent.

Empirical Example

In this subsection we contrast the theoretical arguments outlined above with empirical evidence taking the case of London's New Wembley Stadium, one of the largest soccer stadium construction projects in Europe, as a case in point, whose construction began in 2002. We use data from the Nationwide Building Society and apply empirical specifications where we estimate the conditional relationship of property prices and distance to stadium that correspond to equations (17.3), (17.5) and (17.7).

1. *Individual treatment case*:

$$\log(P_{it}) =$$

$$\alpha_0 + \alpha_1 D_i + \beta_{IND} DIST_i \times D + \sum_o \gamma_o S_{ito} + \sum_q \gamma_q L_{itq} + \sum_t \varphi_t + \varepsilon_{it}, \tag{17.8a}$$

where, D is a 5 km stadium threshold dummy chosen based on existing evidence regarding the range of influence of sports stadiums (Tu, 2005), $DIST$ is the property's distance to the stadium, S is a set of property-specific characteristics (hedonic controls) and L is a set of location-specific characteristics. φ are year fixed effects and ε is the error term which satisfies the usual properties.

2. *Average treatment case*:

$$\log(P_{it}) =$$

$$\alpha_0 + \alpha_1 D_i + \beta_{AV} \min (DIST_{mi} \times D) + \sum_o \gamma_o S_{ito} + \sum_q \gamma_q L_{itq}$$

$$+ \sum_t \varphi_t + \varepsilon_{it}, \tag{17.9a}$$

where m represents the number of stadiums and D now corresponds to 5 km buffer around all stadiums. We use the same stadiums as in Ahlfeldt and Kavetsos (in press), depicted in Figure 17.1. These are all based within the Greater London area and include soccer, rugby, cricket and other stadiums.

3. *Intervention treatment case*:

$$\log(P_{it}) = \alpha DIST_i + \beta_{POST} DIST_i \times POST_t + \sum_o \gamma_o S_{ito} + \sum_q \gamma_q L_{itq}$$

$$+ \sum_t \varphi_t + \sum_q \psi_q + \varepsilon_{it}, \tag{17.10a}$$

where, $POST$ is a dummy variable which, in this case, takes the value of unity at time $t \geq 2002$, coinciding with the demolition of the (old) Wembley stadium and construction of the New Wembley, and ψ are location effects. We restrict estimation of equation (17.10a) for properties within a 5 km radius. In line with equation (17.7), β_{POST} gives the change: $\beta_{POST} = [\log(\overline{P}_{iPOST}) - \log(\overline{P}_{iPRE})]/D_{ij}$.

Table 17.2 presents summarized results of our New Wembley example. The treatment effect coefficient is statistically significant across all three models. For the individual treatment case (column 1), the

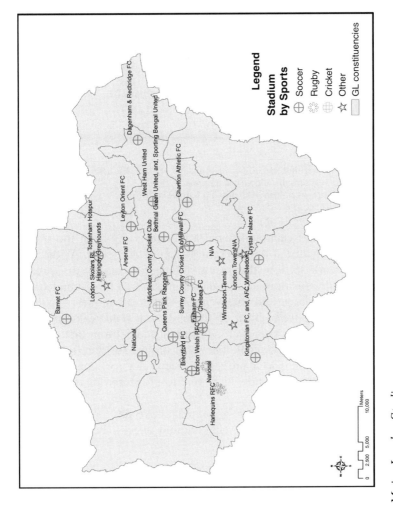

Figure 17.1   Major London Stadiums

Table 17.2   Empirical evidence on stadium impact

	(1) Individual	(2) Average	(3) Intervention
Treatment effect per km distance (β_{IND}, β_{AV}, β_{POST})	0.048[†] (0.004)	−0.027[†] (0.001)	−0.027[†] (0.008)
Year effects	Yes	Yes	Yes
Location effects			Yes
Stadium effects	Yes	Yes	
Location controls	Yes	Yes	Yes
Hedonic controls	Yes	Yes	Yes
Sample period	2002–08	2002–08	1995–2008
Observations	53,492	53,492	5,263
R^2	0.77	0.78	0.90

Notes:
Robust standard errors, clustered on postcode groups, are in parentheses.
Columns (1) and (2) are results of own calculations.
Column (3) results are taken from Ahlfeldt and Kavetsos (2010).
[†] indicates significance at the 1% level.

model suggests that each additional kilometre away from the stadium increases price by about 4.9 per cent (= exp(0.048) − 1). As discussed in the framework section, this result suffers from biases, the direction of which are obvious in this case when compared to the estimated coefficients of the average and intervention treatment models – columns (2) and (3), respectively. Both of these show a remarkable degree of consistency, indicating that each additional kilometre in fact decreases property prices by 2.7 per cent. The most natural interpretation is that the New Wembley lies in a property price crater for reasons that are unrelated to the stadium and which were not captured by the employed location controls.

The empirical specifications presented above are easily generalized to account for non-linearity in the stadium effect. The corresponding equations are the following:

$$\log(P_{it}) = \alpha_0 + \alpha_1 D_i + \sum_n \beta_n X_{ni} + \sum_o \gamma_o S_{ito} + \sum_q \gamma_q L_{itq} + \sum_t \varphi_t + \varepsilon_{it}, \tag{17.8b}$$

$$\log(P_{it}) = \alpha_0 + \alpha_1 D_i + \sum_n \beta_n \min(X_{mni}) + \sum_o \gamma_o S_{ito} + \sum_q \gamma_q L_{itq} + \sum_t \varphi_t + \varepsilon_{it}, \tag{17.9b}$$

where X_n are 250 m ring dummies of n number of radiuses, and

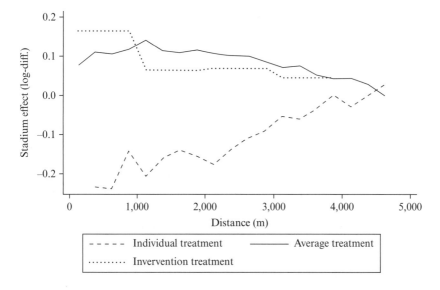

Note: Own illustration. Estimates for the individual and average treatments based on 250 m grid cells and 1,000 m grid cells for the intervention treatment due to a limited number of observations.

Figure 17.2   Estimated results

$$\log(P_{it}) = \beta_n X_i + \sum_n (\beta_{nPOST} X_i \times POST_t) + \sum_o \gamma_o S_{ito} + \sum_q \gamma_q L_{itq} + \sum_t \varphi_t$$
$$+ \sum_q \psi_q + \varepsilon_{it}. \qquad (17.10b)$$

The estimated results of equations (17.8b), (17.9b) and (17.10b) are plotted in Figure 17.2. Their interpretation is not much different from the one offered for the linear case, where the biased estimate of the stadium effect for the individual treatment case is clearly evident. Notably, the estimates and general trend based on the average and intervention treatment equations are fairly similar.

4   CONCLUDING REMARKS AND CHALLENGES

Studies attempting to estimate the impact of sports stadiums on the price of surrounding properties have gained extensive popularity over recent years. This chapter offers a comprehensive summary of existing studies. More importantly, we discuss some of the methodological biases that might arise and represent these using a simple bid-rent model. These are highlighted in an empirical example of London's New Wembley soccer stadium, where we argue that an average or intervention treatment methodology yields unbiased estimates of the stadium effect.

Preference towards which of the two though clearly depends on the availability of data. Under a long time series, with plenty of observations before and after the announcement and/or construction of the stadium, the intervention effect offers an interesting setting to derive the unbiased effect of the stadium under examination. In the UK, however, Land Registry and Nationwide data are only available since 1995, being of little use if one wishes to estimate the effect of a much older stadium. Under such circumstances the investigator might wish to look at a pool of multiple stadiums and estimate the average treatment effect.

All of the studies performed so far are *ex post*, focusing on actual construction or announcement effects. These may not be as useful *ex ante*, where policy makers might wish to know what the neighbourhood effects of a new stadium will be, prior to its construction or announcement. The natural solution to this kind of problem would be to look at a comparable existing stadium as the one intended to be constructed in a similar institutional setting – that is, country, if not city and location. Given the potential difficulty of having an appropriate comparison case, together with the potentially added limitation of data availability, the average treatment effect estimated across comparable existing projects could again be used in this case to offer an *ex ante* estimate of constructing a stadium in a specific location.

The literature yet has to investigate the problem of reverse causality that may arise if sports stadiums are built in high- or low-priced areas on purpose. In fact, neighbourhood regeneration achieved through the construction of a sports stadium is a linkage frequently advanced, as in the case of the 2012 London Olympic Games. This is probably one of the most important challenges which will provide valuable insight in terms of public policy.

Finally, the opportunity cost associated with any investment decision is an area that has also been widely overlooked in the case of stadiums construction. This is especially the case for US-based studies, where taxpayers' contribution to stadium construction is substantial. If property prices (rents) increase by X per cent, say, following a significant amount allocated to stadium construction, the pertinent question is what would the percentage increase on prices (rents) be had the same resources been allocated to other construction projects in the neighbourhood. Although a comparison of multiplier effects can also be applied when comparing alternative projects, this exercise is far more challenging due to the existence of intangible benefits associated with team identification and pride (Kavetsos and Szymanski, 2010).

REFERENCES

Ahlfeldt, G.M. and G. Kavetsos (2010), 'Form or function? The impact of new football stadiums on property prices in London', SERC Discussion Paper 87, available at: http://www.spatialeconomics.ac.uk/textonly/serc/publications/download/sercdp0087.pdf.
Ahlfeldt, G.M. and G. Kavetsos (in press), 'Should I wish on a stadium? Measuring the average effect on the treated', in P. Rodríguez, S. Kesenne and J. Garcia (eds), *The Econometrics of Sport*, Cheltenham, UK and Northampton, MA, USA: Edward Elgar.
Ahlfeldt, G.M. and W. Maennig (2009), 'Arenas, arena architecture and the impact of location desirability: the case of "Olympic arenas" in Prenzlauer Berg, Berlin', *Urban Studies*, **46**, 1343–62.
Ahlfeldt, G.M. and W. Maennig (2010a), 'Stadium architecture and urban development from the perspective of urban economics', *International Journal of Urban and Regional Research*, **34**, 629–46.
Ahlfeldt, G.M. and W. Maennig (2010b), 'Impact of sports arenas on land values: evidence from Berlin', *The Annals of Regional Science*, **44**, 205–27.
Ahlfeldt, G.M. and W. Maennig (in press), 'Voting on a NIMBY facility: proximity costs of an "iconic" stadium', *Urban Affairs Review*, available at: http://uar.sagepub.com/content/early/2011/10/14/1078087411423644.
Carlino, G. and N. Coulson (2004), 'Compensation differentials and the social benefits of the NFL', *Journal of Urban Economics*, **56**, 25–50.
Carlino, G. and N. Coulson (2006), 'Compensation differentials and the social benefits of the NFL: reply', *Journal of Urban Economics*, **60**, 132–8.
Coates, D. and B. Humphreys (2006), 'Proximity benefits and voting on stadium and arena subsidies', *Journal of Urban Economics*, **60**, 285–99.
Coates, D., B.R. Humphreys and A. Zimbalist (2006), 'Compensation differentials and the social benefits of the NFL: a comment', *Journal of Urban Economics*, **56**, 25–50.
Dehring, C., C. Depken and M. Ward (2007), 'The impact of stadium announcements on residential property values: evidence from a natural experiment in Dallas–Fort Worth', *Contemporary Economic Policy*, **25**, 627–38.
Feng, X. and B. Humphreys (2008), 'Assessing the economic impact of sports facilities on residential property values: a spatial hedonic approach', International Association of Sports Economists, Working Paper 0812, available at: http://ideas.repec.org/p/spe/wpaper/0812.html.
Gibbons, S. (2004), 'The costs of urban property crime', *Economic Journal*, **114**, F441–63.
Gibbons, S. and S. Machin (2003), 'Valuing English primary schools', *Journal of Urban Economics*, **53**, 197–219.
Gibbons, S. and S. Machin (2005), 'Valuing rail access using transport innovations', *Journal of Urban Economics*, **57**, 148–69.
Gibbons, S. and S. Machin (2006), 'Paying for primary schools: admission constraints, school popularity or congestion?', *Economic Journal*, **116**, C77–92.
Kavetsos, G. (in press), 'The impact of the London Olympics announcement on property prices', *Urban Studies*, published online doi: 10.1177/0042098011415436.
Kavetsos, G. and S. Szymanski (2010), 'National well-being and international sports events', *Journal of Economic Psychology*, **31**, 158–71.
Kiel, K.A., V.A. Matheson and C. Sullivan (2010), 'The effect of sports franchises on property values: the role of owners versus renters', Department of Economics Faculty Research Series, No. 10-01, College of the Holy Cross, Worcester, MA, available at: http://college.holycross.edu/RePEc/hcx/Kiel-Matheson_NFLStadiums.pdf.

Siegfried, J. and A. Zimbalist (2000), 'The economics of sports facilities and their communities', *Journal of Economic Perspectives*, **14**, 95–114.

Tomkins, J., N. Topham and R. Ward (1998), 'Noise versus access: the impact of an airport in an urban property market', *Urban Studies*, **35**, 243–58.

Tu, C. (2005), 'How does a new sports stadium affect housing values? The case of FedEx Field', *Land Economics*, **81**, 379–95.

18 The BRICS: national and urban legacy agendas

Richard Tomlinson and Orli Bass

1 INTRODUCTION

When visiting the site of the Beijing 2008 Olympic Games on a sunny Sunday afternoon in September 2010, at the entrance to the Olympic Green it was a surprise to find the top half of the 'B' was broken off and the first '0' of the '2008' was missing. In the Green itself were security guards, an ice-cream stand, Mickey and Minnie Mouse posing for pictures, and a person selling toy Chinese soldiers crawling forward with a rifle in one hand and a large Chinese flag in the other. One could buy tickets to enter the 'Bird's Nest' National Stadium, but the forlorn circumstances and the few people dispersed through the mall encouraged one only to leave. There were better things to do in Beijing than waste time in this dead space, located on extremely valuable land close to the city centre.

Question piled upon question. Does this Olympic infrastructure represent wasted investment? What were the opportunity costs at the time of the capital investment? What are the maintenance costs? Who is paying for these costs? What are the opportunity costs of retaining the present land use rather than some higher value and revenue generating land use? Are the questions relevant in the case of China?

Proceeding down this path, are these questions relevant to the BRICS (Brazil, Russia, India, China and South Africa)? Might it be that nowadays it is London that is the outlier – an anomaly in terms of host countries? With the exception of the 2012 London Olympics and the 2022 Qatar World Cup, all recent and future mega events are located in the BRICS.

In pursuing answers to these questions, this chapter elaborates on the research agenda suggested by Tomlinson et al. 2011,[1] with the intention of discerning whether the motivations of the BRICS in hosting mega events differ from high-income countries. Having previously considered issues of identity and image in China, South Africa and Brazil (ibid.), the focus here is on investment in infrastructure and the legacy of such investments. The propositions explored are whether there is a difference between high-income countries and the BRICS that involves (a) mega events being

Source: Photograph by Richard Tomlinson.

Figure 18.1   Entrance to Olympic Green, Beijing, September 2010

of considerably greater significance to the national governments of the BRICS, with the result that the national agenda overshadows opportunities for host cities in the BRICS and, (b) in comparison to cities in high-income countries, diminishes the relative ability of BRICS cities to pursue locally determined urban legacies.

The chapter proceeds as follows. In Section 2, we define mega events and profile the relevant differences between the Olympic Games and (the male version of) the Football World Cup. Section 3 illustrates that most mega events are now located in the BRICS and briefly considers the position of Qatar. Section 4 tackles the question of whether the emergence of the BRICS as global economic and political 'players' creates a different context from that of the high-income countries for bidding for mega events and the analysis of the urban legacy of mega events. Here we consider the BRICS grouping's geopolitical identity and consider the similarities and differences between China and South Africa and cities within them. Section 5 turns to the question of urban legacy and what it means for BRICS cities. Our conclusion (Section 6) is that there are profound differences between high-income countries and the BRICS in the pressures and opportunities arising from hosting mega events, that they pervade the national policy agenda in the lead-up to the event, and that the consequence is to diminish the potential for the host city, or cities, to use the mega event for its own strategic purposes.

2 DEFINITION OF MEGA EVENTS

The definition of mega events in this chapter excludes Expos, although they have previously been classified as mega events along with the Olympic Games and the Football World Cup (Roche, 2000). Expos are notably different from mega sporting events in not providing spectacles that, for a moment in time, create both a global audience and considerable interest from companies serving that audience. In particular, it is argued that it is this global audience that interests the BRICS and causes them to want to host mega events. The definition of mega events therefore centres on the 'sports–media–business alliance', which is based on television rights and corporate partners who acquire marketing rights, and cities (and nations) perceiving mega events as 'promotional opportunities' (Horne and Manzreiter, 2006, pp. 3–8). Expos do not attract equivalent global media moments. Yet from the perspective of urban legacy, while Expos do not create international media moments, they do create opportunities for urban renewal in the host cities themselves (Chalkley and Essex, 1999) and iconic features such as the Eiffel Tower.

Returning to mega events, basing a definition on a combination of television broadcasting income, sponsorships for marketing rights and viewership figures, in other words the Olympics and the Football World Cup, reflects the disregard in which estimates as to the economic benefits of mega events for host countries and cities are held (Baade and Matheson, 2004; Lee and Taylor, 2005; Horne and Manzreiter, 2006; Zimbalist, 2010). Coates (2010, p. 3) contends: 'Over the years, a wide array of independent academic researchers have examined previous World Cups, Olympics, and Super Bowls, so-called "mega- events", and found no evidence that the benefits promised by event organizers have ever materialized'. In effect, the definition of mega events is based on benefits to the IOC (International Olympic Committee) or FIFA (Fédération Internationale de Football Association), and not on benefits to the host country or city.

For both FIFA and the IOC the major source of revenue is broadcasting rights for the event; US$2.4 billion in the case of FIFA and

Table 18.1   FIFA: 2010 event-related revenue*

Event-related activity	Revenue (US$ m)
TV broadcasting rights	2,448
Marketing rights	1,097
Hospitality rights	120
Licensing rights	71
Other (inc. 'Club World Cup')	154
Total	3,890

Note: * Predominantly, but not exclusively, World Cup-related income.

Source: Adapted from 61st FIFA Congress, FIFA Financial Report 2010, Zurich, 31 May and 1 June 2011 (pp. 16–17).

Table 18.2   IOC: Event-related revenue 2008*

Event-related activity	Revenue (US$ m)
TV broadcasting rights	1,737
TOP (partners) marketing programme	437
Royalties	139
Licensing rights	21
(Other)	12
Total (rounded)	2,345

Note: * Predominantly, but not exclusively, Olympic Games-related income.

Source: Adapted from IOC Final Report 2005–2008 (pp. 69, 95).

US$1.7 billion in the case of the IOC (see Tables 18.1 and 18.2). Partners who acquire marketing opportunities are the remaining major source of revenue, albeit more in the case of FIFA (with FIFA generating about twice as much revenue from marketing rights). Based on these tables, in revenue terms FIFA is about 30 per cent larger than the IOC. In some respects, FIFA is also more secure than the IOC because the viewership and advertising revenue is contributed by countries around the world, whereas more than a half of the IOC's broadcasting revenue originates in the USA.

The value of the broadcasting rights and the interests of partners centre on the number of people who view particular events and games. Despite the billions of dollars spent by partners that are premised on projected viewership, the authors are unaware of any authoritative source regarding viewership of the events. While it is clear that both the Olympics and

FIFA command huge audiences, it is unclear how huge the audiences are. Fortunately, the debate regarding viewership is not relevant to this chapter except to note the extraordinary claim that about a billion people watched the India–Pakistan 2011 World Cup cricket match, which was not the final (Marks, 2011).[2] Even if the claim is an overstatement, the numbers rank with the 2006 World Cup final estimated viewership of 638 million (Harris, 2010).

This draws attention to the countries hosting the event and associated politics. Chinese viewership of the Olympics was boosted by considerable government intervention to interest Chinese in the Olympics and in chauvinism surrounding the medal count (Jinxia, 2010; Syed, 2010). Indian and Pakistani viewership of their World Cup cricket match was boosted by the fanatical cricket following in both countries and the rivalry between the world's second- and sixth-largest countries. Were China to become more interested in cricket, a match between China and India would create an unrivalled audience. (The Chinese government is presently promoting the playing of cricket; Maidment, 2005.)

A brief diversion and speculation is that combining the criteria of global audience and broadcasting rights leads to an uncertain future identification of mega events. The reason is that despite having only 14 competing nations, the 'International Cricket Council has sold the rights for broadcasting of 2011 Cricket World Cup for around US$2 billion to ESPN Star Sports. The tournament would be broadcasted all around the world in about 220 countries'.[3] Imprecise as the numbers are, it appears that the 2011 Cricket World Cup will have generated as much as the 2008 Olympics due to the countries within which it has most appeal. In the identification of mega events, if it is not the number of countries participating that matters, but rather what broadcasting companies are willing to pay, then the poster in Indian cities during the Cricket World Cup, '2011. ICC Cricket World Cup. THE CUP THAT COUNTS', may well foretell the future.

Turning to the potential urban legacy differences between the Football World Cup and the Olympics, the obvious difference concerns the dispersion of Football World Cup events among multiple cities (an overstatement in the case of Qatar) and nominally the limited infrastructure implications if accommodation, the transport infrastructure, ITC services and stadiums are already of a world-class level. In comparison to the Football World Cup, the Olympic Games require the creation of an Olympic Park and Village, a stadium designed to a specific format, and many other specialized facilities. Whether one can conclude that, as a result, the Olympics will be more expensive depends on the 'infrastructure backlog' in the host country and also whether apartments in the Olympic

Village and some of the associated facilities will represent profitable investments. While the Olympics might be assumed to be more expensive, if a number of football stadiums are to be constructed and transport investment is required then, in fact, hosting the World Cup may require greater capital investment and lead to greater long-term maintenance costs than the Olympic Games. Thus, while wondering about the accuracy of the data, whereas China reportedly spent US$40 billion on the 2008 Olympics, South Africa reportedly spent US$85.7 billion leading up to the World Cup (Cornelissen, 2010).

Probably the defining question with regard to the Football World Cup and the Olympic Games, both in the BRICS and in high-income countries, is whether infrastructure investment can be incorporated *by* the host city(ies) into *its* (their) strategic plans for managing growth and urban renewal (with emphasis on ownership of the strategic plan). The model repeatedly cited for the Olympics is that of Barcelona. The 'model' involved 'linking city-wide and strategically oriented urban regeneration with the hosting of the Olympics' (Coaffee, 2007, p. 157). In Barcelona, the 1992 Olympic Games was led by the city government in terms of a broader strategic plan to promote economic development and as a catalyst for urban infrastructure projects (Monclus, 2007). To the extent that the Olympic Games brings forward in time needed investment in infrastructure and urban renewal, which is planned for and prioritized by the host city, and also serves as a vehicle for raising funds, generating investment in real estate and transport systems, or obtaining grants from higher levels of government for infrastructure and public housing,[4] a tangible positive Olympic urban legacy is possible. However, the scale of this legacy depends on the perceived infrastructure backlog. London's intended urban renewal legacy for a small area within the city is a drab contrast to the potential legacy that arises from greater investment in cities in the BRICS.

Insofar as the World Cup is located in a number of cities, there is no equivalent model to a single Olympic Games host city using investment in infrastructure to give effect to its strategic plan. This is especially the case if, as in the case of the 2006 German World Cup, stadiums and transport infrastructure were largely in place; with less investment required there is less potential to use infrastructure investment in the pursuit of strategic planning goals. It is to be expected that BRICS cities that are to host World Cup matches will need to undertake considerable additional investment, as proved to be the case in South Africa and is presently occurring in Brazil (Winter, 2011). At the same time, a city's infrastructure needs coupled with a threat to national prestige does create opportunities of a kind. Cape Town (2006, Table 1) projected a contribution of only $10 million to the $2.3 billion funded by grants from central government and investments by the Airports Company of South Africa, South African Railways and also expenditure by the provincial government (Tomlinson, 2009). Were it not for the cost of operating and maintaining the $600 million Green Point stadium, one might conclude that Cape Town, but not the country, benefited handsomely.

The caveat regarding 'the country' arises not only from scepticism regarding benefits, but also the expectation that mega events, both in high-income countries and in the BRICS, exacerbate inequality and may create considerable hardship. This generalization includes examples in high-income countries such as the Barcelona Olympics, which led to the displacement of low-income households (Coaffee and Johnston, 2007) and the 2012 London Olympics which is diverting needed investments in infrastructure from elsewhere in London and throughout the United Kingdom (Fainstein, 2010). Exacerbating inequality through displacement (Greene, 2003; COHRE, 2007), focusing investment in areas that are already well-to-do and creating spaces of exclusion are typical consequences of mega events (Black, 2007). The urban legacies of mega events are many and varied, but when the allocation of resources is considered, one should not anticipate that the poor will benefit, and should anticipate greater inequality.

3 LOCATION OF MEGA EVENTS

The location of mega events and illustrative lesser events is shown in Table 18.3. The information contained in the table demonstrates the point that, aside from the 2012 London Olympics and the still to be announced 2020 Olympics, between 2008 and 2022 all mega events are located in the BRICS, except for the 2022 World Cup in Qatar. The cities thought to intend bidding for the 2020 Olympics include Delhi, Doha, Dubai, Durban, Istanbul, Madrid and Tokyo. Delhi and Durban are, of course, located in the two BRICS countries that have still to be awarded a Summer or Winter Olympic Games.

At the time of the final writing of this chapter (May 2011) Durban, considered to be a favourite (*USA Today*, 26 May 2011[5]), was withdrawn from the list of cities intending to bid for the Olympic Games. The 'Statement on the Cabinet meeting of 25 May 2011'[6] reads:

2.3 Cabinet considered the request by the South African Sports Federation for the country to bid for the hosting of the 2020 Olympic Games. Cabinet has decided that it is better for the country to consolidate the gains of the 2010

Table 18.3   Location of mega and illustrative lesser events

Country	Event		
Brazil	2007 Pan American Games	2014 Football World Cup	2016 Olympics
Russia	2012 Sochi Winter Olympics	2018 Football World Cup	
India	2010 Common-wealth Games	2011 ICC World Cup*	Delhi anticipated 2020 Olympics bid
China	2008 Olympics	2010 Shanghai Expo	2010 Asian Games
South Africa	Earlier African Cup of Nations and rugby and cricket World Cups	2010 Football World Cup	Durban intended 2020 Olympics bid
United Kingdom	2012 London Olympics		
Qatar	2011 Asian Games	Doha intended 2020 Olympics bid	2022 World Cup

Note: * India hosted most of the event, but formally co-hosted the event with Sri Lanka and Bangladesh.

FIFA World Cup for now and rather focus the country's attention to the delivery of basic services to all South Africans.

The authors propose a more complete explanation below.

Qatar's World Cup represents a bizarre exception. Qatar beat the USA in the final round of bidding. The Qatar Statistics Authority reports the population in 2010 as being 1.67 million and 76 per cent male (Qatar Information Exchange, 2006–2010). This reflects the extent of the expatriate population, mostly male migrants. About a third of the population is Qatari. Doha, the capital, accommodates about a million people. How might so small a country need or justify the stadium seating capacity required for a World Cup? The existing seating capacity of 92,564 is modest, but presumably appropriate to so small a country. The total proposed seating capacity, some temporary, is 605,560, with four stadiums in Doha and three in Al Rayyan (Wikipedia, 2011). The utterly spendthrift approach to a World Cup, the oil wealth of the country and the extent of iconic architecture already apparent in Doha belie the need for further 'real jewels', which is how Sepp Blatter, President of FIFA, refers to South Africa's surplus stadiums (KickOff.com, 2008). As noted, Qatar/Doha is preparing a bid for the 2020 Olympics.

4 THE BRICS AGENDA

Having considered the dominance of the BRICS in hosting mega events spanning 2008–2022, here their broad political economic agenda is briefly considered, as well as how this affects the attitude of BRICS towards hosting mega events.

It is clear that the BRICS are asserting a more prominent role in the global landscape. In this regard, the stated rationale for the BRICS cluster is given in the 'Sanya Declaration on BRICS, 13 April 2011' (2011) as:

> It is the overarching objective and strong shared desire for peace, security, development and cooperation that brought together BRICS countries with a total population of nearly 3 billion from different continents. BRICS aims at contributing significantly to the development of humanity and establishing a more equitable and fair world.

Neogy and Anishchuk (2011, no page no.) suggest that 'The main aim of the BRICS is to forge a common emerging-market negotiating stance on issues from climate change to world trade and to act as a counterweight to the West in settings such as the Group of 20 forum of advanced and developing economies'. They quote Dmitry Medvedev: '"Our economic potential, political influence and our development prospects as an alliance are exceptional"', which is indicative of the expanded global position the BRICS hope to achieve.

An aspect of this agenda includes the widespread hosting of mega and other sporting events. Such events, which capture global attention, ostensibly provide ample opportunity for achieving geopolitical goals. Indeed, 'The politics that surround emerging powers' hosting of mega-events overlap in some significant ways with their wider external and internal politics' (Cornelissen, 2010, p. 3022). Moreover,

> [BRICS] countries want to affirm themselves not only in the economic area, but in terms of their global profile. The organization of a sport mega-event exemplifies their economic development but also allows for positive image-making in the context of media coverage and tourism experiences. (Curi et al., 2011, p. 141)

Cornelissen (2010, p. 3021) suggests that sporting events can be employed 'to both place a country more centrally within the international community of states (i.e. to reinforce their international integration) and to highlight the country's distinctions'.

Close (2010, p. 2999, emphasis in original) suggests a pattern of locating mega events in the BRICS:

The choice of Rio fits into a pattern also in so far as, to paraphrase William Kelly, *awarding games to reward or facilitate integration into the world community, or global political economy, is an IOC objective*, a result of which is that games become *coming-out parties*. The 2012 London games aside, it is as if the Olympic torch has been passed from one coming-out party (the 2008 Beijing games) for one *BRIC economy* (the PRC) to another (the 2016 Rio games) for a second *BRIC economy* (Brazil). . . . In the mean time, in 2010, South Africa hosted the biggest *single-sport* mega event, the FIFA World Cup finals, awarded to South Africa as if in recognition of the country's rapid development among the BRICSAM nation-states (Brazil, Russia, India, China, South Africa, ASEAN and Mexico). . . . Perhaps, in effect, the way is being prepared for South Africa to host the Olympic Games, even as early as 2020.

Yet, despite their consolidated purpose, Neogy and Anishchuk (2011) point out that the BRICS 'are a political and economic mosaic'. This insight suggests differing motivations the BRICS might possess in relation to hosting mega events which occur both within and beyond their political borders.

It is proposed that in regard to mega events there are at least two features that are common in the BRICS and one that is unique to each country. One commonality is the much-used reference to a 'coming-out party'. A search of Google, 'coming out party' 'Olympic Games' and 'coming out party' 'World Cup' elicited 60,500 and 153,000 web pages, respectively (28 May 2011). Assuming that England and other high-income countries do not engage in such parties, this sets the BRICS apart from high-income countries. As then Prime Minister Tony Blair said, 'London is already a world city, it always has been'.[7] While Parisians might appreciate a faltering 2012 Olympic Games, if the Olympics fail to be spectacular, there will be little damage to the reputation and economies of London and the United Kingdom. The contrast to Brazil could not be more pronounced. The then President of Brazil, Luiz Inácio Lula da Silva, explained:

> For the US an Olympics is just one more Olympic Games. For Europe an Olympics is just one more Olympic Games. But for us it is something that really will be the reassurance of a continent, a country and its people. Because, here in Latin America, we always feel we have to prove how to do things. (Mackay, 2009)

Lula points to another commonality among the BRICS. Arising from their desire for influence, is a shared need for prestige. The threat to prestige creates common vulnerabilities. The reported expenditure of US$40 billion on the 2008 Beijing Olympics and US$85.7 billion leading up to the 2010 South Africa World Cup reveals the extent to which 'money is no object' when the issue is that of prestige (Cornelissen, 2010). Here lies an answer to the first two questions posed at the outset of the chapter concerning capital investment and opportunity costs. Unfortunately, the BRICS governments have behaved as if these costs were not significant. The difference between the countries arises from their separate and distinct internal politics and histories. In the case of China, the Chinese Communist Party (CCP) could give effect to its internal and global ambitions. For the CCP the two goals of the 2008 Olympics, in order of priority, were legitimizing the CCP and enhancing the image of China (Xu, 2006; Shirk, 2008). Failure would rebound on the CPP and on the prestige of the country, but arguably have little significance for Beijing separate from the overall blow to the national agenda. This would be especially significant since the legitimacy of the CCP no longer rests on communism and has to be constructed from Chinese nationalism (Shirk, 2008), with the Olympics representing an especially prominent opportunity for promoting nationalism and the legitimacy of the CCP.

In this light, an ironic aspect to the Olympics legacy reflects on 'Chairman Hu Jintao telling a group of party propagandists that "We should work hard on overseas propaganda to further display and improve a positive state image"' (Syed, 2010, p. 2867). Remembering that the US broadcasters paid for more than half the IOC Olympic television revenue, Syed (p. 2883) reports that 'Americans became more negative because of the Olympics'. While Beijing constituted the stage, the spotlights shone on China and human rights and Tibet and pollution. Conceding that China can throw a good party does not necessarily create a positive intangible legacy for either Beijing or China.

In the case of South Africa, the legitimacy of the ruling party, the African National Congress (ANC), arises from its having led the liberation movement and its being democratically elected. For the ANC the felt need was that of rebutting the recurring adverse images of Africa in international media and what it means to be African being defined by others through the lens of Afro-pessimism. This provides the backdrop to then Deputy President Thabo Mbeki's 'I am an African' 1996 speech in Parliament:

> We are assembled here today to mark [the masses'] victory in acquiring and exercising their right to formulate their own definition of what it means to be African. . . .
> However improbable it may sound to the sceptics, Africa will prosper!
> Whoever we may be, whatever our immediate interest, however much we carry baggage from our past, however much we have been caught by the fashion of cynicism and loss of faith in the capacity of the people, let us err today and say – nothing can stop us now![8]

The World Cup could not be allowed to fail and, happily, Kgalema Motlanthe (2010), South Africa's Deputy President could say:

> We were made to unleash our imagination and harness the productive energy of our people, while confronting nay-saying, scepticism and lies in various parts of the world.
>
> We were made to do all of this while ensuring that the event would leave a lasting legacy of development and renewed self-belief for our people and our compatriots across the Continent.

Unlike China's success at hosting the Olympic Games as an event attracting negative media scrutiny of human rights abuses and other issues, South Africa's success in hosting the World Cup as an event was accompanied by favourable reporting of the country, its major cities and its peoples (Hammett, 2011; Tomlinson et al., 2011).

As noted, on 26 May 2011, the South African government decided against Durban's bidding for the 2020 Olympic Games. One explanation is that South Africa has had its 'coming-out party' and good sense has prevailed in the light of the estimate that preparing the bid would cost US$45 million and hosting the Olympic Games would cost at least US$4.5 billion (Majavu, 2011). One hopes that these calculations did inform the decision by the South African government, but suspects that the local government elections held earlier in the month, on 18 May, are a significant part of the explanation. Especially significant was the sloganeering of the elections around failures by local governments to deliver housing and services such as water and sanitation. In this light it is no coincidence that the Cabinet statement should include: 'Cabinet has not taken this decision lightly – it has considered the euphoria of the World Cup and the gains we still need to consolidate but, more importantly, cabinet felt it is better to focus the energies of the country on basic service delivery'; hence the headline 'Basic services needed more than Games' (ibid.).

Whereas the internal politics of China is such that the CCP needs to sustain nationalistic fervour, with mega events providing a foremost opportunity of doing so, the internal politics of South Africa, a democratic country, requires that the ANC be seen to put the direct needs of the people before another mega event that cannot carry the weight of another round of false promises of economic development benefits. It is with some surprise that Durban's future bid was edited out of the discussion on urban legacy.

5   MAKING SENSE OF URBAN LEGACY

Concerns with urban legacy and legacy planning have arisen as a more realistic response to past overestimates of the benefits and underestimates of the costs of hosting mega events. MacAloon (2008) explains the origins of the word 'legacy' in the context of mega events. A consulting team was sent by a city preparing its bid to host the Olympic Games to visit the IOC in Lausanne in order to distill the one single issue that most concerned the IOC. The consultant was considered to have succeeded, when he left with the word 'legacy'. With the official languages of the IOC being English and French, it transpires that the word 'legacy' does not fully align with the French meaning of 'heritage'. The IOC's primary concern is with enhancement of the Olympic heritage and culture, but what we are left with now are 'urban project lists' (ibid., p. 2067).

MacAloon (pp. 2067–8) continues that it is 'the inherited cultural capital that distinguishes Olympic from other international sport and is the general source of value that makes anyone want to bid for the Olympics in the first place'. Might this be incorrect? Jinxia and Mangan (2008, p. 2020) describe the considerable efforts the Chinese government made to inculcate the history of the Olympics, but then continue to the inevitable 'publicity China will attract globally' as a 'political exercise'. China, it is argued, will assert itself as a global power and its pride will be expressed in the medal count. This has little to do with Olympic culture and heritage and equally little to do with urban legacy.

In South Africa, Tomlinson (2009, p. 96) notes that in the case of the South African World Cup Bid Book, 'There is no attention to the potential legacy of 2010 for the host cities'. Indeed, he continues to argue in this context:

> When cities use labels such as '2010 legacy projects' and apply them to, for example, the upgrading of a workers' hostel that has nothing to do with 2010, then what stands out is politicians' apparent need to be seen to be spreading the benefits of hosting 2010. It would be a mistake to treat with any seriousness some of the cities' 2010 legacy projects. (p. 96)

Given circumstances in China and South Africa, why did London bid for the 2012 Olympics? When searching the London2012 website using the word 'legacy' one finds:

Legacy
The London 2012 Games offer a unique opportunity to revitalise the Lower Lea Valley, transforming one of the most underdeveloped areas of London into a benchmark 21st century urban environment that reflects the diverse and vibrant population of the area. (London2012, 2011a)

Porter (2009, p. 395) disputes the need for transformation and refers to the London 2012 Olympics as a typical example of mega event planned displacement where the Olympic rhetoric of urban renewal obscures the question of whether renewal is necessary or desirable. Nonetheless, to continue with London2012, a legacy company has been created:

Olympic Park Legacy Company
The Olympic Park Legacy Company is responsible for the long-term planning,
development, management and maintenance of the Olympic Park and its facilities after the London 2012 Games. (London2012, 2011b)

When searching for 'Olympic heritage', in addition to six bullet points,
one finds:

Olympic Heritage
London will host a Games like never before in 2012, drawing on the country's
proud Olympic heritage. (London2012, 2011c)

It really is not all that clear why London is hosting the 2012 Olympics.
These quotes are all so pedestrian and show little regard for the Olympic
culture and heritage. It is suggested that MacAloon is wrong in believing
that 'inherited cultural capital' is the source of value in seeking to host the
Olympics, or indeed the Football World Cup. The joke that London bid
for the Olympic Games because Paris did and that Londoners celebrated
because they had beaten France seems more credible than other explanations. This is especially the case given that in 2004 the future was so well
foretold by England's prime minister at the time:

> There is a very familiar Olympic story, if you look at what happens with every
> other city that has ever hosted this, and it runs something like this – the city
> wins the bid, against the odds, shortly afterwards the recriminations start, the
> preparations are in a poor state, it soon becomes apparent they are hopelessly
> behind schedule, the prices escalate as public money is held up for ransom, the
> various parties to the organisation squabble and fight, the stories creep into
> the press, the race against time begins: will it be ready, will there be a track for
> the 100 metres, will synchronised swimming have to be dropped because the
> Olympic pool won't be built in time? Miraculously then suddenly the mists
> clear, the chaos is abated, the athletes take over and the Games are declared an
> enormous success. Then a month later the recriminations start up again – what
> has been the legacy of the project, what really has been purchased for all that
> investment, why do we have this uninhabited village on the edge of the city,
> does anybody have a use for a big stadium?
> . . . This up to now has been the familiar pattern of the Olympics. But we,
> hopefully, are going to show there is another story to be told.[9]

By 2008 the cost of hosting the Olympics has already increased almost
fourfold, from £2.4 billion to £9.35 billion. In a context where bidding
for the 2012 Olympics occurred before the global financial crisis, in 2008
the minister responsible for the Games expressed regret at having won
the Games (Osborne and Kirkup, 2008). Blair's story remains all too
familiar.
Alert to the history of indebtedness, cost overruns and architecturally

striking white elephants, the IOC (2010, p. 1) urges cities in their bids to minimize such negative outcomes:

> As the Olympic Games have grown to become the world's foremost sporting event, their impact on a host city and country has also increased. This has meant that cities interested in hosting the Games are now placing more and more emphasis on the legacies that such an event could leave for their citizens and, in many cases, they are using the Games principally as a catalyst for urban renewal.

MacAloon (2008) claims that this advice is offset by legacy planning consultants that cause cities to seek to outbid one another; however the IOC (2010) itself profoundly misrepresents urban legacy when it includes airport terminals, subways and other infrastructure that was to be constructed regardless of the Olympics, and also stadiums, which become white elephants as tangible legacies. It appears that when it is not the case that stadiums are refurbished for existing users, for example, the German World Cup stadiums were already used by football clubs in the Bundesliga, or constructed for a specific user, with the Atlanta Braves taking over the Olympic Stadium, white elephants inevitably result. Had Beijing's National Stadium or Cape Town's Green Point stadium been intended for a sports team(s) that requires such a venue, then the conclusion need not be negative.

In a country like South Africa, where poverty remains pervasive and inequality is worsening (Seekings and Nattrass, 2005), the expenditure on the World Cup can only lead to indignation. For example, despite FIFA's having accepted the Newlands rugby stadium as the World Cup venue, Cape Town was offered a quarter-final match if it used Newlands or a semi-final match if it built a new stadium, which it duly did. This largesse is most visible in Durban, where the existing large rugby stadium, also considered a satisfactory venue by FIFA, stands alongside the new stadium.

6 CONCLUSION

This discussion initially leads to a conclusion that is not as sharply defined as one might expect. For all countries and cities, it is to be expected that there will be overestimated benefits and underestimated costs (Coates, 2010). Mega events exacerbate poverty and inequality. Where positives that withstand time are encountered, it is either where little new infrastructure was necessary and the investment was desirable for the public and private operation and management of the city affected, or where the host city can use the new infrastructure to serve the ends of its strategic plan.

The lessons can be summarized as spend as little as possible and let the host city use the capital investment to serve long-term economic and social goals. The 2006 German World Cup and the 1992 Barcelona Olympics stand out.

The notable difference between mega events in BRICS and those hosted in high-income countries arises due to the BRICS context. Whereas the notion of a 'coming-out' party does not apply to high-income countries, it is especially relevant for BRICS – for the country itself and for the credibility of the BRICS concept. In the case of the country itself, the media attention paid to mega events creates considerable opportunities for gaining or losing prestige. There is no equivalent 2012 London Olympics pressure on England. In the case of the BRICS, if countries comprising the BRICS stumble, so too does their political influence.

The outcome is that in China and South Africa, mega events pervaded the national agenda and that this offsets the potential for a city-based agenda. This observation is perhaps redundant in the case of Beijing, which 'is entirely dominated by the central government',[10] but certainly has application in South Africa. Further to the point of a dominant national agenda, with the legitimacy of the liberation party (the ANC) weakened by the failure to deliver services and reduce poverty among the mass of the low-income population, the ANC rejected Durban's intention of bidding for the 2020 Olympics and the conspicuous expenditure needed to host the event.

The outcome of these pressures on the national agenda is that fearful of inadequate infrastructure and poorly managed events, the scale of investment in host cities is extraordinary. Potentially, the city could reap the rewards of this investment by aligning the investment with its strategic planning. However, the investment occurs in the midst of dire time constraints and central controls and sweeps all before it; again to quote Blair, 'one year of blind panic'. In effect, were it possible to incorporate the infrastructure largesse in a city's strategic plans – the Barcelona model – mega events could have enduring positive city legacies. While mega events continue to be driven by national agendas, these legacies are not anticipated to any great extent in cities in the BRICS.

NOTES

1. The chapter is also influenced by the authors' (also in collaboration with others) previous work related to mega events (see Bass, 2009; Pillay and Bass, 2009; Tomlinson et al., 2009; Tomlinson, 2009, 2010; Roberts and Bass, forthcoming 2012).
2. Cricket games last a lot longer than football games and it is to be expected that the viewer will spend more time than the duration of a football game watching the game

and being exposed to advertising. Indeed, cricket provides opportunities for advertising during the course of a game, at the end of each over (usually six balls); many more opportunities than an equivalent period in a football game.

3. See http://www.bdtips.com/Article_Body.php?Article_ID=3195 (accessed 28 May 2011).
4. For example, Atlanta obtained $609 million from the Federal government for this purpose (Andranovich et al., 2001).
5. See http://www.usatoday.com/sports/olympics/2011-05-26-safrica-olympics_N.htm (accessed 28 May 2011).
6. See http://www.info.gov.za/speech/DynamicAction?pageid=461&sid=18598&tid= 33879 (accessed 28 May 2011).
7. See http://www.bdtips.com/Article_Body.php?Article_ID=3195 (accessed 28 May 2011).
8. See http://www.nathanielturner.com/iamanafrican.htm (accessed 28 May 2011).
9. 'Transcript of Opening Statements by the Mayor of London, Mr Ken Livingston and the Prime Minister, Mr Tony Blair in London on Tuesday, 4 April 2006', cited in Fainstein (2010, pp. 134, 135).
10. Email communication from John Logan, 16 May 2008.

REFERENCES

Andranovich, G., M. Burbank and C. Heying (2001), 'Olympic cities: lessons learned from mega-event politics', *Journal of Urban Affairs*, **23** (2), 113–31.
Baade, R. and V.A. Matheson (2004), 'The quest for the Cup: assessing the economic impact of the World Cup', *Regional Studies*, **38** (4), June, 343–54.
Bass, O. (2009), 'Aiming for Africa: Durban, 2010 and notions of African urban identity', in U. Pillay, R. Tomlinson and O. Bass (eds), *Development and Dreams: The Urban Legacy of the 2010 Football World Cup*, Cape Town: HSRC Press, pp. 246–65.
Black, D. (2007), 'The symbolic politics of sport mega-events: 2010 in comparative perspective', *Politikon*, **34** (3), 261–76.
Cape Town (2006), '2010 FIFA World Cup™ Cape Town & Western Cape Business Plan', 31 October.
Chalkley, B. and S. Essex (1999), 'Urban development through hosting international events: a history of the Olympic Games', *Planning Perspectives*, **14** (4), 369–94.
Close, P. (2010), 'Olympiads as mega-events and the pace of globalization: Beijing 2008 in context', *International Journal of the History of Sport*, **27** (16–18), 2976–3007.
Coaffee, J. (2007), 'Urban regeneration and renewal', in J.R. Gold and M. Gold (eds), *Olympic Cities: City Agendas, Planning, and the World Games, 1896–2012*, London: Routledge, pp. 150–62.
Coaffee. J. and L. Johnston (2007), 'Accommodating the spectacle', in J.R. Gold and M. Gold (eds), *Olympic Cities: City Agendas, Planning, and the World Games, 1896–2012*, London: Routledge, pp. 138–49.
Coates, D. (2010), 'World Cup economics: what Americans need to know about a US World Cup bid', available at: http://www.umbc.edu/economics/wpapers/wp_10_121.pdf (accessed 28 May 2011).
COHRE (2007), 'Fair Play for Housing Rights: Opportunities for the Olympic Movement and Others. Mega-Events, Olympic Games and Housing Rights', Centre on Housing Rights and Evictions (COHRE), Geneva, available at: http://www.cohre.org/sites/default/files/fair_play_for_housing_rights_2007_0.pdf (accessed 28 May 2011).
Cornelissen, S. (2010), 'The geopolitics of global aspiration: sport mega-events and emerging powers', *International Journal of the History of Sport*, **27** (16–18), 3008–25.
Curi, M., J. Knijnik and G. Mascarenhas (2011), 'The Pan American Games in Rio de Janeiro 2007: consequences of a sport mega-event on a BRIC country', *International Review for the Sociology of Sport*, **46** (2), 140–56.

Fainstein, S. (2010), *The Just City*, Ithaca, NY: Cornell University Press.

Greene, S.J. (2003), 'Note: Staged cities: mega-events, slum clearance, and global capital', *Yale Human Rights and Development Law Journal*, **6**, 161–87.

Hammett, D. (2011), 'British media representations of South Africa and the 2010 FIFA World Cup', *South African Geographical Journal*, **93** (1), 63–74.

Harris, N. (2010), 'World Cup final "will vie for record of second most-watched event in human history"', *sportingintelligence*, 10 June, available at: http://www.sportingintelli gence.com/2010/06/10/world-cup-final-will-vie-for-record-of-second-most-watched-event-in-human-history-100605/ (accessed 28 May 2011).

Horne, J. and W. Manzreiter (2006), 'An introduction to the sociology of sports mega-events', in J. Horne and W. Manzreiter (eds), *Sports Mega-Events: Social Scientific Analyses of a Global Phenomenon*, New York Blackwell/Sociological Review, pp. 1–24.

International Olympic Committee (IOC) (2010), 'Factsheet: Legacies of the Games', Update January, IOC, Lausanne, available at: http://www.olympic.org/Documents/Reference_ documents_Factsheets/Legacy.pdf.

Jinxia, D. (2010), 'The Beijing Games, national identity and modernization in China', *International Journal of the History of Sport*, **27** (16), 2798–820.

Jinxia, D. and J.A. Mangan (2008), 'Beijing Olympics legacies: certain intentions and certain and uncertain outcomes', *International Journal of the History of Sport*, **25** (14), 2019–40.

KickOff.com (2008), 'Blatter blasts Bafana', 15 September, available at: http://www.kickoff. com/news/4548/blatter-blasts-bafana.php (accessed 28 May 2011).

Lee, C. and T. Taylor (2005), 'Critical reflections on the economic impact assessment of a mega-event: the case of 2002 FIFA World Cup', *Tourism Management*, **26** (4), 595–603.

London2012 (2011a), 'Legacy', available at: http://www.london2012.com/about-us/the-pe ople-delivering-the-games/the-olympic-delivery-authority/oda-priority-themes/legacy.php (accessed 28 May 2011).

London2012 (2011b), 'Olympic Park Legacy Company', available at: http://www.london2012. com/about-us/the-people-delivering-the-games/stakeholders/olympic-park-legacy-company. php (accessed 28 May 2011).

London2012 (2011c), 'Olympic heritage', available at: http://www.london2012.com/games/ games-heritage/olympic-heritage.php (accessed 28 May 2011).

MacAloon, J.J. (2008), '"Legacy" as managerial/magical discourse in contemporary Olympic affairs', *International Journal of the History of Sport*, **25** (14), 2060–71.

Mackay, D. (2009), 'Lula: An Olympics would mean more to Brazil than the US', Inside the Game, 30 April, available at: http://www.insidethegames.com/show-news.php?id=5588 (accessed 28 May 2011).

Maidment, P. (2005), 'China's Cracking Cricket', *Forbes.com*, 10 March, available at: http:// www.forbes.com/2005/09/30/china-india-cricket_cx_pm_1003chinacricket.html (accessed 28 May 2011).

Majavu, A. (2011), 'Basic services needed more than Games', Times Alive, 26 May, available at: http://www.timeslive.co.za/sport/other/article1088086.ece/Basic-services-needed-more-than-Games (accessed 28 May 2011).

Marks, V. (2011), 'India vs Pakistan: ultimate cricket derby brings two countries to a stand-still', *Guardian*, 30 March, available at: http://www.guardian.co.uk/sport/2011/mar/30/ india-pakistan-ultimate-cricket-derby (accessed 28 May 2011).

Monclus, F.-J. (2007), 'Barcelona 1992', in J.R. Gold and M. Gold (eds), *Olympic Cities: City Agendas, Planning, and the World Games, 1896–2012*, London: Routledge, pp. 218–36.

Motlanthe, K. (2010), Address by Deputy President Kgalema Motlanthe at the post-2010 media briefing, South Africa House, London, 15 September, South African Government Information, available at: http://www.info.gov.za/speech/DynamicAction?pageid=461&si d=12986&tid=18459 (accessed 28 May 2011).

Neogy, A. and A. Anishchuk (2011), 'BRICS demand global monetary shake-up, greater influence', *Reuters*, 14 April, available at: http://www.reuters.com/article/2011/04/14/us-brics-idUSTRE73D18H20110414 (accessed 28 May 2011).

Osborne, A. and J. Kirkup (2008), 'Tessa Jowell: Britain would not have bid for 2012 Olympics if we knew about recession', *The Telegraph*, 13 November, available at: http: //www.telegraph.co.uk/sport/othersports/olympics/london2012/3449960/Tessa-Jowell-Britain -would-not-have-bid-for-2012-Olympics-if-we-knew-about-recession.html (accessed 28 May 2011).

Pillay, U. and O. Bass (2009), 'Mega-events as a response to poverty reduction: the 2010 World Cup and urban development', in U. Pillay, R. Tomlinson and O. Bass (eds), *Development and Dreams: The Urban Legacy of the 2010 Football World Cup*, Cape Town: HSRC Press, pp. 76–95.

Porter, L. (2009), 'Planning displacement: the real legacy of major sporting events', *Planning Theory & Practice*, **10** (3), 395–418.

Qatar Information Exchange (2006–2010), 'Population Structure', available at: http://www. qix.gov.qa/portal/page/portal/qix/subject_area?subject_area=177 (accessed 28 May 2011).

Roberts, D. and O. Bass (forthcoming, 2012), 'The World Cup geography of Durban: what will endure?', in P. Alegi and C. Bolsmann (eds), *Africa's World Cup: Critical Reflections on Play, Patriotism, Spectatorship, and Urban Space*, Ann Arbor, MI: University of Michigan Press.

Roche, M. (2000), *Mega-Events and Modernity: Olympics and Expos in the Growth of Global Culture*, London: Routledge.

'Sanya Declaration on BRICS, 13 April 2011' (2011), available at: http://www.dirco.gov.za/ docs/2011/brics0415.html (accessed 28 May 2011).

Seekings, J. and N. Nattrass (2005), *Class, Race and Inequality in South Africa*, Scottsville: University of Kwazulu-Natal Press.

Shirk, S. (2008), *China: Fragile Superpower*, Oxford: Oxford University Press.

Syed, N.A. (2010), 'The effect of Beijing 2008 on China's image in the United States: a study of US media and polls', *International Journal of the History of Sport*, **27** (16–18), 2863–92.

Tomlinson, R. (2009), 'Anticipating 2011', in U. Pillay, R. Tomlinson and O. Bass (eds), *Development and Dreams: The Urban Legacy of the 2010 Football World Cup*, Cape Town: HSRC Press, pp. 96–113.

Tomlinson, R. (2010), 'Whose accolades? An alternative perspective on motivations for hosting the Olympics', *Urban Forum*, **21** (2), 139–52.

Tomlinson, R., O. Bass and T. Bassett (2011), 'Before and after the vuvuzela: identity, image and mega-events in South Africa, China and Brazil', *South African Geographical Journal*, **93** (1), 38–48.

Tomlinson, R., O. Bass and U. Pillay (2009), 'Introduction', in U. Pillay, R. Tomlinson and O. Bass (eds), *Development and Dreams: The Urban Legacy of the 2010 Football World Cup*, Cape Town: HSRC Press, pp. 3–17.

Wikipedia (2011) 'Qatar 2022 FIFA World Cup bid', available at: http://en.wikipedia.org/ wiki/Qatar_2022_FIFA_World_Cup_bid (accessed 28 May 2011).

Winter, B. (2011), 'Special Report: Brazil's Olympic push isn't winning any medals', *Reuters*, 27 March, available at: http://www.reuters.com/article/2011/03/27/us-brazil-infrastructure-idUSTRE72Q18820110327 (accessed 28 May 2011).

Xu, X. (2006), 'Modernizing China in the Olympic spotlight: China's national identity and the 2008 Beijing Olympiad', in J. Horne and W. Manzreiter (eds), *Sports Mega-events: Social Scientific Analyses of a Global Phenomenon*, New York: Blackwell, pp. 90–107.

Zimbalist, A. (2010), 'Is it worth it?', *Finance and Development*, March, 8–11.

19 Mega events and sports institutional development: the impact of the World Cup on football academies in Africa

Jeroen Schokkaert, Johan F. M. Swinnen and Thijs Vandemoortele

1 INTRODUCTION

Mega events such as the Olympic Games (organized by the International Olympic Committee – IOC) and the World Cup (organized by the Fédération Internationale de Football Association – FIFA) require substantial investments in venues and other infrastructure improvements. In order to legitimize the use of public funds to organize these mega events, it is common practice to carry out *ex ante* economic impact studies which, in retrospect, often exaggerate the economic benefits of hosting these mega events (Matheson, 2006). *Ex post* academic analyses are in general marked by strong skepticism, even pointing at negative economic impacts of hosting mega events (see, for example, Baade and Matheson, 2002). Moreover, even when the hosting of mega events generates a beneficial short-term economic impact, this does not necessarily guarantee a positive economic legacy in the long run (Preuss, 2007a).

Over the last years there has been an increase in academic studies that analyze this potential long-term impact of hosting mega events on economic performance. This impact may come about through different channels. For example, Jasmand and Maennig (2008) argue that host cities or countries may experience a valuable 'image' effect which has the potential to increase tourism and investment in the long run. According to Brückner and Pappa (2011), increasing investments in infrastructure and facilities may enhance overall production conditions and hence increase income over a longer time period. Furthermore, the additional international (media) exposure from hosting mega events may provide potential investors with more information, which potentially decreases uncertainty and generates larger international trade flows (Billings and Holladay, 2011). In turn, these increasing trade flows may have a positive impact on economic growth (see, for example, Frankel and Romer, 1999; Barro, 2000).

In general, academic studies on the long-term impact of hosting mega events on economic performance provide mixed evidence about the existence and direction of the effect. For example, several studies provide evidence for positive long-term effects of hosting the Olympic Games on economic performance, both through direct (gross domestic product (GDP) growth, see, for example, Brückner and Pappa, 2011) and indirect measures (for example, trade flows, see, for examle, Rose and Spiegel, 2009, 2011; Song, 2010).[1] However, as Sterken (2006) recognizes, studies on the economic impact of hosting mega events are prone to suffer from endogeneity problems.[2] Candidate cities or countries are in general different from non-candidate cities or countries across several characteristics that influence their ability to host and benefit from the organization of mega events. Studies that correctly account for this selection bias often do not find evidence for a long-term effect of hosting mega events on a country's economic performance (Sterken, 2010; Bayar and Schaur, 2011; Billings and Holladay, 2011). Table 19.1 provides a summary of the studies investigating long-term and nation-wide economic performance effects of hosting the Olympic Games and the World Cup, the two largest international mega events in sports (Fourie and Santana-Gallego, 2011).

Besides hosting mega events, also winning or excelling at mega events could potentially affect economic performance. The academic literature highlights contradictory effects. On the one hand, winning or excelling at mega events may stimulate labor productivity of the winning team's fans, increasing their wage bill and income (Coates and Humphreys, 2002). On the other hand, festivities associated with winning or excelling at mega events might lead to absenteeism by the winning team's fans and/or to violence by the losing team's fans, affecting labor productivity in a negative way (Matheson and Baade, 2005).

In contrast to the relationship between hosting mega events and economic performance, few studies have investigated the potential effects of winning or excelling at mega events on economic performance. In terms of short-run effects, only the economic impact of winning the Super Bowl, the championship game of the National Football League (NFL),[3] has been examined. All studies show that the city winning the Super Bowl experiences a significant increase in real per capita personal income (Coates and Humphreys, 2002; Matheson, 2005; Davis and End, 2010). To the best of our knowledge, there exists only one study on the long-term economic effects of winning or excelling at mega events. Using an instrumental variables approach, Bayar and Schaur (2011) come to the surprising conclusion that winning the World Cup has a positive and significant effect on that country's exports. The authors attribute this result to the existence of

Table 19.1 Literature on long-term and nation-wide economic impacts of hosting mega events

Author(s)	Event	Observation period	Variable of interest	Impact
Sterken (2006)	Summer Olympic Games	1964–1998	Real GDP per capita growth	Positive/none
Sterken (2006)	World Cup	1964–1998	Real GDP per capita growth	Negative/none
Sterken (2010)	Summer Olympic Games	1960–2008	Real GDP per capita growth	Positive
Sterken (2010)	Winter Olympic Games	1960–2008	Real GDP per capita growth	Negative/none
Sterken (2010)	World Cup	1960–2008	Real GDP per capita growth	Negative/none
Brückner and Pappa (2011)	Olympic Games	1950–2006	Real GDP per capita growth	Positive
Brückner and Pappa (2011)	World Cup	1950–2006	Real GDP per capita growth	Negative/none
Billings and Holladay (2011)	Summer Olympic Games	1950–2005	Real GDP per capita	None
Rose and Spiegel (2011)	Summer Olympic Games	1950–2006	Real bilateral exports	Positive
Rose and Spiegel (2011)	World Cup	1950–2006	Real bilateral exports	Positive
Song (2010)	Summer Olympic Games	1950–2006	Real bilateral exports	Positive
Rose and Spiegel (2009)	Winter Olympic Games	1950–2006	Real bilateral exports	None
Rose and Spiegel (2009)	Olympic Games	1950–2006	Real bilateral exports	Positive
Billings and Holladay (2011)	Summer Olympic Games	1950–2005	Trade openness	None
Bayar and Schaur (2011)	World Cup	1950–2006	Real bilateral exports	None

Note: (i) Olympic Games refer to a combined effect of the Winter Olympic Games and the Summer Olympic Games. (ii) Trade openness is defined as the sum of exports and imports as a fraction of total GDP.

a visibility effect on trade: winners of mega events do not incur the costs or infrastructural benefits of hosting but only attract (considerable) visibility.

As this review illustrates, there exists a large literature on the relationship between *nation-wide* impacts and institutional development. However, the academic literature has largely overlooked the link between mega events and sports institutional development at the *local* level (Gratton et al., 2005; Alegi, 2007). Development of local sports institutions is particularly important in developing countries where the sports sector is characterized by financial shortcomings, low participation and a lack of sports facilities (Andreff, 2006).

Football is an interesting sport to study the impact of mega events on the local development of sports institutions in developing countries since the game of football is widespread in Africa (Alegi, 2010). Moreover, African national teams have performed increasingly well at World Cup tournaments in the past decades, with Cameroon, Senegal and Ghana reaching the quarter finals in, respectively, the 1990, 2002 and 2010 editions. Furthermore, in 2010, South Africa was the first African nation to host the World Cup.

The objective of this chapter is to investigate the impact of hosting and excelling at the World Cup on the development of a specific type of local sports institution, namely football academies, which are broadly defined as 'facilities or coaching programs designed to produce football talent' (Darby et al., 2007). For this purpose we analyze case studies on two countries, namely South Africa and Senegal. South Africa was selected as a case study because in 2010, it was the first (and so far only) African country to host the World Cup.[4] Senegal was selected as a case study of an African country that excelled at the World Cup because its national team performed exceptionally well at the 2002 World Cup in Japan and South Korea. Having beaten their former colonial power and defending World Cup champion France in a historical opening game, Senegal eventually reached the quarter finals.

Information on South African and Senegalese football academies was gathered during extensive interviews with directors, coaches and other officials of a variety of football academies in South Africa and Senegal. The South African data were gathered during semi-structured qualitative interviews in September 2010 in the region of Cape Town and Johannesburg. The Senegalese data were gathered during semi-structured qualitative interviews in July–August 2007 in the region of Dakar. Additional information was gathered during interviews with the directors and administrations of the football associations.

Our analysis of various football academies in these countries reveals several interesting findings concerning the effects of hosting and excelling at the World Cup on the development of football academies in South

Africa and Senegal. In South Africa, increased investments in football academies by private companies and FIFA, in combination with domestic spillovers, indicate that organizing the World Cup may have a positive impact on the development of football academies. Nevertheless, a disproportionate concentration of government expenditures on football infrastructure for the World Cup itself rather than on local football institutions and academies tends to increase the inequality between professional football and grassroots football. This could potentially harm the development of South African football in the longer run.

In Senegal, the vast increase in the number of football academies, initially mainly in the less professional sphere but later to some extent also in the more professional sphere, indicates that Senegal's exceptional performance at the 2002 World Cup increased investments in local football institutions. However, our analysis shows that an excellent World Cup performance may also induce governments in developing countries to concentrate on promoting the national team to the detriment of investments in football development at the local level.

We illustrate that there are positive as well as negative impacts from South Africa's hosting of the 2010 World Cup and Senegal's excellent performance at the 2002 World Cup on these countries' development of football institutions at the local level. Hence, there is inconclusive evidence with regard to the final impact of hosting or excelling at the World Cup on local football institutions. While our analysis is the first to document such impacts based on semi-structured qualitative interviews with officials from local football institutions, we do realize that this evidence is limited and should be interpreted carefully.

The remainder of this chapter is organized as follows. Section 2 discusses how a country's hosting or excelling at a mega event may relate to the development of local sports institutions such as football academies. Sections 3 and 4 summarize how, respectively, hosting and excelling at the World Cup was expected to affect the development of local football institutions and academies in South Africa and Senegal, and present the observed impacts on football academies from our fieldwork in South Africa and Senegal. Section 5 presents a more detailed discussion and concludes.

2   MEGA EVENTS AND SPORTS INSTITUTIONAL DEVELOPMENT

As illustrated in the introduction, long-term impacts of hosting or excelling at mega events on a country's economic performance may occur through several channels. One potential channel through which these economic effects may materialize is through nation-wide and local institutional development.[5]

For example, when hosting a mega event, countries undertake substantial infrastructure investments. Studies have shown that if these mainly consist of investments in general economic infrastructure – for example, transportation infrastructure instead of specialized sports facilities – the economic impact of hosting that mega event is more likely to be positive (Matheson and Baade, 2004; Brückner and Pappa, 2011). One could argue that these infrastructure improvements would probably also be undertaken in absence of the mega event. However, as Zimbalist (2010) argues, these much-needed investments in infrastructure could be delayed for (multiple) years in developing countries as a consequence of rigid public policy. Hence, the hosting of a mega event may at least speed up developing countries' investments in public infrastructure and institutions.

The academic literature on mega events has mostly focused on nation-wide institutional development, while it has largely overlooked the link between mega events and (sports) institutional development at the local level (Gratton et al., 2005; Alegi, 2007). One exception to this are the studies on the economic impact of local sports facilities such as large sports stadiums and arenas. Most of these studies do not find an effect of such sports facilities on local economic development (Siegfried and Zimbalist, 2000; Coates, 2007).

Another example of a local sports institution are football academies, which can be broadly defined as 'facilities or coaching programs designed to produce football talent' (Darby et al., 2007). Football academies exist both in developed and developing countries, where in the latter countries football academies have been established in both the formal and informal economy.[6] In general, most academies belonging to the formal sector adopt a professional approach to football training and offer additional services to their trainees. For example, on top of professional football training and decent sports facilities, these football academies frequently provide official academic tuition, requisite football equipment, medical support and physiotherapy, and so on. This contrasts with academies belonging to the informal sector, which are established on an ad hoc basis, have poorly qualified staff and facilities and do not offer additional services such as academic education.

Similarly to studies on the economic impact of professional sports stadiums, some studies have suggested that there is no or even a negative impact of football academies on the development of football and the (local) economy (see, for example, Darby et al., 2007).[7] For example, similar to general concerns that international migration drains developing countries of their human capital (that is, the so-called 'brain drain'), the growing migration of football players, facilitated by the emergence of football academies, has been accused of causing a 'muscle drain' in developing countries by depriving them of their most talented players to the benefit of rich countries' leagues (see, for example, Andreff, 2004; Darby, 2007a, 2007b). However, football academies may have a non-negligible positive impact on the local economy through several channels. For example, their establishment may generate local employment opportunities, stimulate community development (of football) and increase the provision of education to football players. In the longer run, successful football academy graduates may reinvest in their local economy by sending remittances to their families, and/or by financing football projects either during or after their professional football career (Darby et al., 2007; Swinnen and Vandemoortele, 2009).[8] Ad hoc evidence does seem to confirm this, although so far no data are available on these potentially positive economic effects on the local economy, rendering it impossible to assess their magnitude.

Drawing on two specific case studies, the following sections investigate the impact of hosting or excelling at a mega event on local sports institutions, such as football academies, in developing countries.

3   THE IMPACT ON LOCAL FOOTBALL INSTITUTIONS OF HOSTING THE WORLD CUP: THE CASE OF SOUTH AFRICA

In 2010, South Africa was the first African nation to host the World Cup, thus providing a good case study to illustrate the impact of hosting a mega event on football academies in a developing country. South Africa did not perform well at the 2010 World Cup. Being directly qualified as the host country, Bafana Bafana, South Africa's national team, was immediately eliminated in the group stages. Hence, we may reasonably exclude the possibility that the impacts on local football institutions discussed below would be due to excelling at – instead of hosting – the World Cup. This section discusses how hosting the 2010 World Cup was expected to impact the development of local football institutions and academies in South Africa and describes a set of South African football academies that have been affected by the hosting of the 2010 World Cup.

Expectations

Hosting the World Cup increases the hosting country's citizens' affiliation to sports because of factors such as increasing enthusiasm, strengthened networks between politicians and local football federations, and the improvement of a hosting country's image (Preuss, 2007b). For example, in both the US and Germany, the supply of football players increased substantially after organizing, respectively, the 1994 and 2006 World Cup (Giulianotti and Robertson, 2004; Preuss, 2007b). These observations generated expectations that the hosting of the 2010 World Cup would boost the supply of football players in South Africa. Moreover, because there are fewer substitution possibilities for leisure activities in South Africa due to its lower economic development than, for example, the US or Germany (Hoffmann et al., 2002), it was expected that this increase in the inflow of additional football players would be larger in South Africa.

It was anticipated that this expected increase in the supply of football players triggered by the hosting of the 2010 World Cup would generate additional investments in local South African football institutions by different actors, both private and public.

First, the 2010 World Cup was expected to attract additional investments in South African football academies by private companies and individuals. For example, the French ex-international Patrick Vieira expressed his intentions to build on the momentum created by the 2010 World Cup to establish a football academy in South Africa (Morgan, 2007). Another example is the club Thanda Royal Zulu FC, which competes in South Africa's Premier Soccer League (PSL)[9] and is owned by a consortium of Swedish investors. In 2008, the club announced the establishment of a new football academy in addition to their existing Thanda Star Academy. Dan Olofsson, an important partner of the Thanda Star Academy, argued that the 2010 World Cup would drive the development of football in South Africa and in particular their new football academy (Thanda Royal Zulu FC, 2008).

Second, it was expected that the hosting of the 2010 World Cup would spur government expenditure on football institutions and infrastructure. For example, the additional government investment in stadium infrastructure was expected to benefit the development of professional football in South Africa because of improved spectators' comfort and subsequent increased attendance (Alegi, 2007). However, at the same time it was also expected that these stadium subsidies would not benefit the development of football at the local community level. Hence, the announcement that South Africa would host the 2010 World Cup raised expectations that the inequality between elite professional football clubs and local grassroots football clubs and/or academies in South Africa would increase (Kunene, 2006; Alegi, 2007).

Third, FIFA's bid requirements and its communications following the announcement of South Africa as host of the 2010 World Cup created additional expectations about investments in football institutions at the local level in South Africa. For example, each World Cup bidding country is supposed to address how their hosting of the World Cup would benefit football (institutions) at the local level (Guest, 2010b).[10] Another example is that FIFA promoted investments in local football development programs more extensively in the spirit of the first World Cup hosted by an African country (FIFA, 2007).[11] This is well illustrated by the '20 Centers for 2010' campaign, FIFA's official campaign of the 2010 World Cup, which was founded in 2007 in cooperation with non-governmental organizations active in the field of football development. This campaign promised to establish 20 Football for Hope Centers in Africa over the 2007–12 period with the aim of promoting the long-term development of football, healthcare and educational facilities in disadvantaged communities (ibid.).

Observations

In this subsection, we describe a set of South African football academies from the region of Johannesburg and Cape Town of which the foundation and/or performance was influenced by the hosting of the 2010 World Cup.

The Diambars Institute

A professional South African football academy in Johannesburg, the Diambars Institute, is an expansion of the Diambars Institute in Senegal, which was established in 2003. The Diambars Institute is supported by a large group of committed partners. Aside from the involvement of Saer Seck, the vice-president of the Fédération Sénégalaise de Football (FSF), Patrick Vieira and Bernard Lama, two retired French internationals, and Jimmy Adjovi-Boco, a retired Beninese international, the Diambars Institute also attracts sponsorships from large (sports) companies such as Adidas.

All players are resident pupils and are between 13 and 18 years old. The Diambars Institute applies a rotational system such that each year around 20 players graduate and are replaced by new freshmen. Diambars South Africa was formally established in January 2010 with a first intake of 20 players.

Due to a delay in acquiring authorization to set up its own educational and sports infrastructure, the football academy temporarily collaborates with a public school in Boksburg, a city near Johannesburg. All players are currently accommodated at the public school in Boksburg which is also endowed with football training facilities. Academy trainees follow regular classes with the other (non-Diambars) students.

Trainees are recruited only after a rigorous selection procedure and are required to meet criteria of academic proficiency, football talent, and a particular demographic and geographic representation. Admission to the academy is free. The institute's financial sustainability is ensured by revenues from renting out the academy's facilities for activities such as football camps and corporate programs; by FIFA's training compensation; and by fundraising operations.

According to the director of Diambars South Africa, the decision to invest in South Africa was driven by its hosting of the 2010 World Cup and by the availability of a large pool of talented football players in the townships, the (often) poor and underdeveloped urban living areas in South Africa.

Cape United Soccer School of Excellence

Another recently established football academy is the Cape United Soccer School of Excellence (CUSSE) in Cape Town. It was founded in 2009 by the English businessman Mike Steptoe and the former South African football player, coach and manager Colin Gie.

CUSSE was able to acquire its facilities through funds raised with private investors and (former) professional football players such as the English ex-international Ian Wright. CUSSE owns a residential school, where players stay between the age of 15 and 18 years old.

In contrast with the Diambars Institute, CUSSE offers only an unofficial and specific academic curriculum with English and mathematics as core subjects. The main priority of CUSSE is developing football skills of the players.

Currently 32 trainees are registered with the academy, mainly from the Western and Eastern Cape provinces. There are also some players from some other African countries. Selection of the trainees is based on open trials, organized during academic holidays. No registration fee is charged. Concentrating their efforts on establishing transfer networks with European clubs, CUSSE expects considerable revenues from transfer fees of some of their graduates in the near future.

Besides factors such as the good climate, lower investment costs and the availability of a large pool of talent in the townships, the fact that Cape Town would act as a World Cup host city was a decisive factor to invest in South Africa.

The final two South African football academies are examples of less professional football academies. In contrast to the Diambars Institute and CUSSE, the two academies discussed here were established earlier, but benefited from additional investments around the time of South Africa's hosting of the 2010 World Cup.

Dona's Mates Football Development Academy
Located in Orange Farm near Johannesburg, the Dona's Mates Football
Development Academy was established in 1999 by four businessmen.[12]
One of the founders, James Shabangu, is affiliated to the South African
Football Association (SAFA).

The academy provides football training after regular school. Admission
to the academy is free. All players are non-residents and originate from
Orange Farm and surrounding areas. There is no selection procedure and
a total of around 120 players from the age of 6 are registered. There is no
specific age from which players are obliged to leave the academy.

Dona's Mates Football Development Academy has been successful in
transferring one player to the PSL and a few other players to lower-rated
South African clubs and to other, more professional football academies.

The academy lacks decent training fields, but in the spirit of the 2010
World Cup, the project 'Youth Development through Football' (see
further) assisted in acquiring the academy's football facilities and financed
the set-up of a small, surrounded football field.

African Brothers Football Academy
Founded in 2001 in Cape Town, the African Brothers Football Academy
was set up by a South African businessman, Craig Hepburn. The establishment of the football academy was made possible through funds raised
with private investors.

Football training is provided after school but no other services such
as academic education are offered. Trainees are not subject to any trial
to enroll in the academy. A total of around 270 players from the age of 3
until 19 are registered. A monthly contribution of 100 ZAR (about €11)
is charged. Besides revenues from registration fees, daily activities are
financed by renting out the football field and by private sponsorship.

The football academy benefitted from South Africa's hosting of the
2010 World Cup because the company that laid the turf on the new Green
Point Stadium in Cape Town also financed the surfaces for the football
fields of the academy.

4   THE IMPACT OF EXCELLING AT THE WORLD CUP ON LOCAL FOOTBALL INSTITUTIONS: THE CASE OF SENEGAL

Our second case study illustrates the impact of excelling at a mega event
on football academies in a developing country. Senegal performed
exceptionally well at the 2002 World Cup. Having beaten their former

colonial power and defending World Cup champion France in a historical opening game, Senegal ultimately reached the quarter finals. Like the previous section, this section discusses how excelling at the World Cup was expected to affect the development of local football institutions and academies in Senegal and describes some Senegalese football academies that have been affected by the exceptional performance at the 2002 World Cup.

Expectations

In contrast to the somewhat expected event of hosting the World Cup,[13] Senegal's excellent performance at the 2002 World Cup represents a largely unexpected occurrence. As a consequence, no *ex ante* rumors were formed about its potential impact on the development of local football institutions.

However, five graduates of a Senegalese football academy belonging to the formal sector were part of the Senegalese national team that performed exceptionally at the 2002 World Cup (Alegi, 2010). This created the expectation that more formal football academies would have been established after the 2002 World Cup, either from private sector investments or from public sector investments.

Observations

In this subsection, several Senegalese football academies from the region of Dakar are discussed. Fieldwork revealed that academies belonging to the informal sector grew rapidly in Senegal in the wake of the national team's outstanding performance at the 2002 World Cup. According to the FSF, there are nearly 300 such football academies in the region of Dakar alone. Unfortunately, we were unable to structurally survey these informal football academies. In the following we provide information on some formal academies.

Collège Africain Sports-Études
One of the most important professional football academies in Dakar is the Collège Africain Sports-Études (CASE), a football training center that additionally provides basketball and tennis training. The center was established in 1992 as the Center Aldo Gentina by El Hadji Malick Sy, the current president of CASE and former Senegalese Minister of Tourism and former President of the FSF.

Initially, the academy consisted of a partnership between the Senegalese club ASC Jeanne d'Arc and the French club AS Monaco. In exchange for a substantial financial contribution, AS Monaco had the right to select the best players that graduated from the center. In the first decade, the center provided only football training. Since 2004, the center has added academic (secondary) education and other sports training. To emphasize this fundamental change in priorities, the center altered its name to CASE. According to the president, the reason for this turnaround and focus on academic education was that every child, whether he becomes a professional football player or not, needs a decent basic education. First, not all graduated trainees are able to start a professional football career. For these trainees, regular academic education is of foremost importance to successfully enter the regular labor market. Second, those pupils that do become professional football players also need an academic education that allows them to understand and negotiate their future football contracts, and to understand coaches' tactical explanations. Additionally, even professional football players may need to enter the regular labor market at the end of their football career.

Around the time of its priority switch, CASE lost its funding from AS Monaco after some management restructuring at the French club.[14] Due to the subsequent lack of funds, the center entered into some sponsorship deals with foreign and domestic corporations. Furthermore, the academy introduced substantial registration fees.[15] Every year around 30 pupils who lack financial means are selected on the basis of their football talent and offered a scholarship that exempts them from the registration fee. Other players are not subject to selection criteria for admission. In 2007, there were 175 students enrolled (12 to 20 years old). The trainees mainly originate from Dakar and its surroundings but some also from other regions in Senegal or even from other African countries.

Besides revenues from sponsors and registration fees, the transfers of some of their players also generate revenues. CASE has been a major source of talent for clubs overseas and for the Senegalese national team: five graduates were part of the Senegalese national team that reached the quarter finals at the 2002 World Cup (Alegi, 2010).

Kenza Mariste

In the spirit of Senegal's excellent performance at the 2002 World Cup, Kenza Mariste was established in 2005 by an African businessman, Djibril Traoré.[16] The academy does not provide any academic education but compels its pupils to show their monthly school reports.

Until the age of 15, trainees are not subject to any trial to enroll in the academy; older trainees are tested on their football talent before admission.[17] No registration fee is charged and the center has no strategic partnerships or other funds.[18] The academy has no capacity limit – all trainees are non-residents. In 2007, 160 trainees between the ages of 5 and 18 were enrolled, mainly from the Dakar region but also from other parts of Senegal and other African countries.

The academy has a small boarding school to temporarily accommodate those trainees who are accepted to perform trials with a foreign club. Transfers of players to foreign clubs are arranged through official agents.

Kenza Mariste not only operates in Dakar but also in two other, poorer regions in Senegal. In the longer term, the academy's ambition is to establish another set of football academies in other parts of Senegal.

5   DISCUSSION AND CONCLUSIONS

Our case studies yield some insights into whether the expectations concerning the World Cup's impact on football academies have been realized and whether there is a differential impact between hosting and excelling at the World Cup.

A crucial difference between hosting and excelling at a mega event is its anticipation by potential investors (both private and public). Excelling at a mega event – certainly in the case of Senegal in 2002 – is a largely unexpected occurrence. In contrast, it is announced several years in advance which country will be hosting the mega event. Hence, while both hosting and excelling at a mega event may create potential investment opportunities through the increased inflow of football players, they are potentially different with regard to how investors anticipate these occurrences and their related investment opportunities.

This difference in investors' expectations may have important consequences. As has been shown by Marion and Svensson (1984) in the case of large oil price changes, the fact whether an oil price change is expected or unexpected has serious consequences for firms to make adequate investments and to take advantage of these changes. Marion and Svensson demonstrate that, due to rigidities in the capital stocks of firms, their substitution possibilities and hence their opportunities to reap potential benefits (or avoid potential losses) are smaller with unexpected oil price changes than with expected ones. With expected changes, firms are able to anticipate by adjusting investments before the opportunity (or threat) presents itself.

Applied to the impact of mega events on investments in local sports institutions, an important difference may thus exist between how investors are able to capitalize on the additional supply of young football players triggered by a country's expected hosting versus unexpected excelling at a mega event.

In the case of the (anticipated) hosting of a mega event, investors have ample time to raise the necessary funding and to prepare an investment plan that allows them to benefit from the momentum created by the hosting of the mega event. An example in case is the Diambars Institute. Since it was already known in 2004 that the 2010 World Cup would be organized in South Africa, the institute – at that time based only in Senegal – had sufficient time to develop its investment plan for a division of their institute in South Africa. The South African division of the Diambars Institute was finally established in 2010, in time to benefit from the organization of the World Cup to draw in talented young football players. CUSSE serves as another example. Established in 2009, one year before the actual hosting of the World Cup, the fact that Cape Town would act as a World Cup host city was an important factor in the decision to invest in South Africa.

The window of opportunity is different for investing in local sports institutions of a country that excelled at a mega event. Since such an exceptional performance is usually unexpected, investors cannot anticipate that occasion which reduces the potential to capitalize on its momentum. This is for a large part due to capital constraints which are typically high in developing countries, and due to the time required to develop a sound investment plan and raise sufficient capital. As a consequence, those initiatives that are set up in the wake of an unexpected performance at a mega event are typically those that have relatively low capital requirements. An example is the extraordinary performance of the Senegalese national team at the 2002 World Cup. Our field surveys revealed that a huge number of football academies belonging to the informal sector were established in Senegal in the wake of the national team's outstanding performance at the 2002 World Cup. However, typical for these football academies is that they belong to the informal sector, that is, they were established on an ad hoc basis, have poorly qualified staff and facilities (if any at all) and offer no additional services such as an academic education – hence requiring only limited investments. Only recently has Senegal witnessed an increase in the number of football academies belonging to the formal sector where establishing a football academy requires larger investments (Ngan, 2010). This is in line with our argument that in developing countries it takes time to overcome capital constraints to establish a formal football academy. For example, officially launched in 2006, the Center Brésilien de Formation de Football au Sénégal (CBFFS) was created by an ex-Brazilian football player, Aldonilson de Barros Franco, after he had observed the skills and the passion of the Senegalese national football team at the 2002 World Cup (CBFFS, 2007). Moreover, our fieldwork revealed that the football academy Kenza Mariste was also established following Senegal's excellent performance at the 2002 World Cup.

In summary, both hosting and excelling at a mega event have been shown to trigger a surge in the supply of young talented football players. However, these occasions are different in the manner in which investors are able to capitalize on the investment opportunities created by this additional supply of talents. Hence, the impact of hosting versus excelling at a mega event on the development of local sports institutions (football academies) may be quite different, as illustrated by the examples of South Africa and Senegal. This difference between expected hosting and unexpected excelling at a mega event also interacts with the level of development of the hosting or excelling country. The less developed the hosting or excelling country, the more stringent are the credit constraints to invest in formal football academies. Since South Africa is more developed than Senegal,[19] this also contributes to the difference observed between South Africa and Senegal where the World Cup triggered the establishment of relatively more formal football academies in South Africa than in Senegal.

Besides the difference in anticipation by potential investors, a second difference between hosting and excelling at the World Cup relates to potential domestic spillover effects from organizing the World Cup on local football institutions. An example is the African Brothers Football Academy that benefitted from South Africa's hosting of the 2010 World Cup because the company that laid the turf on the new Green Point Stadium in Cape Town also paid for the surfaces for the fields of the academy. Such domestic spillover effects from organizing the World Cup on investments in local football institutions could contribute to the local game's development.

Additionally, organizing mega events such as the World Cup also creates the potential to generate foreign spillovers. Mega events such as the World Cup spur investments in football development projects with spillover effects to neighboring countries as well. The investments in Dona's Mates Football Development Academy serve as an example in this perspective. In the spirit of the 2010 World Cup in South Africa, the 'Youth Development through Football' project assisted in acquiring the academy's football facilities and financially supported the set-up of a small football field. This project is part of the 'South African–German Development Cooperation' between South Africa and Germany and is co-funded by the European Union. The project runs from 2007 until 2012 and is implemented in nine other African countries, the majority of them located in the neighborhood of South Africa, by the Deutsche Gesellschaft für Internationale Zusammenarbeit (GIZ) GmbH on behalf of the German government and the South African Department of Sport and Recreation.[20]

These observations seem to confirm the (positive) expectations about the impact of hosting the 2010 World Cup on investments in South African football academies. Yet, there was also the negative expectation that the 2010 World Cup would amplify the inequality between elite professional football clubs and local football academies and institutions. Guest (2010a) argues that hosting the 2010 World Cup induced a shift from government expenditure on development initiatives at the local level to spending on stadiums.[21] A closer observation of the data on government expenditure seems to confirm this conjecture. While around 8 billion ZAR (about €610 million) was budgeted on upgrading existing stadiums and building new ones, no more than 212 million ZAR (about €16 million) was budgeted on financing programs to stimulate the development of local football institutions (GCIS, 2008). This observation was also confirmed during our field research. The majority of officials from South African football academies highlighted the fact that World Cup revenues were primarily being invested in professional football rather than in local football institutions.

A similar shift in the focus of government expenditure seems to have taken place around the time of Senegal's excellent performance at the 2002 World Cup. Ralph (2006) argues that before and during the 2002 World Cup, Senegalese football officials mainly focused on funding and promoting the national team at the expense of investments in the development of sports institutions at the local level. However, in the first years after the 2002 World Cup, relatively little effort was made to develop the national football team further and few grassroots football academies were established (Ngan, 2010). Only recently have football academies and other football development projects been established in cooperation with the FSF.

With respect to FIFA's promised investments in local football institutions, skepticism among academics and non-academics is high that these positive expectations will not materialize. For example, the '20 Centers for 2010' campaign was followed by rumors that the Football for Hope Centers will eventually not be built (see, for example, Guest, 2010a). By now, centers have opened in South Africa, Mali, Kenya and Namibia, centers are under construction in Rwanda, Ghana and Lesotho, and the future locations of five others have been revealed (Browne, 2011; Geddes, 2011). Since the project does not end until 2012, it is difficult to draw more specific conclusions concerning the credibility of FIFA's promises, but it seems that the World Cup in South Africa has already generated beneficial spillovers for the development of local football institutions in other African countries. In addition, FIFA's World Cup-related investments also create domestic spillovers. After the 2010 World Cup, FIFA launched its '2010 FIFA World Cup Legacy Trust for South Africa'. This project supports a wide range of public benefit initiatives in areas such as football development (FIFA, 2010). Moreover, FIFA's investments in football development programs – equal to around €594 million or 22 percent of total FIFA expenses over the 2007–10 period – increased considerably due to the financial success of the 2010 World Cup in South Africa (FIFA, 2011).

Our analysis is the first to document the impact of hosting and excelling at a mega event on sports institutional development based on semi-structured qualitative interviews with officials from local football institutions, football academies in this case. However, we are aware of the fact that this evidence is limited and should be interpreted with caution. Nonetheless, we find that increased investments in football academies, together with spillover effects, indicate that hosting and excelling at the World Cup may have a positive impact on the development of local football institutions. However, a higher concentration of government expenditures on football infrastructure for the mega event at the expense of expenditures on local football institutions and academies tends to increase the inequality between professional football and grassroots football. This could undermine the development of South African football in the longer term.

NOTES

1. Other studies have examined the long-term effects of hosting mega events on different economic performance indicators such as employment. Examples are Brunet (1995), Baade and Matheson (2002), Madden (2002), Hotchkiss et al. (2003), Hagn and Maennig (2008), Jasmand and Maennig (2008), and Feddersen and Maennig (2010). In contrast to the studies discussed in the text, these analyses focus on regional instead of nation-wide effects. In general, these studies also provide mixed evidence about the existence and direction of the effect of hosting mega events on a region's employment.
2. For more information on the econometric treatment of measuring the economic impact of mega events, see Sterken (ch. 20 in this volume).
3. The NFL is the top league of professional American football in the United States.
4. Before the 2002 World Cup hosted by Japan and South Korea, FIFA applied a continental rotational host policy between Europe and America.
5. There exists a large literature on the relation between institutions and economic development. It has been shown that in general, more developed countries have better institutions (see, for example, North, 1990; Barro, 1999), and that at the same time better institutions also lead to higher economic development (see, for example, Acemoglu et al., 2002; Rodrik et al., 2004).
6. The labor economics literature distinguishes between employment in the regulated, formal economy and employment in the unregulated, informal economy (De Soto, 1989). The presence of an informal economy is a central characteristic of developing countries (Loayza, 1996).
7. Although Darby et al. (2007) do point at potentially positive impacts of formal football academies, the authors are in general skeptical about the objectives and implications of football academies in developing countries.

8. Additionally, a difference between sports facilities (for example, stadiums) and football academies is that stadiums are mostly financed through public subsidies, and hence involve (potentially high) opportunity costs. In contrast, field research documents that formal football academies in developing countries are often privately financed by (former) football players and/or (foreign) companies (Schokkaert et al., 2012).
9. The PSL is the trading name of the National Soccer League (NSL), which is currently composed of 16 clubs in the first tier of South African football (ABSA Premiership) and two leagues of eight clubs in the second tier (National First Division).
10. It should be clear though that this is not the main selection criterion in the bid process for the World Cup. For example, although the Belgium–Netherlands bid and the Japan bid were considered to offer the best programs with respect to the development of football (Guest, 2010b), these two bids ended third out of four candidates in the voting rounds for the 2018 and 2022 World Cup editions.
11. Examples of football development programs run by FIFA are Football for Hope, the GOAL Program, and the Financial Assistance Program (FAP).
12. In the meantime, two businessmen have withdrawn because of their financial problems.
13. For example, the announcement that South Africa was awarded the right to host the 2010 World Cup was made in 2004, six years before the actual hosting took place.
14. Unfortunately, it is unclear whether CASE's shift in priorities influenced AS Monaco's decision to withdraw, or vice versa.
15. Based on the information provided by CASE and our own calculations, the 2007 registration fee varied between 1,140,000 and 1,260,000 CFA francs per year (between 1,740 and 1,920 euros). The IMF estimates that the Senegalese per capita income was slightly lower than €700 per year in 2007 (IMF, 2007).
16. El-Hadji Diouf, a Senegalese former English Premier League player, is the godfather of Kenza Mariste.
17. The center makes this distinction because it believes that older pupils cannot be formed as easily as younger ones, and therefore should have a considerable football aptitude before being admitted.
18. However, a voluntary contribution is demanded from parents with sufficient financial means.
19. Per capita income in South Africa is more than seven times higher than per capita income in Senegal (IMF, 2010).
20. The GIZ GmbH is an organization that is globally active in the domain of international cooperation for sustainable development and international education.
21. Horne (2004) comes to the same conclusions with regard to the 2002 World Cup hosted by Japan and South Korea.

REFERENCES

Acemoglu, D., S. Johnson and J.A. Robinson (2002), 'Reversal of fortune: geography and institutions in the making of the modern world income distribution', *Quarterly Journal of Economics*, **117** (4), 1231–94.

Alegi, P. (2007), 'The political economy of mega-stadiums and the underdevelopment of grassroots football in South Africa', *Politikon*, **34** (3), 315–31.

Alegi, P. (2010), *African Soccerscapes: How a Continent Changed the World's Game*, Columbus, OH: Ohio University Press.

Andreff, W. (2004), 'The taxation of player moves from developing countries', in R. Fort and J. Fizel (eds), *International Sports Economic Comparisons*, Westport, CT and London: Praeger, pp. 87–103.

Andreff, W. (2006), 'Sport in developing countries', in W. Andreff and S. Szymanski (eds), *Handbook on the Economics of Sport*, Cheltenham, UK and Northampton, MA, USA: Edward Elgar, pp. 308–15.

Baade, R.A. and V.A. Matheson (2002), 'Bidding for the Olympics: fool's gold?', in C.P. Barros, M. Ibrahimo and S. Szymanski (eds), *Transatlantic Sport: The Comparative Economics of North American and European Sport*, Cheltenham, UK and Northampton, MA, USA: Edward Elgar pp. 127–51.

Barro, R.J. (1999), 'Determinants of democracy', *Journal of Political Economy*, **107** (6), 158–83.

Barro, R.J. (2000), 'Inequality and growth in a panel of countries', *Journal of Economic Growth*, **5** (1), 5–32.

Bayar, O. and G. Schaur (2011), 'The impact of visibility on trade: evidence from the World Cup', Working Paper, Schroeder Family School of Business Administration, Evansville, IN.

Billings, S.B. and S. Holladay (2011), 'Should cities go for the Gold? The long-term impacts of hosting the Olympics', *Economic Inquiry*, forthcoming.

Browne, T. (2011), '12th Football for Hope Center revealed', available at: http://www.sportanddev.org (accessed 13 May 2011).

Brückner, M. and E. Pappa, (2011), 'For an olive wreath? Olympic Games and anticipation effects in macroeconomics', Research Paper No. 18, University of Adelaide School of Economics, Adelaide.

Brunet, F. (1995), 'The economic impact of the Barcelona Olympic Games, 1986–2004', Working Paper No. 84, Center d'Estudis Olímpics, Barcelona.

Center Brésilien de Formation de Football au Sénégal, (CBFFS) (2007), available at: http://cbffs.blogspot.com (accessed 20 May 2011).

Coates, D. (2007), 'Stadiums and arenas: economic development or economic redistribution?', *Contemporary Economic Policy*, **25** (4), 565–77.

Coates, D. and B.R. Humphreys (2002), 'The economic impact of postseason play in professional sports', *Journal of Sports Economics*, **3** (3), 291–9.

Darby, P. (2007a), 'African football labour migration to Portugal: colonial and neo-colonial resource', *Soccer & Society*, **8** (4), 495–509.

Darby, P. (2007b), 'Out of Africa: the exodus of African football talent to Europe', *Working USA: The Journal of Labour and Society*, **10** (4), 443–56.

Darby, P., G. Akindes and M. Kirwin (2007), 'Football academies and the migration of African football labor to Europe', *Journal of Sport & Social Issues*, **31** (2), 143–61.

Davis, M.C. and C.M. End (2010), 'A winning proposition: the economic impact of successful national football league franchises', *Economic Inquiry*, **48** (1), 39–50.

De Soto, H. (1989), *The Other Path: The Invisible Revolution in the Third World*, New York: Harper & Row.

Feddersen, A. and W. Maennig (2010), 'Mega-events and sectoral employment: the case of the 1996 Olympic Games', Contemporary Economic Discussions No. 35, Faculty of Economics and Social Sciences, Hamburg.

FIFA (2007), '20 Centers for 2010', article available at http://www.fifa.com (accessed 20 April 2011).

FIFA (2010), 'FIFA launches 2010 FIFA World Cup Legacy Trust for South Africa', available at: http://www.fifa.com (accessed 20 April 2011).

FIFA (2011), *FIFA Financial Report 2010*, Zurich: FIFA.

Fourie, J. and M. Santana-Gallego (2011), 'The impact of mega-sport events on tourist arrivals', *Tourism Management*, **32** (6), 1364–70.

Frankel, J.A. and D. Romer (1999), 'Does trade cause growth?', *American Economic Review*, **89** (3), 379–99.

Geddes, M. (2011), 'Three more Football for Hope Centers begin construction', available at: http://www.sportanddev.org 21 (accessed 7 April 2011).

Giulianotti, R. and R. Robertson (2004), 'The globalization of football: a study in the glocalization of the "serious life"', *British Journal of Sociology*, **55** (4), 545–68.

Government Communication and Information System (GCIS) (2008), *2010 FIFA World Cup South Africa*, Pretoria: GCIS.

Gratton, C., S. Shibli and R. Coleman (2005), 'Sport and economic regeneration in cities', *Urban Studies*, **42** (5/6), 985–99.

Guest, A. (2010a), 'Developing soccer in South Africa: where's the game?', available at: http:// pitchinvasion.net (accessed 7 March 2011).
Guest, A. (2010b), 'World Cup bids and saving the world', available at: http://pitchinvasion. net (accessed 15 March 2011).
Hagn, F. and W. Maennig (2008), 'Employment effects of the Football World Cup 1974 in Germany', *Labour Economics*, **15** (5), 1062–75.
Hoffmann, R., C.G. Lee and B. Ramasamy (2002), 'The socio-economic determinants of international soccer performance', *Journal of Applied Economics*, **5** (2), 253–72.
Horne, J. (2004), 'The global game of football: the 2002 World Cup and regional development in Japan', *Third World Quarterly*, **25** (7), 1233–44.
Hotchkiss, J.L., R.E. Moore and S.M. Zobay (2003), 'Impact of the 1996 Summer Olympic Games on employment and wages in Georgia', *Southern Economic Journal*, **69** (3), 691–704.
International Monetary Fund (IMF) (2007), 'World Economic Outlook Database', available at: http://www.imf.org (accessed 1 February 2011).
International Monetary Fund (IMF) (2010), 'World Economic Outlook Database', available at: http://www.imf.org (accessed 1 February 2011).
Jasmand, S. and W. Maennig (2008), 'Regional income and employment effects of the 1972 Munich Olympic Summer Games', *Regional Studies*, **42** (7), 991–1002.
Kunene, M. (2006), 'Winning the Cup but losing the plot? The troubled state of South African soccer', in S. Buhlungu, J. Daniel, R. Southall and J. Lutchman (eds), *State of the Nation South Africa 2005–2006*, Cape Town: HSRC Press, pp. 369–91.
Loayza, N.V. (1996), 'The economics of the informal sector: a simple model and some empirical evidence from Latin America', *Carnegie-Rochester Conference Series on Public Policy*, **45** (1), 129–62.
Madden, J.R. (2002), 'The economic consequences of the Sydney Olympics: the CREA/ Arthur Andersen Study', *Current Issues in Tourism*, **5** (1), 7–21.
Marion, N.P. and L.E.O. Svensson (1984), 'Adjustment to expected and unexpected oil price changes', *Canadian Journal of Economics*, **17** (1), 15–31.
Matheson, V.A. (2005), 'Contrary evidence on the economic effect of the Super Bowl on the victorious city', *Journal of Sports Economics*, **6** (4), 420–28.
Matheson, V.A. (2006), 'Mega-events: the effect of the world's biggest sporting events on local, regional and national economies', Working Paper No. 10, Department of Economics, College of the Holy Cross, Worcester, MA.
Matheson, V.A. and R.A. Baade (2004), 'Mega-sporting events in developing nations: playing the way to prosperity?', *South African Journal of Economics*, **72** (5), 1085–96.
Matheson, V.A. and R.A. Baade (2005), 'The paradox of championships: be careful what you wish for, sports fans', Working Paper No. 04, Department of Economics, College of the Holy Cross, Worcester, MA.
Morgan, B. (2007), 'Visionary Soccer Academy for South Africa', available at: http://www. southafrica.info (accessed 20 December 2010).
Ngan, J. (2010), 'Whatever happened to Senegal?', available at: http://equaliserfootball.com, (accessed 23 February 2011).
North, D.C. (1990), *Institutions, Institutional Change and Economic Performance*, Cambridge: Cambridge University Press.
Preuss, H. (2007a), 'The conceptualisation and measurement of mega sport event legacies', *Journal of Sport & Tourism*, **12** (3–4), 207–27.
Preuss, H. (2007b), 'FIFA World Cup 2006 and its legacy on tourism', in R. Conrady and M. Buck (eds), *Trends and Issues in Global Tourism 2007*, Berlin: Springer, pp. 83–102.
Ralph, M. (2006), '"Le Sénégal qui gagne": soccer and the stakes of neoliberalism in a post-colonial port', *Soccer & Society*, **7** (2–3), 300–317.
Rodrik, D., A. Subramanian and F. Trebbi (2004), 'Institutions rule: the primacy of institutions over geography and integration in economic development', *Journal of Economic Growth*, **9** (2), 131–65.
Rose, A.K. and M.M. Spiegel (2009), 'The Olympic effect', CEPR Discussion Paper No. 7248, Center for Economic Policy Research, London.

Rose, A.K. and M.M. Spiegel (2011), 'The Olympic effect', *Economic Journal*, **121** (553), 652–77.

Schokkaert, J., J.F.M. Swinnen and T. Vandemoortele (2012), 'Football academies and player migration in developing countries', in B. Segaert, M. Theeboom, C. Timmerman and B. Vanreusel (eds), *Sports Governance, Development, and Corporate Responsibility*, London: Routledge, forthcoming.

Siegfried, J. and A. Zimbalist (2000), 'The economics of sports facilities and their communities', *Journal of Economic Perspectives*, **14** (3), 95–114.

Song, W. (2010), 'Impacts of Olympics on exports and tourism', *Journal of Economic Development*, **35** (4), 93–110.

Sterken, E. (2006), 'Growth impact of major sporting events', *European Sport Management Quarterly*, 6 (4), 375–89.

Sterken, E. (2010), 'Economic impact of organizing large sporting events', Working Paper, Department of Economics, Groningen.

Swinnen, J.F.M. and T. Vandemoortele (2009), 'Sport en ontwikkeling: een economische visie op de impact van de Wereldbeker 2010 in Zuid-Afrika', in J. Scheerder and B. Meulders (eds), *Wedijver in een internationale arena. Sport, bestuur & macht*, Ghent: Academia Press, pp. 185–205.

Zimbalist, A. (2010), 'Is it worth it?', *Finance and Development*, **47** (1), 8–11.

20 Economic impact of organizing large sporting events
Elmer Sterken

1 INTRODUCTION

The economic impact of organizing large sporting events is a topic that attracts lively attention (see, for instance, Preuss, 2006, for an overview). Governments (both federal and local), sports federations (National Olympic Committees, international federations such as the International Amateur Athletic Federation (IAAF), the International Olympic Committee (IOC) and FIFA), potential organizers and consultants debate about the total economic value added of such large events. In general, one could consider any sporting event and debate its possible (local) welfare gain, but the scale of the event is relevant to the impact issue if one considers national development. Individual surveys and/or cost–benefit analyses possibly could indicate the welfare improvement and the subjective increase in social returns these major sporting events bring, but do not adhere to the main issue: is it *ex ante* beneficial for a national government to apply for the organization of mega sporting events?

In this study we measure the total economic value added of so-called 'sporadic events' (these are regular but not annually organized events, see Barget and Gouguet, 2007) at the macroeconomic level: that is, we are interested in additional growth of (per capita) gross domestic product (GDP). These major sporting events include multiple sports (such as the Olympic Games) or single sports events (World Cup Soccer). The required scale implies that we need to consider sporting events of a certain minimum size. Barget (2001) defines a large sporting event nowadays to be an event with at least 1 billion viewers and live broadcasting in at least 30 countries. This definition also includes regular large single sports events, such as the Formula 1 racing sequence, the Tour de France, and the major tennis events, for instance. In this chapter we try to analyze the economic impact of organizing irregular events, such as the Olympic Summer and Winter Games and the FIFA World Cup.

It is a fact that at the world level the organization of large sporting events has no impact on GDP growth in the short run (in the long run there might be a growth effect if world productivity increases, but this seems to be unrealistic). At the local level, there might be an impact: there is promotional (not academic) evidence of the economic impact of organizing a smaller event, like the Super Bowl in the US, where estimates vary from a 100 to 400 million US dollars on current year's local GDP (see Matheson and Baade, 2006). For large economies, like the US, the probability that this local impact will affect US GDP growth rates is less likely. For smaller economies, like the Greek economy in 2004, the relative size of the sporting event can become more relevant and the probability of a significant impact increases. Estimates so far do not give a clear and systematic estimate of the economic impact (see, for exceptions, for example, Szymanski, 2002, and Sterken, 2006).

There are many studies, both *ex ante* and *ex post*, of stand-alone events. An early study is for the 1972 Munich Summer Olympic Games by Jasmand and Maennig (2008). For the Summer Olympic Games there is a string of empirical evidence since the Los Angeles Games (see Economics Research Associates, 1984 for the Los Angeles 1984 Games, Kim et al., 1989, for the Seoul 1988 Games, Brunet, 1995, for the Barcelona 1992 Games, Humphreys and Plummer, 1995, for the Atlanta 1996 Games up to Arthur Andersen, 1999, for the Sydney 2000 Olympics and Papanikos, 1999, for the Athens 2004 Games). Recent editions of the Games yield the IOC a profit of about $4 billion for the combined Summer and Winter Games. Most historical studies are based on an input–output model (see Humphreys and Plummer, 1995, for the Atlanta Games, and Ahlert, 2001, for the World Cup Soccer in Germany 2006). More up-to-date analyses use a so-called computable general equilibrium (CGE) approach (see, for example, Arthur Andersen, 1999, for the Sydney 2000 Games). There are also studies that evaluate *ex post* certain aspects of the organization of large events, see, for example, Kim et al., 2006, for the World Cup 2002 in Korea. Other relevant studies for the FIFA World Cup are Baade and Matheson (2004), Hagn and Maennig (2008, 2009) about the impact on unemployment, Allmers and Maennig (2009), Feddersen et al. (2009), Süssmuth et al. (2010), and du Plessis and Maennig (ch. 27 in this volume).

This chapter contributes to the literature in a number of ways. First, it presents systematic evidence on the impact of three large sporting events (the Summer and Winter Olympic Games and the FIFA World Cup) for the whole modern history. Second, we make progress on the important issue of endogeneity of the selection process. In economic growth regressions we estimate the growth rate of real per capita GDP on a dummy variable representing the organization of a specific event in year t. It might be that higher growth economies are more successful in applying for the organization of the event. If so, the impact of the organization dummy on economic growth will be biased. So, generally, impact studies neglect the endogeneity of the organization decision that is highly relevant to the econometric evidence. If high-growth-potential economies are more successful in applying for the organization of large sporting events, neglecting this decision will bias the growth estimates.

We discuss and describe the history of the selection process of the candidate organizers of the three events in Section 2. We estimate a candidacy and a selection model per event. It comes to the fore that higher-growth economies are more likely candidates for organizing the Winter Olympic Games. Economic motives are not found to be relevant to the final selection process by the IOC, contrary to the findings of Feddersen et al. (2008). For the Soccer World Cup, economic growth considerations do not seem to be decisive. In Section 3 we present a simple growth model and analyze the standard results of organizing the Summer or Winter Olympic Games or the FIFA World Cup. We discuss the endogeneity problem and show that for the Summer Olympic Games the alleged impact of organizing is reduced, but still relevant. We summarize and conclude in Section 4.

2   THE SELECTION PROCESS

The main goal of the chapter is to determine the additional growth effects of organizing major sporting events. In order to be able to estimate the added value we have to make an estimate of the normal economic growth rate of organizing countries. Moreover, it might be that, compared to the world level, countries that organize large sporting events are high-growth potentials. This leads to the issue of selection bias. So, an important part of this chapter is on the endogeneity of the selection process. First we describe the selection process for the three types of events. We distinguish two steps: (i) candidacy of cities or countries, and (ii) given official candidacy, election to the hosting city or country. We estimate the impact of economic conditions on the selection process, conditioning for other possible drivers of selection. We have a special interest in the role of economic growth in the selection process. In order to avoid endogeneity problems we include lagged per capita economic growth as a regressor. Further, we include the following types/classes of variables:

- *Geographical data*: we include the latitude of the capital city, an indicator of road density, the total surface area, and so on. Latitude is a proxy for the national risk attitude (the further away from the equator, the more risk averse); road density is a proxy variable for the ability to invest in infrastructure, and total surface is a proxy for size and ability to invest in land development.

- *Indicators of fractionalization*: religion (see McCleary and Barro, 2006), ethnic, and language (see Alesina et al., 2003). A larger degree of fractionalization will reduce the probabilities that a country or city can host the event.
- *Governance indicators*: rule of law, control of corruption, regulatory quality, government efficiency, democracy, voice and accountability, and political stability (see Kaufmann et al., 2006). More stability will lead to a larger probability to host large-scale events.
- *Past candidacies.*

The Selection of the Host of the Summer Olympic Games

Nowadays, the selection of the hosting country of the Summer Olympic Games by the IOC is a long and tedious process. First, one can be considered as an applicant city and reveal one's interest in organizing the event. There can only be one applicant city in each country, supported by its National Olympic Committee. Next, after approval by the IOC a city can turn into a candidate city. About seven years in advance of the event the IOC takes a decision and one of the candidate cities will turn into a hosting city (see Table 20.1). All arrangements are nowadays covered in the so-called Olympic Charter. In the old days though, the selection procedure was not so clear at all. Note that the 1916, 1940, and 1944 editions (though originally planned) were not organized due to the First and Second World Wars.

For all editions from Paris 1900 up to and including Rio de Janeiro 2016 we present the average excess real GDP per capita growth rates (as compared to the world average per capita GDP growth rate) in a window of 9 years in total (four years prior to the selection to four years after the selection date) in Table 20.2. Note that we are interested in economic development and that level differences between countries will be controlled for in the growth model to be estimated.

Averages are for all, pre- and post-Second World War events. We use the data provided by Maddison (2003) for GDP and population series up to and including the year 2006 and extend these using the IMF World Economic Outlook April 2011 edition up to and including 2016. These descriptive statistics give a first indication whether the final organizing countries have shown excess per capita GDP growth rates around the time of the selection. The main assumption could be that the prevailing growth rates have been used as best guesses for the economic development during the event (which we shall show later on). As Table 20.2 shows, the mean excessive growth rates have indeed been positive, but the standard deviations are high. The results before the Second World War seem to be more erratic than the

Table 20.1   Application and selection data for the Summer Olympic Games

Year	Host city	Applicants	Candidates	Date of decision
1896	Athens	1	1	June 1894
1900	Paris	1	1	March 1898
1904	St Louis	1	1	May 1901
1908	London	4	3	May 1906
1912	Stockholm	1	1	May 1909
1916	Berlin	4	4	May 1909
1920	Antwerp	3	3	April 1919
1924	Paris	6	6	June 1921
1928	Amsterdam	2	2	June 1921
1932	Los Angeles	1	1	February 1930
1936	Berlin	2	2	May 1931
1940	Tokyo/Helsinki	13	0	August 1936
1944	London	7	4	June 1939
1948	London	6	3	March 1946
1952	Helsinki	10	6	June 1947
1956	Melbourne	10	5	May 1949
1960	Rome	7	7	June 1955
1964	Tokyo	4	7	May 1959
1968	Mexico	4	7	October 1963
1972	Munich	4	7	July 1966
1976	Montreal	3	3	May 1970
1980	Moscow	2	2	October 1974
1984	Los Angeles	1	1	May 1978
1988	Seoul	2	2	September 1981
1992	Barcelona	6	6	October 1986
1996	Atlanta	6	6	September 1990
2000	Sydney	8	5	September 1993
2004	Athens	11	5	September 1997
2008	Beijing	10	5	July 2001
2012	London	9	5	July 2005
2016	Rio de Janeiro	7	4	July 2009

results after the war. For the later editions of the Summer Olympic Games, the winning of the bid seems to foster growth after the election.

Table 20.2 shows the average excessive growth rates for the countries that finally won the bid process. We take a step back and analyze the candidacy and bid-winning processes. In Table 20.3 we present the estimation results of a logit model to estimate the discrete choice of candidacy for and bid-winning for the Summer Olympic Games. This can be seen as the

Table 20.2   *Excess per capita GDP growth rates for countries that won the bid for the Summer Olympic Games around the selection year: Paris 1900–Rio de Janeiro 2016*

	$t-4$	$t-3$	$t-2$	$t-1$	t	$t+1$	$t+2$	$t+3$	$t+4$
All games	0.24	−1.91	0.87	0.01	0.56	2.09	0.65	0.34	0.50
std dev.	3.55	4.63	5.69	4.61	4.72	4.25	3.62	2.92	2.86
Before WWII	0.14	−4.44	3.04	−0.81	1.35	2.87	−1.40	−0.07	0.64
std dev.	4.40	6.39	9.23	7.69	6.74	5.63	3.04	4.23	3.13
After WWII	0.29	−0.64	−0.22	0.43	0.16	1.70	1.67	0.54	0.42
std dev.	3.20	2.91	2.38	2.05	3.49	3.49	3.52	2.12	2.81

Table 20.3   *Binary logit estimation results: candidacy and bid-winning of the Summer Olympic Games.*

Variable	Candidacy coefficient	Std error	Bid-winner coefficient	Std error
Past candidate	0.623*	0.295	1.538**	0.813
Past bid-winner			−1.236*	0.617
Lagged GDP/capita	0.018	0.015		
Protestant	−0.011*	0.005		
Catholic			−0.012*	0.006
Democracy	0.156*	0.043		
Area	0.089*	0.022		
Intercept	−3.300*	0.325	−1.731*	0.632
Countries	48		48	
Observations = 0	566		83	
Observations = 1	99		18	
Correct prediction rate 0	0.86		0.83	
Correct prediction rate 1	0.21		0.12	
McFadden R^2	0.086		0.061	

Note: Standard errors are Huber/White corrected.
*   Significant at the 95%-confidence level.
**   Significant at the 90%-confidence level.

supply side of the market for selection of hosting cities. In the final model we include real per capita GDP growth the year prior to selection (note that we included all the variables mentioned above, but present only the parameter estimates of the final selection). Past candidacy is an important contributor to current candidacy. Countries with a low democratic tradition and a relative large fraction of people with a protestant religion are less eager to be candidates. Larger countries tend to be more likely candidate organizers. But, by far the most important conclusion is that per capita GDP growth does not affect the decision to become a candidate organizer of the Summer Olympic Games after the Second World War. Next we estimate the final selection process again using a binary logit model. Here we assume that the candidacy process is given (we do not use the Heckman two-step estimator, see Heckman, 1976). So we include 99 candidate cities/countries, of which 18 have been elected. Past candidates have more chance for selection, while countries that hosted the Summer Games in the past have a slight disadvantage. Of all the variables that could possibly be included only the percentage of Catholic people affects the selection process slightly. We do not find any impact of economic indicators. So again in the selection process per capita GDP growth is not an argument.

The Selection of the Host of the Winter Olympic Games

The selection of the host city of the Winter Olympic Games has a history that resembles the selection of the Summer Olympics host city. Like the Summer Games, those in 1940 and 1944 did not take place due to the Second World War (see Table 20.4). The 1976 Games were originally given to Denver, but after a public voting, the city of Denver gave a late notice that it was declining from hosting; Innsbruck took over.

In Table 20.5 we present the average excessive GDP per capita growth rates for the organizing countries. We again observe positive mean excessive growth rates. This can be caused by the fact that richer economies have applied for the organization of the Winter Games, or the fact that the IOC elected the strong economic growth countries. In Table 20.6 we present the estimation results of the binary choice models for candidacy by cities and the results for the bidding process. Here we find that the IOC apparently selects countries with a slightly higher GDP per capita growth.

The Selection of the Host of the FIFA World Cup

The history of the selection of the FIFA World Cup hosting country (or countries) is different from the IOC procedures. Early World Cups were given to countries at the meetings of FIFA's congress. The choice of location was sometimes controversial, given the three-week boat journey between South America and Europe. The decision to hold the first World Cup in Uruguay led to only four European nations competing. The next two World Cups were both held in Europe. The decision

Table 20.4   Application and selection data for the Winter Olympic Games

Year	Host city	Applicants	Candidates	Date of decision
1924	Chamonix	1	1	1921
1928	St Moritz	3	1	May 1926
1932	Lake Placid	8	2	April 1929
1936	Garmisch-Partenkirchen	2	2	June 1933
1940	St Moritz	2	2	August 1936
1944	Cortina d'Ampezzo	3	3	June 1939
1948	St Moritz	2	2	September 1946
1952	Oslo	3	3	June 1947
1956	Cortina	4	3	April 1949
1960	Squaw Valley	5	5	June 1955
1964	Innsbruck	3	3	May 1959
1968	Grenoble	6	6	January 1964
1972	Sapporo	4	4	April 1966
1976	Innsbruck	5	5	May 1970
1980	Lake Placid[1]	3	2	October 1974
1984	Sarajevo	3	3	May 1978
1988	Calgary	3	3	September 1981
1992	Albertville	7	7	October 1986
1994	Lillehammer	4	4	September 1988
1998	Nagano	5	5	June 1991
2002	Salt Lake City	4	4	June 1995
2006	Turin	6	2	June 2005
2010	Vancouver	8	3	July 2003
2014	Sochi	7	3	July 2007
2018	Pyeongchang[2]	3	3	July 2011

Notes:
1. In 1972 the decision to hold the games in Innsbruck was made after the city of Denver declined the organization following a public vote.
2. For 2018, Santiago and Oslo dropped out at an early stage.

to hold the second of these, the 1938 FIFA World Cup in France was controversial, as the American countries had been led to understand that the World Cup would rotate between the two continents. Both Argentina and Uruguay thus boycotted the tournament. After the Second World War, to avoid any future boycotts or controversy, FIFA began a pattern of alternation between the Americas and Europe, which continued until the 2002 FIFA World Cup (see Table 20.7). The system evolved so that the host country is now chosen in a vote by FIFA's executive committee. The main idea is to spread the organization across

Table 20.5   Average excess per capita GDP growth rates for countries that won the bid for the Winter Olympic Games

	$t-4$	$t-3$	$t-2$	$t-1$	t	$t+1$	$t+2$	$t+3$	$t+4$
All games	0.32	0.26	1.51	2.04	0.99	1.22	1.32	0.06	0.91
std dev.	4.73	5.60	4.16	5.96	3.39	4.18	2.42	3.58	3.44
Before WWII	−2.36	−3.35	3.18	3.03	0.02	1.26	1.46	0.70	−2.02
std dev.	4.95	10.31	7.10	6.88	3.47	5.53	2.35	5.54	5.49
After WWII	1.72	1.93	0.71	0.41	0.46	0.62	1.55	0.19	1.54
std dev.	4.60	4.03	3.42	5.93	3.44	4.03	2.50	3.20	2.62

Table 20.6   Binary logit estimation results: Candidacy and bid-winning of the Winter Olympic Games.

Variable	Candidacy coefficient	Std error	Bid-winner coefficient	Std error
Past candidate	1.362*	0.395		
Past bid-winner			0.855	0.602
Lagged GDP/capita	0.043*	0.021	0.178**	0.093
Latitude	0.017**	0.009		
Mountain	2.671*	1.064		
Democracy	0.130*	0.054		
Area	0.071*	0.026		
Intercept	−7.086*	1.161	−2.342*	0.667
Countries	48		48	
Observations = 0	600		60	
Observations = 1	78		18	
Correct prediction rate 0	0.86		0.78	
Correct prediction rate 1	0.30		0.28	
McFadden R^2	0.274		0.061	

Notes: Standard errors are Huber/White corrected.
*   Significant at the 95%-confidence level.
**   Significant at the 90%-confidence level.

all continents. The decision is currently made six years in advance of the tournament.

As is shown in Table 20.8, the countries that have hosted or will host the FIFA World Cup do not show excessive per capita GDP growth rates around the year of decisions with respect to the bids on average. Again, this could be caused by the selection of countries that apply or by the bid selection process run by FIFA. In order to estimate the impact of

Table 20.7   Application and selection data for the FIFA World Cup

Year	Organizing country	Candidates	Date of decision
1930	Uruguay	6	May 1929
1934	Italy	2	May 1932
1938	France	3	August 1936
1942	No World Cup		
1950	Brazil	1	July 1946
1954	Switzerland	1	July 1946
1958	Sweden	1	June 1950
1962	Chile	3	June 1956
1966	England	3	August 1960
1970	Mexico	2	October 1964
1974	West Germany	2	July 1966
1978	Argentina	2	July 1966
1982	Spain	2	July 1966
1986	Mexico	3	May 1983
1990	Italy	4	August 1984
1994	USA	3	July 1988
1998	France	3	July 1992
2002	Korea–Japan	3	May 1996
2006	Germany	5	July 2000
2010	South Africa	5	May 2004
2014	Brazil	1	October 2007
2018	Russia	6	December 2010
2022	Qatar	5	December 2010

Table 20.8   Average excess per capita GDP growth rates for countries that won the bid for the FIFA World Cup

	$t-4$	$t-3$	$t-2$	$t-1$	t	$t+1$	$t+2$	$t+3$	$t+4$
All games	0.36	1.38	0.31	1.24	−0.01	1.06	−1.40	−0.36	−1.16
std dev.	4.54	3.25	4.14	5.42	3.24	4.37	3.28	4.40	4.61
Before WWII	−1.23	2.15	−1.05	−2.81	−1.43	3.48	−5.85	1.36	−9.76
std dev.	7.82	1.49	8.79	3.41	3.86	10.02	6.31	5.30	7.02
After WWII	1.53	1.08	0.65	0.56	−0.20	0.35	−0.76	−0.41	0.35
std dev.	3.28	2.69	3.43	2.28	3.03	1.95	2.09	4.47	1.91

economic growth on the candidacy process we have to determine whether a country is eligible to be a candidate organizer. Remember that FIFA alternated between Europe and Latin America to select the host country. So the sample includes eligible countries only. We also include data on the

Table 20.9   Binary logit estimation results: candidacy and bid-winning of the FIFA World Cup.

Variable	Candidacy coefficient	Std error	Bid-winner coefficient	Std error
Lagged GDP/capita	0.060	0.051	0.141	0.085
FIFA-players	0.203*	0.086	0.089*	0.081
FIFA-rank	−0.125*	0.057		
Intercept	−1.157*	0.575	−1.062*	0.522
Countries	48		48	
Observations = 0	81		23	
Observations = 1	23		14	
Correct prediction rate 0	0.81		0.63	
Correct prediction rate 1	0.33		0.47	
McFadden R^2	0.140		0.078	

Note: Standard errors are Huber/White corrected.
*   Significant at the 95%-confidence level.
**   Significant at the 90%-confidence level.

number of active football players from the FIFA Big Count project in the year 2000. Although we do not have historical data, we assume that the same distribution of players as in 2000 existed in the other years. We call this variable 'FIFA-players'. We also include the FIFA-ranking of the countries (lower rank number implies a stronger team) per decade. Table 20.9 gives the results. We see that GDP per capita is not a key variable to apply for the organization of the World Cup. Countries with many football players and a strong performance are likely to apply more. We also estimate the selection of the host countries. GDP per capita growth does not play a decisive role in the election. The election is generally rather unpredictable: there are hardly any significant regressors.

From the results in Section 2 we can conclude that per capita GDP growth affects the application process for especially the Winter Olympic Games. This implies that the IOC finally chooses from a 'richer' set of countries for the Winter Games than on average. Other selection arguments, such as latitude and the availability of a suitable mountain location seem to play a role for the Winter Games. For both the Summer Olympics and the FIFA World Cup, per capita economic growth does not seem to play a major role in candidacy and election. This implies that we have to deal with endogeneity problems of the application process for the Winter Olympics, but not for the Summer Games or the FIFA World Cup.

3   A GROWTH MODEL OF ORGANIZING LARGE SPORTING EVENTS

The previous descriptive statistical analysis illustrates that sample means of excessive real per capita growth rates of the organizing countries of large sporting events have rather large standard deviations. This implies that it is valuable to condition the means better using an economic growth model. In order to analyze the impact of organizing large sporting events, we estimate a simple growth model that accounts for an explanation of the differences in means of real per capita growth rates. We use the World Development Indicators data produced by the World Bank. This dataset covers the years 1960–2008. We use a rather standard economic growth model. We estimate the three-year moving average of real per capita economic growth GDPCAP in country i in year t (so not the 'for the world average growth corrected' rates) on a set of 'standard' determinants of economic growth: the lagged level of real GDP per capita at $t - 4$ (GDPCAPL: we use four-year lags to adjust for the moving averages in the dependent variable), gross fixed investment as a percentage of GDP (GFCI), general government consumption as a percentage of GDP (GGC), inflation (INF), (quasi-) money growth and openness, measured by exports plus imports as a percentage of GDP (OPEN). We use a three-year moving average of real per capita GDP growth rates in order to approximate the growth momentum which might be due to the organization of the event. The basic model is:

$$\text{GDPCAP}_{it} = \alpha_1 \text{ GDPCAPL}_{it-4} + \alpha_2 \text{ GFCI}_{it} + \alpha_3 \text{ GGC}_{it} + \alpha_4 \text{ INF}_{it} + \alpha_5 \text{ MONEY}_{it} + \alpha_6 \text{ OPEN}_{it} + \delta_i + \delta_t + \varepsilon_{it,}$$

where i indicates the 42 countries included (we are forced to exclude some countries, such as the Soviet Union, because of a lack of data, but do have other centrally planned economies in the sample: Bulgaria, Poland, the Czech Republic, Slovakia, the former Yugoslavia) and t runs from 1960 up to and including 2008. The model is linear in the determinants, as in the standard growth literature, but we do consider a quadratic form in order to test for robustness of the specification. δ_i is a country dummy variable and δ_t is a time dummy variable. ε_{it} is a white-noise residual. The lagged level of real GDP per capita illustrates whether there is convergence among countries: a negative parameter estimate indicates that countries with rather high levels of real GDP per capita tend to have lower growth rates. Gross fixed investment is generally seen to be the standard key determinant of economic growth. Government consumption, representing fiscal policy, is generally believed to have temporary effects on economic development.

We experimented with both the level of government consumption as a percentage of GDP as well with the first-differenced series. The latter allows for the momentum of fiscal expansion. Inflation could be harmful to economic growth in the long run, although there might be a positive correlation in the short term. We include a proxy for monetary policy by including (quasi-) money growth (could be related to inflation in the long run). And finally, openness is important, especially to the smaller countries. Note that we do not include other determinants of growth that have been suggested in the literature, such as school enrollment (due to the lower frequency of data availability), ICT investment, probably an indicator of willingness to invest in future risky developments (no data coverage over our entire sample), market capitalization, credit to the private sector as a percentage of GDP (data available, but with serious breaks for fewer countries), and the GINI-measure of income inequality (low availability and rather constant nature). We include fixed time and country effects (after testing for redundancy of the dummy variables, see the F-test statistic in Table 20.10). The dummy variables for the countries correct for differences in levels (for example, the GINI-coefficient). We estimate the model using the White cross-section (country) correction. Note that we are unable to estimate a dynamic growth model, which would have been interesting due to auto-correlated real per capita GDP growth rates and to the low number of countries (42) included.

In Table 20.10 we give the estimation results of the basic linear model in the first column. The table reveals that the lagged level of GDP per capita, fixed investment, government consumption, and inflation are significant determinants in the basic growth model. Gross fixed investment has a positive impact on economic growth. Government consumption and inflation have a negative impact on growth, which is consistent with a classic view. The first-differences of the government consumption variable did not lead to an improvement of the fit of the model. We do not report the estimates of the dummy variables but give an F-test statistic for fixed effects redundancy. As one can see in all models, the fixed effects are statistically significant. In the second column we include the quadratic terms in order to test for basic nonlinearities. For inflation we find a significant nonlinear effect, which improves the overall fit of the model. We use the quadratic specification to add the organization dummy variables for the Summer Games, the Winter Games, and the World Cup. We test for the common impact of the dummy variables on economic growth using a Wald test (and corresponding p-values). Only the common impact of the Summer Games dummy variables is significant at the 5 percent confidence level. For the Summer Games we do find a positive impact on economic development around the

Table 20.10   Estimation results of the fixed effects economic growth model

	Linear	Quadratic	Summer Games	Winter Games	World Cup
GDPCAPL$_{-4}$	−0.495*	−0.436*	−0.430*	−0.433*	−0.418*
	0.085	0.066	0.066	0.068	0.073
GCFI	0.216*	0.239*	0.241*	0.238*	0.240*
	0.027	0.118	0.119	0.119	0.119
GCFI^2		0.000	0.000	0.000	0.000
		0.002	0.002	0.002	0.002
GGC	−0.165*	0.005	0.014	0.017	0.011
	0.040	0.169	0.170	0.169	0.170
GGC^2		−0.006	−0.006	−0.006	−0.006
		0.005	0.005	0.005	0.005
INF	−0.362*	−1.871*	−1.873*	−1.872*	−1.871*
	0.100	0.534	0.535	0.535	0.541
INF^2		0.055*	0.055*	0.055*	0.055*
		0.020	0.020	0.020	0.020
MONEY	0.001	0.587	0.592	0.588	0.596
	0.001	0.383	0.383	0.384	0.385
MONEY^2		−0.010	−0.010	−0.010	−0.010
		0.011	0.011	0.011	0.011
OPEN	−0.008	−0.019	−0.019	−0.019	−0.020
	0.011	0.020	0.020	0.021	0.021
OPEN^2		0.293	0.290	0.296	0.316
		0.429	0.431	0.432	0.432
Event(−3)			−0.058	−0.312	−0.715
			0.547	0.643	0.584
Event(−2)			0.370	−0.305	−0.200
			0.501	0.645	0.696
Event(−1)			0.867**	−0.210	−0.223
			0.457	0.490	0.807
Event			0.974	−0.263	−1.078
			0.620	0.342	0.965
Event(+1)			1.264*	−0.118	−0.934
			0.573	0.340	0.631
Event(+2)			0.875	0.580	−0.320
			0.740	0.372	0.615
Event(+3)			0.319	0.931**	−0.031
			0.841	0.519	0.477
Countries	42	42	42	42	42
Years	41	41	41	41	41
Observations	950	950	950	950	950
FE-redundancy	4.885	4.502	4.345	4.452	4.409
Wald test			6.544	0.052	1.475

Table 20.10   (continued)

	Linear	Quadratic	Summer Games	Winter Games	World Cup
p-value			0.011	0.821	0.225
SSR	4,685	4,240	4,220	4,231	4,228
Adjusted R^2	0.485	0.532	0.530	0.529	0.529

Notes:
* Significant at the 95%-confidence level.
** Significant at the 90%-confidence level.
Model estimated with the White cross-section correction. Standard errors are below parameter estimates. Fixed effects redundancy tested by an *F*-test. The Wald test indicates the relevance of the event dummy variables. SSR is the sum of squared residuals.

year of the event. Note that we use a moving-average representation of the dependent variable, implying that the growth momentum changes around the organization date of the Summer Games. The additional impact is about a one percentage point of real per capita GDP growth. It should be noted though that the impact of organizing large sporting events is modest at best.

Note that the observed additional growth for the Summer Olympic Games resembles the results presented in Table 20.2 for post-Second World War events. The additional positive growth results do not hold for the Winter Games or the FIFA World Cup, though. The Wald tests on the joint significance of the event dummy variables for the Winter Games and the World Cup indicate that there is no additional effect of organizing these events on real per capita GDP growth.

Above we illustrated that host selection depends in part on GDP per capita growth for the organization of the Winter Olympic Games. For the Summer Games and the FIFA World Cup there is less evidence that selection is endogenous. But since we find only a positive impact for the Summer Games we test for endogeneity of the organization of the Summer Games as well. We estimate a pooled model with instrumental variables correcting for possible endogeneity of the organization dummy variable for the model of the Summer and Winter Games, respectively. We focus on the contemporaneous (that is in the year of the organization of the event) effect. This implies that we need to endogenize the dummy variable that indicates the organization of the event in year *t* by the conditions at year $t - 6$ or $t - 7$ at the date of candidacy and selection. In Section 2 we illustrated that, apart from variables that have a constant nature, like the religious mix and the availability of mountain regions, lagged real per capita GDP growth is the main time-varying determinant of the candidacy and election of the host

Table 20.11   Instrumental variable economic growth model: the Summer and Winter Olympic Games

	Summer Games	Winter Games
$GDPCAPL_{-4}$	−0.342*	−0.344*
	0.053	0.053
GCFI	0.175*	0.176*
	0.024	0.024
INF	−0.786*	−0.785*
	0.159	0.160
INF^2	0.023*	0.023*
	0.006	0.006
Event	0.741	0.805
	0.839	1.793
Countries	39	39
Years	44	44
Observations	1,261	1,261
SSR	3,766	3,768
Adjusted R^2	0.579	0.577

Notes:
* Significant at the 95%-confidence level.
Model estimated with the White cross-section correction. Instruments are the $GDPCAP_{-10}$, $GCFI_{-6}$, INF_{-6}, INF^2_{-6}, and the candidacy dummy variables for the Summer and Winter Games, respectively. Standard errors are below parameter estimates. SSR = sum of squared residuals. Gross sample = 1960–2008; Net sample = 1968–2005.

of the Winter Games. This implies that we need to instrument for real per capita GDP growth and the main determinants are the lagged variables used in the growth model. In order to condition the model we select the significant determinants of our growth model in Table 20.10: the lagged level of GDP per capita, gross fixed capital formation, and the cubic expression for inflation. The instruments used are a dummy variable representing candidate countries (for the Summer and Winter Games, respectively) at year t, the level of real GDP per capita in year $t − 10$, gross capital formation at $t − 6$, and inflation and its quadratic at $t − 6$. Table 20.11 presents the results of the pooled instrumental model of both the Summer and Winter Games. Correction for the endogeneity of the organization dummy leads to the conclusion that the impact of organizing the Summer Games turns out to be insignificant. We experimented by including the lag and the lead of the organization dummy variable, leading to similar results (modest positive parameter estimates, but insignificant). The parameter estimate of the Winter Games organization dummy variable remains insignificant.

4   SUMMARY AND CONCLUSIONS

In this chapter we address the growth impact of major sporting events. We take the example cases of the Summer and Winter Olympic Games and FIFA World Cup Soccer. These three events are mega events in terms of finance, participation, coverage, and attention. On the world scale, organizing large sports events will not affect economic growth. We first present descriptive statistics of economic growth over the whole modern history of the three large sporting events. We find positive excessive growth rates for the Summer Olympic Games (around the event year) only. We do not find any positive impact for the Winter Games or the World Cup Soccer. Considering the literature on the economic impact of organizing large sporting events, we can frame our findings in a general setting of mixed results. Promotional studies tend to present positive estimates of additional growth, while scholarly papers tend to point at lower or no impact. We argue that it is necessary to analyze the additional impact in a growth model and in this chapter we tackle the endogeneity of the selection of candidate cities/countries in an economic growth model in detail. We present historical evidence on the selection process and model applications and selection by the IOC and FIFA. It is evident that high-growth economies tend to apply more often to organize the Winter Olympic Games. The IOC does not use economic criteria to select the host (both the Summer and the Winter Games) though. For the FIFA World Cup there is no strong evidence that GDP growth affects both candidacy and selection.

In our basic model, the Summer Olympic Games appear to lead to slightly higher growth rates. For the Winter Games and FIFA World Cup we do not find significant additional growth effects. If true, the additional growth impact for the Summer Games is about one percentage point additional GDP per capita growth for the year before and the year after the event, although indeed the coefficients in these two years are only significant at the 0.05 and 0.10 levels. The other five years tested do not have statistically significant coefficients. Thus, the statistical evidence is not very strong. Although we do not find that candidacy for the Summer Games depends on economic growth, an instrumental variable estimation of the growth model, correcting for endogeneity of the organization, shows that the additional growth impact is insignificant. For the Winter Games, where we do find support for 'organization endogeneity, the organization impact remains insignificant. Our results therefore support the more scholarly findings in the literature. Future analyses should be focused on *ex ante* experiments in forecasts and modeling of the channels of influence of event organization on economic activity (investment, consumption, tourism).

REFERENCES

Ahlert, Gerd (2001), 'The economic effects of the Soccer World Cup 2006 in Germany with regard to different financing', *Economic Systems Research*, **13**, 110–18.

Alesina, Alberto, Arnaud Devleeschauwer, William Easterly, Sergio Kurlat and Romain Wacziarg (2003), 'Fractionalization', *Journal of Economic Growth*, **8**, 155–94.

Allmers, Swantje and Wolfgang Maennig (2009), 'Economic impacts of the FIFA Soccer World Cups in France 1998, Germany 2006, and outlook for South Africa 2010', *Eastern Economic Journal*, **35**, 500–19.

Arthur Andersen (1999), 'Economic impact study of the Sydney 2000 Olympic Games', Working Paper, Centre for Regional Economic Analysis, University of Tasmania.

Baade, Robert A. and Victor Matheson (2004), 'The quest for the Cup: assessing the economic impact of the World Cup', *Journal of Regional Studies*, **38** (4), 343–54.

Barget, Eric (2001), 'Economics evaluation of sporting events', PhD thesis, Limoges.

Barget, Eric and Jean-Jacques Gouguet (2007), 'The total economic value added of sporting events: theory and practice', *Journal of Sports Economics*, **8**, 165–82.

Brunet, Ferran (1995), 'An economic analysis of the Barcelona '92 Olympic Games: resources, financing, and impact', in Miquel de Moragas and Miquel Botella (eds), *The Keys to Success*, Barcelona: Servei de Publicacions de la UAB, pp. 203–37.

Economics Research Associates (1984), 'Community Economic Impact off the 1984 Olympic Games in Los Angeles and Southern California', Los Angeles Olympic Organizing Committee, Los Angeles.

Feddersen, Arne, André Grötzinger and Wolfgang Maennig (2009), 'Investment in stadia and regional economic development – evidence from FIFA World Cup 2006', *International Journal of Sport Finance*, **4** (4), 221–39.

Feddersen, Arne, Wolfgang Maennig and Ph. Zimmermann (2008), 'The empirics of key factors in the success of bids for Olympic Games', *Revue d'Économie Politique*, **118** (2), 39–55.

Hagn, Florian and Wolfgang Maennig (2008), 'Employment effects of the Football World Cup 1974 in Germany', *Labour Economics*, **15** (5), 1062–75.

Hagn, Florian and Wolfgang Maennig (2009), 'Large sport events and unemployment: the case of the 2006 Soccer World Cup in Germany', *Applied Economics*, **41** (25), 3295–302.

Heckman, James (1976), 'The common structure of statistical models of truncation, sample selection, and limited dependent variables and a simple estimator for such models', *Annals of Economic and Social Measurement*, **5**, 475–92.

Humphreys, Jeffrey M. and Michael K. Plummer (1995), 'The economic impact on the State of Georgia of hosting the 1996 Olympic Games, Studies and Forecasts', Selig Center for Economic Growth, Terry College of Business, University of Georgia, Athens, GA.

Jasmand, Stephanie and Wolfgang Maennig (2008), 'Regional income and employment effects of the 1972 Munich Olympic Summer Games', *Regional Studies*, **42** (7), 991–1002.

Kaufmann, Daniel, Aart Kraay and Massimo Mastruzzi (2006), 'Governance matters V: governance indicators for 1996–2005', Internet Paper, World Bank, Washington, DC.

Kim, Hyun Y., Dogan Gursoy and Soo-Bum Lee (2006), 'The impact of the 2002 World Cup on South Korea: comparisons of pre- and post-games', *Journal of Tourism Management*, **27**, 86–96.

Kim, Jong-Gee, Sang-Woo Rhee, Jaecheon Yu, Kwangmo Koo and Jongduck Hong (1989), 'Impact of the Seoul Olympic Games on Korean economic development', Working Paper 19889-05, Korea Development Institute.

Maddison, Angus (2003), *The World Economy: Historical Statistics*, Paris: OECD.

Matheson, Victor A. and Robert A. Baade (2006), 'Padding required: assessing the economic impact of the Super Bowl', *European Sport Management Quarterly*, **6**, 353–74.

McCleary, Rachel M. and Robert J. Barro (2006), 'Religion and economy', *Journal of Economic Perspectives*, **20** (2), 42–76.

Papanikos, Gregory T. (1999), 'The economic impact of international tourism and the Olympic Games of Athens 2004', Study Series, Athens Institute of Education and Research.

Preuss, Holger (2006), 'Impact and evaluation of major sporting events', *European Sport Management Quarterly*, **6**, 313–16.
Sterken, Elmer (2006), 'Growth impact of major sporting events', *European Sport Management Quarterly*, **6**, 375–89.
Süssmuth, Bernd, Malte Heyne and Wolfgang Maennig (2010), 'Induced civic pride and integration', *Oxford Bulletin of Economics and Statistics*, **72** (2), 202–20.
Szymanski, Stefan (2002), 'The economic impact of the World Cup', *World Economics*, **3**, 169–77.

PART V

CASE STUDIES: ECONOMIC IMPACT OF MEGA EVENTS

21 Tour de France: a taxpayer bargain among mega sporting events?

Judith Grant Long*

1 INTRODUCTION

The Tour de France is a unique case among mega sporting events, offering a relative bargain for host cities especially when compared to the Olympics, FIFA World Cup soccer, and other large-scale global events. In exchange for a relatively modest level of public investment – often a few million euros[1] in fees, road upgrading, and municipal services, the 30 or more towns and cities that serve as 'stage hosts' each year successfully leverage the Tour to promote themselves as tourist destinations, to capture short-term spikes in local spending on hospitality services, to upgrade local cycling infrastructure, and to provide an enjoyable amenity for area residents. Since the Tour passes through more than 600 towns and cities over its approximately 3,500 kilometer length, with its route changing every year to ensure that all of France's regions are featured, these branding, tourism, infrastructure, and amenity benefits are spread across the entire country, achieving a national distribution of benefits rarely achieved in sports or other mega events that are more typically centered on specific metropolitan regions.

Eponymously, the Tour is always held in France, implying that the leverage associated with competitive bidding among aspiring hosts, or the threat to relocate the race in its entirety to another country, is reduced. And while cities and towns compete with one another to host individual stages of the race, the cost of hosting a day of the Tour de France – at least for the time being – is modest compared to that paid by cities hosting other mega sporting events. Moreover, in this era of sustainability, cycling advocates can successfully argue that cycling is not merely a form of recreation, but is also a form of personal transport that offers significant environmental and public health benefits. Thus, when compared to the tens of billions of dollars invested by Olympic and World Cup host cities, and the lack of proportional economic benefits that accompany those public investments, the Tour de France offers a more promising result for its host towns and cities.

This chapter provides an overview of the Tour de France as a mega sporting event, viewed through the lens of economic impacts. It begins with a primer on men's competitive road cycling and its annual tour; an important discussion because competitive cycling is different in many ways from most other major competitive sports. Next it describes the evolution of the Tour's business model since its origins in the early 1900s as the brainchild of newspaper editors hoping to increase circulation and advertising, and onward its current status as the world's premier road cycling event, as well as the crown jewel of the largest multi-media company in France. Against this backdrop, it reviews the overall budget of the Tour, examining in detail the revenues and costs associated with corporate sponsorship of teams, non-team corporate sponsorships and the famed publicity caravan, spectator and broadcast revenues, and the fees paid by cities and towns for the privilege of hosting a stage arrival or departure. Finally, it describes and critiques the findings of the few economic impact studies of the Tour, with examples from the national and local levels, and concludes by discussing the implications for current and future stage hosts.

2   THE TOUR DE FRANCE AND ELITE MEN'S ROAD CYCLING

The Tour de France is the world's oldest and most prestigious multi-stage road cycling race. Launched in 1903, the Tour was soon joined by similar road races in Italy and Spain: the Giro d'Italia (Tour of Italy) in 1909, and the Vuelta a Espana (Tour of Spain) in 1935. Together, these three races are known as the 'Grand Tours' of men's competitive road cycling, and are among the longest multi-stage races in the world,[2] although the last two are less well known outside of continental Europe. In one of the many ways that competitive cycling is different from other major sports, its annual 'world' championships – the UCI Road World Championships – is considered less prestigious than the three grand tours. First held in 1921, the world championships feature one-day contests across a variety of categories (men's, women's, juniors, and so on) that test at most one aspect of a rider's skill such as speed on the flat, or climbing on hills, depending on its location. It also differs from the three grand tours in that participating teams represent their home nations rather than 'trade' or sponsored teams. Perhaps most damning to the cachet of these world championships is that they often fail to attract the best male riders, in stark contrast to the grand tours.

Each July, the Tour de France gathers nearly 200 of the best road cyclists in the world, grouped into 20 or more teams, to engage in a grueling three-week, approximately 3,500 kilometer road race across France, competing against the clock, the terrain, the weather, and one another. The race is 'staged', which means that it is broken down into 20 or more individual day-long races or '*étapes*' (stages), where the primary objective is to win the overall race with the minimum time across these 20-plus stages. Stages can be 'ordinary' meaning the first rider to cross the finish line wins the stage, 'individual time trials' where each cyclist races alone to win the stage with the fastest time, 'team time trials' where the teams compete on the basis of the time their fifth rider crosses the stage finish line, or a 'prologue' stage where short individual time trials determine the starting positions of the first stage.

It is critical to understand that competitive cycling is different from other major sports in that cycling is a *team* sport with *individual* winners. For example, Alberto Contador was the nominal winner of the Tour de France in 2010, notwithstanding doping allegations at the time of this writing. Contador is a great rider, certainly the best stage-rider of his generation, and quite possibly one of the greatest riders of all time, but the real winner of the race was the Astana team on which he rode. No rider can win any professional race without the full support of his team, and in fact, the best rider may not win if his team is inferior to the others: In the 2008 Tour, many believed that Cadel Evans was a better rider than the eventual overall winner, Carlos Sastre, but Sastre's team, Computer Sciences Corporation (CSC), was much stronger than Evans's Davitamon-Lotto team, and was able to lead Sastre to victory.

Each team supports nine cyclists, who among them play several different roles, including the team leader (who is generally considered to be the team's best bet for winning the individual title) and the remaining '*domestiques*' ('servants') who protect the team leader by blocking wind and stopping breakaways by other teams. Generally speaking, there are two kinds of riders, the 'sprinters' who are capable of generating very high speeds (65+ km/hour), and the 'climbers' who leverage their comparatively lower weight to generate proportionally more power on the hills. Team leaders tend to be good at both, as well as individual time trials. Each team is supported by a number of coaches and race officials riding in vehicles following behind the *peloton*.

The team's approach to the race usually includes riding in a group or '*peloton*' ('small ball') during the flat stages, while strategically engaging in 'breakaways', 'chases', 'sprints' to win certain stages of the race. Generally, it is the team that includes the race leader that controls the tempo of the race in a given stage. Most essentially, it is the *domestiques* who sacrifice their chances for individual glory on behalf of the team, providing a break from wind resistance for the team leader (a cyclist riding behind another cyclist requires an estimated 20 percent less energy to ride at a given speed than the cyclist in the lead, in a technique called 'drafting'), by taking breaks to return to the team car that follows behind the *peloton* to get water and nutritional supplements for their teammates, and when the team leader has an equipment malfunction, they are expected to give up their bikes.

The route of the Tour de France changes from year to year, as organizers have pledged to feature all regions of France along its path every five years. During a typical race, the course passes through nearly 600 cities and towns, and across the 20 or so stages, with each stage averaging approximately 100 to 200 kilometers in length. Most races include two or three time trials (both individual and team), three days in the Alps, three days in the Pyrenees, and a half-dozen 'flat' stages culminating in a final, largely ceremonial, stage on the Champs-Elysées in Paris. Among these 600 cities and towns, approximately 30 are official 'stage hosts', meaning locations where arrivals, departures, or both, are celebrated. Stages are increasingly held outside of France – mainly the '*Grand Départ*' – and it is not unusual for the Tour to enter Italy, Spain, Switzerland, and Germany, and more recently sites further afield. The direction of travel along the course each year also alternates between clockwise and counter-clockwise rotations; the first counter-clockwise race was in 1913. The course design includes one or two days of rest, used to transport athletes from the start in one town to the finish in another. Tour fanatics often point to rationales for course design that lay beyond pragmatism and the showcasing of French diversity, with the more generous accounts pointing to the creation of more interesting or challenging routes, and the more skeptical pointing to accommodating the strengths and weakness of particular riders or teams.

The overall winner of the Tour de France is the 'general classification' or 'GC' winner, with the lowest cumulative time over the entire length of the race. A rider's position in the GC competition is normally stated based on the leader's time. For example, Alberto Contador completed the 2010 Tour in 91 hours, 58 minutes, and 48 seconds. The second-place rider, Andy Schleck, finished 39 seconds behind Contador, an unusually close result. The '*lanterne rouge*' or last-place finisher, Adriano Malori, finished four hours and 27 minutes behind Contador; several riders did not finish. The leader in the GC competition after each daily stage earns the right to wear the coveted '*maillot jaune*' (yellow jersey) during the subsequent stage of the race.

Winning a stage of the Tour is extremely prestigious, and once won, riders will compete furiously to keep the jersey for even one additional day. Many riders consider winning the right to wear the yellow jersey as a high point of their career. Thomas Voekler, the French rider who famously kept Lance Armstrong from taking the yellow jersey for 10 consecutive days during the 2004 Tour, has built a very successful career on stage wins. There are also several other prizes awarded for the daily stages that keep riders motivated and spectators interested throughout the race. For example, the green jersey is awarded to the rider with the most cumulative points, where points are awarded based both on finishing position (first, second, and so on). The polka-dot or 'king of the mountains' jersey is worn by winners of climbing stages, based on order of finish, but where points are determined based on the difficulty of the hills. The white jersey goes to the best young rider, and the red numbers (rather than black) are worn by the rider deemed the 'most aggressive'. Riders must also meet pre-established time requirements for each stage, and if they fail to do so, they are disqualified.

The Tour de France is arguably the most important race in the annual world circuit of elite road cycling, but it is only recently that its organizers have agreed to have the sport's premier event formally included as part of an annual calendar of competitions. Historically, the influence of Amaury Sports Organization which owns the Tour (as well as the Veulta a Espana, and many of the other most important cycling events) has been such that its organizers were able to fend off efforts to bring the race under any degree of control by the international cycling federation. More recently, common ground appears to have been found, as the Tour de France and the other grand tours are now part of an official annual calendar of events known as the UCI WorldTour. The UCI WorldTour is governed by the International Cycling Union (Union Cycliste Internationale: UCI) in its capacity as cycling's international federation, and recognized as such by the International Olympic Committee (IOC).

While the UCI is a comparatively weak international sports federation – in cycling the institutional strength lies instead with its national federations – its influence may grow as competitive cycling becomes more globalized. Currently, its mission is to develop and promote the eight disciplines of cycling through collaboration with the national cycling federations in each member country.[3] It operates the UCI WorldTour, the latest organization of the annual racing circuit,[4] aiming to standardize the calendar, to enforce codes of conduct, and to develop cycling's international audience, among other goals. Overall, the UCI WorldTour circuit includes 27 races over the calendar year, the majority of which are held in Europe, but with increasing efforts to broaden the international cycling audience with the introduction of the Tour Down Under in Adelaide, Australia (started in 1999, and became part of the UCI circuit in 2008), the Grand Prix de Cycliste de Québec and the Grand Prix de Cycliste de Montréal in Canada (both started in 2010 as part of the UCI circuit), and for the first time, the

Tour of Beijing (starting in 2011 under a four-year contract with the UCI, and is part of the legacy of the 2008 Olympics).[5]

The UCI also ranks individual cyclists, trade teams, and national teams according to performance in various races. Since only 20 or so teams are invited to participate in the circuit each year, these rankings are critical. For cyclists, team membership is the only path into the marquee events of cycling, now including the Tour de France.[6] In the UCI rankings, individuals earn points based on race results, and team rankings are based on the cumulative scores of their top five cyclists. The Tour de France is the most important race in the ranking point system, followed closely by the two other grand tours. For example, according to the UCI World Rankings for the 2011 season, the overall winner of the Tour would earn 200 points, while winners of individual stages would earn 20 points per stage won; the winner of the Giro d'Italia or the Vuelta a Espana would earn 170 points, and 16 points for winning individual stages; other circuit races award lower point values.

3   ORIGINS OF THE TOUR DE FRANCE: *L'AUTO*, *L'ÉQUIPE* AND THE AMAURY SPORTS ORGANIZATION

Inaugurated in 1903, the Tour de France was the brainchild of French newspapermen Géo Lefèvre and Henri Desgrange, the latter as editor-in-chief of *L'Auto* ('The Car') a daily sports-oriented newspaper circulated in France. The race was conceived as a means to provide new content, improve circulation and ultimately to increase advertising revenues for a newspaper that was struggling to stay afloat. Yet even 100 years ago, the idea to create a sports event as a means to supplementing the revenue model of another business was not new, in cycling or in sports more broadly. In fact, the very same strategy had been deployed by *L'Auto*'s main competitor, *Le Vélo* ('The Bicycle') which at that time had the largest circulation among sports dailies. In the early 1890s, *Le Vélo* owners had started the Paris–Roubaix and Bourdeaux–Paris cycling races; the former is still operating today as one of the classic or '*monument*' one-day races of the UCI WorldTour. It is no coincidence that during the same time period, Frenchman Pierre de Coubertin had the fledging modern Olympic Games underway, and so these new cycling races also tapped into a Western cultural renaissance associated with amateur and elite sport (Reed, 2010).[7]

For *L'Auto*, Lefèvre and Desgrange's fledgling sports daily, the creation of the Tour de France in 1903 did more than boost circulation, its success kept the newspaper from going under. Struggling with poor circulation and an uncertain future after only three years in operation, the Tour breathed new life into *L'Auto* almost immediately, tripling circulation in the first five years, from 25,000 in 1903 to 65,000 in 1906; by the 1920s, circulation passed 250,000 copies, peaking at 500,000 copies per day during the race itself (ibid., p.104). The business model of the Tour de France was simple: it offered content and publicity for *L'Auto*, thereby expanding its newspaper circulation market, while also offering larger audiences for newspaper advertisers as well as providing sponsorship opportunities as part of the race environs. The strategy worked beyond all expectations. Circulation, advertising and sponsorship revenue boomed as race organizers found they had tapped into a triad of conditions favorable to the event: the French and European love of cycling; the burgeoning wealth of the industrial revolution; and growing interest in democracy and French culture. Reed, in his economic history of the Tour, describes this period from 1903 to 1929 as a 'marriage of the bicycle and the press' (ibid., p.104). The race played a critical role in the evolution of that newspaper to its current position, renamed *L'Équipe* after the Second World War, as the largest sports daily in France.[8]

The incredible success of the Tour de France also has a tremendous impact on the business of its current owner, the Amaury Sport Organization (ASO), and its parent company the French media group Éditions Phillippe Amaury (EPA), which purchased *L'Équipe* and the rights to operate the Tour in the 1965. Alongside *L'Équipe*, the ASO owns other print media properties including *L'Équipe* Magazine, France Football, and Vélo Magazine, as well as a television channel, L'Équipe TV. The ASO is also one of the largest operators of sporting events in France. It operates the Vuelta a Espana, the UCI Paris–Roubaix race and other cycling events, as well as the Paris Marathon, the Dakar Rally (annual off-road automobile race, now run in South America due to security concerns), and it is a major partner in the Open de France golf tournament.

4   THE TOUR'S EVOLVING BUSINESS MODEL

Over the past century, the Tour de France has evolved from a national cycling race into one of the world's most recognizable mega sporting event brands. Tour organizers have grown and cultivated the event through a careful balancing act, weighing the interests of the race owners, with those of elite men's road cycling, alongside the business community, and also with great attention to French citizens who themselves feel a strong sense of shared identity with the Tour as an event and as a reflection of French culture. Viewed through the lens of its evolving business model over the past century – an expansive mix of corporate sponsorships, broadcast revenues, host city subventions and general advertising through the publicity caravan – the success of the Tour owners in managing this balance over the past century is a record of checks and balances. At times, the Tour has favored the ethics of competition over profitability, compromising its future viability; at other times, the pursuit of profit has compromised the quality of competition and affected the Tour's brand, mirroring some of the negative impacts associated with increasing commercialization evident at all levels of professional sport.

Corporate Sponsorship of Teams

Although in the present day Tour de France organizers have no control over the sponsorship and licensing of professional cycling teams, and do not receive any direct revenue from the teams aside from race entry fees, this has not always been the case. Since the earliest days of the race, Tour organizers have experimented with both individual and team formats for the race, to maintain interest in the event and to respond to new revenue opportunities. For example, the organizers added time trials and encouraged businesses to sponsor individual prizes such as the 'yellow jersey', first introduced in 1919, and quickly followed by other sponsored prizes.[9]

Among these innovations, the issue of team sponsorship has proven a particularly contentious issue. From 1903 to 1929, bicycle manufacturers were actively serving as team sponsors, a system that allowed the wealthiest of sponsors to attract the most talented riders, and effectively control the outcome of the race. By 1929, Tour organizers sought to distance themselves from the control of the bicycling industry, establishing a 'strict division between the Tour's competitive and publicity structures' (Reed, 2010, p. 110). First, organizers instituted a national team formula, where the top riders would be drawn from and represent their home countries. Second, to compensate for the loss of team sponsorship opportunities, the organizers aggressively courted businesses to serve as sponsors for the race prizes (ibid., p. 106).[10]

Tour organizers were able to maintain these two separate identities, as an athletic contest on the one hand and a business concern on the other, up until after the Second World War, when the recovering French economy meant that many new kinds of businesses were eager to promote their products by attaching them to major sporting events. Early evidence of the importance of these so-called '*extra-sportifs*' (business interests that lay outside those traditionally associated with the cycling industry) first appeared on riders' jerseys and shorts in the 1950s (ibid., p. 108). Over the next decade, the *extra-sportifs* grew so powerful that they were able to lead the charge for a return to the sponsored team format, aiming to maximize their brand identity with specific riders and teams. Their tactics included pressuring Tour organizers by withholding key riders from the race and since most riders were under team contracts for the full racing year, the sponsors were able to bar them from participating if they chose. This challenge came to a head in 1960 when in a show of *extra-sportif* strength the French national team found it had no top-ranked riders able to participate in the Tour. Consequently, in 1962, the race reverted to the sponsored team format.

The increased commercialization of the Tour de France during this era came about despite spirited but short-lived opposition of then-organizer Goddet, who not only felt he had a duty to safeguard the dignity of the race and the sport of cycling, but was also scandalized by the idea of Tour champions serving as sandwich-board men or *'hommes sandwiches'* to the *extra-sportifs* (ibid., p.108). Objections to trade sponsorship also came from some French residents, who opposed the road closures made necessary by the Tour, if it was now to be run for commercial purposes. Thus in 1967 and 1968, the race returned to a national team format, but by 1969 the trade team format was back in place, and has been so exclusively ever since. Not coincidentally, it was during this time that *L'Équipe* was purchased by Emelien Amaury, founder of the Amaury Group (later the ASO), and along with the media company, Amaury acquired the right to operate the Tour de France.

For better or worse, the trade team sponsorship is now fully entrenched in the business model of the Tour. Riders and team brands can be closely linked, such as Raymond 'PouPou' Poulidor for GAN-Mercier during the 1970s, and Lance Armstrong for the US Postal Service in the early 2000s. Sponsoring a UCI pro-cycling team in 2010 was estimated to cost an average of €10 million (US$13 million), offering companies the chance for global exposure throughout the racing year, including during its most valuable promotional property, the Tour de France. Team sponsors pay riders' salaries, their year-round training and race expenses, while also providing coaching, equipment and other benefits. The Tour provides a modest stipend for each competing team, to defray participation expenses, estimated in 2010 at approximately €50,000. Teams can employ between 30 to 50 people over the racing year, including the riders.

Among elite male road cyclists, the average salary for riders contracted to a sponsored UCI team was €190,000 (US$266,000) in 2010, although within each team, rider salaries vary widely according to position and record. These salaries are relatively low when compared to the salaries of professional athletes in other sports, such as the US major leagues, although race prize money is often shared among team members, and for top-performing teams, these earnings can substantially supplement base salaries. In addition, performance bonuses are often pledged by team sponsors, and in some cases, individual riders can pursue sponsorships for endorsing products not controlled by their team contract.

The Tour de France offers the largest purse in professional cycling, valued at over €3.4 million (US$4.5 million) in 2010.[11] The largest individual prize goes to the overall general classification winner, at €450,000 (US$600,000) in 2010, followed by the 2nd and 3rd place riders in the general classification at €250,000 and €100,000 respectively. By tradition, the winner relinquishes his purse to his team and support staff, reflecting the often substantial endorsement opportunities made available to the Tour champion. There are also a variety of stage prizes that are awarded each day of racing: for example, in 2010, the prize for winning the prologue stage was €8,000, €7,000 for a regular stage, and €25,000 for the final stage. There are also daily and overall cash prizes associated with the classification competitions indicated by colored jerseys, as well as small race completion bonuses. Team sponsors, for their part, ensure that when their riders wear a stage prize jersey, it is modified to display their logos.

Tour-wide Corporate Sponsorships and the Publicity Caravan

In addition to the corporate sponsorship opportunities associated with trade teams, the ASO offers a set of event-wide sponsorship opportunities organized in a tiered structure similar to that of other mega sporting events. For the 2009 Tour de France, these tiered sponsorship revenues contributed an estimated €40 million to ASO coffers or an estimated 40 percent of its total revenues: €18 million from the four 'club members' in the first tier (including Skoda), €13 million from the nine or so 'official sponsors' in the second tier (including Nike), and €8 million from the 10 or more 'official suppliers' in the third tier (including PowerBar and other companies that supply goods), and another €8–10 million from the publicity caravan.

Although it accounts for only a small portion of overall revenues from corporate sponsorship, the Tour's publicity caravan is a fan favorite, defining the festive atmosphere associated with viewing the race in person. Introduced in 1930 by Tour organizers as part of the strategy to offer commercial interests displaced from team sponsorship a role that would lie outside of the race itself, the caravan is a parade of business vehicle-based 'floats' that precede the race by an hour or two at the start of each stage, including those occasions when the *Grand Départ* is held outside of France. Businesses pay for the right to participate in the caravan, with performers riding on the vehicles tossing samples of their products and other goodies to spectators along the roadside. While the earliest version of the caravan included only 10 vehicles, by 1935 its membership had increased to 46 businesses.[12]

Today, the publicity caravan is an attraction on its own merits, with Tour organizers estimating that nearly 40 percent of the live spectator audience arrives primarily to take in the show. The caravan includes nearly 200 businesses, in a parade that is almost 20 kilometers long and takes nearly an hour to pass the roadside viewer. In 2009, more than 15 million 'gifts' and product samples were distributed. The cost for major sponsorship in the caravan ranged from between 200,000 and 500,000 euros in 2009, for a total of approximately €8 million in 2009, or less than 8 percent of the total Tour de France budget (Roche and Mercat, 2009, 2010).

Despite the success of the Tour in attracting national and regional sponsors to the publicity caravan, current conditions do not portend growth in the market for corporate sponsors. In large part, the attractiveness of the Tour for sponsors outside of France and Europe can vary depending on the nationality of star cyclists, and other issues in the sports industry. There is perhaps no better example of how the Tour's prospects in international markets are tied to the nationality and performance of individual riders than that of the US viewership levels during and after the Lance Armstrong years. Television ratings for the Tour on the US-based Outdoor Living Network (OLN, aka 'Only Lance Network', now Versus) dropped an estimated 50 percent between 2005, the year of Armstrong's historic seventh consecutive win, and 2006, after Armstrong announced his retirement for the first time. Even during Armstrong's brief return to the Tour in 2009 and 2010, an effort perhaps more centered on raising cancer awareness rather than winning, US viewership increased but did not fully return to 2005 levels, despite expansion in market share for Versus with NBCUniversal/Comcast. Armstrong's appeal is such that he influenced which races were covered in the US and which were not: the Giro d'Italia has never been directly broadcast by a US cable channel, because Armstrong did not race in it during his peak competitive years, although he did so for the first time in 2010. For these events, cycling fans are increasingly turning to pay-for-service internet streaming sites.

Doping scandals have also affected the corporate sponsorship market for the Tour de France. Although prevalent throughout professional sports, allegations about the use of illegal performance-enhancing drugs have a long history in the Tour. Anecdotal reports of doping date back to the 1900s, and drugs are considered to have led to the death of Tom Simpson during the 1967 Tour. Yet the history of doping in competitive cycling predates the Tour itself, and can be traced to the extreme rigors of multi-stage races. As German sports reporter Hans Halter famously wrote in his 1998 article in *Der Spiegel*, 'no dope, no hope', implying that doping was more a requirement than an option. In the early years of the Tour, drugs were often used to combat pain and fatigue so that riders could simply finish the race; now it is common that drugs are used to strengthen their muscles, boost red blood cell production, and to otherwise improve performance, as well as to level the playing field with other riders who are also alleged to be doping. The UCI, and Tour de France officials alongside, are taking a strong stance against doping: they stripped US cyclist Floyd Landis of his title in 2006 for doping, and in 2011, their case against the 2010 Tour champion Spaniard Alberto Contador was under appeal.

Since many companies choose to sponsor the Tour for identity with brand values centered on vitality and competitive success, continuing scandals associated with doping in professional cycling has resulted in a softening in demand for Tour sponsorships. Companies that sponsor teams are most directly affected, since their brand is closely tied with its roster of riders: if one or more of its team members test positive, as was the case with Deutsche Telecom in 2007, the company will often drop the team sponsorship as a way to distance their brand from the scandal. The rapid turnover in team sponsorships can in large part be traced to the fallout and repositioning necessary due to increased testing and surveillance starting in 1998. There is less evidence that doping has impacted the demand for Tour-wide sponsorships, from 'club members', to the 'official sponsors', 'official suppliers' and participants in the publicity caravan, in part because they are more distant from the reputations of individual riders. In this sense, race-wide sponsorships are a safer form of sponsorship; but at the same time, their market is also less valuable as it is primarily national and local in scope, without the access to the global marketplace that team sponsorship can provide. Similarly, there is little evidence that the number of towns and cities interested in serving as stage hosts has declined in response to the increase in doping scandals over the past decade – in fact there are more places bidding to be stage hosts than ever before – perhaps attributable to the distance between their broader civic interests and the performance of specific cyclists.

Taken together, the Tour's reliance on the star power of individuals, the nationality of those individuals, and vulnerability to high-profile doping scandals, suggest that there is limited, or at least unpredictable, potential for growing revenues via corporate sponsorships, at least under the current business model. More broadly, the Tour's fortunes have also been subject to the recent downturn in the European and global economy, resulting in a softening in the market for corporate sponsorships, sports or otherwise.

Spectator and Broadcast Revenues

A defining difference between the Tour de France business model and that of most other mega sporting events is the fact that live spectators are not required to purchase tickets. This curiosity is based in pragmatics, since patrolling the estimated 10 million or more spectators who line the 3,500 kilometer route each year presents a near impossible undertaking, with organizational and security challenges likely to cost more to resolve than that which could be realized from tickets sales. Additionally, the live spectator experience is incredibly short-lived as the entire race often passes a single viewer in a matter of minutes. Moreover, the politics associated with closing public roads for a private event might be far more contentious if area residents were also asked to purchase tickets to watch an event that they were graciously accommodating. Thus, the strategy with regard to ticket sales remains the case today, as race organizers capitalize on this gesture to create the goodwill and carnival atmosphere that characterizes the race to French citizens, to foreign fans, and to the cyclists themselves.

Broadcast revenues, in contrast, are fair game to the Tour owners. In keeping with the origins of the race as a means to provide content for print media, the sale of race broadcast rights has evolved to be the keystone of the Tour business model. By 1929, the rights for radio broadcasts were sold, and by 1948, the first full race television coverage was transmitted by the national French television network. Revenues from these sales were very small, however, in part because of state monopolies in broadcasting, and in part because the full commercial reach of television had not yet emerged. Consequently, the impact on the Tour's profitability was the reverse of the intent: as fans tuned in to their radios and televisions, they no longer need to buy daily newspapers to follow the progress of the race. Revenues from sales of *L'Équipe* (as *L'Auto* was renamed after the Second World War) plummeted, and the modest income from radio and television revenues did not come close to filling the gap. By the 1950s, the race was routinely running at a deficit (Reed, 2010, p. 112).

During this period of financial uncertainty, Tour operators were forced to make peace with the demands of businesses for more access to promotional opportunities. By 1962, the return to trade team sponsorship coincided with changes in television broadcast technology and increasingly widespread television ownership, and the business model of the Tour appeared to be on the precipice of a major shift. In 1965, the owners of the Tour, recognizing that a change from their core competencies was afoot, sold *L'Équipe* and its subsidiary components, which included the race itself, to Émilien Amaury and his Amaury Group – who controlled many of the major sporting events in France and owned many of the facilities in which they were played – and which would later become the Amaury Sports Organization (ASO) (ibid., p. 115).

In 1982, the deregulation of radio and television broadcasting set the stage for the much higher broadcast revenues garnered by the Tour de France today. The number of hours of race coverage expanded as the market for Tour coverage grew both in France and the rest of Europe. The Tour was quickly becoming one of the world's most-watched annual sporting events, and according to most estimates, was the third most-watched overall, behind the Summer Olympics and the FIFA World Cup championships. (Although, as discussed below, this ranking is based on misleading estimates that overstate the Tour's audience size, multiplying the cumulative Tour audience by the 20 or more days it is covered on television; whereas in reality, the average audience size varies markedly from day to day, and hour to hour.) Between 1986 and 1996, coverage by the public television stations in France grew from 38 hours to 112, and accounted for 7.5 percent of all sports content (ibid., p. 117). As the potential audience grew, so did the broadcast fees. Reed (2010) estimates broadcast rights sales, for contracts of varying durations, at 12 million francs in 1990, 32 million francs in 1992, 50 million francs in 1994, €85 million in 1998, and €120 million in a new five-year contract signed in 2007 (Roche and Mercat, 2009, 2010, p. 200). So too did the importance of broadcast revenues in the overall business model, growing from less than 2 percent of the overall Tour budget in 1960, to 26 percent in 1992, to its present-day share at 40 percent of the ASO budget in 2010.

Globally, the television audience of the Tour was estimated at 150 million people in the mid-1980s, and by the late 1990s, estimates of one billion viewers were common (ibid., p. 200). By 2010, estimates often indicated that the global audience had doubled to two billion viewers in more than 180 countries. Critics, however, suggest that these measures vastly overstate the size of the Tour's audience, because they track 'cumulative' viewership, in effect capturing all viewers whether they tune in for one minute or for five hours (Initiative, 2005). A more meaningful measure would be 'average' viewership, capturing the average ratings across the entire length of the broadcast. Using the 'average' measure, the viewership for the last stage of the 2005 Tour – the last stage often yields the highest viewership, and this was the year Lance Armstrong was gunning for his seventh consecutive win – was 16 million viewers across the globe (ibid.). Consequently, a rough estimate of the total audience over the duration of the Tour would be approximately 320 million, although even this more conservative measure is misleadingly generous given that viewership is much higher on the last day of the race. At the same time, this 16 million viewers per stage estimate does not include time-shifted broadcasts, or the increasing importance of internet-based audiences, so yet another adjustment would be needed.

Use of the average viewership measure also affects the common perception that the Tour is the third most-watched mega sporting event in the world, since the cumulative measure distorts total viewership upward due to the three-week duration of the event. Compared to other mega sporting events of 2005 – notably a non-Olympic and non-World Cup championships year – the Tour de France would rank as the 8th most viewed event, after the Super Bowl (93 million viewers), the UEFA Champions League Final (73 million), the Canadian Grand Prix Formula 1 (51 million), the Men's 100 meter final at the World Athletics Championship (23 million), the final games of the MLB World Series (22 million) and the NBA championships (20 million), and the final day of the US Golf Masters Championship (20 million) (ibid.). Of course, the degree to which many of these other events are 'global' is debatable: for example, the Super Bowl, the World Series, the NBA Finals, and even the Masters are mainly watched by US audiences. The Tour's audience, in contrast, is largely European, with the highest levels of viewership in Germany, Belgium, and France, followed by the United States (ibid.).

Regardless of the debates over measuring audience size, it remains that the Tour de France is a mega sporting event of great interest to broadcasters, who are well-equipped to understand the value of their content to advertisers. Today, the Tour is the most broadcast event in France, before the (tennis) French Open, and the Champions League (football). According to the ASO, in 2005, the Tour resulted in 2,965 hours of TV broadcasts in 184 countries, with 1,583 hours in Europe, 504 in America, 502 in Asia, 175 in Africa, 116 in the Middle East, and 85 in the rest of the world (Desbordes, 2007). In 2005, each French TV viewer consumed an average of five hours and 30 minutes of live Tour coverage, against three hours and five minutes for the French Open, two hours and 50 minutes for the Formula 1 auto-racing championship, one hour and 55 minutes for the six-nations nations rugby tournament, and one hour and 20 minutes for the Champions League.[13] The Tour de France brand is also reported to have a 90 percent recognition rate throughout Europe, and is associated with strong values on 'heroism, festivity, generosity, proximity, France, etc' (ibid.).

Stage Host Subventions

A foundational principle of the Tour de France is that it should showcase French culture as well as the French landscape, and consequently the route of the course changes from year to year. As discussed earlier, its route alternates between clockwise and counter-clockwise paths, pledging to highlight all regions of France at least once in every five-year period. Combining this route planning principle with the multi-stage nature of the race, the result is that there are approximately 30 or more possibilities to host a stage arrival or departure, or one of the other special events surrounding the race, such as the *Grand Départ*. For example in 2005, the Tour consisted of 21 stages over 23 days (with two rest days) with arrivals and departures organized in 36 cities and towns, including nine 'stop-over' towns.

Since 1903, cities and towns across France have vied for the opportunity to have the Tour locate an arrival or departure in their town. While their primary motivation likely centered on offering their residents a popular and enjoyable amenity, there was some commercial motivation surrounding giving local businesses the chance to court spectators into visiting their restaurants, shops, and hotels. Almost immediately, Tour organizers realized that aspiring 'stage hosts' would be willing to pay for the privilege of hosting the race. The initial fees or 'subventions' were small, estimated to be between 1,000 and 5,000 francs per host in the 1920s, and increasing to 25,000 francs on average in the 1930s, varying from town to town depending on the prestige associated with particular stages, as well as the logistics of particular locales (Reed, 2010, p. 106). These subventions were an important part of the Tour budget, accounting for 20 percent of the total race budget in the 1930s, increasing to 40 percent by 1947 (ibid., p. 118). The advent of new revenues from selling broadcast rights in the early1970s meant that the Tour could rely less on these subventions, and as a percent of the total budget, subventions decreased to 11 percent in 1999, and 8 percent by 2009 or €11 million.

The process for determining the route of the Tour de France is managed by the ASO, and is an ongoing effort that occurs two to five years in advance of each race. The selection process begins with an expression of intent by a prospective stage host, typically in the form of a letter sent to the ASO. For 2010, more than 250 towns expressed interest in hosting the Tour, an amount far in excess of the 30 or so opportunities. Choices are made based on local geography and road condition, in the context of broader logistics of stage characteristics including duration, desired challenge level and terrain. Prospective hosts also must be able to handle the large number of spectators expected during the stage, as well accommodating the 4,500 people and 2,400 vehicles that accompany the Tour on the road, building and dismantling a temporary infrastructure of bleachers, rest areas, medical facilities, and media tents every day.

The subvention fees charged by the ASO in 2010 were €50,000 for a start, and €100,000 for a finish. In addition, each stage host is expected to invest in road maintenance, signage systems; to provide eight kilometers of safety barriers; to plant yellow flowers in its open spaces; and to pay for the essential municipal services such as police details and garbage collections during the event. These last costs are often far higher than the fee charged by the ASO (CSM, 2010). For example, in 2002, the city of Reims paid €88,000 to the ASO, and invested another €150,000 in preparations (Roche and Mercat, 2009, 2010, p. 198). The average investment ranges between €150,000 and €300,000, but the actual expenditure varies widely among stage hosts, with some running into the low millions.

In an effort to expand the appeal of the Tour outside of France, race organizers have occasionally held a symbolic start, the *'Grand Départ'* (grand start), in locations ranging from Amsterdam (1954) to London and Kent (2007).[14] The *Grand Départ* often includes more than one stage over two or three days, including a *prologue* (a short individual time trial to determine placement in the first stage) and the first stage itself. Looking forward, the ASO has indications of interest in hosting the *Grand Départ* from Corsica for 2013, from Florence for 2014, and Scotland for 2017, among other contenders. The bidding for the *Grand Départ* yields higher fees for the ASO. For example, London paid €2 million to the ASO for the right to host the *Grand Départ* in 2007, paying an additional €3 million in event costs, and according to advocates yielded many multiples of those initial investments in subsequent economic and social impacts. Scotland's bid for 2017 is similarly sunny, anticipating €5 million in fees and local costs, in exchange for anticipated gross economic benefits in excess of €100 million. Since the ASO is able to leverage much higher bid fees from cities outside of France, and because the bidding process increases its brand visibility in a manner similar to the Olympics and the World Cup, it is likely that there will be increasing attention to the potential of globalizing the Tour through the *Grand Départ*.

The Tour's Operating Budget

The annual operating budget of the Tour de France as reported by the ASO was approximately €100 million in 2007, €90 million in 2005, and €77 million in 2003. Most of these annual operating expenses, estimated at €70 million, are paid to the 230 permanent staff of the ASO, who organize the race from year to year, and who also operate a number of other races and events throughout France and beyond. The ASO handles all race logistics, from route selection to media logistics, and onward to drug testing and the management of thousands of volunteers.

It is important to note that this reported €100 million budget does not include the expenses of the teams. For each team, the estimated average annual budget is €7.5 million, of which an estimated 15 percent or €1.1 million per team is spent on the Tour de France for items such as transportation, accommodation, coaches, technicians, and equipment. As an example, the average pro team will need approximately 100 bicycles each year to outfit its riders, although the bikes, or their parts, are often provided in-kind for advertising. Nor does the ASO pay for many of the localized expenses now routinely paid for by the towns and cities that serve as stage hosts, averaging €300,000 across each of the 30 or so cities and towns that host race arrivals and departures for each of the 20 or more stages, for items such as road maintenance, signage, and municipal services. Taken together, the Tour's operating expenses in 2007 total approximately €132 million, with the Tour organizers paying approximately €100 million, the team sponsors together paying approximately €22 million, and stage hosts paying approximately €8–10 million in total (Roche and Mercat, 2009, 2010, p. 198).

On the revenue side, the ASO reports that of its €100 million budget in 2007, it earned approximately €50 million from the sale of broadcast rights, €40 million from sponsor partnerships and €10 million from stage host subventions. For broadcast rights, the importance of this revenue stream to the ASO is increasing: In 1997, broadcast revenues were 30 percent of total revenues, and by 2007, they represented 50 percent of total revenues (ibid., p. 199). France Télévisions, the national French network, paid €20 million to the ASO for the right to broadcast the Tour on their network, with the remaining €30 million earned from foreign networks.

5 ESTIMATING THE ECONOMIC IMPACTS OF THE TOUR DE FRANCE

Compared to other mega sporting events, there are relatively few studies of the economic impacts of the Tour de France, and fewer still in English language journals. It may be that the unique characteristics of the tour compared to the Olympics and Soccer World Cup – ownership by a private company, its reliable profitability and comparatively low costs, its success at showcasing the rich diversity of France, combined with the fact that it is always held in France, and its perception as a local celebration – render it a subject less controversial in terms of measuring economic impacts. For US- and UK-based scholars, concern with sports that dominate our own cultural contexts might also explain the dearth of academic research on the Tour that is available in English. Yet, it appears that there is also relatively little research found in the French and other continental journals, a situation that is likely to change given continuing efforts to globalize the Tour, and burgeoning interest in the economics of sports.

A Snapshot of the Bicycling Industry in France

Bicycling is a €4.5 billion per year industry in France, according to a report prepared for the French government in 2009, with the lion's share of that spending emanating from tourism activities related to cycling at €1.9 billion or 44 percent, followed by bicycle manufacturing at €1.4 billion or 32 percent, and bicycle sales and service at €360 million or 8 percent (ibid., p. 200). The industry is reported to employ over 35,000 people, and is labor intensive, with eight employees per €1 million of spending, compared to 2.4 employees per €1 million in the domestic automobile industry (ibid., p. 200). While the French are not the most avid cyclists in Europe – this honor belongs to the Dutch and the Danes – its ridership is much higher than that in most other parts of the world (ibid., p. 200).[15] More than 40 percent of the French use bicycles, 17 million regularly, and 15 million for recreation. Over 4.4 billion bicycle kilometers are traveled each year in France, for an average of 80 kilometers per resident per year, and representing a 3 percent mode share among all travel (ibid., p. 20).

Cycling is a very important part of the tourism industry in France. France dominates the market for bicycle-based tourism worldwide, capturing one-third of all cycling tourism in Europe. With over 5.5 million stays, cycling is the second most frequent activity of tourists in France. The estimated €1.9 billion spent supports 16,500 employees. In 2007, it is estimated that 7.2 million bike trips were made, of which 5.5 million or 76 percent were made by French residents, and 1.7 million or 24 percent by foreigners. The study also notes that average spending amounts for cycling tourists are higher than the average for other kinds of tourists: €73 per day for tourists moving from place to place (*'itinérant'* – such as cycling tours), versus 61 per day for those staying in one place for their stay (*'en séjour'*), versus all tourist spending on average at €54 per day (ibid., p. 18).

In an effort to capitalize on this comparative advantage in cycling tourism, as well as to capture the public health and sustainability benefits associated with the sport, France is investing in its cycling infrastructure. In 2010, nearly €450 million were spent by city and regional governments in 2010 on creating a 'true national network' of *'véloroutes'*. Spearheaded by coalitions of local governments, over 8,000 kilometers have been created in the past 10 years, with another 5,000 kilometers in the planning stages; the Strasbourg–Ortenau Eurodistrict is a case study in *véloroute* development. In turn, these public contracts have been estimated to return an estimated €144 million to the French government via corporate taxes, and have created 3,700 jobs with an estimated 1,500 jobs in the non-commercial cycling industry, including clubs, federations, and associations (ibid., p. 20).

Several reports, drawing on the same government source data for 2009, point to a list of positive externalities associated with additional investment in developing the cycling industry. These include public health benefits estimated at €5.6 billion, and a series of smaller-scale reductions in some of the negative externalities associated with automobile use, including parking (€42 million), traffic congestion (€24 million), noise (€2 million), climate change (€42 million), and pollution (€50 million) (ibid., p. 24). The main negative externality associated with increases in cycling, both for local trips and tourism, is safety where the impact of an increased number of accidents was estimated to cost €952 million in 2010. The reported net benefit of cycling externalities, or indirect effects, using these estimates is €4.5 billion, although it is not clear if these estimates net out the accidents from alternative modes of transportation (ibid., p. 24).

In the US, by contrast, 60 million or 25 percent of adults ride bicycles with some regularity, defined as at least once per month. The value of the US cycling industry is estimated at US$133 billion dollars, supporting nearly 1.1 million jobs across the country, and generating US$17.7 billion dollars in annual federal and state tax revenue. Cycling in the US produces US$53.1 billion dollars annually in retail sales and services: US$6.2 billion for gear (just over 10 percent) and US$46.9 billion for cycling trip-related expenditures (Outdoor Industry Foundation, 2006).

Economic Impact Studies of the Tour de France

Analyzes of the economic impact of the Tour de France are in short supply, in large part because the ASO is a private company, and is not required to open its books for public examination. Most references draw from data presented in a single source, an annual report on the bicycle economy in France prepared by a private consultant (INDDIGO Altermodal) for the French government over a series of years. The Tour receives specific attention in the 2009 report, and argues that the event delivers net economic benefits to its host country. Specifically, the report states that for 2009, the Tour produced spending in the amount of €272 million, created 2,700 jobs, and plays an important role in regional economic development by spreading this spending across the 600 or so towns and cities that line the race route (Roche and Mercat, 2009, 2010, p. 203).

Breaking down this annual economic impact estimate of €272 million into subcategories, approximately €100 million were spent by the ASO to organize the race, €22 million by the 20 or so teams while participating in the Tour, €16 million on advertising space and airtime, plus the cost of mounting a float for the publicity caravan; €35 million on production of broadcasts during the race; €10 million on stage host subventions; €7 million in value created from image enhancement for stage hosts; €80 million in total tourist spending; and €2 million on organized tours. The jobs estimate is based on the relative high intensity of employment in event management, with an assumption of 10 jobs created for every €1 million spent or approximately 2,700 jobs. Since 230 of these are permanent jobs at the ASO, the report estimates that the net number of jobs created in 2009 was approximately 2,500. While most of these jobs are 'new', they are not a 'net' addition to the job pool: since most Tour spending comes from within France there is a significant substitution effect that is unaccounted for. In addition, many of these jobs are likely temporary and low wage, serving the short-term needs of the Tour during the race as well as short periods immediately preceding and following (ibid.).

Economic Impact Studies of Stage Hosts

Among the few studies that do exist studying the economic impacts of the Tour de France, the majority focus on the impacts on the experience of local stage hosts. The question of local economic impacts is of interest to the ASO as well, since the price that towns and cities pay for the privilege of serving as a stage host is beginning to climb in the presence of a perceived gap between local costs and local benefits. For stage hosts, it is in their best interest to ensure that their bid price or subvention is roughly proportional to the public benefits accruing from the event; ideally the subvention fee would be lower. For the ASO, on the other hand, it may view the purpose of these economic impacts studies as demonstrating the value of the Tour for towns and cities across France, thereby increasing the supply of willing stage hosts, but also the possibility of commanding higher subvention fees in the face of a perceived gap that favors these towns and cities.

Desbordes (2007) compares two economic impact studies analyzing data from 2005, one commissioned by the ASO, and one commissioned by a tour stage host city, in an effort to point out the weaknesses of existing analytical frameworks. Beginning with the ASO report, he reports that the study was commissioned to 'have quantitative and qualitative data about the race, particularly about the economic impact that can be obtained through the race' in an effort to calibrate the local economic impacts in particular so as inform the price paid by stage towns for the privilege of hosting the event (p. 526). Conducted by a private consulting company, the study examined three stage host cities (Nancy, Gerardmer, and Albi), using a supply-side methodology that surveyed vendors (hotels, restaurants, and shops) for indications of transaction volume and composition.

The findings of the ASO commissioned report are not surprising, as Desbordes reports: 'Most vendors experienced short-term spikes in demand for goods and services, with local hotels running at near 100 percent occupancy (compared to seasonal averages of 75 percent, and annual averages of approximately 60 percent), and stores attributing increased sales to visitors, as well as event organizers' (p. 536). While hotel spending was not measured, the report does indicate that hotel occupancy rates on the night of the stage was 94 percent or above, compared to seasonal averages around 76 percent, and annual occupancy rates averaging 60 percent, despite the observation that one-night stays booked a year in advance would interrupt the longer stays typical of business and tourist travelers. The report concludes with survey results indicating that over 90 percent of vendors would wish to host a stage of the Tour again in future. A follow-up survey of local politicians, sponsors, journalists, and so on, indicated that they believed that hosting a stage had increased the image and awareness of their city, bolstering its other tourism development efforts (ibid.). A critical reading of this report suggests that it was structured to deliver a favorable impression of the impact of the Tour on host cities, by measuring known positive impacts such as tourist spending, hotel stays, and media coverage, rather than interviewing local residents and businesses whose interests might be negatively impacted by the Tour, by addressing substitution effects, or assessing opportunity costs, and so on. Thus the report does not meaningfully engage the question of whether hosting a stage is a good thing for the town or city generally.

The other economic impact study highlighted by Desbordes takes the perspective of stage hosts, rather than the ASO. Commissioned by the City of Digne, the study was conducted by a local university, the Universite Pierre Mendes-France of Grenoble. Digne hosted a stage of the tour for the 11th time on July 14th 2005, and paid a reported €75,000 for the privilege, and invested another €75,000 in technical services necessary to support the event (security, access, signage, and communication) for a total direct cost of €150,000. The city aimed to better understand the local economic benefits associated with hosting the Tour, particularly (i) the image of the city (its identity relative to the values of the Tour de France and the link between spectators and the Tour), (ii) awareness of the city outside of its region, and (iii) promotion of the city (expressed as 'social cohesion, economic impact, external communication, animation of a territory'). The methodology involved surveying both local vendors (114 in total), as done for the ASO 2005 study, but also spectators during the event (274), local residents (259), and tour officials (110), with a total of 757 survey respondents (ibid., p. 534).[16]

The results of the Digne study are summarized by Desbordes as follows: the total number of spectators was estimated at 25,000, of whom it was estimated that 64 percent did not live in Digne, and 27 percent were not French, as well as 4,500 others including race officials, teams and riders, sponsors, and the media. The report also suggests that hotels were at 91 percent occupancy on the night of the stage itself, July 14th, and that the average expenditure for non-Digne residents was €23 on food, drink and souvenirs, for a total of €368,000 (ibid., p. 538). (Spending by local residents related to the Tour was estimated at €12 per capita, for a total of €108,000, however this is subtracted from gross spending because of the substitution effect.) The impact of spending on hotels was not reported in the summary, nor are the spending impacts of the non-spectator group, which would be important to any analysis of regional or national economic impact.

For benefits around issues of place-branding, the Digne study as summarized by Desbordes claims 350 articles in the French press (in 78 different journals or magazines) that make mention of Digne, or highlight the 11th stage in 2005. It also estimates that the average television audience on French TV for the 11th stage was 5.72 million, with a bump up to 6.88 million during the arrival, and representing a near 60 percent market share during its time slots, with an average viewing time of three hours and 38 minutes. In terms of the international television audience, the Digne study makes the same errors in estimating broadcast audience size as described earlier in this chapter, with 70 channels outside of France broadcasting the 11th stage, reaching out to the Tour's estimated global audience of 2 billion spectators in over 180 countries. There were 14,763 hits on the city website on July 14th, breaking previous records, and the tourism office received more than double its usual number of email inquiries (+113 percent) during the month of July 2005. As with the ASO study, it is not clear how the measures identified by the City of Digne in their study actually translate to an improved awareness of the city or perception of its brand either within or outside of France.

Existing economic impact studies for the Tour de France, then, are both in short supply, and where they do exist, they tend to be methodologically weak, and subject to the same biases in authorship that often skew similar reports for other kinds of mega sporting events, particularly in cases where reports commissioned by event advocates overestimate economic and other impacts. Desbordes concludes his analysis of these two studies by suggesting a new model that would blend both demand- and supply-side methodologies to capture the true economic impacts of the Tour on stage hosts, although at the time of writing (2011), there did not appear to be any cases where this improved model was executed.

This dearth of studies that evaluate the economic impacts of the Tour de France from the perspective of either the ASO or the towns and cities that serve as stage hosts is perhaps best explained by their symbiotic relationship: the Tour relies on the cooperation and hospitality of cities and towns across France to accommodate the race, and in turn, these cities and towns get affordable access to a mega sporting event. For the 106,000 residents of Nancy, or even for the 17,000 residents of Digne, a subvention of €50,000 or €100,000 may be an indulgence, but is nonetheless possible relative to the size of their municipal budgets. For the Olympics, or even most world championships, these same places would be extreme long-shot host candidates, on both financial as well as operational bases. The Tour requires no stadiums, no athletes' villages, and no media centers; in fact, it requires little in the way of host city participation in the event organization at all. Its non-road infrastructure is portable, carried by huge trucks from town to town, rolled out in a few hours in the departure town, and then quickly packed up and redeployed in the next arrival town. So for a price tag of a few hundred thousand euros, cities and towns from all over France are able to compete for a small piece of a mega event that would otherwise be out of reach.

Another reason why there are so few studies of the impacts of the Tour de France on stage hosts might be that the benefits to the local area – economic, social, cultural and so on – may actually exceed the upfront cost, suggesting that the Tour is not only affordable and accessible, but that it is a good deal, too. Even if economic impacts are modest and tied to a one-shot spike in visitor demand for hotels and restaurants, when taken together with city tourism advertising, infrastructure improvements, and the amenity and social cohesion value for residents, the Tour appears to be a good value compared to other mega sporting events, and provides a more equitable distribution of those benefits across the region.

As if in agreement with this notion – that hosting the Tour de France is a good deal for taxpayers – the number of cities and towns applying to the ASO to be considered as stage hosts is increasing every year. The number of cities outside of France hoping to serve as hosts of the *Grand Départ* is also rapidly growing, fueled in part by larger cities hoping to demonstrate their ability to host world championship events in multiple sports as a means to bolster subsequent bids for the Olympics and/or related events. Of course, what these numbers do not reveal is the political contexts that shape the decision making behind bids to host Tour stages. In parallel with narratives accompanying the competition for franchises in the US major leagues, the fact that there are more cities that want teams than there are teams available should not be interpreted as evidence that hosting major league teams is good for host cities. More typically, these city development strategies reflect the economic interests of specific groups who have sufficient political influence to affect budget decisions and policy making.

Regardless of the overt or tacit rationales underlying bids by cities and towns to host a stage of the Tour de France, the ASO is doubtless mindful of the opportunity to increase subvention fees in response to excess demand, although for the moment they appear to be choosing to wield this leverage outside of France. This increased demand for competitive cycling events outside of Europe is serendipitous, as it allows the Tour to grow its revenues in new markets at the same time as the market for broadcast and sponsorship revenue within France appears to be maturing. Tour stages held in their entirety outside of France – for now limited to the *Grand Départ* – increase the fan base for cycling, and expand the pool of potential corporate sponsors and broadcast partners. When cities offer to pay three or more million euros to host the *Grand Départ*, the ASO collects from this one stage nearly half of what it receives from all subventions fees from the other stages combined.

Viewed domestically, the market for subvention revenues within France also offers growth potential. It is likely that many prospective stage hosts would pay higher subvention fees to the ASO if requested to do so, although there have been no studies on the sensitivity of stage hosts to fee increases. While it may seem a straightforward proposition that the ASO would move to capture excess rents in the domestic market for host subventions – for the ASO, the Tour is a business first and an athletic event second – they would have pursued such a strategy cautiously and incrementally, for both pragmatic and political reasons. Pragmatically, since the subvention fees are flat and not indexed to the size of the locality or its budget, any increase in fees will affect some parts of their host pool more than others. Moreover, since the pool of host cities and towns for a specific stage is geographically determined and thus much smaller than its overall pool for the entire race, any changes to subvention fees will also need to address demand sensitivity in specific regions.

Politically, the ASO relies on these same cities and towns to accommodate the race, and higher subvention fees might diminish the degree of cooperation with local governments that is essential to the production of the Tour de France, from permission for road closures, to preferential treatment in provision of accommodation and other essential on-site services. Tolerance of the many day-to-day nuisances associated with the Tour emanates from the tremendous amount of goodwill associated with the event as means for promoting France and French culture, both within the country and beyond. The ASO has cultivated this goodwill carefully, and there is little evidence to suggest that it would take a more aggressive stance on subvention fees if it would markedly affect the reputation of the Tour as the premier sporting event in France, and the national pride associated with its significant cultural and historical legacy.

For these reasons, the question of whether the Tour de France will continue to offer a comparatively good deal for its host cities and towns remains on the table. Should the ASO pursue a strategy to increase subvention fees for its stage hosts within France, these increases should be weighed in concert with a better understanding of the benefits and costs of hosting different stages of the Tour, and taking a broader perspective than the economic impact studies described above. Moreover, these studies should address the murkier issues associated with the host city experience, enumerating and measuring factors such as the city image, social cohesion, and public health, while at the same time, analyzing the distribution of all benefits and costs across a broader cross-section of the local population.

6   CONCLUSION

The Tour de France may lag the Olympic Games and the FIFA World Cup in audience size and revenue generation, but for France and the hundreds of cities and towns that line the race route each year, the Tour's affordability, combined with its economic, social and health benefits, suggest that it is a bargain for host cities among mega sporting events. Viewed internationally, the Tour is a hallmark sporting event that has built a highly valuable global brand that showcases French culture alongside elite men's road cycling. Within France, the Tour is a much-beloved annual festival, centered on a road cycling race, but encompassing a month-long celebration of national identity, a love of the sport of cycling, and over its 100-year history it has served as a democratizing and globalizing force. French citizens routinely watch one or more stages of the tour in person, enjoying the publicity caravan, following hours of television broadcasts, and travel regionally to watch the *Grand Départ* and other key stages of the race. Especially at the local level, the Tour brings tremendous amenity value to area residents as well as a short-term but significant spike in demand for restaurants, hotels, and related hospitality services.

Almost miraculously, this set of cultural, social, economic and political benefits appears to arrive with very little in the way of direct public investment. Since the Tour de France is privately owned and operated by the ASO, the national government does not provide significant direct subsidies for the operation of the event, although the roads upon which the race is run are publicly owned and primarily maintained for automobile use during the year. The Tour's business model is centered on revenues from the sale of broadcast and print media rights, as well as general sponsorships, and where rider and equipment costs are covered by team sponsorships, with some comparatively small local expenses paid by 'stage hosts'. While the ASO retains full-year staff and manages the complexities of the day-to-day operations of the tour, including mounting security expenses, there are very few of the significant capital expenses typically associated with other mega events including expensive stadiums, athletes' accommodation, and transportation infrastructure. Operating costs are also lower, since spectators are widely dispersed, and there are no costs associated with ticketing or moving athletes around. The profitability of the contemporary Tour, then, suggests that there may be less need for the ASO to pursue public subsidies, and consequently, they are not pressed to cede some of the control that often accompanies these contributions.

Yet signs indicate that the bargain offered by the Tour de France for aspiring host cities and towns may not be available for much longer. Mimicking the sports tourism fervor that accompanies competitive bidding for the Olympics and the Football World Cup, there is evidence that the rent or 'subvention' paid by smaller cities and towns for the privilege of hosting a Tour stage is on the rise, fed by perceptions that local benefits exceed local costs. The ASO, for its part, is beginning to inject a competitive spirit to the stage selection process, particularly the *Grand Départ* stage which is increasingly held outside France, as a means to close the gap between benefits and costs. Within France, however, the potential to increase competition among aspiring stage hosts is moderated by the pragmatics associated with route planning, and by the Tour's century-old legacy as a showcase for French history, culture and landscape. If the dynamics of public subsidies for the Tour shift to align with the competitive bidding models associated with other mega events, then economic impact studies and cost–benefit analyzes will play an important role in future positioning by both its host cities and the ASO.

NOTES

*   I would like to thank Eric Reed of Western Kentucky University for his invaluable guidance as I embarked on this chapter, and for his terrific work on the economic history of the Tour de France; Nicolas Mercat and Emmanuel Roche of INDDIGO/Altermodal for generously providing economic reports on the cycling industry in France; Andrea Smith from USA Cycling for overview data on the US cycling industry; Andrew Long of New York University for providing insights into the business of professional cycling, offered alongside color commentary that only an accomplished amateur cyclist who has taken on *L'Étape du Tour* and a dutiful brother-in-law can provide; and to volume editors Andy Zimbalist and Wolfgang Maennig, for their careful readings and wise counsel. All errors, including those made translating from French, are mine.

1. Since the Tour de France is a French sporting event, the currency used in this chapter is the EU euro. In 2011, the average exchange rate of the EU euro to the US dollar between 2005 and June 2011 is 0.74 (the inverse is 1.35). Since the chapter makes reference to several reports citing economic data for 2005, 2007 and 2009, the average annual EU euro/US$ exchange rate for those years is 0.80 (1.25), 0.73 (1.37), and 0.72 (1.39), respectively.

2. The world's longest bicycle race is the Vuelta Sudamericana, covering over 12,000 kilometers over 130 days while passing through Brazil, Argentina, Uruguay, Chile, Bolivia, Peru and Ecuador. This race is not currently part of the UCI WorldTour.

3. The eight cycling disciplines are road, track, mountain bike, cyclo-cross, BMX, trials, indoor cycling, and para-cycling.

4. The UCI WorldTour was formerly the UCI ProTour, and before that, there were other names for efforts to create a world cycling tour. For a detailed history of the organization of elite cycling, see the UCI website at uci.ch. Also there are several articles and hundreds of newspaper articles that discuss issues related to the organization of competitive cycling including the need to include the grand tours in the world circuit, the conflicts associated with trade or sponsored team, among others.

5. The UCI divides professional teams into three divisions: UCI ProTeams (the highest level), UCI Professional Continental and UCI Continental.

6. Aside from the elite men's division on the UCI WorldTour, there is also a separate division for male riders under the age of 23 in all circuit races, intended to foster development of younger riders. To date, women have not been permitted to participate in the Tour de France, but the UCI has developed the UCI World Cup Women circuit, consisting of eight sanctioned events in 2011, and providing a stage for elite women's road cycling. There is also a series of women's events that mirror the spirit of the grand tours, such as Le Grande Boucle Feminine Internationale (Le Tour Feminin) in France, the Giro Donne in Italy, and the Tour l'Aude in southern France, although the short history of these races has revealed challenges with developing the consistently large audiences necessary to attract sponsors. Despite these challenges, the women's circuit is also expanding into international markets – such as the Tour de Prince Edward Island in Canada, sponsored by the UCI – perhaps under the theory that the market for women's cycling may be greater outside of Europe than within.

7. Delving deeper, historians of the Tour argue that the competition between the owners of *L'Auto* and *Le Vélo* was as much about politics as business, and rooted in the Dreyfus Affair scandal that rocked France at the turn of the twentieth century. The owner of *Le Vélo* was a 'Dreyfusard' (he believed Dreyfus to be innocent of sharing French military secrets with the Germans), whereas *L'Auto* was started during the peak of the scandal by a group of 'Anti-Dreyfusards', notably Count Albert de Dion. The Count did not care for how *Le Vélo* was reporting on the Dreyfus affair, and moreover, one of his car-making rivals, Alexandre Darraqc, was a financial backer of *Le Vélo*. At a horse race in Auteuil in 1899, the Count became so infuriated by then French President Émile Loubet's support of Dreyfus that he hit Loubet over the head with his walking stick, and spent 15 days in jail as a result. When he emerged, the Count and some business associates started *L'Auto* to compete directly with *Le Vélo*, with its first issue released in 1900. Moreover, the appointment of Desgrange as editor-in-chief was strategic, as not only was he was an accomplished cyclist, but he also owned the velodrome at the Parc de Princes in Paris, with partner Victor Goddet. Thus he was well prepared to direct the tour through its infancy. Desgrange would go on to direct the Tour de France for the next 30 years, from 1903 to 1936. Goddet's son Jacques would succeed him, directing the Tour for the next 50 years, from 1936 to 1986.

8. *L'Auto* was disbanded after the war. However, all state assets were returned to the state and then redistributed, once the owners were able to prove that despite printing articles

favorable to the German occupation during the war, they had also used their materials and connections to provide support for liberation efforts. Thus they were able to earn the opportunity to start a new paper after the war, but not under the name *L'Auto*, as it was felt that this would be too much of a competitive advantage over other newpapers. So *L'Équipe* was born. The Tour de France was not run during the war, although the Germans invited Goddet to do so if he chose. He refused. Nonetheless the political left wing in France remained unsympathetic to *L'Équipe* and its subsequent owner Émilien Amaury – when Amaury was killed in a riding accident in 1977, the *Libération* headline read: 'Amaury falls from his horse: the horse is safe'.

9. The origin of the yellow jersey is speculated to lie in the yellow-tinted newsprint used for *L'Auto*. Color-tinted newspapers were conventional at the time; the color of *L'Auto*'s arch rival *Le Vélo* was green, which may explain why there was no green jersey among Tour honors until many years later, when the '*maillot vert*' or green jersey was introduced for the points classification leader in 1950.

10. Desgrange also experimented with corporate sponsorship of individual stages, as a stage in the 1931 tour was (unofficially) referred to as 'The Stage of "La Vache qui Rit"' after the playfully named French cheese product.

11. For a complete breakdown of prize money for 2010, see the 2010 Tour de France regulations, available at http://www.letour.fr/2010/TDF/COURSE/docs/reglement.pdf.

12. Ibid.

13. ASO as reported in Desbordes (2007, p. 527).

14. The Tour *Grand Départ* has been held in Amsterdam (1954), Brussels (1958), Cologne (1965), The Hague (1973), Charleroi (1976) and Leiden (1978) as well as Berlin (1987), Luxembourg (1989), San Sebastian (1992), s'Hertogenbosch (1996), Dublin (1998), Luxembourg (2002), Liège (2004), London (2007), Monaco (2009), and Rotterdam (2010).

15. The highest degree of ridership is found in Demark and the Netherlands, at more than 1,000 kilometers per person per year, followed by the northern Europeans – including Germany, Belgium, and Austria – at 250–500 km/person/year; then France, the UK and others at 50–100; and southern Europe at less than 50.

16. The summary did not explain the determination of the sampling frame or method of sample selection.

REFERENCES

Christian Science Monitor (CSM) (2010), 'How are Tour de France towns picked? Incognito', *Christian Science Monitor*, July 9.

Desbordes, M. (2007), 'A review of the economic impact studies done on the Tour de France: methodological aspects and first results', *International Journal of Sport Management and Marketing*, **2** (5/6), 526–40.

Initiative (2005), Sport + Entertainment, ViewerTrack study.

Outdoor Industry Foundation (2006), 'The active outdoor recreation economy: a \$730 billion annual contribution to the US economy', fall.

Reed, E. (2010), 'The economics of the Tour, 1930–2003', *International Journal of the History of Sport*, **20** (2), 103–27.

Roche, E. and N. Mercat (2009), 'The bicycle economy in France' (L'Économie du vélo en France), INDDIGO/Altermodal.

Roche, E. and N. Mercat (2010), 'The bicycle economy in France' (L'Économie du vélo en France), INDDIGO/Altermodal.

22 Labor market effects of the World Cup: a sectoral analysis

Robert Baumann, Bryan Engelhardt and Victor A. Matheson

1 INTRODUCTION

Every four years the eyes of the world's sports fans turn to the Fédération International de Football Associations (FIFA) World Cup. In the run-up to the 2010 World Cup, 205 national and regional teams competed in qualifying tournaments for the right to be one of the final 32 countries invited to the World Cup finals held in South Africa. Soccer's World Cup is far and away the world's largest sporting event featuring a single sport, and only the Summer Olympic Games can rival the World Cup in terms of scale and popularity. For example, the 2006 World Cup recorded an estimated 26 billion combined viewers over the course of the 64 games of the tournament and the final alone drew an estimated 715 million viewers. By comparison, the opening ceremonies of the 2008 Summer Olympics in Beijing attracted 'only' 600 million viewers, while the 2011 Super Bowl, the annual championship of American football, drew a record 111 million American viewers, the highest ever for an American television broadcast, but few additional non-American viewers, leaving the game far behind the World Cup final's global audience (Telegraph, 2011).

The World Cup is an overwhelming financial success for FIFA itself, which funds over 85 percent of its operations from this quadrennial event. Between 2007 and 2010, FIFA generated $4.189 billion in revenue with $3.655 billion of the total coming directly from sources related to the 2010 World Cup (Australian Broadcasting Corporation, 2011). The event organizers also claim that the World Cup is an overwhelming financial success for the countries lucky enough to be awarded the event. The consulting firm Grant Thornton South Africa predicted that the 2010 World Cup in South Africa would have 'a gross economic impact of $12 billion to the country's economy' with 373,000 international visitors expected (Voigt, 2010). Subsequent revisions placed the economic impact at $7.5 billion along with 198,400 annual jobs (Rihlamvu, 2011).

Previous editions of the event elicited equally rosy predictions. The Dentsu Institute for Human Studies predicted impacts of $24.8 billion and

$8.9 billion for Japan and South Korea, respectively, for the 1998 World Cup hosted jointly by the two countries in 2002 (Finer, 2002). During the bidding process for the 2018 World Cup, the AECOM economics practice predicted that a World Cup based in the US would generate $5 billion for the country and generate 5,000 to 8,000 jobs in each of 12 potential host cities, broadly matching the $4 billion the firm's predecessor estimated for the previous World Cup held in 1994 in the US (Goodman and Stern 1994; Slevison, 2009). The 2006 World Cup in Germany elicited estimates of between $2 and $10 billion in increased income along with up to 10,000 additional jobs (Feddersen and Maennig, 2010).

Of course, the expenses associated with hosting an event like the World Cup are also quite large, and the majority of the costs are typically borne by the host country. Indeed, it is only through passing along the major infrastructure costs that FIFA is able to manage to regularly amass its large surpluses. Just considering the sporting infrastructure, FIFA requires host countries to have at least 12 modern stadiums capable of seating at least 40,000 spectators with one of the stadiums being able to seat at least 80,000 for the opener and the final. Operating costs can also be quite expensive due to the extreme security measures that must be put in place. South Africa's World Cup entailed $3.9 billion in expenses, including at least $1.3 billion in stadium construction costs (Voigt, 2010; Baade and Matheson, forthcoming). The 2002 World Cup required the construction of 10 new stadiums in South Korea at a cost of almost $2 billion and another 10 new or refurbished stadiums in Japan at a cost of between $4 billion and $5.6 billion (Sloan, 2002), while Germany followed in 2006 with €2.4 billion in construction costs of their own (Baade and Matheson, forthcoming). The 2018 and 2022 events in Russia and Qatar figure to be even more expensive due to the lack of existing facilities. Russian officials have stated that they are prepared to spend $10 billion on the tournament (Rianovosti, 2009) while Qatar's bid is likely to be even more costly since it currently has only one stadium of the required size to host tournament matches. Given the enormous costs involved in hosting the tournament, it is reasonable to ask whether the predictions of economic windfall have come true in host countries.

Economists who have analyzed actual data related to the economic performance of host countries before, during, and after the World Cup have typically found identifiable benefits that are a fraction of those claimed by consultants. Using national data, Szymanski (2002) finds that among the world's largest economies, countries hosting the World Cup over the past 30 years experienced lower economic growth during World Cup years. Sterken (2006) also examines national data and instead finds a positive but very small impact from hosting the World Cup.

Baade and Matheson (2004) were the first to undertake an *ex post* analysis of the economic effects of the World Cup using economic data from host cities (as opposed to country-wide data). They examine personal income growth in 13 metropolitan areas that either hosted World Cup games in the United States in 1994 or were directly adjacent to a host site. Their findings suggest that rather than a $4 billion windfall, host cities experienced personal income growth that was below that which normally would have been predicted by a total sum of $5.5 to $9.3 billion. Due to the size of the economies of the metropolitan areas involved, these estimates are subject to a wide degree of variability, but sensitivity analysis performed by Baade and Matheson predicts that economic gains in the cumulative range of $4 billion or more, as suggested by the consultants, can be rejected at a 1 percent significance level, economic gains of $500 million or more can be rejected at a 5 percent significance level, and economic gains above zero dollars can be rejected with a *p*-value of 6.4 percent.

Baade and Matheson (2004), as well as other studies of mega-event analysis such as Crompton (1995), Porter (1999), and Coates and Humphreys (2002) reach similar conclusions: although measurement of changes in net spending in the local economy as opposed to gross spending should be the goal of impact analysis, economic impact predictions almost invariably measure (and publicize) gross rather than net impacts. While major events like the World Cup attract large crowds that spend significant sums of money at the games, spending by local residents typically substitutes for spending elsewhere in the local economy. This results in an increase in gross spending on the event but no increase in net economic activity for the city or country as a whole as money is simply shifting from one sector to another. Even for out of town visitors net spending is lower than gross spending to mega events if it displaces any regular tourists to the city who would rather not arrive during a mega event. Finally, spectator sports and mega events tend to be associated with particularly high levels of leakages, so that the economic multipliers used in impact modeling tend to be unrealistically high (Siegfried and Zimbalist, 2002; Matheson, 2009).

Other examinations of past World Cups appear to support the initial findings of Baade and Matheson (2004). Hagn and Maennig (2008) examine employment in Germany around the 1974 World Cup and find no statistically significant short- or long-term effects. Similarly, Feddersen et.al. (2009) and Hagn and Maennig (2009) both find no short-term labor effects from the 2006 World Cup in Germany, although neither study has an adequate amount of data following the tournament to determine any potential long-term labor benefits.

Allmers and Maennig (2009) point out that previous studies of the economic impact of the World Cup rely primarily on aggregated employment or output data. Even the impact of a large event like the World Cup can be obscured by the regular fluctuations in the large, diversified metropolitan economies in which the games are held, so Allmers and Maennig examine specific sectors of host economies for potential effects. They find no identifiable impact on overnight hotel stays, national tourism income, or retail sales in France during the World Cup in 1998, while in Germany in 2006 they find approximately 700,000 additional hotel nights sold to foreigners and an additional €600–700 million (US$830–970 million) in net national tourism income. While these figures are substantial, they are a fraction of those claimed by event boosters.

Feddersen and Maennig (2010) examine employment in specific parts of the economy, including the hospitality and construction sectors, and find a statistically significant increase in employment in the hospitality sector of roughly 2,000 jobs. This is in line with *ex post* estimates of the sectoral employment impact of the Salt Lake City Winter Olympics in 2002 of an increase of 4,600 jobs in the leisure industry uncovered by Baumann et al. (2010), but a far cry from the *ex ante* estimates of 10,000 new jobs predicted for the German economy in 2006, the 5,000 to 8,000 jobs predicted for each of the 12 potential host cities for the failed US bid for 2022, or the 198,400 new jobs estimated as a result of the 2010 South African World Cup. Feddersen and Maennig also find evidence of a decline in employment in the construction sector possibly as a result of the crowding-out of public sector investment due to World Cup commitments.

Using a similar approach to Feddersen and Maennig and Baumann et al. (2010), this chapter utilizes sectoral employment data in host cities and a sample of control cities to re-examine the effects on local economies of the 1994 World Cup in the United States. This analysis extends and improves upon the previous study of the 1994 World Cup by Baade and Matheson (2004) in several important ways. Most obviously, this chapter examines employment and unemployment, while the previous work looks at personal income. As noted previously, potential employment gains are often used to justify the public expenditures required to host the event.

The use of employment data has two more specific advantages over personal income or GDP data. First, employment data is available monthly, rather than quarterly or annually, for large metropolitan areas in the US. Identifying the economic impact of even a major event like the World Cup is akin to looking for the proverbial needle in a haystack, and the use of monthly data instead of less frequent data reduces the size of the haystack. In addition, the establishment survey provides employment data by industry type, further increasing the chances of finding the elusive 'needle' as well as identifying potential winners and losers among sectors of the economy from hosting the tournament.

2 DATA AND MODEL

We use metropolitan statistical area employment data from the Current Employment Statistics (CES) and the Current Population Survey (CPS). The CES collects payroll data from businesses, and has data for overall employment as well as employment in specific industries. We use the overall employment data as well as employment in three industries: retail trade, professional and business services, and leisure and hospitality. The CPS surveys individuals and provides data on both employment and unemployment but does not have industry-specific data. Each source provides monthly data on employment for several metropolitan statistical areas (MSAs), including all nine of the hosts of the 1994 World Cup: Chicago, Dallas, Detroit, East Rutherford, Foxborough, Orlando, Pasadena, Stanford, and Washington, DC. Some of these locations (East Rutherford, Foxborough, Pasadena, and Stanford) are too small to have employment data, but each is part of a larger MSA that is available in the data. Appendix 22A contains further details on the MSA specification for these cities in each dataset.

We use the other large MSAs (at least 500,000 employed at the beginning of the sample frame) in the data to augment the control group for the World Cup hosts. We choose 500,000 since it is the nearest round number to the smallest MSA in the sample (Orlando). This restriction leaves a total of 44 MSAs in the CES data and 39 in the CPS data, where nine are World Cup hosts. Finally, our sample frame is January 1990 to December 2009. The CES and CPS provide earlier employment data but not for all of the hosts of the World Cup. We present summary statistics of the overall employment and unemployment data in Table 22.1 and summary statistics for the sectoral data in Table 22.2.

It should be noted that some MSAs designated as World Cup hosts also border other MSAs, and it is reasonable to question whether one should expand the definition of a World Cup host to include neighboring MSAs. For example, Dallas borders Forth Worth and some World Cup visitors to Dallas may have engaged in expenditures in neighboring Fort Worth. Similarly, Stanford stadium lies just within the northern border of the San Jose MSA, but is less than a mile from the southern border of the San Francisco MSA. Most notably, Giants Stadium lies within the Bergen-Passaic MSA, but most local accommodation is in next-door Newark or across the Hudson River in New York City. Indeed, Baade and Matheson (2004) include 13 MSAs rather than nine MSAs in their World Cup host variable. This chapter uses a narrower definition of World Cup host than Baade and Matheson (2004), but robustness checks on the regression results show no significant difference in outcomes if the

Table 22.1   Summary statistics

	Mean	Std deviation	Minimum	Maximum
World Cup hosts				
CES employment (000s)	1,846.800	1,157.060	562.900	4,180.400
Change CES employment %	0.055	1.105	−5.762	3.601
CPS employment (000s)	2,472.740	1,555.450	624.000	6,235.200
Change CPS employment %	0.048	0.780	−6.492	2.298
CPS unemployment (000s)	149.800	122.200	22.200	774.300
Change CPS unemployment %	0.650	7.970	−30.420	48.780
Other MSAs				
CES employment (000s)	1,108.400	566.800	514.200	3,838.600
Change CES employment %	0.094	1.064	−5.108	2.592
CPS employment (000s)	1,177.600	567.900	504.500	2,865.600
Change CPS employment %	0.087	0.850	−8.097	5.734
CPS unemployment (000s)	67.810	40.970	17.160	321.560
Change CPS unemployment %	0.700	8.720	−33.550	68.230

Table 22.2   Summary statistics (sectoral data)

	Mean	Std deviation	Minimum	Maximum
World Cup hosts				
Leisure & hospitality (000s)	150.000	1,157.060	562.900	4,180.400
% Δ leisure & hospitality	0.722	1.105	−5.762	3.601
Retail trade (000s)	180.300	113.300	74.000	380.700
% Δ retail trade	0.0246	1.151	−2.620	1.260
Professional & bus. (000s)	251.500	165.600	64.100	525.100
% Δ professional & bus.	0.840	1.410	−1.990	4.720
Other MSAs				
Leisure & hospitality (000s)	112.400	64.600	30.100	410.800
% Δ leisure & hospitality	0.175	0.025	−11.990	11.730
Retail trade (000s)	135.500	73.200	44.800	454.300
% Δ retail trade	0.067	2.312	−10.460	5.990
Professional & bus. (000s)	180.100	129.400	36.400	673.600
% Δ professional & bus.	0.210	1.370	−8.700	11.250

World Cup host variable is expanded to include these additional four neighboring MSAs.

Our *ex post* approach is to estimate the impact on employment from hosting the World Cup. We begin with the following linear model:

$$emp_{it} = \beta_0 + \theta wc_{it} + y_t + m_t + \alpha_i + \varepsilon_{it},$$

where emp_{it} is the employment or unemployment level of MSA i in time t. The dummy variables y_t and m_t are yearly- and monthly-specific controls, which absorb national trends in employment. α_i is a MSA-specific fixed effect that accounts for time-invariant factors of each location. Finally, ε_{it} is the overall error term.

The variable of interest for this chapter, wc_{it}, equals one during the months an MSA hosted a World Cup game, which is either June 1994, July 1994, or both (see Appendix 22A). It is plausible that the employment response is more complicated than a simple dichotomous control (see Box and Tiao, 1975), but we begin here on the assumption that if the World Cup influenced employment at all, it is most likely to have an impact during the event. This assumption is particularly bolstered by the fact that the US bid, unlike more recent World Cups, exclusively utilized existing sports infrastructure. Since no facilities were newly built or significantly refurbished for the games, there is little reason to expect a large increase in employment prior to the start of the tournament. Other specifications for wc_{it} were tested with no significant change in the results; however, it is important to note that this model is really designed to capture only short-run effects of the World Cup. It would be a mistake to extrapolate the results here to make conclusions about any long-run employment effects, positive or negative, from the World Cup.

Similar to other macroeconomic variables, several tests also suggest that the employment and unemployment levels have a unit root. Dickey–Fuller and Phillips–Perron tests on individual MSAs suggest that 39 of the 44 MSAs in the CES data have a unit root at a 10 percent significance level. The Levin et al. (2002) and Im et al. (2003) tests, which are unit root tests for dynamic panel datasets such as ours, also suggest that the level of employment is non-stationary. The same tests on CPS employment and unemployment provide comparable results. In response to these results, we transform the data using the percent change of employment (or unemployment). This transformation passes all three unit root tests above at a 10 percent significance level. Another alternative is the first difference of the data, but we use percent changes here to put all of our MSAs, which have vastly different sizes, on a level playing field.

We also execute the test for autocorrelation within each panel as in Wooldridge (2002) which suggests that autoregressive (AR) terms are necessary in this model. This test estimates $\hat{\varepsilon}_{it} = \rho\hat{\varepsilon}_{i,t-1} + u_{it}$. If the null hypothesis of $\rho = -0.5$ is not rejected, the model likely has autocorrelation. We reject this hypothesis using employment and unemployment levels, first differences, and percent changes. Given the results of the unit root and autocorrelation tests, our model is now:

$$\%\Delta emp_{it} = \beta_0 + \sum_{p=1}^{P} \delta_p(\%\Delta emp_{i,t-p}) + \theta wc_{it} + y_t + m_t + \alpha_i + \varepsilon_{it},$$

where P is the number of lagged values or the AR dimension of the model. We use trial and error to determine the optimal number of AR terms, and found that one lag is sufficient since higher-order lags are highly insignificant.

Unfortunately, including an AR term in a fixed effects model biases the estimates. Since the use of fixed effects is equivalent to de-meaning the data by the MSA-specific means, a correlation is created between the de-meaned independent variables and the error term. Nickell (1981) demonstrates the amount of inconsistency is of order T^{-1} as N approaches infinity. This is a small number given that we have monthly data over 20 years, although at $N = 44$ we cannot assume that this asymptotic figure is accurate for our model.

Kiviet (1995) proposes estimating the amount of inconsistency and uses this result to adjust the estimates. This strategy requires estimation of two unobservable parameters: the AR coefficient and the error variance. Fortunately, consistent estimates are available using the instrumental variable approaches of Anderson and Hsiao (1982), Arellano and Bond (1991), or Blundell and Bond (1998). In addition, the standard error formula in the Kiviet (1995) strategy is asymptotic, so we use a bootstrap technique based on the normal distribution from Bruno (2005). It is also plausible to estimate the model using any of the instrumental variable approaches mentioned above. We choose the Kiviet correction model based on favorable Monte Carlo comparisons (Judson and Owen, 1999; Bun and Kiviet, 2003; Bruno, 2005) and also because there is little difference in our main findings across these techniques. For comparison, we also present estimates of the AR model without the Kiviet correction. These estimations use maximum likelihood since least squares produces inconsistent estimates in AR settings. Finally, we use robust standard errors in all estimations since dynamic panels usually produce heteroskedasticity errors across MSAs.

Table 22.3 presents estimates from three datasets (CPS employment, CPS unemployment, and CES employment) over several econometric specifications. None of the specifications produces a statistically significant effect of hosting in any of the three datasets, nor do the results present a consistency of signs on the coefficients or a pattern in the size of the coefficients that might point to labor market benefits that are not revealed by

Table 22.3   Estimation results

	OLS no fixed effects	OLS with fixed effects	Fixed effects – no Kiviet correction (MLE)	Fixed effects – Kiviet corrected
CES employment				
World Cup host	0.00085	0.00109	0.00112	0.00112
	($p = 0.540$)	($p = 0.450$)	($p = 0.423$)	($p = 0.650$)
Lagged			0.08261	0.08739
employment			($p < 0.001$)	($p < 0.001$)
CPS employment				
World Cup host	−0.00152	−0.00127	−0.00122	−0.00121
	($p = 0.106$)	($p = 0.149$)	($p = 0.173$)	($p = 0.652$)
Lagged			−0.04159	−0.03763
employment			($p = 0.005$)	($p < 0.001$)
CPS unemployment				
World Cup host	0.00110	0.00154	−0.00107	−0.00107
	($p = 0.916$)	($p = 0.812$)	($p = 0.850$)	($p = 0.967$)
Lagged			−0.15496	−0.15143
unemployment			($p < 0.001$)	($p < 0.001$)

Note: All models include yearly and monthly dummy variables. These results are available upon request. (p-values shown in parentheses.)

standard measures of statistical significance. In the CES data, the hosting effect on employment is positive in the four specifications, but the CPS data estimate a negative effect of a similar or even slightly higher magnitude in all four specifications. The CPS unemployment model provides two positive and two negative estimates. All models that include a lagged dependent variable suggest that this term has explanatory power, which is not surprising given the results of our autocorrelation tests. Finally, nearly all of the yearly and monthly dummy variables are statistically significant in every specification, suggesting that MSAs are sensitive to national trends.

Table 22.4 presents estimates from the CES sectoral data for three industries: leisure and hospitality, retail trade, and professional and business services. The estimates for leisure and hospitality and professional and business services are insignificant. All four coefficients for the retail trade model, however, are significant at the 5 percent level, but the sign is negative, suggesting that employment in retail trade actually decreased by 0.42 percentage points during the World Cup. At the average size of

Table 22.4 Estimation results for sectoral data

	OLS no fixed effects	OLS with fixed effects	Fixed effects – no Kiviet correction (MLE)	Fixed effects – Kiviet corrected
Leisure & hospitality				
World Cup host	−0.00254	−0.00245	−0.00158	−0.00133
	($p = 0.310$)	($p = 0.446$)	($p = 0.518$)	($p = 0.428$)
Lagged			0.37142	0.37099
employment			($p < 0.001$)	($p < 0.001$)
Retail trade				
World Cup host	−0.00450	−0.00426	−0.00425	−0.00421
	($p = 0.020$)	($p = 0.028$)	($p = 0.027$)	($p = 0.030$)
Lagged			0.00768	0.00673
employment			($p = 0.473$)	($p = 0.567$)
Professional & business serv.				
World Cup host	0.00055	0.00071	0.00084	0.00085
	($p = 0.869$)	($p = 0.850$)	($p = 0.803$)	($p = 0.817$)
Lagged			0.05594	0.05529
unemployment			($p < 0.001$)	($p < 0.001$)

Note: All models include yearly and monthly dummy variables. These results are available upon request. (*p*-values shown in parentheses.)

a World Cup host in 1994, this translates to a loss of roughly 750 retail trade jobs per month, or 1,500 total over the two-month event. The retail trade estimation is also unique because the lagged dependent variable term has little or no explanatory power. While testing employment in the construction sector would also be of potential interest as a comparison to Feddersen and Maennig (2010), data on construction employment were available only for a fraction of the cities in the sample (22 out of 44), so this test was not undertaken. In addition, since no stadium construction occurred in the United States as a consequence of hosting the tournament, one would not expect public investment to crowd out private construction as potentially occurred in Germany in 2006.

The fall in retail trade employment is perhaps somewhat surprising on the surface, but is in fact consistent with both economic theory and past studies of mega events. An influx of visitors could cause a fall in retail trade (and hence employment in that sector) for several reasons. First, local residents could leave the area during the period of the World Cup to avoid the crowds and congestion associated with the event or at the very least could change their shopping patterns to avoid the environs around the stadiums or other World Cup-related activities. Second, local residents could have spent money on World Cup tickets and events which substituted spending away from regular retail establishments. Third, World Cup visitors could have crowded out other tourists who would have been more likely to spend money on retailers instead of sporting events. This pattern has been observed in previous scholarly studies of mega events. Baade et al. (2010), for example, found that during the 2002 Salt Lake City Winter Olympics, retail sales at restaurants and hotels surged but sales at department stores fell, more than offsetting the gains in the other sectors of the economy. Taken together, the results suggest either zero or negative employment effects of hosting the World Cup. Even for the largest point estimate for overall employment (CES Kiviet corrected lagged dependent model), which again it should be noted is highly statistically insignificant, the 'World Cup effect' translates to an increase in employment of about 0.1 percent or roughly 1,900 jobs for each World Cup host city per month. Since the World Cup lasted over two months for all but one city (Detroit, see Appendix 22A), this represents an increase in employment of 3,800, roughly half that of AECOM's predictions for the 2022 US World Cup. Even bending over backwards to put the most optimistic spin on the data fails to produce the employment surge claimed by the boosters.[1]

These results are also broadly in line with other studies that compare *ex ante* predictions with *ex post* reality, including Allmers and Maennig (2009) and Feddersen and Maennig (2010). All told, there is no evidence in the US data during the 1994 World Cup to support a claim that the event will increase employment and economic activity at the levels suggested by event promoters.

3   CONCLUSIONS

It is often claimed that the World Cup is a golden opportunity for a country to showcase itself to the world while also generating a substantial economic return. *Ex ante* estimates of the economic impact of the World Cup typically start in the billions and rise from there. The predictions of economic gains coincide with large predicted employment effects ranging from 10,000 new jobs well into six-figure increases. These promises of a large financial windfall prompt countries to bid vigorously to host the event and to provide substantial funding to subsidize the tournament, often including billions of dollars of spending on sports-related infrastructure. Do *ex ante* predictions match *ex post* reality?

Our analysis of labor markets in the US during the 1994 World Cup generally finds no statistically significant change in employment or unemployment in host cities compared to cities that did not host the World Cup games. Estimates of economy-wide changes in employment in host cities, under four different estimation techniques, are all statistically insignificant, and the signs on the coefficients are as likely to suggest a fall in employment as a rise in employment. Even the most optimistic spin on the data suggest that the employment gains from the tournament were a fraction of that claimed by the event boosters. Furthermore, an analysis of sectoral labor data shows that even in the industry most likely to be affected by the tournament, leisure and hospitality, no increase in employment can be identified. Indeed, the only industry in which the World Cup appeared to have a statistically significant impact on employment was the retail trade, and in this sector of the economy the effect was negative with the presence of the tournament associated with a fall in employment of roughly 1,500 jobs per city in the sector.

The results in this chapter further reaffirm the conclusions of other researchers who have examined the economic impact of mega events, and we conclude that cities should be cautioned from making expensive promises based on inflated predictions. From a short-run employment standpoint, at least, the World Cup fails to live up to its billing as the world's greatest sporting event, and the excitement on the field fails to translate into jobs in local economies. Indeed, in the retail trade employment sector, the Golden Cup appears to be more of a poisoned chalice.

NOTE

1. Given the size of the host cities and the relatively high standard error on the coefficient a 95 percent confidence interval on the CES overall employment effect of the World Cup produces a range of – 12,600 to 20,000, which would include the AECOM estimates. That being said, while the model does not allow us to conclusively reject an hypothesis of 5,000 to 8,000 new jobs, the evidence is decidedly against any conclusion suggesting significant job gains.

REFERENCES

Allmers, S., and W. Maennig (2009), 'Economic impacts of the FIFA Soccer World Cups in France 1998, Germany 2006, and outlook for South Africa 2010', *Eastern Economic Journal*, **35** (4), 500–519.
Anderson, T.W. and C. Hsiao (1982), 'Formulation and estimation of dynamic models using panel data', *Journal of Econometrics*, **18**, 47–82.
Arellano, M. and S.R. Bond (1991), 'Some tests of specification for panel data: Monte Carlo evidence and an application to employment equations', *Review of Economic Studies*, **58**, 277–97.

Australian Broadcasting Corporation (2011), '2010 World Cup "a huge financial success"', available at: http://www.abc.net.au/news/stories/2011/03/03/3154951.htm (accessed March 31, 2011, posted March 4, 2011).

Baade, R. and V. Matheson (2004), 'The quest for the Cup: assessing the economic impact of the World Cup', *Regional Studies*, **38** (4), 343–54.

Baade, R. and V. Matheson (forthcoming). 'Financing professional sports facilities', in Zenia Kotval and Sammis White (eds), *Financing Economic Development in the 21st Century*, 2nd edn, NewYork: M.E. Sharpe.

Baade, R., R. Baumann and V. Matheson (2010), 'Slippery slope: assessing the economic impact of the 2002 Winter Olympic Games in Salt Lake City, Utah', *Region et Développement*, no. 31, 81–91.

Baumann, R., B. Engelhardt and V. Matheson (2010), 'Employment effects of the 2002 Winter Olympics in Salt Lake City, Utah', Working Paper Series No. 10–02, Department of Economics, College of the Holy Cross, Worcester, MA.

Blundell, R. and S. Bond (1998), 'Initial conditions and moment restrictions in dynamic panel data models', *Journal of Econometrics*, **87**, 115–43.

Box, G. and G. Tiao (1975), 'Intervention analysis with applications to economic and environmental problems', *Journal of the American Statistical Association*, **70**, 70–79.

Bruno, G. (2005), 'Estimation, inference and Monte Carlo analysis in dynamic panel data models with a small number of individuals', *Stata Journal*, **5** (4), 473–500.

Bun, M. and J. Kiviet (2003), 'On the diminishing returns of higher-order terms in asymptotic expansions of bias', *Economics Letters*, **79** (2), 145–52.

Coates, D. and B. Humphreys (2002), 'The economic impact of post-season play in professional sports', *Journal of Sports Economics*, **3** (3), 291–9.

Crompton, J. (1995), 'Economic impact analysis of sports facilities and events: eleven sources of misapplication', *Journal of Sport Management*, **9** (1), 14–35.

Feddersen, A., A.L. Grötzinger and W. Maennig (2009), 'Investment in stadia and regional economic development – evidence from FIFA World Cup 2006', *International Journal of Sport Finance*, **4** (4), 221–39.

Feddersen, A. and W. Maennig (2010), 'Sectoral labour market effects of the 2006 FIFA World Cup', Hamburg Contemporary Economic Discussions, No. 33.

Finer, J. (2002), 'The Grand Illusion', *Far Eastern Economic Review*, March 7, 32–6.

Goodman, R. and R. Stern (1994), 'Chicago hosts opening game of World Cup', *Illinois Parks and Recreation*, **25** (3), 34.

Hagn, F. and W. Maennig (2008), 'Employment effects of the Football World Cup 1974 in Germany', *Labour Economics*, **15** (5), 1062–75.

Hagn, F. and W. Maennig (2009),. 'Labour market effects of the 2006 Soccer World Cup in Germany', *Applied Economics*, **41** (25), 3295–302.

Im, K.S., M.H. Pesaran and Y. Shin (2003), 'Testing for unit roots in heterogeneous panels', *Journal of Econometrics*, **115** (1), 53–74.

Judson, K.A. and A.L. Owen (1999), 'Estimating dynamic panel data models: a guide for macroeconomists', *Economics Letters*, **65**, 9–15.

Kiviet, J.F. (1995), 'On bias, inconsistency, and efficiency of various estimators in dynamic panel models', *Journal of Econometrics*, **68**, 53–78.

Levin, A., C.F. Lin and C.S.J. Chu (2002), 'Unit root tests in panel data: asymptotic and finite-sample properties', *Journal of Econometrics*, **108**, 1–24.

Matheson, V. (2009), 'Economic multipliers and mega-event analysis', *International Journal of Sport Finance*, **4** (1), 63–70.

Nickell, S. (1981), 'Biases in dynamic models with fixed effects', *Econometrica*, **49**, 1417–26.

Porter, P.K. (1999), 'Mega-sports events as municipal investments: a critique of impact analysis', in J. Fizel, E. Gustafson and L. Hadley (eds), *Sports Economics: Current Research*, Westport, CT: Praeger, pp. 61–74.

Rianovosti (2009), 'Putin orders sports minister to prepare bid for 2018 World Cup', available at: http://en.rian.ru/sports/20090505/121448011.html (accessed March 31, 2011, posted May 5, 2009).

Rihlamvu, Edwin (2011), '2010 FIFA Soccer World Cup', *Africa Travel*, available at: http://www.africa-ata.org/sports.htm (accessed March 31, 2011).

Siegfried, J. and A. Zimbalist (2002), 'A Note on the local economic impact of sports expenditures', *Journal of Sports Economics*, **3** (4), 361–6.

Slevison, Andrew (2009), '$5 billion economic impact if World Cup hits U.S. shores', available at: *TribalFootball.com* (accessed March 31, 2011, posted October 30, 2009).

Sloan, D. (2002), 'Cup offers Japan economic free kick', *XtraMSN*, available at: http://xtramsa.co.nz/sport/0,,3951-1071885,00.html (accessed February 20, 2002, posted January 25, 2002).

Sterken, E. (2006), 'Growth impact of major sporting events', *European Sport Management Quarterly*, **6** (4), 375–89.

Szymanski, S. (2002), 'The economic impact of the World Cup', *World Economics*, **3** (1), 169–77.

Telegraph, The (2011), 'Super Bowl set U.S. TV record audience', avialable at: http://www. telegraph.co.uk/sport/othersports/americanfootball/8310107/Super-Bowl-set-US-TV-record-audience.html (accessed March 31, 2011, posted February 8, 2011).

Voigt, Kevin (2010), 'Is there a World Cup economic bounce?', CNN.com, available at: http://edition.cnn.com/2010/BUSINESS/06/11/business.bounce.world.cup/index.html (accessed March 31, 2011, posted June 11, 2010).

Wooldridge, J. (2002), *Introductory Econometrics: A Modern Approach*, 2nd edn, New York: South-Western College.

APPENDIX   22A

Table 22A.1   MSA data

City	CES MSA	CPS MSA
East Rutherford,NJ	Bergen-Hudson-Passaic, NJ	Newark-Union, NJ-PA
Foxborough, MA	Boston-Cambridge-Quincy, MA-NH	Boston-Cambridge-Quincy, MA-NH
Pasadena, CA	Los Angeles-Long Beach-Glendale, CA	Los Angeles-Long Beach-Santa Ana, CA
Stanford, CA	San Jose-Sunnyvale-Santa Clara, CA	San Jose-Sunnyvale-Santa Clara, CA

In the cases of World Cup hosts that are too small to have MSA data in the CES or CPS, we use MSAs for each city as in Table 22A.1.

In general, we use the smallest MSA possible that contains each city in order to produce the best possible chance of identifying employment effects of the World Cup. Choosing larger MSAs, say the New York City metropolitan area for East Rutherford, produced no substantial changes in the results.

World Cup games were hosted in June and July 1994 with one exception: Detroit hosted only in June 1994.

23 Not-so-mega events
Dennis Coates

1 INTRODUCTION

Enter 'world championships' into Google and you will get over 36 million results. On the first page of 10 links are the World Air Guitar Championships and the World Beard and Moustache Championships. The World Air Guitar Championship will occur for the 16th straight year in the summer of 2011. The event lasts four days with contestants from 20 countries. The 2011 event is in Oulu, Finland. Beard and Moustache competition fans have attended the event every other year since 1995. The event began, in its current organization, in Germany in 1990. The Italian beard competitors claim to have started the event in the 1970s. Since the 1990 event, host cities have included Carson City, Nevada, Anchorage, Alaska, and Berlin, Germany. The 2009 event, in Anchorage, saw the US team dominate, winning 12 of the 18 categories.

Adding 'sports' to the Google search reduces the results to a mere 11 million. Near the top of this dramatically pruned list is the Lumberjack World Championships, held for 52 years in Hayward, Wisconsin. The event attracts competitors from at least five countries to go head to head in 20 events over three days. As many as 12,000 spectators attend the competition, in a county with fewer than 20,000 inhabitants. The arena serves duty for Fred Sheer's Lumberjack Shows five days a week throughout the summer when not in use for the World Championship event. John Deere and NorTrax, the farm and heavy equipment manufacturer and seller, sponsor the event. Not to be outdone, Stihl, the maker of chainsaws and other outdoor tools, sponsors the Timber sports series, including world championships. The Stihl timber sports website reports news on the competitions from around the world, including the Benelux Championship and the regional qualifying events across the United States.

Few people would consider the Air Guitar, Beard and Moustache, or Lumberjack and Timber sports competitions to be mega events. Nonetheless, for the cities and towns that host at least some of these events, the influx of visitors and the spending they bring with them may be substantial relatively speaking. On the other hand, everyone would likely agree that the term 'mega event' applies to the Winter and Summer Olympic Games and the Football World Cup. Despite huge live audiences and worldwide television viewership in the billions, the evidence that these events have substantial economic impact on the host communities is mixed, at best.

Not so clearly mega events are events like the European Football Championships, Commonwealth Games, the Pan American Games, or the Asian Games or world championships in sporting disciplines such as track and field, swimming, or gymnastics, and the Tour de France. Moreover, one might dispute that the Winter Olympics is a mega event in the same sense as the Summer Olympic Games or the Football World Cup. I shall make more of this point below. Where events such as the Women's Football World Cup, the Rugby World Cup, and the Cricket World Cup fall on the scale of mega to not-mega events is debatable. Surely below these types of events in likely mega-event status are Grand Prix car races such as the Toyota Grand Prix of Long Beach and the Macao Grand Prix. On an absolute scale, the Lumberjack, Air Guitar, and Beard and Moustache World Championships are surely several notches below these on the mega-event scale and may be more on a par with the Men's Softball Fastpitch Championship (Turco and Navarro, 1993) or the Red Bull Big Wave Africa professional surfing event (Ntloko and Swart, 2008). For all of these events, whether they meet one's definition of a mega event or not, an important question is the extent to which they bring economic benefits to their host communities and, in the event that they are publicly subsidized, whether they generate a positive return on the public funds.

Before turning to the sporting events that will be the focus, it is important to note that there is a vast literature on the benefits of hosting non-sporting events. The most obvious of these sorts of events are the array of conventions and conferences for which cities across the United States build convention centers. Baade et al., (2009) examine the impact of national political conventions on a variety of measures of economic activity, including employment and income per capita, and find no discernible impact. Coates and Depken (2011) include the 1992 Republican National Convention among the events considered in their analysis of sales tax collections in Texas counties, and find that the event reduced sales tax revenues in Houston by about $1.4 million. Less obvious than the large conventions and conferences are numerous festivals. Research on the impact of festivals is common in journals related to tourism and the arguments for hosting such events would sound very familiar to students of mega sporting events. Indeed, with only slight editing, the following quote from Felsenstein and Fleischer (2003, p. 385) would be a common justification for sports events:

> The most obvious reasons for the popularity of the local festival as a tourism promotion tool are that (1) festivals increase the demand for local tourism

(Smith and Jenner 1998), and (2) successful festivals can help recreate the image of a place or contribute toward the exposure of a location trying to get on the tourism map (Kotler, Haider, and Rein 1993).

Despite this similarity in justification for festivals and sporting events, this chapter focuses on the sporting competitions.

In their introduction to this volume, Maennig and Zimbalist discuss several means of classifying an event as a mega event, one of which is the economic impact. Among their contenders are also the number of athletes, attendance and television viewership, and 'international significance'. An additional factor they include is location, though the context for location is as a determinant of television viewership. Against these possible determinants of mega-event status consider the Winter Olympic Games and compare them to one of the questionable mega events, the Commonwealth Games. The 2010 Vancouver Winter Olympics lasted for 17 days with the participation of 2,566 athletes from 82 countries.[1] The 2010 Delhi Commonwealth Games lasted 12 days, with the participation of 7,000 athletes from 71 countries.[2] While the Vancouver Winter Olympics website boasts of 3 billion television viewers, over a billion are reported to have watched the opening ceremonies to the Delhi Commonwealth Games.[3] Under any of these comparisons, athletes, nations represented, or TV audience, there is no clear distinction that makes the Winter Olympics a mega event and the Commonwealth Games not one. Indeed, both may be mega events, though the Commonwealth Games are rarely mentioned as such in the literature. For this reason, the Winter Olympics are included among the not-so-mega events in this study.

In this chapter, location will play a key role, but one not related to TV. Instead, here location is important as it defines the baseline against which the event is compared. An event that may be small in attendance, lacking in television audience, and irrelevant or trivial internationally, may nonetheless have considerable economic impact on the local community that stages it. For example, Coates and Depken (2011) asked 'Is Baylor Football to Waco what the Super Bowl is to Houston?'. Their answer is that '[a single Baylor football] game has about one third the relative impact (on sales tax collections) to the Waco economy as the Super Bowl did to the city of Houston's economy'. In other words, a college football game in a small to moderately sized city may not be nearly as big as the Super Bowl, but it can still be a very significant economic influence on its home city.

Indeed, the literature that looks at the impact of stadium construction and the presence of professional sports franchises has regularly addressed location, or geographic, considerations. Noll and Zimbalist (1997) note that if one focuses on a sufficiently narrow geographic location, then the construction of a stadium or arena is likely to generate a large economic impact. The smaller the area around the facility under consideration, the more that events at the facility will attract spending and activity from outside its borders, and the less the decision is based on global net benefits and the more it is based on redistribution to the narrow jurisdiction. The earliest work on sports team and facility impact focused on the metropolitan area or the city (see Baade and Dye, 1988, 1990; Baade, 1996; Coates and Humphreys, 1999). More recent work has examined localized impact around the stadium or arena. Tu (2005), Feng and Humphreys (2008), and Ahlfeldt and Maennig (2010) estimate the impact as a function of distance from the stadium, finding larger impact nearer to the facility. Coates and Humphreys (2006) and Ahlfeldt et al. (2010) assess the influence of proximity to stadiums or proposed sites of new stadiums on voting behavior. The evidence is clear that proximity matters.

Extending this argument to the mega-event context, the issue is how large the reach of the event into the countryside away from the official host city. With events like the Summer Olympics and the Football World Cup, games and competitions are often spread not just across the metropolitan area of one city but across the country. Smaller events, with fewer participants, may not need to hold competitions outside of the host city, concentrating the impact in that city. Of course these smaller events will also draw fewer spectators and a smaller television audience, so even with the concentration of the impact it may still be small. Indeed, the smaller the event, the more like a regular sporting event, and the less like a mega event, it may be.

Moreover, in Chapter 2, Maennig and Zimbalist compare mega events to regular sporting events saying 'In contrast, mega events tend to bring in more dollars from outside the local economy'. One goal here is to consider whether these not-so-mega events bring in more dollars from outside the local economy than they cost to stage. Perhaps the most significant issue in this context is the extent to which these events are able to generate net increases in tourism, both at the time of the event and persisting into the future. Consequently, this chapter examines evidence on tourism related to sports events, particularly the not-so-mega events.

Issues that do not seem to matter for whether an event is or is not a mega event may also be important, particularly as this relates to the success of the event at bringing in more outside money than is spent by the host community. The typical examples of mega events are one-off experiences. Cities do not host the Olympics in successive cycles. Likewise, cities cannot expect to host the Football World Cup repeatedly. However, other events occur in the same location each year. Among these events are the Boston Marathon, the Macao Grand Prix, and the Daytona 500 and all the other automobile races held by the National Association for Stock Car Auto Racing, NASCAR. These annual events are different from both the 20 days of the Olympics once in a lifetime and the eight, 15, 41 or 81 home game seasons of the National Football League (NFL), Major League Soccer, National Hockey League (NHL) and National Basket ball Association (NBA), and Major League Baseball (MLB) of the US professional sports leagues.

An additional issue that Maennig and Zimbalist do not mention in their introduction is the nature of the organizer of the event. Many of the events studied in this volume are organized by international organizations such as the International Olympic Committee or the Fédération Internationale de Football Associations (FIFA). Smaller events may be organized by regional international organizations or the governing bodies of the individual sport disciplines. The Commonwealth Games are an example of the former, organized by the Commonwealth Games Federation; the International Association of Athletics Federations, governing body of track and field (known as athletics outside the United States) competitions, is an example of the latter. But there are other sports events organized outside these groups by business organizations. The most visible example of these is the X Games, a product of ESPN. Stock car racing organized by NASCAR is like this as are the Tour de France,[4] and the Lumberjack and Timber Sports competitions, all of which are organized by corporate entities. A question that has not been raised in the literature is whether the nature of the organizer of the event matters. For example, if no public funds are being requested by the organizing committee, then there would likely be little objection by economists to hosting the events. The rub is when organizing committees request public support and produce economic impact statements suggesting large benefits from doing so. If a completely privately funded event can produce large social benefits, then the claim of event sponsors on public funding is less compelling. Consequently, a second goal for this research is to consider the privately organized events.

Before continuing, it is important to note two points about research on the not-so-mega events, particularly of the international variety. First, most of the research that has been done on these smaller events focuses on a single event in a single location; these studies are almost case studies, so drawing inferences from them for the universe of such events is problematic. Second, research on the general impact of these events is difficult because of a lack of comparable, high-quality data over time and across countries. For example, Coates and Depken (2011) are able to compare sales tax collections connected to events in different counties in Texas with reasonable confidence that the data are comparable across counties and across time. One cannot be so confident that data about metropolitan areas, to say nothing of smaller political or administrative jurisdictions, from myriad countries ranging from highly industrialized to less developed are equally accurate or similarly defined. Indeed, such data may not exist for many less-developed countries. But to truly assess the impact of these not-so-mega events on the cities that host them, comparable time-series data across cities and countries is necessary.

The next section is organized around literature related to the Winter Olympic Games. The suggestion that the Winter Olympics are not a mega event is developed, considering the impact of the Games on the economy of the host communities, including the tourism affects and the success at building a brand. Section 3 reviews literature related to other smaller events beginning with the most commonly studied of these, various motorsports competitions. This section also discusses research on the impact of non-World Cup Football events, the Rugby World Cup, and the X Games. Section 4 looks into the site selection process for the Commonwealth Games. The goal of the section is to provide some background on the efforts to which cities go to attract an event. Section 5 presents some empirical results on the impact of the Commonwealth and Pan American Games. A discussion and summary concludes (Section 6).

2 WINTER OLYMPICS

Aside from the Summer Olympic Games and the Football World Cup, perhaps the most likely mega event is the Winter Olympics. As noted above, the Winter Olympics are not obviously or clearly larger than the Commonwealth Games. In fact, the research that has been done on hosting Winter Olympics suggests that they are poor investments in terms of their long-term economic impact. Perhaps this is not surprising, as the host cities for Winter Olympics are often quite small, think of Lake Placid, New York or Lillehammer, Norway, remote, and with tourism that is highly seasonal.

Lillehammer is a clear example of a failed long-run economic development benefit from hosting a Winter Olympics. Teigland (1999, p. 305) 'compares ex ante theories and predictions with ex post reality'. His general conclusion is that predicted tourism growth following the 1994 Winter Olympics was not achieved and much of what growth there was could be traced to alternative coincidental factors affecting the broader Norwegian economy. Moreover, growth in capacity in Lillehammer prior to the event has dramatically exceeded the demand since the event.

The weak impact of the Lillehammer Olympics is not unique. Teigland presents results of the tourism impacts of the 1988 Calgary Games and cites research on tourism effects from the 1992 Albertville Winter Olympics (Richard and Friend, 1995; Barbier, 1996) that reach similar conclusions; namely, any increase in tourism following the Games is all or nearly entirely explained by broader macroeconomic factors, while none of it is linked to the occurrence of the Games. Porter and Fletcher (2008) studied the 2002 Salt Lake City Winter Olympics. Their results indicate that proponents of the Games wildly overstated the real impact the Games would have on the local economy. For instance, because hotel capacity is unresponsive to one-time short-term boosts to demand, hotel room rates rise dramatically while the number of rooms booked rises much less. Porter and Fletcher report that the price of a room increased by 141 percent in and around Salt Lake City during the Winter Olympics while hotel occupancy rose 31 percent. Interestingly, Porter and Fletcher find no evidence of increased air passenger traffic at the Salt Lake City Airport during the months of the Games.

The lack of an increase in air traffic suggests that the number of visitors to Salt Lake City was not meaningfully larger during the Olympic Games period than otherwise. Indeed, the Salt Lake City Olympics may have been more beneficial for the neighboring state of Colorado than it was for its home state Utah. Michael Leeds (2008) provides evidence that ski resort communities in Colorado benefitted by an increase in net taxable sales of $160 million in 2002. The finding documents one of the main criticisms of pre-event impact studies, namely that they inadequately account for sub-stitution behavior by consumers. Leeds's results make a good case that the Winter Olympics in Salt Lake led to people avoiding Utah ski resorts by taking their ski vacations to Colorado.

Rose and Spiegel (2009) and Song (2010) provide evidence that countries that host mega events have more international trade than countries that do not host such events. Rose and Spiegel find a very large impact on exports of hosting the Olympic Games and the Football World Cup. The Summer Olympics are linked to a 30 percent increase in the host country's exports; the FIFA World Cup effects are the same as the Summer Olympics.[5] Interestingly, the Winter Olympic Games have a smaller effect and one which is usually not significantly different from zero. In other words, the Winter Olympics are different from the Summer Olympics and the Football World Cup. Rose and Spiegel develop a theoretical model in which hosting, or indeed seeking to host, a large international event like the Olympics serves as a signal that a country intends to liberalize. They 'assume that countries that intend to pursue liberal trade policies in the future can signal this intent by engaging in the costly activity of bidding to host the Olympic Games' (p. 19). In fact, Rose and Spiegel extend their empirical analysis to bidding for the Games, and still find a positive and significant impact on the level of exports. The empirical results that indicate either seeking to host or actually hosting the Summer Olympics or the Football World Cup are connected to greater trade are consistent with the theory. On the other hand, the insignificance of hosting the Winter Olympics is not. Rose and Spiegel explain the insignificance of the Winter Olympics based on the host cities being small, remote, resort locales, particularly in the earlier years of the data. They provide no explanation for why hosting the Winter Olympics is not a signal of the intent to liberalize.[6]

Song (2010) extends the Rose and Spiegel data and includes an analysis of bilateral tourist flows. Focusing on the Summer Olympics, Song finds that the permanent effect of hosting the Summer Olympics is a reduction in tourism. That is, of course, counter to expectations, so Song examines the effects for different lengths of time starting both before the event and continuing after. Further analysis of the data led to the conclusion that the impact on exports is slow to develop but persists over a long time period while the impact on tourism is positive for a short period and then turns negative over the long run. Song's evidence regarding the Winter Olympics suggests that these Games have little impact on either exports or tourism.

A recent study by du Plessis and Maennig (2010) examined the short-run impact of the 2010 Football World Cup in South Africa on tourism there. Using data on arrivals of international flights and hotel occupancy they find that the net increase in tourists during the World Cup was a disappointing 91,000 (65,000 from outside Africa and 26,000 from other African nations). Fourie and Santana-Gallego (2010) also address tourism, examining the impact of the Summer and Winter Olympics, the Football World Cup and the Rugby World Cup on tourism. They find that neither the Rugby World Cup nor the Winter Olympics has an impact on tourism. Based on the existing literature, there is no evidence of a significant and sustained economic development impact of the Winter Olympic Games. An argument made by proponents of events is that they raise awareness of the host city. Of course, part of that added awareness is expected to pay off in terms of tourism and other economic impacts on the city, so the indirect evidence on this improved awareness is not encouraging. The direct evidence is equally unsupportive. Ritchie and Smith (1991) surveyed people from 20 areas in the United States and Europe about their perceptions of Calgary, Canada. The survey was conducted over a period of four years, beginning in 1986 and continuing through 1989. Calgary hosted the Winter Olympics in 1988. Prior to the Games, 10 percent to 12 percent of European survey respondents named Calgary as a Canadian city. The number jumped to 40 percent during 1988 but declined to 31.9

percent in 1989. The pre-Games numbers were a bit higher in the United States, but the Games and post-Games numbers are quite similar to those from Europe. In other words, roughly a third of the gains in recognition brought by hosting the Winter Olympic Games in 1988 had dissipated by the end of 1989. Ritchie and Smith raise the fundamental issue in their concluding remarks. 'For those cities that do experience a marked increase in awareness (such as Calgary), it is not immediately obvious that this will translate into increased visitation levels, tourism receipts, and/or other forms of economic development' (p. 9). Nonetheless, cities do chase after this awareness and recognition urged forward by event promoters. And they do so using events that are frequently far less visible than the Winter Olympics. It is to the research on these other not-so-mega events that I now turn.

3 OTHER EVENTS

This section will review literature on the impact of other not-so-mega sports events. Among these, the type of events with the largest existing body of literature is the numerous motor sports competitions. Motor sports are different from most of the other competitions considered because (i) they recur in the same location at the same time of year, and (ii) they are governed by explicitly for-profit enterprises. These get the lion's share of the attention before we move on to discuss other sports events.

An important difference between many of the events in this section is that they are held annually in the same location. Motor sports events are the most numerous of these. In the United States, NASCAR puts on races around the country with most tracks hosting one or at most two of the premier races in a season. Many of the tracks are in small cities in the southern United States, and these events draw tens of thousands of spectators. The track in Dover, Delaware, population 36,000, is Dover International Speedway with a seating capacity of 135,000; Bristol Speedway seats 165,000 in Bristol, Tennessee whose population is about 26,000; Darlington Speedway in Darlington, South Carolina seats 65,000, the population of Darlington is 67,000. Attendance at races is clearly large relative to these communities. Whether these events bring substantial economic impact is another question.

Bernthal and Regan (2004) evaluated the impact of races at Darlington Speedway. Their estimated impacts are substantial, but of questionable accuracy. For example, they find that two race weekends in Darlington generate a total of over $6 million in lodging expenses and over $520,000 in lodging taxes. Coates (2009) examined accommodation taxes in South

Carolina by county and month over a period of eight years and found little evidence that the taxes were higher in race than in non-race months. In only one county was there a statistically significant increase in accommodation tax revenues in race versus non-race months. Interestingly, that county, Dillon, is not the home to the track, though it is adjacent to it, and the boost was only $1,740, a boost of 35 percent over the non-race month average of $5,006. A large stretch of Interstate 95, the main north–south highway on the east coast of the United States, does pass through Dillon County. It may be that hotels and motels along the interstate see some increased traffic associated with races at Darlington, but it could also be that rental rates are increased for that time period.

Coates and Gearhart (2008) considered the impact of NASCAR tracks and events on housing rents with the conclusion that there is no strong evidence either that tracks or events raises or reduces rents. Baade and Matheson (2000) found that the impact of NASCAR's premier race, the Daytona 500, on Volusia County, Florida, and environs was an increase in taxable sales of about $40 million, far less than the $1.8 billion of impact reported in the press.

Cities around the world also host other types of automobile races. In the United States, the most famous race may be the Indianapolis 500. Other races include the Los Angeles Grand Prix, the St. Petersburg Grand Prix, and beginning Labor Day weekend 2011, the Baltimore Grand Prix. Grand Prix races outside the US have been the focus of several studies. For example, the Macao Grand Prix is the subject of research by McCartney (2005); Chen (2008) cites Eason (2007) and Quinonez (2008) on the Bahrain Grand Prix; the Singapore Grand Prix was discussed by Henderson et al. (2010); a possible South Africa Grand Prix is the subject of Bessit's (2006) Master's thesis; the Melbourne Grand Prix has been researched by Gamage (1997), Applied Economics (2006) for the State of Victoria, and Dwyer and Forsyth (2009).

The three studies of the Grand Prix in Melbourne are quite different in intent and in conclusions. Gamage (1997) is interested in the choice of the location of the race and the application of input–output analysis to the issue. He suggests that locating the event in the metropolitan area will be favored over more distant venues because of larger multipliers in the former compared to the latter. He reports an increase in household income of AU$20 million from a metropolitan location versus AU$18 million from the non-metropolitan venue. Gamage's analysis is dated and methodologically weak. He does not, for example, recognize that input–output models of the sort he uses effectively assume infinitely elastic resource supplies (see Porter and Chin, ch.15 in this volume). Dwyer and Forsyth (2009) is largely a methodological paper. Their discussion also points out criticisms of the input–output method for analyzing events. They show that the different methods of analysis lead to vastly different implications about the value of the Melbourne Grand Prix. Traditional cost–benefit analysis produced a net loss from the event of AU$6.7 million[7] while a computable general equilibrium (CGE) analysis indicates an increase in gross state product (GSP) of over AU$62 million. The CGE model also shows a reduction in the GSP of the other Australian states of AU$60.5 million so that the net impact of the Grand Prix is only AU$1.9 million, barely noticeable in Australian gross domestic product (GDP).

Some studies report impacts from Grand Prix races that are not such trivial contributions to the local economy, though those that do are generally flawed. According to Chen (2008), Eason (2007) reports that the 2006 Bahrain Grand Prix produced an impact of US$394 million, fully 3 percent of Bahrain's GDP, while the 2007 event produced US$594 million according to Quinonez (2008). The latter is clearly not an academic study, as it is published in the *Gulf Daily News* under the title 'Businesses urged to cash in on F1'. Evaluation of Eason (2007) has not been possible as I have not found it.

Consider the economic impact report (Baltimore Racing Development, 2010) for the Baltimore Grand Prix, an IndyCar Formula 1 race to be held for the first time in September, 2011. The report projects $70 million of impact on the Baltimore regional economy, with the 'multiplier effect' raising this to $119 million of 'yearly benefits'. The impact report projects 100,000 visitors to the city of Baltimore, with 60,000 of them staying at least one night. The analysis underlying this report leaves much to be desired. As one example, the 'multiplier effect' is equated to 'indirect costs and induced costs', suggesting a lack of understanding on the part of the authors both of a multiplier and that costs are not benefits (see Kesenne, ch. 16 in this volume). Bessit (2006) evaluated the possibility of a South Africa Formula 1 Grand Prix. Bessit's analysis was hampered by a lack of information from the government, the promoters (SA F1 Bid Company), or the Formula 1 organization, particularly that there was no detail on the project's economic impact analysis on which to judge the accuracy of assumptions and conclusions. One conclusion was clear to Bessit, that the government was being asked to contribute in the form of both infrastructure and a direct payment to Formula 1 Motorsports for the right to host the race, but that the decisions regarding the race were not necessarily how to best organize it for the benefit of South Africans.

Several issues stood out in this regard. First, one of the motivations for introducing a Formula 1 race in South Africa was to increase tourism, yet the intended location for the Grand Prix was Cape Town which was the principal tourist destination already. Bessit asked about alternative cities, such as Johannesburg, as potential sites. The SA F1 Bid Company CEO David Gant indicated that Formula 1 Motorsports CEO Bernie Ecclestone was adamant that Cape Town be the host. Bessit suggests that Johannesburg as host would both increase its tourism and likely lead to spillover tourism to the destinations in Cape Town, while people visiting Cape Town for the race would be unlikely to visit Johannesburg. Second, Bessit notes that government is asked to contribute 75 million rand toward infrastructure improvements. He notes that this figure does not include upgrades to roads near the track or to the Cape Town International Airport. Finally, Formula 1 Motorsports would receive $20 million as a host fee in the first year with the fee rising 10 percent each year. The national government was asked to contribute to this fee, though its share would ostensibly decline over time.

McCartney (2005) evaluates the Macao Grand Prix from the perspective of an attraction for visitors. McCartney surveyed people in the lobby of a hotel with high occupancy during the weekend of the Macao Grand Prix. Interestingly, he found that 13 percent reported not knowing that the event was taking place despite it happening annually at the same time of year for 50 years. Moreover, 57 percent of the sample reported not traveling to Macao for the Grand Prix. About 30 percent said they would not have traveled to Macao during the race period had they known of the race. Of those that were in Macao explicitly for the Grand Prix, nearly 41 percent said they did not intend to participate in other activities while in Macao. Eighteen percent of visitors who were there for the race indicated that they would not come to Macao if there were no race. Well over half of the respondents there for the race had been to the race before.

Henderson et al. (2010) conducted a survey about the impact of the Singapore Grand Prix. Their survey was conducted two months after the race, randomly selecting individuals at two light rail stations in Singapore. Respondents were in substantial agreement that putting on the race resulted in an increase in government spending; about the same percentage agreed that the race had increased business opportunities. There was less agreement on whether tourism benefitted, but still a majority felt that it had. The race increased the pride in Singapore of a majority of the respondents, and a majority also agreed that the race had disrupted their lives.

What one learns from surveys of the type conducted by McCartney (2005) or Henderson et al. (2010) is unclear.[8] Survey questions about people's willingness to return to Macao in the future for the event involve no real commitment and may simply be the natural tendency to tell the questioner what one thinks they want to hear. People's perceptions or opinions about whether the Singapore Grand Prix was good for tourism may bear no resemblance to the facts, especially two months after the event and given that the government agency in charge has declared the event a success. The objective information that exists with respect to Grand Prix races suggests that they may be beneficial to the host city/region but that much of that gain comes at the expense of other regions. The net effect for the hosting country is, therefore, likely to be small.

Two studies have evaluated the Union of European Football Associations (UEFA) Football Championships. Humphreys and Prokopowicz (2007) consider the impacts on the Ukraine and Poland of hosting the 2012 event; Pestana Barros (2006) measured the willingness to pay of Portuguese citizens to host the 2004 event. Humphreys and Prokopowicz concluded:

> Although the event will attract a large number of spectators and television viewers, a simple cost benefit analysis indicates that the costs of hosting the event will exceed the direct economic impact related to increased tourist spending by a wide margin and the presence of positive benefits depends on benefits from factors like improvements in the transportation infrastructure. (p. 496)

Pestana Barros (2006) concludes that hosting Euro 2004 'is not a Pareto improvement of the public good, since the aggregated willingness-to-pay is lower than the estimated total cost' (p. 400).

Three studies focus on the impact of the Rugby World Cup. Before considering them, however, it is important to see how the event is portrayed in the popular press. Reporting about a Deloitte Sport Business Group study, *The Press* (March 18, 2009) from Christchurch, New Zealand, says that 'the Rugby World Cup could boost the New Zealand economy to the tune of $1.25 billion, as well as laying the foundation for significant future tourism'. Jones (2001) sought to determine 'the true worth of the 1999 Rugby World Cup'; Charrier and Jourdan (2009) and Barget and Gouguet (2010), each published in French, examine the 2007 Rugby World Cup held in France. Jones (2001) studies the Rugby World Cup held in Wales in 1999. He concludes that there were benefits to the region though they were not as large as they might have been. He contends that the fault lay with the bidding process and organizational problems. Among the issues is the fact that four of the six matches held in Wales featured the Welsh team, limiting the amount of visitor spending in the Principality.

Charrier and Jourdan (2009) focused specifically on the effects of the Rugby World Cup on three communities in the Île-de-France region. They found that 'the impact of the Rugby World Cup on visitor numbers at tourism sites in the Paris region was negligible or negative' (p. 45). In one community, Saint-Denis, they found a 22 percent reduction of tourist visits relative to the norm for that time of year. The shortfall was attributed to some tourists avoiding the region during the Rugby World Cup and others substituting World Cup-related activities for traditional tourism.

Barget and Gouguet (2010) also examined the economic impact of the 2007 Rugby World Cup in France. They report finding positive impact in every French region, but with substantial variation among the regions. Moreover, the positive impacts are attributed to spending on stadiums and by spectators viewing the giant television screens.

Turco and Navarro (1993) computed a return on investment for the 1992 Amateur Softball Association Men's National Fastpitch Softball Championship held in Bloomington, Illinois. Determining the rate of return on government funds invested in putting on an event is uncommon in the literature. There are numerous reasons for this, one of which is that many of the benefits are non-pecuniary. Putting a dollar value to the increased pride felt by Singapore residents from hosting the Singapore Grand Prix, for example, would be arbitrary and could easily bias the results. Turco and Navarro report a return of 123 percent, quite an amazingly successful investment by any standard. Unfortunately, they also count the money spent both as the investment and as part of the return on the investment. Following their method of computing return, few investments would be bad ones.

One final event to mention is the X Games produced by ESPN and the Anshutz Entertainment Group. Independent studies of the impact of the event have not been done. ESPN has commissioned an economic impact study (Weinstein et al., 2010) of the event held annually in Los Angeles. It is useful to consider this event, however, because it is largely funded privately; largely, but not entirely, as the city of Los Angeles, California also contributes financially toward the event. The impact report identified $50 million of benefits to Los Angeles from X Games 16. Benefits include $12 million linked to tourism increases, $6 million from 'setting up, staging and television broadcast production' (p. 1). There were also 'roughly $12 million in multiplier effects flowing from direct spending associated with the X Games' (p. 1). The broadcast of the Games went to '175 countries and more than 380 million homes' (p. 1). The report estimated the value of the broadcasts to Los Angeles at 'approximately $20 million'. The report argues that '[t]hese estimates are conservative since they do not include incremental expenditures by local residents on X Games activities', nor do they include 'the value of corporate sponsorship or community outreach programs associated with the X Games' (p. 1).

By the standards of the Olympics, Football World Cup, or the Commonwealth Games, the X Games are clearly not a mega event. The report accounts for the hotel room nights associated with 261 athletes, 138,000 spectators and broadcasts reaching 380 million homes. Contrast that with the Vancouver Winter Olympics which had 2,566 athletes and (claimed) television viewership of 3 billion. The estimated impact of the X Games also pales in comparison to that for the Olympics or even the

Commonwealth Games. Even if the benefits of the X Games to Los Angeles are accurately measured, and despite assurances that they are conservative, they still may be exaggerated, the impact on LA is tiny. For example, data on 2009 GDP for the Los Angeles metropolitan area from the Bureau of Economic Analysis website indicates a value of $730,941,000,000; for just the Arts, Entertainment, and Recreation Industry, the GDP of Los Angeles metro area in 2009 was $13,719,000,000. That means that the X Games contribute 0.007 percent, that is seven thousandths of 1 percent, to total GDP for the LA area, and only 0.36 percent, or thirty-six hundredths of 1 percent, to the Arts, Entertainment, and Recreation sector.

But even these effects may be overstated. Included in the benefits are spending on venue rentals, scaffolding rentals and set-up and other costs associated with putting on the X Games. To include them assumes that the venues would have been idle, that the scaffolding would have been unrented, and so on, had the event not occurred. Perhaps that is true, but it is by no means obvious or necessary that such is the case. Likewise, spending by ESPN staff on hotels and meals while in LA for the event is included as a benefit. This assumes that those rooms would have remained idle and that the seats at restaurants taken by ESPN staff would not have been filled by other patrons. Again, perhaps that is true, but it is by no means necessary.

Of course, the argument that media coverage of the Games from Los Angeles provided $20 million worth of benefits to LA is also suspect. The suggestion is that viewers will be enticed to visit Los Angeles at some point in the future because of what they saw of the city during the X Games broadcast. The idea that people who would watch the X Games, which have been held in LA for a decade, have never heard of the city or its attractions before watching the broadcast seems rather unlikely. Moreover, one has to wonder how much of the 27 hours of coverage focused on the city and its environs as opposed to the Games and the participants. One wonders how many 30-second advertisements aired during the broadcast the city could purchase for $20 million and if those focused ads would not have greater impact than the short showing of vistas from the area. In short, the value of the broadcast may be overstated.

Clearly, the economic impact of the X Games may be quite small. Unlike many of the events described above, there is relatively little in the way of public subsidy. How much the city of Los Angeles contributes is unknown, but relatively speaking this must be small. There are no new facilities to construct, for example. Moreover, ESPN has chosen Los Angeles as the home for the event, settling on it after having early events in other locations. Alex Rizos, Senior Manager, Communications, at ESPN, said that Los Angeles was the ideal location because it is the home of the types of sports events that the X Games features. Perhaps the chief advantage of the

X Games, therefore, is that the organizers do not have to bid for the right to host the event. The bidding process is discussed in the next section.

4   BIDDING TO HOST AN EVENT

For most of the events discussed above, cities must bid to the international governing body to be designated host. The bid process is similar across events, requiring participation of various levels of government as well as the local organizing committee. The international sports federations that grant host status want guarantees that: facilities will be up to standard and ready on time for the event; spectators and participants will have comfortable lodgings and easy travel to the venues; broadcast and print media facilities will be modern and capable of providing high-quality coverage of the events. This section examines the host bid process for the Commonwealth Games including a review of the two competing bids to host the 2018 Games, Hambantota, Sri Lanka and Gold Coast, Australia, and the scandal when one city, Halifax, Nova Scotia, backed out of the bid process to host the 2014 Games.

The Commonwealth Games Federation provides a detailed guide book for the bid process, the *Candidate City Manual* (2011). The manual is 153 pages long. Highlights of the manual include the requirements for design of a Commonwealth Games logo by the host city candidates, including stipulations about the nature of the logo, format of the submissions, and the list of questions to be answered by candidate cities in their application form. Rules governing visits by the Commonwealth Games Federation Evaluation Commission (2003) and by visitors from other national Commonwealth Games Association members restrict the giving of gifts and the accommodations and provision of food and drink. 'A sense of moderation should particularly prevail concerning hospitality and accommodation'. Indeed, '[m]oderation should prevail, concerning all hospitality and entertainment offered by Candidate Cities to CGAs and their delegates, at all times'. Clearly, the Commonwealth Games Federation wants to avoid the appearance of impropriety throughout the bid process. The cost of applying to host the 2018 Games is a non-refundable fee of £60,000 sterling. Paid-up applicants receive the documents and information produced for the candidate cities by the Commonwealth Games Federation, participation in two programs intended to help candidate cities navigate the bid process, and evaluation of their bid by the Commonwealth Games Federation Evaluation Commission. Not covered by the £60,000 is travel and accommodations of the commission. The local bid committee covers that expense, as described above.

The Candidate City Questionnaire addresses 15 themes. The first theme is called 'Vision and Concept', and candidate cities are asked why they wish to host the Commonwealth Games. Candidate cities are also expected to explain how the event fits into the city's long-range planning, how they selected locations for venues, their plans for integrating youth outreach into the program, and plans for opening and closing ceremonies, medal ceremonies and cultural events, including how to maximize the broadcast appeal of these ceremonies.

Additional themes cover political organization and support for the Games, including implementing and enforcing necessary laws to protect the Games logo and intellectual property, to protect the participants through customs and immigration, and evidence of public support for the bid. Themes also address the ability of Commonwealth Games personnel to enter and exit the host country and to move materials for the Games into and out of the country without import or export duties; the required immunizations and other health regulations; restrictions or limitations on the press; the plans for marketing; the plans for security of the participants and the spectators; the quality and proximity of medical and health facilities; the quality of the athlete accommodation and accessibility to the training and competition venues; and the sports venues. Theme five concerns the likely weather conditions at the time of the event and other natural hazards that might affect the Games. This theme also asks the candidate city to discuss environmental protection and sustainability with regard to venues and transportation. Environmental impact studies are to be summarized in this section.

Theme 6 addresses '[t]he reasonableness of the financial plan/budget developed to support the operations of the Commonwealth Games'. Candidate host cities must explain and describe '[t]he relevance of the financial guarantees provided to ensure the financing of all major capital infrastructure investments required to deliver the Commonwealth Games' and to 'cover a potential economic shortfall of the' local organizing committee. Among the guarantees are price controls, particularly over hotel rates, new and special taxes implemented for the Games, and travel expenses of delegations from Commonwealth Games Associations representing non-host countries. The candidate city is expected to '[p]rovide a financial guarantee from the competent authorities covering a potential economic shortfall of the [organizing committee]'.

The *Candidate City Manual* provides a budget template which is reproduced in Table 23.1. Note that the template accounts for broadcast revenues which go to the Commonwealth Games Federation, not the host city or its organizing committee. The budget template also includes a line for national, regional and local government subsidies. Tables 23.2 and 23.3 reproduce the budget tables from the Gold Coast, Australia, and

Table 23.1 Budget Template 6.10: detailed Commonwealth Games budget (OC budget)

A – REVENUES	GBP (000)	%	B – EXPENDITURE	GBP (000)	%
1 Broadcast Rights (CGF)			B1 Capital Investments		
			11 Sports facilities		
			Commonwealth Games		
			Village and other villages		
			MPC & IBC		
			Other (specify)		
			Sub-total		
2 Local sponsorship					
3 Official suppliers			B2 Games Operations		
4 Ticket sales			12 Sports venues		
5 Licensing			Commonwealth Games		
Licensing merchandise			Village & other villages		
			MPC		
Coin programme			IBC/HBO		
Philately			13 Games workforce		
Sub-total			14 Information systems		
			Telecommunications &		
6 Lotteries			other technologies		

418

7 Donations

   Sub-total

8 Disposal of assets

9 Subsidies

   National government

   Regional government

   Local government

   Sub-total

10 Other revenues

25 SHORTFALL

12 TOTAL

   Internet

15 Ceremonies and culture

   Opening Ceremony

   Closing Ceremony

   Medal award ceremonies

   Cultural programme

   Baton relay

   Other programmes

16 Medical services

17 Catering

18 Transport

20 Security

21 Advertising & promotion

22 Administration

23 Test events & meetings

24 Other

   Sub-total

25 SURPLUS

TOTAL

Note: Indicate GBP/local currency exchange rate used in preparing the budget.

Source: Commonwealth Games Federation (2011).

Table 23.2   Budget 6.10: detailed Commonwealth Games Budget

A	REVENUES	£GBP millions	%
1	Broadcast Rights (CGF)	37.80	3.04
2	Local Sponsorship	50.40	4.06
3	Official Suppliers	0.00	0.00
4	Ticket Sales	34.65	2.79
5	Licensing	3.15	0.25
6	Lotteries	0.00	0.00
7	Donations	0.00	0.00
8	Disposals of Assets	0.00	0.00
9	Subsidies		
	– State Government	698.67	56.23
10	Other (Games Village)	417.93	33.63
	TOTAL REVENUES	1,242.60	100.00

B	EXPENDITURE	£GBP millions	%
B1	CAPITAL INVESTMENTS		
13	Sports facilities	171.92	30.06
	Games Village	399.03	69.77
	Main Press Centre (MPC)	0.63	0.11
	International Broadcast Centre (IBC)	0.32	0.06
	Other	0.00	0.00
	TOTAL CAPITAL INVESTMENTS	571.90	100.00
B2	OPERATIONS		
14	Sports and Venues	122.16	18.21
	Games Village	78.06	11.64
	MPC and IBC	1.89	0.28
15	Games Workforce	72.70	10.84
16	Telecommunications and Other Technologies	70.56	10.52
16	Internet/Website	6.30	0.94
17	Ceremonies and Culture		
	Opening and Closing Ceremony	15.75	2.35
	Medal Award Ceremonies	6.30	0.94
	Cultural Programmes	11.03	1.64
	The Queen's Baton Relay	3.15	0.47
	Other Programmes	9.45	1.41
18	Medical Services	3.15	0.47
19	Catering	12.73	1.90
20	Transport	34.65	5.17
21	Security	69.30	10.33
22	Advertising and Promotion	37.17	5.54
23	Administration	45.36	6.76

Table 23.2   (continued)

24	Pre-Games Events and Coordination	1.89	0.28
25	Other and Contingency	69.10	10.30
	TOTAL OPERATIONS	670.70	100.00
	TOTAL EXPENDITURE	1,242.60	100.00
	DEFICIENCY	0.00	0.00

Note: Federal government and Gold City Council have committed significant contributions to the Games and discussions are continuing to determine the level of cash contribution.

Source: Gold Coast City (2011).

Hambantota, Sri Lanka, candidate files, respectively. As these files make clear, government subsidies comprise the lion's share of the funding for the event; the Australian bid is supported by £698.67 million from the state government, fully 56 percent of the revenues in the budget; the government of Sri Lanka pledges support of £272.77 million, or 66 percent of the revenues for the Hambantota bid. Hamilton, Ontario, Canada and Delhi, India competed to host the 2010 Games, a competition won by Delhi. For the Hamilton bid, Canada, Ontario, and the city of Hamilton pledged grants of CDN$580 million; McMaster University added another CDN$50 million. Public support amounted to 88 percent of the revenues for the Hamilton bid. The governments of India and the city of Delhi proposed to support the Delhi bid with US$234.8 million of grants, about 56 percent of the revenues from the event.

The budget documents make clear that government at some level will provide a great deal of money to support the Games. Much of the money goes to construction, expansion, or renovation of sport venues. Gold Coast, for example, budgeted £571.9 million for capital investment, with £399 million going toward the Games Village and £171.92 million toward sport venues. Following the Games, the Games Village will become 'a master-planned, transit-oriented, knowledge-based community', with retail and office spaces replacing Commonwealth Games Association and Games Health facilities. The Village will house 2,100 residents after the event. In Hambantota, the Games Village will become a residential area for a new sports university and for a nearby business and IT park. It is not clear if the business and IT park exists or is also part of the intended legacy of the Games.

As has been described above, the evidence of benefits from these events is weak. The costs, on the other hand, can be substantial. One city, Halifax, Nova Scotia, Canada, started the process of bidding for the 2014

Table 23.3 Detailed Commonwealth Games budget (OC budget) (currency rate 1 GBP = 177.32 LKR as at 1 April 2011)

A	Revenues	GBP (000)	%	B	Expenditure	GBP (000)	%
1	International Broadcast Rights	29,569	7	B1	Capital Investments		
				10	Sports facilities	20,369	5
				10	Commonwealth Games Village and other villages	0	0
				10	MPC & IBC	0	0
				10	Other (specify)	11,866	3
2	Local sponsorship & official suppliers	102,216	25			32,235	8
3	Ticket sales	4,898	1	B2	Operations		
4	Licensing	1,058	0	11	Sports venues	53,290	13
				11	Commonwealth Games Village and other villages	48,345	12
				11	Other Non Competition Venues	6,282	2
				11	IBC/MPC[1]	5,955	1
				12	Games workforce	27,086	7
				13	Information systems	15,937	4
				13	Telecommunications & other technologies	12,919	3
				13	Internet	1,895	0
		137,741	34	14	Ceremonies and culture		0

5 Disposal of assets	0	0		Opening Ceremony	14,545	4
				Closing Ceremony	6,113	1
		0	0	Medal award ceremonies	1,273	0
				Cultural programme	4,789	1
				Baton relay	4,236	1
				Other programmes	9,136	2
6 Subsidies				15 Medical services	1,361	0
National government	272,774	66		16 Catering	10,583	3
Regional government				17 Transport	17,965	4
Local government	272,774	66		18 Security	30,874	8
				19 Advertising & promotion	20,910	5
				20 Administration	16,994	4
				21 Pre-Commonwealth events & coordination	2,912	1
7 Other	0	0		22 Other[2]	64,881	16
					378,280	92
8 SHORTFALL	0			23 SURPLUS	0	
9 Total	410,515	100		Total	410,515	100

Notes:
1. Host broadcasting services to be provided at no cost to the OC by state owned television broadcaster, Sri Lanka Rupavahini Corporation (SLRC). SLRC to independently formulate suitable sub-contract arrangements with local private sector broadcasters in order to recover associated host broadcaster costs.
2. Other costs include amount for contingency (GBP 46.20 million), Sponsorship rights and Host Fee payment to the CGF (GBP 10.60 million) and committed amount for the Athlete Training and Development Support Programme (GBP 5.00 million).

Source: Hambantota (2011).

Commonwealth Games, but withdrew after an independent evaluation found the proposed budget to be unrealistic. The documents were unavailable to the public for months after the withdrawal, as they 'contain information that may compromise the commercial interests of a third party' (Montgomerie, 2007). However, the decision by the Halifax government to withdraw, after learning that the Province would cap its contribution at CDN$400 million, is based on several factors. Duff Montgomerie, Nova Scotia's Provincial Deputy Minister of Health Promotion, listed the issues in his letter to the Province's Standing Committee on Public Accounts which requested he appear to discuss the matter. Among the factors are a discrepancy of about CDN$300 million between the estimated budget from the domestic bid and the budget for the final bid;[9] a budget gap in revenues of over CDN$1 billion which would be funded by Halifax and Nova Scotia governments; a consultant report that indicated the Province of Nova Scotia was at risk of exposure to costs in addition to those estimated in the budget. The decision to withdraw was motivated by the principle of 'never compromising the Province's fiscal position'. An article in *The Times and Transcript* (New Brunswick) from July 2008 reported that the Halifax Games would have cost CDN$2.2 billion had that city won the right to host the 2014 Commonwealth Games. The bid process, even though it was not completed, reportedly cost CDN$9.5 million (*The Globe and Mail*, November 17, 2007). Preparation of the bid book alone cost CDN$3.4 million. Another million dollars was spent on travel by bid officials traveling to Commonwealth countries to lobby for Halifax's bid. Clearly, bidding on an event is an expensive endeavor.

The decision to withdraw was criticized severely in Nova Scotia and in other parts of Canada. In an article reflecting back on the decision, *The Halifax Daily News* (December 30, 2007) reported that Bid Chairman Fred MacGillivray referred to the withdrawal as 'a dark day for Halifax, a dark day for Nova Scotia and a dark day for Canada'. He also said the withdrawal was a 'severe blow to the province'. That same article quoted two individuals; according to Philip Croucher the bid would have got Halifax 'out of the sports infrastructure dark ages'; while Adam Richardson said, 'We looked silly, and boy, did I want that outdoor stadium for a CFL [Canadian Football League] team'. Pat Connolly of *The Halifax Daily News* opined on the withdrawal in an article entitled 'Our World Class Embarrassment'. To Connolly, the withdrawal from the Commonwealth Games bidding caused the illusion that Halifax was becoming a world class city to die 'in infamy' (Connolly, 2007). In Hamilton, Ontario, Halifax was accused of making a bid in the domestic competition that was 'low-balled and misleading', The editorial page of *The Guardian* from Charlottetown, Prince Edward Island, called for an apology from Halifax 'for botching its bid for the 2014 Commonwealth Games, plus compensation for the opportunities the city wrongly took from us' (Ottawa Citizen, 2007).

Whether the original bid by Halifax was low-balled or misleading, that the provincial and city governments were willing to pull out because the costs exceeded the benefits ought to be a good thing. One can only imagine how the citizens of Nova Scotia would have reacted to building a number of highly specialized sport facilities that later sat idle. The real question is whether and to what degree events like the Commonwealth Games generate legacy benefits to the community. The next section uses the Rose and Spiegel data on bilateral trade patterns described above to assess the impact of the Commonwealth Games.

5 TRADE AND GROWTH EFFECTS OF THE COMMONWEALTH AND PAN AMERICAN GAMES

The data in this analysis are those used by Rose and Spiegel (2009). They constructed a dataset that paired countries as trading partners covering the years from 1950 through 2007. Included in their analysis are variables on common language, common colonial power, distance between the countries, real GDP per capita in both countries, and other variables. For a complete discussion of the variables they include in their gravity model of international trade one should consult their paper. They also constructed variables that indicated the year in which a country hosted the Summer or Winter Olympics and all subsequent years. To this I have added analogous variables for the Commonwealth Games and the Pan American Games. These last variables have simply been added to the regression equations estimated by Rose and Spiegel, who provided their data and programs.

Rose and Spiegel estimate a variety of models to assess the sensitivity of their results to alternative approaches. They allow for year fixed effects, trading partner fixed effects, originating country fixed effects, and destination country fixed effects. In some specifications they have year and originating country dummy variables and destination country fixed effects. They also allow for originating country-specific time trends. Their Olympic variables are included in the model in two ways. First, they simply include a dummy variable for the year that a country first hosted the Summer Games and a dummy variable for the year a country first hosted the Winter Games. In some regressions they use a dummy variable that identifies the year a country first hosted any Olympic Games. Second, they estimate the model using a variable that takes a value of one in any year of or subsequent to hosting the first Summer Olympic Games. They also construct an analogous variable for the Winter Games. To each of these alternative specifications, I have added similarly constructed Pan American and Commonwealth Games variables. The results from Rose and Spiegel concerning the Summer and Winter Olympic Games are unchanged by the addition of the Commonwealth and Pan American Games variables.

Of interest here, however, is the estimates of the effects of the Commonwealth and Pan American Games variables. The general conclusion is similar to that of Rose and Spiegel regarding the Winter Olympics, that is, that the effects are not robust across specifications and are not generally positive and statistically significant. The results are different in nature between the Commonwealth Games and the Pan American Games, however. In every specification, the estimated impact of the Pan American Games is negative, and in most cases statistically significant. The year of the event dummies are implausibly large, with coefficients of –0.77 and –0.16, or nearly a 54 percent and 15 percent reduction in trade in the year of the event, respectively.[10] The Commonwealth Games effect is not robustly estimated. The coefficient on the Commonwealth Games variable is estimated to be positive and statistically significant in two specifications, but insignificant in four models, with three of those estimates negative. The Commonwealth Games variable is not significant in the models with year and country effects, the most reliable of the models. The implication from these results is that the Pan American and Commonwealth Games cannot be relied upon to boost a country's trade. If hosting an international event is the signal of intended openness as Rose and Spiegel suggest, then hosting either the Commonwealth or the Pan American Games is an ineffective, misleading, or misinterpreted signal. In other words, the results with regard to these games are not consistent with the Rose and Spiegel signaling hypothesis.

The lack of robustness in the Commonwealth Games effects, like those for the Winter Olympics reported by Rose and Spiegel, needs some explanation. The positive and significant results come from models with no host country or trading pair effects. Accounting for trading partner effects, or originating and destination country effects makes the Commonwealth Games variable statistically insignificant, with the point estimate sometimes positive but more often negative. In other words, when it is positive and statistically significant, the Commonwealth Games variable is proxying for influences that are more accurately attributed to host country and trading partner specific effects.

One final piece of evidence on the impact of the Commonwealth Games and the Pan American Games concerns the impact on the year to year

Table 23.4 Descriptive statistics

Variable	Mean	Std dev.	Min	Max
Log Real GDP per capita	8.425	1.104	5.750	11.148
Summer Olympics	0.080	0.271	0	1
Winter Olympics	0.055	0.228	0	1
Pan American Games	0.054	0.226	0	1
Commonwealth Games	0.045	0.207	0	1
Log Population	8.878	1.790	3.657	13.879

Note: Number of observations is 4,408.

growth rate in real GDP per capita of the sports events. Rose and Spiegel's variables include real GDP per capita for each country by year. Restricting that data to include a single time series of real GDP and population for each country in the data reduces the number of observations dramatically, but it also allows one to estimate a type of growth equation, in which the dependent variable is the change in the log of real GDP per capita and whose explanatory variables are the Olympic, Commonwealth, and Pan American Games variables as well as the lagged natural logarithm of real GDP per capita and the natural log of population. The estimated equation is: [11]

$$\ln rgdppc_{it} - \ln rgdppc_{it-1} = \beta_0 + \beta_1 \ln rgdppc_{it-1} + \sum_k \delta_k m_{itk} + \sum_j \gamma_j D_{itj} + \mu_{it}$$

The βs, γs, and δs are parameters to be estimated and μ is a random error term with mean zero and variance that may differ by country i. The D_{itj} are a list of country- and year-specific effects and country-specific time trends; m_{itk} are the event dummy variables taking value of 1 in every year from the first time an event is hosted through the end of the data, and zero for all prior years. There are four events in the analysis, the Summer and Winter Olympics and the Commonwealth and Pan American Games. The δ_k are the parameters of interest.

Before reporting the results, a further discussion of the data is in order. Table 23.4 reports descriptive statistics for the variables other than country dummies and country-specific time trends. There are 147 countries in the analysis, with the number of years of data for each country ranging from a minimum of three to a maximum of 51. The data contain 57 years of observations, 1950 through 2007, but the model was estimated with six lags of the log of real GDP per capita because the lag length is unknown. The Bayes Information Criterion statistic was smallest for a single lag, indicating that that is the number of lags which best fit the data, so that is the estimation that is reported.

Table 23.5   Growth regression

Variable	Base model	Japan separate
Lagged log real GDP per capita	−0.149	−0.151
	0.000	0.000
Summer Olympics	0.026	0.015
	0.061	0.322
Winter Olympics	0.018	0.012
	0.336	0.527
Pan Am Games	0.023	0.023
	0.186	0.182
Commonwealth Games	−0.006	−0.005
	0.776	0.783
Log population	−0.095	−0.096
	0.005	0.005
Japan Summer Olympics		0.074
		0.059
F-statistic (137,4140) [F(138,4139)]	5.670	5.660
	0.000	0.000
Country fixed effects (131)	5.330	5.350
	0.000	0.000
Country-specific time trends	Yes	Yes
F-statistic(4,4140) [F(4,4139)]	1.510	0.770
Null: Summer, Winter, Pan Am, and Commonwealth Games coeffs all zero	0.198	0.543

Table 23.5 provides the parameter estimates for a base model and for a second model in which Japan's hosting of the 1964 Summer Olympics is treated separately. In both models, the estimated impact of lagged real GDP per capita on the year to year change in real GDP per capita is negative and statistically significant. The estimate implies a rate of convergence to the steady-state level of the real GDP per capita of about 0.161. This is a high rate of convergence, but the model pools very dissimilar countries as well as omits important variables, such as human capital and political and economic institutions, in standard growth equations.[12] The results also indicate that populous countries have slower growth rates in real GDP per capita. For both models, an F-test of the overall significance of the regression easily rejects the null hypothesis that none of the included regressors is statistically significant.

The variables of interest are the event host variables. Their coefficients indicate the impact of hosting the events on growth in real GDP per capita. In the base model, the Summer and Winter Olympics and the

Pan American Games all have positive coefficient estimates, while the Commonwealth Games coefficient is negative. None of the coefficients is statistically significant at the 5 percent level, and given there are over four thousand degrees of freedom, use of higher-level cut-offs may not be justified. Nonetheless, the Summer Games variable is significant at the 6.1 percent level, suggesting very weakly that hosting the Games has a permanent effect on economic growth. However, as a group, one cannot reject the null that all the host variable effects are equal to one another and equal to zero.

Further exploration, shown in the second model, reveals that the impact of the Summer Olympics on the growth rate of real GDP per capita is driven almost entirely by Japan, the coefficient for which is 0.074. The *p*-value on the Japan Summer Olympics variable is 0.059. The Summer Olympics coefficient drops from 0.026 to 0.015 and the *p*-value rises from 0.061 to 0.322; the coefficient is cut nearly in half and the probability of this coefficient arising under the null hypothesis that the coefficient is zero climbs by a factor of five. As before, one cannot reject the null hypothesis that the Summer and Winter Olympic Games coefficients and the Pan American and Commonwealth Games coefficients are all zero. In sum, the evidence here strongly suggests that the growth rate of real GDP per capita is not raised by hosting any of these events.

6   CONCLUSION AND DISCUSSION

The impact of not-so-mega events on local economies is difficult to gauge. The evidence is sparse, as most of the events have not been studied systematically. One reason for this lack of study is the enormous variety of possible such events. A second reason is that data are hard to get for the small international events. The end result is that most of the work on these events focuses on a single event, possibly one that occurs in the same location repeatedly. Some of these events, particularly those that are held in very small cities and towns and do not involve the use of public subsidies, are likely to be significant sources of local economic activity. The Lumberjack World Championships are an example of this. The evidence that exists regarding the large international events that are a step or two below the Summer Olympics or the Football World Cup does not support arguments that these events are enormously successful means of enhancing the local economy.

This chapter adds to the literature on these not-so-mega events by examining the impact of two of them, the Commonwealth and the Pan American Games, on the level of trade and on the growth rate of real GDP per capita. The results in both cases indicate that hosting these events does not increase trade and will not increase the rate of economic growth. Nothing in this analysis indicates that there are no benefits from hosting not-so-mega events, as often hosting these events is more about city or national pride than it is about economic growth and development. It is also possible, as the case of Halifax, Nova Scotia, indicates, that hosting an event may be a means by which a community can justify investing scarce resources in improving its public sports infrastructure. The Halifax case also makes clear that public officials from any city or region that contemplates a bid to host one of these events must do so in the knowledge that costs may explode and that pulling out, even when well justified, may expose them to public scorn.

NOTES

1. Information comes from the website http://www.olympic.org/vancouver-2010-winter-olympics, (accessed June 15, 2011).
2. Delhi Commonwealth Games information comes from the website http://www. cwgdelhi2010.org/news/delhi_promised_delhi_delivered (accessed June 15, 2011). The BBC reports 71 countries but only 4,300 athletes at the Delhi games, see http://news. bbc.co.uk/sport2/hi/commonwealth_games/delhi_2010/9052926.stm (accessed June 6, 2011).
3. Press reports from Australia indicate that viewership in that country was down, and quite substantially, compared to the 2006 Melbourne and 2002 Manchester Games, see http://www.news.com.au/business/ten-under-fire-over-poor-commonwealth-games-audience/story-e6frfm1i-1225935764816 (accessed June 6, 2011).
4. See ch. 21 by Long, in this volume.
5. The Rose and Speigel (2009) results are suspect because the impact is so large. Preliminary analysis using their data and programs adding the lagged value of exports between trading pairs as a regressor reduces the impact of the Summer Games and the Football World Cup from their estimated level of 30 percent to 8 percent or less. The Winter Games effect is negative and statistically significant.
6. A further problem in the Rose and Speigel results concerning signaling is that when hosting the Winter Olympics and having a failed bid to host those Olympics are both in the model, the host variable is negative and statistically significant while the failed candidacy variable is positive and significant. The relative sizes of the coefficients implies that a country would do better to put in an uncompetitive bid for the Winter Olympics than to win the rights to host them.
7. Applied Economics (2006) produced a value of AU$3.8 million of net loss to Victoria of the 2005 Grand Prix.
8. Additional survey-based studies are Bull and Lovell (2007), who examined the perceptions of residents of Canterbury, England of hosting the first stage of the 2007 Tour de France; Ritchie et al. (2009) who consider the perceptions of the London 2012 Olympics of residents of two non-host British cities; and Maennig and Schwarthoff (2010) who surveyed residents of Durban, South Africa about what they expected from that city hosting games from the 2010 Football World Cup and construction of a signature stadium for that purpose.
9. Halifax had won a domestic competition to make the bid over Hamilton and Oakville, Ontario.

10. Percentages are calculated as 100*[exp(coefficient estimate) – 1].
11. This specification is developed in Barro and Sala-i-Martin (1999). The model assumes that every country has the same steady-state, or long-run equilibrium, levels of GDP per capita and capital–labor ratio. The implication is, therefore, that poorer countries will grow faster than richer ones, but that these growth rates will also converge over time. The parameter β_1 is a function of the speed of convergence. If countries do not have the same steady state, then the model above does not hold. This suggests that empirical analysis should be done on as homogeneous a group of countries as possible if the interest is in testing convergence. The goal here is to assess whether hosting a mega, or not-so-mega, event influences a country's growth rate of GDP per capita. Consequently, the discussion and analysis focus on the event effects.
12. If the data are split into the original members of the OECD and all other countries, the coefficient on lagged GDP per capita for the OECD countries is about –0.06 while that for the non-OECD countries remains about –0.15. Both coefficients are statistically significant at conventional levels.

REFERENCES

Ahlfeldt, Gabriel and Wolfgang Maennig (2010), 'Impact of sports arenas on land values: evidence from Berlin', *Annals of Regional Science*, **44** (2), 205–27.
Ahlfeldt, Gabriel, Wolfgang Maennig and Michaela Olschlager (2010), 'Lifestyles and preferences for (public) goods: professional football in Munich', Hamburg Contemporary Economic Discussions, No. 30.
Applied Economics (2006), '2005 Australian Formula One Grand Prix Cost–Benefit Analysis for the State of Victoria', September.
Baade, Robert A. (1996), 'Professional sports as catalysts for metropolitan economic development', *Journal of Urban Affairs*, **18** (1), 1–17.
Baade, Robert A., Robert Baumann and Victor A. Matheson (2009), 'Rejecting "conventional" wisdom: estimating the economic impact of national political conventions', *Eastern Economic Journal*, **35**, 520–30.
Baade, R.A. and Richard F. Dye (1988), 'An analysis of the economic rationale for public subsidization of sports stadiums', *Annals of Regional Science*, **22** (2), 37–47.
Baade, Robert A. and Richard F. Dye (1990), 'The impact of stadiums and professional sports on metropolitan area development', *Growth and Change*, **21** (2), 1–14.
Baade, Robert A. and Victor A. Matheson (2000), 'High octane? Grading the economic impact of the Daytona 500', *Marquette Sports Law Journal*, **10** (2), 401–15.
Baltimore Racing Development (2010), 'Economic Impact Report: Baltimore Grand Prix'.
Barbier, B. (1996), 'Problems of the French Winter Sport resorts', *Tourism Recreation Research*, **18** (2), 5–11.
Barget, E. and M. Gouguet (2010), 'Measuring the economic impact of hallmark sporting events: the case of the Rugby World Cup 2007', *Revue d'Économie Régionale et Urbaine*, **3**, 379–408.
Barro, Robert and Xavier Sala-i-Martin (1999), *Economic Growth*, Cambridge, MA: MIT Press.
Bernthal, M.J. and T.H. Regan (2004), 'The economic impact of a NASCAR racetrack on a rural community and region', *Sport Marketing Quarterly*, **13**, 26–34.
Bessit, C.S. (2006), 'South African Formula One Grand Prix: a dream or nightmare', University of Johannesburg.
Bull, Chris and Jane Lovell (2007), 'The impact of hosting major sporting events on the local residents: an analysis of the views and perceptions of Canterbury residents in relation to the Tour de France 2007', *Journal of Sport and Tourism*, **12** (3–4), 229–48.
Charrier, D. and J. Jourdan (2009), 'The local tourism impact of major sporting events:

a qualitative approach to the Rugby World Cup in Île-de-France', *Teoros, Revue de Recherche en Tourisme*, **28** (2), 45–54.

Chen, Na (2008), 'What economic effect do mega-events have on host cities and their surroundings? An investigation into the literature surrounding mega-events and the impacts felt by holders of the tournaments', Master's dissertation in Finance and Investment, University of Nottingham, UK, available at: http://edissertations.nottingham.ac.uk/2358/1/08MAlixnc3.pdf.

Coates, Dennis (2009), 'Hotel tax collections and a local mega-event', IASE/NAASE Working Paper Series, Paper 09-01, available at: http://college.holycross.edu/RePEc/spe/Coates_SouthCarolina.pdf.

Coates, Dennis and Craig A. Depken, II (2011), 'Mega-events: is Baylor Football to Waco what the Super Bowl is to Houston?', *Journal of Sports Economics*, **12** (6), 599–620.

Coates, Dennis and David Gearhart (2008), 'NASCAR as a public good', *International Journal of Sport Finance*, **3**, 42–57.

Coates, Dennis and Brad R. Humphreys (1999), 'The growth effects of sports franchises, stadia and arenas', *Journal of Policy Analysis and Management*, **18** (4), 601–24.

Coates, Dennis and Brad R. Humphreys (2006), 'Proximity benefits and voting on stadium and arena subsidies', *Journal of Urban Economics*, **59** (2), 285–99.

Commonwealth Games Federation (2003), 'The Report of the Commonwealth Games Evaluation Commission for the 2010 Commonwealth Games, available at: http://www.thecgf.com/media/games/2010/2010_eval_report.pdf, (accessed July 8, 2011).

Commonwealth Games Federation (2011), *Candidate City Manual: 2018 Commonwealth Games*, London: Commonwealth Games Federation.

Connolly, Pat (2007), 'Our world-class embarrassment', *The Halifax Daily News*, March 10.

Du Plessis, Stan and Wolfgang Maennig (2010), 'The 2010 FIFA World Cup high-frequency data economics: effects on international tourism and awareness for South Africa', draft paper, Department of Economics, University of Stellenbosch and University of Hamburg.

Dwyer, Larry and Peter Forsyth (2009), 'Public sector support for special events', *Eastern Economic Journal*, **35**, 481–99.

Felsenstein, Daniel and Aliza Fleischer (2003), 'Local festivals and tourism promotion: the role of public assistance and visitor expenditure', *Journal of Travel Research*, 41 (May), 385–92.

Feng, Xia and Brad R. Humphreys (2008), 'Assessing the economic impact of sports facilities on residential property values: a spatial hedonic approach', IASE/NAASE Working Paper Series, Paper 08-12, available at: http://college.holycross.edu/RePEc/spe/FengHumphreys_PropertyValues.pdf.

Fourie, Johan and Maria Santana-Gallego (2010), 'The impact of mega-events on tourist arrivals', Stellenbosch University Working Paper 171.

Gamage, A. (1997), 'Economics of venue selection for special sporting events with special reference to the 1996 Melbourne Grand Prix', available at: http://eprints.vu.edu.au/868/1/grandprix-event.pdf (accessed July 8, 2011).

Gold Coast City (2011), 'Candidate City File', Vol. 2, available at: http://www.thecgf.com/games/2018/Gold_Coast_VOL_2.pdf (accessed July 8, 2011).

Halifax Daily News, The (2007), 'Game over for Halifax', *The Halifax Daily News*, December 30.

Hambantota (2011), 'Together from the heart: Hambantota 2018 Commonwealth Games Candidate City File', Vol. 2, available at: http://www.thecgf.com/games/2018/Hambantota_2018_Candidature_File_Volume_2.pdf (accessed July 8, 2011).

Henderson, Joan C., Ken Foo, Hermes Lim and Serene Yip (2010), 'Sports events and tourism: the Singapore Formula One Grand Prix', *International Journal of Event and Festival Management*, **1** (1), 60–73.

Humphreys, Brad R. and Szymon Prokopowicz (2007), 'Assessing the impact of sport mega events in transition economies: Euro 2012 in Poland and Ukraine', *International Journal of Sport Management and Marketing*, **2** (5–6), 496–509.

Jones, Calvin (2001) 'Mega-events and host region impacts: determining the worth of the 1999 Rugby World Cup', *International Journal of Tourism Research*, **3** (3), 241–51.

Kotler, P., D.H. Haider and I. Rein (1993), *Marketing Places: Attracting Investment, Industry and Tourism to Cities, States and Nations*, New York: Free Press.

Leeds, Michael (2008), 'Do good Olympics make good neighbors?', *Contemporary Economic Policy*, **26** (3), 460–67.

Maennig, Wolfgang and Florian Schwarthoff (2010), 'Stadiums and urban development: International experience and the plans of Durban, South Africa', draft paper, University of Hamburg and GMP von Gerkan Marg & Partners International, Berlin.

McCartney, Glenn James (2005), 'Hosting a recurring mega-event: visitor *raison d'être*', *Journal of Sport Tourism*, **10** (2), 113–28.

Montgomerie, Duff (2007), Letter to Rhonda Neatt, Standing Committee on Public Accounts Clerk, available at: http://www.halifax.ca/halifax2014archives/Documents/H2014LettertoPublicAccounts_March26_07.pdf (accessed June 10, 2011).

Noll, Roger G. and Andrew Zimbalist (1997) 'The economic impact of sports teams and facilities', in Roger G. Noll and Andrew Zimbalist (eds), *Sports, Jobs and Taxes: The Economic Impact of Sports Teams and Stadiums*, Washington, DC: Brookings Institution Press, pp. 55–91.

Ntloko, Ncedo Jonathan and Kamilla Swart, (2008), 'Sport tourism event impacts on the host community: a case study of Red Bull Big Wave Africa', *South African Journal for Research in Sport, Physical Education and Recreation*, **30** (2), 79–93.

Ottawa Citizen (2007), 'We want an apology, Halifax', *The Guardian* (Charlottetown, Prince Edward Island), March 14.

Pestana Barros, Carlos (2006), 'Evaluating sport events at the European level: the Euro 2004', *International Journal of Sport Management and Marketing*, **1** (4), 400–410.

Porter, P. K. and D. Fletcher (2008), 'The economic impact of the Olympic Games: *ex ante* predictions and *ex post* reality', *Journal of Sports Management*, **22** (4), 470–86.

Quinonez, N. (2008), 'Businesses urged to cash in on F1', *Gulf Daily News*, Bahrain, June 26.

Richard G. and K. Friend (1995), 'The UK ski holiday market', *Journal of Vacation Marketing*, **1** (3), 259–64.

Ritchie, Brent W., Richard Shipway and Bethany Cleeve (2009), 'Resident perceptions of mega-sporting events: a non-host city perspective of the 2012 London Olympic Games', *Journal of Sport and Tourism*, **14** (2–3), 143–67.

Ritchie, J.R. Brent and Brian Smith (1991), 'The impact of a mega-event on the host region awareness', *Journal of Travel Research*, **30**, 3–10.

Rose, Andrew K. and Mark M. Spiegel (2009), 'The Olympic Effect', National Bureau of Economic Research Working Paper 14854, Cambridge, MA.

Smith, C. and P. Jenner (1998), 'The impact of festivals and special events on tourism: occasional studies', in *Travel and Tourism Analyst*, 4, London: Economist Publications.

Song, Wonho (2010), 'Impacts of Olympics on exports and tourism', *Journal of Economic Development*, **35** (4), 93–110.

Teigland, Jon (1999), 'Mega-events and impacts on tourism; the predictions and reality of the Lillehammer Olympics', *Impact Assessment and Project Appraisal*, **17** (4), 305–17.

Tu, C.C. (2005), 'How does a sports stadium affect housing values? The case of FedEx Field', *Land Economics*, **81** (3), 379–95.

Turco, D.M. and R. Navarro (1993), 'Assessing the economic impact and financial return of a national sporting event', *Sport Marketing Quarterly*, **2** (2), 17–23.

Weinstein, Roy, Jeremy DeGracia and Edna Lin (2010), 'Economic impact of the 2010 X Games 16 on Los Angeles County', report provided by Alex Rozis, Senior Manager, Communications, at ESPN.

24 Reflections on developing the 2010 FIFA World Cup™ research agenda
Kamilla Swart and Urmilla Bob

1 INTRODUCTION

Since South Africa's readmission to international sport more than a decade ago, it has increasingly used sport tourism events, and mega events in particular as a catalyst for socio-economic development and as part of the broader transformational and development agenda. The 2010 FIFA World Cup™ is used as an illustrative case study to examine the challenges of conducting mega-event research, with a specific focus on examining economic impacts. The focus on economic impacts is justified because mega events require massive private and public sector investments (especially in developing contexts such as South Africa where resources are limited and socio-economic challenges are widespread) and the economic long-term spin-offs remain the key reason for justifying bidding and hosting for mega events. Yet, undertaking economic impact assessments poses several methodological and logistical challenges as this chapter illustrates. The need to broaden the research agenda to incorporate social, environmental and political aspects is highlighted as well as the contestations and debates that emerged in relation to developing the 2010 research agenda. This chapter reflects on this research agenda, specifically with regard to the importance of formulating and undertaking research to evaluate impacts associated with the 2010 FIFA World Cup™ and to inform planning and policy developments, especially for developing countries interested in bidding and hosting future mega events.

Mega sporting events have become highly sought-after commodities for both developed and developing countries as they move towards event-driven economies (Swart and Bob, 2009). For South Africa, the allure of mega events was especially attractive to signal international recognition at the end of the apartheid era as well as to advance the developmental and transformational agenda. Having already successfully hosted the 1995 Rugby World Cup, the 1999 African Nations Cup and the 2003 Cricket World Cup, the South African government sought to host the 2006 FIFA World Cup™ (van der Merwe, 2009). Van der Merwe further notes that the bid for the 2006 Cup had three main objectives: first, it would encourage capital construction and enhance the country's profile to attract tourism; second, it would induce international pride; and third, it would present local sport powerbrokers with an opportunity to consolidate their role in the 'new' South Africa. However, South Africa lost the bid by one vote to Germany and FIFA introduced the continent-wide rotational system whereby only African countries could bid for the 2010 FIFA World Cup™. South Africa continued its bid, along similar lines for the 2010 event, and secured the right to host this event. Van Der Merwe (p. 31) asserts that South Africa's hosting of the 2010 World Cup promises 'a crowning achievement of not only South Africa's re-entry into the international community, but also Africa's journey to a more equitable and just global order'. Moreover, then President Thabo Mbeki in his letter to President Sepp Blatter of FIFA, said: 'We want, on behalf of our continent, to stage an event that will send ripples of confidence from Cape to Cairo – an event that will create social and economic opportunities throughout Africa' (Mail & Guardian Online, 2010).

It is therefore not surprising that there was a tremendous amount of excitement (and apprehension) associated with the hosting of the 2010 FIFA World Cup™ in South Africa. In particular, it was anticipated (and publicized) that the World Cup would contribute significantly to job creation, infrastructural development and social enhancement. For South Africa, of particular importance is the fact that the FIFA World Cup was seen as an important component of contributing to South Africa's transformational and development agenda. Critical questions remain in relation to what extent socio-economic and sport-related (especially in relation to football) benefits were achieved and who were the likely beneficiaries. Therefore it was imperative that perceptions, needs and aspirations of different key stakeholders (such as the local communities, business sector, public sector and so on) be integrated into the World Cup processes, including the planning, implementation and post-event phases. This required critical research to be undertaken among different stakeholders to examine key issues and impacts.

It is important to consider, as underscored by Tomlinson et al. (2009) and many of the chapters in this book, that economic projections of the World Cup are often flawed, with the overestimation of benefits and underestimation of costs. Moreover, there is considerable debate as to whether previous World Cups had a positive impact on the host country's economy (ibid.). Given the South African government's intention to leverage the 2010 event for economic (and social) development and considering that the South African government budget for the World Cup had increased substantially since 2004 (du Plessis and Maennig, 2009), critical questions remained in relation to what extent these laudable intentions would be achieved and who would be the likely beneficiaries of the potential benefits to be accrued, especially in relation to direct and indirect economic and social gains. Therefore, it was considered imperative that perceptions, needs and aspirations of different key stakeholders (such as the local communities, business sector, public sector and so on) be integrated into the 2010 FIFA World Cup™ processes, including the planning, implementation and post-event phases. This required critical research to be undertaken at different levels and among different stakeholders to examine key issues and impacts.

This chapter reflects on the proposed and implemented 2010 research agenda articulated by several academics, specifically in relation to the importance of formulating and undertaking research to examine critical aspects pertaining to South Africa hosting the 2010 FIFA World Cup™ and how research can inform future planning and policy developments. Furthermore, it critically focuses on the use of mega events to promote and enhance sport development efforts in developing countries such as South Africa. Specifically, the chapter undertakes a critical analysis of two workshops aimed at developing the 2010 research agenda, the research priorities and methodological approaches identified as well as challenges encountered. In terms of the research priority areas, the importance of going beyond economic impacts is emphasized together with the need to utilize both top-down and bottom-up approaches to assess economic impacts. The methodological approaches adopted are critiqued. The chapter also reflects on lessons learned and best practices. The importance of national and international collaborative efforts are emphasized together with the unique resources and skills that academia can leverage. The importance of academics developing and driving research agendas on mega events is deemed to be critically important given that this sector provides the crucial lens to assess sport events and provide rigorous research to inform future decision making and planning. To this end, the chapter presents a coordinated and integrated approach to developing and implementing a research agenda when resources are limited.

2   THE 2010 RESEARCH AGENDA

The 2010 research framework or model was developed during two workshops and in consultation with several academics and stakeholders to maximize benefits to key stakeholders in terms of World Cup legacies and to ensure participation at all levels. The workshops (the first was held in July 2008 and was the 2010 Research Agenda Workshop hosted by the 2010 Organizing Committee (OC) South Africa while the second was held in December 2009 in conjunction with the Sport Mega Events and their Legacies Conference) were attended by a range of stakeholders, including academics and individuals from the government and private sectors. In both workshops, attendees reinforced the importance of systematically undertaking research in relation to the 2010 FIFA World Cup™. This was deemed to be particularly important given the unique opportunities and challenges faced in relation to Africa hosting its first mega event. From a research perspective, the 2010 FIFA World Cup™ provided an opportunity to clarify whether trends and patterns emerging from research on previous mega events (specifically the FIFA World Cup™) would be discernible in 2010 and how these relate to development efforts in South Africa specifically and Africa more generally.

Prior to and during the July 2008 workshop a research audit of current research being undertaken in relation to the 2010 FIFA World Cup™ was conducted. The audit revealed that a significant amount of research was being undertaken across several themes and by a range of researchers, primarily academics and consultants. The main focus areas were economic and tourist projections and concerns (especially debates related to government spending given the enormous development challenges South African society faced), resident perceptions, impacts of crime and readiness to host. However, there was a lack of coordination and research was undertaken on an ad hoc basis. There was evidence of duplication and researchers generally experienced several resource constraints, the most important of which was funding to conduct rigorous and continuous research. However, the research audit identified a range of indicators that informed the development of the 2010 FIFA World Cup™ research agenda and flagged key issues of concern in the South African context.

The initial 2008 workshop also identified a range of research areas and supported the continued relevance of the research agenda in order to maximize limited resources and engender collaboration. Some of these included:

- baseline research to determine stakeholder needs, expectations, challenges and opportunities relating to the hosting of the 2010 FIFA World Cup™;
- the identification and evaluation of previous research initiatives and best-practice case studies (local and international) that could be relevant and which could provide a frame of reference for planning, decision making and further research relating to the hosting of mega events;

- a strategic audit and evaluation of infrastructure and facilities, with a view to identifying gaps, challenges and opportunities;
- a survey of current and potential key stakeholder roles, relationships and current and potential coordination mechanisms;
- a strategic audit of the reality and perceptions of key enabling environmental factors (for example, safety, security and health issues) from a destination and community development perspective;
- a comprehensive review and systematic monitoring of relevant policies, strategic planning frameworks and guidelines;
- identifying relevant benchmarking, monitoring and evaluation guidelines and criteria;
- development of guidelines and criteria to determine capacity levels, gaps and opportunities in host cities;
- a strategic assessment of sponsorship opportunities and challenges related to the hosting of mega events;
- a strategic assessment of the skills development needs and training offerings related to the hosting of mega events;
- a comprehensive evaluation of the event (for example, socio-economic impact assessment, service quality, residents' perceptions, marketing and media impacts, business leveraging and so on, as well as post-event impacts, including long-term impacts); and
- development of systems to secure the learning which the event engenders so that it can be built into the management of local enterprise and the governance of host communities.

However, given the timeframes and the lack of political will to allocate the necessary resources to implement a coordinated research agenda that emanated from the OC workshop, the participants at the December 2009 workshop focused on highlighting key research priority areas for 2010. The two main research thrusts related to the economic and social/political issues or impacts. Additionally, environmental aspects were highlighted. As will be elaborated on later, as part of the Department of Environmental Affairs (DEAT) Green Volunteer Programme, a Green Survey was conducted which provides a basis to examine selected environmental issues as well. The rest of the chapter focuses on the three main components of research undertaken during the World Cup: the economic, social and environmental aspects. This is followed by an examination of gaps and challenges experienced in relation to implementing the research agenda.

3 ECONOMIC IMPACT ASSESSMENTS: 'BOTTOM-UP' VERSUS 'TOP-DOWN' APPROACH

While there is a bias towards economic impact assessments of mega sporting events, there is no doubt that this aspect is central in relation to examining whether the key objectives of bidding for and hosting a mega event have been met. The main aspect identified that required research was to ascertain economic impacts in relation to initial and current forecasts. Several critiques of economic impact forecasts reveal that they tend to overestimate benefits and underestimate costs, as mentioned previously. Forecasts on the 2010 FIFA World Cup™ in South Africa is a case in point. Du Plessis and Maennig (2009) indicated that US$1.35 billion invested by government on stadiums was much higher than the initial US$105 million budgeted for at the time of the bid in 2004. Moreover, Grant Thornton (2003), forecast a net economic gain of US$3 billion for the South African economy, based on 230,000 foreign tourists staying in South Africa for an average of 15 days. While the OC did not officially update its forecasts in the years leading up to 2010 notwithstanding many changes in the plans (for example, 13 stadiums were proposed in the bid book and a new stadium in Cape Town was never part of the initial plans), Grant Thornton revised their forecasts in 2008, with even more optimistic direct expenditure figures of US$3.9 billion, and a consequent economic impact of $6.58 billion (cited by du Plessis and Maennig). In April 2010, Grant Thornton noted that they revised their figures down from 483,000 visitors (2007) to 373,000 visitors (2008) but with an extended length of stay from 14 days to 18.7 days. They further noted that the gross economic impact was projected to be higher, however government spending had also increased substantially. Tolsi (2010) further underscores that the 2010 bid book was not in the public domain until recently and 'is a curious mélange of hyperbole and underestimation' and argues that the figures represent gross miscalculations of taxpayers' money on infrastructure such as stadiums.

Another concern raised with economic impact studies is that they tend to adopt the 'top-down' approach which uses national economic data. While this approach is likely to be less costly, the quality and accessibility of South African data is an important consideration. In addition, the 'top-down' approach uses aggregated data, and identifies only additional visitor nights, which are statistically counted (Preuss and Kursheidt, 2009). To address this limitation, it is imperative to also use the bottom-up approach to assess the event's economic impacts which include the administration of questionnaire surveys to spectators during the event. Preuss (2005) contends that while there are many models to assess the economic impacts derived from event spectators, their limitation is that they consider the consumption of tourists as a part of the overall economic impact. Moreover, he argues that the consumption patterns of these tourists are not often precisely evaluated and concludes that the accurate determination of money streams from event-affected persons are the basis for reliable assessments of economic impacts of events.

A brief outline of the different consumptions patterns of event visitors as identified by Preuss (2005, pp. 287–8) is detailed next. Casuals, timeswitchers and residents represent a redistribution of economic impacts. 'Casuals' are visitors who attend a sport event but were in the host community primarily for other reasons, that is, visiting friends and/or relatives, business, and so on. 'Timeswitchers' are those who purposely schedule their visit to coincide with the sport event but who would have visited at another time anyway. 'Residents' are sport event attendees in their home community. 'Resident spending' represents a switching of transactions from one local business that is, dining out, cinema, theatre, and so on, to another, in this case the sport event. In contrast, event visitors, extensioners and homestayers represent positive potential economic impact. 'Event visitors' are those visiting the host community specifically because of the sport event in question. 'Extensioners' are visitors who would have come anyway but extended their stay due to the event. 'Homestayers' are residents who purposely stay in the host city during the event due to the event. Any positive impact from these groups would then have to be offset by the negative impact from casuals, timeswitchers, runaways, and avoiders. 'Runaways' are residents who purposely leave the host city during the event due to the event. 'Avoiders' are tourists who stay away but would have come without the event. Avoiders can either be 'cancellers' – tourists who totally cancel their trip – or they can be 'pre/post-switchers' – tourists who will come earlier or later. It is thus evident that event attendees' places of origin and local spending influence the economic impacts of the event.

This 'bottom-up' methodology was used for the 2010 FIFA World Cup™ study and builds on the model developed by Preuss for the 2006 FIFA World Cup in Germany and Euro 2008 in Austria (visitor surveys only conducted in Austria). While the bottom-up approach is more costly since primary data need to be collected and analysed, it is extremely useful since it allows for more precise assessments. The spectator surveys, as well as the resident surveys although not the focus of this chapter, were highlighted as being priority areas, especially given the level to which it entails the collection of primary data and the logistics involved in collecting and analysing the data. The lessons from developing the research agenda clearly reflect the importance of critically thinking about what aspects need to be studied, what methodological approach should be used and who should be involved in undertaking the research.

Additionally, to ensure that economic assessments are undertaken rigorously, academics from South Africa worked with (and are still working with) colleagues (specifically sport tourism specialists and sport economists) from the USA and Germany to develop the survey instruments, formulate the sampling framework and analysing the data collected. In order to ensure that comparative analyses could be undertaken with the 2006 studies, the German approach was adopted and similar surveys (with changes to ensure that unique South African aspects are included) were implemented in South Africa. In addition, researchers (both academics and consultants) teamed up with partners in their respective cities and regions to deliver research in five host cities, namely, Cape Town, Durban, Johannesburg, Port Elizabeth and Pretoria, in order to assess city-level as well as national impacts. In total, 9,192 visitor surveys were conducted across these host cities, in the stadium precincts and official FIFA Fan Parks. Key aspects in the survey included visitor information, consumer behaviour, previous attendance/visits, perceptions of the host destination and demographic profile. Surveys were conducted primarily in English, however they were also available in Dutch, French, German, Italian, Korean, Portuguese and Spanish. It was anticipated that the national- and city-level economic impact analyses would be completed in August 2011. The length of time required to undertake a proper economic analysis is one of the key challenges faced since several stakeholders would like estimations immediately after the event.

This methodology also allows for comparative research to be extended to the 2014 FIFA World Cup™ in Brazil. This is an important consideration since a major limitation of mega-event research is that comparisons cannot be made given the different methodological approaches used. This is significant since Brazil is also a developing country and comparisons are likely to be more relevant. Identifying best practices and learning from the South African experience is therefore critical.

It is important to note that the research agenda proposed emphasized the importance of undertaking both bottom-up and top-down economic assessment approaches. Given the complexities, importance and unresolved methodological challenges that undertaking economic studies face, it is suggested that a mega-event research agenda should incorporate both top-down and bottom-up approaches which could complement and/ or challenge each other. This will permit a more analytical approach to examining mega events since the difference in results could be the basis for debate and reflection.

Additional economic research themes/aspects identified during the workshop were tourist flows during the event, that is, mobility within South Africa and the region (the South African Development Community: SADC); economic impacts and perceptions of local businesses; direct and induced benefits of tourist income (during and after the event); an examination of projected versus actual government spending related to the 2010 FIFA World Cup™ (public expenditure), procurement processes and Black Economic Empowerment; and investment patterns and trends linked to the World Cup. Linked to economic aspects is infrastructural research. The main issues identified during the workshops were capital expenditure patterns in relation to urban infrastructural renewal projects, transport and ICT development, and stadium development. Business surveys were undertaken in Cape Town and Durban. However, the other aspects were not addressed due to limited resources.

4   SOCIAL ASPECTS

Chappelet and Junod (2006, p. 85) indicate that social impacts often relate to the intangible, subjective experiences associated with the event, the 'collective memory'. Research on social aspects tends to focus on locals and visitors using resident perception and visitor surveys, respectively. Often linked to social benefits are the more intangible considerations. As Poynter (2006) states, mega-event effects could include intangible aspects such as enhanced city/host country images, more efficient local governance practices or improved communal well-being. The workshops specifically highlighted the positive image of South Africa, profiling host cities and destination awareness exposure as key research aspects. Examining the 'feel-good' effects was also deemed to be critical and workshop attendees generally supported Cornelissen and Maennig's (2010) assertion that the 'feel-good' factors linked to a once-in-a-lifetime experience such as hosting the FIFA World Cup™ and nation building are the key benefits associated with hosting mega events. Their examination of the FIFA World Cups in Germany 2006 and South Africa 2010 reveal how political and socio-cultural processes influence a sense of national pride and promote nation building. In addition to visitor and resident surveys to track these aspects, media analysis was highlighted as an appropriate research approach.

   Resident surveys were conducted before and after the World Cup to examine social aspects in relation to perceptions and experiences. The focus was on residents living in close proximity to the completion venues in Durban and Cape Town. Furthermore, two rural communities in KwaZulu-Natal (Makhowe and Izibukwana) as well as a small town (Gansbaai) in Western Cape were surveyed to assess non-host perceptions and experiences. Furthermore, the visitor surveys undertaken during the World Cup to collect economic data also included questions pertaining to perceptions and experiences. The workshops highlighted the need to focus on both positive and negative social impacts which the surveys included.

The resident surveys at best provide case studies. Unfortunately, there was inadequate funding and capacity to undertake resident surveys throughout the country in both host and non-host locations. However, in Durban and Cape Town surveys were undertaken 3–6 months before and after the event. This will permit an examination of perception changes as a result of the event, a neglected field of research. The analysis is currently being undertaken. However, it needs to be noted that an important aspect of local responses to mega events and social impacts relates to protests and demonstrations which are reflective of the concerns of residents and workers. This aspect should be incorporated in future research.

Another component of mega-event research in relation to social objectives deemed to be important is participation in the sport itself and skills development opportunities. Particular aspects identified in the workshop in relation to sport development were: raised public awareness in the sport, increased interest and participation, attendance, media coverage/viewership, competence in ability to host future events, exposure of footballers and skills development. Some of these aspects (public awareness, interest and participation, attendance and viewership) were covered in the visitor and resident surveys. Voluntarism was an important component of skills development associated with the event. Mega events generally require a huge number of volunteers and thus provide a range of training opportunities. Volunteer surveys are often used to examine volunteer perceptions and experiences that can be used to inform operational planning for future events. While this aspect was identified in the workshop, volunteer surveys were undertaken only in Cape Town, by a group of researchers from the USA who used a local researcher to facilitate the research study.

5 ENVIRONMENTAL IMPACTS

There is a growing body of literature that examines the environmental impacts associated with hosting mega sporting events (Wood, 2005; Davenport and Davenport, 2006; Schmied et al., 2007; Ahmed and Pretorius, 2010; Bob, 2010). The larger the event, the greater are the impacts likely to be experienced in terms of extent and geographical scope. They underscore that mega events have a widespread global footprint and an activity of this scale is likely to have substantial impacts on the environment. However, these impacts are rarely reviewed, evaluated or quantified.

Furthermore, environmental concerns have been largely ignored in relation to mega-event planning and design. Davenport and Davenport (2006) specifically illustrate that the greatest ecological threats that any form of mass tourism such as mega sporting events create are linked to the significant infrastructural and transport arrangements required to support it which accrue into substantial, often irreversible, environmental degradation as well as social consequences. These include: the physical development of resorts and stadiums; consumption of fuel by buildings, aircraft, trains, buses, taxis and cars; and overuse of water resources, pollution by vehicle emissions, sewage and litter. The underuse of facilities after the event is also a broader sustainability concern.

Existing research highlights the importance of increased awareness on sustainability imperatives in relation specifically to minimizing and mitigating against negative environmental impacts associated with hosting mega events such as increased pollution, traffic congestion, environmental degradation, solid waste management, as well as water and energy consumption. Mega events also provide an ideal opportunity for promoting environmental awareness (the focus of the FIFA World Cup™ Green Goal programme) and ensuring a carbon-neutral event. This has seen an increased interest in the 'greening of events' which can be the basis for assessing whether mega events can be viable and sustainable.

During the 2010 FIFA World Cup™, Green Surveys were conducted nationally as part of the DEAT's Green Volunteer Programme. A survey was conducted with visitors and locals during the World Cup period (11 June to 11 July 2010) to ascertain visitor and resident perceptions of the environmental impacts of the 2010 FIFA World Cup™. Three hundred green volunteers were trained and placed in specific locations in all nine provinces and the programme included the implementation of a survey which was aimed at assessing environmental awareness and behaviour among respondents, their perceptions about the environmental impacts of the 2010 FIFA World Cup™, awareness of greening programmes associated with the World Cup™ and perceptions and experiences of foreign visitors in relation to South Africa specifically. In total 15,066 surveys were completed. It is hoped that ecological and carbon footprint analysis will be used in addition to the Green Surveys to assess the environmental impacts of the 2010 FIFA World Cup™.

6   KEY LESSONS LEARNED

The importance of comparative research is stressed. Mega events are viewed as having differential impacts in developed and developing contexts.

As indicated in the discussion, attempts were made in the visitor survey to ensure that similar data were collected in South Africa as was the case during the 2006 German World Cup. Comparative analysis will unpack impacts in greater detail and assess the nature and extent of the differences. Empirical data can be used to provide a more rigorous understanding of assumptions prevalent in the literature. For example, Cornelissen (2010) illustrates that developing nations such as China, South Africa and Brazil have become significant players in the mega sporting event industry and these countries hope that the hosting of the event will promote long-term legacies in relation to economic and social benefits. How different are these aspirations from developed countries and are the benefits anticipated and accrued dissimilar?

The South African researchers experienced major challenges in terms of coordinating the 2010 research agenda, and partnered with host cities and tourism organizations who recognized the value of this study. It is unfortunate that national endorsement could not be achieved and can be perceived as a missed opportunity to conduct comparative research across the host cities using the same methodology. Our experience reflects that key event stakeholders (host cities, national governments, organizing committees, businesses and so on) do not always understand the importance of undertaking research and are often hesitant to share information or to allocate the necessary resources for research. This is extremely short-sighted since it is rigorous and consistent research that permits monitoring and evaluation to take place. The lack of buy-in and support for a national research agenda is also reflective of the poor research culture that prevails in South Africa.

While several research areas and concerns were identified, only limited research was undertaken based on priority areas and research capacity (included areas of interest) of the academics involved. Mega-event organizers must be encouraged to plan for research and commit appropriate resources. Almost all the research undertaken and identified in the discussion above was funded by academics based at South African universities. In some instances, organizations (for example, the City of Cape Town and Tourism KwaZulu-Natal in Durban) supported the research efforts by providing financial assistance. Furthermore, the National Research Foundation provided a grant to undertake specific aspects of the research. This was complemented by individual academics' research funds. To emphasize, partnerships are critical to leverage the necessary resources required to undertake mega-event research when primary data collection is required. Our experience with developing the 2010 research agenda shows that an important aspect is to identify existing institutional, infrastructural and resource issues that are likely to impact on related research efforts. To this end, identifying appropriate partners is critically important and it is this broad network that is enabling research to be conducted across the country despite research funding not being available nationally. In fact, as indicated earlier, the main funding was from the researchers themselves, with additional support from a few host cities and provincial tourism organizations. It is therefore imperative that mega-event research be budgeted for sufficiently to provide a comprehensive analysis in relation to aspects identified in this chapter. This will permit an integrated and holistic assessment.

Post-2010 it is hoped that this collaborative endeavour will result in the development of a database of research relevant to the 2010 FIFA World Cup™ including international best practice and current research being undertaken in relation to it. This will permit a critical examination of the advantages and disadvantages of hosting the World Cup and prospects for bidding for future mega/major events.

7   CONCLUSION

This chapter illustrates that despite significant resource constraints, it was possible to undertake a significant amount of research during the 2010 FIFA World Cup™ on several components. A challenge faced currently is to develop a publications and information dissemination plan as part of a knowledge management strategy to ensure that the information is examined critically and that it informs mega-event knowledge production as well as relevant policies and future bidding and hosting efforts. It is imperative that a mega-event research agenda includes what the findings will be used for and who are the potential targeted groups. This will entail continued collaboration among researchers as well as the private and public sectors. Special journal issues have emerged as a key avenue to disseminate information in the academic arena. Furthermore, workshops are planned to develop a publications strategy.

It was clear that there was a willingness and commitment to undertake research from national and international researchers and organizations. However, the issue of accessing the necessary resources/funding was a major challenge experienced. Lessons from the 2010 FIFA World Cup™ research agenda indicate that the research required for mega events of this nature necessitates partnerships and interdisciplinary capacity from a range of stakeholders. Furthermore, the mobilization of the necessary resources to undertake the research needed and attempt to leverage buy-in at a national level and among host cities to ensure consistency in the research approaches and data collected is required.

A coordinated and integrated approach to research pertaining to the 2010 FIFA World Cup™ is well-suited for collaborative and interdisciplinary research and critically important to ascertain developmental impacts. The 2010 research agenda is intended to draw from a wide range of experiences and perspectives. Focusing on bringing researchers together from different sectors and institutions not only facilitated the field research component but also permitted a more substantive analysis of the issues under consideration. Additionally, capacity building and empowerment of younger researchers, especially from historically disadvantaged backgrounds, will contribute significantly to skills development in the areas of research, sport tourism and sport management in the country. The successful hosting of a mega event, and more importantly achieving a positive legacy, is grounded in the acquisition, production and dissemination of information and knowledge and should not be overlooked. However, research requires sufficient planning, high levels of interdisciplinary cooperation, commitment and resources.

REFERENCES

Ahmed, Fatima and Leon Pretorius (2010), 'Mega-events and environmental impacts: the 2010 FIFA World Cup in South Africa', *Alternation*, **17** (2), 274–96.

Bob, Urmilla (2010), 'Sustainability and events design', in Dimitri Tassiopoulos (ed.), *Events Management: A Development and Managerial Approach*, Claremont, Western Cape: Juta & Co., pp. 207–24.

Chappelet, Jean-Loup and Thomas Junod (2006), 'A tale of 3 Olympic cities: what can Turin learn from the Olympic legacy of other Alpine cities?', in Diego Torres (ed.), *Major Sport Events as Opportunity for Development*, Proceedings of a Workshop, Valencia, Spain, 14–16 June.

Cornelissen, S. (2010), 'The geopolitics of global aspiration: sport mega-events and emerging powers', *International Journal of the History of Sport*, **27** (16–17), 1–18.

Cornelissen, S. and W. Maennig (2010), 'On the political economy of "feel-good" effects at sport mega-events: experiences from FIFA Germany 3006 and prospects for South Africa 2010', *Alternation*, **17** (2), 96–120.

Davenport, John and Julia L. Davenport (2006), 'The impact of tourism and personal leisure transport on coastal environments: a review', *Estuaries Coastal and Shelf Science*, **67**, 280–92.

Du Plessis, Stan and Wolfgang Maennig (2009), 'South Africa 2010: initial dreams and sobering economic perspectives', in Udesh Pillay, Richard Tomlinson and Orli Bass (eds), *Development and Dreams: The Urban Legacy of the 2010 FIFA World Cup*, Pretoria: Human Sciences Research Council Press, pp. 55–75.

Grant Thornton (2003), 'South Africa 2010 World Cup Bid Executive Summary', available at: http://wiredspace.wits.ac.za/bitstream/handle/10539/5950/Appendix.pdf?...2 (accessed 22 May 2011).

Grant Thornton (2010), 'Updated economic impact of 2010', available at: http://www.gt.co.za/files/grant_thornton_updated_2010_economic_impact_210410.pdf (accessed 22 May 2011).

Mail & Guardian Online (2010), 'The bid book for our bucks', 11 June, available at: http://www.mg.co.za/article/2010-06-11-the-bid-book-for-our-bucks (accessed 12 June 2010).

Poynter, Gavin (2006), 'From Beijing to Bow Creek: measuring the Olympics effect', London East Research Institute Working Papers in Urban Studies, University of East London, available at: http://www.uel.ac.uk/londoneast/research/FromBeijingtoBowBells. pdf (accessed 15 June 2011).

Preuss, Holger (2005), 'The economic impact of visitors at major multi-sport events', *European Sport Management Quarterly*, **5** (3), 281–301.

Preuss, Holger and Markus Kursheidt (2009), 'How crowding-out affects tourism legacy', Sport Mega-events and Their Legacies Conference, Stellenbosch, South Africa, 2–4 December.

Schmied, Martin, Christian Hochfeld, Hartmut Stahl, Ralf Roth, Frank Armbruster, Stefan Türk and Christa Friedl (2007), 'Green champions in sport and environment: guide to environmentally-sound large sporting events', Federal Ministry for the Environment, Nature Conservation and Nuclear Safety (BMU), Berlin and German Olympic Sports Confederation (DOSB), Division Development of Sports, Frankfurt.

Swart, Kamilla and Urmilla Bob (2009), 'Venue selection and the 2010 FIFA World Cup: a case study of Cape Town', in Udesh Pillay, Richard Tomlinson and Orli Bass (eds), *Development and Dreams: The Urban Legacy of the 2010 FIFA World Cup*, Pretoria: Human Sciences Research Council Press, pp. 114–30.

Tolsi, Niren (2010), 'The World Cup bid book fiasco', Mail & Guardian Online, available at: http://www.mg.co.za/article/2010-06-13-the-completely-miscalculated-world-cup-bid-book-that-cost-us-a-bundle (accessed 12 June 2010).

Tomlinson, Richard, Orli Bass and Udesh Pillay (2009), 'Introduction', in Udesh Pillay, Richard Tomlinson and Orli Bass (eds), *Development and Dreams: The Urban Legacy of the 2010 FIFA World Cup*, Pretoria: Human Sciences Research Council Press, pp. 3–17.

Van der Merwe, Justin (2009), 'The road to Africa: South Africa's hosting of the "African" World Cup', in Udesh Pillay, Richard Tomlinson and Orli Bass (eds), *Development and Dreams: The Urban Legacy of the 2010 FIFA World Cup*, Pretoria: Human Sciences Research Council Press, pp. 18–32.

Wood, Emma (2005), 'Measuring the economic and social impacts of local authority events', *International Journal of Public Sector Management*, **18** (1), 37–53.

25 The economic impact of the golf Majors
Stephen Shmanske*

1 INTRODUCTION

Professional golfers compete in tournaments year round and all over the world. Traditionally, four tournaments have attained a special status, becoming known as the Majors. They are: the Masters, played each year at the same course in Augusta, Georgia; the US Open Championship, played at a different course in the United States each year; the Open Championship or 'British Open', played at a different course in the British Isles each year; and the Professional Golfers Association (PGA) Championship, played at a different course in the United States each year. These tournaments do not approach the magnitude of the NFL's (National Football League) Super Bowl, however, among the community of golfers and golf fans they are anticipated with equal fervor. The golf Majors have among the largest purses, and carry extra monetary significance for the players because of endorsement possibilities for the winners. Because of the money and prestige, the Majors attract the top talent, consequently attracting large crowds of spectators.

The sporting significance of the golf Majors is undeniable, but quantifying the economic significance for the local community is not nearly as straightforward. Sports boosters will always point to the additional spending by visitors who come to attend sports competitions. There is also extra spending by those staging an event in terms of lighting and power, crowd control, parking, and preparing the course beforehand. Some of this spending takes place weeks or even months in advance of the event itself. This extra demand for local goods and services increases income in the local community and may lead to further increases in future spending, thus having a 'multiplied' effect in the local economy.

For example, a local association forecast the impact of the 2009 US Open held at Bethpage Black on Long Island (Kamer, 2009). This report estimates the direct spending by the US Golf Association (USGA), the sponsor of the tournament, and its vendors to be $24.5 million. Using multipliers from the RIMS II[1] input–output model of the Long Island economy, the direct spending leads to indirect spending of $23.5 million for a total of $48 million even before spending by the participants and spectators. The USGA itself predicts that its gross revenues from tickets, concessions, logo'ed merchandise, and the like to be $37.4 million. Albeit most of this revenue stream does not stay in the local community, but close to 9 percent skimmed in sales taxes does remain. Furthermore, these expenditures are in addition to local lodging, food and transportation expenditures by attendees.

To get a feel for the expenditures in the local economy by attendees consider a report done on the economic impact of the 2008 US Open Championship at Torrey Pines Golf Course in San Diego ('2008 US Open Economic Impact Analysis', 2008). Using surveys of spectators to get demographic characteristics and spending patterns this report estimates direct expenditure of spectators at $73.6 million. Again, multipliers from the RIMS II model, this time for Southern California, were used to estimate additional indirect expenditures of $68.5, for a total of over $142 million. As a ballpark estimate, totaling the direct spending by the sponsors, the direct spending by the spectators, the indirect spending, and the repatriated taxes gives a total of nearly $200 million.

The analyses of the 2008 and 2009 US Opens notwithstanding, there are many critics of the basic methodology of adding up 'direct' expenditure and applying an input–output table to estimate additional 'indirect' expenditures. Some of the direct expenditures are not additional, and would have taken place anyway, in the local economy, but perhaps elsewhere in place or time. Some 'new' direct expenditures may displace or crowd out other local expenditures. After the event, some, or even most, of the direct expenditure 'leaks' out of the local economy and the indirect expenditures are thus overestimated. Proponents of the use of this methodology attempt to make adjustments for these effects but boosters often uncritically accept the rosiest of unadjusted forecasts in advocating for local political and economic support for a prospective event. These problems and adjustments are covered in other chapters in this volume and elsewhere (Matheson, 2011; Simmons and Deutscher, 2011; von Allmen, 2011).

One could probably get a near unanimous consensus that the rosiest estimates are overstated. This is because the rhetoric surrounding the rosiest estimates comes from project supporters who are not disinterested in the outcome of a decision to host a mega event. However, this does not mean that there is no net local economic spillover benefit. Thus, it becomes an empirical question to measure the existence and extent of the local economic impact of hosting a mega event. Unfortunately, it is not an easy question. It is much more involved than an uncontrolled year-to-year comparison of economic activity as Victor Matheson humorously points out:

[T]he NFL reported that, 'Thanks to Super Bowl XXXIII, there was a $670 million increase in taxable sales in South Florida compared to the equivalent January–February period in 1998'. (NFL Report, 1999) . . . Unfortunately for the NFL, their study is woefully inept as the league neglected to account for factors besides the Super Bowl, such as inflation, population growth, and routine economic expansion, that could account for the rise in taxable sales. As noted by Baade and Matheson (2000), over 90% of the increase can be accounted for by these variables. . . . Finally, it is worth noting that taxable sales in the area during January–February 2000, the year after the game, were $1.26 billion higher than in the same months during the Super Bowl year. Strangely, the NFL never publicized a story announcing, 'Thanks to the lack of a Super Bowl, there was a $1.26 billion increase in taxable sales in South Florida compared to the equivalent January–February period in 1999'. (Matheson, 2011, pp. 480–81)

The unsophisticated comparison that the NFL trumpets cries out for a more systematic, more inclusive look at the data. Ideally, comparisons of the level of economic activity should be made for multiple years and for multiple locations. A study of the American rotating golf Majors, namely the US Open Championship and the PGA Championship, allows us to undertake exactly this type of analysis. In a multiple regression setting with fixed yearly effects and fixed county effects, one can isolate the effect on the local economy in the year of (and the years following) the staging of a Major golf tournament. This is precisely the goal of this chapter.

2 MODELS AND DATA

Consider Figure 25.1 which illustrates several possible patterns of economic activity associated with hosting a mega event. In each panel year T represents the treatment year in which the golf Major was staged. Up until T there is a baseline of economic activity. For ease of illustration this baseline is pictured as stationary but in the fixed effects model to be estimated below, the baseline will follow whatever average trend in the data actually exists. In Panel A there is a one-year increase associated with the event. This effect would be captured in a regression model by the inclusion of a dummy variable which would single out the treatment year in question. But if hosting a Major golf tournament had a lasting effect as illustrated in Panels B or C, the one-time dummy variable would fail to pick it up.

Panel B illustrates the possibility that there is a lasting effect of hosting a Major. For example, the publicity and good will associated with hosting a Major could lead to a permanent shift in the level of economic activity in the area. This effect could be picked up by the inclusion of an indicator

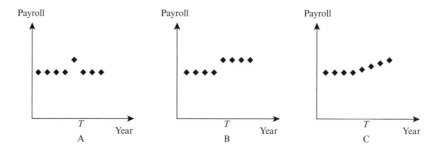

Figure 25.1   Economic activity patterns

variable that separated the post-treatment economic activity from that occurring before the event.[2]

Panel C illustrates the case in which a one time shift is not the proper specification because the event causes a lasting increased trend in economic activity above the baseline. In such a case a post-treatment trend variable must be added to properly capture the effect.[3]

Ultimately, the patterns in Panels A–C can be combined. A change in activity due to hosting a Major golf tournament could take the form of a one time or lasting shift with or without a lasting increased trend. Indeed, any pattern could follow the hosting of a mega event. With limited data, one must impose a specific functional form in a regression model to test whether such a pattern explains the data better than the null hypothesis that hosting the event has no effect. The beauty of looking at multiple Majors in different locales over multiple years is that it allows testing for the existence of any pattern of economic activity by the inclusion of indicator variables tied to the number of years following the hosting of the event itself. One need not impose a conjectured pattern beforehand. A description of the data will make this point clearer.

Counting both the US Open and the PGA Championship, for the years 1991 to 2008 there were 36 tournaments contested on a total of 24 different golf courses. These 24 locales and 18 years, listed in Table 25.1, form the dataset for the analysis. Payroll data by year for each of the relevant counties were retrieved from the County Business Patterns data available online.[4] Yearly data are used to get the closest comparison across the different tournaments and to avoid picking up a spiking of economic activity around the event that is ultimately offset by a lull in activity elsewhere in the year. If there is a large enough true gain to the local economy it should persist and show up in the yearly data.[5]

Two dependent variables will be explored. The first, total annual payroll, is a good measure of overall economic activity in a county. This

Table 25.1   US Open and PGA Championships 1991–2008

Year	Sponsor	Golf course	City, State	County
1991	USGA	Hazeltine National Golf Club	Chaska, MN	Carver
1992	USGA	Pebble Beach Golf Links	Pebble Beach, CA	Monterey
1993	USGA	Baltusrol Golf Club	Springfield, NJ	Union
1994	USGA	Oakmont Country Club	Oakmont, PA	Allegheny
1995	USGA	Shinnecock Hills Golf Club	Southampton, NY	Suffolk
1996	USGA	Oakland Hills Country Club	Bloomfield Hills, MI	Oakland
1997	USGA	Congressional Country Club	Bethesda, MD	Montgomery
1998	USGA	The Olympic Club	San Francisco, CA	San Francisco
1999	USGA	Pinehurst Resort & Country Club	Village of Pinehurst, NC	Moore
2000	USGA	Pebble Beach Golf Links	Pebble Beach, CA	Monterey
2001	USGA	Southern Hills Country Club	Tulsa, OK	Tulsa
2002	USGA	Bethpage State Park	Farmingdale, NY	Nassau
2003	USGA	Olympia Fields Country Club	Olympia Fields, IL	Cook
2004	USGA	Shinnecock Hills Golf Club	Southampton, NY	Suffolk
2005	USGA	Pinehurst Resort & Country Club	Village of Pinehurst, NC	Moore
2006	USGA	Winged Foot Golf Club	Mamaroneck, NY	Westchester
2007	USGA	Oakmont Country Club	Oakmont, PA	Allegheny
2008	USGA	Torrey Pines Golf Course	San Diego, CA	San Diego
1991	PGA	Crooked Stick Golf Club	Carmel, IN	Hamilton
1992	PGA	Bellerive Country Club	St. Louis, MO	Saint Louis City
1993	PGA	Inverness Golf Club	Toledo, OH	Lucas
1994	PGA	Southern Hills Country Club	Tulsa, OK	Tulsa
1995	PGA	Riviera Country Club	Los Angeles, CA	Los Angeles
1996	PGA	Valhalla Country Club	Louisville, KY	Jefferson
1997	PGA	Winged Foot Golf Club	Mamaroneck, NY	Westchester
1998	PGA	Salhalee Country Club	Redmond, WA	King
1999	PGA	Medinah Country Club	Medinah, IL	Du Page
2000	PGA	Valhalla Country Club	Louisville, KY	Jefferson
2001	PGA	Atlanta Athletic Club	Duluth, GA	Gwinnett
2002	PGA	Hazeltine National Golf Club	Chaska, MN	Carver
2003	PGA	Oak Hill Country Club	Rochester, NY	Monroe
2004	PGA	Whistling Straights	Kohler, WI	Sheboygan
2005	PGA	Baltusrol Golf Club	Springfield, NJ	Union
2006	PGA	Medinah Country Club	Medinah, IL	Du Page
2007	PGA	Southern Hills Country Club	Tulsa, OK	Tulsa
2008	PGA	Oakland Hills Country Club	Bloomfield Hills, MI	Oakland

measure should pick up any growth in employment or wages due to added economic activity. It will also pick up gains in part-time, overtime, or temporary added employment, that may be necessary to deal with special problems posed by staging a mega event. Total annual payroll should also pick up gains coming from the indirect spending part of the story. For example, the US Open is held in June, potentially creating a bump up in economic activity that will start to filter through the rest of the economy for the rest of the year.

Second, this chapter looks at the payroll in the hotel/motel sector of the economy which should be especially sensitive to the influx of visitors coming for the mega event.[6] These visitors include contestants and spectators, who may need housing for the week of the event, and also employees of the sponsoring association and its out of town vendors who may visit weeks or months in advance of the event. Keep in mind that the direct spending for temporary housing is only part of the direct expenditure stream associated with the event, so the coefficient estimates should be appropriately smaller when the second dependent variable is used.

The following equation is estimated with ordinary least squares (OLS) using the robust standard errors subprocedure:[7]

$$\text{PAYROLL} = a_0 + A_1\text{MAJOR} + A_2\text{YEAR} + A_3\text{COUNTY} + e.$$
$$(25.1)$$

Each observation of PAYROLL refers to a given county's payroll in a given year measured in constant 2008 \$US.[8] As discussed above, PAYROLL is either the total yearly payroll or the yearly payroll in the hotel/motel sector. The As are vectors of coefficients associated with the matrices of data.

The main variables of interest are in the matrix, MAJOR, which is composed of vectors of dummy variables denoted, M_i, for $i = 0$–4. M_0 is the dummy variable equal to one for an observation where the county hosted a Major in the year in question. Its coefficient will allow us to test the hypothesis that hosting a Major golf tournament is good for the local economy in the year in question, at least in the sense of its effect on payrolls, against the null hypothesis that hosting a Major golf tournament has no contemporaneous effect. The variables M_1 through M_4 pick up the effects in the first through fourth years following the hosting of the tournament. Using the five variables, M_0–M_4 allows for any pattern of effects on economic activity coincident with and following the hosting of a Major golf tournament.[9]

The matrix, YEAR, is composed of dummy variable vectors which isolate the effect of each year. The pattern of these fixed effects coefficients in A_2 should coincide with the general level of economic activity for the year.

Table 25.2   Summary statistics

Variable	Mean	Standard deviation	Minimum	Maximum	n
Total county payroll (2008 US$)	28.4 billion	37.6 billion	574 million	187.4 billion	432
Hotel/motel county payroll (2008 US$)	210 million	278 million	641,000	1.1 billion	370

The matrix, COUNTY, is composed of dummy variable vectors which isolate the effect of each locale. The pattern of these county effects coefficients in A_3 should coincide with the overall size (or industry-specific size) of the county. Some interesting comparisons should show up in the coefficients. For example, consider Monterey county in California, which is small compared to many of the counties in the data, but which is a resort area with a large hospitality industry sector. When overall payroll is used, Monterey county will be below average in magnitude, but when payroll in the hotel/motel sector is used, Monterey will be above average in size.

To avoid singularity in the estimation, one county and year must be left out of the fixed effects, to be picked up in the constant term, a_0. Therefore, the dummy variables for Allegheny county, which includes the Oakmont Country Club in Oakmont, Pennsylvania, and for 1991, the first year of data, are omitted. Consequently, the yearly fixed effects represent the differences between the year in question and 1991. Meanwhile, the county effects measure differences between the county in question and Allegheny county.

Summary statistics for the two dependent variable payroll measures are listed in Table 25.2. Useable figures for the hotel/motel sector are not available for all counties for all years so the dataset is correspondingly smaller. There are no omissions for the overall county payroll.

3   RESULTS

The statistical results are listed in Table 25.3. Unfortunately for the boosters of the golf Majors, I was unable to identify any significant increase in county payrolls timed with hosting a US Open or a PGA Championship. The coefficients of the main variables of interest, M_0–M_4, are statistically insignificant in both regressions. The problem is not due

Table 25.3   Coefficient estimates (t-statistics)

Dependent variable	Total payroll (1,000 US$2008)	Hotel/motel payroll (1,000 US$2008)
Constant	2.40E7 (21.05)***	104,392 (7.81)***
M_0	40,162 (0.06)	4,968 (0.62)
M_1	43,545 (0.06)	5,764 (0.65)
M_2	381,747 (0.54)	9,898 (1.15)
M_3	443,625 (0.74)	2,197 (0.29)
M_4	246,317 (0.46)	1,254 (0.12)
1992	−461,138 (−0.31)	−8,796 (−0.61)
1993	−641,034 (−0.40)	−8,918 (−0.61)
1994	−489,552 (−0.30)	−9,836 (−0.64)
1995	303,292 (0.20)	−8,064 (−0.56)
1996	1,211,624 (0.87)	−2,046 (−0.16)
1997	2,364,686 (1.85)*	4,212 (0.35)
1998	4,347,068 (3.65)***	17,820 (1.56)
1999	5,885,534 (4.75)***	31,931 (2.60)***
2000	7,487,080 (5.26)***	55,157 (3.33)***
2001	7,008,526 (5.32)***	31,080 (2.80)***
2002	5,911,673 (4.85)***	18,562 (1.77)*
2003	6,021,792 (4.82)***	19,903 (1.73)*
2004	6,315,584 (4.96)***	29,790 (2.66)***
2005	6,446,777 (4.94)***	35,181 (3.00)***
2006	7,445,771 (4.94)***	46,619 (3.08)***
2007	7,832,549 (4.95)***	45,026 (2.87)***
2008	7,359,993 (4.84)***	43,098 (2.50)**
Carver	−2.71E7 (−33.87)***	−120,179 (−8.06)***
Cook	8.86E7 (50.96)***	639,657 (25.89)***
Du Page	−736,399 (−1.49)	−3,858 (−0.33)
Gwinnett	−1.72E7 (−44.62)***	−91,886 (−6.21)***
Hamilton	−2.50E7 (−38.40)***	−127,973 (−9.91)***
Jefferson	−1.33E7 (−23.12)***	−56,350 (−4.93)***
King	2.31E7 (13.37)***	184,681 (14.88)***
Los Angeles	1.39E8 (50.36)***	828,920 (33.96)***
Lucas	−2.03E7 (−25.48)***	−103,162 (−9.26)***
Monroe	−1.32E7 (−14.76)***	−82,095 (−6.87)***
Monterey	−2.45E7 (−33.15)***	35,140 (3.09)***
Montgomery	−8.85E6 (−20.69)***	−41,395 (−3.92)***
Moore	−2.69E7 (−23.32)***	−91,754 (−5.90)***
Nassau	−3.90E6 (−6.90)***	−60,707 (−5.31)***
Oakland	7.59E6 (9.22)***	−45,915 (−3.94)***
Saint Louis City	−1.60E7 (−22.62)***	−43,480 (−3.54)***

Table 25.3 (continued)

Dependent variable	Total payroll (1,000 US$2008)	Hotel/motel payroll (1,000 US$2008)
San Diego	1.42E7 (8.64)***	476,283 (20.59)***
San Francisco	3.77E6 (5.71)***	509,764 (26.36)***
Sheboygan	−2.63E7 (−31.15)***	−108,754 (−9.79)***
Suffolk	−6.27E6 (−15.80)***	−69,449 (−5.69)***
Tulsa	−1.65E7 (−27.70)***	−83,365 (−7.18)***
Union	−1.67E7 (−25.22)***	−93,268 (−7.63)***
Westchester	−7.84E6 (−18.19)***	−27,369 (−2.20)**
R^2	0.989	0.977
n	432	370

to multicollinearity. In regressions that include only M_0, its coefficient is statistically insignificant in both regressions and the point estimate is even negative for the case of total county payroll.[10]

There does not appear to be any problem in the data or the calculations. The overall fit is good in both equations. The use of robust standard errors did not change any of the inferences that would have been drawn from OLS. Given the good fit and the lack of evidence of any severe problem with heteroskedasticity, additional specification searches were forgone.

With respect to the general trends in the data, the pattern of the fixed effects coefficients tracks what we know about the US macroeconomy. There were slight, relatively short recessions in the early 1990s and in the early 2000s, and the start of a major recession in 2008. All three of these are picked up in the results. Compared to the starting year of 1991, the coefficients show a decline in payrolls in 1992 through 1994, followed by strong growth in payrolls from 1995 to 2000. In 2001 and 2002 payrolls dipped again, then grew steadily through 2006 or 2007 before dipping again slightly in 2008.

Meanwhile, the county effects coefficients are of plausible magnitude and related, as they should be, to the relative size of the county. Compared to the omitted Allegheny county, counties such as Los Angeles in California and Cook in Illinois are orders of magnitude larger, while others such as Sheboygan in Wisconsin or Moore in North Carolina are significantly smaller. The regressions were even able to pick up the significant negative coefficient for Monterey county in California in the total payroll regression due to its small size, while still picking up a significant positive coefficient for hotel/motel payroll regression because of the resort nature of the county. The polar opposite of California's Monterey county is Michigan's Oakland county, the home of the Oakland Hills Country Club. Oakland county is above average in size and has a significant positive coefficient in the total payroll regression, but has a small presence in the hospitality sector and, therefore, a significant negative coefficient in the hotel/motel payroll regression. Monterey and Oakland are the only two counties in the data with such sign reversals.

With respect to the main variables of interest, can the lack of significant effects on payroll be reconciled with the obvious intuitive notion that people are attracted to an area to attend a Major golf championship event, and while there, spend money in the local economy? There are several possible ways to answer this question but perhaps crowding-out and time shifting of demand are the most straightforward.[11]

For example, suppose the counties in the sample host a Major golf tournament once every dozen years or so. What happens in the other 11 years? One could imagine an area that hosts some sort of special festival (perhaps even a different one) every year. For one year it just happens to be the PGA Championship. When looked at in the data, the year with the golf Major does not stand out from the rest of the data. What has really happened is that the golf tournament has crowded out some other event that would have occurred in the year in question. So it is not all of the direct spending associated with the golf tournament that is added; it is only the amount above and beyond what would have happened that year anyway. Unfortunately it is impossible for any research design to pick up what would have happened in the absence of hosting a Major golf tournament. In any one year, an area either does, or does not host a Major and it is impossible to say what would have happened in the counter-factual case. Controlling through time and across different areas is the best that can be done. Hosting a tournament may be nice, but no one can ever know what would have happened that week if the tournament did not take place. The data seem to indicate that something of similar magnitude would have taken place in absence of the tournament and was crowded out that year and perhaps time shifted to another year in the data.

Notwithstanding the crowding-out and the lack of the ability to document the effects of added direct expenditure and the indirect secondary expenditure, resident and nearby golf fans clearly benefit from the presence of the tournament. These people may seem incredulous that such an event does not cause a positive blip in economic statistics. But much of their gain might be captured as consumer surplus from the ability to attend the event and, thus, not show up in employment data or any other data. As a possible testament to this explanation consider that, in many cases, local resident golf fans volunteer to help stage the event. And in some cases there is a waiting list to volunteer or even a payment made to 'volunteer' at the tournament. These people are clearly better off due to the presence of the golf tournament, but their gains do not show up in the data. Therefore, it follows that the desirability of hosting such an event need not be dependent upon showing a gain in local employment, income, or production. However, by the same token as the crowding-out scenario in the preceding paragraph, these obvious gains for the golf fans should be offset by the consumer surplus lost by non-golf fans who may lose the opportunity to do something else that week and who may suffer from added congestion. And in some cases it is even golfers themselves who lose out, as was the case when a local public-access, municipal golf course nearby the Olympic Club in San Francisco was closed to provide parking for the 1998 US Open. Data on gains and losses in consumer surplus are simply not available, so the use of measurable series is the next best thing. When the measurable data on county payrolls are used, it appears that staging a Major golf tournament has no significant effect.

NOTES

* I acknowledge technical assistance from Jed DeVaro and comments from the editors which have prompted me to consider additional tests.
1. The RIMS II models are developed by the Bureau of Economic Analysis of the US Commerce Department and are available at: http:www.bea.gov/bea/regional/rims/.
2. Alternatively, a difference-in-differences model can also capture the effect with a single dummy variable for the treatment year. If the dependent variable is the year-to-year change in economic activity, only the treatment year stands out differently from the rest of the time series. Forming first differences comes with the cost of reducing the number of observations.
3. I am indebted to the editors for pointing out the possible relevance of the effects illustrated in Panels B and C. See also, Hotchkiss et al. (2003); Hagn and Maennig (2008); and Feddersen and Maennig (2011).
4. See http://www.census.gov/econ/cbp/index.html.
5. Or maybe not. If the $200 million figure mentioned in the introduction is the correct magnitude, its influence may be swamped. It is a lot of money, but in many of the counties involved it represents less than 1 percent of the total annual payroll. Averaging out the fixed effects for each county will put all counties on the same scale, but still, a $200 million amount will be large qualitatively in some counties while seeming like random measurement error in others.
6. The County Business Patterns data are also broken down by NAICS (formerly SIC) industry codes allowing examination of particular sectors of the economy.
7. The panel is short and wide so that problems that might arise in time-series estimation are not a major concern. Unit root tests would be insignificant. Fixed effects take care of any non-stationarity on average. Although it would be possible to interact the county dummies with prespecified trend patterns to catch the possibility that different trends exist in different counties, there is no prior reason to suspect that any county differs from the general macroeconomic pattern.
8. The regressions are done on payroll levels. Logarithms of earnings are often used in salary regressions to correct for the heteroskedasticity usually present in individual salary regressions, but are not appropriate in the present context. Using levels, the

regression seeks to find a fixed dollar addition to economic activity in the county-year in question because the tournaments themselves are roughly the same size regardless of the size of the county in which they are staged. Using logarithms would be testing for a fixed percentage effect across counties for which expectation there would be no basis in theory. Thus, a regression using logarithms of payrolls as the dependent variable would be theoretically biased against rejecting the null hypothesis of no effect. At the urging of the editors such a regression was run and, as expected, returned insignificant coefficients.

9.   Experimentation with other time periods, including looking only at M_0, the contemporaneous effect, did not alter the inferences.
10. The F-tests for inclusion of all five M_i variables are insignificant at the 0.10 level in both equations.
11. Sports economists have looked intensively at the crowding-out issues at least as early as Noll and Zimbalist (1997). A recent excellent survey of empirical work is Coates and Humphries (2008). The theoretical issues are explained thoroughly in von Allmen (2011).

REFERENCES

'2008 US Open Economic Impact Analysis' (2008), Center for Hospitality and Tourism Research, San Diego State University, San Diego, CA.

Baade, Robert and Victor Matheson (2000), 'An assessment of the economic impact of the American Football Championship, the Super Bowl, on host communities', *Reflets et Perspectives*, **30**, 35–46.

Coates, Dennis and Brad R. Humphries (2008), 'Do economists reach a conclusion on subsidies for sports franchises, stadiums, and mega-events?', *Econ Journal Watch*, **5** (3), September, 294–315.

Feddersen, Arne and Wolfgang Maennig (2011), 'Mega-events and sectoral employment: the case of the 1996 Olympic Games', Hamburg Contemporary Economic Discussions No. 35.

Hagn, F. and Wolfgang Maennig (2008), 'Employment effects of the Football World Cup 1974 in Germany', *Labour Economics*, **15** (5), 1062–75.

Hotchkiss, J.L., R.E. Moore and S.M. Zobay (2003), 'Impact of the 1996 Summer Olympic Games on employment and wages in Georgia', *Southern Economic Journal*, **69** (3), 691–704.

Kamer, Pearl M. (2009), 'The 2009 U.S. Golf Open at Bethpage Black: its impact on the Long Island economy', Research Report from the Long Island Association.

Matheson, Victor A. (2011), 'Economics of the Super Bowl', in Leo H. Kahane and Stephen Shmanske (eds), *The Oxford Handbook of Sports Economics, Volume 1: The Economics of Sports*, Oxford: Oxford University Press, pp. 470–84.

National Football League (1999), 'Super Bowl XXXIII generates $396 million for South Florida', NFL Report, 58.

Noll, Roger G. and Andy Zimbalist (eds) (1997), *Sports, Jobs, and Taxes*, Washington, DC, Brookings Institution Press.

Simmons, Rob and Christian Deutscher (2011), 'The economics of the World Cup', in Leo H. Kahane and Stephen Shmanske (eds), *The Oxford Handbook of Sports Economics, Volume 1: The Economics of Sports*, Oxford: Oxford University Press, pp. 449–69.

von Allmen, Peter (2011), 'Multiplier effects and local economic impact', in Stephen Shmanske and Leo H. Kahane (eds), *The Oxford Handbook of Sports Economics, Volume 2: Economics Through Sports*, Oxford: Oxford University Press, pp. 321–34.

26 People's perception of the social impacts of the Beijing Olympic Games before and after 2008

Yingzhi Guo, Chun Zhou and Yuansi Hou

1 INTRODUCTION

The 121st Session of the International Olympic Committee (IOC) was held in Copenhagen on 2 October 2009 and voted for the host city of the 2016 Summer Olympics. Rio de Janeiro, the capital of Brazil, was announced as the host city, attracting worldwide attention.

Some years earlier, on 13 July 2001, Juan Antonio Samaranch, president of the IOC had announced Beijing, China as the host city of the 2008 Summer Olympic Games thus ensuring the country increased attention from around the world (*Heilongjiang Daily*, 2007).

The slogan for the Beijing Olympic Games, 'One World, One Dream' and three core concepts, 'Green Olympics', 'High-tech Olympics' and 'People's Olympics', became a focus for the Chinese government and people (Yuan, 2008). The Beijing Olympic Games Committee carried out surveys with regard to designing an emblem and a mascot as well as planning and constructing the Olympic venues. Community residents participated enthusiastically by volunteering to help in the preparation and implementation of the Games (Zhang, 2009). Since it was the first time China had hosted this kind of mega event, the whole nation paid considerable attention (Yang, 2007).

This study uses social perception as the breakthrough point, analyzing the impact of the 2008 Beijing Olympic Games. Based on an analysis of the social perception of the Beijing Olympics, we hope to derive theoretical and practical implications for the future development of the Olympic Games. The research is significant in the following two ways. First, most of the previous studies of the Olympic Games at home and abroad are inclined to choose one aspect to study. However, taking the Beijing Olympics as an example, this study comprehensively probes into all ways in which the Olympic Games had an influence in society and the degree of social perception, hoping to draw general rules by making a case analysis of the impact of the Games. Second, by studying the perceived impact of the Games, the chapter analyzes the attitudes of people from different walks of life. From the viewpoint of the Chinese people, the research takes into account benefits and motivation levels. Research results will be of a practical significance for future Olympic Games.

2 LITERATURE REVIEW

Several studies focusing on the impact of the Olympic Games have already been carried out. Because of the wider spread and greater number of participants, the international impact has become more prominent. The Olympic Games have become an activity with a long history of development and receive considerable attention. In the academic field, previous studies have also focused on this field and many of them have taken the impact of the Olympic Games as an entry point of research.

Review of Chinese Literature on the Olympics

In terms of impact-relevant literature, most studies focus on the economic effects of the Olympic Games and the effect on related industries.

With regard to the economic impact, Zhou and Huang (2002) divided the economic benefits generating from the Games into direct and indirect economic benefits, and conducted empirical research into both types of economic impact. By comparing the input and output of the Olympic Games, Dong (2004), and Lin and Yu (2006) studied the economic impact on its host city. Wang and Chen (2005) and Sun (2007) discussed the economic value of the Games. Based on the analysis of the economic impact on its host city, Yan (2010) discussed the basic strategy of post-Olympic economic development. Xu and Ding (2009) evaluated the relative efficiency of the short-term economic impact on the host city. By integrating the case studies of several countries, Feng (2009) analyzed the influence of the Olympic Games to the regional economy. Zhao and Wu (2009) proposed a macroeconomic development strategy for post-Olympics China.

From the perspective of industry association, Luo (2003), Tao (2004), Liu (2007), and Zou and Peng (2005) looked at the tourism industry as the main sector affected by the Olympics. From the perspective of a non-host city, Zhang and Sun (2009) discussed the follow-up impact of the Beijing Olympics on China's tourism industry. Guan (2005) and Zheng and Ding (2006) analyzed the impact of the Games on cultural industries. Dong (2009) discussed the positive impacts of the Olympics on China's sports industry. Wu et al. (2009) carried out an analysis and interpretation of several basic issues concerning the effects of the Games on China's leisure sports. Xu (2009) and Li et al. (2010), studied the post-Olympic sustainable development of the sports industry of Guangxi and Hebei, respectively. Shi et al. (2002) summarized the impact on industry from both vertical and horizontal angles.

With regard to the social impact, Peng and Zhou (2010) explored the history of the modern Olympic Games management philosophy and the sociological causes of the changes. Wang and Li (2009) carried out research on the impact of the Beijing Games on gross national happiness (GNH) and discussed its evaluation system. Li (2007) and Peng and Chang (2009) studied the relationship between the Beijing Olympics and the happiness index of Beijing citizens. Li et al. (2007) analyzed the impact of the 2008 Olympic Games on the cultural environment. Wang (2010), taking the Beijing Olympics as the example, analyzed the influencing factors of residents' support for large-scale events. Researchers have also been concerned about the impact of the Games on urban development. Li et al. (2009) investigated the research of the relationship between urban development and big urban events, such as the Olympic Games. Zhang and Nie (2010) focused on the social and cultural follow-up impacts of the Beijing Olympics on China's non-host cities. Ding and Yuan (2010) focused on the urban marketing impact of the Games and proposed recommendations. Chen (2009) studied the impact of the Beijing Olympics volunteers on the community volunteer service system. In addition, Du et al. (2009) analyzed the heritage value of the Beijing Olympic Games and its development and utilization. Cui (2009) carried out a comprehensive analysis of the impact of the Olympic Games on 'soft powers', such as national cohesion, cultural and educational links and the construction of a harmonious society.

With regard to the sports impact, based on the experience of other countries, Lv and Li (2008) warned that Chinese sports may decline. Fu (2010) recommended seizing the opportunity to promote Olympic sports in China's mass development. From the perspective of physical education resources in higher education, Liu (2009) inspected the impact of the Beijing Olympic Games on China's sports undertakings. Guo et al. (2010) focused on an analysis of the impact of the Beijing Olympics on the sports development of Chinese village farmers.

Methods of Literature Review

Previous scholars are inclined to use both qualitative and quantitative methods to study the impact of the Olympic Games, first determining the factors to be examined in advance, and then using quantitative methods to measure the selected factors. With regard to choosing Olympic Games cases, most studies used the Beijing Olympics as a case study and introduced theories borrowed from other disciplines (for example, economics) to build the model of the impact.

3   OBJECTIVES OF THIS RESEARCH

Using the Beijing Olympics as the focus, Games-related aspects of research appear to be meaningful. From the 'angel of society' perception of impact, this study aims to achieve the following objectives.

First, from a macro perspective, the study examines the social perception among Chinese people of the Beijing Olympics. From the aspect of the publicity for the Games, the research analyzed the awareness and reputation produced by the Beijing Olympics. At the same time, this study also analyzed the social perception of the Olympics regarding public and economic benefits, social promotion and the social costs of the Olympic Games.

Second, from the micro point of view, this research examines the impact of the Beijing Olympics on its participants and the impression it created on respondents. The research explores seven aspects of the respondents' motivations for coming to the Games: social interaction, increasing cultural knowledge, promoting feelings of society members, pursuit of novelty, escape from daily life, the attractiveness of the Olympic Games and Olympic Games souvenirs.

Third, the study examines the social perception of the Games. Based on the existing literature and residents' perception, this research seeks to accomplish a systematic analysis of the impact of the Beijing Olympics.

4   METHODOLOGY

We conducted quantitative research on the perception of the Olympic Games. After obtaining data regarding society's perception of the impacts of the Olympics, we used factor analysis to determine the social impact of the Games in all aspects of the different degrees of attention.

Finally, we analyzed the sampling data from different years to observe the changes in perception and motivation for participating before and after the Games, which can be a reference point for future large-scale events such as the Olympics.

5 DATA SOURCES

Based on evidence, this study used a questionnaire to obtain relevant data. Respondents were asked to indicate their responses on a 5-point scale, with 1 indicating no agreement and 5 indicating strong agreement. We conducted large-scale sampling, stratified by geographical area and income level.

To ensure a sufficient number of respondents, a total of 2,600 questionnaires were distributed to investigate the perception of the Beijing Olympics. Of these 2,506 questionnaires were valid (data reliability was checked through data verification and mathematical testing).

To ensure representation of the sampling, the questionnaires were distributed according to regional districts, including samples from provinces in eastern, western and central China. Further, the respondents were subdivided according to their standard of living – metropolises (Shanghai, Beijing), and small urban and rural locations (Hubei, Sichuan, Inner Mongolia, and so on).

To ensure that the sampling results can be compared with some degree of validity, the sampling survey was conducted from 2007 to 2010. Of the 2,506 valid questionnaires, 669 were from 2007, 656 from 2008, 625 from 2009 and 556 from 2010.

The study used simple random sampling to collect data and then used SPSS software to carry out the analysis.

6 RESEARCH RESULTS

Social Demographic Characteristics

The respondents' profile is summarized in Table 26.1. In terms of gender, the table shows that there were a slightly higher proportion of males than females in 2007, 2009 and 2010, and in 2008, there were more female respondents. With four-year data available, it is obvious that males and females displayed the same degree of attention toward the Beijing Olympics while different occupational social groups showed different degrees of attention. Students, sales/service staff, professional technical personnel, civil servants and teachers were the main occupation divisions for respondents. Taking students as an example, there were 157 students out of a total sample of 669 in 2007, accounting for 23.5 percent. In 2008, the number of students was 221 out of a total population of 656 respondents, accounting for 33.6 percent. In 2009, the number of students was 118 out of a total sample of 625 respondents, accounting for 30.1 percent.

Table 26.1   Comparison of social-demographic characteristics (N=2,506)

	2007 samples (N=669) (%)	2008 samples (N=656) (%)	2009 samples (N=625) (%)	2010 samples (N=556) (%)
Gender				
Male	50.8	41.2	50.7	51.8
Female	49.2	54.9	49.0	46.9
Age				
Below 16	1.9	1.7	1.0	2.2
16–25	29.9	48.9	36.7	29.5
26–35	24.6	25.0	28.8	32.4
36–45	19.7	15.4	18.7	20.7
46–55	13.4	7.9	11.6	7.7
56–65	7.4	0.9	1.9	5.0
Above	3.1	0.2	1.3	1.1
Occupation				
Civil servants	10.9	3.0	7.5	4.9
Professional technical personnel	9.4	11.0	10.4	17.9
Sales/service staff	9.4	9.9	9.5	11.7
Student	23.5	33.6	30.1	23.4
Agriculture/fishing	2.8	2.0	2.2	2.0
Teacher	5.4	6.4	9.6	12.3
Housewife	6.0	3.1	4.5	2.4
Soldiers	1.6	0.0	1.4	0.2
Hospitality	3.3	2.1	2.3	2.5
Travel agency	3.4	3.5	2.6	1.5
Restaurant	5.1	1.4	3.2	2.7
Mass media	3.6	0.5	2.1	3.6
Businessman	4.5	4.6	3.9	9.5
Transportation	4.6	0.3	2.9	0.6
Others	6.1	7.3	5.6	6.2
Education				
Junior high school or below	7.6	2.9	5.0	4.0
Senior high school	17.3	11.0	13.4	10.1
Secondary technical school	9.7	4.4	8.8	5.8
Junior college	19.7	17.5	17.1	19.2
University	37.1	49.4	42.1	47.7
graduate or above	8.1	10.5	12.3	10.1

Table 26.1   (continued)

	2007 samples (N=669) (%)	2008 samples (N=656) (%)	2009 samples (N=625) (%)	2010 samples (N=556) (%)
Monthly income(RMB)				
Less than 2,000	34.6	23.8	23.5	16.8
2,000–3,999	30.5	33.2	33.3	25.6
4,000–5,999	16.0	13.0	14.6	18.2
6,000–7,999	6.1	9.9	7.7	16.0
8,000–9,999	5.7	5.8	7.5	12.6
>10,000	6.9	9.1	10.7	9.0

In 2010, the number of students was 130 out of a total sample of 556 respondents, representing 23.4 percent of the total sample population. The study also divided the respondents into different levels of average monthly income from 2,000 Chinese YMB yuan to 10,000 Chinese YMB yuan, in order to observe the economic level and ascertain whether there is a correlation between the perception of the Beijing Olympic Games and the income level. In addition, the questionnaire respondents differ by educational background and age. The proportions of low-level students (junior high school or lower) and graduates (master's degree and above) were smaller than other education groups. Most respondents were located at the high school to university education stages. The number of the sample population with a university degree was greatest in 2008 and 2010 (324 and 265, respectively), and accounted for 49.4 and 47.7 percent, respectively, within the total population. With regard to age, the largest group was aged below 35, and especially in 2008 the sample comprised mostly young people.

Perception of the Beijing Olympic Games

Certainly the Beijing Olympics would have had an impact on society, but to what extent and in which specific areas the impact can be felt are what this study aims to find out. The study used 28 items to conduct factor analysis to investigate the possible impacts of the Olympics. By applying to the Kaiser–Meyer–Olkin (KMO) and Bartlett's test of sphericity, the validity of the research can be tested. The KMO value is 0.935, greater than 0.9, which shows that there is no great difference among the degree of correlation between variables, so the data are suitable for factor analysis. The result of Bartlett's test of sphericity demonstrates the

Table 26.2   KMO and Bartlett's test results

Test results		
KMO		0.935
Bartlett's test of sphericity	Approx. chi-square	29,369.190
	df	378
	Sig.	0.000

independent relationship between different variables, which proves the proper application of principal factor analysis (Table 26.2).

After the principal factor analysis, five main factors were extracted from the 28 items: social improvement impact, social cost impact, publicity impact, impact on local citizens, and life and employment impact. According to the different social impact perceptions, the factor loadings of 28 factors and five principal factors are listed in Table 26.3. The extracted five main factors can explain 61.28 percent of the overall variance of the perception scale, which shows that the analysis can largely explain the perception of the impacts of the Olympic Games. Among them, the cumulative percentage of variance of only two factors – the social improvement impact and the social cost impact – reached 40.90 percent. Further, the eigenvalues of five main factors are greater than one (Table 26.3). For example, the eigenvalue of the social improvement impact factor was 3.873 and the social cost impact factor reached 3.712, indicating that the five extracted main factors are sufficient to explain the phenomenon.

From the social perception of the impacts of the Beijing Olympics, it is generally considered that the positive impacts brought about by the Games far outweighed the negative effects. Respondents have given a relatively positive evaluation of how the Olympics impacted on society, such as social improvement, an improvement in living conditions and employment, and the provision of participating opportunities (the averages of the social improvement impact factor, the impact on local citizens factor and the life and employment impact factor were all more than 3.5). However, in terms of the social cost impact factor, respondents indicated a low degree of concern – the average of the perception of the social cost impact was 2.81, a relatively low value. In general, this study shows that the whole of society was optimistic about the impact of the Beijing Olympics.

The Beijing Olympics could influence social improvement, which is an ideal accepted by the whole society (the mean of the social improvement impact factor is 4.05). In detail, the Games are thought to enhance the image of the local society, promote people's understanding of China and bring a variety of development opportunities to China (to increase business

Table 26.3 Impact perception of the Beijing Olympic Games

Perception of impacts	Mean	Factor loading	Eigenvalue	% of variance	Cumulative %	Reliability (α)
Social improvement impact	4.146		3.873	13.832	13.832	0.847
Increasing business opportunities	4.09	0.594				
Promoting social image	4.18	0.657				
Enhancing social pride	4.21	0.699				
Economic benefits for municipal works	3.98	0.681				
Making the world better understand China	4.39	0.677				
Expanding publicity to promote trade	4.01	0.541				
Protecting and promoting Chinese culture	4.16	0.603				
Promoting construction of local new infrastructure	4.15	0.443				
Social cost impact	2.81		3.712	13.257	27.089	0.854
Not increase the pressure on services and facilities (fire alarms, roads and so on)	2.78	0.844				
Not increase the degree of congestion	2.74	0.806				
Not cause a deterioration in the local environment	3.25	0.620				
Not increase crime rate	3.12	0.773				
Not increase local price levels	2.95	0.790				
Not disturb the peace of local residents	2.93	0.801				

Table 26.3 (continued)

Perception of impacts	Mean	Factor loading	Eigenvalue	% of variance	Cumulative %	Reliability (α)
Publicity impact	3.68		3.410	12.177	39.266	0.805
Innovative sporting concepts	3.77	0.738				
Distinctive theme	3.87	0.721				
Rich sports content	3.95	0.708				
Extensive publicity of mass media	4.17	0.610				
Good food and accommodation	3.91	0.634				
Superior location	3.90	0.549				
Leave a big impression	4.10	0.555				
Impact on local citizens	3.60		2.773	9.904	49.169	0.786
Helping to improve relationships among citizens, athletes and tourists	3.67	0.726				
Providing local residents with family entertainment	3.62	0.727				
Increasing local tourism	4.05	0.551				
Having an educational meaning for Chinese residents	3.77	0.576				
Increasing physical and recreational opportunities	3.79	0.514				
Life and employment impact	3.58		2.267	3.58	52.749	0.690
Raising living standards	3.52	0.724				
Increasing employment opportunities	3.83	0.694				

470

opportunities, protect and publicize Chinese culture, promote international trading, and so on). Concerning social cost, respondents focused on the increasing deterioration of the local environment (the mean of the item is 3.25) and the increasing crime rates (3.12), but it was not widely believed that the Olympic Games brought an excessive social burden to its host city. Obviously, the Beijing Olympics left a deep impression on the respondents (the mean of the publicity impact factor is 3.68). The publicity impact can be attributed to the influence of mass media, rich sports content, innovative sporting ideas and a unique theme. Specific to the individual, the Games are also considered to provide a variety of opportunities, including: increasing local tourism (the mean is 4.05), having an educational meaning for Chinese residents (3.77), and increasing physical and recreational opportunities (3.79).Further, the respondents had a relatively good impression of Beijing and believed that the host city was a good location and could provide good food and accommodation. In addition, the Beijing Olympics is also considered to increase employment opportunities for local citizens (the mean is 3.83) and improve local living standards (3.52).

Comparison Analysis of Respondents' Perception of Social Improvement, Pre- and Post-Olympic Games

Using ANOVA analysis, this subsection compares the means, *t*-values and *p*-values of the items in the social improvement impact perception factor (Table 26.4). After comparing the data from the four years, it was found that the respondents showed a stronger perception of the social improvement impact of the Games in 2009 and 2010 (the means are 4.28 and 4.12, respectively), compared with the results in 2007 and 2008. The reason for this situation is the improvement and changes in all aspects of social life caused by the Olympics were reflected in 2009 and 2010, after the 2008 Olympics. However, when comparing the perception situation in 2009 and 2010, the 2009 sample data express a stronger perception of the social improvement impact of the Games than was the case in 2010, indicating that during the post-Olympic period, the perception of the social improvement impact was gradually weakening. When comparing the data from 2007 and 2008, the perception is slightly higher in 2008 (the mean is 4.12) than in 2007 (4.05). Through analyzing and comparing the demographic data from 2007 and 2008, the 2008 data have a higher proportion of women (13.7 percent higher than men), the proportion of young respondents in the 16–25 year-old range is up to 48.9 percent and the respondents' ratio with a university degree or above is 59.9 percent, indicating that young and highly educated people were more likely to perceive the positive social improvement impact of the Olympic Games.

Table 26.4   Comparison analysis of tourists' perception of social improvement, pre- and post-Olympic Games

Perception of impacts	Mean				*t*-value	*p*-value
	2007	2008	2009	2010		
Social improvement impact	4.05	4.12	4.28	4.12	11.49	0.000
Increasing business opportunities	4.06	4.06	4.17	4.12	2.50	0.082
Promoting social image	4.08	4.14	4.35	4.19	13.78	0.000
Enhancing social pride	4.12	4.18	4.35	4.21	8.06	0.000
Economic benefits for municipal works	3.94	3.91	4.12	4.01	7.59	0.000
Making the world better understand China	4.34	4.30	4.51	4.37	8.56	0.000
Expanding publicity to promote trade	3.82	4.02	4.20	4.02	19.10	0.000
Protecting and promoting Chinese culture	4.01	4.25	4.27	4.14	4.94	0.007
Promoting construction of local new infrastructure	4.06	4.12	4.28	4.16	8.43	0.000

Eight items are listed under the principal social improvement impact factor. The 2007 data show that two items: 'economic benefits for municipal works' and 'expanding publicity to promote trade' have lower means (3.94 and 3.82, respectively). In the 2008 sampling results, the former drops to 3.91, and the latter rises to 4.02. In 2009, the sampling results show that the means of these two items rise to 4.12 and 4.20, respectively, which demonstrates that in 2007, before the Olympics, people were doubtful about the potential economic benefits that would be brought about by municipal construction projects, the possible effects of publicity and the trade promotion caused by the Olympic Games. The 2008 respondents had a more negative attitude toward the outcomes of municipal construction than those in 2007, but the 2008 perception of 'expanding publicity to promote trade' was greater than in 2007. After Beijing successfully hosted the Games in August 2008, in 2009 and 2010, the positive social improvement impact of the Olympics was revealed, leading to means of 4.12 and 4.20, respectively, in 2009, and 4.01 and 4.02, respectively, in 2010 – that is, higher than in 2007 (3.94 and 3.82, respectively) and 2008 (3.91 and 4.02, respectively). However, the mean of 'economic benefits for municipal works' was still the lowest among all the items in 2009 and 2010.

Table 26.5   Comparative study of tourists' perception of social cost impact, 2007–2010

Perception of impacts	Mean				*t*-value	*p*-value
	2007	2008	2009	2010		
Not increase social cost	2.81	2.91	3.18	2.98	62.98	0.000
Not increase pressure on services and facilities (fire alarms, roads, etc.)	2.65	2.75	2.95	2.76	9.94	0.000
Not increase the degree of congestion	2.54	2.77	2.94	2.80	15.61	0.000
Not cause a deterioration in the local environment	3.07	3.11	3.57	3.13	17.04	0.000
Not increase crime rates	3.01	3.03	3.34	2.95	16.27	0.000
Not increase local price levels	2.78	2.88	3.22	2.96	21.08	0.000
Not disturb the peace of local residents	2.82	2.92	3.07	3.22	5.57	0.004

Comparative Study of Respondents' Perception of Social Cost Impact, 2007 to 2010

Using ANOVA analysis, this subsection compares the means, *t*-values and *p*-values of the items in the social cost impact perception factor (Table 26.5). After comparing the data from the four years, it was found that the respondents showed a stronger perception of the social cost impact of the Beijing Olympics in 2009 and 2010 (the means of these two years are 3.18 and 2.98, respectively), compared with the results in 2007 and 2008 (2.81 and 2.91, respectively).

Looking through all of the items under the social cost impact factor, it can be seen from the four-year sampling data that the trend of this factor is almost the same as the trend of the social improvement impact factor. Before the 2008 Olympics, the perceived social cost impact is not strong in 2007 and the mean is only 2.81. Of all of the items, the perception of 'not cause a deterioration in the local environment' (the mean is 3.07) is slightly stronger than other items. The perception of 'not increase the degree of congestion' is the lowest (2.54), indicating that the majority of respondents were more concerned with the social costs related to daily life and most of the respondents believed that the Olympic Games would increase the pressure on the city traffic situation.

During the Games, all of the assumed social cost impact items exercised an influence over society, so all of the means of the items in 2008 were higher than those of the sampling results in 2007. Generally respondents agreed that the Games put the greatest pressure on social service facilities among all of the social costs (the mean is 2.75), followed by transportation (2.77). It is also perceived that the Games had a great impact on price levels and the peace of local residents (means are 2.88 and 2.92, respectively).

During the post-Olympic period, in 2009 the data showed that the means of respondents' perceived social costs increased. With the positive impact of the Olympics on the socio-economic, cultural and other aspects of life, the respondents' previous concerns were alleviated. Some of the issues of the social costs that were intensified during the Games were weakened by the end. Except for 'not increase the degree of congestion' and 'not increase the pressure on services and facilities (fire alarms, roads and so on)', whose averages are still less than 3, the averages of all other items increased.

In 2010, sampling results showed that the respondents' perceived social costs of the Olympic Games as a whole was somewhat lower than in 2009, but still higher than the 2007 and 2008 results. The mean of the item 'not disturb the peace of local residents', continued to rise on the basis of the level of 2009. After the Olympics ended, respondents ceased to have concerns about further disturbance caused by the Games.

Comparative Study of Respondents' Perception of Publicity Impact, 2007 to 2010

Using ANOVA analysis, this subsection compares the means, t-values and p-values of the items in the publicity impact perception factor (Table 26.6). After comparing the data from the four years, it was found that the respondents showed a stronger perception of the publicity impact of the Games in 2009 and 2010 (the means are 4.22 and 3.99, respectively), compared with the results in 2007 and 2008 (3.71 and 3.94, respectively).

Before the 2008 Games, the means of the items under the perceived Olympic Games publicity impact factor ranged from 3.4 to 3.5 in 2007. The item which has the biggest mean is 'extensive publicity of mass media', whose mean is 3.90, followed by 'leaves a big impression' (3.89). The item which has the smallest mean is 'innovative sporting concepts' (3.52). The means of the remaining items are around 3.70.

From the mean value analysis, the majority of respondents believed that the publicity in the mass media was comprehensive. Advertisements and publicity content were likely to impress visitors. For most respondents, their perception is that Beijing, the Olympic host city, has a superior

Table 26.6   Comparative study of tourists' perception of publicity impact, 2007–2010

Perception of impacts	Mean				t-value	p-value
	2007	2008	2009	2010		
Publicity impact	3.71	3.94	4.22	3.99	5.20	0.006
Innovative sporting concepts	3.52	3.78	3.99	3.82	36.67	0.000
Distinctive theme	3.57	3.83	4.21	3.92	57.62	0.000
Rich sports content	3.72	3.94	4.20	4.00	36.70	0.000
Extensive publicity of mass media	3.90	4.16	4.46	4.19	51.68	0.000
Good food and accommodation	3.70	3.92	4.13	3.91	28.14	0.000
Superior location	3.69	3.87	4.15	3.94	24.46	0.000
Leaves a big impression	3.89	4.05	4.40	4.12	40.66	0.000

location, good food and comfortable accommodation. Furthermore, most of the respondents believed that the Beijing Olympics has a clear theme, with rich content. However, the inadequacy of the Games may lie in the innovation of sporting concepts.

The results of the 2008 data show that the means of items have increased compared with the 2007 data. The 'extensive publicity of mass media' and 'leaves a big impression' items still have the highest means, matching the 2007 sample results. It is noteworthy that 'innovative sporting concepts' and 'distinctive theme' have the largest increase rate in 2008, confirming that the success of the 2008 Games left a profound impression on the sporting concept.

In the 2009 sample data, most items have a mean higher than 4.0 except for 'innovative sporting concepts', whose mean is 3.99. An overall comparison of the data from 2007 to 2009 shows that the means of every item display the same increasing trend. Among all the items, 'distinctive theme' shows the largest increase, indicating that the respondents' understanding of the 2008 Olympics continued to deepen. Further, 'extensive publicity of mass media' and 'leaves a big impression' still obtained the most agreement from the respondents.

The 2010 sampling results show that the means of each item declined slightly compared with the data of 2009, but they were still higher than in 2007 and 2008. This phenomenon shows that with the end of the event and the passage of time, respondents' perception of the publicity will gradually weaken.

Table 26.7   *Comparative study of tourists' perception of impact on local citizens, pre- and post-Olympic Games*

Perception of impacts	Mean				t-value	p-value
	2007	2008	2009	2010		
Impact on local citizens	3.60	3.81	3.96	3.81	10.51	0.000
Helping to improve relationships among citizens, athletes and tourists	3.50	3.71	3.82	3.71	14.86	0.000
Providing local residents with family entertainment	3.42	3.62	3.86	3.70	12.78	0.000
Increasing local tourism	3.87	4.11	4.19	4.06	9.91	0.000
Having an educational meaning for Chinese residents	3.63	3.80	3.91	3.78	10.71	0.000
Increasing physical and recreational opportunities	3.59	3.80	4.00	3.82	10.48	0.000

Comparative Study of Respondents' Perception of the Impact on Local Citizens Pre- and Post-Olympic Games

Using ANOVA analysis, this subsection compares the means, *t*-values and *p*-values of the items in the impact on local citizens factor (Table 26.7). After comparing the data from the four years, it was found that the respondents showed a stronger perception of the impact on local citizens of the Games in 2009 (the mean of this year is 3.96), compared with the results in the 2007 and 2008 (3.60 and 3.81, respectively), and the results of the 2010 data are generally the same as those of 2008.

In the 2007 sampling data, 'increasing local tourism' has the highest mean (3.87) and 'providing local residents with family entertainment' has the lowest mean (3.42).The remaining items are as follows: 'having an educational meaning for Chinese residents', 'increasing physical and recreational opportunities', and 'helping to improve relationships among citizens, athletes and tourists'. The 2007 data indicate that respondents were more concerned about the role of the Olympics in promoting the education of residents and in educating local citizens; however respondents were less aware of the opportunities that the Olympic Games can bring the residents in the form of participatory entertainment activities.

The 2008 data are consistent with the 2007 data with the means of the items slightly increasing and the ranking of the means are the same as the

2007 data. Among all of the items, only 'increasing physical and recreational opportunities' has a slightly higher rate than other items, indicating that as time goes by, the Olympics preparation, organizing and follow-up work in 2008 became more mature and the Games can provide more and more sports and entertainment opportunities. In addition, 'providing local residents with family entertainment' still has the lowest mean among all of the items, indicating that the family-oriented entertainment requirements were not satisfactory for respondents.

Overall, comparing the 2007, 2008 and 2009 data, it can be seen that the means of every item of the 2009 data are higher than those of 2007 and 2008 and the ranking of all the item means are almost the same, indicating the stability of the sampling result. With the ending of the Beijing Games, the means of all the items have risen. But the 2009 sampling results are different in some respects: 'providing local residents with family entertainment' has a mean of 3.86, exceeding that of 'helping to improve relationships among citizens, athletes and tourists' (3.82). This result suggests the added value that the Games brought to the local community and changed the citizens' evaluation from negative to positive. This point is indicative of the potential impact on the livelihood of the local citizens brought by the Games, and should be noted by all the future Olympic host cities and international Olympic researchers.

However, in the 2010 sample data, the perception of the principal component factor and the perception of the various items mostly fell back to the 2008 levels. This situation demonstrates that for the Olympic event itself, the impacts on tourists and local tourism reached their highest level in the year after the event was held, but the impacts are relatively temporary and their sustainability is weak. On the other hand, the means of 'providing local residents with family entertainment' and 'increasing physical and recreational opportunities' retain their higher position (3.70 and 3.82, respectively), and are higher than the 2007 and 2008 corresponding levels, indicating that the Beijing Games brought significant added value for the daily fitness and recreational activities of ordinary people.

Comparative Study of Respondents' Perception of the Life and Employment Impact, Pre- And Post-Olympic Games

Using ANOVA analysis, this subsection compares the means, t-values and p-values of the items in the life and employment impact factor (Table 26.8). After comparing the data from the four years, it was found that respondents showed the strongest perception of the life and employment impact of the Games in 2009 (the mean of this year is 3.91), compared with the results in 2007, 2008 and 2010 (3.73, 3.89 and 3.74, respectively). But

Table 26.8   Comparative study of tourists' perception of life and employment impact, pre- and post-Olympic Games

Perception of impacts	Mean				*t*-value	*p*-value
	2007	2008	2009	2010		
Life and employment impact	3.73	3.89	3.91	3.74	0.932	0.394
Raising the living standards	3.39	3.66	3.54	3.57	7.32	0.001
Increasing employment opportunities	4.06	4.12	4.28	3.90	3.08	0.046

of special concern is that in 2008 the mean of 'raising living standards' is 3.66, higher than the mean of the 2009 sampling data (3.54). Before the Beijing Olympics, respondents generally believed that the Games would provide more employment opportunities and improve people's standard of living, but the great number of jobs created were only temporary and cannot fundamentally solve the country's employment shortages. After the Games, as many temporary positions were withdrawn, the employment issue re-intensified. Further in terms of an improvement in living standards, the goal cannot be attained in one step. This appears to be the reason for the declining mean of 'raising living standards' and a decline in the increase rate of the mean of 'increasing employment opportunities' in the 2009 sampling results. Based on the comprehensive effects of many international and domestic macroeconomic factors, in the 2010 sampling data, the means of these two items are significantly lower than in the 2008 sampling data. These all show that the impact of the Games on overall employment is not apparent, at least in the short term. Further, the impact of the Olympics itself is not as strong as elements such as the economic environment, political policies and systems, and other macro factors.

7   CONCLUSIONS

Through conducting questionnaires and related data analysis, this study observed the perception of the impacts of the Beijing Olympic Games, the motivation and the relationship between perception and motivation, and then drew the following conclusions. The impacts of the Games mainly include the following five aspects: social improvement impact, social cost impact, publicity impact, impact on local citizens, and life and employment impact. On the whole, people were looking forward to the Beijing

Olympic Games before they were held – its positive perception was much higher than the negative perception. Further, its favorable factors have generally been recognized with a high evaluation. The study conducted a survey of respondents' perceptions on the possible impacts of the Games and at the same time analyzed the motivation of participating in the Olympics. However, there are still some limitations to this study: First, the study investigated only the perceived impacts of the Beijing Olympics, but did not conduct in-depth research into the reasons behind the perceptions. Second, it has been more than two years since the end of the Games, and a number of follow-up effects are gradually becoming clear. In addition to some impacts shown in the sampling results of the 2009 and 2010 sampling data, there may be some long-term effects that have not yet been revealed.

REFERENCES

Chen, X.Q. (2009), 'Voluntary activities of the Olympic Games and establishment of the Beijing social voluntary service system', *Social Science of Beijing*, **24** (3), 29–33 (in Chinese).

Cui, P. (2009), 'Impact of the Beijing Olympic Games on Chinese "soft power"', *Sports Tribune*, **16** (5), 19–23 (in Chinese).

Ding, L.Y. and Y.H. Yuan (2010), 'Research in city marketing based on the Olympics Games', *Journal of Nanjing Institute of Physical Education (Social Sciences)*, **24** (4), 53–5 (in Chinese).

Dong, J. (2004), 'The economic impacts on the Olympic host cities', *China Sport Science and Technology*, **40** (1), 34–37 (in Chinese).

Dong, X.S. (2009), 'The positive impacts of the Beijing Olympic Games on the sports industry in China', *Market Modernization*, **566** (5), 257 (in Chinese).

Du, W., A.H. Yang and H. Jun (2009), 'Evaluation of the value and development strategy of the legacy of the Beijing Olympic Games', *Journal of Jilin Institute of Physical Education*, **25** (4), 5–6 (in Chinese).

Feng, R. (2009), 'The study of the Olympic impacts on regional economics', *Market Modernization*, **565** (4), 217–18 (in Chinese).

Fu, B. (2010), 'Research on the Beijing Olympic Games' influence upon the mass PE development of our country', *Journal of Taiyuan University*, **11** (2), 49–52 (in Chinese).

Guan, Y.S. (2005), 'Development of the 2008 Olympic Games economy in Beijing and the Olympic culture industry', *Sports and Science*, **26** (1), 36–9 (in Chinese).

Guo, M.G., T.Y. Liu, Q.S. Hu and J. Wang (2010), 'Effects of the Beijing Olympic Games on village peasant sports in China', *Journal of Physical Education*, **17** (5), 26–9 (in Chinese).

Heilongjiang Daily (2007), 'Beijing Olympic countdown – the whole world pays attention to Beijing, expecting the Chinese to create miracles', available at: http://2008.sohu.com/20070809/n251502070.shtml (accessed 9 August 2007) (in Chinese).

Li, H.X., Y.T. Wang and X.D. Wan (2009), 'Review of the Beijing Olympic Games and urban development', *Beijing Planning Review*, **24** (3), 63–74 (in Chinese).

Li, W.P. (2007), 'Research on the relations between the 2008 Olympic Games and the gross national happiness', *Journal of Beijing Sport University*, **30** (2), 160–62 (in Chinese).

Li, W.P., G.Q. Long and X.M. Li (2007), 'Research of the 2008 Olympic Games/cultural environment effects in Beijing', *Sports and Science*, **28** (1), 44–6 (in Chinese).

Li, Y. L., S.P. Zhang and B Feng. (2010), 'The sustainable development of the sports industry in Hebei after the Beijing Olympic Games', *China Business and Trade*, **19** (2), 205–6 (in Chinese).

Lin, X.P. and C.G. Yu (2006), 'Influence of and law research about the modern Olympic impacts on host city economic development', *Journal of Shanghai University of Sport*, **30** (2), 1–7 (in Chinese).

Liu, F.M. (2007), 'Influence factors of Olympic tourism and its inspiration to the Beijing Olympic Games', *Journal of Beijing University of Physical Education*, **30** (7), 884–6 (in Chinese).

Liu, P.L. (2009), 'The influence of the Beijing Olympic Games to PE class resources in higher education', *Science and Technology Information*, **25** (27), 20–71 (in Chinese).

Luo, Q.J. (2003), 'Effects of world mega events on the tourism industry and enlightenment to China: a case study of the Olympic Games and the World Cup', *Commercial Research*, **271**, (11), 150–52 (in Chinese).

Lv, S.T. and L.D. Li (2008), 'Competitive sports of China would be ready for a decline: a kind of reverse thought after the Beijing Olympic Games', *Journal of Wuhan Institute of Physical Education*, **42**, (9), 5–11 (in Chinese).

Peng, X. and X.M. Zhou (2010), 'Historical changes of the concept of the modern Olympic Games and its sociological factors', *Journal of Southwest University of Political Science and Law*, **12** (1), 77–83 (in Chinese).

Peng, Y.C. and L. Chang (2009), 'Research about the impact of the 2008 Olympic Games on the resident happiness index', *Sports and Science*, **30** (1), 24–27 (in Chinese).

Shi, B., K. Zhang and X.P. Zhang (2002), 'Discussion on the conductive effect of the Olympic economy', *China Sport Science and Technology*, **38** (8), 18–20 (in Chinese).

Sun, K.C. (2007), 'Analysis and research on modern Olympics economic benefits', *Group Economics Research*, **233** (6), 30–31 (in Chinese).

Tao, Y. (2004), 'Research on problems of entry visas for the host country in Olympic Games', *China Sport Science and Technology*, **40** (1), 38–40 (in Chinese).

Wang, J.Q. (2010), 'Analysis of the influential factors of residents' support for mega events: based on the data of the 2008 Beijing Olympic Games', *Tourism Science*, **24** (3), 63–74 (in Chinese).

Wang, J. and Z.L. Chen (2005), 'Analysis of the economic value of the Beijing Olympic Games', *Enterprise Economy*, **293** (1), 16–17 (in Chinese).

Wang, Z.H. and W.P. Li (2009), 'Effects of the Beijing Olympic Games on national happiness indexes and construction of an evaluating system', *Journal of Shanghai University of Sport*, **33** (3), 10–15 (in Chinese).

Wu, S.B., Y.T. Jing and Y.L. Bi (2009), 'Impacts of the 2008 Olympic Games on recreational sports in China', *Market Modernization*, **566** (7), 246 (in Chinese).

Xu, C.M. and H.X. Ding (2009), 'Relative efficiency evaluation of the Olympic Games' short-term economic influence on the host city', *China Sports Science*, **29** (4), 76–9 (in Chinese).

Xu, S.J. (2009), 'The sustainable development of the sports industry in Guangxi after the Beijing Olympic Games', *Market Modernization*, **566** (1), 254–5 (in Chinese).

Yan, B.F. (2010), 'Discussion of sports economic development in China', *Sports Culture Guide*, **28** (4), 65–8 (in Chinese).

Yang, S.A. (2007), 'Good luck Beijing: serious sports competition preparation; press statement, 2007', available at: http://www.beijing2008.cn (accessed 21 March 2007) (in Chinese).

Yuan, M.S. (2008), 'Green Olympics, high-tech Olympics and people's Olympics are the intangible heritage of the Olympics', *Social Science of Beijing*, **23** (3), 14–17 (in Chinese).

Zhang, C.P. (2009), 'Effects of the Beijing Olympic Games on soft strengths of China', *Journal of Physical Education*, **16** (5), 19–23 (in Chinese).

Zhang, Y. and X.F. Nie (2010), 'The follow-up social and cultural influence to non-host cities after the Beijing Olympic Games', *Sport*, **1** (6), 144–9 (in Chinese).

Zhang, Y. and Y.T. Sun (2009), 'The influences of the 2008 Beijing Olympic Games to the non-host cities tourism industry', *Journal of Nanjing Institute of Physical Education (Social Sciences)*, **23** (2), 53–55 (in Chinese).

Zhao, C.J. and W. Wu (2009), 'Macro strategies for developing the Chinese economy after the 2008 Olympic Games', *Sports and Science*, **30** (3), 24–6 (in Chinese).
Zheng, G.H. and S.Y. Ding (2006), 'The effect of the Beijing Olympic Games on China's culture industry', *Journal of Tianjin University of Sport*, **21** (5), 397–400 (in Chinese).
Zhou, J.M. and X.B. Huang (2002), 'Analysis of the economic impacts of Olympic marketing', *Journal of Wuhan Institute of Physical Education*, **36** (3), 22–9 (in Chinese).
Zou, T.Q. and H.J. Peng (2005), 'Analysis of tourism effects of the Olympic Games – case study of the Sydney Olympic Games and the Athens Olympic Games', *Journal of Business Economics*, **162** (4), 45–50 (in Chinese).

27 The 2010 FIFA World Cup high-frequency data economics: effects on international tourism and awareness for South Africa*

Stan du Plessis and Wolfgang Maennig

1 INTRODUCTION

The 2010 FIFA World Cup was clearly successful as a tournament and as an advertisement for South Africa's capacity to host a global event. Expectations were high prior to the tournament regarding the home team's performance and the tournament's magnitude as a major event with the potential to benefit the South African economy.

The home team's strong performance, better than could reasonably have been expected, was the source of much local pride. Further, the tournament was an organizational and logistical success despite the sometimes pessimistic forecasts in the international media. An otherwise critical international press did not contradict the 'summa cum laude' grade assigned to the World Cup by FIFA president Sepp Blatter (Reeves, 2010).

An economic analysis of the 2010 FIFA World Cup should be conducted at the micro or managerial level of the local organizing committee (LOC) and of FIFA. The financial outcomes of the LOC are not yet known. FIFA, which earned US$3.4 billion in total commercial revenues, provided the LOC with US$423 million, an amount that is considered to have been sufficient to ensure that the tournament was within budget (Pedroncelli, 2010). The costs of the stadiums and the transport infrastructure were almost entirely publicly financed, but these costs should not be attributed solely to the 2010 FIFA World Cup, since many of these investments have long-term benefits. It is too early to assess the ultimate impact of these public investments on the long-term growth path of the economy.

On a micro level, there are always winners, losers and those who are unaffected by a major event of this kind. On the one hand, there are reports of increased demand for vuvuzelas, travel in luxury coaches, tour operators and tourist attractions close to the stadiums (personal communication, Mariette du Toit-Helmbold, CEO, Cape Town Tourism, 25 June 2010). On the other hand, South African manufacturers seem to have been largely unaffected by the event (personal communication, Denny Thaver, Coface, SA's trade credit protection company, 2 July 2010).

But there was also controversy. Many South Africans experienced the tournament preparations as disruptive (for example, Tolsi, 2010). FIFA's prescriptive approach and the LOC's plans were also controversial. Cornelissen (2009), for example, raises the concern that the plans would entrench existing spatial inequality in the country, and Darkey and Horn (2009) point out that owners of guesthouses were discouraged by the rigidity of the FIFA and LOC requirements for accreditation.

To appreciate the total economic impact of a major sporting event, it is necessary to move beyond data on individual enterprises and sectors to investigate the effect of the tournament using meso- and macroeconomic data. These data have the advantage of aggregating possible increases in the incomes of individuals with the losses of others, thereby presenting a general economic picture.

This chapter starts with a discussion of the net tourist increase to South Africa during the FIFA World Cup, as this is the major source of short-term economic benefit. We used high-frequency data to estimate the likely tourist flow. After this follows a discussion of possible reasons for the disappointing number of actual tourist arrivals after the optimistic estimates. But there have been other short-term benefits, including a feel-good effect and longer-term gains in the form of image and improved international perception of the economy. Evidence for these effects is discussed in the final section.

2   INTERNATIONAL TOURISM: THE ORIGIN OF SHORT-TERM INCOME AND EMPLOYMENT EFFECTS

Optimistic Expectations and Their Impact on Tournament Preparations

The additional impact on local income and employment of a major sporting event results only from expenditures by non-residents visiting the event region. Expenditures by domestic residents on the event do not typically contribute to the impact of the event beyond the immediate duration of the tournament; even if individuals purchase televisions and other items used in relation to the event, the event usually affects the timing of the consumption decisions rather than the overall level of consumption and savings. Any increased consumption by residents during the tournament is typically counterbalanced by reduced demand in other months and other sectors. Nor did the public investment in stadiums and infrastructure for

Table 27.1   Supply of hotel beds in South Africa

Level	2007	2010	Av. growth p.a.
5 star	8,013	10,295	8.7
4 star	12,585	21,049	18.7
3 star	23,714	26,698	4.0
2 star	3,559	4,185	5.5
1 star	3,156	3,645	4.9
Total	51,027	65,872	8.9

Source: Pam Golding (2010).

the occasion of the tournament necessarily imply an expenditure boost: with limited public finances, any additional spending on stadiums will be compensated for by reduced spending on other public purposes, if not immediately, then over time as the government's intertemporal budget constraint comes into play.

This explains the emphasis on international tourism in *ex ante* impact studies of the effect of the 2010 FIFA World Cup. The event raised high expectations: 230,000 foreign tourists were predicted to stay for an average of 15 days (Grant Thornton, 2004), and this projection was later increased to 380,000 overseas visitors (Grant Thornton, 2008). To estimate the impact of the tournament it is important to distinguish between 'international tourists' and 'overseas tourists' since differences are to be expected between the spending patterns of tourists from other countries in Africa and those from Europe, Asia and the Americas.

The optimistic forecasts with respect to tourist inflows were well received on the basis of the perceived effects of previous large sporting events hosted in South Africa in the low tourist season months, including the rugby and cricket world cups (Spronk and Fourie, 2010). By contrast, early warnings (for example, du Plessis and Maennig, 2007; Allmers and Maennig, 2009) from World Cup host nations such as France (1998) and Germany (2006) and from European Cup organizers that the net increase in the number of tourists that accompanies such events is typically small or even insignificant received no attention in the optimistic *ex ante* impact studies (for example, Grant Thornton, 2004, 2008). The optimistic expectations were reflected in the considerable private sector investment in the tourism sector in the years leading up to the tournament. Table 27.1 compares the number of hotel beds available in the various categories of hotels in 2007 and 2010.

While there was considerable expansion over this period, especially at the luxury end of the market, it would not be appropriate to attribute this solely or even largely to the approaching 2010 FIFA World Cup. Instead, rising demand had long necessitated investment in extra capacity. Nevertheless, the approaching 2010 FIFA World Cup affected the timing of these projects, advancing their completion dates in anticipation of the tournament. Some of this investment was of doubtful long-term viability, and there was a risk that some of the new hotels would fail when room occupancy and rates per room dropped after the tournament (Cokayne, 2010).

The available hotel beds listed in Table 27.1 exclude the many guesthouses in the South African tourism sector. Regrettably, there is no formal estimate of the number of these establishments and their available beds. However, the Department of Tourism reported that prior to the tournament approximately one third of the accommodation pre-booked through FIFA's MATCH system was non-hotel accommodation (DoT, 2010). The role of FIFA's MATCH system was a major concern for the owners of guesthouses. Even before the tournament, Darkey and Horn (2009) reported survey evidence of these owners' misgivings about the manner in which the FIFA and the LOC arranged accommodation, and 60 per cent of the long-term bed-and-breakfast proprietors expected the tournament to have a negative impact on their business.

Divergent Estimates of Tourist Arrivals

Official data on tourist arrivals for the months covered by the tournament have been released by Statistics South Africa. The data are shown in Table 27.2 for June and July 2009, and for the same months in 2010, covering the tournament which started on 11 June 2010 and lasted until the final on 11 July 2010.

The data in Table 27.2 are intended to reflect only tourist arrivals. However, the ability to assess the purpose of a visit is imperfect and especially in the case of arrivals from mainland Africa these data include very substantial numbers of migrant workers in addition to tourists. For that reason StatsSA published a separate monthly total excluding arrivals from Africa (as well as 'unspecified' arrivals) – a convention we have repeated in Table 27.2. Since the data in the table are shown per calendar month, the final two columns create a 'tournament month' from the 2009 and 2010 data, by adding the number that arrived in June starting on the 10th to the number that arrived in July until the 11th. According to StatsSA's data, 109,621 more 'overseas' visitors arrived in South Africa during the tournament month than during the comparable days of 2009.

A number of alternative and notably divergent estimates of tourist arrivals are available (Lapper and Blitz, 2010). High forecasts were on the order of 350,000, such as the Grant Thornton prediction of 373,000 made

Table 27.2   Official tourist data for June and July 2009 and 2010: number of visitors and their country of origin

Region	June 2009	July 2009	June 2010	July 2010	Benchmark month*	Tournament month*
Europe	72,144	91,904	123,702	98,113	80,707	117,282
North America	25,502	28,951	50,902	32,068	27,274	45,314
Central & S. America	4,605	5,699	47,188	11,731	5,092	35,621
Australasia	7,813	9,464	18,450	8,911	8,567	15,462
Asia	13,999	15,704	30,914	26,209	14,905	29,909
Middle East	2,794	5,124	6,189	6,010	3,681	6,259
Africa	376,280	461,630	421,074	494,815	414,658	456,296
Unspecified	2,294	4,938	22,892	2,557	3,282	16,169
Total	505,431	623,414	721,311	680,414	558,165	722,311
Total ex-Africa & unspecified	126,857	156,846	277,345	183,042	140,226	249,847
Increment						109,621

Note: * The benchmark and tournament months were constructed to match the number of days the tournament lasted in June and July 2010, assuming that tourists would have arrived no later than 10 June 2010 and counting arrivals until 11 July 2010.

Source: StatsSA (2010).

shortly before the tournament (Baumann, 2010; Business Day, 2010). Some estimates even exceeded 500,000, such as the estimate reportedly made by the LOC midway through the tournament (Naidu and Piliso, 2010). Estimates at the lower end were close to 200,000 (du Plessis and Venter, 2010). On a regional level, a survey conducted by Cape Town Tourism indicated that occupancy levels in Cape Town for the first two weeks of the tournament averaged 34 per cent in the first week of the 2010 FIFA World Cup and 40 per cent in the second week, with positive effects for accommodation in the neighbourhood of Green Point stadium. However, establishments that were further afield were disappointed in the number of reservations (personal communication, Mariette du Toit-Helmbold, 25 June 2010).

High-Frequency Data on Tourist Arrivals

This chapter compares such numbers with evidence from two sources. We use data first on actual arrivals at the international airports and second on

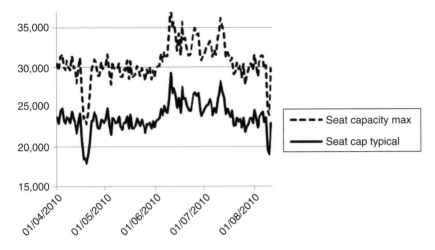

*Figure 27.1   Seat capacity of international flights to South African
international airports, 1 April to 2 August 2010*

occupancy rates in the hotels of the major cities. To begin the analysis, we
note that the number of international plane landings did not increase substantially between June 2009 and June 2010. Daily data on plane landings
at the three South African international airports in Johannesburg (where
the vast majority of international flights arrive), Cape Town and Durban
were collected from the ACSA (Airports Company South Africa) website
(www.acsa.co.za/). Baumann et al. (2009) used similar data in an earlier
paper.

The average number of international arrivals per day for all three
airports on the dates of 10 June (the day before the opening ceremony
and the first day with a visible increase in arrivals) and 11 July (the day
of the 2010 FIFA World Cup final) increased to an average of 133 from
an average of 125 international arrivals in the time period from 22 April
(first normal flight day after Easter) to 9 June: an average addition of eight
plane arrivals per day (+6 per cent).

To calculate the transport capacities, the specific types of planes landing
in South Africa were taken from the ACSA daily observations and combined with the 'typical' and 'maximal' seat capacities (taken from http://
flug.airego.de/, the Aircraft Encyclopaedia – www.flugzeuginfo.net/).

Figure 27.1 shows an increase in the daily seat capacities during the 2010
FIFA World Cup period of some 11 per cent, compared to the time period
from 22 April 2010 to 9 June 2010, before the Cup. In this April–June
period, daily capacity was at about 29,980 seats, whereas it increased to

Table 27.3   Hotel occupancy rates in major cities and regions

	Cape Town	Durban	Gauteng
June 2006	52.5	79.6	68.2
June 2007	55.0	74.2	73.1
June 2008	48.1	74.6	72.5
June 2009	49.5	67.3	54.9
June 2010	51.7	61.8	77.3
Benchmark month*	45.7	70.9	53.9
Tournament month*	64.1	60.0	85.0

Note: * The tournament month was calculated as in Table 27.2.

Source: STR Global.

some 33,350 seats (+3,370) per day in the period from 10 June 2010 (the day before the opening ceremony and the first day showing a significant increase) to 11 July (the day of the World Cup final). Assuming that the available capacity was fully utilized, this implies a maximum increase in capacity of some 107,800 seats.

This modest estimate is consistent with those made by Cape Town Tourism indicating that the number of international arrivals in Cape Town was 44 per cent higher in June 2010 than in June 2009 (personal communication, Mariette du Toit-Helmbold, 25 June 2010). Some observations are necessary. First, the base period is modest: the number of international tourists visiting South Africa in 2009 was sharply down from previous years. Total quarterly arrivals from the USA, Great Britain and Germany, which make up approximately 45 per cent of total air arrivals, reached more than 250,000 visitors during the high season from 2004 until the summers of 2007 and 2008 before dropping (during the first two quarters of 2009) to levels not seen since 2003. Second, Cape Town Tourism's estimate of international arrivals seems to include tourists who initially landed in Johannesburg; thus, their numbers appear to be inflated by double counting.

We now turn to the second method of estimating additional tourism from the 2010 FIFA World Cup, that using hotel occupancy rates. Table 27.3 shows the hotel occupancy rates for the three major centres of Cape Town, Durban and Gauteng for each month of June since 2006 and includes a tournament (2010) and benchmark month (2009) calculation, following the method used in Table 27.2. Figure 27.2 shows the same data, but in terms of the daily frequency for June and July 2010.

The data in Figure 27.2 should be read alongside the information on

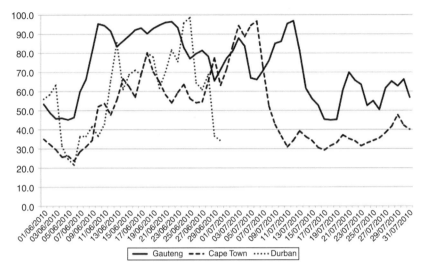

Source: STR Global.

Figure 27.2   Hotel occupancy rates (%) in the major cities, June/July 2010

capacity expansion in Table 27.1, which indicates that growth especially occurred in high-end accommodation. Figure 27.2 shows the extent to which 2010 FIFA World Cup visitors used the Gauteng region as their base for the tournament because of the number of stadiums in close proximity and the easy access by road and air to more distant stadiums. The tournament month is a useful abstraction for the purposes of identifying those tourists who arrived for the FIFA World Cup. The daily hotel occupancy data for Gauteng showed an increase over the comparable day in 2009 only from 10 June onwards. In Cape Town the difference only emerges from 11 June onwards. The Gauteng hotels were fully booked on the day of the finals, but within two days had returned to the level of 2009. As mentioned above, the data on seat capacity for international flights support the same abstraction.

Combining the occupancy rates for the tournament and benchmark months with the number of available hotel rooms in the major cities[1] gives a figure of 11,684 additional hotel rooms occupied on an average day during the tournament (and an additional 5,842 occupied guest-house rooms). To complete the calculation we need an assumption about the average duration of stay for international visitors. We base our assumption on survey data from the 2006 FIFA World Cup in Germany, showing that European visitors stayed on average six days while other overseas international guests stayed 11.4 days on average. For the South African tournament we assume that African visitors stayed on average for six days, other overseas visitors 11.4 days, and that South African visitors who stayed in hotels did so for two nights on average. Finally, we assume that 80 per cent of the rooms were occupied by two persons and the remainder by single occupants. With these data and assumptions, the estimated number of additional overseas arrivals is 65,000, with another 26,000 African arrivals and 72,000 South African tourists.

Explanations for the Lower than Expected Turnout

A number of factors are likely to have played a role in the disappointingly small tourism impact of the 2010 FIFA World Cup. The first is the international recession. Our data on arrivals compare the 2010 FIFA World Cup period to the days before and after the event, which were affected by the crisis in the same manner. Without the crisis, the number of tourists before, during and after the event could have been substantially larger. The effect of the recession may have been accentuated by South Africa's geographic location, being a long-haul (and therefore higher cost) destination for Europeans, Asians and Americans.

The scholarly literature lists other potential reasons for major sporting events having only a limited impact on tourism (for example, Coates and Humphreys, 2000; Baade and Matheson, 2004; Allmers and Maennig, 2009; du Plessis and Maennig, 2009; Maennig and du Plessis, 2009): One important reason is the crowding-out of 'normal' tourists due to the noise, traffic jams and other disturbances. In the South African case, there was considerable crowding-out in the hunting sector, a market whose peak season is typically June (The Star, 2010), because overseas hunters found that flights to South Africa were now more expensive and some were fully booked, and that transport facilities were now catering for the tournament and were thus very expensive to divert to the game lodges.

Two other reasons may apply in the special case of South Africa. First, the international perception of the country as a dangerous location may have had a higher than expected negative effect on the increase in tourist arrivals. Second, price crowding-out is sometimes mentioned in the scholarly literature but rarely supported with data. In the case of South Africa, a special form of price crowding-out may have been at work: self-defeating expectations, that is, the adverse impact on actual arrivals of exaggerated price rises in the tourist sector, where these price rises were based on the *ex ante* anticipation of massive tourist arrivals.

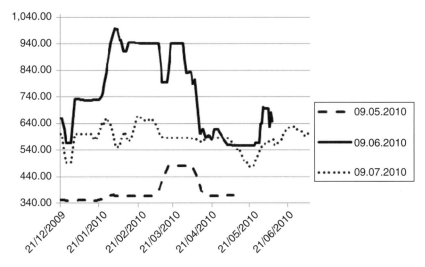

Figure 27.3a   Prices for Frankfurt–Johannesburg flight connections for flight dates 9 May, 9 June and 9 July (seven-day moving average of the cheapest prices between 15 December, 2009 and 3 August, 2010, €)

Figures 27.3a and 27.3b show the seven-day moving averages (to adjust for systematic weekly fluctuations) of prices for flights from Frankfurt, London, Madrid, Paris and Rome to Johannesburg on fixed days during, before and after the 2010 FIFA World Cup. These airports are the international hubs of the nations that were expected to have the most influential soccer teams in the tournament.

The cheapest prices of such flights were collected on a daily basis beginning on 15 December 2009 via the publicly available internet portal www.billigflieger.de/, a German online booking site. In the case of the flight connection between Frankfurt and Johannesburg on 9 May 2010 (a date well before the 2010 FIFA World Cup) the supply price between 15 December 2009 and 8 May 2010 varied between €350 and €480, with an average of €387.2. For the same flight on 9 June 2010, prices were over €900 during the period between end of January and the end of March. From that time forwards, there was a downward correction in flight prices, possibly due to a combination of an intervention by South Africa's Competition Commission and the airlines' realization that they would not be able to reach sufficient bookings for their flights at the inflated fares. However, even after this correction, prices for flights were consistently at least 50 per cent higher than in the non-World Cup periods.

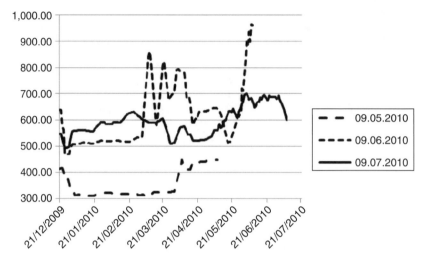

Figure 27.3b   Prices for London–Johannesburg flight connections for flight dates 9 May, 9 June and 9 July (seven-day moving average of the cheapest prices between 15 December, 2009 and 3 August, 2010, €)

Flight prices for the other connections between the major European airports and Johannesburg had similar developments to the one described for Frankfurt. We restrict ourselves to providing an additional Figure 27.3b for London.[2] The price crowding-out effect indicated by these figures may have been biased downwards because our statistics exclusively use the cheapest flights and do not control for the number of seats available at this price.

An additional factor that could have constrained demand was the relatively high local tourist sector prices (in dollar terms). To illustrate this factor, Figure 27.4 shows the Econex/Portfolio real price index in rand and dollar terms.[3] Rand appreciation over recent years also led to higher dollar prices for international tourists.

Further, higher than normal hotel prices may have affected the number of tourists visiting the 2010 FIFA World Cup. As with the 2006 FIFA World Cup, there is clear evidence that the inflexibility of the tournament schedule improved the pricing power (in local currency) of hotels more than is usual for the season, and that improvement is reflected in the average room rates (in rand, adjusted for inflation) reported in Table 27.4. Figure 27.5 shows the room rates on a daily basis for the tournament month. The table shows the actual average rand amount charged in these cities per room.

Although the hotel prices reported above were the actual prices, the decision to visit South Africa was made weeks and months ahead of

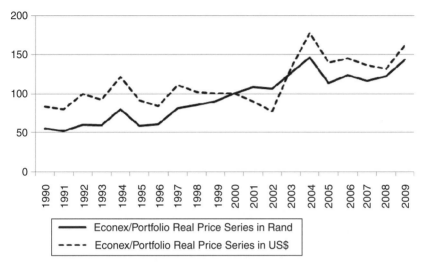

Source: Econex.

Figure 27.4   Rand and dollar tourist sector price index

Table 27.4   Average room rates per day (in rand constant 2006 prices)

	Cape Town	Durban	Gauteng
June 2006	649	549	544
June 2007	724	626	670
June 2008	805	733	810
June 2009	909	832	959
June 2010	1,983	1,429	2,182
Benchmark month*	1,275	827	1,461
Tournament month*	2,670	1,254	3,075

Note: * The tournament month was calculated as in Table 27.2.

Source: STR Global.

time based on prices quoted at that time. We recorded the lowest-quoted prices for hotel rooms collected on a daily basis since 30 April 2010 via the publicly available internet portal www.hrs.de (the data from this site are similar to these obtainable from www.hotels.com). Figure 27.6 shows that the lowest prices for accommodation in Johannesburg for 9 May (this date near to but outside of the 2010 FIFA World Cup period) was more or

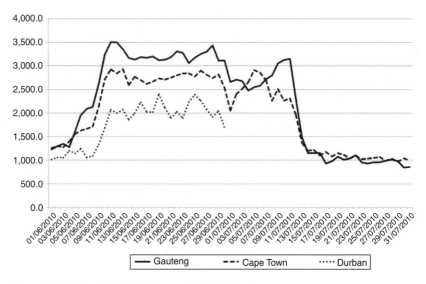

Note: Daily data for July 2010 not available for Durban.

Source: STR Global.

*Figure 27.5   Average room rates (current rand on a daily basis for June/
July 2010)*

less constantly between €45 and €50 per night over the entire data period. By contrast, during the World Cup period it was not possible to book accommodation for less than €120 per night at any point after late April. Advertisements for the cheapest accommodation increased to approximately €700 for the night of 25 June if booked one month in advance. Accommodation suppliers then obviously realized that they would not find sufficient bookings at such a high price and reduced supply prices, but subsequently it was still not possible to book accommodation for 25 June for less than approximately €260. Similar observations are available for the other 2010 FIFA World Cup cities. The same applies to the price quotations for car rentals.[4]

Air carriers, car rental agents and hoteliers enjoyed an enhanced price environment during the 2010 FIFA World Cup, with rates doubling and tripling. Restaurants are also likely to have profited handsomely, though we have no data to confirm this.

The negligible increase in the capacities of air carriers in combination with the sharp price increases depicts an inelastic supply and high windfall profits for the sector. It remains unclear, however, whether the modest supply reaction by airlines was due to (i) internal information that, on

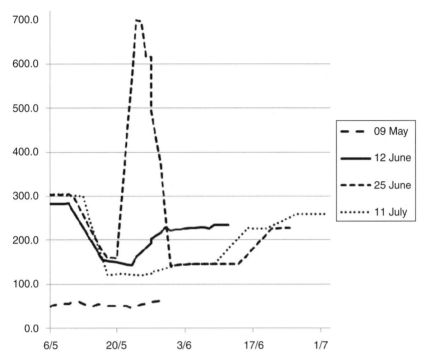

Figure 27.6   *Prices for hotel accommodation in Johannesburg for the dates 9 May, 12 June, 25 June and 11 July (seven-day moving average of the cheapest prices between 30 April, 2010 and 3 August, 2010, €)*

the basis of their pricing strategies, no additional supply would be needed or (ii) that the inherent logistical costs of changing the flight schedules would have been too high to increase supply (personal communication, Mrs Weber, the personal assistant to Joachim Hunold, CEO, Air Berlin, 29 July 2010).

The economy of a host nation may well experience increased income from such price effects, that is, higher prices may be accompanied by higher salaries. But slack labour market conditions made it unlikely that labour would benefit greatly. Indeed, non-agricultural wages in South Africa increased on average by only 1.4 per cent during the second quarter of 2010, compared with an average quarterly increase of 3.4 per cent over the preceding four quarters using seasonally adjusted data from the South African Reserve Bank's quarterly bulletin.

In the case of airfares, most of the profit (with the exception of South

African Airways flights) clearly went abroad. In the case of the hotel industry, no data on the capital shares of foreign investors are available, but at least in the case of the international hotel chains a high proportion of the profit did not stay in South Africa (Matheson, 2009). A similar argument applies for car rental firms.

The modest and sector-specific economic benefits mentioned above are especially frustrating given the urgent need for poverty alleviation in a society with deep inequalities and widespread underdevelopment (see Van der Berg, 2010, for a description of these socio-economic challenges). Against this background, winning the bid to host the tournament raised expectations of a significant impact on poverty and inequality. So optimistic were these expectations that Czeglédy (2009) identifies indications of millenarianism.

Pillay and Bass (2009), among others, also cautioned against raising expectations and articulating the expected benefits of the tournament exclusively in pro-poor terms. Cornelissen (2009) added the concern that the legacy of the tournament would reinforce existing spatial inequalities. But these words of caution did not resonate widely, and the result was frustration with the ultimately modest impact on poverty and inequality in South Africa.

In summary, according to our data on additional international plane landings, we do not see any evidence for a net increase in World Cup-related overseas tourism beyond approximately 90,000 to 118,000 persons. This range is consistent with StatsSA's estimated increment of 109,600 for the tournament month shown in Table 27.2. Even in 2010 FIFA World Cup cities, occupancy rates were far from 100 per cent during the event period, implying that the South African economy could not make full use of its resources.

Additionally, even this modest positive effect in June and July does not prove that the tournament had a positive tourism effect because 'time-switcher' effects have to be considered. In the cases of the 2004 European Cup in Portugal and the 2006 FIFA World Cup in Germany, increased numbers of international tourists in the event months of June and July were partly or fully offset by lower numbers in other months. It is conceivable that tourists who would otherwise have travelled to the host nations during May or August transferred their stay in a utility-maximizing way to the FIFA World Cup months (Allmers and Maennig, 2009).

Our results confirm previous studies on the effects of mega sporting events which, almost without exception, find that the *ex post* measurable sport events effects are significantly below the effects claimed *ex ante* by their organizers and sponsors, and that these events generate scarcely any significant tourism, income or employment impact (for example, Baumann et al., 2009, and the literature cited therein).

However, our results go a step further. They make it clear that the overly optimistic forecasts themselves may have contributed to the smaller than expected tourism effect. The over-confident expectations of the tourism industry, as reflected in its pricing behaviour, were self-defeating because they dampened the enthusiasm of potential visitors and thus also the potential increase in the number who visited South Africa for the Cup.

3 OTHER SHORT-TERM ECONOMIC EFFECTS AND POTENTIAL LONG-TERM EFFECTS

A feel-good effect might be the most evident positive outcome of a mega sporting event. Nevertheless, only a few studies attempt to evaluate this phenomenon of benefiting from an event without active attendance at the stadium, and they do so using the concept of willingness to pay. Before the 2006 FIFA World Cup, only one out of five Germans surveyed revealed a 'willingness to pay' (WTP) greater than zero for the 2006 FIFA World Cup to take place in Germany (Heyne et al., 2010). On average, the WTP was €4.26 per person which, with 82 million inhabitants, corresponds to approximately €351.5 million. After the 2006 FIFA World Cup, the proportion with a positive WTP had increased to 42.6 per cent and the average was €10.0, amounting to €830.8 million for the whole country. It follows that this feel-good effect was one of the largest effects of the World Cup.

While the feel-good effect refers most obviously to the impact on locals, there is a related potential impact on foreigners due to an improved international perception of the host country (du Plessis and Maennig, 2007), which Matheson (2006) argues is one of the 'major intangible benefits of mega-events claimed by sports boosters'. Although the host country enjoyed extensive media coverage during the tournament, it remains difficult to quantify such awareness effects. We propose to use two innovative sources of information, drawing on the rising importance of the internet as a source of news and information, on the one hand, and social networks as an increasingly important platform for expressing interest and association, on the other. Both are examples of a new computational social science that uses the data spontaneously generated by macro social networks as an alternative to data collected purposefully by a statistical agency or researcher (Lazer et al., 2009).

Figure 27.7 uses the number of Google hits as a proxy for awareness and plots the index of the number of Google hits for the search words 'South Africa', 'Germany', 'Namibia' and 'World Cup 2010' for each day from

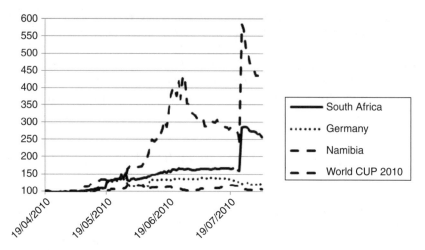

Figure 27.7   Index of the number of Google hits, 19 April 2010 to 3 August 2010

19 April 2010 to 3 August 2010. The data are a visual representation of the rising international awareness of South Africa, showing an increase of approximately 60 per cent during the 2010 FIFA World Cup period compared with April 2010. The same measure of awareness for Germany, possibly due to its national team performance, increased by up to approximately 40 per cent, whereas for Namibia it did not increase by more than 20 per cent for any day in the observation period. The biggest increase in awareness was for the 2010 FIFA World Cup tournament itself, which might suggest that only part of the awareness of major events is directed towards the host country.

Google hits are a supply-side indicator, however, because Google records the number of webpages relevant to a given keyword. From a media economics perspective, the demand side is also interesting.

As a proxy for the demand side, we counted the number of members of the Facebook groups 'South Africa 2010', 'My South Africa', 'Namibia' and 'Super Bowl'. Figure 27.8 plots the index of the number of members of these Facebook groups for each day from 19 April to 3 August 2010 and shows that the number of members of 'My South Africa' increased by approximately 20 per cent, well above the near-to-zero increase of the Facebook group 'Super Bowl'. It must be mentioned, however, that the number of members of the group 'Namibia' increased by nearly the same amount. In addition, the number of members in the group 'South Africa 2010' increased by more than 170 per cent, again relativizing the awareness effect for the host country.[5]

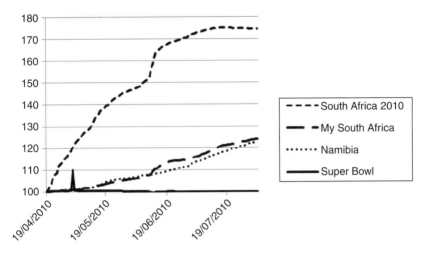

*Figure 27.8   Index of the number of members in Facebook groups,
19 April 2010 to 3 August 2010*

4   CONCLUSION

The central claim of this chapter is that the economic impact of international tourist arrivals during a FIFA World Cup, such as the 2010 tournament in South Africa, will be considerably smaller, at least in the short term, than was widely expected prior to the event. This phenomenon is not unique to South Africa, but is the general result of most *ex post* analyses of FIFA World Cups. Our focus was on accurately estimating tourist arrivals during the 2010 FIFA World Cup, because any immediate economic impact must derive from these arrivals. We found a modest number of arrivals – a net increase in tourists of some 90,000 to 108,000 persons, which was much lower than the forecasts. This result is consistent with du Plessis and Venter's (2010) estimated tourist arrivals, which they used to calculate that the likely short-term impact of the tournament was 0.1 per cent of GDP.

It seems plausible that higher supply prices, in anticipation of very high demand during the event, contributed to the modest number via a crowding-out effect. Prices for flights to South Africa during the 2010 FIFA World Cup period were three times higher than normal for bookings made between the end of January and the end of March 2010. Although these prices dropped closer to the tournament, they remained at least 50 per cent higher than normal. A similar observation can be made for hotel prices and for price quotations for car rentals. Partly because of South Africa's elastic labour supply and the near-zero capacity effects of the 2010 FIFA World Cup, the price increases translated less into higher salaries than into higher profits for capital owners and foreign investors.

Overly optimistic forecasts of *ex ante* impact studies of approximately 400,000 overseas visitors may have induced this pricing behaviour that damped down the potential increase in the number of tourists. This is not an argument against the appropriate use of *ex ante* impact studies. On the contrary, *ex ante* quantitative forecasts or measurements play an important role in sport event economics as in other economic areas. But it is a warning that *ex ante* economic impact studies with overly optimistic claims may induce self-defeating expectations. At present, it is not possible to determine the likelihood of positive medium- or long-term effects of the 2010 FIFA World Cup; on the basis of empirical studies of comparable sporting events, it appears that such effects cannot be guaranteed (for example, Jasmand and Maennig, 2007; Hagn and Maennig, 2008; Matheson, 2009; Zimbalist, 2010, and various chapters in this book).

Although the 'core' criteria of economic performance (such as income and employment) are usually the focus of impact studies, modern economics recognizes other effects as well, such as awareness and image effects. Our study indicated a rising awareness of South Africa that may well be one of the largest short-term economic effects of the tournament. There is widespread agreement that the 2010 FIFA World Cup was successfully hosted by friendly, relaxed and committed South Africans. The country takes pride in having passed such an important test under the scrutiny of the world (Schifferle, 2010). The positive media coverage and visual documentation of an incident-free 2010 FIFA World Cup has given South Africa a chance to reintroduce itself to the rest of the world. The depressing stories about crime, racial tension, HIV and power shortages have been displaced by a host of positive new images. This could translate into increased tourism and increased trade and attract foreign direct investors.

A channel by which the tournament could raise the long-term growth of the South African economy is through the impact on local self-confidence. This new self-confidence is manifested in sporting affairs, as the revived plans to host the Olympic Games may indicate. Beyond this, a poll conducted among 400 South Africans shows that 85 per cent of South Africans now have more hope for a positive future for all South Africans than they did before the tournament (Rasmussen, 2010). In a 2011 poll, 70 per cent of South Africans said they now believe the World Cup actually brought the country economic disadvantages, but 78 per cent think that the World Cup also brought social cohesion, gave people the opportunity to socialize with other race groups and unified South Africa.[6]

While the authors have little doubt about the potential for long-term positive economic effects, it is too early to find supporting statistical evidence. If our expectations also prove to be too sanguine, then South African Minister of Sport Mankenkhesi Stofile may have been correct when he said in 2007: 'The memory of that tournament will be a lasting legacy'; in other words, we shall have to look to less tangible benefits of such events rather than hope for substantial economic enrichment.

NOTES

* An earlier version of this chapter was published in *Development Southern Africa*, **28** (3), September 2011, 349–65.
1. The data in Table 27.1 were aggregated at the national level, while the occupancy rates related to Gauteng, Cape Town and Durban. During June 2010 there were 23,518 hotel beds available in Gauteng, 16,245 in Cape Town and 10,546 in Durban.
2. However, European data are available from the authors on request.
3. The Econex/Portfolio price index reflects the price of accommodation in the tourist sector in South Africa.
4. Details available from the authors on request.
5. The absolute starting numbers on 19 April 2010 were 'South Africa 2010' = 9,496, 'My South Africa' = 23,216, 'Namibia' = 8,801 and 'Super Bowl' = 21,012.
6. See http://www.hsrc.ac.za/HSRC_Review_Article-245.phtml (accessed 26 July 2011).

REFERENCES

Allmers, S. and W. Maennig (2009), 'Economic impacts of the FIFA Soccer World Cups in France 1998, Germany 2006, and outlook for South Africa 2010', *Eastern Economic Journal*, **35**, 500–519.
Baade, R.A. and V.A. Matheson (2004), 'The quest for the Cup: assessing the economic impact of the World Cup', *Regional Studies*, **38** (4), 343–54.
Baumann, J. (2010), 'Fewer World Cup visitors than expected', *Business Day*, 23 June, p. 4.
Baumann, R.W., V.A. Matheson and C. Muroi (2009), 'Bowling in Hawaii: examining the effectiveness of sports-based tourism strategies', *Journal of Sports Economics*, **10** (1), 107–23.
Business Day (2010), 'The numbers don't add up', *Business Day*, 23 June, p. 1.
Coates, D. and B.R. Humphreys, (2000), 'The stadium gambit and local economic development', *Regulation: The Cato Review of Business and Government*, **23** (2), 15–20.
Cokayne, R. (2010), 'Hotels may go bust as room rates fall', *The Star*, 18 June, p. 4.
Cornelissen, S. (2009), 'Sport, mega-events and urban tourism: exploring the patterns, constraints and prospects of the 2010 World Cup', in U. Pillay, R. Tomlinson and O. Bass, (eds), *Development and Dreams: The Urban Legacy of the 2010 Football World Cup*, Cape Town: HSRC (Human Sciences Research Council) Press, pp. 131–52.
Czeglédy, A.P. (2009), 'Urban dreams: the 2010 Football World Cup and expectations of benefit in Johannesburg', in U. Pillay, R. Tomlinson and O. Bass (eds), *Development and Dreams: The Urban Legacy of the 2010 Football World Cup*, Cape Town: HSRC (Human Sciences Research Council) Press, pp. 225–45.
Darkey, D. and A. Horn (2009), 'Homing in(n) on the economic benefits of 2010 FIFA World Cup: opportunities for and misgivings of bed-and-breakfast operators in Gauteng, South Africa', *Urban Forum*, **20** (1), 77–91.

DoT (Department of Tourism) (2010), *Quick Facts: Government Preparations. 2010 FIFA World Cup South Africa*, Pretoria: Government Printer.

Du Plessis, S. and W. Maennig (2007), 'World Cup 2010, South African economic perspectives and policy challenges informed by the experience of Germany 2006', *Contemporary Economic Policy*, **25** (4), 578–90.

Du Plessis, S. and W. Maennig (2009), 'South Africa 2010: initial dreams and sobering economic perspectives', in U. Pillay, R. Tomlinson and O. Bass (eds), *Development and Dreams: The Urban Legacy of the 2010 Football World Cup*, Cape Town : HSRC (Human Sciences Research Council) Press, pp. 55–75.

Du Plessis, S. and C. Venter (2010), 'The home team scores! A first assessment of the economic impact of World Cup 2010', Proceedings of the 10th International Hamburg Symposium on Sport and Economics, Hamburg, Germany, 16–17 July.

Grant Thornton (2004), '2010 Soccer World Cup facts you should know', Grant Thornton, Johannesburg, available at: www.gauteng.net/research/pdf/soccer1.pdf (accessed 22 July 2006).

Grant Thornton (2008), 'The economic impact of the 2010 Soccer World Cup', Grant Thornton, Johannesburg.

Hagn, F. and W. Maennig (2008), 'Employment effects of the Football World Cup 1974 in Germany', *Labour Economics*, **15** (5), 1062–75.

Heyne, M., W. Maennig and B. Süssmuth (2010), 'Induced civic pride and integration', *Oxford Bulletin of Economics and Statistics*, **72** (2), 202–20.

Jasmand, S. and W. Maennig (2007), 'Regional income and employment effects of the 1972 Munich Olympic Summer Games', *Regional Studies*, **42** (7), 991–1002.

Lapper, R. and R. Blitz (2010), 'South Africa prove wrong World Cup sceptics', *Financial Times*, 9 July, p. 5.

Lazer, D., A. Pentland, L. Adamic, S. Aral, A.L. Barabasi, D. Brewer, N. Christakis, N. Contractor, J. Fowler, M. Gutmann, T. Jebara, G. King, M. Macy, D. Roy, and M. Van Alstyne (2009), 'Computational social science', *Science*, **323** (5915), 721–3.

Maennig, W. and S. du Plessis, (2009), 'Sport stadia, sporting events and urban development: international experience and the ambitions of Durban', *Urban Forum*, **20** (1), 61–76.

Matheson, V.A. (2006), 'Mega-events: the effect of the world's biggest sporting events on local, regional, and national economics', AIES Working Paper series, No. 06-22, Department of Economics, College of the Holy Cross, Worcester, MA.

Matheson, V.A. (2009), 'Economic multipliers and mega-event analysis', *International Journal of Sport Finance*, **4** (1), 107–23.

Naidu, B. and S. Piliso (2010), 'World Cup's R6.5 bn bonanza', *The Sunday Times*, 20 June, p. 1.

Pam Golding (2010), Newsletter, Pam Golding Tourism & Hospitality Consulting, Johannesburg, June.

Pedroncelli, P. (2010), 'The LOC is pleased with preparations for the World Cup', available at: www.goal.com/en/news/1863/world-cup-2010/2010/04/09/1870139/world-cup-2010-organising-committee-set-to-deliver-world-cup (accessed 12 July 2010).

Pillay, U. and O. Bass (2009), 'Mega-events as a response to poverty reduction: the 2010 World-Cup and urban development', in U. Pillay, R. Tomlinson and O. Bass (eds), *Development and Dreams: The Urban Legacy of the 2010 Football World Cup*, Cape Town: HSRC (Human Sciences Research Council) Press, pp. 75–95.

Rasmussen, K. (2010), 'World Cup afterthoughts', available at: www.playthegame.org/news/detailed/world-cup-afterthoughts-4888.html (accessed 18 July 2010).

Reeves, N. (2010), 'Champions Spain back home: Blatter praises South Africa', *The Sydney Morning Herald*, 12 July, available at: http://news.smh.com.au/breaking-news-world/champions-spain-back-home-blatter-praises-safrica-20100712-107t1.html (accessed 13 July 2010).

Schifferle, T. (2010), 'Spain: Champion of an ambivalent World Cup', *Sport Intern*, **42** (20100712), 1.

Spronk, K. and J. Fourie (2010), 'South African mega-events and their impact on tourism', Stellenbosch Economic Working Papers 03/10, Stellenbosch University.

Star, The (2010), 'Hunting industry maimed by pricey tourism event', *The Star*, 23 June, p. 17.

StatsSA (Statistics South Africa) (2010), 'Tourism and migration, April 2010', Statistics South Africa, Pretoria, available at: www.statssa.gov.za/publications/statsdownload. asp?ppn=P0351andSCH=4681 (accessed 25 July 2010).

Stofile, M. (2007), 'Opening address' by Sport and Recreation Minister M. Stofile at the International Year of African Football and 2010 World Cup workshop, Pretoria, 7 March.

Tolsi, N. (2010), 'Field of shattered dreams', *Mail & Guardian*, 13 May, p. 10.

Van der Berg, S. (2010), 'Current poverty and income distribution in the context of South African history', Stellenbosch Economic Working Papers 22/10, Stellenbosch University.

Zimbalist, Andrew (2010), 'Is it worth it?', *Finance and Development*, **47** (1), March, 7–12.

28 For a monsoon wedding: Delhi and the Commonwealth Games
Nalin Mehta and Boria Majumdar

1 INTRODUCTION

Delhi's Tihar Jail is reputed to be the largest prison in South Asia. Among its more famous inmates, at the time of writing, is Suresh Kalmadi, Chairman of the Organizing Committee (OC) of the Delhi Commonwealth Games (CWG) 2010, Member of Parliament from Pune and head of the Indian Olympic Association (IOA). He is being prosecuted by India's Central Bureau of Investigation as the 'main accused' in a corruption case for irregularly awarding a time-scoring-result system for the Games to a Swiss company, and has separately been charged with money laundering (Kumar, 2011; Thakur, 2011).[1] Eight other senior officials from the OC's top management, including its former Secretary General and Director General, are also in Tihar Jail and being prosecuted for similar charges of corruption, criminal conspiracy, forging documents and passing them off as genuine in order to fix lucrative contracts they were awarding (Agencies, 2011).[2] The now suspended head of Prasar Bharti, the host broadcaster, and the then head of Doordarshan, the state TV network, have similarly been accused by a government-appointed high level committee (HLC) investigating the Games of providing 'undue benefit' to key private companies, resulting in large losses to the exchequer (High Level Committee, 2011a, pp. 3, 5, 53–4).

Probing the massive infrastructure building that went into the Games, the same government committee, appointed after a public outcry and led by senior auditors, also found Delhi's state government and its various civic agencies guilty in many cases of bad planning, approving ill-conceived estimates and manipulation of contracts. This ultimately translated into 'undue gains' for private contractors in city beautification projects such as street lighting and streetscaping. Among the higher-profile cases is that of the construction of the Games Village where delays are estimated to have led to losses over Rs 2 billion. It was built by a private construction company which, despite delays and cost overruns, was awarded a controversial financial bailout in 2009 by the Delhi Development Authority (DDA). The project was beset by such irregularities that the HLC has advised the prime minister to take action not only against the contractor but also against several key public servants (High Level Committee, 2011b).

Politically, the CWG were a disaster. At the federal level, the United Progressive Alliance coalition government of Prime Minister Manmohan Singh which, against most predictions, had won a renewed and stronger mandate for a second term in the 2009 national elections, found itself beset by major corruption allegations by the end of 2010. Although the federal government did not directly run the Games, the public spectacle of shoddy organization and the brazenness of some of the organizers in making money had turned into a major political embarrassment well before the Games took place in October 2010. By early 2011, separate scandals such as kickbacks in allocating telecom spectrum contributed to the image of a government overrun by graft and it became the target of a major civil society campaign to bring in a new Anti-Corruption Bill in Parliament. The clear misuse of public funds in the CWG was a key element of the discourse. Similarly, the provincial government of Delhi too found itself enmeshed in similar charges, with the Opposition demanding the resignation of the Chief Minister (Pandey, 2011).[3]

The investigations into wrongdoing by the organizers will go on for a long time but it was not supposed to end like this. For their organizers, the Games were meant to be about projecting the capital city as a shining beacon of India's global power play, a notion that was at the heart of Delhi's bid for the CWG from the beginning. Internal OC documents are unambiguous on the 'bidding rationale' of Delhi 2010:

> *These Games will showcase, New Delhi, the capital of India, to the world and promote it as a global city of an emerging economic power.* These Games will act as a medium for the development of the country. (OC, 2007, p. 14; added italics)

Delhi wanted to do a Beijing, albeit on a smaller scale. One of the key missions of the OC is to project India as 'an economic superpower' (OC, 2006, p. 53) and in late 2006, its officials made a presentation to Prime Minister Manmohan Singh. Describing this presentation, the Committee's official newsletter listed six points, in a slide entitled 'impact of hosting the Games'. Only one made a cursory reference to sport. The rest of the listed aims, laid down in those pre-global recession days, are revealing: 'enhance the image and stature of India', 'project Delhi as a global destination', 'act as a catalyst for sustained development of infrastructure', 'add to the prevailing upbeat mood in the Indian economy' and 'create opportunities for trade, business and investment for Delhi and India' (*Games News*, 2006, p. 10). It could have been written by the Ministry of Tourism or Commerce.

Yet, the enduring image of the CWG in 2010 for most observers in Delhi was the pictures of filthy toilets in the athletes' village that flashed around the world just before the Games started. Such was the public anger that the OC chairman was booed at the opening ceremony in Delhi. By the time the Games ended, most Indians were simply relieved that no bridges had collapsed, like the pedestrian bridge outside a stadium that collapsed just days before the Games started. After a year of only bad news in the lead-up to the Games, the simple fact that nothing went overtly wrong during the 12 days of the Games, that the sporting events went off without a hitch and that India did well on the medals tally, convinced many that the Games were indeed successful.

Yet, the legacy of waste, corruption, tremendous cost overruns and bad planning speaks for itself. This is what this chapter seeks to delineate in order to shed light on why the Delhi Games became so contentious.

2   'MANY THINGS WERE NOT FACTORED IN': THE COSTS

How much did the 2010 CWG cost? That is the first big question this chapter examines. It is not an easy question to answer because the work was spread across diverse sectors and the money was being spent by a bewildering morass of multiple agencies. To enter the story of the CWG is to enter into a labyrinth of overlapping controls – Ministry of Sports, Ministry of Home Affairs, Ministry of Urban Development, Ministry of Tourism, Delhi government, Planning Commission, New Delhi Municipal Corporation (NDMC), Municipal Corporation of Delhi (MCD), Sports Authority of India (SAI), the DDA and so on. There are several HLCs to coordinate their work[4] but many things remain unclear to the very end.[5] The result is that even many among those involved in the Games organization did not have the full financial picture in front of them, with each government agency pursuing its own targets.

Parliamentary records show that at the time of government approval for the Games, the Games budget estimate had been only INR[6] 6.17 billion.[7] This was a very preliminary original estimate and the Vajpayee government agreed to fund any future shortfalls between revenue and expenditure.[8] It was a virtual blank cheque. By March 2003, when Delhi submitted its official bid, the Games costs estimates had tripled to INR 18.9 billion ('Updated Bid Document', 2003, pp. 174–8). As the then Sports Minister Sunil Dutt told Parliament in 2004, even at the time everybody knew that these were only early projections that could only go up later.[9] What is shocking is just how much they went up by. Table 28.1 shows how the budgets have kept on rising, sector by sector ever since.

Table 28.1 CWG estimated costs (2003–08) (in INR billion)

Year	Operating expense	Infrastructure	Publicity in Melbourne (Bollywood show)	Security/services	Pune Youth Games	Athletes	Others/overlays	Broad-casting	Total
Dec. 2002	3.990	2.180							6.17
Mar. 2003	6.555	10.850		1.548					18.95
Dec. 2005	8.960	33.764							42.72
Nov. 2006	7.670	26.690	0.29	2.640	1.100	3.00			41.39
Aug. 2007	7.670	27.070	0.29	2.640	1.100	6.61			45.38
Dec. 2008	16.280	41.090	0.29	2.770	3.514[1]	6.78	4.00	4.63	79.36
Jul. 2009	16.280	97.640	0.29	2.770	3.514	6.78[2]	4.05[3]	4.63	135.95
Final 2009 – incl. Delhi govt infrastructure cost estimates	16.280	671.810	0.29	2.770	3.514	6.78		4.63	706.08

Notes: 2006 figures were estimated by Government of India with a variation of 10–25% under various heads. Government of India provided flexibility of up to 15 per cent in OC budget of Rs 6.76 billion to Ministry of Youth Affairs and Sports, up to 10 per cent to Sports Authority of India budget of Rs 10 billion and 25 per cent variation to DDA in its Rs 3.25 billion budget for the Games Village. In May 2007, a flexibility of Rs 3.0 billion was envisaged in the overall budget.

1. This includes cost of civic infrastructure (Rs 1.34 billion) and security (Rs 0.07 billion) for Commonwealth Youth Games.
2. CAG 2009 did not have a separate category for expenditure on 'Athletes' in its activity breakdown (though it did note it in its funding sources) and this figure is from parliamentary records cited above.
3. CAG 2009 listed a total of Rs 7.49 billion in the 'Others' column. We assume that it included Rs 3.44 billion that were spent on the Pune Youth Commonwealth Games as CAG noted this figure in a separate chart on funding sources. Since we have a separate column for the Pune Games here, we have subtracted that amount from said column.

Table 28.1 (continued)

Sources: OC data for 2003 are from 'Updated Bid Document' (2003, pp. 174–8). The 2002 and 2003 government data are from Prithviraj Chavan, Unstarred Question No. 1261 4 August.

Data for 2005 are from Oscar Fernandes, Minister of State (Independent Charge) Statistics & Programme Implementation, Youth Affairs and Sports and Overseas Indian Affairs, Government of India, Rajya Sabha Unstarred Question No. 3347 (asked by E.M. Sudarsana Natchiappan), answered on 22 December 2005, 'Plan for Commonwealth Games'. Rs 8.96 billion (US$199 million) was the Games operating budget worked out in 2005 by the OC. This was based on CGF Manuals/Regulations, Host City Contract Obligations and key inputs such as air fares, hotel/transport costs, catering costs, and so on from service providers. The OC first submitted its budget for recommendations by the sports and finance ministries in September 2005. On 30 May 2006, the Finance Ministry, laid down some parameters to appraise the proposal for the consideration of the Expenditure Finance Committee (EFC). On 13 September 2006, the EFC arrived at a revised expenditure figure of US$177.4 million (Rs 7.67 billion), with a provision for escalation up to 15 per cent as against US$199 million (Rs 8.96 billion). See OC (2006, pp. 46–47, 200).

Data for 2006 are from Mani Shankar Aiyer, Minister of Panchayati Raj, and Youth Affairs and Sports and Development of North-East Region, Government of India, Rajya Sabha Unstarred Question No. 239 (asked by C. Perumal and Janardhana Poojary), answered on 23 November 2006, 'Creation of Infrastructure for the Commonwealth Games'. Annexure II; Mani Shankar Aiyer, Minister of Panchayati Raj, Youth Affairs and Sports and Development of North-Eastern Region, Government of India, Rajya Sabha Unstarred Question No. 2722 (asked by Rajeev Chandrashekhar), answered on 26 April 2007, 'Status of Preparation for the Commonwealth Games'. For more information also see Oscar Fernandes, Minister of State (Independent Charge) Statistics & Programme Implementation, Youth Affairs and Sports and Overseas Indian Affairs, Government of India, Lok Sabha Unstarred Question No. 70 (asked by Virendra Kumar, Chandrakant Bhaurao Khaire, Sanat Kumar Mandal and Virchandra Paswan), answered on 23 November 2005, 'Commonwealth Games 2010'; Mani Shankar Aiyer, Minister of Panchayati Raj, and Youth Affairs and Sports and Development of North-Eastern Region, Government of India, Lok Sabha Unstarred Question No. 2153 (asked by Salarapatty Kuppusamy Kharventan), answered on 6 December 2000, 'Preparation for Commonwealth Games'; Mani Shankar Aiyer, Minister of Panchayati Raj, and Youth Affairs and Sports and Development of North-East Region, Government of India, Rajya Sabha Unstarred Question No. 1788 (asked by Vijay Jawaharlal Darda), answered on 10 August 2006, 'Programme to Showcase India at Melbourne Commonwealth Games'; Mani Shankar Aiyer, Minister of Panchayati Raj, and Youth Affairs and Sports and Development of North-East Region, Government of India, Rajya Sabha Unstarred Question No. 413 (asked by Ram Jethmalani, Shri Ravi Shankar Prasad), answered on 3 May 2007, 'Amount Sanctioned for Commonwealth Games'.

Data for 2007 are from Mani Shankar Aiyer, Minister of Panchayati Raj, Youth Affairs and Sports and Development of North-Eastern Region, Government of India, Rajya Sabha Unstarred Question No 413 (asked by Ravi Shankar Prasad and Ram Jethmalani), answered on 3 May 2007, 'Amount Sanctioned for Commonwealth Games'; Mani Shankar Aiyer, Minister of Panchayati Raj, Youth Affairs and Sports and Development of North-Eastern Region, Government of India, Lok Sabha Unstarred Question No. 4766 (asked by Ramji Lal Suman and Sri Chinta Mohan), answered on 9 May 2007, 'Expenditure for Commonwealth Development, Government of India, Rajya Sabha Unstarred Question No. 3953 (asked by Dara Singh), answered on 10 May 2007, 'CPWD S Blueprint to Facelift Stadium for Commonwealth Games'; Mani Shankar Aiyer,

Minister of Panchayati Raj and Youth Affairs and Sports, Government of India, Rajya Sabha Unstarred Question No. 1358 (asked by Nirmala Deshpande), answered on 23 August 2007, 'Training of Youth for Commonwealth Games'; Mani Shankar Aiyer, Minister of Panchayati Raj and Youth Affairs and Sports, Government of India, Rajya Sabha Unstarred Question No. 1361 (asked by Jai Parkash Aggarwal), answered on 23 August 2007, 'State of Preparedness for Commonwealth Games'; Mani Shankar Aiyer, Minister of Panchayati Raj and Youth Affairs and Sports, Government of India, Rajya Sabha Unstarred Question No. 1980 (asked by T.T.V. Dhinakaran), answered on 30 August 2007, 'Sites for Commonwealth Games'.

Data for 2008 are from Dr M.S. Gill, Minister of State (Independent Charge) for Youth Affairs and Sports, Government of India, Rajya Sabha, Unstarred Question No. 1234 (asked by Jai Prakash Aggarwal), answered on 11 December 2008, 'Expenditure on Commonwealth Games'; Mani Shankar Aiyer, Minister of Panchayati Raj, Youth Affairs and Sports and Development of North-Eastern Region, Government of India, Rajya Sabha Unstarred Question No. 292 (asked by Rajeev Chandrashekhar), answered on 28 February 2008, 'Preparation for Commonwealth Games'; Mani Shankar Aiyer, Minister of Panchayati Raj, Youth Affairs and Sports and Development of North-Eastern Region, Government of India, Rajya Sabha starred Question No. 202 (asked by Dr Vijay Mallya), answered on 13 March 2008, 'Status of Commonwealth Games'; Mani Shankar Aiyer, Minister of Panchayati Raj, Youth Affairs and Sports and Development of North-Eastern Region, Government of India, Lok Sabha starred Question No. 35 (asked by Asaduddin Owaisi and K. Dhanaraju), answered on 27 February 2008, 'Preparation for Commonwealth Games'.

July 2009 data, unless marked otherwise (and except for expenditure on Melbourne Games), are from CAG (2009, pp. 5, 57–58).

Final 2009 cost estimate for infrastructure is from Delhi government, internal note on Commonwealth Games, handed to author by a senior government officer on condition of anonymity, May 2009. The note, we were informed, was prepared by the Office of the Chief Secretary. Subsequently published as Directorate of Information and Publicity (2009).

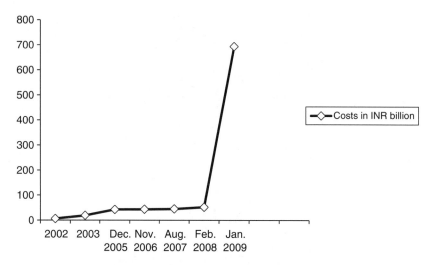

Figure 28.1   CWG 2010: escalation in cost estimates (2003–09) *

By 2005, the estimated costs had shot up by more than six times from the original figure. By February 2008, the then Minister of Sports was estimating a figure of over INR 70 billion and in 2009, the Comptroller and Auditor General provided an estimate of about INR 130 billion. This was more than 20 times the original cost estimate and even this figure did not include spending by many agencies (see Table 28.1 and Figure 28.1).[10] If you were running a company, such sharp cost overruns would, in most cases, be seen as management failure. But this is only half the story.

In early 2009, one of us was discussing these rocketing estimates – INR 51.87 billion in 2008 – with a senior Delhi government official when he dropped a bombshell. We had met about something else over lunch on a lazy Sunday afternoon. The Games came up in passing and he listened to our calculations before calmly pointing out, 'The total Games spending on city infrastructure is INR 65,550 crores [655.50 billion]'. It did not square at all with any of the other financial data. But he was high up in the Chief Minister's inner circle and clearly knew what he was talking about. So we asked him for a detailed breakdown and there it was in fine print:

655.50 billion clearly marked in an internal Delhi government note on what it calls 'Commonwealth Games-related work'. The state government subsequently published these figures officially and when added together with other costs, they pushed the total amount to more than INR 700 billion.

Our problem was that between 2003 and 2008, this estimate on infrastructure spending by the provincial government did not figure in any of the data submitted by successive sports ministers in Parliament or in internal OC records that were made available to us. This new information, prepared by the Delhi Chief Secretary's office, had us completely flummoxed. Why was it invisible?

A close analysis of the financial data reveals that the Games infrastructure budgets submitted in Parliament between 2003 and 2008 had listed only a little over INR 13 billion (for building civic infrastructure) against the Delhi government's name. This was the amount that the Delhi government said it needed extra funding for, asking the Planning Commission[11] for a grant. This was the amount that was reflected in budget estimates by sports ministers in Parliament, instead of the state government's total Games-related estimate. The Delhi government has been spending far more from its own coffers – the Comptroller and Auditor General also pointed this out – only this spending was not noted in any other reporting. The OC and central government budget records, therefore, never reflected the rest of the INR 655.5 billion that was being spent on the Games. If you include this budget, overall Games expenditure shoots up to INR 706 billion. (Table 28.1 and Figure 28.1). This is more than 114 times the original calculation made in 2002.

In a sense, Table 28.1 and Figure 28.1 also illustrate the problems in any budget tabulation of this massive endeavour. Further, the Delhi government is just one of many stakeholders in this whole enterprise. Imagine if there were hidden numbers in other places too. Table 28.2 further breaks up the 655.50 billion that the Delhi government says was spent on CWG-related work.

Some might say that much of the money being spent by the Delhi government would have been spent anyway. Projects such as new power stations account for nearly half of this budget and is it misleading to account for these in a CWG estimate? No, it is not. There is good reason why the Delhi Chief Secretary's office chose to put all these costs under the heading 'Projects Related to CWG 2010'. This is their language, not ours. The fact is that most of this infrastructure construction was fast-tracked only because of the Games and the kind of money that is being spent on Delhi's infrastructure would not have been possible in ordinary times. Power, for instance, was fast-tracked due to the lofty promise to showcase a capital

Table 28.2   Approximate cost of the projects related to CWG 2010 (Delhi government data)*

S.No.	Project	Cost (in INR billion)
1.	Flyovers & Bridges	57.00
2.	Road Over Bridge (ROB)/Road Under Bridge (RUB)	5.20
3.	Stadiums	6.50
4.	High Capacity Bus System (HCBS)	15.18
5.	Augmentation of DTC Fleet	18.00
6.	Construction of Bus Depots	9.00
7.	Widening of Roads Strengthening + Resurfacing	7.00
8.	Street Lighting	6.50
9.	Street-scaping	5.25
10.	Improved Road Signages	1.00
11.	Metro Connectivity	168.87
12.	New Power Generation Plants (instrument from NTPC, DVC, THDC, PPCL, Aravali Power Corporation)	350.00
13.	Water Supply (STP, WTP, Munak Canal etc.)	9.50
14.	Health	0.50
15.	Parking Facility by covering nallahs	4.0
16.	Communication & IT	2.00
	TOTAL	665.50

Note: * Internal note on Commonwealth Games, handed to author by a senior government officer on condition of anonymity, May 2009. The note, we were informed, was prepared by the Office of the Chief Secretary. Subsequently published as Directorate of Information and Publicity (2009).

city with 24-hour power during the Games. As V.K. Verma, Director General of the OC put it:

> For all the huge infrastructure projects which either would have been really slowed down or there would have been a huge time over-run on those projects, we now know that there is a timeline to it. This is a huge legacy advantage for Delhi.
> Now whether it is creation of world class venues or it is the widening of roads and new flyovers or metros or general sprucing up of the city or cityscaping, in every facet – building of new hotels, hospitals, everything is like as if a city is being rebuilt. So that is the big legacy advantage of the Commonwealth Games.[12]

Why does all this matter? Well, for one thing, most of this money is the taxpayer's. The Vajpayee government in 2003 had guaranteed the

Commonwealth Games Federation (CGF) that it would pay for any shortfalls between revenues and expenditure of the OC.[13] We have already seen the huge cost overruns outlined. Remember that even these escalated costs do not cover the entire expenditure. For instance, the billions being spent on building new hotels, on the Games Village by Emaar and elsewhere by the private sector on its own or in public–private partnerships are not part of the budgets reproduced here.[14] Remember also that the Central government has given funds to the OC as an unsecured loan to be repaid only after revenues start coming in. Under the terms of the Games contract, the schedule and other details of this governmental loan 'will be worked out later' (Ministry of Youth Affairs and Sports, 2008, p. 41). The OC, a private non-profit body, has a virtual blank cheque in perpetuity. Suresh Kalmadi, the OC's now arrested chief defended himself, saying:

> We will return every penny we've received from the government by collecting money . . . We will only return the amount given to the Organising Committee. Why should you count the expenses incurred on infrastructure, airport, flyovers, metro, Games Village, malls etc. This will be a legacy from the Games. All these developments move the city 5–10 years forward. (Masand, 2009)

It is a plausible enough assertion, but given the OC's track record and unfulfilled claims so far, it is difficult to be sanguine on when the money would be returned to the government treasury.

There are some who say that cost overruns always happen in big sporting events like this one. The Beijing Olympics was a good example of this and London, which is preparing for the 2012 Olympics, is another. If these cities got their fiscal management so wrong, why is it necessary that Delhi should do so well?

A pertinent example here is Melbourne, which hosted the 2006 Commonwealth Games. Unlike Delhi, Melbourne's total spending of $2,913,157,000 was just 0.6 per cent above its estimate.[15] In contrast, just look at the yawning gap between Delhi's projections and its reality.

The big question is why were the cost estimates so far off the mark? Was it because of mismanagement or because of unavoidable circumstances? Delhi's Chief Minister Sheila Dikshit has a plausible point when she argues that the global downturn is partly responsible: 'There are many stakeholders. The estimates given were approximations but because of the current economic situation things have changed. Both cement and steel are costlier' (Ghosh, 2009).

But see what the Director General (DG) of the OC has to say in his defence. Speaking to us in January 2009, he admitted that the costs had escalated so sharply because the original estimates were based on total ignorance. It was such a chilling admission that it deserves to be reproduced in full:

All of us made a budget. We, the OC made a budget. The Delhi government made a budget, we all made a budget. The first budget was made two years back [so, four years after the Bid was submitted!]. At that time the OC was a fledgling organization. It was finding its feet. Nobody had the past Games' experience. Watching the Games, seeing the Games is one thing but nobody was inside it. The budget was made on very basic things. So if you want to present a very basic Games, the budget was made like that [sic]. Similarly the other arms, the Delhi government – all the budgets were very rudimentary budgets. As you really take the plunge, as you get more and more into it, you begin to look at the other websites, you begin to get more documents as to what was done. Then your estimations also keep going up, so now a more detailed exercise has been done. [sic]

We are in the process of revaluating our budgets and of course input costs have gone high – steel has become more expensive, cement is a problem. These are normal escalations which happen. *But many things were not factored in, to which one has become wiser because everybody is into the Games more, everybody has read more about the Games.* Everybody has got more data and information about the previous Games. So now we are benchmarking with respect to that. [sic][16]

Frankly then, the OC had no idea what it was doing. Delhi hosted the Asian Games in 1982 but there was no institutional memory of it, or if there was, it was not tapped into. The Government of India signed a blank cheque based on unreliable budget estimations made by amateurs who did not seem to know what they were doing.

3   SAME AS PUTTING A MAN ON THE MOON? THE DELHI VERSUS INDIA DEBATE

This brings us to the second big question we seek to address: did Delhi really need the Games at all? If the Delhi government's figures are correct, then the amount being spent on CWG-related development projects in Delhi is more than four times the amount being spent annually on the entire National Rural Health Mission![17] It is a sobering thought. India would have been better off putting these vast resources where they were really needed.

For all its great power pretensions, can a country where 28.3 per cent of its people still live below the poverty line[18] really afford this magnitude of expenditure on a sporting event of this kind? These are important questions, especially for a government that came back to power on the vote of the *aam aadmi* (the common man). The heavy spending on Delhi came at a time when the Manmohan Singh government was dealing with a fiscal deficit of 6.8 per cent of GDP in 2009. Between 2007 and 2009, it was estimated by at least one eminent economist, that total government spending was as much as nine times its income.[19] For a government whose first priorities are to sustain India's high growth trajectory, to focus on social development programmes such as the National Rural Employment Guarantee Scheme, the National Rural Health Mission, the National Rural Livelihood Mission, the new National Food Security Act and so on, does the heavy CWG spending not appear to be too expensive a diversion?

Even before the Games, India's capital city was already one of the most developed regions in the country. Outside the city, many would be justified in thinking that Delhi has always been a favoured place. For instance, the capital already had 1,749 km of road length per 100 sq km area in 1996–97 compared to the national average of 73 km per 100 sq km area in 1995–96 ('Updated Bid Document', 2003, p. 165). Writing in 2000, the social anthropologist Anita Soni (2000, p. 79) pointed out, 'As the supreme centre of political power, Delhi has assured itself of preferential treatment in the allocation of national resources. The Central Plan Outlay for Delhi is more than for the entire State of Assam, for instance'. The capital was already one of the best-funded and most-developed places in India before the Games. Now, it is even more so.

But the Games are more than just a simple arithmetic calculation about resource allocations. They are about a rising India and its global power projection. As the Indian Finance Minister Pranab Mukherjee told Parliament in 2009, 'The Commonwealth Games present the country with an opportunity to showcase our potential as an emerging Asian power'. Therefore, he added another INR 13.6 billion into the Games budget (Majumdar and Mehta 2010, p. 19). International power projection, however badly done, does not happen for free.

The overwhelming impression one gets while sifting through the Games records is of power elites who bought into the idea of the Games without really thinking through its implications and detailed costs. They successfully sold the notion of development through the Games and once that was done, the rest was a *fait accompli*. The 'Games train' had left the station. Studying similar sporting events in the past, sport historian David Black (2008, pp. 472–3) has shown that once such Games are set in motion, the costs of failure 'become too ghastly to contemplate'. This has a dynamic of its own, weighing 'particularly heavily on emerging and/or smaller centres, often hosting second-order events, who do not have an established reputation for successful event management and who may be subject to more or less prejudicial doubts about their ability to do so, particularly in postcolonial contexts'.

Delhi is certainly not a small centre but the argument holds true. It was terrified of failing before the glare of the world's cameras and in that sense, India fell prey to what Havana did for the Latin American Games in 1991,

Kuala Lumpur for the 1998 Commonwealth Games and Athens for the 2004 Olympics.

Social historians of sport have a word for what Delhi is going through: the 'winner's curse' (Cashman et al., 2004, p. 26, Andreff, ch. 4 in this volume). Every city that wins an event like the Commonwealth Games, talks up its benefits, while talking down the downside. This becomes part of a narrative that is progressively enriched, without critical examination. It does benefit a few – but does that really translate into the greater good? (see Black, 2008, p. 473).

Responding to this criticism, the OC's DG has an interesting response, drawing an analogy with India's ongoing moon mission:

> See, it is like saying that whatever money we [India] are spending on putting a man on the moon, from that standard that should not be done. Because what relevance is there for putting a man on the moon when there is poverty? One-third of the country is quite poor. These are extreme notions. The country has to move forward on all facets . . . Everything has to move together.[20]

The mission to the moon, however, is part of a larger scientific thrust with deep-seated strategic and defence implications. India's space programme is run rather well and has had significant successes. If the CWG were so important, why were they run so badly? It is to this question we now turn.

4   OF THE PEOPLE, BY THE PEOPLE BUT 'NOT RESPONSIBLE TO THE PEOPLE'

In December 2008, a lawyer representing the CWG OC made an astounding statement before a Delhi court. Refusing to provide information under the Right to Information Act (RTI), Advocate B.P. Singh, appearing for the committee, argued, '*We are not responsible to people. We get loans from the governments so we are responsible only to them and the government [is in turn] responsible to the public*' (IANS, 2008). The OC was refusing to reveal information about its affairs even though it is funded almost entirely by the government and *despite* strictures from the Sports Ministry (Sood, 2008).

It was an extraordinary argument to make, and rather revealing about the proprietary mindset of those who were running the show. The Games are ostensibly about bettering Delhi but here were its organizers arguing that they did not think they were responsible to the city's people. As their lawyers argued in the Delhi High Court:

The committee does not fulfil the criteria of being declared a State under article 12 of the Constitution and hence it cannot be declared a public authority. The committee has not been established or constituted as an institution of self government or under the Constitution. It has not been created under the law made either by Parliament or state legislature. (Times News Network, 2008).

The OC had no qualms about taking billions of rupees in public money but refused to be bound by the rules that govern public institutions. The Central Information Commission's definition of public authorities, subject to the RTI Act, clearly includes organizations substantially financed by the Central government or State governments. Its manual states clearly that the 'financing of the body or the NGO by the Government may be direct or indirect'. The organizers claimed exemption because their funding was in the nature of government loans but why this extreme reticence for any transparency with the public? Whose interest does it serve? Eventually, the Delhi High Court dismissed the OC's claims but if it had been performing well, would it have opposed the requests for information so vehemently? There was, perhaps, too much to be embarrassed about.

The discord between the Ministry of Sport and the OC over the disclosure of information also reveals a great deal about the complex management structure put in place for the Games. Even though the Games have always enjoyed the support of Delhi's ruling governments – both at the federal and the provincial levels – there is a clear distinction between the government *per se* and the OC. It was created in February 2005 as a registered society vested with the authority of delivering the Games. Its Executive Board is a 15-member body which includes the chairman and vice chairman, two nominees each of the federal and provincial governments and the IOA, four nominees from national sports federations and three nominees of the CGF.

Despite the presence of dozens of other governmental committees to oversee the Games effort, in practice, the OC's Secretariat virtually ploughed its own furrow until the Prime Minister's Office decided to act in October 2009 and get the Sports Ministry to take greater control.

5   THE BID AND THE REALITY

In *The Great Indian Novel*, Shashi Tharoor famously observed that India is not 'an underdeveloped country' but 'a highly developed one in an advanced state of decay'. It was a phrase that captured the overwhelming despair and shabbiness that had come to characterize the worst excesses of what came to be called 'the license-permit raj'. The rise of the Azeem Premjis and Narayan Murthys in the 1990s shattered that grand narrative of fallen greatness, ushering in a new era of self-belief. This is an India that is fast emerging as one of the new pillars of the world economy; an India that gives billions of dollars to the International Monetary Fund in return for a greater say on the global high table (IANS, 2009). Delhi certainly has the talents and the abilities, yet it made such a mess of the Commonwealth Games. As always, in India, opposites co-exist. The story of the CWG in its first few years is a case in point.

Delhi's organizers flew in Bollywood stars to dance to the drumbeats at the Closing Ceremony of the 2006 CWG. No one quite understood why but the ten-minute Bollywood trailer cost the Delhi government Rs 290 million. The stars were meant to showcase Delhi, to somehow put it on the map. In contrast, the entire Indian sports contingent at the Melbourne Games cost the government less than Rs 30 million.[21] In a sense, though, this lopsided spending was rather symbolic of the Games effort. When they should have been focusing on the script, the organizers have often seemed to focus on the gloss.

Delhi's glossy 2003 bid document had proudly promised that 'all major Games facilities either exist or would be created by 2007, except for the Games Village' ('Updated Bid Document', 2003, pp. 44, 49, 64). This included a grand commitment from the central and state governments to 'complete' new venues (one outdoor and two indoor stadiums) by 2007.[22] The Evaluation Committee of the CGF did push the original timelines a little forward. Even according to this, however, most venues were to be delivered by 2008, some even by 2005.[23]

The reality on the ground has been way different. The prime minister was eventually forced to intervene in 2009 but things were so bad that *The Hindustan Times* (Murali and Singh, 2009) summed up the collective fear that seemed to be building up just over a year before the Games:

> *What is actually needed for it [the Games] to materialise without our embarrassing ourselves, is a miracle.* And even more money . . . What we face is a race against time . . . The venues are officially 40 per cent complete, but walk by them and all you can see is a mess. (Added italics)

The Problem

To begin with, Delhi got off the starting blocks rather late. Beijing 2008 and London 2010, for instance, followed a seven-year time cycle: two years for planning and approvals, four years for construction and development and the last year for test events and trial runs (CAG, 2009, p. 10). In the case of Delhi, though, the first few years were utterly wasted. As per the contract with the CGF, Delhi's OC was to be in place by May 2004, but it was not formed until as late as February 2005. In contrast, the OC for the 2014 Games in Glasgow was formed even before the award of the Games (ibid., p. 9).

This rendered most of the original timelines redundant. The bid document had four phases: 2004–06 for planning, 2006–08 for creating, 2008–10 for delivering and 2010–11 for concluding. The CAG's auditors found 'no evidence of the four-phase approach being translated into action during the first phase years of 2004 to 2006'. Planning only really commenced from late 2006 (ibid., pp. 9–10). Part of the problem was the serious lack of expertise within the OC for organizing an event of this magnitude. It had set itself a target for recruiting key functional heads by April 2007 (OC, 2006, p. 60). Yet, several posts at this level were only being advertised and filled up by the end of 2008. An important unit like Communications did not get an Additional Director General (ADG) untill mid-2009. The first steps to fill the gaps were only taken with the appointment of technical consultants in 2007 (CAG, 2009, p. 9). The OC's DG was quite candid about the learning curve his organization had been on:

> Most of us have been to several Olympic Games, several Asian Games. When you go to these Games, you are not really becoming a part of their work force. You are not becoming an insider. What you are experiencing is much more than a spectator but you are still a guest. So you are seeing the brighter side, the happier side of the Games. The toll, the sweat that is inside, you have not been a part of . . .
>
> We also have consultants . . . but again consultants can only take you that far . . . then you have to run.[24]

But the Games effort did not run. It crawled. There was a serious problem of coordination between a virtual jungle of government agencies. The OC's own SWOT analysis in 2007 had highlighted a 'general apprehension' about the problem of 'inadequate formal or established protocols' to coordinate between multiple stakeholders and government agencies (OC, 2007, pp. 22–3). This is exactly what went wrong. Twenty-one major organizations and agencies were involved, each with different roles, budgets and reporting lines. According to CAG (2009, p. 10), 'Many agencies were either unaware of their role or refuted the role expected of them'. Many even had different timelines for the same project.

Even though the government set up a Core Group of Ministers to coordinate the work, in practice pulling together so many moving parts proved to be a bureaucratic quagmire with as many as 22 subcommittees.[25] The Prime Minister's Office was involved at sporadic intervals, taking status updates in 2006 and 2008,[26] but one gets the overwhelming impression that the entire impetus lacked a strong centre of the kind that Rajiv Gandhi gave to the 1982 Games.

In 1982, the prime minister's young son, cutting his political teeth, had spearheaded the effort, giving the Buta Singh-led OC a focused coherence from the highest level. In contrast, 2010 seemed to lack such a concentrated direction – leaving it all to the now disgraced Suresh Kalmadi and his team – until the Sports Ministry began taking charge in 2009.

Cumulatively, this caused serious problems. For instance, the OC submitted its budget to the government in November 2006, but it received approval only in April 2007. Similarly, basic planning documents were way behind schedule. The Games Organization Plan and Games Master Schedule were to have been ready by May 2004. These were only finalized for the CGF's approval in August 2007 and May 2008. The test event strategy was to be ready by October 2008 but it was not even ready by mid-2009. Out of 34 functional areas in the General Organization Plan, draft operational plans had been prepared for only 16 functional areas by March 2009 (CAG, 2009, p. 11, appendix IV).

One has to ask just what was happening? The managerial limbo translated into chaos at the venues. Until February 2009, construction had not begun on lawn balls and archery sites. Construction on the velodrome only began in January 2009 (Times News Network, 2009). As the CAG pointed out, on the ground this laxity meant that 'OC had given only conditional approval to the final designs for most venues'. Shockingly, in 13 cases, at 11 venues, agencies began construction even before conditional approval by the OC of the final designs. With the government failing to evolve a single window clearance system, a great deal of construction activity got stuck in a bureaucratic swamp. In five major venues – Jawaharlal Nehru stadium, the National Stadium, IG stadium, SPM aquatic complex and Karni Singh shooting range – applications for 24 no-objection certificates were submitted by up to 11 months after the stipulated date of completion of the related consultancy work of which they were supposed to be part. Jamia Milia Islamia had still not applied for clearances for Rugby 7s and TT training venues in March 2009 (CAG, 2009, pp. 23–4).

Not surprisingly, the old chestnut of national pride became the last defence for infrastructural delays. Time and time again, when the administrators were accused of not following the rules, they responded with the same basic argument – forget the rules now, the nation's pride is at stake. As a Delhi Urban Arts Commission (DUAC) member told the *Times of India* (Verma, 2009), 'There is no overall planning and they want us to clear projects in a hurry before the Games and compromise the city ultimately'. When the DUAC protested, it was accused of blocking CWG projects. As DUAC Chairman K.T. Ravindran said,

Suddenly the government bodies like PWD seem to have woken up to a Commonwealth Games deadline and there is time pressure. So, they want DUAC clearance at the earliest. These projects should have been planned years in advance. There is simply no planning strategy . . . In any foreign country, projects are completed much before the deadline and trials are also run on them. (Quoted in Verma, 2009)

By the end of 2009, then, Delhi's great white hope lay in what North Indians call *jugaad*, that wonderful yet utterly untranslatable word that roughly means a propensity to improvise. In the end, improvisation enabled India to deliver the Games without inherently solving the great divides that had underpinned this effort since the beginning.

6   CONCLUSION

India is not the first nor will it be the last country to attempt to use sports to project its power. Dubai's ruler Sheikh Mohammad bin Rahid al-Makhtoum has long used sport as part of a multi-billion dollar 'charm offensive'. The Gulf states have amassed a number of sporting events for precisely this reason: golf (four events), tennis (Qatar and the Dubai Open), the WTA Championship 2008–2010, horse racing (the Dubai World Cup), motorsport (Bahrain GP, Qatar Moto GP, Abu Dhabi GP) and soccer (2011 AFC Asian Cup in Qatar). All kinds of governments, representing every type of political ideology, have endorsed international sporting competition as a testing ground for the nation or for a political system – German Nazis, Italian Fascists, Soviet and Cuban Communists, Chinese Maoists, Western capitalist democrats, Latin American juntas – all have played the game and believed in it (Jackson and Haigh, 2008, p. 351).

Sporting events are so important for national pride that when Paris lost the bid to host the 2012 Olympics, *Le Monde* predicted that 'the current malaise in France is likely to get worse' (quoted in Black, 2008, p. 467). We do not doubt that big sporting events have an appeal for cities and nations – that is why they are so popular. There are, indeed, benefits but as one study (Black, 2008, pp. 467, 468, 472) of big games warns:

Their benefits continue to be chronically oversold and their opportunity costs minimised and overlooked. Their continued – indeed growing – popularity therefore presents a puzzle that can at least partly be accounted for by the particular appeal and usefulness of such events as a strategic response to the conditions of globalisation . . .

[T]here are predictable patterns of hyperbolic promotion, collective gullibility and underappreciated opportunity costs and distributional impacts that deserve much closer attention from responsible policy-makers than they typically receive.

These words ring true for Delhi. With India looking to graduate from 'developing country status' with these Games, and the organizational effort moving only by fits and starts, the organizers constantly resorted to appeals to patriotism.

India's Sport Minister sought to allay concerns about the delays in 2009 by comparing the disorganization with the spectacle of the traditional Indian wedding. 'Never mind the delays', he promised. 'Like a seemingly disorganized arrangement in an Indian marriage – just like in the movie *Monsoon Wedding* – we will have a grand Games' (PTI, 2009).

In the end, Delhi did have its monsoon wedding. Embarrassing problems – such as unclean toilets in the Games Village – kept cropping up until the opening ceremony itself but the fact that the sporting events themselves went off without a hitch once they started convinced many Indians and much of the mainstream press that the Games were somehow a success. The opening and closing ceremonies seemed grand enough in this narrative. There was relief that things did not break down midway and the two weeks of the Games passed without any further embarrassing headlines. After a year of depressing news and foreboding about the Games, the national media discourse now turned triumphalist – a mood helped along by the fact that India eventually stood second on the medals tally, a position it had never achieved before. In the final analysis though, the Delhi Games have left behind what can only be called a sellotape legacy and a train of corruption investigations that will forever cloud its memory.

NOTES

1. The company, Swiss Timing, has vehemently denied the charges and in early 2011 published full page advertisements in major Indian newspapers with its rebuttal. See for instance, its full page advertisement in *The Times of India* (9 March 2011), New Delhi, p. 2.
2. All the main accused have publicly denied any wrongdoing.
3. The charges of wrongdoing were denied by Delhi Chief Minister Sheila Dixit. Her government has submitted a detailed 14-volume 3,400 page rebuttal to the HLC reports on the management of the Games to the Ministry of Home Affairs.
4. The OC itself consists of two governmental nominees, two IOA appointees, two state government nominees and four national federation nominees.
5. For example, the Commonwealth Games have been the subject of parliamentary scrutiny since 2003 with successive sports ministers laying out consolidated Games budgets in response to probing questions by members of parliament. Given that most funding and a great deal of the implementation is being done by government agencies, these parliamentary records should be the most comprehensive. Yet, not until May 2007 was the Rs 2.64 billion estimated for security arrangements in the Games included in the overall budget figures produced in Parliament by various sports ministers. This, despite the fact that the OC had always factored these costs and the Delhi Police have

been party to discussions since the very beginning. It had provided the CGF a pre-liminary estimate of its plans even before Delhi won the bid! Even this Rs 2.64 billion security budget, when it was ultimately reported in Parliament, did not include the cost of CCTV cameras, perimeter security and a PA system. The security costs were reported to Parliament in Mani Shankar Aiyer, Minister of Panchayati Raj, Youth Affairs and Sports and Development of North-Eastern Region, Government of India, Rajya Sabha Unstarred Question No. 413 (asked by Shri Ravi Shankar Prasad, Shri Ram Jethmalani), answered on 3 May 2007, 'Amount Sanctioned for Commonwealth Games'. The breakdown of the cost is referred to in OC (2007, p. 88).

6. INR stands for Indian rupee. By way of comparison, in mid-July 2011, US$1 equalled approximately INR 44.5.

7. This included Rs 3.99 billion estimated by the IOA as operating expenditure for the Games, Rs 1.86 billion estimated by the Delhi government for the Games Village and Rs 32 million estimated by the DDA for creating new infrastructure and upgrad-ing existing facilities. Annexure 1, Sunil Dutt, Minister of Youth Affairs and Sports, Government of India, Lok Sabha Unstarred Question No. 3180 (asked by Shri Salarapatty Kuppusamy Kharventhan, Shri Ananta Nayak and Shri Ajit Jogi), answered on 20 December 2004, 'Commonwealth Games'. Also, Sunil Dutt, Minister of Youth Affairs and Sports, Government of India, Rajya Sabha Unstarred Question No. 454 (asked by Shri E.M. Sudarsana Natchiappan, Shri Janardhana Poojary and Shri R.P. Goenka), answered on 3 March 2005, 'Preparation for Commonwealth Games'. Prithviraj Chavan, Minister of State in Prime Minister's Office, Government of India, Rajya Sabha Unstarred Question No. 1261 (asked by Shri Eknath K. Thajur), answered on 4 August 2005, 'Funds for Commonwealth Games'.

8. Sunil Dutt, Unstarred Question No. 454 (see note 7).

9. Sunil Dutt, Unstarred Question No. 3180 (see note 7).

10. The Comptroller and Auditor General's budget calculation did not include cost of DMRC, Airports Authority of India and several other agencies (CAG, 2009, p. v).

11. Oscar Fernandes, Minister of State (Independent Charge) Statistics & Programme Implementation, Youth Affairs and Sports and Overseas Indian Affairs, Government of India, Rajya Sabha Unstarred Question No. 3347 (asked by Shri E.M. Sudarsana Natchiappan), answered on 22 December 2005, 'Plan for Commonwealth Games'. By August 2007 the Delhi government's action plan had gone up to Rs 13.52 billion for spending on health, transport, roads, horticulture, water, electricity and infrastruc-ture according to records submitted in Parliament. Mani Shankar Aiyer, Minister of Panchayati Raj and Youth Affairs and Sports, Government of India, Rajya Sabha Unstarred Question No. 1361 (asked by Shri Jai Parkash Aggarwal), answered on 23 August 2007, 'State of Preparedness for Commonwealth Games'.

12. Interview with V.K. Verma, Director General, Commonwealth Games, President, Badminton Federation of India, January 2009.

13. Mani Shankar Aiyer, Minister of Panchayati Raj and Youth Affairs and Sports, Government of India, Rajya Sabha Unstarred Question No. 1930 (asked by Shri Prasanta Chatterjee and Shri Tarini Kanta Roy), answered on 9 March 2006, 'Cost of Commonwealth Games'.

14. Mani Shankar Aiyer, Minister of Panchayati Raj and Youth Affairs and Sports, Government of India, Rajya Sabha Unstarred Question No. 3030 (asked by Shrimati S.G. Indra), answered on 24 August 2006, 'Private Sector Contribution for Organizing Commonwealth Games'.

15. Melbourne had estimated an expenditure of $2,895,021,000 and ended up spending only $18,136,000 more than this. In actual operations in Melbourne, they spent *less* than they had estimated ($938 million), as opposed to an estimate of $1,036 million. It was only in construction that they went majorly over the estimates: an extra $45 million was spent under this head. KPMG (2006, pp. 47–9).

16. Emphasis is ours. Interview with V.K. Verma (see note 12).

17. The allocation of the National Rural Health Mission, the Union Health Ministry's

flagship programme in the Union Budget of 2009–10 was Rs 141.27 billion. Of this, Rs 120.70 billion were provided in the Interim Budget and 20.57 billion later by the Finance Ministry in its Budget. PIB Press Release, 'Budget 2009–10', 6 July 2009.

18. The poverty figures are Planning Commission estimates.
19. The estimate was made by Shankar Acharya, former chief economic advisor. Quoted in Aiyar (2009).
20. Interview with V.K. Verma (see note 12).
21. Figures from Mani Shankar Aiyer, Minister of Panchayati Raj, and Youth Affairs and Sports and Development of North-East Region, Government of India, Rajya Sabha Unstarred Question No. 1788 (asked by Shri Vijay Jawaharlal Darda), answered on 10 August 2006, 'Programme to Showcase India at Melbourne Commonwealth Games'.
22. The Games' operational plan in the bid was based upon data and study conducted by M/S A. Sharma & Co. The first schedule was drawn up in the original bid document, which laid down a timeframe of 1 Jan 2004 to 1 May 2006 to complete the planning process (framework of systems and infrastructure and accurate cost estimates) and stipulated 1 May 2006 to 1 May 2008 to 'create' the Games. The delivery timeline was May 2008 to December 2010 ('Updated Bid Document', 2003, pp. 172, 18, 38).
23. The Evaluation Committee estimates for delivery of venues were as follows: 2005: Jawaharlal Nehru Sports Complex (lawn bowls), Indoor Stadium at Saket; 2006: Yamuna Sports Complex (Rugby 7s); 2007: Yamuna Sports Complex (boxing), Indira Gandhi Stadium sports complex (wrestling); 2008: Jawaharlal Nehru stadium (athletics), Indira Gandhi Indoor Stadium (netball), the Dr Shyama Prasad Mukherjee Swimming Pool (diving and swimming), the training facilities at the Village; 2009: Yamuna Velodrome Indira Gandhi Sports Complex, the Dhyan Chand National Stadium (CGF, 2003, pp. 67–72, 75).
24. Interview with V.K. Verma (see note 12).
25. Figure from Suresh Kalmadi, Chairman, OC, CWG Delhi 2010, 'A Word from the Chairman', *Annual Report 2008 Organising Committee Commonwealth Games Delhi 2010*. For details on the governmental structures set up to monitor the Games effort, see Mani Shankar Aiyer, Minister of Panchayati Raj, Youth Affairs and Sports and Development of North-Eastern Region, Government of India, Rajya Sabha Unstarred Question No. 2722 (asked by Shri Rajeev Chandrashekhar), answered on 26 April 2007, 'Status of Preparation for the Commonwealth Games'; Mani Shankar Aiyer, Minister of Panchayati Raj, Youth Affairs and Sports and Development of North-Eastern Region, Government of India, Rajya Sabha Unstarred Question No. 510 (asked by Shri Jai Prakash Aggarwal), answered on 10 May 2007, 'Preparations for Commonwealth Games'; Sunil Dutt, Minister of Youth Affairs and Sports, Government of India, Rajya Sabha Unstarred Question No. 1063 (asked by Shri Raju Parmar, Shri P.K. Maheshwari), answered on 10 March 2005, 'Arrangements for the Commonwealth Games'.
26. Mani Shankar Aiyer, Minister of Panchayati Raj, Youth Affairs and Sports and Development of North-Eastern Region, Government of India, Rajya Sabha Unstarred Question No. 292 (asked by Shri Rajeev Chandrashekhar), answered on 28 February 2008, 'Preparation for Commonwealth Games'.

REFERENCES

Agencies (2011), 'CWG scam: CBI files chargesheet against Kalmadi, others', *The Indian Express*, 20 May, available at: http://www.indianexpress.com/news/cwg-scam-cbi-files-chargesheet-against-kalmadi-others/793615/ (accessed 21 May 2011).

Aiyar, Swaminathan S. Anklesaria (2009), 'One-night stand or a prolonged affair?', *Sunday Times of India*, New Delhi, 12 July.

Black, D. (2008), 'Dreaming big: the pursuit of "second order" Games as a strategic response to globalisation', *Sport in Society: Cultures, Commerce, Media, Politics*, Special Issue: Sport and Foreign Policy in a Globalising World, **11** (4), July, 467–80.

Cashman, R., K. Toohey, S. Darcy, C. Symons and R. Stewart (2004), 'When the carnival is over: evaluating the outcomes of mega sporting events in Australia', *Sporting Traditions*, **21** (1), 1–32.

Commonwealth Games Federation (CFG) (2003), 'The Report of the Commonwealth Games Evaluation Commission for the 2010 Commonwealth Games', CFG, London, October.

Comptroller and Auditor General of India (CAG) (2009), 'A Report on the Preparedness for the XIX Commonwealth Games, 2010', New Delhi, July.

Directorate of Information and Publicity, Delhi Government (2009), 'Creating Commonwealth for All: Status Report on Infrastructure', New Delhi.

Games News: Commonwealth Games Delhi 2010 (2006), 1 (2).

Ghosh, Abantika (2009), 'Games security is a big concern', *The Times of India*, 3 January, New Delhi.

High Level Committee for Commonwealth Games 2010 (2011a), 'First Report of HLC on Host Broadcasting', First Report, New Delhi, Vigyan Bhawan Annexe.

High Level Committee for Commonwealth Games 2010 (2011b), 'Report on City Infrastructure', Third Report, New Delhi, Vigyan Bhawan Annexe.

IANS (2008), 'Court pulls up Commonwealth Games organising panel', New Delhi, 23 December.

IANS (2009), 'India to Invest $10 billion in IMF: Pranab', 4 September, available at: http://timesofindia.indiatimes.com/india/India-to-invest-10-billion-in-IMF-Pranab/articles how/4973685.cms (accessed 10 October 2009).

Jackson, Steven J. and S. Haigh (2008), 'Between and beyond politics: sport and foreign policy in a globalising world', *Sport in Society: Cultures, Commerce, Media, Politics*, Special Issue: Sport and Foreign Policy in a Globalising World, **11** (4), July, 349–58.

KPMG (2006), 'Office of Economic Impact Study of the Melbourne 2006 Commonwealth Games: Post-event Analysis' (Office of Commonwealth Games Coordination) October.

Kumar, Vinay (2011), 'CWG Scam: Kalmadi Named "Main Accused" in First CBI Charge Sheet', *The Hindu*, 20 May, available at: http://www.thehindu.com/news/national/article2035048.ece (accessed 21 May 2011).

Majumdar, B. and N. Mehta (2010), *Sellotape Legacy: Delhi and the Commonwealth Games*, New Delhi: HarperCollins.

Masand, Ajai (2009), 'We will return every penny to the government', *The Hindustan Times*, New Delhi, 21 February.

Ministry of Youth Affairs and Sports (2008), *Outcome Budget 2008–2009*, New Delhi: Government of India.

Murali, Kadambari and Shivani Singh (2009), 'Trailing badly in final lap', *The Hindustan Times*, 18 Febraury.

Organizing Committee (OC) Commonwealth Games 2010 Delhi (2006), 'Progress Report on Status of Games Planning By Organising Committee Commonwealth Games 2010', Organising Committee, CWG 2010, New Delhi.

Organising Committee (OC) Commonwealth Games 2010 Delhi (2007), 'General Organisation Plan', OC 2010, New Delhi, August.

Pandey, Sidharth (2011), 'CWG swam: where is Shunglu Report? asks BJP', 25 March, available at: http://www.ndtv.com/article/india/cwg-scam-where-is-shunglu-report-asks-bjp-94086 (accessed 30 May 2011).

PTI (2009), 'Gill: CWG is like the "Great Indian Wedding"', *The Times of India*, New Delhi, 20 February.

Soni, A. (2000), 'Urban conquest of Outer Delhi: beneficiaries, intermediaries and victims the case of Mehrauli countryside', in Denis Vidal, Emma Tarlo and Veronique Dupont (eds), *Delhi: Urban Spaces and Human Destinies*, New Delhi: Manohar, CSH, pp. 75–94.

Sood, R. (2008), 'Accountability issues put games' organising panel, Sport Min on collision course', *The Financial Express*, New Delhi, 30 December.

Thakur, Pradeep (2011), 'ED charges Kalmadi with money laundering', *The Times of India*, 19 May, available at: http://articles.timesofindia.indiatimes.com/2011-05-19/india/29559941_1_suresh-kalmadi-games-contracts-oc (accessed 20 May 2011).

Times News Network (2008), 'Games Panel Moves HC Against Public Body Tag', *The Times of India*, New Delhi, 11 December.

Times News Network (2009), 'Underfire Organisers Present Brave Face' *The Times of India*, New Delhi, 25 February.

'Updated Bid Document: Delhi 2010 Commonwealth Games', (2003), December.

Verma, R. (2009), 'Games-Bound Govt. Finds DUAC in Slow Lane', *The Times of India*, New Delhi, 1 February.

29 The case of Brazil 2014/2016

Luiz Martins de Melo

1 INTRODUCTION

Brazil and the city of Rio de Janeiro have earned what appears to be an excellent opportunity to strengthen their development process and improve their image before the world by gaining the right to host the 2014 World Cup and the 2016 Olympic Games. However, hosting these events is not a panacea for solving problems such as environmental degradation, poor public transport, growth of slums and urban violence. These problems cannot be overcome by magic. On the other hand, it is fair to expect that the planned investments and the expectations produced by promoting the city will generate an increase in growth rate and leave a lasting legacy.

A legacy is what these events can leave the host country. Hosting a mega event can be a catalyst for change in a region (city, state or country). Hosting the two largest mega sporting events in the world is especially exciting. Both events have the potential to transform the lives of the poorest citizens in Brazil, especially in the city of Rio de Janeiro, which will not only host the 2016 Olympic Games but is also the main venue of the World Cup 2014. However, it remains doubtful whether the changes will be for better or worse, given the bid that was projected for the Olympic Games.

Although both of these mega events can engender significant environmental and economic change, they each leave a distinct legacy. The Olympic Games take place in large cities surrounded by metropolitan areas and they last no more than two weeks. These characteristics imply the possibility of profound changes in the urban condition and the logistics of such cities. Investments involve the construction of new facilities and the revamping of old ones, and entail a strong impact on urban mobility, the environment, tourism and lodging. The legacy of the Olympic Games cannot be measured solely by the modern sports facilities built, which are subject to technical standards of excellence, but mainly through the improvements of social and urban conditions in the host cities. The FIFA World Cup is a widespread event that takes place in many cities and regions. Its legacy is much more related to the investments made in modern sports stadiums, which have to meet FIFA specifications, and in urban mobility, in order to facilitate access to the matches.

The literature on the economic impact of mega sporting events is very careful to evaluate the benefits of investments made for their realization. Analyzing these papers, Zimbalist (2010, p. 11) states:

> These studies present the following picture of the economic impact of hosting the Olympic Games: although a modest number of jobs may be created as a result of hosting the games, there appears to be no detectable effect on income, suggesting that existing workers do not benefit (Hagn and Maennig, 2009; and Matheson, 2009). Moreover, the impact of hosting the games depends on the overall labor market response to the new jobs created by the games and might not be positive (Humphreys and Zimbalist, 2008). The economic impact of hosting the World Cup appears, if anything, to be even smaller (Hagn and Maennig, 2008 and 2009).

Although the economic impact of these investments can be considered negligible, the intangible asset that is formed by the expectation of improving the living conditions of the population cannot be disregarded. Even if difficult to measure, these positive expectations can be a powerful tool for generating intangible assets.

Barcelona is an example of a positive social and urban transformation process. Even though the Olympics have left a high fiscal and financial deficit, the impacts of such a mega sporting event cannot be assessed exclusively from this point. Wouldn't the outcomes of the intangible assets formed by the implementation of the 1992 Summer Olympic Games be bigger than the financial costs? To invest in these assets wouldn't it be necessary to get loans? Aren't loans debt? The capitalist system is a system based on credit (debt), public or private. The debt precedes the realization of any investment, hence the centrality of the financial and banking system for its operation. Of course, from time to time, the excesses must be corrected, especially when the ideology of free markets and financial deregulation becomes hegemonic (Cassidy, 2009).

This chapter is structured as follows. Section 2 provides an overview of the Brazilian economy mainly based on its infrastructure conditions. Section 3 analyzes the projected investments for the realization of the 2014 World Cup. The focus here is on Brazil's ability to afford the construction of the stadiums in the 12 cities selected for the event. Section 4 focuses on the 2016 Olympic Games in Rio de Janeiro and the planned urban interventions to host this mega event. Finally, Section 5 offers some concluding remarks.

The methodology used in the chapter is described in Nelson (1995, p. 50):

> But economists also need to be understood as 'theorizing' when they are trying to explain what lies behind the particular phenomena they are describing, even when they are not advertising their account as a 'theory'. Winter and I have

called this kind of analysis 'appreciative' theorizing. While starting with the empirical subject matter, the accounts put forth by economists of the development of an industry, or the evolution of a technology, focus on certain variables and ignore others, just as is the case with formal theory. Quite complex causal arguments often are presented as parts of these accounts, if generally in the form of stories.

2   BRAZIL ECONOMIC OUTLOOK

There has been no growth cycle in Brazil since the 1970s. The average annual growth rate of the country's gross domestic product (GDP) has been very low since the end of the 1970s, as shown in Table 29.1. Between 1980 and 2010, it remained below Brazil's average growth rate in the twentieth century, 6.5 percent.

The income per capita growth in Brazil has been very slow (Table 29.2). In the 1990–2010 period, income per capita average growth rate was just 1.3 percent. In 2010, with the economy running at a 7.5 percent growth rate, per capita income grew 6.5 percent. But in 2011, due to growing inflationary pressures, the Brazilian Central Bank decided to implement a tighter monetary policy and raise the interest rate. Currently, Brazil's economy has already cut its growth to below 4 percent per year and has the highest basic real interest rate in the real world, 8.6 percent per year. The nominal prime rate is 12.25 percent annually. So, the economic outlook is not so positive.

The long stagnation of the Brazilian economy for almost three decades has caused investments in infrastructure to fall sharply. Infrastructure investment, which had averaged 5.4 percent of GDP in the 1970s, fell to 2.3 percent of GDP in the 1990s. In the 2001–08 period, it remained on average 2.0 percent of GDP. It is well known that investment in infrastructure must be made upfront, that is, the supply must be higher than the demand.

Table 29.1   Average growth rate

Years	GDP %
1961–1970	6.17
1971–1980	8.63
1981–1990	1.57
1991–2000	2.54
2001–2010	3.58

Source: Brazilian Central Bank (BACEN).

Table 29.2   Brazil income per capita

Period	$ current prices	$ real growth rate
1990	3.201.5	−7.1
1991	2.721.0	−0.7
1992	2.555.6	−2.2
1993	2.790.4	3.3
1994	3.471.7	4.2
1995	4.848.8	2.6
1996	5.208.6	0.6
1997	5.319.8	1.8
1998	5.076.5	−1.5
1999	3.477.1	−1.2
2000	3.765.7	2.8
2001	3.186.1	−0.2
2002	2.860.7	1.2
2003	3.097.2	−0.2
2004	3.665.2	4.3
2005	4.812.0	1.9
2006	5.867.3	2.7
2007	7.282.7	4.9
2008	8.705.7	4.1
2009	8.347.6	−1.6
2010	10.814.0	6.5

Source: http://www.ipeadata.gov.br, author's own elaboration.

When we analyze the past decade, it seems that the country has been making a recovery. From 2000 to 2005, the real annual GDP growth rate was 3.0 percent. In the second half of the decade, growth increased to 4.4 percent per year. The annual growth rate of investment rose from 1.3 percent (2000–05) to 9.9 percent (2006–10). This recovery had positive implications, such as reducing poverty, increasing formal employment, income growth and the expansion of economic boundaries, the bottle-necks that had been preventing the country's sustainable growth, espe-cially those related to logistics.[1] But the Brazilian current investment rate is still below the sustainable level for a fast-growing economy.

During the National Economic Forum at the National Bank for Social and Economic Development (BNDES), the former president of Brazil's central bank, Arminio Fraga, said that the investment rate in Brazil, 18.5 percent of GDP, is insufficient to achieve a sustainable economic growth rate of 5 percent per year (Abdala, 2011). Among BRIC countries (Brazil, Russia, India and China) Brazil has the lowest ratio of investment to

GDP. In 2010, China reported an investment rate of 43 percent, India 34 percent and Russia 20 percent. According to the Institute for Applied Economic Research-IPEA[2] to achieve a GDP growth rate of 5 percent per year, Brazil needs to achieve an average investment rate of 25 percent annually (Table 29.3).

Brazil has a dire need for investment in infrastructure. Increasingly, infrastructure bottlenecks are an impediment to economic growth. Also the successful completion of the 2014 World Cup and 2016 Olympic Games depends on substantial improvements in transportation infrastructure, urban mobility and airport capacity. In major metropolitan areas, where the main activities of the World Cup and the Olympics will be concentrated, lies both the greatest demand for housing and also many social problems.

Road transportation accounts for more than 60 percent of the movement of production, but 70 percent of the roads are in poor or bad condition. In Rio de Janeiro, road transportation accounts for 75 percent of freight and passenger runs. The travel time between home and work averages two and a half hours (Melo and Dominato, 2010). This situation degrades the quality of life of the poorest members of the population, who are the main users of public transport. In São Paulo, the largest and most important city of the country, traffic jams extend hundreds of miles daily.

The Growing Acceleration Program (PAC), launched by the Federal government, mainly aimed at solving the logistic bottleneck of the Brazilian economy, should have prioritized railway, subway and commuter railway surface transport. These types of infrastructure improvements expand the potential building area and decrease public transport cost through the operational effect of scale and scope.

To keep focusing on road transportation – buses and other vehicles powered by an internal combustion engine – as set up in the planning bid of the 2016 Olympic Games, will only worsen the living conditions of the entire population, including the middle class, whose vehicles regularly get stuck in huge traffic jams when traveling to and from work. Intra- and intercity transport by rail is negligible. The overwhelming majority of travel is done by motor vehicles powered by petroleum derivatives. Only the wealthy few can escape in helicopters from the worsening situation in metropolitan areas.

About 80 percent of the Brazilian population is urban and more than 50 percent live in one of the 10 largest metropolitan areas – the same areas that will host the mega sporting events. In those metropolitan areas, the number of motor vehicles is growing faster than investment in transportation systems. In the words of Lessa (2009, p. 19):

Table 29.3　Nominal investment rate

Period	Percent of GDP
1991	17.0
1992	18.7
1993	20.8
1994	21.4
1995	18.2
1996	17.7
1997	17.3
1998	15.5
1999	15.8
2000	16.7
2001	15.7
2002	15.5
2003	15.8
2004	16.2
2005	16.8
2006	17.6
2007	18.8
2008	17.2
2009	19.2
2010	18.5

Source:　http://www.ipeadata.gov.br, author's own elaboration.

Nothing is more important for the development of Brazil than changing the transport matrix and increasing railway and waterway participation in the transportation of goods. Brazil should restore coastal shipping – we have 7,500 km of coastline and three river basins – and establish inter-regional railway routes integrating the north and northeast to the mid-south and southeast, as well as install systems implementation modalities. Road transport would enhance the supply network of the major rail and waterways. Therefore, it will take five years for the logistics cost to be reduced from the current 13% of GDP to 8.9% (US standard). This 'technological revolution' will increase the productivity of all economic activities in Brazil.

The rate of investment in infrastructure over the next four years is expected to reach between 2.5 and 3.0 percent of GDP, which is a 25–30 percent increase on previous investments (Table 29.4).

Brazil's GDP in 2010 reached $2.089 trillion. An investment rate of 18.5 percent of GDP amounts to $386 billion. Stadium and infrastructure investment for the 2014 World Cup and the 2016 Olympic Games has been estimated at $35.0 billion for a five-year period, an average investment of

Table 29.4   Planned infrastructure investments, 2011–2014

Sector	$bn	%
Electricity	86.9	36.6
Telecommunications	45.0	18.8
Sanitation	25.6	10.7
Logistics	80.6	33.9
Railroads	37.5	15.9
Highways	31.8	13.3
Ports	11.3	4.7
Infrastructure	238.1	100.0

Note: Exchange rate: $1.00 = R$1.60.

Source: Puga and Borça (2011); author's elaboration.

$7.0 billion per year. This is 1.84 percent of the investment rate per year in Brazil. Table 29.4 shows that investment in infrastructure for the 2011–14 period is estimated at $238.1 billion. The 2014 World Cup and the 2016 Olympic Games infrastructure investment is estimated at $20.0 billion, so these figures are perfectly affordable for the Brazilian economy.

Logistics integration is essential for Brazil. One example of bad investment is the planned bullet train between Rio, São Paulo and Campinas. Its estimated cost is $21.5 billion. With these resources it would be possible to build 48 km of subway in São Paulo or Rio de Janeiro. It would be possible for Supervia (Urban Train Company of Rio de Janeiro) to install a high-quality train system, by restoring old tracks of extinct railroads in Rio de Janeiro, in order to reach 60 percent of the total population that live in the suburbs. All metropolitan regions have similar conditions for installing urban railroad services. The successful completion of mega sporting events has a lot to do with good logistics systems.

Despite logistics setbacks, income distribution in Brazil has improved consistently. In 2001, the Gini index was almost 0.6. In 2010 it improved to 0.53. In the last decade the real income per capita accumulated growth rate of the 10 percent wealthiest was 10 percent, for the 50 percent poorest it was 67.9 percent. Adjusting for inflation and population growth, the 50 percent poorest income growth was 577 percent higher than that for the 10 percent richest in that period.[3]

This process brings momentum to the economy and generates externalities in all directions. It strengthens mass production modernization, introduces new consumption patterns and empowers the poorest with democratic rights.

The impact of hosting mega sporting events varies according to the level of development in the host city and country. Evidence shows that the size of the impact is directly linked to the focus of the planning. When directed at revamping less-developed areas that house the poorest people it can have a very positive impact. In order to have such a positive impact, investment in transport infrastructure should be made before the construction of sports stadiums and should focus in areas of greatest social impact. In Rio de Janeiro, the planning for the construction of Olympic sporting venues has not followed that framework. The planning in the 2016 Rio Olympic bid has focused in Barra da Tijuca, one of the wealthiest areas of the city. By doing this, the planning for the Olympic Games is guiding the way in which the city's future is being laid down, exactly the opposite of what it should be in order for it to leave a lasting legacy to the city: Olympic Games planning should be integral to the city planning.

3   THE WORLD CUP 2014

Transportation costs are very important for the World Cup logistic system because there are very long distances between the host cities. Table 29.5 shows the distances between São Paulo, the most important political and economic city in Brazil and the other 11 host cities.

It is clear that the only way tourists and journalists could travel between host cities is by plane. This fact highlights a problem common to the 12 host cities: the lack of airport capacity to cope with the visitor influx anticipated for 2014. Airports have undergone a process of low investment in modernization and expansion. Domestic air traffic has developed rapidly as the average income increased and a low pricing system was enforced on Brazilian air companies. Some airports are operating close to their full capacity and others above.

Strong growth in demand in recent years was not followed by an increase in airport operational capacity. This situation is reflected in the fact that 14 of the 20 largest passenger terminals are operating above the limit in 2010. In 2003, the average number of passengers passing through airports was 71 million. In 2010, this figure jumped to 154 million, a 117 percent increase in eight years (Neto and Souza, 2011).

Aiming at holding the World Cup, the Federal government assured the Brazilian Airport Infrastructure Company – Infraero – that it would provide funds to invest R$3.5 billion in 13 airports during the 2011 to 2014 period. That accounts for R$875.0 million annually, a figure higher than the average amount invested in 2003/10 (R$268.9 million) and 2010 (R$403.5 million) (ibid.). If Infraero has the operational capacity to

Table 29.5   Distance between host cities (km)

To/from	São Paulo
Cuiabá	1,634
Curitiba	408
Porto Alegre	1,119
Recife	2,672
Rio de Janeiro	429
Salvador	1,979
Manaus	3,971
Brasília	1,029
Belo Horizonte	586
Fortaleza	3,127
Natal	3,015

Source: Ministry of Transport.

achieve that level of investment, airport infrastructure in Brazil will be operating at its full capacity (ibid.). But, in the last few years, Infraero has been unable to invest all available resources. It will be extremely difficult for passenger terminal modernization to meet the 2014 World Cup demand. Given the average time to implement infrastructure projects in Brazil, 10 out of the 13 terminals of the host cities will not have full operational capacity by 2014 (ibid.). For the 2016 Olympic Games further investment would be necessary. It seems that infrastructure investments barely cover the needs of the World Cup and the Olympic Games and do not even come close to responding to the country's or the cities' needs. How can these events leave a lasting legacy like that?

The Brazilian population and surface area transport infrastructure play a crucial role, and Table 29.6 shows data that allow a comparative analysis between Brazil and some developed countries. The Brazilian population and surface area are larger than those of all developed countries, except the USA. This evidence poses very hard challenges in building quality infrastructure because of the country's size and population. Nonetheless, quality infrastructure, especially transport, is critical for the success of the World Cup. Perhaps setting up an effective infrastructure system is the most crucial factor in organizing the competition. If the infrastructure does not work well for the Brazilian population, it is not going to work well for visitors.

The logistics gap between Brazil and developed countries is overwhelming – more so, when this underdeveloped logistic has to deal with a large population and surface area. There is no way to gain scale

Table 29.6   Population and surface area

Country	Population	Brazil/country	Surface area (sq. km)	Brazil/country
Brazil	191,971,506	1.0	8,514,880	1.0
USA	304,375,000	3.9	9,831,510	1.2
France	62,277,432	3.1	549,190	15.5
Germany	82,110,097	2.3	357,050	23.9
UK	61,414,062	3.1	243,610	35.0
Portugal	10,622,413	18.1	92,120	92.4
Italy	59,832,179	3.2	301.340	28.3
Ireland	4,425,675	43.6	70.280	121.2
Greece	11,237,094	17.1	131.960	64.5
Spain	45,555,716	4.2	505.000	16.9

Source: World Bank (2009).

and scope to reduce costs, unless the investment rate in infrastructure had been higher than in the 1980s. To overcome this shortfall in four or five years is almost impossible.

Another problem is the difference in income between Brazil and developed countries, or to put it bluntly: can Brazil afford expensive football stadiums? The income gap is shown in Table 29.7.

Developed countries have built a modern infrastructure of transport, telecommunications, energy and sanitation. Further, they have modern sporting venues which are compatible with their high-income society. They have set up a welfare state that provides healthcare, a good public education system and social security for their citizens. They are more or less ready to host mega events.

Developed countries have private firms and organizations that can afford to maintain those facilities after the mega event. Inhabitants in high-income countries can afford to pay £50 for a football ticket in England or US$100 for a National Basket Association (NBA) ticket in the USA.[4] In Brazil there is no demand for these kinds of sophisticated sports facilities because the investment does not pay. The difference in income explains why it is very difficult to have modern sports facilities to meet FIFA's requirements (Melo, 2007).

The 2009 season of the Brazilian Championship, including its three divisions, took 10.06 million fans to stadiums, resulting in $100.0 million in gross revenues, with the first division accounting for 72 percent of the total. This amount represents an average ticket cost of $10.0 per supporter. The average stadium attendance in the first division football

Table 29.7   Economic indicators

Country	GNI per capita, PPP (current international $)		GDP per capita (current US$)	
	2008	Country/Brazil	2008	Country/Brazil
Brazil	10,080	1.0	8,205	1
USA	47,100	4.7	47,209	5.8
France	33,280	3.3	44,508	5.4
Germany	35,950	3.6	44,446	5.4
UK	36,240	3.6	43,541	5.3
Portugal	22,330	2.2	22,923	2.8
Italy	30,800	3.1	38,492	4.7
Ireland	35,710	3.5	60,460	7.4
Greece	28,300	2.8	31,670	3.9
Spain	30,830	3.1	35,215	4.3

Source: World Bank (2009).

National Championship was 15.5 thousand in 2009 and 14.3 thousand in 2010. The average ticket price was $15. Therefore, the total turnover of the three football divisions does not cover the cost of modernizing even one stadium for the 2014 World Cup.

The total cost of modernizing the most important football stadium, Maracanã, located in Rio de Janeiro, has been estimated at $625.0 million. In São Paulo, the Morumbi stadium, home of the three times FIFA world champion, São Paulo Football Team, has been excluded from the World Cup because it falls short of technical specifications. The local organizing committee for the World Cup have decided to build a new stadium in order to meet FIFA's technical requirements. After FIFA's overview visit to Brazil in May 2011, they demanded that the stadium project should be modified. The new project has an estimated cost of $650.0 million, a 30 percent increase in the total cost. As the construction work has not started yet, it is quite possible that this stadium, chosen to be the inauguration venue, will not be ready.

In May 2009 the 12 host cities for the 2014 World Cup were chosen. At that time the total investment projected for building and modernizing stadiums was $3.0 billion. During this period inflation was 9 percent and the total budget project now is $4.7 billion, an increase of 56 percent (Bastos and Mattos, 2011). All host cities claimed that FIFA's technical requirements were mainly responsible for such an increase. Along with the increasing costs are delayed works and extended deadlines.

The majority of Brazil's football stadiums are old and crumbling. Their modernization is well overdue. Nine of the 12 grounds are publicly owned and more than 90 percent of total expenditure is expected to come from public funds. Stadiums in the larger and richer cities, Rio de Janeiro, São Paulo, Belo Horizonte, Curitiba, and Porto Alegre, are less of a concern. However, in cities such as Brasilia, Cuiabá, Manaus, and Natal, where there is no football team in the first division of the Brazilian National Championship, it is going to be very difficult to fill the stadiums on a regular basis after the Cup. Even in cities such as Fortaleza, Recife and Salvador, which have football teams in the first division, the population does not have the purchasing power to pay ticket prices high enough to maintain those stadiums. Therefore, at least half of the stadiums that are being built or revamped for the World Cup are likely to become 'white elephants' (Downie, 2010).

Furthermore, why spend money on lavish sports facilities that have little use after the World Cup? Why do countries like Brazil, which have manifold social problems, have to have the same sophisticated and complex sports facilities as the developed countries? Is it worth it?

4   2016 OLYMPIC GAMES

First, it is important to remember the results of the technical evaluation made by the International Olympic Committee (IOC) of the Rio de Janeiro bid to host the 2016 Summer Olympic Games. The report submitted by the Brazilian Olympic Committee (COB) received the lowest score among the finalists: 6.8. Tokyo scored highest, with 8.6, followed by Madrid (8.4) and Chicago (7.4). Rio de Janeiro's bid actually reached fifth place, behind Doha, which received a rating of 7.4. Doha was eliminated, since it could only host the event in October, a situation that was not acceptable to the IOC.

The technical evaluation undertaken by the IOC considered 11 items. For each, a range of grades was applied by different judges. The highest scores reached by Rio were 'governmental support and public support' (ranging from 7.3 to 8.8) and 'experience at hosting sporting events' (6.6 to 7.9). The lowest scores were: 'security' (4.6 to 7), 'transport infrastructure' (5.3 to 7.2) and 'lodging' (5.5 to 6.4).

The final phase of the evaluation process allowed the development of the initial bid, the correction of some weak points and the diffusion of the main aspects of the final bid to the media and public opinion. In this bidding phase estimated outlays range from $42.0 million to $50.0 million, but there is no official financial report yet.

The bid proposed investment budget was $18.0 billion. The three spheres of government, federal, state and municipal, will be responsible for $15.3 billion or 87.5 percent of the total. But, as is well known, those projected budgets are much underestimated. This is not a feature unique to underdeveloped countries trying to make up budgets to win sporting events bids. London's estimated cost of the 2012 Olympic Games was $4.0 billion. Now costs are expected to reach $19.0 billion, even with some projects being scaled back and others partially dismissed (Zimbalist, 2010). The 2007 Pan American Games in Rio had its initial proposed budget multiplied by 10, and left behind underused sporting venues and almost no urban legacy.

The 2016 Rio de Janeiro Olympic Games Organizing Committee (RJ OCOG) proposed project located most sports venues in Barra da Tijuca Olympic Park. This neighborhood is expected to receive 56 percent of all facilities that need to be built. It will hold 10 venues, three of which are already built: the Maria Lenk Aquatic Park, the Velodrome and the Multipurpose Arena. The other seven still need to be built, including the future Brazilian Olympic Training Center. They will occupy an area of 45 hectares. The two Media Villages, the Main Press Center (MPC), the International Radio and Television Center (IBC) and the official hotels of the IOC are also to be located there.

To tackle the problems of public transport and the environment, the proposed budget assumes that it will require investments of $3.5 billion. The main improvements would be: cleaning up the Barra da Tijuca lagoon system and implementing the Bus Rapid Transit (BRT), bus services with special reserved road lanes, connecting Barra da Tijuca to other parts of the city. Three BRT lines are proposed. The first is the Transcarioca line, linking Barra da Tijuca to the International Airport, with an estimated cost of $0.5 billion. The second is the Transolympic line, linking Barra da Tijuca to Deodoro, a neighborhood with an Olympic center. This line has an estimated cost of $0.35 billion. The third is the Transwest line with an estimated cost of $0.5 billion. The buses would use biofuel to reduce pollution, thereby providing an Olympics environmental legacy. There was no subway line construction projected in the winning bid. However, after the result was publicized, the Rio de Janeiro state administration government heralded the extension of the metro from Ipanema to Barra da Tijuca, 13.5 km (8.4 miles) away and at a cost of $2.5 billion. In spite of this, bus lines would continue to be the basis of the public transportation system.

Urban mobility must be understood as the movement of people and vehicles in a city or metropolitan area. This process of displacement acquires relevant proportions in cities which have been incorporating a number of suburbs and satellite cities. The metropolitan area requires the means of transport to be diverse and integrated.

In Rio, the most obvious negative consequence of public transportation is that it is mainly a system operated by regular bus lines. The population wastes hours stuck in traffic jams. To minimize these problems, a portion of the population regularly resort to unsafe transportation in vans – not always legalized – in the knowledge that they are running serious risks.

There is a consensus that the most effective solution to the problem of urban mobility in cities with high population densities such as Rio de Janeiro is a diversified and integrated subway network. However, the only subway expansion planned to be built for the Olympic Games is the one from Ipanema to Barra da Tijuca. To make matters worse, the extension runs in a single continuous line and does not allow connections to other lines.

The problem is that there seems to be no integration between the city urban planning and its transportation needs. Without an integrated approach to the city's urban planning, such fragmented solutions will not provide any effective improvements. An illustrative example of this lack of understanding is the Barra da Tijuca urban development. No public infrastructure such as a sewage network and public transport was provided. The circulation of buses and private cars was prioritized without providing any alternative public transport. The result of this kind of approach is daily traffic jams and the pollution of the lagoon system, which has already reached the beach.

Hosting the Olympic Games is a unique opportunity for the development of any city. Few have made good use of this opportunity. The 1992 Barcelona Olympic Games is the paradigm of positive evaluation in the literature of mega sporting events. The basic feature of this assessment is a consensus that the development plan for hosting the Summer Games must be included in the urban developing plan of the city. This is to say that hosting the Olympics must primarily be a favor to the city and not to the Olympic Games.

The Barcelona legacy of urban modernization, economic and social development extended much further than just sports venues. The city and the organizing committee decided to locate the main facilities for the Games near the historic city center, in its old port. At the time, the cost of expropriating land and transferring families in order to release space in the city for the Olympic facilities and urban improvements was considered too expensive. However, years after the Olympic Games, it has proved to be very cheap compared to the revenues that accrued to the city. The projects were selected by public tender, in which only Catalan architects could participate. There was no loss of quality with this procedure. After the Olympics the international recognition of the technical quality of the Catalan architecture and technical services related to it became an important asset to the city. The public management of the entire process and the political approval of the majority of the population was another decisive point in the success of the endeavor (Moragas and Botella, 1996). The hearts and minds of the population were won over by a decision-making process that considered their needs and interests. This is the kind of management that turns what can be considered an expensive short-term project into effective results in the long run. Munich 1972 is also mentioned in one of the few econometric studies that finds a long-term positive effect of the Olympic Games, at least partly (Jasmand and Maennig 2008).

Rio de Janeiro has to decide which way it wants to go, it has to choose between making the Games for Barra da Tijuca or for the City of Rio de Janeiro. Facing the challenge of integrating the historic port and downtown area means primarily recovering the historical city center and allocating investments in infrastructure to the most degraded region, the North Zone, the old suburban area of the city.[5] In this region live almost 60 percent of the population who have to travel to and from work every day. The smaller part of the population, no more than 30 percent, live in Barra da Tijuca and in the South Zone. Despite this, the majority of the modern urban facilities are concentrated in the location of the wealthiest residents. Barra da Tijuca is located 40 km (25 miles) from the historical center and has a low population density. Since the rate of population growth in Rio de Janeiro has been very low in the last few years, population density is the basic element for efficient operation of urban infrastructure. High density allows the scale and scope of the infrastructure investment to reduce operational costs.

It is important to note that there is a diagnostic error in the urban planning of Rio de Janeiro: the urbanization of the Barra da Tijuca region is regarded as a model for the whole city. If that model prevails, the city will become more and more disjointed, with some low-density better-off regions, and other worse-off regions concentrating most of the population.

Planning for the London 2012 Olympic Games illustrates its concerns about the legacy of mega sporting events to society. The facilities have been concentrated in the eastern part, the most degraded area of the city largely occupied by low-income immigrants. The water and soil in this area were contaminated by four centuries of careless use by industry and oil refineries. The 2012 London OCOG set up a planning process that included the participation of the population most directly involved through committees comprising community members. The aim of these committees was to discover whether there would be a demand for the sports facilities after the Games. In accordance with what they discovered, some of them have become temporary facilities. The investment focused on improving the neighborhood infrastructure, and the urban and social planning will go beyond 2012. London has incorporated into its planning the rotation of arenas during the Games to prevent the construction of unnecessary sporting venues.

Security has been a huge problem for the people living in Rio de Janeiro. However, it has not been a problem for the realization of mega events, of any kind, in the city. During those mega events, as in the Pan American Games, police and army troops flooded the streets, thereby acting as a huge deterrent to criminal activities.

To avoid having to use the Army in security control of civil areas during the 2014 World Cup and the 2016 Olympic Games, the Rio de Janeiro government is fighting crime through the creation and implementation of Police Peacekeeping Units (UPPs) in areas dominated by crime. UPPs take over these territories, arresting and expelling the criminal lords in order to free the local communities from the illegal power that has pre-vailed in the absence of formal authorities. The security policy in progress through the UPPs is one of the most successful ones, and has contributed most to the growing climate of confidence in the city. In the last election, the Governor of Rio de Janeiro was re-elected in the first ballot with more than two-thirds of the votes. His political victory was mainly achieved by the population's approval of the security policy. The electorate was almost unanimous about this point.

Accommodation is another problem for Rio de Janeiro. According to the Brazilian Association of Hotels (ABIH), at the time of the bidding victory there were only 28,000 rooms in the city, a shortage of 30,000 rooms. The RJ OCOG is committed to creating 49,750 rooms in hotels, hostels, ocean liners and in the two villages to accommodate visitors, the media and ref-erees. The ABIH is committed to increasing hotel rooms to 34,000. The RJ OCOG projection of hotel rooms is probably somewhat overstated, as is commonly the case with projected figures aimed at producing future outcomes. The mega sporting events literature is used to registering overly positive figures that ultimately are not realized[6] (Hagn and Maennig, 2008, 2009; Zimbalist, 2010). What is already occurring is an increase in hotel daily rates and housing prices as well as in the price of urban land. The reasons for this increase are various: incomes are rising after many years of very low economic growth, the UPPs have improved the political climate, and the population's perspectives about the World Cup and the Olympic Games are mostly positive. In regions where UPPs have been implemented, such as Tijuca, Vila Isabel and Copacabana, land, rent and property values have appreciated more than 50 percent (Cirilo and Valone, 2011).

Thus the success of the 1992 Barcelona Games and the planning for the 2012 London Summer Olympics are good examples of the ways in which the Olympic Games bring advantages to a city, rather than vice versa.

5   CONCLUSION

As discussed in this chapter, the cost to Brazil is an important feature to consider when analyzing World Cup and Olympic Games planning. The cost of hosting for a country relates both to national and urban logistics. In the case of Brazil, for decades the country has been lagging in infrastructure investment and its transportation system is mainly based upon travel by road and does not meet the current needs of a great part of the population. Compared to developed countries, transport, telecommunications, energy and sanitation infrastructure differs greatly, and Brazil has an income per capita three to four times lower than high-income countries such as the UK and the USA. Also, Brazil has yet to set up a welfare state that provides healthcare, a good public education system and social security for all its citizens. These conditions make hosting a mega sporting event much more demanding on the country's resources than in developed countries. So, with so much still lacking with regard to basic needs, why should Brazil have the same sophisticated and complex sports facilities as the developed countries? Is it worth it?

The answers to these questions differ greatly depending on who is to gain and who loses with building these facilities. What this chapter has tried to show is that in order for the mega events and facilities to make a difference to the living conditions of the population, planning has to focus on providing a positive long-lasting legacy. In Barcelona this was successfully accomplished. In London, it seems to be in the process of being achieved.

In Brazil and in Rio de Janeiro in particular, the economic and political climate have changed positively in the last decade or so. The performance of the economy, the improvements in social conditions, the successful security strategy of the Rio government and new discoveries of oil reserves in offshore deep waters, mostly in the coastal area of Rio de Janeiro, are the main motors of that change. Being awarded the World Cup and the Olympic Games can also play an important role in building a more confident scenario for the future.

However, for someone who witnessed the realization of the 2007 Pan American Games in Rio, there is no reason to believe that the promises made for the World Cup and the Olympic Games will be fulfilled. Despite the fact that its technical and sporting organization was very good, nothing that had been promised with regard to the urban legacy to the city was realized. The Pan American Games held in Rio in 2007 reportedly cost 10 times the official budget, and left behind underused arenas. Since the 2016 Olympic Games planning has enjoyed the same technical background as the 2007 Pan American Games, what can be expected of its completion? And what can be expected of the 2014 World Cup?

With the World Cup, it may be argued that even if the only reward it leaves behind is Brazil's sixth world championship, it will still be worth it. After all, in a country of football what could be more important, especially after spending over 60 years ruminating over what was lost in the 1950 World Cup in Brazil?

With the Olympic Games the story is quite different. Brazilians cannot really dream of beating the US in gold medals. Hosting the Games was advertised as a panacea for solving the city's problems. But the best it can do, when properly planned, is to help solve some of the city's problems. However, this seems not to be the case of Rio de Janeiro's bid. The current planning includes redeveloping the dilapidated port area and cleansing Guanabara Bay after 20 years of sewage and industrial pollution. Yet, whereas Barcelona built its main Games venues and facilities in run-down areas of its port, Rio de Janeiro will concentrate its main sporting venues in Barra da Tijuca, an upper-middle-class neighborhood located in the wealthiest part of the city.

With such a disjointed approach to the Olympic Games planning, the expected legacy may well be limited to the massive broadcasting of Rio's image all over the world for a brief period. This is certainly an intangible asset that may enhance the city's position in tourism and as a host of international sporting events. At least, in this way, a use will be found use for the 'white elephants' left behind. In brief, we can be sure that the party will be great; however, the hangover could be even greater.

NOTES

1. In Brazil it is assumed that each increase of 1 percent in infrastructure investment will produce a 0.2 percent increase in GDP (Puga and Borça, 2011).
2. See http://www.ipeadata.gov.br.
3. The data are available at www.fgv.br/cps/dd.
4. The Brazilian average monthly wage in 2010 was $931.63. If the ticket price were $100, how could Brazilians afford it? For Brazilian economic and social data, see www.ibge. gov.br.
5. After several meetings with the IOC technical staff, Rio de Janeiro's mayor decided to move the Media Village and Referees Village to the Port neighborhood which is in the process of being revamped. This is an improvement in the bid, but a minor one.
6. The number of expected visitors for the World Cup is very high. More than one million tourists are expected. In the last three years Brazil received 6.5 million tourists, on average, per year. These figures also point to a lack of hotel rooms with hotel daily rates skyrocketing. But these tourist figures have been exaggerated and have caused negative effects with regard to the number of tourists (self-defeating tourists) as discussed in du Plessis and Maennig (2011).

REFERENCES

Abdala, V. (2011), 'Taxa de investimento do país é insuficiente para manter ritmo de crescimento', *Agência Brasil*, May 17.

Bastos, M. and R. Mattos (2011), 'Esportes', *Folha de São Paulo*, São Paulo, 19 May.

Cassidy, J. (2009), *How Markets Fail*, New York: Farrar, Straus & Giroux.

Cirilo, J. and G. Vallone (2011), 'Rentabilidade de imóvel dispara no país' (Return of building fires in the country), Folha de São Paulo, 6 June.

Downie, A. (2010), 'World Cup 2014: march of the white elephants', *Financial Times*, July 5.

Du Plessis, S. and W. Maennig (2011), 'The 2010 World Cup high-frequency data economics: effects on international awareness and (self-defeating) tourism', Economic Discussions No. 37, University of Hamburg/Faculty Economics and Social Sciences.

Hagn, F. and W. Maennig (2008), 'Employment effects of the Football World Cup 1974 in Germany,' *Labour Economics*, **15** (5), 1062–75.

Hagn, F. and W. Maennig (2009), 'Large sport events and unemployment: the case of the 2006 Soccer World Cup in Germany', *Applied Economics*, **41** (25), 3295–302.

Humphreys, B. and A. Zimbalist (2008), 'The financing and economic import of the Olympic Games', in Brad Humphreys and Dennis Howard (eds), *The Business of Sports*, Vol. 1, Westport, CT: Praeger.

Jasmand, S and W. Maennig (2008), 'Regional income and employment effects of the 1972, Munich Summer Olympic Games', *Regional Studies*, **42** (7), August, 991–1002.

Lessa, C. (2009), 'Potencialidades da matriz de transporte para o Brasil' (Matrix of potential transportation to Brazil), Valor Econômico, 26 August.

Matheson, V. (2009), 'Economic multipliers and mega-event analysis', *International Journal of Sport Finance*, **4** (1), 63–70.

Melo, L.M. (2007), 'Brazilian football: technical success and economic failure', in R.M. Miller and L. Crolley (eds), *Football in the Americas: Fútbol, Futebol, Soccer*, London: Institute for the Study of the Americas, pp. 193–208.

Melo, L.M. and V. Dominato (2010), 'Políticas de apoio, logística e infraestrutura', in Renata Lebre La Rovere and Mauro Osorio da Silva (eds), *Desenvolvimento Econômico Local da Zona Oeste do Rio de Janeiro e de seu Entorno*, Rio de Janeiro: PoD Editora, pp. 103–19.

Moragas, M.and M. Botella (eds) (1996), *Las Claves Del Éxito, Impactos sociales, deportivos y comunicativos de Barcelona'92*, Barcelona: Centro de Estudios Olímpicos y Del Deporte/ Universidad Autónoma de Barcelona.

Nelson, R.R. (1995), 'Recent evolutionary theorizing about economic change', *Journal of Economic Literature*, **33** (1), March, 48–90.

Neto, C.A.S.C. and F.H. Souza (2011), 'Aeroportos no Brasil: investimentos recentes, perspectivas e preocupações', Nota Técnica no. 5, IPEA, Brasília, April.

Puga, F.P. and G. Borça Jr. (2011), 'Perspectiva de investimentos em infraestrutura 2011–2014', *Visão do Desenvolvimento*, No. 92, Banco Nacional do Desenvolvimento Econômico e Social (BNDES).

World Bank (2009), 'World Development Indicators database', September, available at: www.databank.worldbank.org.

Zimbalist, A. (2010), 'Is it worth it?', *Finance & Development*, March, 9–11.

30 The employment effects of London 2012: an assessment in mid-2011

Dan Brown and Stefan Szymanski

1 INTRODUCTION

In this chapter we investigate the employment effects of the London 2012 Olympics in the run-up to the Games. Employment levels at the Olympic site have been published by the Olympic Delivery Authority on a quarterly basis since September 2008. London's bid for 2012 was notable for its emphasis on the legacy benefits of the Games and its impact on the surrounding areas. Therefore we review related and unrelated infrastructure projects that have occurred in the areas around the site, notably the five 'host' London boroughs (Greenwich, Hackney, Newham, Tower Hamlets, and Waltham Forest). Finally, we review overall employment trends at the level of the London boroughs over the past decade using data published by the Office of National Statistics (ONS).

The legacy impacts of London 2012, in particular the regeneration of the Lower Lea Valley region, constituted a major argument in favour of London's successful Olympic bid. London's candidate file reads: 'the most enduring legacy of the Olympics will be the regeneration of an entire community for the direct benefit of everyone who lives there'. If London 2012 is to make a real difference in the lives of those in its most deprived area, we should expect significant local employment effects. Indeed, London's candidate file states: 'The biggest economic legacy from the games will be the creation of wider employment opportunities and improvements in the education, skills and knowledge of the local labour force in an area of very high unemployment'.

Thus far, however, we find that the employment impact of the Games is small. In April 2011 there were 12,343 people employed directly at the site, this figure representing peak employment to date, and well in excess of the average since 2008 when employment reached a significant level. This represents just over 2 per cent of total employment in the host boroughs and less than one-third of 1 per cent of total employment in London.

In the next section we discuss the nature of the economic impact that might be expected due to the Games. Section 3 examines employment levels on the Olympic site itself, Section 4 reviews some of the other recent infrastructure projects in the region, and then Section 5 looks at employment trends in the host boroughs and London in general. Section 6 concludes.

2   THE ECONOMIC IMPACT OF THE GAMES

One of the strengths of the UK's approach to hosting the Olympic Games has been the detailed analysis before the event of objectives and outcomes. While the Games are technically controlled by the city in which they are held (via the London Organising Committee of the Olympic Games: LOCOG), the necessity of government support for funding of infrastructure investment (under the auspices of the Olympic Delivery Authority: ODA), financial guarantees and enabling legislation means that in reality the host government needs to decide its overall strategy. In 2008 the Department of Culture, Media and Sport (DCMS), the relevant government ministry, set out the following 'National commitments':[1]

G1.   To make the UK a world-leading sporting nation;
G2.   To transform the heart of East London;
G3.   To inspire a generation of young people;
G4.   To make the Olympic park a blueprint for sustainable living;
G5.   To demonstrate the UK as a creative, inclusive and welcoming place to live in, visit and for business;
G6.   To draw on the unique and inspirational power of the Games to promote inclusion, positive attitudes towards, and the active participation of disabled people.

Note that objectives G2 and G4 relate specifically to the local area in which the Games will be held. In addition, the Mayor of London laid down five legacy commitments in January 2008:

L1.   To increase opportunities for Londoners to become involved in sport;
L2.   To ensure Londoners benefit from new jobs, businesses and volunteering opportunities;
L3.   To transform the heart of East London;
L4.   To deliver a sustainable games and develop sustainable communities;
L5.   To showcase London as a diverse, creative and welcoming city.

In this chapter we are focused primarily on the pre-Games employment effects, which are part of objective L2.

It is important to set the development of the Olympic site in its broader context (Figure 30.1). The Olympic site is in the Stratford[2] area of East London, a region characterized by severe deprivation.[3] The host boroughs formed part of the hinterland of London's docklands, which largely closed

Figure 30.1   London boroughs, the host boroughs and the Olympic site

down in the 1960s and 1970s, during which period the region is estimated to have lost in the region of 150,000 jobs, some 20 per cent of total employment in the area (Poynter and MacRury, 2009). The host boroughs and their surrounding areas have not recovered from this economic shock, and now count among the most deprived boroughs in the country. Based on a national index of deprivation the five host boroughs ranked 2nd, 3rd, 6th, 23rd, and 27th out of 354 English boroughs (ibid., p. 17).

The government has devoted significant resources to encouraging redevelopment of the area, most notably through support for the Docklands development project in the 1980s, turning part of the region (mostly located within Tower Hamlets) into an extension of the financial district (the eastern border main financial district the 'City of London' – also known as the 'Square Mile' – is located less than four miles from the Olympic site). A number of long-term transport projects have also received government support (for example, the Dockland Light Railway and the Jubilee Line Extension), while the Millennium Dome project in Greenwich also attracted significant public funding.

In 1996, the government awarded a contract to London and Continental

Railways (LCR), a private sector consortium, to build a high speed rail track from the Channel Tunnel to London St. Pancras. As well as providing a public subsidy, the government gave LCR development rights around the London terminal and at Stratford which lay along the route. In 1997, LCR started working on plans for a mixed retail, commercial and residential development to be named Stratford City. Thus, by 2003, when the government decided to support a London Olympic bid, plans for development of the site were already well advanced, and much of the development would have occurred even if London had not won the Games.

Winning the Games in 2005 was a highly unexpected event, since Paris was the runaway favourite. Kavetsos (2011) shows that this unexpected event had a significant impact on property prices, with properties within a three-mile radius of the Olympic site enjoying a 5 per cent increase in value, (over and above the average increased property values in greater London) while properties within a nine-mile radius increased in value by 2.2 per cent on average (both increases statistically significant). These increases presumably reflected the increased amenity value (although to the extent that these effects reflect any interaction with complementary development projects, the value may not be fully attributable to the Olympics).

3   OLYMPIC SITE EMPLOYMENT

Table 30.1 provides a timeline for construction activities related to the Olympic site.

On-site Olympic expenditure was minimal prior to winning the Games. After the Games were awarded to London in 2005, a number of projects had to be carried out before the construction of Olympic facilities could start. This mainly involved the remediation of contaminated land and burying electric power cables which were previously carried on overhead pylons. This work was funded by the London Development Agency and cost in the region of £1 billion.

Table 30.2 presents the published employment data provided by the ODA since September 2008.

The figures show that employment on the Olympic site has risen from 2,539 in September 2008 to 12,343 by April 2011 (see also Figure 30.2). These are relatively modest figures. Thus, the total employment in the host boroughs in 2010 was 495,000, and, hence, employment on the Olympic site represented only 2.1 per cent of employment, at what was in all probability the peak period of construction employment. Over the 2½-year period for which we have data, total employment on the Olympic site is

Table 30.1   Olympic site construction timeline

Date	Activity
11/07/03	The British Olympic Association informs the IOC that London is bidding for the 2012 Olympic Games
06/07/05	London's Olympic bid is announced as winner, London is to host the 2012 Olympic Games
05/06	Construction work on two 6 km underground tunnels (to supply power to the Olympic site underground) begins. Construction was completed June 2007
14/12/06	Demolition work on the Olympic Park (OP) site begins at Eton Manor
04/08	Construction on the Primary Substation begins (OP). Construction was completed October 2009
22/05/08	Construction on the Olympic Stadium begins (OP)
03/06/08	Construction on the Olympic Village begins
07/08	Construction on the Aquatics Centre (OP) begins
09/08	Construction on the Energy Centre begins (OP)
03/09	Construction on the Velodrome (OP) begins
04/09	Construction on the International Broadcast Centre/Main Press Centre (OP) begins
07/09	Construction on the Handball Arena (OP) begins
09/09	Construction on the Olympic Fringe (the development of the town centres of Stratford, Hackney Wick and Leyton, and the construction of 13,000 new housing units) began
10/09	Construction on the Basketball arena begins

equivalent to 16,420 person years, compared to a total of 1,232,450 person years in the host boroughs in total, that is, 1.3 per cent. In the context of total employment in all London boroughs of around 3.6 million per year, these figures are clearly negligible.

The employment may also be considered disappointing in the light of the commitment to create jobs for local people, given that the five boroughs suffer from unusually high unemployment rates. On average, less than a quarter of those employed on the Olympic site are resident within the five boroughs, and, indeed, it is possible that even many of these have migrated into the area at least temporarily to take advantage of the temporary employment opportunities. It is striking to note that between one-third and one-half of the Olympic site workforce are not even resident in London, despite the obvious inconvenience of having to commute to the middle of London to work. The ODA is satisfied that it has met its target of employing at least 15 per cent of its workforce from local residents.

Table 30.2 Olympic Park employment

Date	Olympic Park contractors				Olympic Village contractors				Total			
	Host boroughs	Other London boroughs	Outside London	Total	Host boroughs	Other London boroughs	Outside London	Total	Host boroughs	Other London boroughs	Outside London	Total
Sep-08	637	929	973	2,539					637	929	973	2,539
Jan-09	751	1,131	1,238	3,120					751	1,131	1,238	3,120
Apr-09	826	1,351	1,657	3,834					826	1,351	1,657	3,834
Jul-09	866	1,503	1,938	4,307					866	1,503	1,938	4,307
Oct-09	1,009	1,668	2,165	4,842					1,009	1,668	2,165	4,842
Jan-10	1,230	2,060	2,987	6,277					1,230	2,060	2,987	6,277
May-10	1,272	2,185	2,985	6,442				3,228	1,909	3,280	4,481	9,670
Oct-10	1,289	2,088	2,866	6,243	1,008	1,571	1,511	4,090	2,297	3,659	4,377	10,333
Jan-11	1,346	2,200	2,953	6,499	1,468	2,121	1,792	5,381	2,814	4,321	4,745	11,880
Apr-11	1,339	1,971	2,724	6,034	1,771	2,523	2,015	6,309	3,110	4,494	4,739	12,343

Source: ODA Employment and Skills Update.

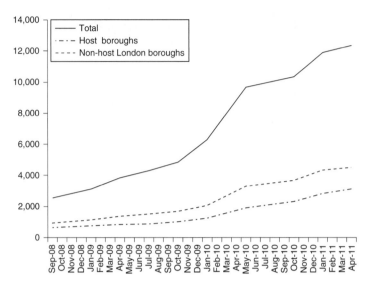

Figure 30.2   Olympic Park employment (employed for 5 days or more in a month)

4   OTHER REGENERATION PROJECTS IN THE HOST BOROUGHS

The need for the regeneration of areas of East London has been recognized ever since its industrial decline dating from the 1960s. Numerous regeneration projects have been implemented under the direction of a number of organizations and partnerships, starting with the London Docklands Development Corporation set up in 1981. The London Thames Gateway Development Corporation, born in 2004, was the government's lead regeneration agency for the Lower Lea Valley and London Riverside, but in 2011 the government announced that it would be abolished and its functions returned to local government by 2013. Other large-scale construction work has been ongoing in the host boroughs throughout the period discussed here, and may account for the residual between Olympic employment and the total construction sector employment change.

Since information on the number of jobs created by these development projects is not available, we have simply listed the start and end dates of construction, the sums of money invested (to gain an idea of the scale of the projects), and the boroughs in which construction is taking place, where this information is available. It should be noted that some of the 'Olympic' transport infrastructure construction (see Appendix 30A) would have taken place in the absence of the Olympics, and is only partly funded by the ODA. Thus, some of the employment on the Olympic transport infrastructure projects also represents 'other regeneration project' employment. (Table 30.3.)

These projects are separate from the Olympics; they are not funded or coordinated by the ODA. Employment on the construction of these projects cannot be considered a direct effect of the Olympics. Nonetheless, many of these projects may be taking place as a consequence of London's hosting of the Olympics. There are complementarities between the Olympic investments and these other development project investments.

Olympic advocates argue that these other development projects have only become financially viable in the presence of the Olympic investments, in line with 'Big Push' theories of development. The most widely cited example is the Westfield group development of what is claimed to be Europe's largest shopping Mall in Stratford City, a £1.45 billion investment whose owners claim has created 25,000 construction jobs (without specifying over what period) and 18,000 permanent jobs in retail and related services. Stratford City was a planned development before London decided to bid for the Games, but it is at least arguable that the plans might not have been realized, or would have been realized in a lesser form, if London had not won the Games.

Without transcripts of discussions undertaken within government agencies, London borough councils and private sector companies (such as Westfield), we cannot know for sure whether the Olympics figured significantly in the decision to go ahead with these projects. However, some comments from the associated organizations imply the Olympics have been important. Westfield's Group Managing Director Steven Lowy, considering the progress of Westfield Stratford City, noted, 'We wouldn't be doing this in this time scale without the Olympics'. He has also stated that Westfield could 'anticipate significant transformation flowing from the 2012 Olympics, with Stratford City becoming the metropolitan centre of East London'. The Green Grid Initiative Area Framework 1 (Lea Valley) document states that 'the design and delivery of these new open space areas (those outside the Olympic Park site) will be brought forward over the coming years in parallel with the Olympic Park'. The ExCel centre is to be used as an Olympic venue, although the London 2012 website mentions 'there is no construction needed to create ExCel's five arenas', suggesting that this expansion may have taken place without the Olympics.

Set against this, there are some construction projects that have been significantly delayed as a result of the Olympics. In 2003, the government supported the completion of the Crossrail Project, a major east–west rail link which is expected to have significant development potential for East

Table 30.3 Details of major non-Olympic regeneration projects in host boroughs 2007/08–2008/09

Project	Project details	Construction dates	Estimated total project cost	Location
Royal Arsenal	Construction of 1,400 homes, 350,000 square feet of industrial premises, and two museums	2000–18	Not known	Greenwich
East London Green Grid Initiative	The construction of 50 small projects, including open spaces and natural landscaped	2006–10	£110 million	6 project areas, covering all five host boroughs, and extending to other East London boroughs
Westfield Shopping Centre, Stratford City	The construction of a 5 million square foot commercial office district, 2.9 million square feet of retail and leisure space, 1.3 million square feet of hotel space as well as new homes and community spaces	July 2008	£1.45 billion	Newham
ExCel expansion	A 50% increase in the size of the facility equivalent to 14 football pitches (7), including a 5,000 seated auditorium and 20 new conference rooms	11 August 2008–2010	£160 million	Newham
Woodberry Down Estate	Construction of 4,412 new homes and 38,500 square feet of community facilities. Phase 1 involves the construction of 117 social rented new homes	Phase 1 construction began in March 2009	Not known (Homes and Communities Agency contributed £16 million to start Phase 1)	Hackney
Ferrier Estate, Kidbrooke	Removal of 1,906 homes, construction of 4,000 new homes alongside improvements to local facilities such as schools	Demolition began March 2009	£1 billion	Greenwich

London, by 2012/13, but once it became clear that completion could not be guaranteed before 2012, it was postponed. The first section of track is now scheduled for completion in 2018, some five years later than planned in 2003. It is possible that there are other infrastructure projects with positive rates of return that will be completed later, or may now have been shelved, due to the commitment to fund the Olympics.

5   EMPLOYMENT TRENDS IN LONDON

Estimating the employment impact simply by adding up recognizable Olympic projects is not completely satisfactory. The 2012 Olympics may contribute positively to employment in the host boroughs both directly and indirectly. Direct employment effects of the Olympics are those which result immediately from the construction work on the Olympic site. The most obvious direct employment effects are those in the construction sector. Construction sector job creation results from the demolition and remediation work on the Olympic Park site in preparation for construction; the construction work undertaken on the Olympic Park and Olympic Village sites themselves; as well as work on local transport infrastructure (see Appendix 30A).

The *direct effects* extend beyond the construction sector. To give an example: if food vendors set up close to the Olympic construction sites to provide for the construction workforce, the employment created is a direct result of Olympic construction work. Complementary jobs may be created in any number of different sectors to cater for an inflow of construction workers, from grocers to hairdressers. The non-construction direct effects can be very wide ranging.

The timing of the direct employment effects will tie in closely with the important dates of Olympic construction work. Some job creation could have begun before the start of construction work, with businesses rationally locating in the area anytime after the Olympic announcement in anticipation of an increasing construction workforce. In fact, if it was expected that the International Olympic Committee (IOC) would announce London as winner before its formal announcement on 6 July 2005, this direct Olympic effect may even predate the announcement. Kavetsos (2011) takes betting odds as the best gauge of these expectations; with London priced at 11–4, and Paris at 1–4 prior to the announcement, we reasonably expect to see little effect before July 2005. We hypothesize that direct employment effects occur fairly immediately from the announcement onwards, and are very closely tied to the volume of Olympic construction activity taking place at any time.

The *indirect employment effects* of the 2012 Olympics are more complex. Some indirect channels can be identified explicitly. First, we expect employment linked to tourism to increase significantly. At the time of the Games, local travel agents may see a surge in demand as tourists look for assistance planning their East London holiday; more receptionists, catering staff and cleaners will be required as hotels fill out; while businesses may set up in host boroughs to sell a variety of different goods to tourists. Second, a wealth effect on household consumption or on investment of local businesses may result from house-price increases in the host boroughs.

However, ultimately the indirect effects may be very wide ranging, and cannot be neatly separated into distinct channels in this way. The ambition of the Games is to dramatically regenerate this deprived East London region. If the Olympics succeeds in breaking the Lower Lea Valley out of its relative poverty trap, if it stimulates investment, consumption and a virtuous cycle of increasing prosperity, a range of economic activities suddenly become viable that were not when the region was not so prosperous. Job creation in any number of different sectors may thus be attributed indirectly to the Olympics.

Understanding the timing of the indirect effects is as complex as the identification of the effects themselves. Some indirect employment effects may occur immediately at the time of the announcement of London's successful bid. If businesses rationally anticipate the future increase in prosperity and tourist numbers at the time of the announcement they may find it profitable to move to the region immediately. The house-price effect was found to occur at the time of the Olympic announcement; associated wealth effects may also be quick to impact. If businesses take time to relocate to host boroughs, for example reflecting the time taken to sell fixed factors of production, invest in new capital or hire new workers for the new location, there will be a lag associated with some employment creation. The legacy impacts on employment through increased prosperity will occur in the future once those substantial increases in prosperity have materialized, if in fact they do. To summarize, we should expect the majority of the indirect employment effects to occur later than the direct employment effects. The more substantial the legacy effects, the more significant will be the proportion of indirect employment created after the Games.

The Annual Population Survey (APS) provides figures for total employment numbers and rates, and employment numbers disaggregated by sector, for each local authority area in the UK. Since London boroughs are classified as local authority areas, this provides employment numbers and rates at a London borough level. Individuals are assigned to London boroughs in accordance with their place of residence. The APS is published quarterly, with statistics measured annually ending in each respective quarter. The APS is available from January–December 2004 to January–December 2009. Before January–December 2004, dating back to March 1999 to February 2000, comparable information was collected in the Annual Local Area Labour Force Survey (ALALFS). The ALALFS data are only available for periods dating from March one year to February the following year. We combined the two datasets to provide a measure of employment from 1999/00–2008/09, as described in Appendix 30A. We use April–March data for the APS since it fits closest with the March–February ALALFS data.

There exist some differences between the two datasets. They differ first in sample size, the APS comprising the ALALFS and an 'APS boost' sample, to achieve a minimum of 450 economically active adults in each London borough. The method to produce annual figures from the quarterly Labour Force Survey data (the foundation of both datasets) differs (see the 'Labour Force Survey User Guide – Volume 6' for more information). For both datasets we use the total working-age population. The APS dataset changed after August 2008, measuring women aged 16–64 rather than the previous working-age definition for women – aged 16–59. The APS figures dating back to 2004/05 were modified, but our ALALFS dataset still uses the original working-age definition for women. Nonetheless, for the purposes of this chapter we believe that the two datasets are sufficiently compatible.

Our measure of economic activity rates is compiled from the ALALFS and APS datasets (see Appendix 30A), just as with our employment measures. We consider the total economic activity rate among those of working age in each London borough.Throughout our analysis we consider 32 London boroughs, consistently excluding the City of London. Employment numbers and rates are not available for the City of London before 2003/04. Employment numbers by sector are not available for the City of London for any sector other than Banking, Finance and Insurance and Manufacturing, on the grounds that the number sampled in these other sectors was too small. The industrial structure of the City of London is so different from the 32 London boroughs that it can be considered an outlier for our purposes.

Figure 30.3 compares employment rates on average in the host boroughs and the non-host London boroughs. This shows that employment rates in the host boroughs have been consistently between 5 per cent and 10 per cent lower in the host boroughs, reflecting their relatively high levels of deprivation. However, while employment rates have continued to fall across London over the last decade, rates have started to rise again since 2005, when the Games were won.

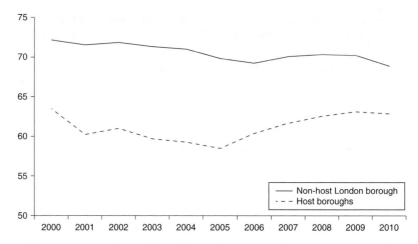

Figure 30.3   Host borough employment rates against the average non-host borough employment rate (%), 1999/00–2009/10

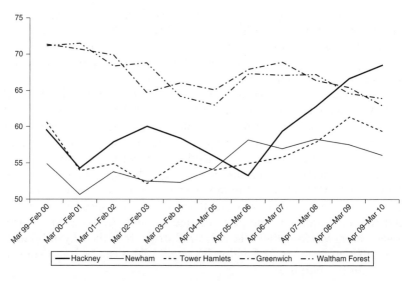

Figure 30.4   Host borough employment rates (%) 1999/00–2009/10

Figure 30.4 shows the employment rates for each of the host boroughs. This shows that while employment rates have been trending downwards in Greenwich and Waltham Forest, in line with the rest of London, rates have been rising consistently in Newham, Tower Hamlets and especially Hackney.

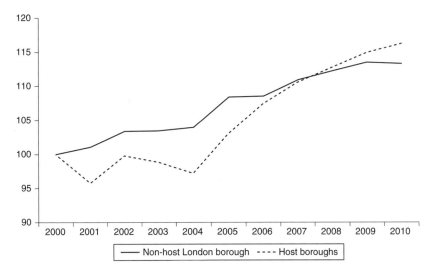

*Figure 30.5   Average host borough employment growth against average
non-host borough employment growth, 1999/00–2009/10*

Next we consider the total increase in employment since 2000 (Figure 30.5). It is striking that employment in London has sustained continuous growth, not only during the boom period of the middle of the decade but also during the minor recession of 2001/02 as well as the major recession that started in 2008. Employment growth in the host boroughs has been particularly strong since 2004, coinciding with the period following the award of the Games to London.

Figure 30.6 disaggregates the employment growth figures by host borough. While all the host boroughs have experienced employment growth over the period, there is evidence of strong growth in Hackney, Newham and Tower Hamlets since 2004.

Table 30.4 ranks London boroughs according to their employment growth rates since 2005. While the growth rates of employment in London generally have been lower since 2005 than in the five years before 2005, the pattern is reversed in the host boroughs, This effect is largely accounted for by the rapid growth in employment in Hackney and Tower Hamlets, which top the rankings. The remaining three boroughs are only average in their employment growth rates since 2005.

The London employment data are disaggregated into seven categories based on the Standard Industrial Classification: manufacturing, construction, distribution hotels and restaurants, transport and communications, banking finance and insurance (BFI), public administration education and

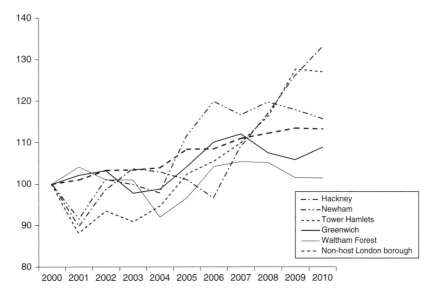

Figure 30.6   Average host borough employment growth, 1999/00–2009/10

health (PAEH), and other services. The calculation in Table 30.5 shows the total cumulative additional employment years created relative to the baseline of 2004/05.

The pattern of employment growth is striking. The two sectors that dominate the increase in host borough employment years since 2004/05 are BFI and PAEH. BFI makes the largest positive contribution to employment increases in two host boroughs, Greenwich and Hackney, and the second-largest positive contribution in Tower Hamlets and Newham. Overall, the BFI sector created more jobs than any other in the host boroughs over the period. PAEH makes the largest positive contribution to increases in employment years in three of the five boroughs: Tower Hamlets, Newham and Waltham Forest, and the second-largest positive contribution to increases in employment in Hackney. These two sectors accounted for 91 per cent of employment growth in the host sectors. Neither sector has any clear association with the construction phase of the Olympic project.

By contrast, employment in the construction sector decreases across the period in three of the five boroughs – Greenwich, Hackney and Tower Hamlets – and in aggregate falling in the host boroughs by around 9,000. It is difficult to reconcile these findings with the hypothesis that direct Olympic effects have driven the relative increase in employment rates in host boroughs identified above. While direct Olympic employment effects cover sectors

Table 30.4   Employment rate growth ranks

Borough	Average annual growth rate of employment 2000–2010	Average annual growth rate of employment 2005–2010
Hackney (host)	2.91	5.66
Tower Hamlets (host)	2.42	4.39
Southwark	2.60	3.31
Lambeth	2.64	3.15
Camden	3.83	3.04
Islington	2.68	2.63
Hounslow	1.20	1.70
Westminster	3.94	1.53
Richmond upon Thames	1.78	1.47
Wandsworth	1.80	1.47
Brent	0.93	1.40
Sutton	0.18	1.35
Merton	0.84	1.17
Kingston upon Thames	1.86	1.11
Barking and Dagenham	0.17	1.05
Waltham Forest (host)	0.14	0.97
Greenwich (host)	0.85	0.86
Hillingdon	0.47	0.80
Kensington and Chelsea	2.76	0.75
Newham (host)	1.48	0.74
Bromley	0.86	0.66
Croydon	1.04	0.48
Barnet	0.04	0.20
Harrow	0.46	0.16
Havering	−0.28	0.15
Lewisham	1.48	0.02
Haringey	0.44	−0.21
Hammersmith and Fulham	1.45	−0.27
Redbridge	0.48	−0.59
Bexley	0.34	−0.72
Enfield	0.12	−0.78
Ealing	1.00	−1.03
Non-host London borough	1.25	0.88
Host boroughs	1.52	2.44

Table 30.5 *Cumulative increase in employment 2004/05–2009/10 by sector*

	Greenwich	Hackney	Newham	Tower Hamlets	Waltham Forest	Host boroughs	Non-host boroughs
Total	21,300	59,600	27,000	57,300	33,200	198,400	450,500
Manufacturing	−5,000	−6,600	−2,300	6,900	3,100	−3,900	−15,500
Construction	−16,200	−5,000	6,800	−1,900	7,000	−9,300	69,000
Distribution, hotels and restaurants	9,700	4,300	6,600	−3,200	12,500	29,900	−148,400
Transport and communications	8,800	−1,200	−9,400	1,500	−14,400	−14,700	−21,000
Banking, finance and insurance	36,200	32,300	9,500	29,400	−14,700	92,700	290,900
Public administration, education and health	−13,700	29,000	18,300	29,600	24,800	88,000	185,600
Other services	4,500	−900	−6,400	−3,300	5,900	−200	14,000

other than construction, we can reasonably expect the construction sector to be the greatest recipient of direct Olympic employment. Changes in employment years in the construction sector are of a smaller scale than changes in the BFI and PAEH sectors, and are negative in three of the five boroughs. This is particularly interesting in the context of the increases in construction sector employment in non-host boroughs over the same period. The construction sector was the third-largest positive contributor to increases in employment years in non-host boroughs, creating 69,000 additional years of employment in total. The limited contribution of the construction sector to overall increases in employment years in host boroughs therefore cannot be explained as the result of a downturn in construction sector employment more widely. It is intuitively difficult to believe that a large proportion of the PAEH and BFI employment increases were the direct effect of the construction activities taking place on the Olympic site, and so the importance of direct Olympic employment effects appears questionable.

The employment increases in non-host boroughs were driven primarily by the PAEH and BFI sectors, just as in the host boroughs. If there were a significant indirect employment effect of the Olympics, we may expect the pattern by sector of those host borough employment increases to differ from the non-host boroughs more markedly. The host boroughs seem to have benefited from the same factors that have generated London-wide employment increases in the PAEH and BFI sectors. This does not necessarily mean that there have been no indirect Olympic effects, even if it is suggestive.

6   CONCLUSIONS

Comparing increases in construction sector employment years with total increases in employment years since 2004/05, the construction sector accounts for little of the additional employment years generated in host boroughs. Comparing employment years created on the Olympic Park with overall increases in construction sector employment years, Olympic construction accounts for little of additional construction sector employment years created in host boroughs since 2007/08. Construction sector employment changes do not seem to be driving total employment changes, and Olympic construction employment does not seem to be driving these construction sector employment changes. While the employment on the Olympic Park site does not fully represent Olympic construction sector work, and construction sector employment does not fully represent the total direct employment effect of the Olympics, our findings still cautiously suggest that the direct employment effects of the Olympics are small.

NOTES

1. DCMS (2008), 'Before, during and after: making the most of the London 2012 Games', London.
2. This Stratford has no relationship with Stratford-Upon-Avon, the birthplace of Shakespeare, which is more than 100 miles away in the midland county of Warwickshire.
3. The site is also often referred to as the Lower Lee Valley (alternatively 'Lea' – either spelling is accepted).

REFERENCES

Kavetsos, G. (2011), 'The impact of the London Olympics announcement on property prices', *Urban Studies*, published online doi: 10.1177/0042098011415436, August 22.
Poynter, G. and I. MacRury (eds) (2009), *Olympic Cities and the Reshaping of London*, Aldershot: Ashgate.

APPENDIX 30A

Table 30A.1 lists here the major transport infrastructure construction projects undertaken by the ODA in the host boroughs. Some of these projects may have gone ahead in the absence of the Olympics, and are part funded from sources other than the ODA. Where the information is available we have listed the dates of construction, and the proportion of funding coming from the ODA.

Table 30A.1   Olympic transport projects

Project	Project description	Date	ODA funding
Railway Depot	Construction of a new 12 track Railway Depot at Orient Way	December 2006 to December 2010	Not known
Stratford Regional Station	Upgrade of Stratford Regional Station: improvements to platform access, construction of a new westbound Central Line platform, construction of nine new lifts, lengthening and widening of platforms and construction of a new entrance	Due to be finished by the end of 2010	£125 million investment, fully funded by the ODA
North London Line (being converted from National Rail to Docklands Light Railway)	Extension from Stratford Regional station to Stratford International station	Not known	Not known
Docklands Light Railway	2.6 km track extension from King George V to Woolwich Arsenal station	2005–09 (opened January 2009)	£80 million investment by ODA. The project is part funded by ODA. The total estimated cost of the project is £145 million

Table 30A.1   (continued)

Project	Project description	Date	ODA funding
Stratford International Station Bridge	Construction of a 36 m bridge at Stratford International Rail Station to form a new exit and entrance to the station	Completed at the time of the July 2010 'Connected' publication	Not known
Walking and cycling paths	Resurfacing paths, implementing clearer signs and improving exit and entrance points	Due to be finished by Summer 2011	£10 million investment by ODA

Sources: 'Transport Plan for the London 2012 Olympic and Paralympic Games Summary', October 2007, ODA; 'On Track', Issue 2, December 2009, ODA; and 'Connected', July 2010, ODA.

Table 30A.2   *Methods used to compile datasets*

Dataset	Source	Method to compile data	Further information on source
Employment rate 1999/00– 2009/10	Annual Local Area Labour Force Survey and Annual Population Survey, ONS	We took the 'Annual Population Survey Employment Rate – aged 16–64', for the dates April 04– March 05 to April 08–March 09 for the 32 London boroughs. The ALALFS provides only the number of 'Persons of Working Age In Employment'. This was divided by the total 'Persons of Working Age', to provide the employment rate for the years March 1999–February 2000 to March 2003–February 2004. This is the same methodology as has already been carried out in the APS dataset to provide the employment rate. These two datasets are combined to give our overall series	ONS: 'Annual Population Survey' (article) ONS: 'Labour Force Survey User Guide – Volume 6: Local Area Data'

Table 30A.2 (continued)

Dataset	Source	Method to compile data	Further information on source
ODA Employment numbers by borough, September 2008 to April 2011	ODA 'Employment and Skills Update – September 2008' to 'Employment and Skills Update – April 2011'	Employment numbers by borough were taken from Table 3 in these publications	–
Economic activity rate 1999/00–2009/10	Annual Local Area Labour Force Survey and Annual Population Survey, ONS	We have combined the 'Annual Population Survey Economic Activity Rate – aged 16–64' for the dates April 04–March 05 to April 08–March 09, with a measure of the economic activity rate derived from the ALALFS 'Persons of Working Age Economically Active' dataset. Just as with the employment measure, the ALALFS does not provide rates; we divide the number economically active by the total 'Persons of Working Age' consistent with APS methodology, to obtain a measure of economic activity rates for the years March 1999–February 2000 to March 2003–February 2004. These two datasets are combined to give our overall series	ONS: 'Annual Population Survey' (article) ONS: 'Labour Force Survey User Guide – Volume 6: Local Area Data'
Employment numbers by sector 2004/05–2009/10	Annual Population Survey, ONS	Employment numbers were taken from the 'Employment Numbers by Industry' dataset (available on the Nomis website)	

PART VI

CONCLUSION

31 Future challenges: maximizing the benefits and minimizing the costs
Wolfgang Maennig and Andrew Zimbalist

1 INTRODUCTION

It is characteristic for the scholarly analyses of mega sporting events to make the assumption that the governing bodies wield monopoly power. In the case of mega events, the sporting federations use their monopoly power in order to try to extract the maximum of benefits, profits, or, in economic terms: 'rents'. The International Olympic Committee (IOC), for instance, auctions off the right to host the Winter and Summer Games in a multi-stage competition. Prospective host cities/countries bid against each other to purchase a unitary product. The competitive bidding, in turn, leads the would-be hosts to bid up to the point where the expected marginal social utility of benefit from the Games equals the expected marginal social cost; or worse, if the winner, due to imperfect information, is subjected to a curse and bids beyond the benefit (see Andreff, ch. 4 in this volume).

Or worse still, the bidding cities may suffer from a principal–agent problem. That is, a city's (principal) campaign to host a mega event may be initiated and driven by private interests (agent) that have individually to gain from the construction, design, fanfare, financing, and so on of the event. The private interests of these individuals or companies may only be congruent with the broader development interests of the city by coincidence. If the private interests form a coalition and, from their base of economic power and political connections, then enlist local politicians, the resulting campaign may have little to do with benefitting the city's economy. If the agent is not acting in the city's interests, then the theoretical formulation of bidding up to the point where the marginal expected social benefit equals the marginal expected social cost may have little to do with reality. In such a case, the calculus in practice is then approximated by the marginal private benefit versus marginal private cost, the latter being small for the agent(s). When the vast bulk of the social cost is borne by the public, this criterion will lead to massive overspending.

2   MARKET POWER AND COST OVERRUNS

To be sure, the possibility of such a principal–agent problem may also help to explain why the advertised social costs often bear small resemblance to the final price tag for hosting a mega event. The private interests promoting the event are motivated to present a scaled-down budget to ease the proposal's way through the city council and/or the state legislature. Once passed at this level, the agent then, and particularly under competitive pressure during the bidding process, finds new facilities to be built or new bells and whistles to be added.

Many prospective hosts see the mega event as an opportunity to overcome political differences and institutional bottlenecks, and gain approval for long-needed infrastructural improvements in the areas of transportation, energy or telecommunications. Also, the host cities try to outdo each other with more and more architecturally impressive facilities in order to maximize any image effects. And sometimes mega events can work in this way; however, the same countries that are in dire need for such investments are often the same ones that lack the institutional capacity and skilled labor to effectively carry out the necessary construction. Typically, organizers fall behind in their timetable and, ultimately, must pay premiums and/or even bribes to get the work done (see Burbank et al., ch. 10 and Mehta and Majumdar, ch. 28, in this volume). Together with other inflationary elements, some of them out of reach of the organizers (for example, rising raw material prices), the project's costs begin to balloon, and Games with an initial budget of, say, $5 billion may become a final expenditure of $15 billion.[1] The *ex post* costs of Athens (over $16 billion for preparing and operating the Summer Olympics 2004); China (more than $40 billion for the Games in 2008)[2] and South Africa for the 2010 World Cup also far exceeded the planned costs (see Tomlinson and Bass, ch. 18 in this volume). Of course, when planned properly the overhead/construction costs can be substantially reduced, especially in already developed countries, as was true, for example, for the Los Angeles Olympics of 1984 and the German World Cup in 2006.

3   WHITE ELEPHANTS

The seemingly inevitable outcome of the competitive bidding process is the production of white elephants.[3] The competition to win the bidding process for host selection often leaves in the dust rational city planning for long-term land use and financial prudence. Olympic stadiums are proposed with seating capacities of some 80,000 that will be too large for any regular future use. Swimming arenas, velodromes, bobsled tracks,[4] elaborate, oversized soccer facilities in countries where rugby is the leading sport, surplus hotel construction and so on seem to be telltale characteristics in a city that the Olympics or the World Cup has been there. The notorious Bird's Nest Olympic Stadium in Beijing is now commonly described as abandoned. Similarly, many of the sporting edifices from the Olympic Stadium in Sydney, Green Point Stadium in Cape Town, or the Water Cube in Beijing go unused or underutilized for most or all of the year, while they require millions of dollars of maintenance and operations expense, and they occupy valuable urban land.

Athens, host of the 2004 Summer Olympic Games, is particularly tragic. While many of the Olympics sports facilities sit idle, half of the 10,000 apartments in the Olympic Village are unoccupied, most of the 27 commercial properties on the site have closed and promised schools were never finished. A recent article in London's *The Telegraph* told part of the story (Govan, 2011):

> Despite grand plans for an Olympic legacy, municipalities ran out of money and the political will to maintain them.
>
> 'We had some very good plans, well-laid plans,' said Athanasios Alevras, a socialist MP from the ruling PASPOK party and former deputy minister of culture in the run-up to the Games. 'The idea was to build sites that could be then converted to benefit the lives of Atheneans afterwards. The Olympic Village was a great plan to regenerate an area.'
>
> But, he admits, it went wrong. 'We promised infrastructure and facilities that then weren't delivered. The plans were not respected. Basically, it's a disaster.'
>
> He blames a change in the government and a lack of vision. 'It isn't just that we ran out of money but that the administrative system just wasn't prepared to do what was needed,' said Mr Alevras.
>
> Many on the streets of Athens see state overspending on the Olympics as a major contributor to Greece's runaway financial problems. Sofia Sakorafa, an MP thrown out of George Papandreou's ruling PASOK party after voting against the bailout package a year ago, estimates the Games cost Greece €27bn, vastly over the given €5.5bn budget. She added that no official figure for the cost has ever been published.
>
> 'It was a hugely wasted opportunity and one that sticks in the throat of many people. We are left with installations that are rotting away because we don't even have the money to maintain them. A lot of entrepreneurs and property developers got rich very quickly,' said Ms Sakorafa.

For the 2014 World Cup, Brazil is building new stadiums in Brasilia, Cuiaba, Manaus and Natal; all cities without a team in the domestic soccer leagues (Zimbalist, 2011 and de Melo, ch. 29 in this volume).These modern-day architectural wonders are not built with natural materials and they will not last for centuries like medieval churches or palaces (Cartwright, ch. 8 in this volume).

Further, winning the bid also costs more and more. South Africa reportedly spent $45 million to win the right to host the 2010 World Cup. The cost of Chicago's failed bid to host the 2016 Summer Games has been estimated at $100 million. The bidding process has been virtually transformed into a sporting competition of its own.

4   DO MEGA EVENTS COMPETE?

Still, it makes sense to return to the question of whether mega events wield monopoly power. Take the largest mega event, the Olympics. Does it compete with other mega sporting events? Are the various mega events substitutes for each other? If the Olympics raises its prices too much, will consumers, that is, cities, countries or spectators, migrate to other mega sporting events?

For instance, can NBC, which will pay the IOC a US rights fee of $4.38 billion to televise the four Olympic Games between 2014 and 2020, extract higher advertising revenues per viewer delivered (CPMs)[5] than other mega events? If an advertiser pays $1 million for a 30-second spot on prime-time Olympics which has five million US households, the CPM is $200. The same advertiser may pay $50,000 for a spot during the Daytona 500 which might have 300,000 viewers, for a CPM of $167. Why wouldn't the advertiser substitute spots on the Daytona 500 (which yields more viewers per dollar) for spots on the Olympics until the price went up to equilibrate the CPM between the Olympics and the Daytona race? And if the CPMs are the same (and if similar competition yielded equal CPMs across all television programming), can we really say that the Olympics has market power, at least in the television market? In fact, there are several reasons why the CPMs may not equalize: the audience demographics may differ with one group of viewers being more valuable to the advertiser than another, the seasonal timeframe may be different, the advertiser may not be able to reach as many different viewers with multiple spots on non-Olympic programming due to an inadequate aggregate number of spots, and the cost per viewer of producing the advertisement will be lower for the show with more viewers.

Of course, one would also want to assess the opportunities for the IOC to set higher prices in the sponsorship market, in the ticket market, in the market for internet rights, and so on. It seems reasonable to us to conclude that the US Department of Justice's Antitrust Division's standard for monopoly power (ability to increase prices 5 percent or more without decreasing profits) applies to the major mega sporting events, such as the Olympics and the World Cup, as well as several others. Generally, the organizers of mega events do exercise market power.

5 ARE MARKETS FOR MEGA EVENTS CONTESTABLE?

If the IOC possesses monopoly power, is the market of the Olympics contestable? That is, can other firms enter the market to produce a rival Olympic Games? There are many reasons to believe that new entry is not feasible: the Olympic brand dates back at least to 1896, if not Ancient Greece, and is exceptionally strong; television networks would balk at dedicating air time to show rival games, let alone offering hundreds of millions of dollars in rights fees; corporations would not shell out big bucks for unproven competitions; cities would be reluctant to invest in infrastructure and sports facilities; fans would not pay top dollar for tickets, and so on. In fact, back in 1986, US media mogul Ted Turner created the Goodwill Games and televised them on his own network. He lost over $26 million in that year and another $40 million in 1990, after which the Goodwill Games died a slow death and were last played in Brisbane, Australia in 2001. The market for Olympic Games is probably the least contestable among mega sporting events, but others, such as the Soccer World Cup, the Cricket World Cup, the Super Bowl or Wimbledon, appear close to impregnable.[6]

In economic theory natural monopolies can be justified because they are associated with decreasing long-run average costs. Setting aside the question of whether there is a declining long-run average cost curve, the more telling feature of mega sporting events is that consumers appear to have a strong preference for only one product. Part of the allure, after all, of the World Cup is that the country with the world's best soccer team is at stake; likewise, the Olympics have the best individual athletes in the world, and so on. In boxing, when competition began between sanctioning bodies, the determination of the world champion became ambiguous, and many fans lost interest. Below we shall return to the question of what can be done to improve consumer welfare in the face of the monopoly power of the organizers of mega sporting events.

It remains to observe that, like any good monopolist, the IOC seeks to expand its terrain, lest another producer takes advantage of nearby markets. Such nearby markets may be contestable, especially if the IOC behaves indifferently. Thus, in 2010 the IOC started the first Youth Olympic Games in Singapore. On the one hand, the Youth Games are a potential new market to exploit and commercialize, and to extend the Olympic brand. On the other, there are some concerns that youth champions will dilute the uniqueness of Olympic champions, especially in sports like gymnastics. There is a further concern that preparing young (or pre-) teenagers for the rigor, discipline, specialization and intense competition of playing high-profile sports before the world audience is seriously detrimental both to their emotional and physical development. Of course, this latter concern is playing itself on different stages internationally (for example, the Little League World Series) in any event.

6   WHAT IS THE ECONOMIC IMPACT OF MEGA SPORTING EVENTS?

Do mega events produce a positive economic impact in the host cities or countries? The media attention and size of mega events, together with the fact that, unlike games in a national sports league, they attract hundreds of thousands of visitors, lead to the view that mega events promote local job creation and increase local income. The reality is more complex.

As summarized by Baumann et al. (ch. 22) and by Coates (ch. 23) in this volume, the existing empirical scholarly literature on the economic impact of mega events is virtually unanimous: a host city/country should not anticipate a benefit on 'hard core' economic variables such as income, employment, taxes and so on. A few studies have identified a small boost in hospitality or leisure sector employment from hosting the World Cup or the Olympics, but an increase in one sector may be offset by losses in another. Sterken (ch. 20 in this volume) finds only weak evidence of a possible, modest economic impact from hosting the Summer Games, and no evidence of a positive impact from hosting either the Winter Games or the World Cup. Most studies have found no statistically significant economic effect from hosting and a few have found a negative effect. Feddersen and Maennig (2010) test the 1996 Atlanta case with more disaggregated data and employ a different empirical strategy; they find smaller economic effects than HotchKiss et al. (2003).

By this time, the reasons for these somber outcomes are well understood. First, during mega events many local residents are prompted to leave the area to avoid the crowds, congestion and higher prices. Second, those locals who stay and spend money at the sporting events are not spending their money at other local retail or entertainment venues. Third, visitors to the mega event may crowd out others who would visit the host city, but cannot obtain transportation or hotel space. Fourth, some visiting attendees at the mega event are in the city for other reasons and would be spending their (or their local host's) entertainment dollars elsewhere in the local economy. Alternatively, the visitors may have been planning a trip to the host city anyway, but decided to change the time of their visit to coincide with the mega event. In such a case, only the timing of the expenditure, not the expenditure itself, has been affected. Fifth, the majority of the money spent at mega events either is repatriated back to the sanctioning body (such as FIFA or the IOC) or is purchasing goods that were not produced locally. Sixth, the financing costs associated with the construction, operations and security costs of the mega event can be onerous, as we have seen, and may compel the host government to raise taxes or reduce other services, either of which would produce a drag on the local economy.

7 PSYCHIC AND INDIRECT BENEFITS

As discussed by Süssmuth (ch. 14 in this volume), however, there is another, emerging body of literature that identifies what can be appreciable psychic benefits for the local population associated with hosting a mega event. These benefits may be supplemented by a sustained increase in property values near the new facilities that were constructed for the mega event, as discussed by Ahlfeldt and Kavetsos (ch. 17) and by Brown and Szymanski (ch. 30) in this volume. Another possible indirect benefit is the advertising effect of such events. Many Olympic host metropolitan areas and regions view the Olympics as a way to raise their profile on the world stage. In this sense, the intense media coverage before and during the Olympic Games or other big events is a form of advertising, possibly attracting tourists who would not have otherwise considered the city or region, and who may generate significant, broad, and long-lasting economic benefits. Any such benefits should, of course, appear in the econometric studies on the growth impact of mega events, and those studies have not been encouraging. In this regard, the comment by Graham Matthews, a former forecaster for the Australian Federal Treasury, is instructive: 'While having the Olympics may have made us feel warm and fuzzy and wonderful, in cold hard terms it's actually hard in international experience to determine if there has been a positive, lasting impact on tourism from having that brief burst of exposure' (Zimbalist, 2010a, p. 11).

Public awareness of past Olympic host sites in both Europe and North America was the subject of a 1991 study by Ritchie and Smith (1991, pp. 3–10). Based on several thousand telephone interviews carried out over 1986–89, less than 10 percent of the North American residents surveyed and less than 30 percent of the Europeans could recall that the 1976 Winter Olympic Games had been held in Innsbruck, Austria. Only 28 percent of the North Americans and 24 percent of the Europeans surveyed remembered that the 1980 Winter Games took place in Lake Placid, New York. Other research showed that recognition of Calgary having hosted the 1988 Winter Games had almost entirely faded by 1991 (Matheson,

2008). And if the Games are accompanied by bad weather, pollution, unsavory politics, or terrorist acts, the Games may actually damage a location's reputation. Indeed, Wonho Song (2010) finds that the long-term impact on tourism from hosting the Summer Olympics is negative, while the Winter Games show no impact on either tourism or exports.

8   THE IMPACT OF IMPACT STUDIES

Given the consistent and clear conclusion of scholarly studies of the economic impact of mega sporting events, it remains to ponder why so little attention has been paid to these *ex post* studies by prospective host cities. Indeed, prospective hosts invariably pay hundreds of thousands of dollars to consulting companies to produce studies that conclude substantial economic benefits will ensue from hosting the mega events. In May 2011, LOCOG (the London Organising Committee for the Olympic Games) put out a request for proposal (RFP) seeking to identify a group to produce such a promotional economic impact study. The RFP even stipulated that LOCOG was anticipating significant public criticism prior to the 2012 Games around the massive budget that will have been expended on the preparation for the Games, and that LOCOG felt the need to have strong propaganda to respond to the anticipated critiques. These promotional efforts notwithstanding, the cumulative scholarly work has found its way into the public discourse and begun to exert an inevitable impact.

9   FUTURE CHALLENGES

Some Basic Considerations

If the economic gains from hosting mega events are small, or perhaps non-existent, what can host cities and regions do to optimize the benefits (or minimize the costs) of hosting events like the Olympic Games?

Hosting the Olympic Games requires a significant amount of land for facilities, housing for athletes, media, staff, and spectators, and parking. Host cities or regions need to make careful decisions on usage of land which is increasingly scarce both in the large urban areas that typically host the Summer Games and in the mountainous areas that host the Winter Games. Unsuccessful Games leave behind legacies of seldom- or never-used structures that take up valuable land and are expensive to maintain. In contrast, events like the Los Angeles Summer Olympics use existing facilities as much as possible, consuming as little additional urban land as possible. The stadium used for the opening and closing ceremonies in the 1996 Atlanta Games was reconfigured to a baseball stadium immediately after the Games. Olympic planners need to design facilities that will be useful for a long time after the Games are over and that are constructively integrated into the host city or region.

The impact of hosting major sporting events may vary according to the level of development in the host city and country. Properly planned, hosting a large event can serve as a catalyst for the construction of modern transportation, communications, and sport infrastructure, which generally benefit less-developed areas more. The catch, however, is that the lower the level is a country's development, the more difficult it is to overcome the organizational challenges to plan adequately, build efficiently, and pull off successful operations.

While hosting the Olympics, for example, requires a significant outlay of public funds for improvements that could have been made without hosting the Games, public policy is often so gridlocked that needed infrastructural investments could be delayed for years or even decades if not for the Olympics or other mega sporting events. And on occasion the IOC does provide some funding to facilitate the completion of desirable projects.

In more-developed regions, where land is more scarce during the initial bidding and planning period, and destined to become scarcer still over the 7–10-year period of Olympic selection and preparation, hosting the Games can occasion a gross misuse of land.

The value of hosting a major event like the Olympic Games is likely to vary from one situation to another. The bidders for future mega events would do well to steer clear of any Olympic hype and to take a long, hard, and sober look at the long-run development goals of their regions.

This is easier said than done, particularly when there are structural impediments which stack the cards against prospective hosts. Hence, the obvious next question is whether these structural impediments will be overcome by evolutionary, automatic changes or whether a policy debate is needed.

The Changing Technological and Human Landscape

There are indeed transformations that are occurring or will occur that will affect the organization and outcomes of mega sporting events.

First, technological progress will proceed apace, and, as it does, it will continue to change the way fans watch sports. Presumably, more and more sports will be available on the internet, as new niches for live streaming multiply, on mobile phones, on tablets and even on the lenses of eyeglasses. Exactly how this will impact rights fees and viewership is next to impossible to discern, both because the institutional rules for developing and sending these video streams will change and because consumer habits will change – and, undoubtedly, in different ways in different countries. Technological change will enable more ubiquitous viewership and it will promote fragmentation as new sports (and other programming) become available. From the vantage point of mid-2011, the only thing that we know for certain is that there will be a proliferation of delivery modalities and, hence, of opportunities for sharing live video signals.[7]

Another factor closely related to technological change is the growing individuation of life. Many of the innovations, for example, TV set, the computer, mobile phones, and tablets, have enabled us to spend more time alone and less time together in groups or community. Sports serve as an antidote to this tendency. Whether it is soccer fans from a country rooting for their team in the World Cup, gymnastics fans rooting during the Olympics, or New Yorkers rooting for the Yankees, it is something that people share with their friends, neighbors and fellow city or country residents. It is a common subject to discuss that unites the lawyer, the business executive, the dentist, the laborer, and the taxi driver in a community. It is the exhilaration of standing, cheering and high-fiving at a stadium with 50,000 other fans when a player on your team scores a goal or scores a touchdown. Thus, the growing attenuation of community spawned by technology creates a void that sporting events can fill. For these reasons, among others, the growing role of sport and mega sporting events is likely to continue.

Policy Issues

Globalization and gender

Globalization is not new to mega sporting events; to the contrary, mega sporting events are a constituent part of globalization. In certain areas though, (mega) sporting events might have to reconsider their role. Two issues must be raised. First, today's Olympic sports are Euro-centered; American, Asian, and African sports are underrepresented. The Olympic Family has to rethink its selection process for the sports disciplines to be included in the Olympics. Second, the ability of women to actively participate in mega sporting events on an equal opportunity basis is not only a human right, but also an economic issue. Without the full integration of female talents, the world is not making use of its full production capacities. (Mega) sporting (events), when successful in the full integration of women, from athletes to high-profile sports officials, can be a blueprint for developments in other areas of human development. Many sport federations, including the IOC and FIFA, have successfully opened their competitions to women and even have pressed members to select more female delegates to international sports administrative bodies. It appears, however, that further opportunities exist to promote women's participation and interest. For instance, concepts such as 'mixed teams' are rarely to be found at mega events, though they are well tested at the Youth Olympic Games. Another striking exception, of course, is the mixed doubles competition found at Wimbledon and other tennis tournaments. Surely, other team sports would be amenable to this model and, if they were introduced, there would not only be more participation opportunities for women, but this participation would likely increase fandom among the female audience. It would also potentially apply pressure in those countries where women's role has been subordinate to break down some traditional social roles. Interestingly, mixed doubles at Wimbledon has a long history and also serves as a model to engage more athletes from smaller and less-developed countries. In 1925, for instance, at Wimbledon a mixed doubles team, consisting of Umberto de Morpurgo of Mexico and Elizabeth Ryan of the United States went all the way to the finals; in 2010, the team of Cara Black of Zimbabwe and Leander Paes of India won the mixed doubles competition. In addition, it would also make eminent sense for mega events to revisit restrictions on dress code that make it difficult for women from some cultures to participate in certain events.

Globalization in the long run may reduce the value of 'nation', which may, in turn, question the endurance of 'national teams'. The finding of David Forrest et al. (ch. 13 in this volume) on the influence of the size of a country's population, GDP, and home advantage on medal wins implies that equally talented athletes from less-advantaged nations have less chance to win medals. Why not reserve some wild cards in certain team sports for international teams, consisting of athletes from nations too small to be able to compete? Why not, for instance, reserve at least one rowing eight a starting position for athletes from smaller nations like Belgium, Peru, Tunisia, and Singapore, who otherwise would never have a chance to compete in an eight? Any innovative concept, any future change in the design of mega events that would allow a balancing of national advantages and disadvantages could be truly path breaking for globalization beyond sports.

Demographic change

Along with globalization, demographic shifts might become a major driving force not only in societal development, but also in sports. Fewer young people in many Western countries may lead to fewer athletes and fewer medals; this is not a problem for those countries which do not have the problem of low birth rates (and which, in many cases, belong to the group of nations that heretofore has been disadvantaged). It might become a problem, however, if the older population becomes less interested in high performances by younger people. The IOC has, for other reasons, introduced the Youth Olympic Games. It could be time to start discussing 'Masters Olympic Games'. In many sports, masters competitions already successfully exist.

This is not a call against the interest of younger persons. To the contrary, the repeated emphasis on sustainability, especially ecologically sound and durable constructions for mega events, adapted to local needs, is a call for younger generations to take on more responsibility. And because 'white elephants' engender operating and maintenance costs that can threaten local financial stability and local economic growth, this is also an economic issue.

Doping and corruption

Two of the major threats to the sustainability of mega sporting events are doping and corruption. Doping and corruption are not easily defined and not easily detected. With the ongoing development of new compounds and masking agents, the complicated protocols for testing and a plethora of logistical problems, effective testing is a difficult and costly proposition (Zimbalist, 2010b, ch. 8 passim). The average cost of catching one doped athlete easily reaches six figures in US dollars (see, for instance, Maennig, 2002). The problems of doping and corruption obviously both have a high degree of economic determination and consequence. Nevertheless, in both cases relatively little use has so far been made of economic instruments in elaborating countermeasures. Economic analysis suggests that additional and more efficient instruments are available. An initial principle is that it makes sense to extend anti-doping and anti-corruption measures only as long their marginal social utility exceeds their marginal social cost. From an economic point of view, there is an optimal (or 'to be accepted') degree of delinquency which must not be zero. Yet, with the high losses in credibility, both for the delinquent athletes and for the sport, the 'optimum' cannot be far from zero.

Evidently for too many athletes the expected benefit from doping (additional victory honors, additional income) is greater than the expected additional costs (potential loss of honor on discovery as well as financial losses resulting from competition bans). In particular, older athletes, who are in any case at the end of their career, are hardly affected by temporary competition bans. An economic solution could increase the expected costs of doping by agreeing more often on financial penalties of a sufficiently high level. More fines of this kind also have the advantage of being protected by contract law. They would thus be easier to implement on a deterrent level than temporary competition bans, which have often fallen foul of the law relating to work and personal rights.

Such a policy of financial penalties must be directed at all those found guilty of doping and facilitating doping, and should not be restricted to the athletes alone. For their part, the athletes could also insure themselves against unwanted manipulation on the part of trainers and others via contracts containing similar penalties. The recipients of the money from the penalties could be those parties who were damaged by the external effects of doping. The implementation of this principle, of course, also requires a number of refinements.

Regarding corruption in the bidding process, it would make straightforward sense to render the bidding/selection process more transparent by placing greater emphasis on sport-related criteria and less on non-sport-related ones, such as geopolitical factors. The incentive for corruption-free behavior on the part of the applicant cities and the IOC members should be increased via enhanced controls and greater potential punishments.

Institutional reform

Although there is obviously no shortage of ideas for future modifications, innovations and reforms, one has to admit that efficient structures of international sports would ensure an ongoing process of self-checking and self-optimization. One such institutional reform might entail a restructuring of the governing institutions of mega-sport sanctioning bodies, so that they could be more responsive or behave more like benevolent monopolies. For instance, the selection of candidate cities as well as the winning city by the IOC is performed by a group of up to 115 people, called the IOC members. This group was reformed in 2006, following the revelation of extensive corruption in connection to the awarding of the 2002 Winter Games to Salt Lake City. But the reforms could be carried considerably further. The 115 members include: 15 active athletes who are elected by their peers at the Olympic Games; 15 individuals selected from National Organizing Committees (NOCs); 15 individuals from the International Federations (IFs); and 70 individual members who are self-regenerating. Each member is assumed to represent the Olympic Movement, rather than a particular country or sport. Clearly, a healthy majority of members belong to the self-generating aristocracy who are accountable to no one, other than the Olympic Movement and the president of the IOC.

If the IOC's voting structure were made more democratic, say, by having the voting body itself be elected every four years by the 200-plus NOCs and the international sport federations that belong to the Olympic Movement, then it would be more likely to respect the planning needs and financial constraints of the prospective host cities. The current members of the IOC are not going to give up their power voluntarily, but their power comes from the loyal participation of the NOCs in the Olympic Movement. The NOCs, if organized, have some latent power. A pipe-dream perhaps, but it cannot hurt to float the idea.

A related reform might be to make IOC voting transparent; that is, to end the anonymity of the voting process. At the very least, transparency would make it easier to connect voting patterns with payoffs, and should provide a powerful disincentive to IOC members not to sell their votes. Failing such a full transparency reform, in order to increase levels of responsibility and improve control, voting on the host of Olympic Games, World Cups and other mega events should be open to inspection for a small circle of notaries who, while sworn to silence, would be able to match names to voting if necessary. If an allegation of corruption should arise, it would be a simple matter to check how any suspects may have voted or whether their votes were decisive for the vote as a whole (Maennig, 2002).

Yet another reform that could combat the excessive resources lavished on mega sporting events would be to designate a permanent host of the Games. For example, if Athens hosted the Summer Olympics every four years, then there would not be the duplication of unsustainable facilities every quadrennium. The arguments against such a reform are twofold: one, it would potentially decrease the globalizing effect of the Olympics that follows from moving the Games to different continents from cycle to cycle; two, for some the expression of architectural creativity that comes with new Olympic stadiums and arenas would be muted. Of course, the counter arguments to this latter point are poignant to many observers – namely, that market forces and private demand should govern the pace and magnitude of artistic expression, and that mega-building duplication is not ecologically sound.

10   CONCLUSION

The foregoing discussion attempts not only to provide an overview of the economic and social issues facing mega sporting events today, but also to engage a debate about (a) the technological, social and economic forces shaping the future of these events and (b) the relevant policy options that might be applied to improve their popularity and performance. The chapters collected herein represent the current research of scholars who have been actively investigating mega events over the last two decades. Like sports itself, mega events have grown to be a key component of how people and countries relate to each other and enjoy the benefit of leisure time. Understanding the dynamic forces that shape these events is a serious and important challenge. We hope that this book has provided a useful foundation for advancing that understanding.

NOTES

1. The initial budget for the London 2012 Games was £2.4 billion; by 2008 it had increased almost fourfold to £9.35 billion. The initial budget for the Sochi, Russia Winter Games in 2014 was $12 billion and the latest estimate is $33 billion. The most remarkable of all cost overruns belongs to the 2010 Commonwealth Games in Delhi, India, where the initial budget from December 2002 was 6.2 billion rupees while the final budget from 2009 was over 11 times that, or 706 billion rupees. See Mehta and Majumdar (ch. 28 in this volume) and Andrew Zimbalist (2010a).

2. Note that these *ex post* figures do not represent Olympic specific costs. Indeed, the accounting of Olympic costs is muddled by several factors. In general, the costs published by the local organizing committee of the Games (the OCOG) represent only the operating costs for the Games and capital costs are not included in the OCOG budget. To be sure, many of the capital costs, particularly those for infrastructure and sometimes for permanent sporting facilities, by economic logic should not be attributed to the Olympic Games. For instance, if the Games induce Beijing to modernize its airport, a project that was needed in any event, then the investment in the airport should be amortized or prorated with only a small share of the expenditure attributed to the Games. A similar accounting logic would apply to other infrastructural or facility expenditures, provided that they continue to be fully used after the 17 days of Olympic competition are over.

3. Of course, if the governing bodies put pressure on the bidders to present sustainable plans and this pressure went beyond convenient rhetoric, then we might see a constructive change in this pattern.

4. In Turin, for example, the bobsled-run venue cost $108 million to construct, and Deputy President of the Turin Games, Evelina Christillin commented to a *Wall Street Journal* reporter: 'I can't tell you a lie. Obviously, the bobsled run is not going to be used for anything else. That's pure cost' (Zimbalist, 2010a, p. 10).

5. CPM stands for cost per thousand viewers; it is a standard metric of efficiency in television advertising.

6. Many mega events are organized by so-called non-profit institutions, such as the IOC or FIFA; others are organized by for-profit institutions, such as Formula 1 or NASCAR. Although efforts to organize rival mega events have foundered, in some instances there have been successful efforts to take over the existing sanctioning body. As we write in July 2011, for instance, both the News Corporation of Ruppert Murdoch and Exor of the Agnelli family are independently seeking to gain control of Formula 1 racing, which is currently majority owned by CVC Capital.

7. Another feature of technological change is the digital video recorder. The DVR allows viewers to record any show and watch at a later time, skipping over commercials. Since sports fans generally want to view their sport live, yet viewers of TV drama or comedy shows are happy to watch them at any convenient time, the relative value of advertising on sports shows increases with the DVR. This development is partially offset by virtual advertising at the bottom of the screen or integrated advertising in the event, but standing alone the DVR increases the relative value of sporting events.

REFERENCES

Feddersen, Arne and Wolfgang Maennig (2010), 'Mega-events and sectoral employment: the case of the 1996 Olympic Games', Hamburg Contemporary Economic Discussions, No. 35.

Govan, Fiona (2011), 'Greece's Olympic dream has turned into a nightmare', *The Telegraph*, 29 June.

Hotchkiss, Julie, R.E. Moore and S.M. Zobay (2003), 'Impact of the 1996 Summer Olympic Games on employment and wages in Georgia', *Southern Economic Journal*, **69** (3), 691–704.

Maennig, Wolfgang (2002), 'On the economics of doping and corruption in international sports', *Journal of Sports Economics*, **3**, 61–89.

Matheson, Victor (2008), 'Caught under a mountain of Olympic debt', *The Boston Globe*, August 22.

Ritchie, J.R. Brent and Brian H. Smith (1991), 'The Impact of a mega-event on host region awareness: a longitudinal study', *Journal of Travel Research*, **30**, 3–10.

Song, Wonho (2010), 'Impacts of Olympics on exports and tourism', *Journal of Economic Development*, **35** (4), 93–110.

Zimbalist, Andrew (2010a), 'Is it worth it?', *Finance and Development*, March, 8–11.

Zimbalist, Andrew (2010b), *Circling the Bases: Challenges and Prospects for the Sports Industry*, Philadelphia, PA: Temple University Press.

Zimbalist, Andrew (2011), 'Brazil's long to-do list', *America's Quarterly*, Summer, 56–62.

Index